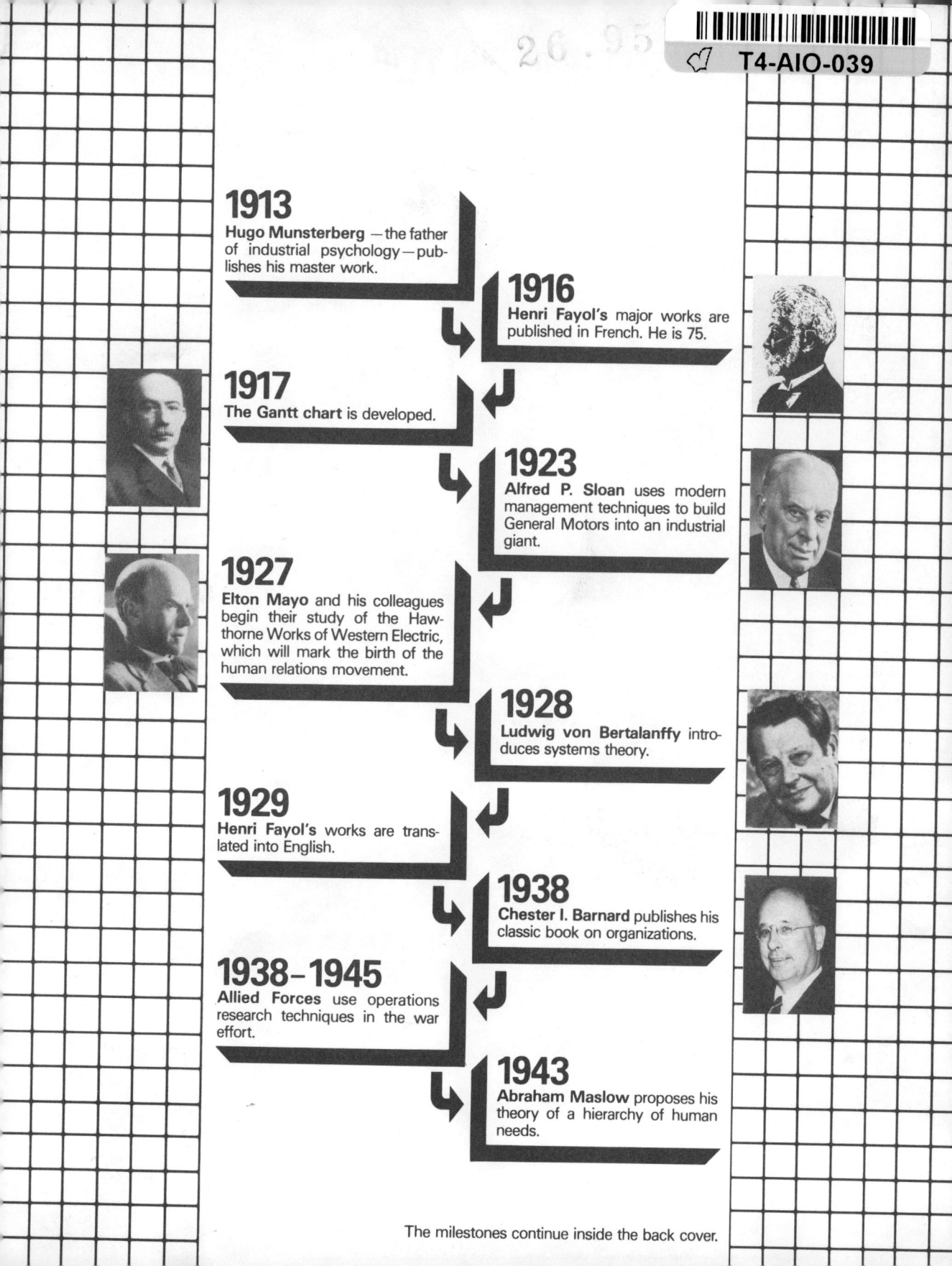

1913
Hugo Munsterberg —the father of industrial psychology—publishes his master work.

1916
Henri Fayol's major works are published in French. He is 75.

1917
The Gantt chart is developed.

1923
Alfred P. Sloan uses modern management techniques to build General Motors into an industrial giant.

1927
Elton Mayo and his colleagues begin their study of the Hawthorne Works of Western Electric, which will mark the birth of the human relations movement.

1928
Ludwig von Bertalanffy introduces systems theory.

1929
Henri Fayol's works are translated into English.

1938
Chester I. Barnard publishes his classic book on organizations.

1938–1945
Allied Forces use operations research techniques in the war effort.

1943
Abraham Maslow proposes his theory of a hierarchy of human needs.

The milestones continue inside the back cover.

PRINCIPLES OF
MANAGEMENT

SECOND EDITION

About the Authors

LOUIS E. BOONE (B.S., M.S., Ph.D.) holds the Ernest G. Cleverdon Chair of Business and Management at the University of South Alabama. He formerly chaired the Division of Management and Marketing at the University of Tulsa and has taught management in Greece and the United Kingdom.

Professor Boone has authored or coauthored a number of books, including the widely acclaimed *The Great Writings in Management and Organizational Behavior* (PennWell Books, 1980; Donald D. Bowen, coauthor). His research interests include the areas of management information systems and executive behavior, and he has published articles in such journals as *Business Horizons, Journal of Business Strategy, MSU Business Topics, Business,* and the *Journal of Business of the University of Chicago.*

Professor Boone is a member of the Academy of Management and of the editorial review boards of the *Journal of Experiential Learning and Simulation* and the *Southern Business Review.* He is advisory editor in management for Penn-Well Books.

DAVID L. KURTZ (B.A., M.B.A., Ph.D.) currently holds the Thomas F. Gleed Chair in Business and Finance at the Albers School of Business, Seattle University. He was formerly a professor and head of department at Eastern Michigan University. During 1974, Professor Kurtz was the Ian Potter Foundation Visiting Fellow at the Caulfield Institute of Technology (Melbourne, Australia). He also previously taught at the University of Arkansas and Davis and Elkins College.

Professor Kurtz is the author or coauthor of numerous books, and more than forty articles, monographs, cases, book reviews, invited papers, and computer simulations. Professor Kurtz's textbooks, including *Contemporary Business,* coauthored with Louis E. Boone, are widely used in collegiate schools of business.

A member of numerous professional associations, Professor Kurtz has also served in editorial capacities with three academic journals in business administration. He was also advisory editor for the General Learning Press.

Professor Kurtz has been involved in consulting and training activities in business and has been the president of a small corporation.

PRINCIPLES OF
MANAGEMENT

SECOND EDITION

LOUIS E. BOONE

Ernest G. Cleverdon Chair of
Business and Management
University of South Alabama

DAVID L. KURTZ

Thomas F. Gleed Chair of
Business and Finance
Seattle University

RANDOM HOUSE
BUSINESS DIVISION
NEW YORK

To
Seib and Paul

For their friendship, advice,
and assistance over the years.

Second edition
987654321
Copyright © 1981, 1984 by Random House, Inc.

Library of Congress Cataloging in Publication Data

Boone, Louis E.
   Principles of management.

   Includes index.
   1. Management.   I. Kurtz, David L.   II. Title.
HD31.B619   1984   658   83-22956
ISBN 0-394-33625-9

Manufactured in the United States of America

COVER ART: Alexander Calder's *The Red Oval
Counterweight.* Photograph, courtesy Perls Galleries, New York

Designed by Levavi and Levavi
Part title art drawn by Charles Hess

Additional acknowledgments and credits appear on pp. 645–46.

Preface

The 1980s are exciting times in which to begin a study of management. Never before have organizations ranging from business firms to government agencies placed greater importance on effective management in achieving organizational objectives. Capable managers are needed in both giant corporations and in neighborhood businesses, in hospitals and in financial institutions, in cultural organizations and in the National Football League. Management concepts have universal applications for both profit and nonprofit organizations. Both large and small organizations operate by utilizing human and other resources in the pursuit of objectives.

Principles of Management is a student-oriented text for the 1980s. It may be the only truly student-oriented text in the discipline, with a focus on aiding student *learning* while helping the instructor *teach* the subject matter.

The second edition of *Principles of Management* has been thoroughly updated and revised. While it retains the features that made it one of the most widely adopted texts in management, a number of major changes have been made as a result of extensive feedback from users of the first edition.

PRINCIPLES OF MANAGEMENT PROVIDES MORE THOROUGH TREATMENT OF ESSENTIAL MANAGERIAL FUNCTIONS. Certainly the most noticeable feature in the new edition of *Principles of Management* is the major strengthening of the discussion of universal management functions. A separate five-chapter section, "Planning and Decision Making," is markedly improved with the addition of a new chapter on strategic planning. A second chapter on motivation has been added to the leadership section. In addition, a new chapter on control techniques now appears in Part V, "The Control Function." These new chapters provide more detailed treatment of planning, motivation, and controlling in response to the many management professors who requested added emphasis on managerial functions in the new edition.

PRINCIPLES OF MANAGEMENT INCLUDES LONGER, MORE COMPREHENSIVE CASES AT THE END OF EACH PART. These cases are especially useful for instructors who want to utilize cases to emphasize the *applications* of management concepts. In addition, shorter cases in the form of *managerial incidents* appear at the end of every chapter.

IMPORTANT MANAGEMENT SUBJECTS ARE COVERED IN SEPARATE CHAPTERS. While many textbooks neglect emerging areas of management, making occasional passing references or lacking coverage altogether, the authors of *Principles of Management* feel that the areas of international management, operations management, management information systems, the systems approach to planning and decision making, ethics, management of nonprofit organizations, and careers in management are too important to ignore. Each of these subjects is treated in detail in separate chapters.

MANAGEMENT IS EXPLAINED IN BOTH PROFIT AND NONPROFIT SETTINGS. Management is a universal concept. *Principles of Management* employs cases, examples, and applications from nonprofit as well as business settings to reflect the growing importance of effectively managing nonprofit organizations in today's society—a subject often neglected in other texts.

PRINCIPLES OF MANAGEMENT PROVIDES ACCEPTED, ORTHODOX COVERAGE. The study of organization and management is characterized by a number of different "approaches," each focusing on specific aspects of management thought. A review of current textbooks shows the popularity of a variety of approaches—systems, behavioral, classical, contingency, quantitative. Instead of reflecting a single school of management thought, *Principles of Management* stresses the contributions of each in the management discipline. *Principles of Management* provides a "mainstream" treatment of organization and management, matching the subject coverage of most introductory courses. Instructors will not have to spend hours adjusting their course to the text.

THE TEXT STRESSES PEDAGOGICAL SOUNDNESS. The emphasis on student learning in *Principles of Management* is evident on the first page of each chapter. Specific learning objectives and important management terminology open each chapter. A short case precedes the text material and illustrates in a novel fashion the application—correct or incorrect—of the subject matter of the chapter. Vocabulary-building is further stressed by the inclusion of definitions in the margins and by a comprehensive glossary at the end of the book. Each chapter ends with a summary, a set of review questions, applications exercises, and a longer "managerial incident" describing actual applications of the chapter subjects in a profit or nonprofit organization.

READER INTEREST IS STRESSED. Instructors who used the first edition of *Principles of Management* reported that students actually enjoyed reading and studying the text! Unlike some other texts that either lack substance or use technical jargon to report research study after research study, *Principles of Management* incorporates research findings in a clear manner and focuses on real managers facing real situations and decisions. Hundreds of examples from the real world breathe life into a text that is both comprehensive and rigorous. The cases and examples are designed to illustrate the *application* of fundamental management concepts discussed in the text. *Principles of Management* avoids sexist language and portrays women in realistic roles.

RESEARCH FINDINGS ARE DOCUMENTED IN THE TEXT. The management discipline is populated with many writers, researchers, and philosophers who are continuing to contribute to its understanding. Much of their work is carefully documented in this text. Pioneer management writers—Fayol, Barnard, McGregor, Taylor, and Drucker, among others—are profiled in the text.

A COMPLETE INSTRUCTIONAL SUPPORT PACKAGE IS AVAILABLE. *Principles of Management* is a complete teaching/learning package for the introductory management course. In addition to the text, the instructional support package, already the most comprehensive ever assembled for this course, has been revised and expanded for the second edition. The package includes a comprehensive Student Course Mastery Guide with Mini-Cases new to this edition, a computer simulation (DECIDE), four-color acetate transparencies, and a test bank, in addition to a comprehensive instructor's resource manual.

The authors gratefully acknowledge the following authors who prepared the ancillary items of the *Principles of Management* package:

STUDENT COURSE MASTERY GUIDE
James W. Baird, *Community College of the Finger Lakes*
Israel B. Markowitz, *Metropolitan State College*

TEST BANK
Israel B. Markowitz, *Metropolitan State College*
Nobert M. Graham, *Arapahoe Community College*

DECIDE
Thomas F. Pray, *Rochester Institute of Technology*
Daniel R. Strang, *SUNY College at Geneseo*

ACKNOWLEDGMENTS. *Principles of Management* would not have been possible without the concerted efforts of a number of dedicated professionals. Our innovative and energetic editor, Paul Donnelly, and the fine staff at Random House were responsible for assembling a team of reviewers whose suggestions, criticisms, and advice markedly assisted in the book's development. The authors are deeply grateful for the efforts of Mildred E. Buzenberg, *Kansas State University*; Franklin Cantwell, *Texas Wesleyan College*; Wayne Cioffari, *Mercy College*; James Conley, *Eastern Michigan University*; Jagdish Danak, *Eastern Michigan University*; William C. Feldbaumer, *Trenton State College*; Marjorie M. Gilmore, *Community College of Denver—Auraria*; Douglas Gordon, *Arapahoe Community College*; J. Kenneth Graham, *Rochester Institute of Technology*; Michael F. Heil, *Miami University*; Robert W. Higgins, *Middlesex County College*; John W. Lloyd, *Monroe Community College*; Vincent P. Luchsinger, *Texas Tech University*; Earl F. Lundgren, *University of Missouri*; Daniel W. McAllister, *University of Nevada—Las Vegas*; George R. McDonald, *University of North Alabama*; Israel B. Markowitz, *Metropolitan State College*; Ina Midkiff-Kennedy, *Amarillo College*; Stuart Murray, *The University of Tulsa*; David L. Short, *Lansing Community College*; Jeffrey C. Susbauer, *Cleveland State University*; Glen L. Tischer, *Bergen Community College*; H. Ralph Todd, Jr., *American River College*; Jay Todes, *Northlake College*; Jerry L. Wall, *Western Illinois University*; Irving Wechsler, *Borough of Manhattan Community College*; Bert W. Weesner, *Lansing Community College*.

Finally, we would like to acknowledge and thank the following contributors of original material: Edgar T. Busch, *Western Kentucky University*; K. Tim Hostiuck; Thomas F. J. Pipal, *Eastern Oklahoma Legal Aid Services*; Phillip K. Sherwood, *Oral Roberts University*.

January 1984

LOUIS E. BOONE
Mobile, Alabama

DAVID L. KURTZ
Seattle, Washington

Contents

ix

PART V   The Control Function   408

PART VI   Additional Dimensions   479

PART VII   Your Future in Management 580

Chapter 22: FUTURE TRENDS IN MANAGEMENT 582

Chapter 23: CAREERS IN MANAGEMENT 598

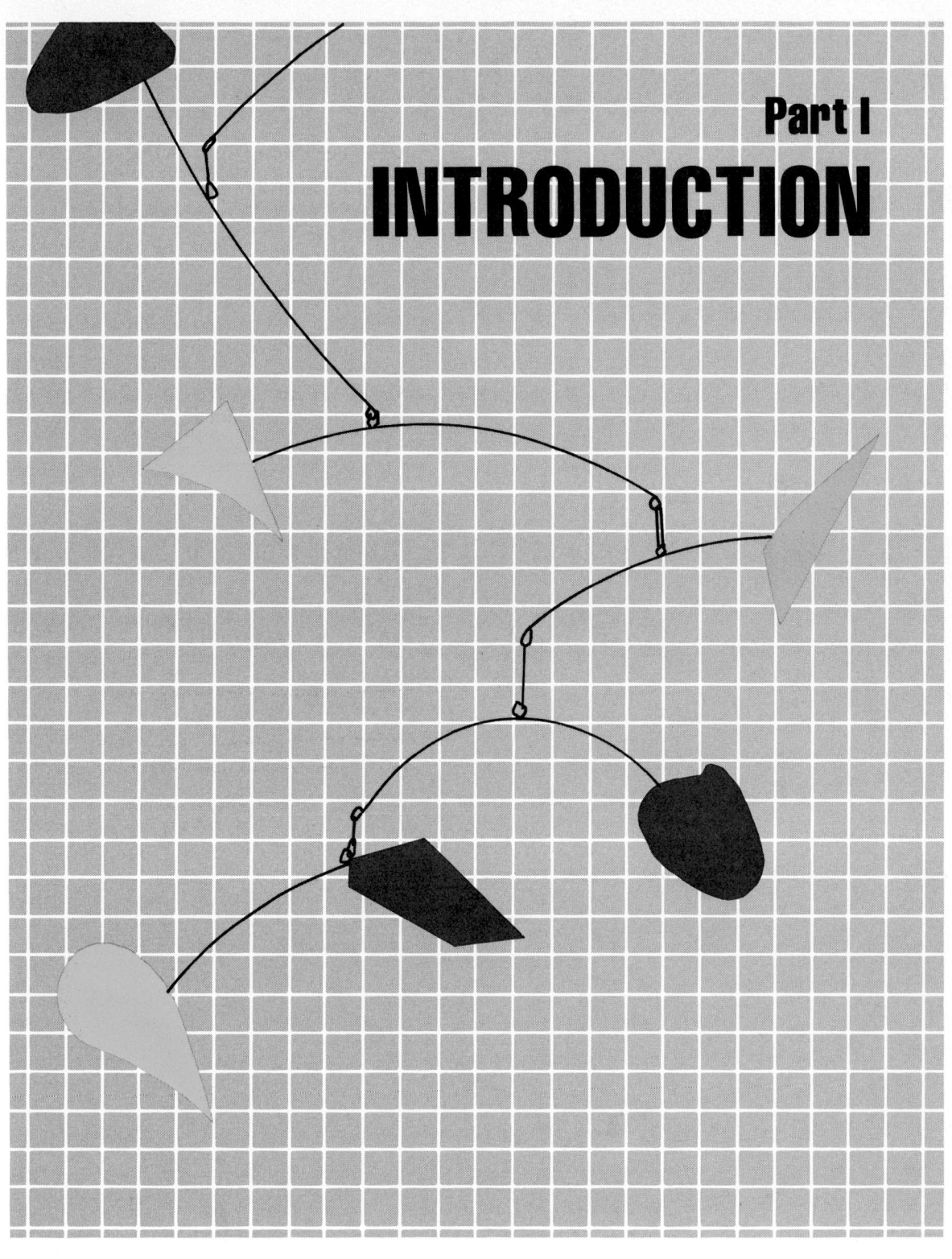

Part I
INTRODUCTION

1.
An Overview

Learning Objectives

AFTER STUDYING THIS CHAPTER YOU SHOULD BE ABLE TO

1. Define management.
2. Identify the functions of management and how they are applied in practice.
3. Demonstrate that management concepts have universal application to both profit-oriented and nonprofit organizations.
4. Describe the managerial hierarchy.
5. Draw a capsule profile of top management.
6. Discuss whether management is an art or a science.
7. List and explain the various approaches to management theory.

Key Terms

management

planning

organizing

leading

controlling

bottom line

stakeholders

By working faithfully eight hours a day,
you may eventually get to be boss and
work twelve hours a day.
> ROBERT FROST

The important thing to recognize is that
it takes a team, and the team ought to
get credit for the wins and the losses.
Successes have many fathers, failures
have none.
> PHILIP CALDWELL
> *Chairman of the Board, Ford*
> *Motor Company*

I t is 8 A.M. when Barbara D. Capsalis arrives at her downtown Manhattan office. Capsalis is a senior vice president of the Chemical New York Corp., the nation's sixth largest commercial bank. With a staff of nearly 1,000 and an annual budget in excess of $50 million, she has back-office responsibility for corporate and correspondent bank deposit, loan, and funds transfer operations worldwide. Like most managers, Barbara Capsalis is accustomed to long hours. A quick glance at her daily schedule might show the following:

8:00–8:30	Arrive at office Review previous evening's work with secretary
8:30	Bi-weekly meeting with division head and four peer area heads to discuss divisional planning and policy issues
10:00	Presentation by staff members analyzing errors and describing plans to reduce error ratios and increase customer inquiry turn-around time
11:30	Legal Department briefing Review of legal options and customer relations implications associated with processing error reported after contractual cut-off period
12:30	New York Clearing House Funds Transfer Committee Luncheon Industry Association Committee
2:00	Meeting with marketing, data processing, and internal staff to review status, priorities, schedule, and costs of major automation project

4:00	Discussion of clerical staff issues and concerns with corporate human resources staff
5:30	Brooklyn Navy Yard Board of Directors Meeting
7:00	Jog and dine with husband
8:30	Work on keynote speech for Association of Women in Computing annual meeting

Capsalis' job is that of a professional manager. As such, she is responsible to Chemical's shareholders, customers, and senior management both for the work of officers and clerical employees reporting to her and, with other managers, for shared activities. In addition, she represents Chemical Bank in both industry and community affairs. Her appointment schedule illustrates the variety of tasks and responsibilities involved in the field of management.[1]

This textbook discusses the theory and practice of management. Readers will explore not only what managers like Barbara Capsalis do but also the theoretical foundations on which her actions are based.

What Is Management?

Management is a difficult term to define. It has a variety of applications and interpretations—all correct within a given set of parameters. Sometimes it is used to describe the executives and administrators of an organization, as when one talks of labor–management negotiations. In other cases, it suggests the professional career path aspired to by most business administration students. And in still other cases it refers to a system for getting things done.

Management is the use of people and other resources to accomplish objectives.

This textbook follows a systems-type definition. *Management* is the use of people and other resources to accomplish objectives. This definition is applicable to all organizational structures, both profit-oriented and not-for-profit for the process of management is as important to the effective functioning of a hospital or fire department as it is to Procter & Gamble.

Management by necessity involves the creation of an environment in which people can use other resources to reach stated goals. It also involves the implementation of the functions of management—planning, organizing, leading, and controlling. Management is a pervasive aspect of the operation of all organizations. Barbara Capsalis' position with Chemical New York Corp., her career path, and the duties she actually performs can all be classified as management. Capsalis must use people and other resources to accomplish the bank's objectives. This is the very essence of management.

---

[1] An excellent article on how general managers actually spend their time is John P. Kotter, "What Effective General Managers Actually Do," *Harvard Business Review* (November–December 1982), pp. 156–167.

"I have bad news for you, Gibson.
I've hired another gopher!"

MANAGEMENT IS THE USE OF PEOPLE AND OTHER RESOURCES TO ACCOMPLISH OBJECTIVES

SOURCE: From *The Wall Street Journal* (June 24, 1982), p. 27, by permission of Cartoon Features Syndicate.

The Functions of Management

The managerial process consists of four functions that must be performed by every manager: planning, organizing, leading, and controlling.[2] Henri Fayol, the distinguished French management theorist and practitioner, is usually credited with identifying these basic functions of the managerial process. Fayol's contributions to the study of management are discussed in detail in Chapter 2 and elsewhere in the text.

The four functions of management may be defined as follows:

Planning: The process by which managers set objectives, assess the future, and develop courses of action to accomplish the objectives.

---

[2] The various functions of management are discussed in articles such as Richard B. Robinson, Jr., "The Importance of 'Outsiders' In Small Firm Strategic Planning," *Academy of Management Journal* (March 1982), pp. 80–93; Henry Mintzberg, "Organization Design: Fashion or Fit?" *Harvard Business Review* (January–February 1981), pp. 103–116; John E. Oliver, Jr., "An Instrument for Classifying Organizations," *Academy of Management Journal* (December 1982), pp. 855–866; Melvin Blumberg and Charles D. Pringle, "The Missing Opportunity in Organizational Research: Some Implications for a Theory of Work Performance," *Academy of Management Review* (October 1982), pp. 560–569; Terrance R. Mitchell, "Motivation: New Directions for Theory, Research and Practice," *Academy of Management Review* (January 1982), pp. 80–88; and Douglas Cederblom, "The Performance Appraisal Interview: A Review, Implications, and Suggestions," *Academy of Management Review* (April 1982), pp. 219–227.

Organizing: The process of arranging people and physical resources to carry out plans and accomplish organizational objectives.

Leading: The act of motivating or causing people to perform certain tasks intended to achieve specified objectives. It is the act of making things happen.

Controlling: The process by which managers determine whether organizational objectives are being achieved and whether actual operations are consistent with plans.

Figure 1-1 is a model of the managerial process that is based on these four functions. It is important to note that these functional activities must be performed within a general framework for management. This framework can be subdivided into four separate categories:

1. Historical framework
2. Organizational framework
3. Environmental framework
4. Technological framework

The various components of the managerial framework are discussed in detail in Chapter 2.

Applying the Functions of Management

While Figure 1-1 provides an overview of the managerial process, it is important to see how these functions operate in actual practice. In this section we discuss how four executives have each applied one of the functions to a real-world situation. It is especially worth noting that while the illustrations cited here are of top management, the functions of planning, organizing, leading, and controlling are performed by all levels of management—from a first-line supervisor to the company president.

Planning is the process of setting objectives for the future and developing courses of action to accomplish them.

PLANNING: JOSEPH S. GAZIANO

Joseph S. Gaziano has planned for a number of years to turn Tyco Laboratories, Inc., the New Hampshire-based company he heads, into a billion-dollar corporation. His plan is twofold: first, to build his company through acquisitions; and second, to increase the growth of Tyco's existing businesses in electronics and electrical equipment, fire protection systems, and flexible materials used mainly in packaging. Gaziano has made rapid headway toward his goal. His acquisitions have helped increase Tyco's annual revenues from $44 million in 1974 to over $600 million. In addition, Gaziano's high-yield investments in other companies have paid off at a handsome profit, sometimes providing cash for other acquisitions and at other times leading to the addition of the company

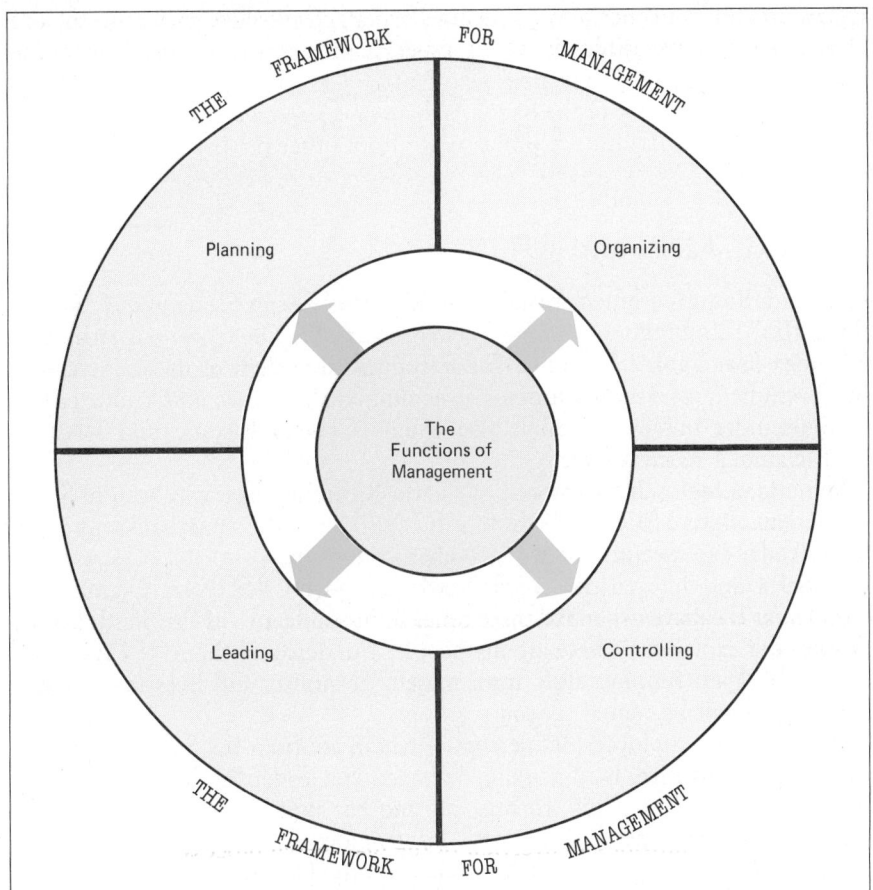

Figure 1-1
A MODEL OF THE
MANAGERIAL
PROCESS

itself to Tyco's rapidly expanding base. Gaziano's dream of building a billion-dollar enterprise now appears to be within his grasp.[3]

ORGANIZING: J. ROBERT FLUOR

J. Robert Fluor's firm—Fluor Corp.—is a leading process engineering and construction outfit with annual sales of more than $3 billion. The company also has major natural resource holdings worldwide. Fluor takes on huge projects like the $5 billion Saudi Arabian gas-conservation project to convert wellhead gases burned off as wastes into fuel. In developing his company, Fluor had to make major changes in the organizational structure of process construction. Realizing that organizational size, advanced technology, and the far-flung nature of big construction projects made the horizontal structure of his company inefficient, Fluor reorganized his personnel by projects. Now each job has its own set of de-

Organizing is the process of arranging people and physical resources to carry out plans and accomplish organizational objectives.

[3] See Aimee L. Mornier, "The Man Who Would Be Geneen," *Fortune* (March 12, 1979), pp. 108–110. The 1982 update was provided by Tyco Laboratories.

signers, procurement specialists, personnel experts, controllers, and so forth, and job captains are responsible for getting a specific project through each step in the process and out to field personnel who handle the actual construction. In the case of a project the size of the Saudi Arabian one, several teams are used. Fluor labels his efforts to keep each job separate from other projects "our basic religion."[4]

LEADING: JOHN MARIOTTA

Leading is the act of motivating or causing people to perform certain tasks intended to achieve specific objectives. It is the act of making things happen.

John Mariotta runs a much smaller firm than does Joseph Gaziano or J. Robert Fluor. His $12 million operation—Welbilt Electronic Die Corp.—is located in the Bronx near Yankee Stadium. The firm does 80 percent of its business with the government, making such items as cooling kits for tanks and stabilizer fins for Sidewinder missiles. Welbilt also counts General Electric and Western Electric among its customers.

Mariotta, a high school dropout of Puerto Rican heritage, was born in Spanish Harlem. Before Welbilt became a success, Mariotta went bankrupt three times. Today his executive style personifies leadership.

Mariotta and his partner, Fred Newburger—who fled Nazi Germany in World War II—have expanded three times in the same area of the South Bronx. As Mariotta explains, "These are my people. I understand them. If I run from my people, I am running away from myself." Mariotta still lives in the same Bronx apartment he rented sixteen years ago.

Welbilt's 250 employees, 90 percent of whom are from the South Bronx, see Mariotta as a sensitive, hard-working manager. His leadership has inspired considerable loyalty among his workers; no one has quit Welbilt for two years. Mariotta keeps in close contact with his employees. He even loans workers money to cover emergencies, medical bills, and the like. Raises and promotions are frequent. Productivity bonuses have been used in the past. And employees know they can go to the chief about job-related problems. John Mariotta may have dropped out of high school, but he knows a lot about leading and motivating people.[5]

CONTROLLING: HARRY PHILLIPS

Controlling is the process by which managers determine whether organizational objectives are achieved and whether actual operations are consistent with plans.

Harry Phillips probably knows as much about trash collection as anyone. Phillips is chairman of Browning-Ferris Industries, a $661 million trash hauler that serves 260,000 customers. Browning-Ferris handles anything from garbage to chemical wastes. Its customers are worldwide. For example, Browning-Ferris is now hauling trash in Riyadh, Saudi Arabia. The company is also involved in building a garbage-to-energy plant outside of New York.

---

[4] Walter McQuade, "Bob Fluor, Global Superbuilder," *Fortune* (February 26, 1979), pp. 54–61. The 1982 update was provided by Fluor Corp. Another interesting discussion of Fluor appears in Nick Gallucio, "The Growth Engineer," *Forbes* (March 30, 1982), pp. 62–63.

[5] Cheryl Morrison, "It's People That Count," *Inc.* (December 1982), pp. 84–88.

Browning-Ferris is a very profitable firm with an operating margin in excess of 35 percent. Much of its success should be credited to Harry Phillips' efforts to control costs. Phillips explains:

> Your costs in this business are associated with time. If it costs $9.42 per hour to operate a garbage truck, and if you have enough market share to make a stop every 7 minutes instead of 15, then your cost per stop drops from $10.50 to $4.90.

As a result, Browning-Ferris drivers are paid according to the number of stops they make, rather than by the hour. Phillips also closely monitors parts and fuel costs. Engines and gear ratios are selected according to the terrain and type of driving that characterizes each market. Sales personnel are expected to sign up to 80 to 100 net new clients annually. Drivers are given extensive safety training in order to control insurance costs, which average 3 percent of revenues. Harry Phillips clearly recognizes the importance of control even in the garbage business.[6]

Management Concepts Have Universal Application

Donald Regan, Robert McNamara, Roy Ash, and countless other top managers have illustrated how basic management concepts have universal application to problem-solving situations.[7] All of these people were top corporate executives leading major firms like Merrill Lynch, Ford, and Litton before accepting such important government positions as secretary of the treasury, secretary of defense, and head of the Office of Management and Budget.

George Shultz provides an excellent illustration of this transferability. Shultz has been a top manager in three different environments. He was dean of the University of Chicago's business school, secretary of the treasury, and then president of the Bechtel Group, a major construction company. But he gave up his $500,000 a year post at Bechtel to become secretary of state in 1982, a job that pays about one-seventh as much![8]

Although the problems and organizational constraints vary widely between private enterprises and nonprofit organizations and between small firms and industrial giants, the functions performed by managers are nearly the same. All managers operate in organizations with specific objectives. They must plan, organize, lead, and control so that these organizational objectives are met. The functions of planning, organizing, leading, and controlling are similar regardless of the ownership or type of organization that is involved. The universality of management is a well-known concept in both the private and public sectors.

[6] Toni Mack, "Browning-Ferris Cleaning Up," *Forbes* (July 5, 1981), pp. 101–102.
[7] A questioning viewpoint is expressed in Myron D. Fottler, "Is Management Really Generic?" *Academy of Management Review* (January 1981), pp. 1–12.
[8] See Michael Kolbenschlag, "Bechtel's Biggest Job Constructing Its Own Future," *Forbes* (December 7, 1981), pp. 139, 142.

To Lillian Evelyn Gilbreth, life was a managerial challenge. Her home, her family, and the world of business and industry were the laboratories Gilbreth used to show that almost anything could be done quickly and efficiently if a systematic, organized approach were applied.

Known as the consummate home and industrial efficiency engineer, Lillian Gilbreth graduated from the University of California in 1900 with a degree in psychology and the intention of becoming a dean of women. Instead, she married industrial engineer Frank Bunker Gilbreth, who shared her interest in time-efficiency management, and embarked on the road to creating the "one best marriage."

Working as a team, the Gilbreths pioneered the study of time-saving techniques for both the home and industry. Their rambling Montclair, New Jersey, house was a model of precision and efficiency. Assembly calls, family council budget meetings, and a system that awarded household jobs on a contractual basis to the lowest bidder were all part of the family routine for the Gilbreths and their twelve children, two of whom described the Gilbreth family life in *Cheaper by the Dozen*. Charts and follow-up systems determined the flow of work, and work centers and work surfaces turned the house into a kind of well-oiled family factory. What could have been a chaotic child-rearing situation became a model of what Lillian Gilbreth could accomplish if she put her mind to it.

Using many of the same techniques that proved successful in their home, the Gilbreths applied their motion studies to factory routines and to the design of model nurseries and kitchens. After Frank's death in 1925, Lillian continued their work. She took over control of Gilbreth, Inc., consulting engineers in management, where she concentrated on what she knew best: improving the efficiency of

Environmental circumstances change from one managerial situation to another. Government organizations, for example, require an executive to adjust to a different set of environmental parameters than would be common in business.[9] Management styles have to adjust to the particular factors confronting the decision maker. This adaptive approach is referred to elsewhere in this text as *contingency management.*

Consider the following remarks about the similarities and differences between management in the private and public sectors.

> One very important thing you have to learn in Washington is the difference between appearance and reality. At Bendix, it was the reality of the situation that in the end determined whether we succeeded or not. In the crudest sense, this meant the bottom line. You can dress up profits only for so long—if you're not successful, it's going to be clear. In government there is no bottom line, and that is why you

[9] Management problems faced by executives entering government service are discussed in "For Businessmen in the Bureaucracy, Life Is No Bed of Roses," *U.S. News & World Report* (September 25, 1978), pp. 56–58.

the American home. She conducted detailed analyses of how American home-makers could make kitchens more efficient. At a National Organization of Better Homes in America meeting, for example, she interrupted the work of 4,000 busy women to measure the distance from their elbows to the floor, obtaining figures she needed to calculate the optimum height for stoves and sinks.

Lillian Gilbreth's mission to streamline the operation of the home and factory could not have been accomplished without a keen sense of effective planning, organization, leadership, and control. Her commitment to creating a truly effective managerial system pervaded her entire life—surmounting even the grief she felt after her husband's death. Two days after Frank Gilbreth's funeral, Lillian boarded an ocean liner bound for Europe. There she took Frank's place at a convention, delivered his speeches, and attended committee meetings. She explained her ability to overcome her grief in this way: "I am only adhering to my husband's principles—the elimination of waste motion." *

Lillian Gilbreth, who received her Ph.D. from Brown University, taught management science and industrial engineering at Purdue University and Bryn Mawr College. Her life-long contributions to the sciences of industrial engineering and psychology were recognized by the American Management Association, the Society for the Advancement of Management, and the Society of Industrial Engineers, all of which made her an honorary member.

Lillian Gilbreth died in 1972, but her contributions to taking the waste out of human labor are still a vital aspect of modern management science.

* *Current Biography* (1940), p. 336.

Sources

"Dr. Lillian Gilbreth," *Fortune* (September 1935), p. 82.

Current Biography (1949), S.V., "Gilbreth, Frank Bunker (Jr.), and Carey, Ernestine (Moller) Gilbreth," pp. 224–226.

Current Biography (1940), S.V., "Gilbreth, Lillian Evelyn," pp. 336–337.

can be successful if you appear to be successful—though, of course, appearance is not the only ingredient of success.
W. MICHAEL BLUMENTHAL[10]

(Blumenthal now heads Burroughs Corp. He served as secretary of the treasury after being Bendix's board chairman.)

Many of the similarities stem from size, and there are certain things unique to big organizations. They require a variety of competencies, along with intricate planning and budgeting. However, planning in a business is more analytical and thoughtful than in government. You are in a less reactive mode.
DONALD RUMSFELD[11]

(Rumsfeld is now chief executive at G. D. Searle & Company. He was previously a member of Congress, secretary of defense, and White House chief of staff.)

[10] "Candid Reflections of a Businessman in Washington," *Fortune* (January 29, 1979), p. 36.
[11] Donald Rumsfeld, "A Politician-Turned-Executive Surveys Both Worlds," *Fortune* (September 10, 1979), p. 91.

Managing a Nonprofit Organization

Nonprofit organizations provide an excellent illustration of the concept of the universality of management.[12] Effectively managed nonprofit organizations accomplish their goals, while poorly managed ones do not. Good management is a key ingredient in the success of any organization—profit or nonprofit.

The not-for-profit sector of our society is exceedingly diverse. Nonprofit organizations include hospitals, government agencies, unions, art and cultural institutions, colleges and universities, and cooperatives, among others.[13] The following features often characterize nonprofit organizations and constrain the managerial approaches and techniques that are employed:

1. *Service is intangible* and hard to measure. This difficulty is often compounded by the existence of multiple service objectives.
2. *Customer influence* may be weak. Often, the enterprise has a local monopoly, and payments by customers may be a secondary source of funds.
3. *Strong employee commitment* to professions or to a cause may undermine their allegiance to the enterprise.
4. *Resource contributors* may intrude into internal management—notably fund contributors and government.
5. *Restraints* on the use of rewards and punishments result from 1, 3, and 4 above.
6. *Charismatic leaders* and/or the "mystique" of the enterprise may be important means of resolving conflict in objectives and overcoming restraints.[14]

Considering a few examples, the second characteristic in this list—"Customer influence may be weak"—might be illustrated by a public health agency. The customer, or patient, may pay only a minor portion of the cost of treatment. In fact, the nonprofit organization, the health agency, may be more attuned to satisfying the government officials who provide the bulk of the funding. Characteristic 6—"Charismatic leaders"—might be demonstrated by the immense importance of Ralph Nader to the consumerism movement. While consumerism may be considered a broad social movement consisting of numerous nonprofit organizations, Nader's key role is seldom questioned.

The unique characteristics of nonprofit organizations create obstacles to effective operation. Two primary problems in such operations are:

---

[12] Managing nonprofit organizations is discussed in articles such as David W. Young, " 'Nonprofits' Need Surplus Too," *Harvard Business Review* (January–February 1982), pp. 124–131; Thomas J. C. Raymond and Stephen A. Greyser, "The Business of Managing the Arts," *Harvard Business Review* (July–August 1978), pp. 123–132; Frederick J. Turk, "Some Management Tips for Arts Organizations," *World* (Summer 1978), pp. 30–33; and Thomas E. Copeland and Keith V. Smith, "An Overview of Nonprofit Organizations," *Journal of Economics and Business* (Winter 1978), pp. 147–154.

[13] The diversity of the not-for-profit sector is noted in William H. Newman and Harvey W. Wallender III, "Managing Not-for-Profit Enterprises," *Academy of Management Review* (January 1978), pp. 25–26.

[14] Reprinted by permission from *ibid.*, p. 26.

1. Lack of direct-line responsibility
2. Lack of a *bottom line,* industry jargon for a measurement of performance such as profitability[15]

Bottom line reflects
company profitability on
the income statement.

Nonprofits typically do not possess a direct line of responsibility similar to the owner–board of directors–management hierarchy that characterizes profit-oriented institutions. A nonprofit (with the exception of government agencies, where the taxpayer might loosely be given this designation) has no true owners. Management levels are also often confused. In some not-for-profit enterprises there can be three separate management hierarchies—administrative, professional (such as doctors or curators), and voluntary. All impact on the overall management of the organization.

Nonprofits also suffer from a lack of a clearly identified bottom line. The output of the entity's activities goes to its customers, rather than providing benefits to the organization itself. A related issue concerns the nonprofit's lack of some work incentives such as bonuses and stock option plans. Thus, a sense of personal satisfaction and accomplishment becomes an important motivator in the not-for-profit sector.

The Managerial Hierarchy

Management acts as a catalyst for getting things done within an organization. In some cases, these organizational objectives can be accomplished through a simple management–subordinate hierarchy. In many small businesses, the owner–manager is the only member of the management team. But as the organization becomes larger and more complex, a more sophisticated structure is required.

Figure 1-2 illustrates the three basic levels of management:

1. Top management
2. Middle management
3. Supervisory management

Many people describe this hierarchy as a pyramid since there are relatively fewer positions as one progresses to higher levels of management. Similar hierarchies exist in both profit and nonprofit organizations.

Top management is usually appointed, elected, or designated by the organization's *stakeholders*—those to whom the organization is dedicated to serving—or their representatives. The president of the United States is elected by the general public, or the nation's stakeholders. The president of General Foods is selected by the firm's board of directors, representing the stockholders. The president of a college or university is appointed by the institution's board of trustees, regents, or governors. Top management is concerned with overall management policy and strategy, and ultimately it is responsible for all decisions made within the managerial hierarchy.

Stakeholders are the
persons whom the
organization is
dedicated to serve.

[15] The remainder of this section is based on Cecily Cannon Selby, "Better Performance for Nonprofits," *Harvard Business Review* (September–October 1978), pp. 93–95.

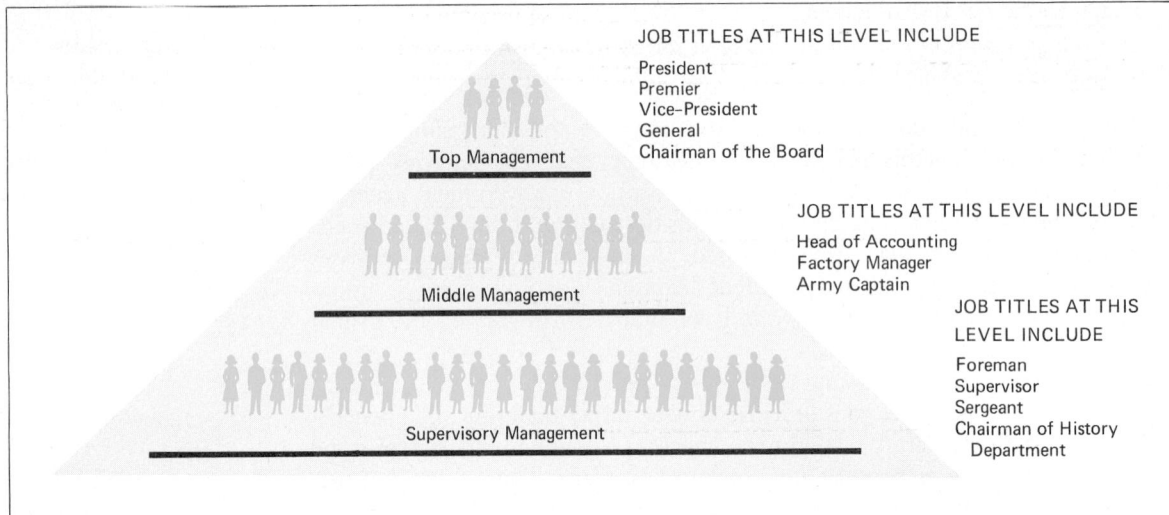

JOB TITLES AT THIS LEVEL INCLUDE
President
Premier
Vice-President
General
Chairman of the Board

Top Management

JOB TITLES AT THIS LEVEL INCLUDE
Head of Accounting
Factory Manager
Army Captain

Middle Management

JOB TITLES AT THIS
LEVEL INCLUDE
Foreman
Supervisor
Sergeant
Chairman of History
    Department

Supervisory Management

**Figure 1-2
THE MANAGEMENT
HIERARCHY**

Middle management deals with the actual administration and operation of the organization's activities. As Figure 1-2 suggests, the head of the accounting function and an army captain are examples of middle management. These people possess considerable responsibility and authority in the performance of their assigned missions. But they look to top management for direction and guidance and are responsible to these higher ranking executives.

Supervisory management includes the managers who have ongoing, direct contact with subordinates. Typically, a supervisor is the leader of some type of work group, such as a college's history department or the paint shop in a factory. These managers are often involved in the actual tasks carried out by the unit. For instance, a district sales manager will often call on key accounts with his or her local representatives.

The management hierarchy provides an overall framework for the accomplishment of objectives. Chapter 9 describes the organizational function in detail, noting how management uses the hierarchical structure to reach its goals.

Managers—A Capsule Profile

Heidrich and Struggles, a management consulting firm, reports that managers are a hard-working occupational group. Those at the top of the nation's largest corporations work long hours. Nearly 62 percent of the chief executive officers of companies with earnings over $2 billion spend at least sixty hours a week at their jobs[16]—but the rewards are also high for those who succeed. In 1980 the typical chief executive officer earned $285,000 in salary and bonus, had stock options, a company car, club membership, and extra life insurance paid for by the company. The rewards of a management career are examined further in Chapter 23.

[16] Heidrich and Struggles, Inc., *Profile of a Chief Executive Officer,* © copyright 1980 by Heidrich and Struggles, Inc.

What are the basic characteristics of those who go on to become managerial successes? What are their family backgrounds? Where were they born? How did they get to the top? How old are they? What is their employment history?

A PROFILE OF THE CHIEF EXECUTIVE

A recent study by the authors and C. Patrick Fleenor provides a comprehensive profile of a modern chief executive's background.[17] The study, based on *Forbes* data about 798 top managers, revealed that most chief executives were born in the Midwestern and Northeastern states (see Figure 1-3). New York headed the list with 109 chief executives. It was followed by Illinois (50), Pennsylvania (49), Texas (48), and Ohio (44). Fifteen or more chief executives were born in the following states: California, Indiana, Iowa, Massachusetts, Michigan, Minnesota, New Jersey, and Oklahoma. It is also interesting to note that 35 of the top executives were foreign-born.

The typical chief executive is a mature person who has extensive experience

[17] This section is from C. Patrick Fleenor, David L. Kurtz, and Louis E. Boone, "The Changing Profile of Business Leadership," *Business Horizons* (July 1983). The *Forbes* data is from "Who Gets the Most Pay?" *Forbes* (June 7, 1982), pp. 74–78, 82–86, 88, 90, 94–97, 99–100.

Figure 1-3
DISTRIBUTION OF U.S.-BORN CEOs AMONG THE VARIOUS STATES

SOURCE: Reprinted from C. Patrick Fleenor, David L. Kurtz, and Louis E. Boone, "The Changing Profile of Business Leadership," *Business Horizons* (July 1983). Based on data in "Who Gets the Most Pay?" *Forbes* (June 7, 1982), pp. 74–78ff.

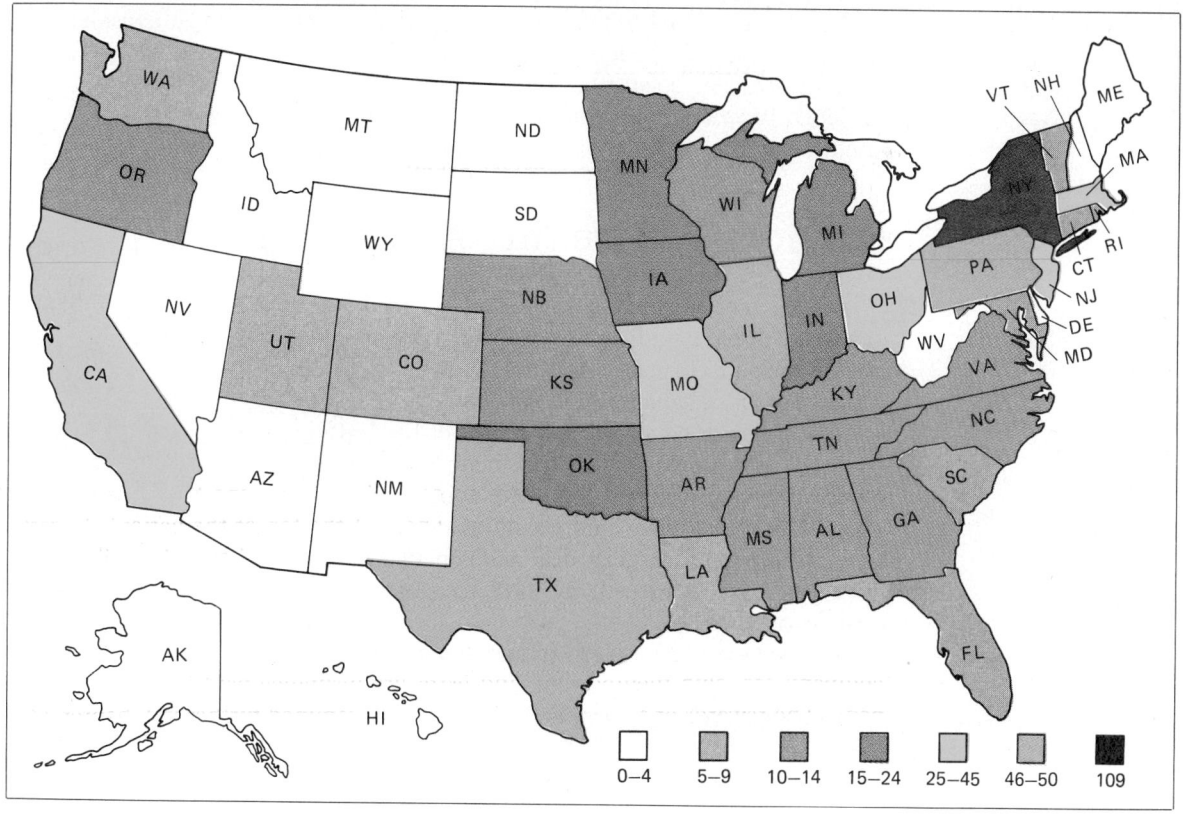

Figure 1-4
THE FUNCTIONAL
BACKGROUNDS OF
CHIEF EXECUTIVES

SOURCE: Reprinted from C.
Patrick Fleenor, David L.
Kurtz, and Louis E. Boone,
"The Changing Profile of
Business   Leadership,"
Business Horizons (July
1983). Based on data in
"Who Gets the Most Pay?"
Forbes (June 7, 1982), pp.
74–78ff.

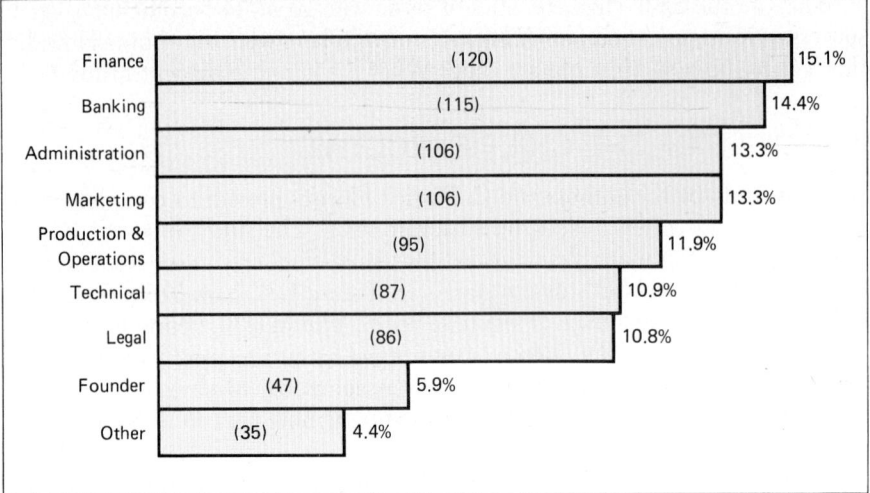

with the company. While ages ranged from thirty-seven to eighty-four, only three of the chief executives were under forty. Over 84 percent were between fifty and sixty-nine. The route to the top took between 5.9 and 20.2 years.

Data on functional backgrounds were also analyzed. Although considerable diversity was found, the most common background was finance. Banking was in second place. The diversity of backgrounds shown in Figure 1-4 suggests that a particular functional background is not an essential requirement for those who reach the apex of their company's hierarchy.

Management: An Art? A Science?

The question of whether management is an art or a science or both is a common one in the discipline's literature. A basic understanding of this issue is crucial to the discussion of management that follows.

Science is a systematic study that leads to a general body of knowledge about a subject. The discussion in Chapter 2 of the historical framework of management clearly indicates that management has been the target of systematic study for centuries and that general principles or concepts have been derived from this effort. Most observers would classify management as a developing science. Society already knows a great deal about management science, but considerably more needs to be learned. By most recognized standards, then, management qualifies as a science.[18]

Management is also an art. In fact, one source has even defined management

---

[18] The conclusion that management should be classified as a science is supported by papers such as Ronald F. Gribbins and Shelby D. Hunt, "Is Management a Science?" *Academy of Management Review* (January 1978), pp. 139–144.

as the "art of making decisions with insufficient information."[19] The artistic process is generally seen as having three vital aspects: craft, vision, and communication.[20] The process of management qualifies as an art form in all instances. Managers must have the tools (craft) to accomplish their tasks. They must possess vision in order to implement innovative strategies, and they must be able to communicate effectively in the work environment and elsewhere. AT&T's director of corporate planning, Henry M. Boettinger, puts it this way: "To manage is to lead, and to lead others requires that one enlist the emotions of others to share a vision as their own. If that is not an art, then nothing is."

A balanced perspective suggests that management is both an art and a science. The management process follows the general scenario for the artistic process. But its craft or tool aspects are clearly based on a scientific body of knowledge that has been accumulated over time. It seems likely that the discipline of management will always maintain both scientific and artistic components.

Approaches to Management Theory

A number of schools or approaches to management thought have developed over the years as scholars and practitioners have attempted to develop explanations and generalizations concerning organizational and managerial activities. Over time, so many different approaches developed with their own unique emphases that one writer characterized them as a management theory "jungle."[21] The various approaches include the following:

1. The *Empirical, or Case, Approach*—based on the practical experience of managers of various enterprises, but with more emphasis on distilling fundamentals from case experience.
2. The *Interpersonal Behavior Approach*—the study of management centered on interpersonal relations and heavily oriented toward individual psychology.
3. The *Group Behavior Approach*—closely related to the interpersonal behavior approach, but concerned primarily with behavior of people in groups. It varies all the way from the study of small groups to characteristics of large groups. It is often called *organization behavior.*
4. The *Cooperative Social System Approach*—focuses on the study of man-

---

[19] Roy Rowan, "Those Business Hunches Are More Than Blind Faith," *Fortune* (April 23, 1979), p. 111.

[20] The discussion of management and the artistic process is based on Henry O. Boettinger, "Is Management Really an Art?" *Harvard Business Review* (January–February, 1975), pp. 54–64. The concluding quote is from p. 64.

[21] See Harold Koontz, "The Management Theory Jungle," *Journal of the Academy of Management* (December 1961), pp. 174–188. Koontz expressed similar views in "Making Sense of Management Theory," *Harvard Business Review* (July–August 1962), pp. 24–26, 31–32, 34, 36, 38, 40, 42, 46. See also Harold Koontz, "The Management Theory Jungle Revisited," *Academy of Management Review* (April 1980), pp. 175–187.

agement as one of human relationships in cooperative social systems. Its emphasis is on system.

5. The *Sociotechnical Systems Approach*—the study of management as a combination of social systems and technical systems (machines and methods), particularly with an emphasis on how the technical system influences the social system.

6. The *Decision Theory Approach*—this approach expresses the belief that, since managers make decisions, the study of management must be a study of decision making.

7. The *Systems Approach*—having seen scientists and practitioners utilize systems thinking and analyses in other fields, an increasing number of scholars and writers in management have attempted to employ the systems approach in this field.

8. The *Mathematics*, or *"Management Science," Approach*—attempts to reduce management theory to the solution of a mathematical model deemed appropriate for a particular situation. But it has become increasingly apparent that the use of mathematical techniques represents a tool and is no more management than it is physics, biology, or geology.

9. The *Contingency*, or *Situational, Approach*—this approach has tended to take academicians by storm in recent years. Actually, it is not a new approach to management thinking. Essentially, this approach emphasizes the fact that what managers do in practice depends upon a given set of circumstances, or the "situation." All this is, of course, nothing more than a realization—long held by practitioners in all fields from mechanics to baseball—that practice demands the application of knowledge (science) to realities.

10. The *Management Roles Approach*—sparked by the research and writing of Professor Henry Mintzberg, this approach is to observe what managers actually do and study management as a number of roles (for example, interpersonal, informational, and decisional) that managers act in practice.

11. The *Operational Approach*—this approach was developed from the idea of management process and attempts to draw together the pertinent knowledge of management by classifying it according to the function of managers. Like other operational sciences, it endeavors to put together for the field of management the concepts, principles, theory, and techniques that underpin the actual practice of managing. The operational approach includes a central core of science and theory unique to managing plus knowledge eclectically drawn from various other schools and approaches. This approach is interested only in that knowledge in the various fields that is pertinent to management.[22]

These approaches clearly show the diversity of viewpoints about management theory. The disentanglement of the management theory jungle is an important

[22] Adapted by permission from Harold Koontz, "Retrospective Comment," in Louis E. Boone and Donald D. Bowen (eds.), *The Great Writings in Management and Organizational Behavior* (Tulsa, Okla.: PennWell Books, 1980), pp. 272–273.

need. Organizational mistakes are costly, and management needs a clear vision of how it should proceed. Elements of these approaches are evident throughout *Principles of Management*, but the overriding emphasis in this text is on providing students with a balanced perspective of the field of management.

Summary

Management is a difficult term to define because it has a variety of applications and interpretations. In this text we define it as the use of people and other resources to accomplish objectives. The managerial process consists of four functions: planning, organizing, leading, and controlling. Chapter 1 develops a model (Figure 1-1) illustrating how these functions are performed within a general framework for management.

Management concepts have a universal application to all problem-solving situations. The concepts of effective management are as appropriate to the Red Cross, a church, or a public agency as they are to a major corporation. Nonprofit organizations have characteristics different from those of the profit-oriented sector, but the management concepts are similar.

There are three basic levels of management:

1. Top management
2. Middle management
3. Supervisory management

This hierarchy is often described as a pyramid since there are relatively fewer slots at each higher level. These levels of management are common to both profit-oriented and not-for-profit enterprises.

Chapter 1 also presents a capsule profile of top management. The general conclusions are that this group is most likely from the Midwest or Northeast, possesses a variety of functional backgrounds, and is relatively mature.

The management literature often discusses whether management is an art or a science. A balanced view of this argument implies that management has both artistic and scientific components.

Chapter 1 concludes with a discussion of the various approaches to management theory. An analysis by a leading management writer suggests that these approaches have become more numerous during the past two decades.

REVIEW EXERCISES

1. Define the following terms: (a) management (b) planning (c) organizing (d) leading (e) controlling (f) bottom line (g) stakeholders.

2. Why is management a difficult concept to define?

3. Explain the model of the managerial process presented in Figure 1-1.

4. Does management have universal application? Discuss.

5. How is the management of a nonprofit organization both similar to and different from the management of a profit-oriented organization?

6. Outline the basic levels of management.

7. Develop a capsule profile of top management.

8. Is management an art or a science?

9. Discuss the various approaches to management theory.

10. How does the diversity of managerial approaches affect business?

ASSIGNMENTS/PROBLEMS/ DISCUSSION QUESTIONS

1. "In terms of functional aspects, I didn't find all that much difference between heading a large corporation and the Federal Reserve Board. That surprises my friends in business. Coming here, I feel, was a very easy transition. Here, we deal in defining issues through objectives, and priorities, mobilizing information, convincing ourselves, including whoever is chairman, of the correct decision and dealing with such outside constituencies as Congress, the banks and the public. A corporation is much the same. There objectives have to be in terms of bringing a product to production or to market or acquiring a company or spinning off a company. And then you have to convince your organization to implement it because you can't just order them to do it. If they don't believe in it, they'll make it hard." *

G. WILLIAM MILLER

(Miller, now an international financial consultant, once headed the Federal Reserve Board. He later became secretary of the treasury. Miller was also formerly chief executive officer of Textron.)

Comment on the viewpoint expressed by Miller.

* Miller is quoted in Gary F. Schuster, "Decision Number Six," *Detroit News Magazine* (March 11, 1979), p. 46.

2. Consult three other texts in your library and develop a list of definitions of management. What do these definitions have in common? How are they different?

3. Select one of the following not-for-profit organizations and prepare a brief report on the management of the organization:

    a. Your college or university
    b. The Girl Scouts or Boy Scouts
    c. A local hospital
    d. The local police department
    e. A public school system
    f. The United Way

4. Request permission to observe the daily routine of a manager of a local firm. Record what he or she does during the day. How would you categorize the various tasks performed by the manager?

5. Write a brief essay on your conceptualization of management. File the essay until the completion of the course you are now taking. Then make an analysis of whether, and how, your views have changed.

A MANAGERIAL INCIDENT

The Prekhanov Institute of the National Economy

The Prekhanov Institute of the National Economy is a business school with an extensive program for educating practicing managers. The school is part of the Soviet Union's attempt to introduce modern management practices to its ineffective industrial sector.

Many of the courses at Prekhanov Institute would be familiar to business students in North America. The school offers classes in organizational design, management psychology, information processing, and decision making. Lectures are the usual teaching method, but cases and business games are also used.

Management science has always been popular with Soviet leaders. In fact, Lenin believed that Frederick Winslow Taylor's work would shortly allow Russia to surpass the Western nations in productivity. Systems theory, which tries to integrate the various aspects of the organization, is well received today. By contrast, the students at Prekhanov Institute—most of whom have technical or engineering backgrounds—seem most interested in management psychology.

The management education received by these executives, all members of middle or top management, is often in conflict with Marxist philosophy. For example, Marx believed that class motivated individual behavior. But today's Soviet business student is also taught about informal group behavior, and Soviet academics debate whether a theory of personal leadership is acceptable to a Communist state.

So far, the results of Soviet management education are mixed. While techniques are learned easily, it does not appear that management practice has changed significantly. Apparently, management science will not be the panacea that Lenin had hoped.

SOURCE: Mark R. Bessinger, "Soviet Factory Directors Go to Business School," *The Wall Street Journal* (November 2, 1981), p. 26.

Questions and Problems

1. Relate the above discussion to the material presented in Chapter 1.

2. Why has management education had such a minimal impact on management practice in the Soviet Union?

2. The Framework for Management

Business will be better or worse.
                    CALVIN COOLIDGE

Once you get into this great stream of
history, you can't get out.
                    RICHARD NIXON

T he late Samuel Irving Newhouse started what is now the nation's biggest privately held media enterprise. The Newhouse chain includes

Twenty-eight newspapers—read by 3.2 million people—including the New Orleans *Times–Picayune,* Newark *Star-Ledger,* Cleveland *Plain Dealer,* and the St. Louis *Globe Democrat.*

Cable television units that make Newhouse the eighth largest such operation in the United States.

Eight magazines, including *Vogue, Glamour, Parade, Self,* and *House & Garden.*

Random House, the publisher of this textbook, which Newhouse acquired from RCA.

It is estimated that Newhouse enterprises generate a $100 million–$140 million profit on $1.5 billion of sales annually, a remarkable accomplishment for a privately held company that does not have a headquarters office. The Newhouse company is a family-run operation. In fact, twenty Newhouses work for the organization. Four senior Newhouses maintain their offices at different publications. They each visit a set group of operations and report their findings to other family members through memos. Professional managers at their diverse enterprises deal only with the Newhouse assigned to their operation.

The management framework of the Newhouse organization is characterized by a strong historical perspective. Samuel Irving Newhouse, the founder, prepared an outline entitled "A Memo to the Children of S. I. Newhouse" that described how he built the company. The first newspaper was bought with funds borrowed from family members, whom he later hired. The message was clear that "the ties that matter are the ties to each other."

**Figure 2-1
RELATION BETWEEN
MANAGERIAL
FUNCTIONS AND THE
FRAMEWORK FOR
MANAGEMENT**

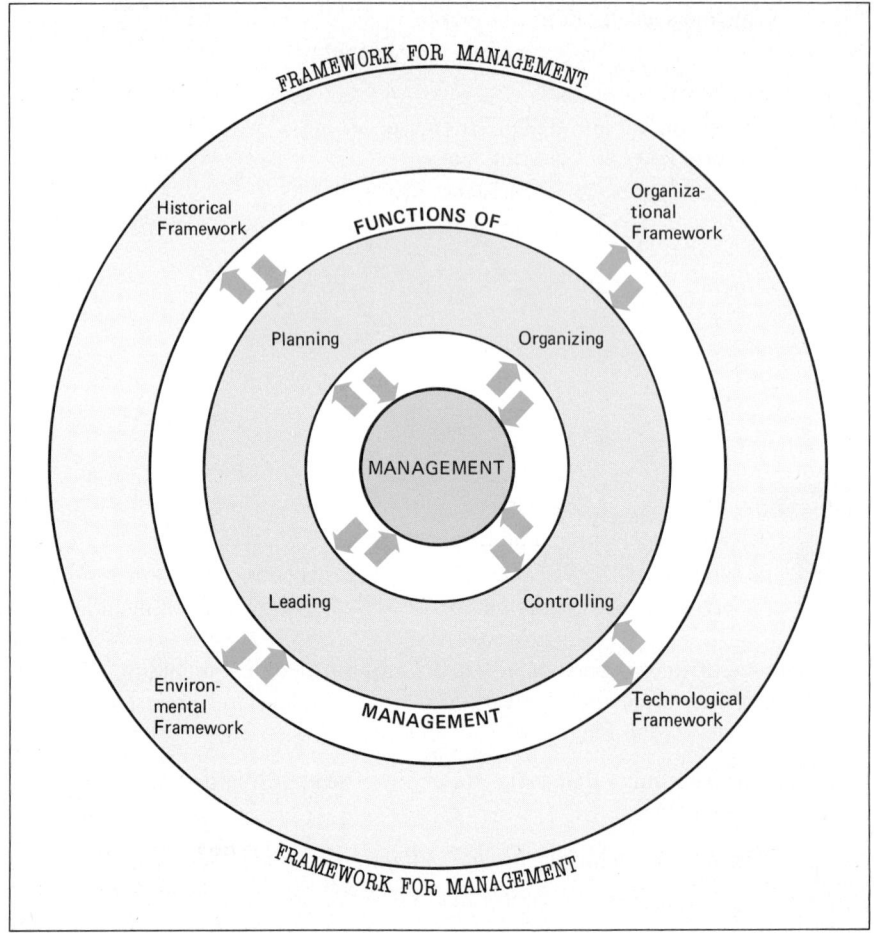

**Framework for
management** consists
of the historical,
organizational,
environmental, and
technological factors
that affect managerial
functions

The memo is an integral part of the managerial framework of Newhouse.[1] Other factors, too, make up this framework. Chapter 2 explains how such factors influence managerial decision making.

The essential managerial functions—planning, organizing, leading, and controlling—were identified in Chapter 1. Effective managers perform these functions in their pursuit of the goals that have been specified for their organizations. However, the performance of these functions is affected significantly by a number of partially or totally uncontrollable factors. These factors—historical, organizational, environmental, and technological—comprise what has been referred to as the *framework for management.* Figure 2-1 identifies the components of the framework for management and suggests their relation to the performance of managerial functions.

[1] Daniel Machalaba, "Newhouse Chain Stays with Founder's Ways, and with His Heirs," *The Wall Street Journal* (February 12, 1982), pp. 1, 22.

The Historical Framework for Management

Like most modern disciplines, contemporary management thought rests on a historical framework enriched by the many significant contributions of earlier theorists and practitioners. Many of these contributors—Henri Fayol, Chester I. Barnard, Elton Mayo, Douglas McGregor, A. P. Sloan, Jr., and Frederick W. Taylor—are featured in the profiles in each chapter of this textbook. Still others are discussed in the following section.

Management's historical framework has both theoretical and applied components. Important management contributions have come from both groups. The rich diversity of management's contributions was clearly illustrated by a plan to request that the U.S. Postal Service honor people who made outstanding contributions to business and management practice and thought by issuing a series of commemorative stamps. Nominations were sought from the Business History Conference, the History Division of the Academy of Management, and a random sample of other Academy of Management members. Each group's candidates reflected its own biases. The Business History group favored entrepreneurs and practicing managers; the Academy's History Division was oriented toward academicians from the scientific management school; and the Academy of Management sample also favored academicians, but with less bias toward the scientific management school. The composite of these surveys is shown in Table 2-1.

RANK	CONTRIBUTOR	NUMBER OF VOTES	POINTS	TOTAL POINTS	FIRST-PLACE VOTES
1	Taylor, Frederick W.	108	850	958	51
2	Barnard, Chester I.	81	516	597	9
3	Gilbreth, Frank	70	414	484	0
4	Mayo, Elton	61	368	429	3
5	Gilbreth, Lillian	61	348	409	2
6	Sloan, Alfred P., Jr.	55	313	368	3
7	Follett, Mary Parker	55	302	357	2
8	Ford, Henry	48	262	310	4
9	Maslow, Abraham	45	209	254	3
10	Gantt, Henry L.	40	211	251	2
11	Roethlisberger, Fritz	41	203	244	2
12	Wharton, Joseph	40	196	236	0
13	Lewin, Kurt	33	172	205	2
14	Edison, Thomas A.	27	171	198	6
15	Du Pont, Pierre	28	148	176	0
16	Carnegie, Andrew	32	143	175	2
17	Whitney, Eli	21	123	144	3
18	Rockefeller, John D.	23	114	137	1
19	Slater, Samuel	19	116	135	3
20	Watson, Thomas	18	102	120	2

Table 2-1 OUTSTANDING CONTRIBUTORS TO MANAGEMENT THOUGHT AND PRACTICE: A COMPOSITE RANKING

SOURCE: Daniel A. Wren and Robert D. Hay, "Management Historians and Business Historians: Differing Perceptions of Pioneer Contributors," *Academy of Management Journal* (September 1977), p. 476. Reprinted by permission.

Frederick Taylor headed the list for each survey as well as the composite rank-ing.[2]

EARLY CONTRIBUTORS

Most management students of the 1980s think of management as a business- or industry-related discipline. But historically, people were more concerned with the management of other organizations such as the state, church, military, tribe, or household. The very earliest examples of management come from nonbusi-ness entities.[3] These management techniques were later adapted to commercial applications.

The list below identifies some of the most important of the numerous ancient and medieval contributors.[4]

The Sumerians were concerned with record keeping in 5000 B.C.

By 4000 B.C., the Egyptians were aware of the importance of planning, or-ganizing, and controlling.

Staff advice existed in Egyptian management by 2000 B.C.

Socrates discussed the universality of management in 400 B.C.

Xenophon recognized management as a separate art in 400 B.C.

Plato described specialization in 350 B.C.

Alexander the Great used a staff organization extensively during his military campaigns from 336 to 323 B.C.

Alfarabi listed the traits of a leader in A.D. 900.

Ghazaei suggested the traits of a manager in A.D. 1100.

EARLY INDUSTRIAL ERA CONTRIBUTORS

The movement of manufacturing to a factory system (where products are pro-duced in a centralized location) from a craft-like cottage system (where produc-tion was contracted to a family living/work unit) had a significant impact on management history. This movement, which occurred in Europe (particularly the United Kingdom) in the mid-1700s, is usually called the *industrial revolu-tion*.

Management had to be adapted from its public administration applications to

Industrial revolution was the mid-eighteenth century movement of English manufacturing to a factory system (where products are produced in a centralized location) from a cottage system (where production was contracted to family living/work units).

---

[2] Daniel A. Wren and Robert D. Hay, "Management Historians and Business Historians: Differing Perceptions of Pioneer Contributors," *Academy of Management Journal* (September 1977), pp. 470–476.

[3] Daniel Wren, *The Evolution of Management Thought* (New York: Ronald Press, 1972), p. 14.

[4] Claude S. George, Jr., *The History of Management Thought* (Englewood Cliffs, N.J.: Prentice-Hall, 1968), pp. xiii–xiv, 20–21. Reprinted by permission of Prentice-Hall, Inc.

use within the developing factory systems.[5] The industrial revolution had launched an industrial era within which modern management concepts had to be developed.

Four major contributors can be identified in this era of management thought: Robert Owen, Charles Babbage, Andrew Ure, and Charles Duprin. All were forerunners of later developments in management. Owen's concern for human welfare preceded the behaviorist school; Babbage was a pioneer in scientific management, operations research, and management science; and Ure and Duprin were early advocates of management education.[6]

ROBERT OWEN—HUMAN RESOURCES MANAGEMENT PIONEER

A successful factory owner at eighteen years of age, Robert Owen (1771–1858) became an early advocate of improved management of human resources. He attempted to better the situation of the pauper children employed in his Scottish factory (a common practice of the era). He proposed legislative reform that would limit the hours and usage of child labor. Owen's proposals were viewed as radical at the time.

Owen used what he called the *silent monitor* to encourage productivity. Blocks of wood were painted in four different colors, with each color signifying a different level of accomplishment. The blocks were then attached to each machine in the factory. Employees were graded daily; and the appropriate color was turned so that all could see.

Owen urged other manufacturers to adopt his concern over improving the human resources they employed. He claimed that returns from investments in human resources would far exceed those in machinery and equipment.

Later, Owen suggested the establishment of "villages of cooperation" based on communal sharing of the output of their inhabitants. In 1824, he set up the first such village at New Harmony, Indiana. Still later, in 1834, Owen's socialist views were evident in his direction of the British trade union movement. While Owen's reforms failed, his concern for human welfare has to be considered a precedent for the behaviorist school.

CHARLES BABBAGE—INVENTOR AND MANAGEMENT SCIENTIST

Charles Babbage (1792–1871) was an early pioneer in areas that now are known as scientific management, operations research, and management science. In 1822, Babbage produced the first practical calculator, which he termed his *difference machine*. He also produced a rudimentary computer—termed the *analytical machine*—that included the various aspects of contemporary computer hardware. Babbage also developed gaming programs that were precedents of more modern quantitative methods.

Babbage published his views on management and manufacturing processes, including his belief that the division of labor was a necessary aspect of all devel-

---

[5] The problems involved in this adjustment are described in Wren, *The Evolution of Management Thought*, pp. 43–52.

[6] The discussion of Owen, Babbage, Ure, and Duprin is based on Wren, *The Evolution of Management Thought*, pp. 63–79.

oped economic systems. He also proposed observational procedures for studying manufacturing operations.

The inventor realized the importance of the human factor. He believed that management and employee interests were closely linked. Thus, Babbage advocated use of profit-sharing and employee suggestion plans.

ANDREW URE AND CHARLES DUPRIN—MANAGEMENT EDUCATION PIONEERS

Andrew Ure and Charles Duprin were early proponents of management education: Ure in the United Kingdom and Duprin in France. Ure, who taught in Glasgow, published a book outlining various principles and concepts of manufacturing. He was responsible for educating many of the managers of his day. Ure argued that the factory system produced numerous advantages for society, far offsetting its problems.

Duprin was a French engineer. He was impressed with Ure's work, which he came to know when visiting the United Kingdom from 1816 to 1818. Shortly thereafter, Duprin's appointment to a professorship in Paris commenced a long career. Duprin's writing and curriculum, well known throughout France, may have influenced Henri Fayol's subsequent contribution to management thought.

THE CLASSICAL SCHOOL

The classical school of management thought includes administrative theory[7] and scientific management concepts. The classical school includes those early contributors to an overall theory of management. The two major components of this school of thought are best represented by the work of Henri Fayol and Frederick W. Taylor.

Administrative Theory

Henri Fayol and Max Weber are cited here as pioneers in administrative theory. Many others could be mentioned. For example, Fayol is usually credited with the development of the functional or management process school. But R. C. Davis of Ohio State University probably did more to popularize this school than anyone else in the United States.

HENRI FAYOL—DEVELOPER OF MANAGEMENT'S FIRST GENERAL THEORY

Fayol (1841–1925), who is profiled in Chapter 5, was Europe's most distinguished management theorist and the first to develop a general theory of management.[8] He was born to a well-to-do French family in 1841 and was educated as an engineer. Fayol spent his entire career with a mining company, eventually becoming the managing director of the enterprise.

Fayol was a practitioner whose ideas and theoretical contributions evolved from his own experiences in industry. His major contribution to management

---

[7] Wren's terminology—*administrative theory*—has been adopted to describe the contributions of Fayol and Weber.

[8] Except as otherwise noted, the section on Fayol follows George, *The History of Management Thought*, pp. 105–111.

thought was not published until he was seventy-five.[9] Even then his work was little noted outside of France until it was translated and published in the United States years later.

The basis of Fayol's theory was that industrial undertakings consisted of six separate activities: (1) technical (production, manufacture, adaptation); (2) commercial (buying, selling, exchange); (3) financial (search for and optimal use of capital); (4) security (protection of property and persons); (5) accounting (stocktaking, balance sheets, costs, statistics); and (6) managerial (planning, organizing, command, coordination, control).

Fayol concentrated on the last of these activities, the managerial activities. He went on to create the first general theory of management with his identification of fourteen basic principles of management:

1. *Division of work* (specialization belongs to the natural order)
2. *Authority and responsibility* (responsibility is a corollary to authority)
3. *Discipline* (discipline is what leaders make it)
4. *Unity of command* (people cannot bear dual command)
5. *Unity of direction* (one head and one plan for a group of activities having the same objectives)
6. *Subordination of individual interest* to the general interest
7. *Remuneration* (fair, reasonable rewarding of effort)
8. *Centralization* (centralization belongs to the natural order)
9. *Scalar chain* (line of authority, gang-plank principle)
10. *Order* (a place for everyone and everyone in his place)
11. *Equity* (results from combination of kindliness and justice)
12. *Stability of tenure of personnel* (prosperous firms are stable)
13. *Initiative* (great source of strength for business)
14. *Esprit de corps* (union is strength)[10]

In addition to the development of a comprehensive management theory, Fayol is credited with enunciating the universality of management concept discussed in Chapter 1. He also advocated teaching management in school and college and believed that his own theory could serve as an instructional model in such an effort.

MAX WEBER—FOCUSING ON AUTHORITY

Max Weber (1864–1920) was a German contemporary of Fayol who was concerned with the study of organizational sociology. As a result of his conceptual work in this area, Weber is considered part of the classical school of management. His wide-ranging contributions, however, make it difficult to limit him to any given discipline.[11]

[9] Noted in Wren, *The Evolution of Management Thought*, p. 212.

[10] Henri Fayol, *General and Industrial Management* (London: Pitman, 1949), pp. 19–20. Quoted in George, *The History of Management Thought*, p. 109. Reprinted by permission of Pitman Publishing Limited.

[11] See Kenneth McNeil, "Understanding of Organizational Powers: Building on the Weberian Legacy," *Administrative Science Quarterly* (March 1978), p. 65; and Wren, *The Evolution of Management Thought*, p. 229.

Weber believed that there were three types of authority: *charismatic*, based on the peculiar powers of the leader; *traditional*, based on loyalty to the individual; and *rational-legal*, based on a system of formal, explicit rules—typically a bureaucracy. *Bureaucracy* refers to a management approach based on a formal organizational structure with set rules and regulations. Unfortunately, the concept is now held in low regard because of its association with inefficiency and incompetence in many organizations.

Bureaucracy refers to a management approach based on a formal organizational structure with set rules and regulations.

Weber's thoughts on organizational behavior were based on his analysis of capitalism as it exists in the modern Western world. Capitalism had existed in earlier eras, but the important point for Weber was that the modern form was characterized by a bureaucratic organizational structure. He believed that the combination of bureaucracy and the capitalistic framework created the current economic system.[12]

Bureaucracy required various specialists. Weber believed that the use of specialists in a bureaucracy provided advantages over other forms of organization. He also specified various requirements for an effective bureaucracy:

Technical training for its personnel

Appointment on the basis of merit

Set salaries and retirement benefits

Guaranteed careers

Divorce of people's private lives and their organizational positions

Set hierarchy of jobs and offices

Implementation of an adequate control system

Rational rules and regulations within the organization

Certain obedience to a superior's command[13]

Like Fayol, Weber's conceptual developments were not widely known to American management for several decades. It was not until years after his death that the importance of Weber's studies was widely recognized. His work is now considered an integral part of classical organizational and management theory.[14]

Scientific Management

Scientific management is a school of management popularized during the early 1900s that is based upon the application of the scientific method to the workplace and other management activities.

Scientific management refers to a school of management thought that became popular in the early 1900s. It was based on the notion that the scientific method could be applied to the workplace and the related management activities. Among its major early contributors were Frederick W. Taylor, the Gilbreths, and Henry L. Gantt.

[12] McNeil, "Understanding of Organizational Powers," pp. 67–68.

[13] Victor A. Thompson, *Modern Organization* (New York: Knopf, 1961), p. 11

[14] Earlier neglect of Weber's contributions is suggested in Wren, *The Evolution of Management Thought*, p. 234.

FREDERICK W. TAYLOR—FATHER OF
SCIENTIFIC MANAGEMENT   *494*

Frederick W. Taylor (1856–1915), who is profiled in Chapter 17, is credited
with the development of scientific management. An engineer and inventor,
Taylor first began to experiment with new managerial concepts in 1878 while
employed at a steel company. He went on to work in a variety of other capacities. He retired in 1901 to devote full time to the dissemination of scientific
management techniques.[15]

Taylor outlined four principles that constitute scientific management:

First: Develop a science for each element of a person's work, which replaces the
old rule-of-thumb method.

Second: Scientifically select and then train, teach, and develop the worker,
whereas in the past he chose his own work and trained himself as best he
could.

Third: Heartily cooperate with the workers so as to insure all of the work being
done in accordance with the principles of the science which has been developed.

Fourth: There is an almost equal division of the work and the responsibilities between the management and the workers. The management take over all work
for which they are better fitted than the workers, while in the past almost all
of the work and the greater part of the responsibility were thrown upon the
workers.[16]

Taylor differentiated these principles from the mechanisms of management
such as time study, standardization of tools, time-saving devices, and so forth.[17]
His comprehensive system of scientific management had five basic features:

1. Organizational and technical improvements such as better machine operations, cost accounting, purchasing, and stock and tool room control
2. A planning department that was responsible for coordinating the overall
   operation and assigning jobs
3. The use of functional foremen who were responsible for a single functional activity within the manufacturing process
4. Time study to determine the rate at which a job should be done
5. An incentive wage system[18]

**FREDERICK TAYLOR
OBSERVING WORK
ACTIVITY**

[15] Taylor's career is discussed in Daniel Nelson, "Scientific Management, Systematic Management, and Labor, 1880–1915," *Business History Review* (Winter 1974), pp. 482–483; and in
George, *The History of Management Thought,* p. 87.

[16] Frederick W. Taylor, *Principles of Scientific Management* (New York: Harper, 1911), pp.
36–37. Copyright 1911 by Frederick W. Taylor; renewed 1939 by Louise M. S. Taylor. Reprinted by permission of Harper & Row, Publishers, Inc.

[17] These mechanisms are listed in Taylor, *Principles of Scientific Management,* pp. 129–130. Cited
in George, *The History of Management Thought,* p. 91.

[18] These features are listed in Nelson, "Scientific Management," p. 490.

Scientific management became the accepted management philosophy largely because it provided a response to the labor unrest and problems that prevailed at the time. The incentive wage system advocated by Taylor was the accepted remedy for labor problems during the early 1900s. While Taylor's system was a far more comprehensive approach to management, its labor-oriented features facilitated its acceptance by management.[19]

Taylor's views were an important step in the evolutionary development of management thought. One management writer put it this way: "Considering that it has been over 65 years since Taylor's death and that a knowledge explosion has taken place during these years, Taylor's track record is remarkable. The point is not, as is often claimed, that he was 'right in the context of this time' but is now outdated, but that most of his insights are still valid today."[20]

THE GILBRETHS—TIME AND MOTION STUDY PROPONENTS

The Gilbreths—Frank B. (1868–1924) and Lillian M. (1878–1972)—were responsible for many contributions to management theory and are generally identified with the scientific management era. Frank Gilbreth is considered the father of motion study because of his early studies of bricklaying. *Motion study* refers to the determination of the best set and number of motions to accomplish a specified task. Gilbreth's modification of the bricklaying process increased hourly output from 120 to 350 bricks.[21]

> **Motion study refers to the determination of the best set and numbers of motions to accomplish a specified task.**

Lillian Gilbreth was active in much of the research concerning motion studies. Later, she became a widely recognized industrial psychologist, management consultant, and professor of industrial engineering.[22] Frank and Lillian were the parents of twelve children, and their family life became the subject of a book, *Cheaper by the Dozen*, which was written by two of their children.[23]

During the course of their studies, the Gilbreths identified seventeen basic hand motions which they called *therbligs* (except for the transposition of the *t*

> **Therbligs is the term coined by the Gilbreths to refer to the seventeen basic hand motions they identified in the course of their studies.**

[19] Nelson, "Scientific Management," pp. 479, 486. Also W. Jack Duncan, "The History and Philosophy of Administrative Thought," *Business and Society* (Spring 1971), p. 29.

[20] Edwin A. Locke, "The Ideas of Frederick W. Taylor: An Evolution," *Academy of Management Review* (January 1982), pp. 22–23.

[21] Frank Gilbreth's early work in motion study is described in George, *The History of Management Thought*, pp. 96–98.

[22] Lillian Gilbreth's contributions are described in John E. Burns, "A Biographical Memoir of Lillian Moller Gilbreth," *Industrial Management* (September–October 1978), pp. 28–32.

[23] Noted in Wren, *The Evolution of Management Thought*, p. 158.

THE GILBRETHS WOULD BE PROUD OF THE GOVERNMENT INSPECTORS

U.S. Department of Agriculture inspectors now use mirrors to check the backsides of slaughtered chickens. The procedures eliminated the hand motions involved in "positioning the carcass for inspection." The government claims the mirror saves money because a team of three inspectors can examine 70 chickens per minute versus 54 to 60 without the mirror.

SOURCE: "Chicken Testers to Use Mirrors," *Detroit News* (April 15, 1979), p. 2-E (AP story).

and *h*, and the addition of the *s*, therbligs is Gilbreth spelled backward). The Gilbreths were also responsible for such management tools and techniques as the process chart, flow diagrams, and a merit-rating system for employees.[24]

HENRY LAURENCE GANTT—FATHER OF THE GANTT CHART[25]   444

A teacher and an engineer, Henry Laurence Gantt (1861–1919) joined, in 1887, the steel company that employed Frederick W. Taylor. Gantt later followed Taylor to other employers and became one of his best known disciples. He was a prolific writer and an extremely successful consultant.

[24] George, *The History of Management Thought*, p. 98.

[25] This section is based on Wren, *The Evolution of Management Thought*, pp. 148–158. For an interesting account of one of Gantt's consulting assignments, see Daniel Nelson and Stuart Campbell, "Taylorism Versus Welfare Work in American Industry: H. L. Gantt and the Bancrofts," *Business History Review* (Spring 1972), pp. 1–16.

A TYPICAL PROGRESS CHART PREPARED BY HENRY GANTT

EXPLANATION OF PROGRESS CHART

When the machines are running, it is necessary to know whether or not they are doing the work which is most needed and also at what rate they are doing it.

Our chart system for presenting these facts is based on the following principles, and is very effective:

1. The fact that all activities can be measured by the amount of time needed to perform them.

2. The space representing the time unit on the chart can be made to represent the amount of activity which should have been performed in that time.

Bearing these two principles in mind the whole system is readily intelligible and affords a means of charting all kinds of activities, the simplest as well as the most complex.

These charts force us to make a schedule: They show how the schedule is being lived up to, by showing at a glance a comparison between what has been done, and what should have been done.

Charts of this kind, if kept in sufficient detail, also indicate with great accuracy the probabilities of future performance, and enable a manager to anticipate his needs and make preparations therefor.

In a manufacturing establishment the schedule portions of the charts are taken from whatever promises have been made. Performance is charted at intervals against the schedule. If these charts are kept entered to date they will enable a manager to concentrate his efforts on those operations which are being delayed.

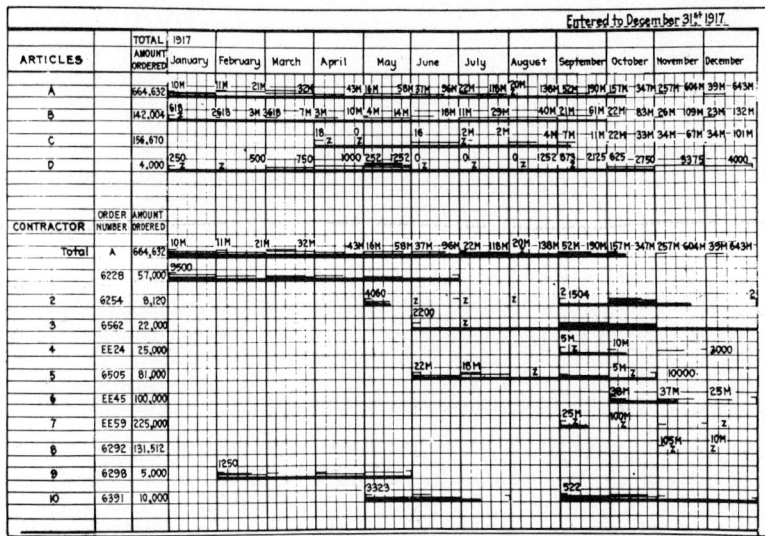

KEY TO PROGRESS CHART

At the left of the chart is a list of articles to be procured. The amounts for which orders have been placed are shown in the column headed "Amount Ordered." The dates between which deliveries are to be made are shown by angles. The amount to be delivered each month is shown by a figure at the left side of the space assigned to that month. The figures at the right of each space indicate the total due at that date.

If the amount due in any month is all received, a light line is drawn clear across the space representing that month. If only half the amount due is received, this line only goes half way across. In general, the length of the light line indicates the amount delivered during that month.

The heavy line shows cumulatively the amount delivered up to the date of the last entry. It will be noted that, if this line is drawn to the scale of the periods through which it passes, the distance from the end of the line to the current date will represent the amount of time deliveries are behind or ahead of the schedule. It is thus seen that the short lines are the ones which require attention as they are farthest behind schedule.

A, B, C, and D are summaries.

A is a summary of the orders shown on the lower part of the chart.

Gantt made several contributions of his own to the scientific management school. He dropped Taylor's piece-rate pay system for a "task work with a bonus system." In Gantt's plan, workers received a bonus for completing all of their daily tasks. He also awarded bonuses to supervisors who were successful in getting all of their subordinates to meet the output goal.

Another of H. L. Gantt's contributions was the Gantt Chart for controlling the nation's supply system during World War I. At the time, Gantt was serving the government as a dollar-a-year management consultant. His charting procedures had ready application to industrial management and were the forerunners of today's PERT (program evaluation and review technique) discussed in Chapter 17. Gantt is profiled in Chapter 17.

OTHER DISCIPLES OF SCIENTIFIC MANAGEMENT

F. W. Taylor had many disciples. Gantt, Carl E. Barth, Morris L. Cooke, H. K. Hathaway, Hollis Godfrey, Royal R. Kelly, C. Bertram Thompson, and Frank B. Gilbreth were some of the better known proponents of Taylor's scientific management concepts. These people played a major role, particularly after Taylor's retirement in 1901, acting primarily as consultants to firms interested in installing scientific management. In many cases, they had to make changes in Taylor's original system.[26] Taylor's disciples had a decided impact on management thought; in fact, one, Morris L. Cooke, has recently been credited with preparing a portion of Taylor's book, *The Principles of Scientific Management.*[27]

THE BEHAVIORAL SCHOOL

Behavioral school is an approach to management thought that emphasizes effective employee motivation as a primary determinant of organizational and managerial effectiveness.

The behavioral school in management thought is nearly as diverse as the classical school. Essentially, behaviorists believe that those involved in the organization are the prime determinants of organizational and managerial effectiveness.

Behaviorists moved away from supervisory procedures and industrial engineering techniques and focused their attention instead on the motivation of people. Members of this school see human behavior as a complex subject but as the most vital aspect of management.

MARY PARKER FOLLETT—FOCUSING ON GROUP INFLUENCE[28]

As a political philosopher, Mary Parker Follett (1868–1933) believed that the group itself is more important than the individuals included. Follett, who argued that the true person emerged only as part of a group, was a devotee of

---

[26] See Nelson, "Scientific Management," pp. 488–500.

[27] This interesting account appears in Charles D. Wrege and Anne Marie Stotka, "Cooke Creates a Classic: The Story Behind F. W. Taylor's Principles of Scientific Management," *Academy of Management Review* (October 1978), pp. 736–749.

[28] This section is based on Wren, *The Evolution of Management Thought*, pp. 300–310.

Gestalt psychology (the premise of which is that the whole—the group—is more important than the total of its parts—the individuals).

After being asked to lecture before a management audience, Follett began to shift her orientation to business. Here she suggested that the group—the business enterprise—should be a joint effort, rather than a conflict between separate interest groups like management and labor. One management historian put it this way: "For her, the essence of good human relations was creating the feeling of working *with* someone rather than working *under* someone."[29]

HUGO MÜNSTERBERG—FATHER OF INDUSTRIAL PSYCHOLOGY[30]

Hugo Münsterberg (1863–1916) was a German-educated Harvard psychologist and an early advocate of applying psychological concepts to business. His many newspaper and magazine articles helped popularize his views with management.

Münsterberg's concepts were published in *Psychology and Industrial Efficiency* (Boston: Houghton Mifflin, 1913). In this book, he suggested that psychologists could best assist management by determining the people most appropriate for a job; describing the psychological conditions that maximized output by employees; and assisting in the motivation of people to achieve management's goals.

ELTON MAYO—APPLYING BEHAVIORAL APPROACHES TO MANAGEMENT[31]

Elton Mayo (1880–1949) is featured in the profile in Chapter 12. An Australian who ended up at Harvard, Mayo went on to direct the famous Hawthorne studies which are described in detail in Chapters 12 and 13.

This research effort was conducted at Western Electric's Hawthorne plant. The Hawthorne studies were a milestone in the development of the behavioral school. They emphasized the impact of human motivation on productivity and output. Mayo's work pointed out the existence of a workplace culture that sets its own productivity standards, and it is considered a cornerstone in the evolution of management thought.

ABRAHAM H. MASLOW—FOCUSING ON HUMAN NEEDS

Abraham H. Maslow (1908–1970), a Brandeis University psychologist, suggested that a number of different human needs exist and that organizations relying solely on money as a motivator may be ignoring important needs. He felt that human needs could be arranged in the following hierarchy.[32]

1. Physical and physiological needs
2. Safety or security needs

---

[29] *Ibid.*, pp. 305–306.
[30] This section is based on George, *The History of Management Thought*, pp. 102–103; and Wren, *The Evolution of Management Thought*, pp. 197–199.
[31] This section is based on George, *The History of Management Thought*, p. 143.
[32] See Abraham H. Maslow, "A Theory of Human Motivation," *Psychological Review* (July 1943), pp. 370–396.

3. Love or social needs
4. Ego or status needs
5. Self-actualization, self-realization, self-fulfillment

Maslow believed that people went from the most basic needs in the hierarchy to the next higher level needs. He saw this conceptualization as a general model that was subject to certain deficiencies and constraints, for example, the tendency of some people to fixate at a given level. Maslow's hierarchy of needs model, which is described in detail in Chapter 13, has played a key role in the acceptance of behavioral science in management.

DOUGLAS MCGREGOR—CHALLENGING TRADITIONAL ASSUMPTIONS ABOUT EMPLOYEES[33]

Douglas McGregor (1906–1964) spent most of his career at the Massachusetts Institute of Technology, with a six-year stint as president of Antioch College. His primary contribution to management thought is the now famous dichotomy of the two alternative management views of subordinates. According to McGregor, *Theory X* managers believe that their subordinates are uninspired workers who seek to avoid responsibility and work assignments. By contrast, *Theory Y* managers hold that all subordinates view work as rewarding if given the chance by their superiors.

McGregor thought that management's perception of subordinate behavior played a significant part in determining the type of leadership style that was employed. Theory X suggested supervision and evaluation as the key management functions. On the other hand, a Theory Y conceptualization implied that improved communications and greater employee participation in decisions would be the most desirable format for management. McGregor's theories are discussed in detail in Chapters 13 and 15.

CHRIS ARGYRIS—MATCHING HUMAN AND ORGANIZATIONAL DEVELOPMENT[34]

Chris Argyris is a contemporary advocate of the behavioral school of management thought. The Yale University professor believes that people normally progress from a stage of immaturity and dependence to maturity and independence and that many modern organizations keep their employees in a dependent state, thus preventing the individual from achieving his or her fullest potential. Further, Argyris believes that several of the basic concepts and principles of modern management—such as specialization—inhibit the natural development of a "healthy" personality. He feels that the incongruence between the organiza-

---

[33] McGregor's work is outlined in Wren, *The Evolution of Management Thought*, pp. 448–452. His theory is presented in Douglas McGregor, *The Human Side of Enterprise* (New York: McGraw-Hill, 1960).

[34] The material on Argyris is from Wren, *The Evolution of Management Thought*, pp. 446–448. Wren cites Argyris's book *Personality and Organization: The Conflict Between the System and the Individual* (New York: Harper & Row, 1957) as his source.

tion and personal development can be alleviated through such management actions as *job enlargement,* where a person is given greater work-related responsibilities, for example, increasing the number of different tasks to be performed by the individual or allowing employees more opportunity to participate in the decision-making process.

OTHER CONTRIBUTORS TO THE BEHAVIORAL SCHOOL

The great diversity of the behavioral school makes it impossible to discuss all of its contributors. People like Levin, Homans, Whyte, and Festinger did much to assist its development and will be discussed in detail elsewhere in this text.

THE QUANTITATIVE SCHOOL: DECISION THEORY, MANAGEMENT SCIENCE, AND SYSTEMS THEORY

The quantitative school consists of several major branches such as decision theory, management science, and systems theory. Each of these components is described later. Although the diversity of the branches makes precise definitions difficult, the school is generally characterized by attempts to systematize the decision-making process. The goal is to better understand how decisions are made and how they can be improved.

The quantitative school had its origins in military applications. One of the earliest examples occurred in 212 B.C. when Archimedes assisted the City of Syracuse with military strategy when the Romans attacked the city.[35] Quantitative research was employed by both the United Kingdom and the United States during World War I. And this approach became widely accepted during World War II when it was used to plot strategies for protecting troopships and the like. After the war the benefits of using quantitative methodology in industry became readily apparent. Today, the quantitative school is an established part of management thought.

CONTINGENCY THEORY

Contingency theory is one of the more recent attempts to synthesize earlier management thought. The earliest studies with a contingency orientation can be dated in the immediate post–World War II era. Contingency theory—sometimes termed *situational management*—simply says that management actions and styles should be dependent upon the circumstances of the situation confronting the manager. Environmental factors such as public opinion might have impact on the decision-making process. So might employee and management attitudes. The appropriate decisions to make in a given situation or the proper management style may be determined only after these and other situational factors are carefully considered.

Contingency theory, often called situational management, is an approach to management that emphasizes adjusting managerial actions and styles to the specific circumstances of the situation confronting the organization.

[35] Will Durant, *The Story of Civilization* (New York: Simon and Schuster, 1939), II, p. 632. This is cited by George, *The History of Management Thought,* p. 150.

The historical evolution of contingency theory is described in Chapter 13. The development of contingency theory, like that of the other schools, suggests the rich historical framework upon which the study of management is based.

The Organizational Framework for Management

An organization's background, culture, and structure can have a major impact on the decisions that management must make.[36] These factors constitute what can be termed *the organizational framework for management.*

All organizations go through a process of evolutionary development that can have a profound impact on the managerial framework at any given time. Consider the case of Saga Corp., the largest contract food service organization on college campuses. Saga was formed by Harry W. Anderson, William F. Scandling, and W. Price Laughlin when they took over the food service at Hobart College in 1948.

Saga now provides food service management at 845 schools, hospitals, and businesses. The firm later diversified into the restaurant business with the Black Angus, Straw Hat Pizza, The Refectory, and Velvet Turtle operations. In 1979, Saga decided to divest itself of The Refectory chain and today its three restaurant divisions operate a total of 300 units.

The founders operated as a troika in managing the company. Each person specialized in a particular functional area: Laughlin in marketing, Scandling in

---

[36] An interesting volume discussing this general topic is Terrence E. Deal and Allan A. Kennedy, *Corporate Cultures: The Rites and Rituals of Corporate Life* (Reading, Mass.: Addison-Wesley Publishing Company, 1982).

SOME FIRMS EVOLVE FROM VERY HUMBLE BEGINNINGS

SOURCE: *The Saturday Evening Post* (July-August 1982), p. 83. Reprinted with permission from The Saturday Evening Post Society, a division of BFL & MS, Inc. © 1982.

"It all started out with a garage sale."

finance, and Anderson in personnel and operations. The founders even began rotating the chief executive officer's responsibilities during recent years.

While the founders accepted many advanced managerial concepts, they had difficulties with the troika format in daily operations. Twice they tried to pull back and restrict themselves to policy roles dealing with major corporate-wide problems in an attempt to delegate operational decisions to others. In each case, they returned to the troika format and their involvement in day-to-day operations. The founders also tried to divide and organize the company geographically as well as functionally. Anderson went to Oberlin, Ohio, and Laughlin to Kalamazoo, Michigan, with Scandling remaining in Geneva, New York, where Saga was founded. Later, the offices were rejoined, and the headquarters was moved to California.

In 1978 the founders decided once again to limit their roles. This time they called their new roles *founder–directors.* While the three men are supposed to function as other directors do, their continued control of 32 percent of Saga's stock suggests their dominant roles on the board. Ernest C. Arbuckle, the retired chairman of Wells Fargo, was enlisted as Saga's board chairman, and an outside chief executive officer, Charles A. Lynch, was hired to run Saga.[37]

The new organization survived its early tests, and there has been a significant improvement in results during the last two fiscal years. Whether or not these results continue depends on the effectiveness of yet another management change. In 1982 Lynch was appointed chairman of the board and chief executive officer (CEO). Arbuckle was named chairman of the executive committee of the board prior to his retirement in 1983.

ENTREPRENEURSHIP—THE BEGINNING OF AN ORGANIZATIONAL FRAMEWORK

The Saga story illustrates the evolutionary process that occurs in all organizations. While the Saga situation is somewhat more dramatic than most, the traditional change process still existed. Anderson, Scandling, and Laughlin were the entrepreneurs in this venture. The term *entrepreneur* refers to those who take financial and other risks to start a business entity. Richard Cantillon, an eighteenth-century French economist, coined the term, and it has remained an important ingredient of both the economics and management literature.[38]

Entrepreneurs are profit seekers who willingly accept risks in order to reach their financial goals. They tend to be involved in every phase of the business and make most decisions, even relatively minor ones. As long as the organization re-

An entrepreneur is a person who takes financial and other risks to start a business entity.

---

[37] "Saga Tries Management Pros," *Business Week* (November 20, 1978), pp. 162, 164–165, 167. See also "Following the Corporate Legend," *Business Week* (February 11, 1980), p. 65. The 1982 update was provided by the Saga Corp.

[38] Frederick Arthur Webster, "Entrepreneurs and Ventures: An Attempt at Classification and Clarification," *Academy of Management Review* (January 1977), p. 55.

mains relatively small, the direct involvement offers the important advantage of a close attention to details and often fosters a sense of personal loyalty among subordinates. In the Saga case, Lynch, the new chairman and CEO, commented, "There is a personal commitment in this company that I've never seen anywhere else."[39] Similarly, Peter Engel, former president of Helena Rubinstein, observed, "When Madame Rubinstein ran the company everybody got up each morning wondering, 'What does Madame Rubinstein want me to do today?' and since she ran the company until she was 94, people intuitively knew what she wanted."[40]

Sometimes entrepreneurial success breeds problems. The organization often grows until it exceeds the managerial capacity of the entrepreneur. While many entrepreneurs can make the transition from personal management to a stage of professional management, others cannot. But all organizations, sooner or later, lose their original entrepreneurial orientation. The timing of this transition varies. For Saga the fact that there was a troika of entrepreneurs meant that the successful initial stage could go on almost indefinitely. But in other firms continued dominance by the original entrepreneur can create severe problems. Henry Ford's domination of his firm nearly ruined it, until Ford Motor Company was rescued by his grandson and a professional management team was assembled.

THE SHIFT TO PROFESSIONAL MANAGEMENT

Professional management refers to persons who are hired for their training and skills in managerial techniques but who were not involved in establishing the enterprise.

The term *professional management* is often loosely applied to a multitude of managerial situations and personnel. Within the context of organizational evolution, *professional management* refers to people who are trained and skilled in managerial techniques but who were not involved in originally establishing the enterprise. Professional managers must have a detached perspective that is impossible for many entrepreneurs. Since they were not involved in the original establishment, they can objectively analyze the firm's current position and plan for the future. Arbuckle and Lynch represent the professional management stage at Saga.

Mennen Co. is another firm that has undergone such a shift in recent years. The Morristown, New Jersey, toiletries manufacturer is a family-owned company with a 103-year history. But for the first time, Mennen is now headed by professional managers rather than family members.

The new management is pursuing an aggressive, growth-oriented strategy. This approach is in marked contrast to the traditional course pursued by the Mennen family. For the most part family members were content to collect dividends rather than expand the company. This orientation often put operating management and the family owners in conflict. In fact, during one eight-year pe-

[39] "Saga Tries Management Pros," p. 167.
[40] "Peter Engel: Facelift at Helena Rubinstein," *MBA Executive* (September 1978), p. 7.

The board chairman of Joseph Cohn & Son, Inc., a Connecticut contract painting firm, is *Betsy* D. Henley-Cohn. Ms. Cohn's father, realizing that he was terminally ill, turned to his daughter after his son declined interest in succeeding him at the family's company. Ms. Cohn exemplifies a growing trend for daughters to succeed their fathers in family-owned businesses.

In fact, an official of the Center for Family Business expects the number of women taking over such firms to escalate rapidly from the current 500. It is estimated that about 50 percent of the nation's two million family businesses will soon experience a generation change. This would mean that there are probably a half million new female chief executives waiting to take over for Mom or Dad!

SOURCE: ''When Daughter Takes Over the Family Business,'' *Business Week* (March 29, 1982), pp. 172–173.

JOSEPH COHN & SON, INC.?

riod, three chief operating officers were dismissed or quit. But today both the board chairman and president are non-family members.[41]

Once professional management has been established, the next evolutionary stage is to arrange for succession so that quality decision making can be maintained. Some professional managers have been known to be reluctant to give up their leadership position, thereby falling into some of the same traps that the original entrepreneurs did. In sum, it is important to remember that the organizational framework of management is an evolutionary process; the only thing permanent about an organization is change itself.

The Environmental Framework for Management

A variety of environmental factors can—and do—influence the managerial process. In some cases the impact is minor. But in other situations, an environmental factor can significantly alter management decisions.

Some important environmental factors affecting management include (1) external and internal expectations, (2) competitive environment, (3) legal environment, (4) economic setting, and (5) social and ethical factors.

EXTERNAL AND INTERNAL EXPECTATIONS

There are numerous external and internal expectations that impact on the framework of management. Executives tend to take actions that fulfill the expectations of people both inside and outside the firm. Tradition, the customary way of doing something, plays a major role in management decision making.

[41] "The Outsiders' Touch That's Shaking Up Mennen," *Business Week* (February 1, 1982), pp. 58–59.

Walt Disney Productions zealously guards its reputation as the dominant movie maker for the family and the five- to thirteen-year-old markets. Disney has only recently worked on a movie that could possibly receive a PG (Parental Guidance) rating. Walt Disney was an innovator in this particular segment of the entertainment industry, and his firm continues to work on plans that he conceived (Disney died in 1966). Donn B. Tatum, chairman of the executive committee of Walt Disney Productions, commented on the traditions existing within the firm: "There was a time after Walt died that I wondered whether the Disney spirit could be transmitted to succeeding generations. But I have now seen it transmitted through four generations with no apparent diminution."[42] This tradition is seen in such recent Disney Production releases as *Night Crossing* and the animated feature *The Fox and The Hound.*

While tradition is primarily an internal expectation, a firm's image with the public influences external expectations. The image of firms like Bloomingdale's and Neiman-Marcus as prestige retailers could impact on a variety of management decisions. These could range from employee training decisions to merchandising practices. Similarly, McDonald's board chairman Ray Kroc's motto "quality, service, and cleanliness" is the cornerstone of much management decision making at the offices of the fast-food giant.

COMPETITIVE ENVIRONMENT

The competitive environment refers to the firm's relative situation in the marketplace. It includes such factors as how the firm rates in market share, technological innovation, financial strength, involvement in growth industries, and the development of its human resources. All of these factors can play a major role in management decision making.

A firm might be financially strong, have good personnel, and dominate its industry; yet if the company is positioned in a declining industry, management may have to take aggressive action to move the firm into new, expanding markets. Similarly, a firm in a growth industry may lack the financial strength to compete in the long run. So management might consider a merger with another enterprise in order to correct this deficiency.

One of the major lessons any manager must learn is that the competitive environment is not set; it is dynamic. To paraphrase the classical maxim of the TV weather forecaster: "If you don't like the competitive environment that exists— just wait, it will change soon!" The real question for management is whether or not the new setting will be more favorable than the previous one.

LEGAL ENVIRONMENT

All societies have some sort of formal or informal legal system that regulates activities. The set of legal mandates facing business is exceedingly complicated

---

[42] "Can Disney Still Grow on Its Founder's Dreams?" *Business Week* (July 31, 1978), p. 67. The 1982 update was provided by Walt Disney Productions.

and in some cases perhaps contradictory. Sears, for instance, suggested such a claim in a suit it filed against the federal government a few years ago.

The legal environment for management consists of federal, state, and local regulations, as well as those of foreign nations in which the business may operate. Some aspects of the legal environment have very broad goals, such as the preservation of the competitive environment. The Sherman and Clayton acts, which ban efforts to restrict competition or to monopolize a market, are examples. Others, like the legislation setting up the Occupational Safety and Health Administration, may deal with issues as specific as the storage height of fire extinguishers.

Effective managers must be cognizant of the legal factors that can impact a particular situation. This environment forms the parameters within which the managerial process must operate if it is to continue to receive public sanction.

ECONOMIC SETTING

Reaganomics, a term coined to describe the economic policies of the Reagan administration, clearly illustrates the effect that the economic setting has on management decisions. A 25 percent tax cut was implemented over a three-year period, thus offsetting the increased tax collections for social security and the effects of inflation. This and other tax incentives for both individuals and businesses have impacted decisions made by many executives. But Reaganomics has also meant that tax cuts had to be partially balanced by spending cuts. So managers have had to reassess the vitality of some government markets.

The recent recession is another feature of today's economic setting. While inflation declined from the double-digit levels common at the beginning of the decade, unemployment became more widespread. This situation influences staffing and other managerial decision making. Today's management is well aware of the importance of the economic setting.

All management decisions must reflect the economic realities of a given situation. Some markets should be avoided because of minimal profit opportunities. A product refinement may price the item too high relative to its competition. Resistance to higher wage demands may reflect management's inability to pass increased costs along to the consumer. The economic setting is clearly a key influence on the management process.

SOCIAL AND ETHICAL FACTORS

Management decisions should go beyond mere compliance with legal standards. Decisions should be socially responsible and within the ethical norms of society. Social and ethical factors are among the most important aspects of the environmental framework for management. Chapter 19 is devoted to social responsibility and executive behavior.

The importance of this aspect of the environmental framework is derived from the fact that society tends to judge management critically on whether it has met its socially responsible and ethical obligations. A management that does otherwise invites a harsh assessment of the organization, its people, and the products it represents. The importance of social and ethical factors will be highlighted throughout this text.

The Technological Framework for Management[43]

When Carlo DeBenedetti took over as the chief operating officer of the Olivetti group, Olivetti was carrying a debt burden of $1.1 billion and had incurred losses on $1.9 billion in worldwide sales in one year. DeBenedetti realized that technological advances would be the key to turning around the Italian office equipment company; he had to quickly move the firm away from its traditional mechanical equipment and into electronic products. He also recognized the importance of the United States market. Olivetti was an important factor in many European markets, getting 56 percent of its revenues from such customers. But even though the United States was the world's biggest office equipment market, it accounted for only 12 percent of the Italian firm's income at that time. Olivetti therefore moved to capture some of the U.S. market, extensively surveying U.S. office equipment needs because DeBenedetti believed that the American market was more advanced than the European customers upon which Olivetti relied. DeBenedetti also expanded Olivetti's research and development facility in California's "Silicon Valley" (industry jargon for an area noted for its concentration of electronics firms).

Olivetti's financial situation influenced DeBenedetti to budget research and development at only half the level of some competitors. But the new executive took decisive steps in other areas. He introduced new accounting controls designed to identify nonprofitable products. This was the first time such an analysis had been conducted at Olivetti. The fast-paced technological changes in office equipment made such a pruning a necessity at Olivetti. Another important decision was the creation of a new product screening and development system, which DeBenedetti believes will cut the lead time for the introduction of new products to one year from the three years common to the Italian manufacturer.[44]

[43] Excellent articles on this subject include Don Gervin, "The Comparative Analysis of Structure and Technology; A Critical Appraisal," *Academy of Management Review* (January 1979), pp. 41–51; Frederick Rossini and Barry Bozeman, "National Strategies for Technological Innovation," *Administration & Society* (May 1977), pp. 81–110; and two articles in the January 1977 issue of *Academy of Management Review*: David F. Gillespie and Dennis S. Mileti, "Technology and the Study of Organizations; An Overview and Appraisal," pp. 7–16; and Mariann Jelinek, "Technology, Organizations, and Contingency," pp. 17–26.

[44] "Olivetti: Its Growth in Europe Will Rely on U.S. Technology," *Business Week* (February 12, 1979), pp. 86, 88. The 1982 update was provided by Olivetti Corp. of America.

To reach its internal growth objectives, DeBenedetti also acquired major shares in technologically innovative companies whose products enhanced Olivetti's growth. Investments were made in point-of-sales systems (Data Terminal Systems, TMI, and Telxon); office automation (Syntrex and Compuscan): automative bank tellers (Docutel); specialized minicomputers (Stratus and Ithaca); magnetic memories (Irwin and Lanx); telecommunications (Intecom); and integrated circuits (AMCC).

Carlo DeBenedetti is a manager prepared to deal with the technological framework that envelops his company. The dictates of a changing technology are a critical aspect of the contemporary management environment, and all effective managers must understand technology and the methods for coping with technological change.

WHAT IS TECHNOLOGY?

Technology may be defined as the science of applying information and knowledge to problem-solving situations. Much information becomes a part of human knowledge without being applied to the solution of problems. Technology refers to the process of putting knowledge to work for humanity.

The technology of most industries of the 1980s is relatively advanced, at least in developed nations. But much more can be done.

It is difficult to anticipate the impact of technology. For instance, a 1930s government study of technology failed to foresee television, jets, organ implants, laser beams, and the ballpoint pen.[45] Nevertheless, technology has provided significant breakthroughs in the past, and improved technology is seen as the answer to many of today's business and societal problems. Many people see technological innovation as a way to improve America's productivity, a measure of the nation's output of goods and services. The 1981 gain of 2.3 percent was the biggest increase since 1976, and in 1980 the United States actually suffered a 4.3 percent decline. Between 1973 and 1981, U.S. productivity increased at a rate of only 1.7 percent annually. This was far behind the average annual gains posted by Japan (6.8 percent), the Netherlands (5.1 percent), France (4.6 percent), Germany (4.5 percent), and Denmark (4.1 percent).[46] It is interesting to note that a *Fortune* magazine review of the productivity lag attributed much of the problem to excessive government regulation and to the inability of some industries to switch their production to electronic technology.[47] Clearly, techno-

Technology is the science of applying information and knowledge to problem-solving situations.

[45] President Reagan made this point at the 1982 Versailles summit. See "The Uneasy Partnership," *Newsweek* (June 14, 1982), p. 27.

[46] Patricia Capdevielle, Donato Alvarez, and Brian Cooper, "International Trends in Productivity and Labor Costs," *Monthly Labor Review* (December 1982), pp. 3–14. The data reported here are from a table on p. 4 of this article.

[47] Edward Meadows, "A Close-Up Look at the Productivity Lag," *Fortune* (December 4, 1978), pp. 82–85, 88, 90.

/>

When industrial sociologist Joan Woodward (1917–1971) began her organizational studies of manufacturing firms in the early 1950s, she broke new ground. Up until then, management theorists believed that certain general management principles could be applied to any manufacturing business, no matter what its technological base. Woodward proved that they could not. In addition, Woodward's pioneering studies caused management theorists to reappraise their views on just how organizations are structured. For the first time, they were forced to consider factors they never considered before.

Woodward's research took place in South Essex, England, where she studied 100 manufacturing firms employing at least 100 people each. The data that resulted from her work showed no clear relationship between a firm's size, type of industry, or profitability and its organizational structure. However, an unsuspected relationship did emerge between a firm's organizational structure and its manufacturing technology. Woodward was able to place all the firms in the study into three broad technological categories: *small batch and unit production,* which, for example, characterized furniture manufacturing; *large batch and mass production,* which characterized automobile manufacturing; and *long-run process production,* which characterized oil refineries.

Woodward found that as the technical complexity of a firm increased, so did the number of managerial levels and the breadth of the chief executive officer's span of control (that is, the number of people reporting directly to him or her). In addition, the data showed that first level supervisors in unit and small batch production firms had smaller spans of control than their counterparts in large batch and mass production industries, who had the largest spans of control. Wood-

logical innovation is important to the economic health of industry, and it is important for managers to be aware of some of the empirical research related to technology.

THE WOODWARD STUDIES[48]

The impact of technology in determining the appropriate organizational structure was discovered in an investigation of 100 English firms by Joan Woodward and her research associates that is described in this chapter's profile. The researchers concluded that technology was the key in relating different organizational formats. In other words the firms in each technology group tended to have similar organizational patterns.

[48] This section is based on Joan Woodward (ed.), *Industrial Organization: Behavior and Control* (London: Oxford University Press, 1970), pp. v–vi, ix–xiii, 234–243. The South Essex studies are described in Joan Woodward, *Industrial Organization: Theory and Practice* (London: Oxford University Press, 1965). Woodward's classifications have been used in more recent studies. See, for example, Yezdi M. Godiwalla, Wayne A. Meinhart, and William D. Warde, "Environment and Technology: Strategic Contingency Mixes for Overall Corporate Strategy," *University of Michigan Business Review* (March 1979), pp. 26–32.

ward's research also showed that operational procedures increase at the middle-range mass production level. These firms have a far greater number of rules, controls, and specific job definitions, a more rigid chain of authority, and less flexible employee-employer relationships than either unit and small batch or process production firms.

These findings had broad implications for the study of the basic structure of organizations. By establishing a link between the technology of production and the organizational structure of a company, they challenged established theories of formal organization and spurred the development of new approaches to organizational structure. Woodward's findings also showed that in order to be effective, management style had to be linked to the organization's production technology.

Joan Woodward continued to expand this approach to organizational structure until her untimely death at the age of 54. As a full professor in the Industrial Sociology Unit of the Department of Mechanical Engineering at Imperial College in England, she taught industrial sociology to both graduate and undergraduate science and technology students, who she believed must understand the social environment in which jobs exist if they were to succeed. As an academician who insisted on basing her studies on sound empirical data, she also helped develop a new respect and trust between industry and those researching its practices. And her findings increased industry's recognition that industrial sociologists like Woodward had something valuable to contribute—indeed, something that could improve the very success of their business operations.

Sources

Andrew D. Szilagyi, Jr., *Management and Performance* (Santa Monica, Calif.: Goodyear Publishing Co., 1971).

Joan Woodward, *Industrial Organization: Behavior and Control* (London: Oxford University Press, 1970).

Editorial review of Joan Woodward, ed., *Industrial Organization: Behavior and Control* in *Industrial and Labor Relations Review* (July 1971), pp. 644–645.

Terry Bishop, "Joan Woodward," *Personnel Management* (December 1971), pp. 31–32.

As a result of these studies, a research unit was established at the Imperial College of Science and Technology (Great Britain) in 1962. The initial Woodward studies stimulated considerable research into the relationship between technology and management. The research was extended into such areas as the degree of uncertainty involved and managerial control systems. Joan Woodward's work is considered a pioneering effort in research on the technological framework for management.

TRIST AND BAMFORTH'S RESEARCH ON THE COAL MINING INDUSTRY

A classical study of the impact of changing technology on the workplace was conducted by researchers from Great Britain's Tavistock Institute of Human Relations. E. L. Trist and K. W. Bamforth investigated the effect of the introduction of new technology on the British coal mining industry following its nationalization shortly after World War II. Bamforth, a coal miner for eighteen years, brought considerable personal experience to the research effort.

Traditionally, the British mining industry used what was called a *hand-got* method. Coal was extracted by groups of two to eight miners who made separate contracts with management. These groups worked at their own pace and developed considerable cohesiveness. The work groups were highly stable and closely knit. The miners were even known to take on the care of a co-worker's family if that person were injured or killed.

Then new technology was introduced. The longwall production unit was implemented. The miners no longer worked in small groups on relatively small coal faces. The longwall method called for mining a coal face 180 to 200 yards long. Three shifts totaling forty miners were employed, and each individual performed a specific function like boring holes, operating a coal cutter, or loading coal on a conveyor. Many jobs were dependent upon other functions that were done by persons on other shifts. The close group relations of the hand-got method disappeared. Instead, failure to accomplish an assigned task was often blamed on others. Considerable productivity and morale problems developed.[49]

The Trist and Bamforth study suggests that improved technology is not a guaranteed approach to improving efficiency. Too often, technology is introduced without considering its impact on the people involved. The human component may be the most critical aspect of the productivity puzzle.

[49] E. L. Trist and K. W. Bamforth, "Some Social and Psychological Consequences of the Longwall Method of Coal-Getting," *Human Relations* (February 1951), pp. 3–38.

Summary

The framework for management includes a variety of perspectives, all of which influence the decision-making process. The perspectives discussed in this chapter include (1) historical, (2) organizational, (3) environmental, and (4) technological perspectives.

The historical framework can be described in terms of the evolution of management thought. Chapter 2 explores a variety of factors in this evolution: (1) ancient contributors; (2) early industrial era contributors; (3) the classical school; (4) scientific management; (5) the behavioral school; (6) the quantitative school: decision theory, management science, and systems theory; and (7) contingency theory.

Organizations also go through a process of evolutionary development that can have a profound impact on the managerial framework at any given time. Organizations are started by entrepreneurs—people willing to take the necessary risks. But entrepreneurial success often leads to problems as the organization grows beyond the managerial capacity of the entrepreneur. Eventually, professional managers take over from the entrepreneurs. Professional managers are people trained and skilled in managerial techniques who were not involved in the original establishment of the organization. They can offer a detached perspective that is impossible for many entrepreneurs. The next stage in this evolutionary process is to arrange for succession in order to provide continuity.

The environmental framework for management includes such factors as (1) external and internal expectations; (2) competitive environment; (3) legal environment; (4) economic setting; and (5) social and ethical factors.

Technology is the science of applied information and knowledge. It is the process of putting knowledge to work for humanity. The technological framework within which management operates can be crucial, particularly now, when U.S. productivity has declined. Chapter 2 examines various elements of the technological framework for management, including the Woodward studies and the research by Trist and Bamforth.

REVIEW EXERCISES

1. Define the following terms: (a) industrial revolution (b) bureaucracy (c) scientific management (d) motion study (e) therbligs (f) behavioral school (g) contingency theory (h) entrepreneur (i) professional management (j) technology (k) productivity.

2. Why do you think Frederick W. Taylor was rated so highly in the survey reported in Table 2-1?

3. Trace the historical evolution of management thought.

4. Explain Henri Fayol's contributions to management.

5. Describe the evolutionary process that characterizes the organizational framework of management.

6. Discuss the various environmental factors impacting on management.

7. What is technology? How does it impact on management?

8. Why has American productivity lagged behind that of other industrialized nations in recent years?

9. Outline Joan Woodward's contributions to management thought.

10. Describe the research by Trist and Bamforth.

ASSIGNMENTS/PROBLEMS/ DISCUSSION QUESTIONS

1. The Economic Recovery Tax Act of 1981 provided a tax credit for research and development expenditures. Discuss the implications of this tax provision on the technological framework of management.

2. The U.S. Census Bureau reports that the hours an urban dweller devoted to "work for pay" were down. By contrast, the time spent sleeping and on personal care, organizations, media, and other leisure activities was up. *

Assess the impact of these changes on the framework for management.

3. A Michigan firm, Donnelly Mirrors, has guaranteed its 600 employees that no jobs will be cut because of technological changes or efforts to trim costs. Donnelly is not unionized.†

Relate the Donnelly Mirrors illustration to the section dealing with technology.

* "What's Up in the Use of Time?" *Detroit News* (March 12, 1978), p. 9-C (from Newspaper Enterprise Association).
† Nancy Foy and Hermon Gadon, "Worker Participation Contrasts in Three Countries," *Harvard Business Review* (May–June 1976), p. 81.

4. An analysis of South Carolina manufacturers revealed that firms with less than one hundred employees had to spend $810.19 per employee to comply with the provisions of the Occupational Safety and Health Act. The study concludes that OSHA requirements could cause the deterioration of the "competitive position" of these small manufacturers.**

Discuss this report within the context of this chapter.

5. Prepare a brief report on an individual who made a major contribution to management thought and practice.

A MANAGERIAL INCIDENT

No One Wanted to Help Haloid Company

Some years back, a small firm named Haloid Co. began working with Battelle Memorial Institute, a research organization, to develop a new copying process. Outside financial help was needed, so firms like IBM, Lockheed, Eastman Kodak, and AM International (formerly Addressograph-Multigraph)

** John W. Ray, "Some Financial Implications of OSHA Compliance for Small Businesses in South Carolina," *Business and Economic Review* (March, 1979), pp. 15–18.

were invited to join the new venture. All these firms refused, and Haloid had to undertake the venture by itself. Along the way, the small firm changed its name to Xerox Corp., and the new process became one of the most successful technological innovations of the century.

As the years went by, Xerox grew rapidly. Some executives like Chairman C. Peter McColough began to worry that the transition from a small entrepreneurial company to a major corporate enterprise had caused Xerox to become too bureaucratic and unresponsive. McColough remarked:

> Some of us were concerned that some of the syndromes of a large company were creeping in, that the decision making was getting ponderous, that the business had not been decentralized as it should have been as we had gotten bigger and therefore more impersonal. We decided we'd better take a look at our general style of management, the whole life-style of the company——and so we called together people from around the world.

Panels of employees from throughout the organization were assigned to look at various aspects of the operation. Eight months were spent in this self-analysis. The culmination of the exercise was a conference in Acapulco attended by 90 to 100 employees. Problems were analyzed, proposals studied, and an action list of changes developed. This organizational renewal process became known within Xerox as the "Spirit of Acapulco." McColough credits many improvements at Xerox to the Acapulco conference. Efforts were initiated to reduce the problems and centralization that had developed as Xerox grew.

In recent years the Spirit of Acapulco has grown at Xerox. As part of a reorganizational effort to further decentralize the decision-making process, substructures called *strategic business units* were formed. These units operate relatively free of central corporate control.

SOURCES: "The Corporation and Its Obligations" (an interview with C. Peter McColough), *Harvard Business Review* (May–June 1975), pp. 132–33. The McColough quotation is from p. 132. George R. White and Margaret B. W. Graham, "How to Spot a Technological Winner," *Harvard Business Review* (March–April 1978), p. 146. The 1982 update was provided by Xerox Corp.

Questions and Problems

1. Describe the organizational framework for management at Xerox.

2. Discuss how the firm's technological background might affect Xerox management.

3. The Systems Concept in Management

Learning Objectives

AFTER STUDYING THIS CHAPTER YOU SHOULD BE ABLE TO

1. Explain the systems approach to management.
2. List the three fundamental concepts of systems theory.
3. Identify the components of a system.
4. Distinguish between closed and open systems.
5. Explain the major characteristics of open systems.

Key Terms

suboptimization

system

boundary

synergy

inputs

transformation

outputs

closed system

open system

cycle of events

negative entropy

feedback

dynamic homeostasis

differentiation

equifinality

The system is the solution.

Off the system!

STUDENT RADICAL, 1968

Borneo's steamy lowlands are the residence of some of the world's fiercest mosquitoes. The insects are carriers of malaria, a disease that regularly threatens the Borneo villagers. In an attempt to reduce the mosquito population in Borneo, the World Health Organization supervised the spraying of homes with DDT. The pesticide was effective in controlling mosquitoes and also killed the cockroaches. Unfortunately, the poisoned cockroaches were eaten by cats, which also died. Then the real problems began.

The death of the cats was followed by an explosion in the rat population. The rats threatened local food supplies and even attacked sleeping villagers. Only after Royal Air Force personnel collected and air-lifted stray cats from remote areas to the newly malaria-free, catless, rat-infested villages was the ecosystem brought back into balance.[1]

Similar problems on a much smaller scale resulted when the traffic manager of a Canadian manufacturer decided to reduce transportation costs. By switching from trucks to rail transportation, the traffic manager was able to reduce annual shipping costs by $4,150. But rail shipments took three days, as compared with truck transport time of eight hours. The difference required an added inventory investment of $16,900 a year to cover the three additional days of lead time before an order arrived. The traffic manager's actions had resulted in *suboptimization*—a condition in which attempts to optimize the operations of one component result in less than optimal operations of the overall organization due to the interactions of the various components. The traffic manager had succeeded in cutting transport costs, but *total* costs actually increased $12,750 a year. As soon as the traffic manager's superiors became aware of the situation, the firm's products were back in trucks.[2]

Suboptimization occurs when attempts to optimize the operations of one component result in less than optimal operations of the overall organization.

Thinking in Terms of Systems

What lessons are to be learned from these examples? Is it that insecticides should not be used when cats are present? Is it that highway transportation is generally preferable to shipment by rail? Not at all. The moral is that when many variables interact with each other in different and complex ways, it is fre-

[1] Douglas H. Haden, *Total Business Systems* (St. Paul, Minn.: West Publishing Co., 1978), p. 3.
[2] F. R. Denham, "Making the Physical Distribution Concept Pay Off," *Handling and Shipping* (October 1967).

In the late 1920s young biologist Ludwig von Bertalanffy began to concentrate his attention on the organism as a system. The concepts he derived from this new approach resulted in the publication of his first book, *Modern Theories of Development* (1928), in which he developed the systems theory of the organism. Not content to limit his theory to the realm of biology and the natural sciences, he went on to demonstrate its application to the social sciences in *Robots, Men, and Minds* (1967) and *Organismic Psychology and Systems Theory* (1968).

In von Bertalanffy's work lay the beginnings of the systems revolution that has spread through the academic world and into business and industry. A scholar's scholar, von Bertalanffy quickly recognized the widespread application of the theory he had pioneered, and he summarized its far-reaching relevance in what was to become the Bible for the systems movement, *General Systems Theory* (1969). His definition of systems theory provides insight into the breadth of this new "interdisciplinary discipline":

> Systems theory is a broad view which far transcends technological problems and demands, a reorganization that has become necessary in science in general and in the gamut of disciplines from physics and biology to the behavioral and social sciences to philosophy. It is operative, with varying degrees of success and exactitude, in various realms, and heralds a new world view of considerable impact.

quently impossible to predict the outcome by focusing on individual factors. Instead of analyzing parts, the effective manager must focus on the whole. These wholes are termed *systems*, and the parts that make them up are called *components*.

A MILITARY BEGINNING

This broad focus on the total organization and the environment in which it operates that eventually acquired the label *systems approach* can be traced to World War II. Associated with this approach were such problems as how to bomb strategic targets located deep in Germany more effectively from British air bases and investigations of optimum search patterns for use by destroyers in locating U-boats in the North Atlantic. The systems approach was employed for the Manhattan Project, which led to the development of the atomic bomb, and was used after the war to overcome the Berlin blockade. It was at work in the development of the Polaris and Minuteman military systems,[3] and it enabled the National Aeronautics and Space Administration to land a man on the moon.

[3] Glen McDaniel, "The Meaning of the Systems Movement to the Acceleration of the American Economy," in *Proceedings of the 1964 Systems Engineering Conference* (New York: Clapp & Poliak, 1964), p. 1; quoted in Lee Adler, "Systems Approach to Marketing," *Harvard Business Review* (May–June 1967), pp. 105–118.

Von Bertalanffy was born in Vienna in 1901. In 1926 he received his doctorate from the University of Vienna, where he attained the rank of professor in 1934. He moved to Canada in 1949 and became professor of theoretical biology at the University of Alberta. A founder of the Society for the Advancement of General Systems Theory and of the Center for Advanced Study in Theoretical Psychology, von Bertalanffy's contributions range across the fields of physiology, biophysics, the philosophy and methodology of the natural sciences, and historic-methodological research. He is famous for his equations for animal growth, which are used in fisheries around the world; for his development of fluorescence cytodiagnosis in early cancer detection; and for his research on the origin of the postal service in fifteenth-century Italy.

It is fitting that a man whose gifted mind embraced so many branches of learning should have been instrumental in leading the academic world to the discovery of holism as a methodology—or, in other words, to the discovery that complex phenomena "must be explained not only in terms of their components, but also in regard to the entire set of relations between their components." Aldous Huxley aptly characterized Ludwig von Bertalanffy as "one of those strategically placed thinkers, whose knowledge in many fields permits them to strike at the joints between the various academic disciplines . . . and so to penetrate to the quick of living reality in a way which the specialists, however learned and gifted, can never do."

Sources

"Ludwig von Bertalanffy, *General Systems Theory* (New York: Braziller, 1969).

Ludwig von Bertalanffy, *Robots, Men, and Minds: Psychology in the Modern World* (New York: Braziller, 1967).

Brockhaus Enzyklopadie, vol. 2. s.v., "Bertalanffy, Ludwig von."

Ervin Laszlo. "Introduction: The Origins of General Systems Theory in the Words of von Bertalanffy," in Ervin Laszlo (ed.), *The Relevance of General Systems Theory: Papers Presented to Ludwig von Bertalanffy on His Seventieth Birthday* (New York: Braziller, 1972).

What Is a System?

Systems thinking, viewpoints, and terminology have been adapted from the military by many diverse organizations—both profit and nonprofit—and have come to assume a central role in the modern world. Words like *feedback, input,* and *synergy* have found their way into the language of many academic disciplines and are a part of the manager's vocabulary.

The basic notion of a system is simply that it is a set of interrelated parts. A person might be considered a system of organs, a molecule may be thought of as a system of atoms, and a group as a system of individuals. Implicit in these concepts is a degree of totality or "wholeness" that makes the whole something different from, and more than, the individual units considered separately.[4]

The term *system* comes from the Greek word *systema*, which refers to an organized relationship among components. It denotes plan, order, arrangement, and method. The human body is a system made up of circulatory, skeletal, and nervous subsystems. Only when each of these subsystems is functioning properly is the total system effective. A firm's components might include such interrelated areas as production, marketing, and finance. Coordination of these subsystems allows the business to achieve its objectives.

---

[4] Seymour Tilles, "The Manager's Job: A Systems Approach," *Harvard Business Review* (January–February 1963), p. 73.

System is an organized group of parts, components, or subsystems linked together according to a plan in order to achieve specific objectives.

A *system* may be defined as an organized group of parts, components, or subsystems linked together according to a plan to achieve specific objectives.[5] The system's components may be as simple as a single machine or a complex assemblage of both people and clusters of machines.

The opposite of systematic is chaotic. An orderly coordination of components is required if the system is to function efficiently. Just as the traffic manager must consider speed of alternative transportation modes in choosing the most efficient distribution system, so also must the manager consider all components in developing an optimum business system.

FUNDAMENTALS OF SYSTEMS THEORY

While systems thinking has been applied to many subjects, there exists a conceptual core common to all systems approaches. Before applying systems thinking to management, it is essential to identify these basic concepts.

**Figure 3-1
PETROLEUM
REFINING AND
DISTRIBUTION
SYSTEM**

SOURCE: Richard A. Johnson, William T. Newell, and Roger C. Vergin, *Operations Management: A Systems Concept* (Boston: Houghton Mifflin, 1972), p. 71. Copyright © 1972 by Houghton Mifflin Company. Reprinted by permission.

System Components: Attributes and Interactions

First, a system is defined in terms of the entities or components that compose it, their attributes or characteristics, and the interrelationships among them. For example, a public school system would be defined in terms of students and teachers, books and blackboards, buildings and classrooms. The petroleum refining and distribution system depicted in Figure 3-1 illustrates this concept of

[5] Elias M. Awad, *Systems Analysis and Design* (Homewood, Ill.: Irwin, 1979), p. 4. See also August W. Smith, *Management Systems: Analysis and Applications* (Hinsdale, Ill.: Dryden, 1982), p. 3.

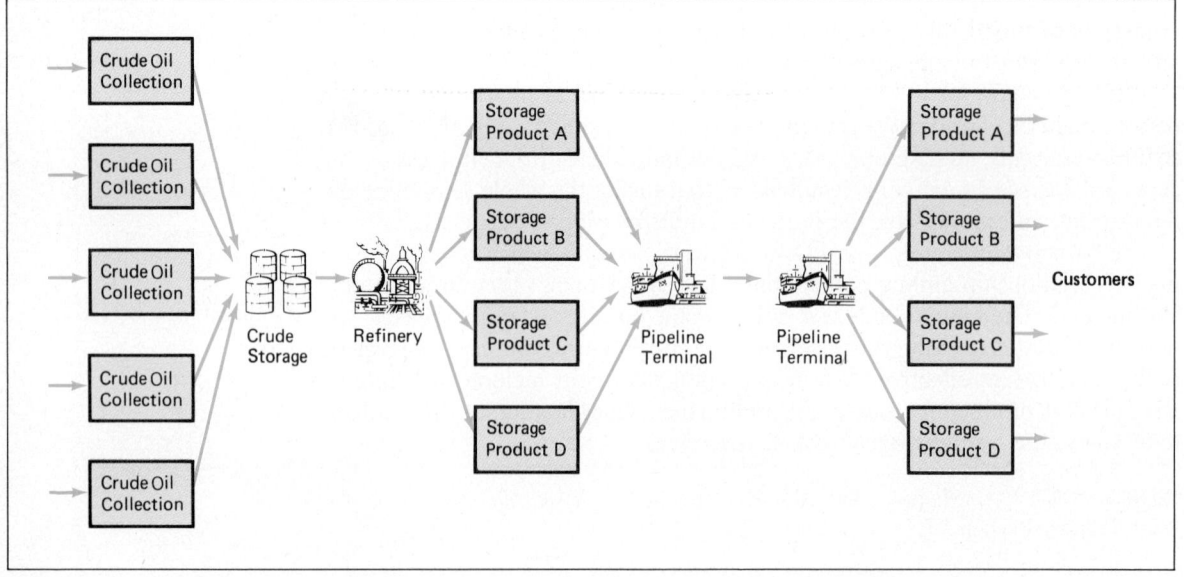

system entities, characteristics, and interrelationships by focusing on the collecting, refining, shipment, and storage of petroleum products.

Boundary: Dividing Line Between System and Environment

The system is also affected by the environment in which it exists. In order to determine what is included as part of the system and what is thought of as the system's environment, it is necessary to define the system's boundary. A system's *boundary* may be thought of as an arbitrary line drawn between the system and its environment to clarify issues in analyzing a particular problem. In considering a public school system, should the Parents–Teachers Association (PTA) be included as a component of the system or as part of its environment? The correct answer depends upon the subject under analysis. If the subject under discussion is curriculum reform, the PTA would probably be included. Should the subject involve the scheduling of existing classes, it might not be included.

> **Boundary separates the system and its environment; it can help to clarify issues in analyzing a particular problem.**

The concept of a system's boundary leads to the second fundamental premise of the systems approach. Every system is part of a larger system, or suprasystem, and is itself composed of two or more smaller systems, or subsytems. A partial listing of the subsystems of a school system might include the classroom, library, the various academic departments (chemistry, English, and history, among others), physical education, extracurricular activities, and administration. On the other hand, the public school system is itself a subsystem of the overall educational system. Figure 3-2 shows the human system.

Synergy—More Than the Sum of Its Parts

The third fundamental premise of systems theory is contained in the term synergy. *Synergy* is used to describe the idea that a system is more than the sum of its individual parts. It is not simply the components and their characteristics that compose the system; it is also their interrelationships and interdependencies. To the extent that these interrelationships are positive and supportive, the system will benefit. However, if they are nonsupportive, the system will suffer greatly. For this reason, most applications of systems theory take into account the critical factors of the process between and the interchanges among system components.

> **Synergy is a term used to describe the idea that a system is more than the sum of its individual parts.**

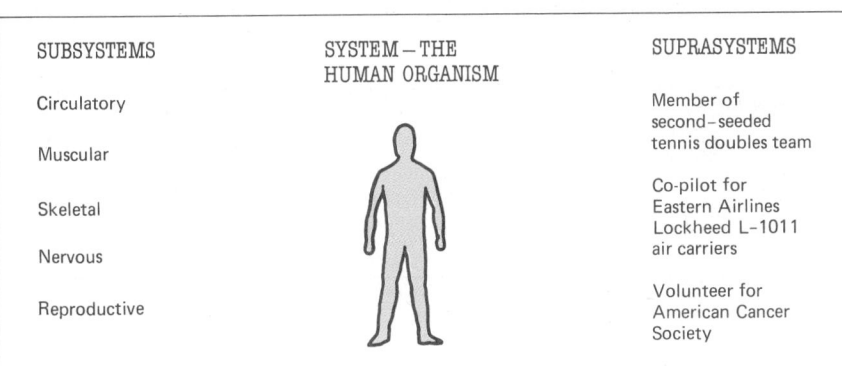

SUBSYSTEMS	SYSTEM – THE HUMAN ORGANISM	SUPRASYSTEMS
Circulatory		Member of second-seeded tennis doubles team
Muscular		
Skeletal		Co-pilot for Eastern Airlines Lockheed L–1011 air carriers
Nervous		
Reproductive		Volunteer for American Cancer Society

Figure 3-2 EXAMPLE OF SYSTEMS, SUBSYSTEMS, AND SUPRASYSTEMS

SYSTEM COMPONENTS

Systems are often drawn in the shape of flow charts or block diagrams. An elementary system generally takes the form shown in Figure 3-3. The system is a combination of inputs, transformations, and outputs. This input–transformation-output chain is sometimes called the *cycle of events.*

Inputs are human and other resources—energy, machinery, raw materials, component parts, and information—that are necessary to operate and maintain the system or subsystem. People provide both physical and mental energy required to operate business systems. Petroleum, natural gas, coal, or other fuels may be required for a Schwinn Bicycle Company production facility. Large amounts of data serve as inputs for conversion into information by the firm's accounting system.

Inputs may be divided into two general categories. *Production inputs* are those inputs that undergo transformation and become a part of the system's outputs. Glass, metal, and rubber are some of the production inputs for Nissan's Smyrna, Tennessee, production facility. Crude oil is a production input for a petroleum refinery. *Maintenance inputs,* in contrast, are those inputs that facilitate the functioning of the system but do not directly become a part of the system's output. Coolant is a maintenance input in the operation of an automobile engine. Maintenance inputs are often crucial for human resources, since these are the factors that motivate the members of the organization to remain with the organization and to perform their tasks in an efficient manner.

Transformations are the operations involved in converting inputs into outputs. All systems exert influence upon and typically change the inputs they receive. A manufacturing facility such as Republic Steel has complex mechanisms for converting iron ore, coke, and limestone into finished steel. The telephone subscription department for *Working Woman* magazine transforms telephone change-of-address requests by subscribers into written instructions for its mailing department. This process of change is sometimes labeled the *throughput* of the system.

Outputs are the products of the system. They are the results of the transformation process. Two forms of outputs exist: direct and indirect. Both must be considered in assessing an organization. The *direct outputs* are those for which the system was originally established. General Motors Corp. produces automo-

Inputs are human and other resources that are necessary to operate and maintain the system or subsystem.

Transformations are the operations involved in converting inputs into outputs.

Outputs are the products of the system.

Figure 3-3
COMPONENTS OF AN ELEMENTARY SYSTEM

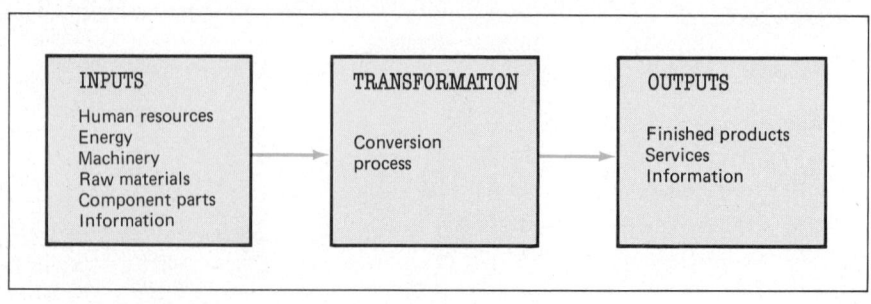

INPUTS	TRANSFORMATION	OUTPUTS
Human resources Energy Machinery Raw materials Component parts Information	Conversion process	Finished products Services Information

biles; Gulf Oil Corp. produces gasoline; General Mills produces cereal. However, there are also additional or *indirect outputs* that can be equally important. Organizations occupy a place in their physical, economic, and social environments; and their activities affect these environments. Gulf Oil, in the process of producing petroleum products, employs thousands of people, provides financial support to television programming on the Public Broadcasting System, and seeks to avoid polluting the physical environment. Thus providing jobs, aiding public broadcasting, and trying to practice conservation are indirect outputs at Gulf. To understand a system totally, it is necessary to know both its direct and indirect outputs.

The system for brewing beer is shown in Figure 3-4. Although the direct outputs are bottled and canned beers, such indirect outputs as *spent grain* utilized in the brewing process are present. Some brewing companies have been successful in using this waste product as an input in other systems producing animal feeds.

Open and Closed Systems

Systems may be classified as open or closed based upon the nature of their boundaries. *Closed systems* are sets of interacting elements operating without any exchange with the environment in which they exist. Such systems require no inputs—human, mechanical, or otherwise—from the outside environment. Very few systems—and no organizations—are totally closed. Systems vary in their dependence on material, information, and energy inputs from the outside environment. Even a relatively closed system such as a windup alarm clock periodically requires outside intervention when it runs down.

Closed systems thinking is the older approach and dates to the Renaissance and research in the physical sciences (notably chemistry and physics). Truly closed systems possess two defining characteristics. First, no exchange occurs between the system and its environment across the system's boundaries. Second, such a system becomes perfectly deterministic or predictable. In a closed system, if the initial conditions are known and a stimulus is introduced, the terminal condition can be predicted with certainty. Consider a pool table as a system. If the following conditions and stimuli are known, it should be possible to predict exactly where each ball will come to rest:

Closed systems
sets of interacting
elements operating
without any exchange
with the environment in
which they exist.

1. the position of every ball on the table;
2. the elasticity of the bumpers;
3. the coefficient of friction between the balls and the table;
4. how hard the cue ball is hit;
5. the direction of the cue ball; and
6. the type of spin on the cue ball.

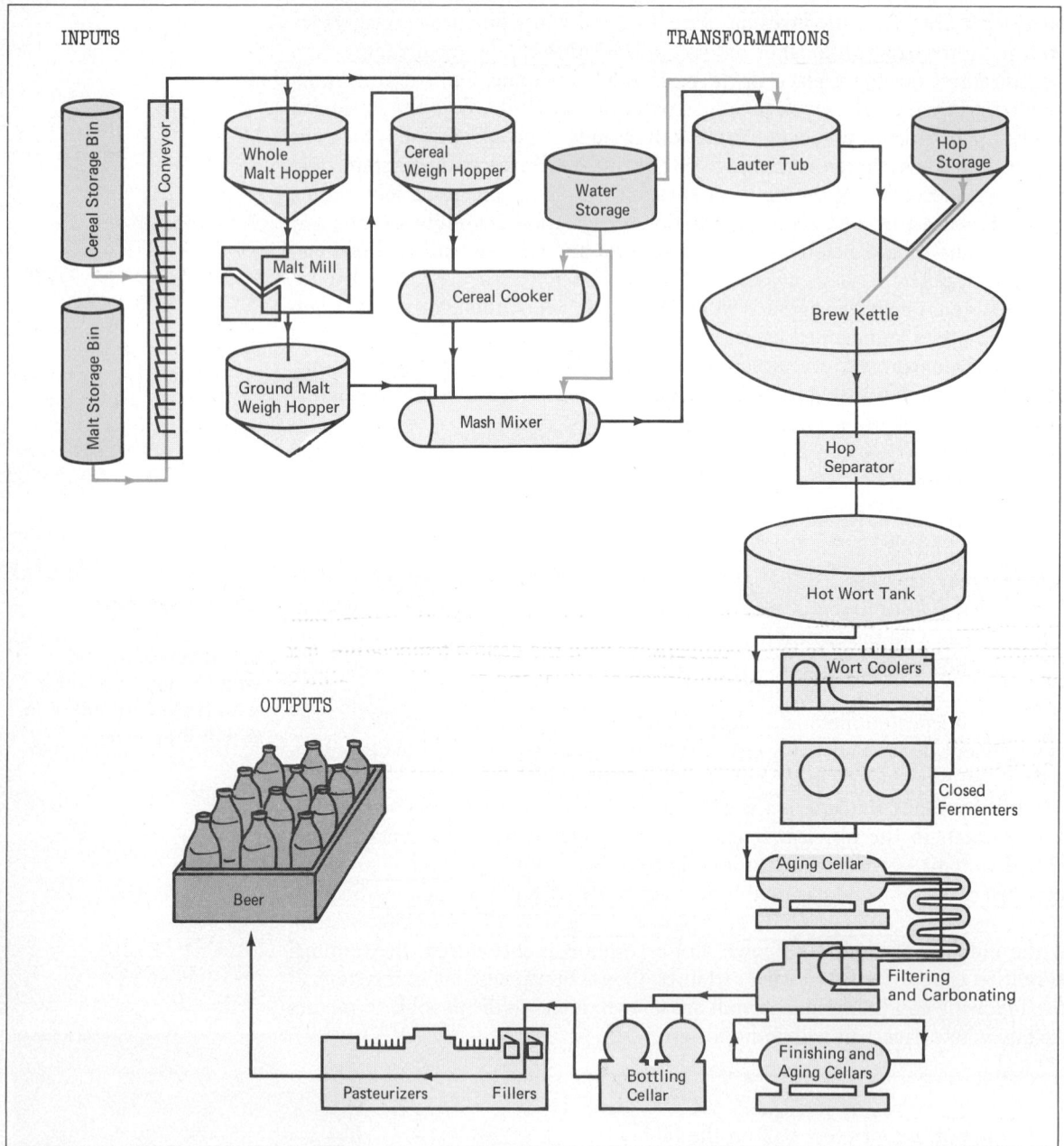

Figure 3-4
INPUTS, TRANSFORMATIONS, OUTPUTS—COMPONENTS OF A BREWING SYSTEM

Many concepts of the natural sciences were adopted by social scientists. When the classical management writers such as Weber, Fayol, and Urwick began to develop their ideas about organizations, it was natural for them to borrow from the closed systems perspective then popular in the physical sciences. This resulted in an emphasis on structure and in an attempt to eliminate any disruptions from the environment influencing their studies of planned system activities.

Open systems approaches, by contrast, are of more recent origin and emphasize the interdependence of the system with its environment. Based primarily on a biological rather than a physical model, open systems allow for the evolution of structure over time and interaction with their environment. Such systems are based upon the knowledge that no system is totally deterministic. Open systems thinking can be illustrated by further consideration of the pool table example. As the player strikes the cue ball, she closes her eyes, reaches out, and picks up one ball from the table. This change is analogous to the impact of the environment on a system. It has now become impossible to predict just where the balls will ultimately come to rest.

Open systems emphasize the interdependence of the system with its environment; they allow for the evolution of structure over time and interaction with the environment.

AN OPEN SYSTEM IN THE FACTORY

Figure 3-5 illustrates a heating/air conditioning system for a factory. Since the system continually interacts with its environment by measuring the actual temperature in the building to make comparisons with the desired temperature, it is an open system. Based upon this comparison of actual and desired temperatures, a decision is made. Should the temperature rise above the desired temperature, the decision would be made to activate the air conditioner units until it reaches the desired range. On the other hand, a low temperature may result in a decision to turn off the air conditioners. Such a system is characterized as open not only

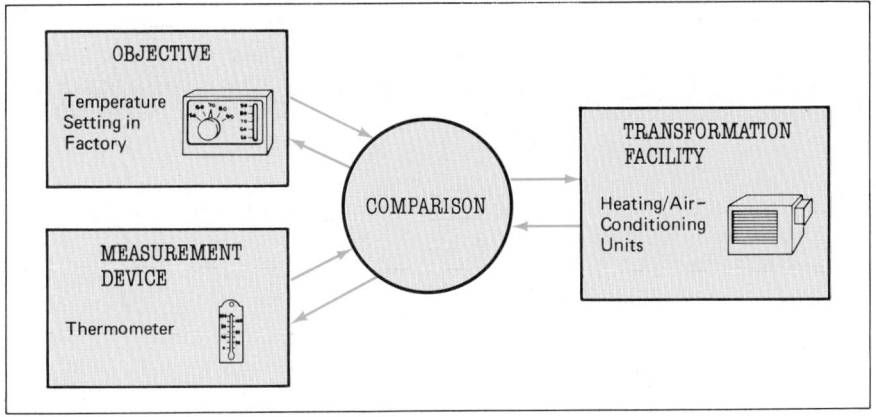

**Figure 3-5
HEATING/AIR
CONDITIONING
SYSTEM**

as a result of its obtaining temperature readings from its environment, but also as a result of environmental forces determining the desired temperature setting. Such settings may differ over time, with perhaps 75° Fahrenheit used during the summer and a lower temperature used during the winter months.

USING CLOSED SYSTEMS THINKING IN AN OPEN SYSTEM

Although organizations are clearly open systems, it is often useful to use closed systems thinking in focusing on specific parts of the overall organization. Managers may choose to consider a specific department such as accounting as though it were a closed system in order to improve productivity or attempt to solve bottlenecks that have developed. Managers must always recognize, however, that the department is one subsystem in a larger system. Any recommendations for that part of the organization may greatly affect the overall organization.

Characteristics of Open Systems

Cycle of events refers to the process by which the open system receives inputs from its environment, transforms them, and generates output.

Daniel Katz and Robert Kahn have identified several common characteristics of organizations as open systems.[6] First, every organization is involved in a *cycle of events*. It receives inputs from its environment, transforms them, and generates output for individuals or other organizations. Then the cycle is repeated.

A second characteristic of open systems is called *negative entropy*. Entropy is the tendency for systems to run down, become disorganized, or even disintegrate. By continuing to import and transform resources from its environment, the open system can fight this tendency toward entropy, and it may grow rather than decline. Systems capable of remaining healthy over long periods of time are said to exhibit negative entropy. All open systems must be able to repair themselves, survive, and be capable of growth. For a business firm, one widely used criterion of negative entropy is long-run profitability.

Feedback mechanisms, characteristic of open systems, inform the organization of deviations from objectives and may lead to adjustments in activities.

Feedback mechanisms are a third characteristic of open systems. Feedback is information used by the system to monitor its performance. Feedback informs the organization of deviations from objectives and may lead to adjustments in activities. The thermostat of the heating/air conditioning system shown in Figure 3-5 is a feedback mechanism.

Dynamic homeostasis is the process whereby the open system maintains equilibrium over a period of time.

A fourth characteristic is *dynamic homeostasis*. All organisms exhibit a tendency toward homeostasis or *balance*. Human body temperature is 98.6° Fahrenheit. Some deviations from the norm are possible, but the acceptable range is small and a temperature outside this range is likely to result in permanent brain damage or even death. The body is equipped with certain physiological mecha-

---

[6] Daniel Katz and Robert L. Kahn, *The Social Psychology of Organizations* (New York: Wiley, 1966), pp. 19–26.

**HEALTHY SYSTEMS
EXHIBIT NEGATIVE
ENTROPY**

SOURCE: *The New Yorker*
(June 14, 1982), p. 41.
Drawing by Donald Reilly; ©
1982. The New Yorker
Magazine, Inc.

nisms for maintaining the optimum temperature, despite variations in the temperature of the immediate environment. If the temperature is too low, the person shivers; if the temperature is too high, he or she perspires. In addition to physiological adjustments, people maintain an optimal temperature by both adjusting themselves to the environment (amount of clothing) and by adjusting the environment to themselves (installing air conditioners and central heaters). This process whereby an organism maintains itself in an optimal state is called *homeostasis.*[7]

Organizations must also maintain equilibrium if they are to continue to perform their tasks. Since organizations change over time, this equilibrium must be dynamic if the system is to maintain a steady state during the input-transformation-output cycle of events.

A fifth characteristic of open systems is *differentiation.* This is the tendency toward increased specialization of functions and differentiation among the various components that comprise the system. This differentiation occurs in response to the characteristics of the environment and becomes increasingly complex as the system grows. In the medical profession, the number of specialists has increased as a result of the growth of medical knowledge. In fact, the American Medical Association has more members who are specialists than general practitioners.

Differentiation is achieved as the open system develops specialized functions among its various components; as the system grows in response to its environment, it differentiates into increasingly complex components.

[7] W. Lambert Gardiner, *Psychology: A Story of a Search* (Belmont, Calif.: Brooks/Cole, 1970), p. 13.

Equifinality is the principle that open systems can achieve their objectives through different courses of action.

Equifinality is the final characteristic of open systems. The general principle is that open systems can achieve their objective through different courses of action. It is not necessary that a single method exist for achieving an objective. As Katz and Kahn point out, "A system can make the same trial state from differing initial conditions and by a variety of paths."[8] The characteristic of equifinality requires flexibility in choosing the appropriate means to achieve systems objectives. Rather than an endless search for the "one best way," the manager may choose from a variety of satisfactory alternatives. The decision maker in an open system recognizes, like Huckleberry Finn, that there are "more ways than one to skin a cat."

[8] Katz and Kahn, *The Social Psychology of Organizations*, p. 25.

RULES FOR EFFECTIVE DECISION MAKING, BY BENJAMIN FRANKLIN

Although Benjamin Franklin was never heard to utter the term *equifinality*, his recommendations for making tough decisions certainly reflect the concept. The following letter was written to Joseph Priestley in 1772:

Dear Sir,

In the affair of so much importance to you, wherein you ask my advice, I cannot, for want of sufficient premises, advise you what to determine, but if you please I will tell you how. When those difficult cases occur, they are difficult, chiefly because while we have them under consideration, all the reasons pro and con are not present to the mind at the same time; but sometimes one set present themselves, and at other times another, the first being out of sight. Hence the various purposes of informations that alternatively prevail, and the uncertainty that perplexes us. To get over this, my way is to divide half a sheet of paper by a line into two columns; writing over the one Pro and over the other Con. Then, during three or four days consideration, I put down under the different heads short hints of the different motives, that at different times occur to me, for or against the measure. When I have thus got them all together in one view, I endeavor to estimate their respective weights; and where I find two, one on each side, that seem equal, I strike them both out. If I find a reason pro equal to some two reasons con, I strike out the three. If I judge some two reasons con, equal to three reasons pro, I strike out the five; and thus proceeding I find at length where the balance lies; and if, after a day or two of further consideration, nothing new that is of importance occurs on either side, I come to a determination accordingly. And, though the weight of the reasons cannot be taken with the precision of algebraic quantities, yet when each is thus considered, separately and comparatively, and the whole lies before me, I think I can judge them better, and am less liable to make a rash step, and in fact I have found great advantage from this kind of equation, and what may be called moral or prudential algebra.

Wishing sincerely that you may determine for the best,
    I am ever, my dear friend, yours most affectionately.

B. Franklin (signed).

SOURCE: Benjamin Franklin, "Letter to Joseph Priestley (1772)," *The Benjamin Franklin Sampler* (New York: Fawcett, 1956).

The Systems Approach to Management

The decision maker of the 1980s should be cognizant of systems thinking and its contributions to more effective operations. The modern manager needs a new approach for three reasons:

1. A new way of thinking about managerial problems and activities is necessary to permit the manager to take account of the tremendous amount of new knowledge that is appearing.
2. A framework is needed that permits the manager to relate one specialty in the organization to another.
3. The manager must be able to raise his or her sights above the day-to-day in-company operations and understand how the firm relates—in its complex environment—to the other great systems of which it is a part.[9]

A systems approach to management promises to do this. This focus upon the organization as a unified system made up of dozens of interrelated parts provides the necessary perspective for the manager in the planning, organizing, leading, and controlling functions that must be accomplished in any organization.

[9] These reasons are discussed in Tilles, "The Manager's Job: A Systems Approach," p. 81.

Summary

Systems are organized groups of parts, components, or subsystems linked together according to a plan to achieve specific objectives. Thinking in terms of total systems lessens the possibilities of suboptimization, whereby one component of the system seeks to optimize its operations, but its actions adversely affect the operations of the overall organization.

Three basic concepts provide a conceptual core for systems thinking. First, a system is defined in terms of the entities or components that comprise it, their attributes or characteristics, and the interrelationships among them. Second, every system is part of a larger system and is itself composed of two or more smaller subsystems. The third concept is synergy—recognition that a system is more than the sum of its individual parts.

A system is composed of inputs, transformations, and outputs. This chain is sometimes called the *cycle of events*.

Systems may be classified as closed or open. Closed systems are sets of interacting elements operating with no exchange with the environment in which they exist. Open systems are characteristic of today's organizations and emphasize the interdependence of the system with its environment. The primary characteristics of open systems include the concepts of the cycle of events, negative entropy, feedback mechanisms, dynamic homeostasis, differentiation, and equifinality.

REVIEW EXERCISES

1. Define the following terms: (a) suboptimization (b) system (c) boundary (d) synergy (e) inputs (f) transformation (g) outputs (h) closed system (i) open system (j) cycle of events (k) negative entropy (l) feedback (m) dynamic homeostasis (n) differentiation (o) equifinality.

2. Briefly explain the systems approach to management.

3. Distinguish between systems, subsystems, and suprasystems.

4. Explain the origin of the systems approach to organizational problems.

5. List the three fundamental concepts of systems theory.

6. Explain the concept of system boundaries.

7. Identify the components of a system.

8. Identify and briefly explain the two types of inputs to a system. What are the two types of systems outputs?

9. Distinguish between closed and open systems.

10. Explain the major characteristics of open systems.

ASSIGNMENTS/ PROBLEMS/ DISCUSSION QUESTIONS

1. Identify the inputs, transformations, and outputs for the following organizations:
   a. A local hospital
   b. Pizza Hut retail outlet
   c. San Francisco Forty-Niners National Football League club
   d. A local bank

2. Consider your college or university as a system. Identify its subsystems and suprasystems.

3. Give two examples from your experience that reflect the operation of suboptimization.

4. Robert Townsend reports an interesting case in his book *Up the Organization:*

> The British created a civil service job in 1803 calling for a man to stand on the Cliffs of Dover with a spyglass. He was supposed to ring a bell if he saw Napoleon coming. The job was abolished in 1945.*

Explain how systems thinking in the British civil service might have prevented this job from lasting 142 years.

5. Why is a temperature control system considered to be an open system? How might a heating system be considered a closed system?

A MANAGERIAL INCIDENT

Applying Systems Concepts to Social Problems

Traditionally, we have examined community and other social problems one at a time. There were traffic problems, garbage disposal problems, smoke abatement problems, educational problems, juvenile delinquency problems, housing

* Robert Townsend, *Up the Organization* (New York: Knopf, 1970), p. 93.

problems, law enforcement problems, and so on. Private citizens, business firms, other private organizations, and public agencies did what they could to deal constructively with these various problems. Many of the solutions were ingenious, and the public welfare was greatly enhanced by the public and private efforts to deal with these matters of mutual concern.

The usual approach in all of these programs, however, was to treat each problem as an isolated problem. As long as social relationships and community life were simple, this approach was satisfactory. But economic growth, increasing population, congestion, and an increasing mutual interdependency of the citizenry revealed flaws in the simple, direct, and effective approaches of the past. Smog, for example, was caused by domestic trash burning and auto exhausts as well as by industrial smokestacks. Control of juvenile delinquency and other crimes required consideration of housing, education, and law enforcement programs.

To some extent, these interrelationships were recognized all along. But an increasingly complex society made more explicit acknowledgement necessary if viable solutions were to be achieved. Current experimentation and developments in the solution of social problems suggest the direction that we are moving in applying the systems concept.

SOURCE: David J. McLaughlin, ''Systems: Semantics and Significance,'' *Advanced Management Journal,* April 1970 (New York: Society for Advancement of Management, 1970).

Questions and Problems

1. What problems are present in applying systems thinking to social problems that are less significant in business problems? What steps would you recommend in reducing these problems?

2. Relate each of the following characteristics of open systems to this incident:

   a. cycle of events
   b. negative entropy
   c. dynamic homeostasis
   d. differentiation
   e. equifinality

THE CITY OF SAGEVIEW: THE MANAGEMENT PROCESS
AT WORK IN THE PUBLIC SECTOR

At 3:30 the Sageview team is to hold its first meeting. The team consists of Dave Foster, director of the Municipal Assistance Center (MAC) at Western State University, and three Western State MBA students. The purpose of the team's meeting is to find ways to respond to Steve Morris, Sageview's city manager of six months. Morris has asked MAC to assist in improving employee productivity and satisfaction in the Sageview city organization.

Dave especially wants the Sageview team's efforts to be successful for two reasons. First, Steve Morris is an old and close friend. Second, Morris enjoys a high reputation for innovation and effectiveness among other city managers. Many city managers will thus watch with interest MAC's efforts in Sageview. If a low-cost, high-benefit program can be implemented in Sageview, many other cities should fund similar work with MAC.

A week ago Dave visited Sageview and gathered preliminary information on Sageview and its problems. He sifted through it in preparation for the team's meeting.

DEMOGRAPHICS

Sageview is a prosperous western city with a population of approximately 100,000. Its economy is diversified among energy production and agribusiness. One manufacturer accounts for 10 percent of the employment. This manufacturer is expanding, and two medium-sized, high technology firms have located in the city in the past three years. Unemployment is less than 4 percent. Housing is adequate but falling behind and becoming very expensive.

This case was prepared by William R. Fannin, assistant professor of management at the University of Maine at Orono; Don C. Moore, department head of Market Development with Lockwood, Andrews, and Newnam, Inc.; and Lisa C. Guinn, research associate, and Rebecca Thacker, graduate assistant, at Texas A & M University. Adapted and reprinted by permission of the authors.

The city is politically homogeneous. Few political divisions have been exhibited in city elections in two decades. Like most western cities, Sageview is very conservative fiscally. Its property tax rate is low for a city of its size in the West. Sageview, however, is not without problems. New growth is demanding expansion of city services and the creation of new programs.

PREVIOUS CITY MANAGERS

During the thirteen years that preceded Steve Morris' arrival in Sageview, two city managers had served the city. Jim Lynch was the first of Morris' predecessors. Having managed several prominent western cities—one three times the size of Sageview—Lynch was well respected by other city managers.

Lynch told Dave several years ago that he had come to Sageview to retire. He wanted to make no major changes. Changes, Lynch felt, stirred up things, and he was tired of the hassle from public furor. Thus, his unwritten policy was that no major changes were to be proposed to him by his staff. This policy was well understood by the city staff and was in effect throughout Lynch's tenure in Sageview. When Lynch retired he was comforted by the knowledge that he had done a good job in Sageview. No major public protests had occurred while he was city manager.

Lynch was followed by Bill Jones. A civil engineer by training, Jones came to Sageview from a city half its size. He prided himself on keeping taxes down. His standing order was "no new programs, no new taxes."

The net result of these two management styles was the stifling of change. Fred Henderson, who served as the planning director under both, found this very frustrating. "For years I tried to get improvements in our zoning ordinance. The response was 'There's no money in the budget'; 'We're not going to get into that mess right now.' Now we're paying the price. Today, we have real problems with development."

The Sageview City Council usually preferred not to ask for new taxes, but now the council recognized that needed changes had been put off too long. City hall rumors circulated that the council "encouraged" Jones' early retirement. During the initial interview with the council, Steve Morris was told in no uncertain terms that changes had to be made. No specific demands were made except that his administration bring the city into the "last half of the twentieth century."

MORRIS' MANAGEMENT STYLE

Morris was thirty-eight years old and known to city management professionals as a "progressive, effective" city manager. Before coming to Sageview, he served four years each as city manager in two cities with populations of 30,000 to 50,000. Both these cities had been facing serious financial and development problems before Morris began his tenure. Both were in strong fiscal shape when he left, and Morris believed both were also progressing well on the development of new or better city services.

In each city Morris felt that he had done a good job and had the support of the city council. Each time he changed jobs, it was to accept a position with a larger city that he felt would offer new professional challenges for him.

Steve Morris sees his management style as having three key components. First, he emphasizes providing opportunities for individuals to reach their full potential and grow in their jobs. "I believe in hiring good people and giving them freedom to try new ideas."

The team concept is the second major part of Morris' style. Upon reaching Sageview he formed his assistants and division heads into a top management team (see Exhibit 1). He holds frequent team meetings where any major problems facing the city as a whole are thoroughly discussed. Division heads are encouraged to bring up problems from their specific areas to the team, and when appropriate, several divisions work together on a common problem.

The last component of Morris' style is the use of task forces to solve city problems. A task force may be headed by a division head, but its members are drawn from all levels and departments in the organization. Memos are sent to employees describing the problem and soliciting volunteers for a task force. Those employees selected for the task force are given time off from regular duties to work with the task force. Morris thinks that this broadens the scope of employees' jobs and lets the city avail itself of the talents and interests of many more individuals than a rigid structure allows.

Morris believes all three components of this management style have worked well for him. He believes that they have started to improve how Sageview employees view their jobs. He hopes Sageview employees see him as a city manager open to suggestions, concerned for the welfare of all employees, and equally concerned with the efficiency and quality of city services.

SAGEVIEW'S ORGANIZATION

The City of Sageview employs approximately 860 employees. It is structured into forty-seven departments grouped into nine divisions (see Exhibit 2). The nine division heads, safety officer, the assistant city manager, and city manager make up the top management team.

FIRE AND POLICE UNREST

Before Morris' arrival in Sageview, the police and firefighters had petitioned for formal collective bargaining rights. Under the city charter, a public referendum had to approve the granting of collective bargaining rights to any municipal employees wanting to unionize. Ten months before Morris' arrival, the vote was held, and Sageview citizens turned down the proposition.

More recently, the police petitioned for a referendum to grant police officers an immediate 25 percent pay raise. This petition was submitted after the police in another city won a similar referendum.

The Sageview Police Officer's Association (SPOA) conducted a well-organized publicity campaign modeled after that in the other city. TV ads showed police officers willing to lay down their lives for citizens and asked, "How much is law and order worth to you?"

Several council members openly opposed the

**Exhibit 1
CITY OF
SAGEVIEW—THE
TOP MANAGEMENT
TEAM**

Below is a short description of the people who make up Sageview's top management team and Steve Morris' perceptions of their views on recent changes.

Henry Williamson—Chief of Police. Graduated from Sageview High School; joined the Sageview PD immediately after army service in World War II; became the chief in 1963. He is now 61 years old. Henry generally favors Morris' changes.

Fred Henderson—Planning Director. Masters of Urban and Regional Planning; began working for the city in 1969; became director in 1973. Fred is very excited about the opportunities to expand the scope of his department's operations under Steve Morris.

Rob Byers—City Attorney. Started to work for the city in 1977 right out of law school; became city attorney in 1980; sees some of his authority as having been challenged because Steve has asked that he be kept informed of the legal office's activities. Ron likes to remember that formally he is appointed by the council, not the city manager.

Bill Briggs—Safety Officer. Masters of Educational Administration; was hired by Steve Morris in August 1983 and is very favorable to the changes Steve has made.

David Wilkes—City Engineer (Acting Public Works Director). B.S. in Civil Engineering; started with the city in 1956; became city engineer in 1966. David feels that recent changes have produced too much work. A division director cannot worry about others' problems and adequately handle his own.

Frank Tuttle—Utility Director. B.S. in biology; started working for Sageview in 1967; became director in 1981. Frank shares many of Wilkes' views about recent organizational changes.

Sam Shilling—Director of Community Services. M.A. in Parks and Recreation; started with Sageview in 1974; made director in 1980. He is very positive toward Morris' management style.

Allen Fleet—Fire Chief. Associate of Arts in Fire Technology; joined the Sageview FD in 1957; made chief in 1982; doesn't see any reason for everybody to know what other departments are doing; running the fire department is as much work as he needs.

Bob Billingworth—Finance Director. B.B.A. in Finance; came to Sageview as finance director in 1982, having been an assistant finance director in a smaller community. He is generally positive toward Morris' management style but is uncertain of the real impact of organizational changes.

Dick Marlin—Traffic Director. M.S. in Civil Engineering; came to Sageview as traffic director in 1979. Dick is very concerned over how proposed organizational and pay scale changes will affect his department.

Tom Harris—Assistant City Manager. M.A. in Urban Studies; came to Sageview with Steve Morris, having worked with him in his previous city. Tom works closely with Steve, so closely that it is often hard to tell which one originated a particular idea or action.

Ted Filler—Administrative Assistant to the City Manager. Masters of Public Administration; Sageview is his first job since graduating and he came to the position two months ago. Predictably, he is very supportive of Steve's and Tom's ideas.

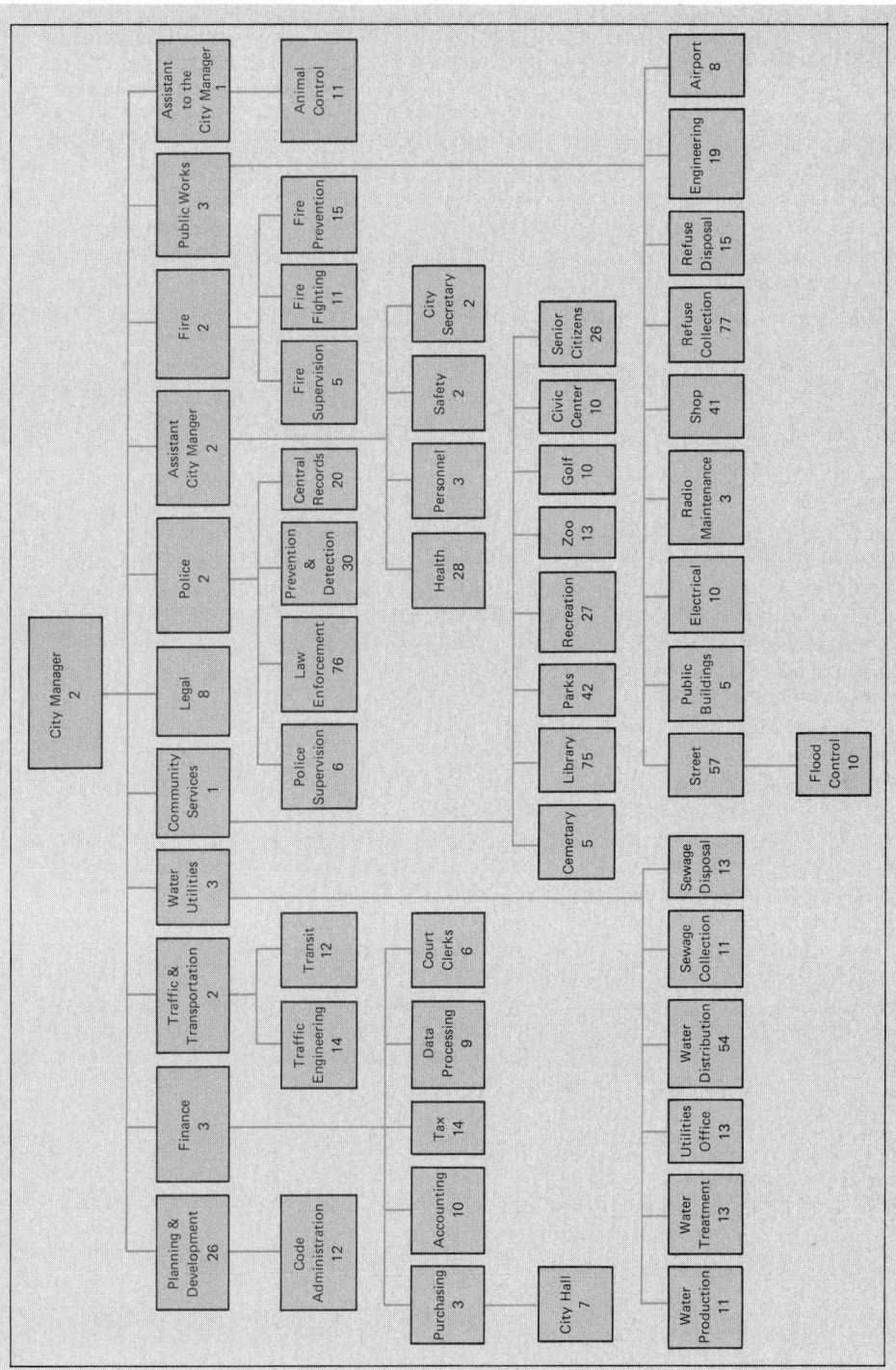

**Exhibit 2
CITY OF
SAGEVIEW—CITY
ORGANIZATION
CHART**

SPOA campaign, and the city's only daily newspaper carried an editorial against the pay raise. In one of Morris' first actions, the city manager's office released to the press a wage and salary study showing that Sageview's police salaries were about average for other western cities.

The propositions lost at the polls. Morris, however, knew his problems with the police and fire fighters were not over. Resentment had developed between police and fire officers and city management.

OTHER PROBLEMS

Police and fire disputes were not the only problems facing Steve Morris. The public works director was fired four months after Morris took office. He had been with the city for fifteen years and openly opposed changing his operations. For example, he refused to allow the Engineering Department to work on the Planning Department's new flood plan even though Morris had directed him to provide engineering assistance to Planning.

The firing had an unknown impact on the rest of the staff. Morris sensed that most employees understood why the firing occurred, but there was some evidence that a few "old-timers" were apprehensive about contradicting Morris' ideas. Morris didn't want the firing to build a wall between him and the staff.

Dave found that a wall was already developing. During a coffee break, Sageview's shop foreman responded to Dave's question on what he thought of his new city manager this way: "Well, I guess Mr. Morris is all right. Bill (the former manager) was a pretty good manager, too. He'd just drop by and chew the fat with you. I seldom see Mr. Morris."

The apprehension of many city employees toward Morris was also increased by a new wage classification program he instituted. Salaries and job classifications had not been analyzed in many years. Morris felt that a wage study was essential to insure that equal work received equal pay. Such a study, however, takes time and while it was being conducted, employees voiced interest and concern over its possible effects on their jobs and salaries.

Morris told Dave, "I'm worried that my management style, personnel changes I've made, the police and fire agitation, and the other new things we're working on could have lowered the staff morale. This is especially likely given the previous administration's 'go slow' policies. Dave, I don't want to wait for some of our people to catch up before we start to make more improvements. But I don't want to lose their participation either."

With his thoughts collected, Dave walked into the conference room. The Sageview team meeting was about to start.

Questions

1. What should Foster say at the team meeting?

2. Evaluate the decision-making approach used by the City of Sageview.

3. How can Morris introduce the changes demanded by the city council within the city's existing managerial framework?

Case I-2

HOOKER CHEMICAL AND PLASTICS:
THE LOVE CANAL STORY

Hooker Chemical and Plastics Corp. found itself in the middle of complex legal maneuverings involving $2.3 billion worth of filed intents-to-sue in 1979 as a result of its dumping chemical wastes sealed in steel drums near the Love Canal during the period of 1942 to 1953. In 1978 New York State declared a health emergency when eighty-two chemicals, eleven of them suspected carcinogens, were identified on the surface near the Love Canal. Abnormally high rates of birth defects, miscarriages, and liver disorders have been reported by Love Canal residents. Hooker officials deny any legal liability.

LOVE CANAL

The canal is adjacent to the Niagara River about four miles from the famous falls. It is in the city of Niagara Falls. The canal was dug in the 1890s to provide water and power for William J. Love's visionary scheme for a model industrial city. The canal was never finished and the model city never materialized. The immediate area ultimately did become heavily populated with industrial chemical plants. Carborundum, Union Carbide, Olin, Du Pont, Hooker, and a city water treatment plant were operating in the area in 1978.

In 1942 the old canal appeared to be an ideal dump site for waste from Hooker's Niagara Falls plant. The area was sparsely populated and the canal was 10 feet deep, 60 feet wide, and 3,000 feet long and surrounded by an impervious clay soil. (Water transmission through clay is ⅓ inch in twenty-five years.) Hooker obtained permission to use the canal for dumping in 1942 and subsequently acquired a strip of land 2,000 feet wide with the canal approximately in the center. The chemical wastes were sealed in steel drums and

dropped in the old canal and covered with a layer of clay. Approximately 22,000 tons had been deposited by 1953.

In 1953 Hooker closed the dump and sold the land to the city's Board of Education for one dollar. The dump was overfilled with clay. The board subsequently constructed a school on part of the land and sold the remainder to a developer who built and sold homes for families. None of the homes was built directly over the canal but it is believed during the process of road construction some of the overfill was removed and distributed in the area.

In 1976, after abnormally heavy rains, the canal overflowed its underground banks and quantities of various chemicals oozed to the surface. Apparently, the steel drums had corroded and leaked their contents, which leaked through the soil. In some places pools of chemicals sat on the surface. Near the canal chemicals such as Mirex and Lindance, banned for use as pesticides, plus Choloroform, Benzane, Trichloroethane, Toluene, Tetrachloroethane, and 1,3,5 Trichlorobenzene leaked into basements. EPA air monitors recorded 250 to 5,000 times the safe level of some chemicals.

The New York Times (August 2, 1978, p. B-9)[1] made this report:

> Karen Schroeder's backyard seems to be the lowest draining point for the waters leeching out of the fill. Her swimming pool popped out of the ground by the rising water table, her whole garden killed. The redwood posts of her backyard fence eaten away, and local authorities pumped 17,500 gallons of chemical filled water out of her yard in two days this year, water that even Chemtrol, the country's biggest waste disposal company, refused to handle, she said. So it was

This case was prepared by Professor Gary Whitney of the University of San Diego as a basis for class discussion rather than to illustrate either effective or ineffective handling of an administrative situation. Adapted and reprinted by permission of the author.

trucked to Ohio and poured down a deep-well disposal site.

Her dog died young and now her husband, Timothy, jokes that their daughter's rabbit has become the miner's canary. "If it dies, we'll know to move away."

One expert, Dr. Beverly Paigen of Buffalo's Roswell Park Memorial Cancer Center, noted that there were definitely elevated "rates of miscarriages, increased risk of birth defects, increased urinary tract problems, and a striking effect on the central nervous system." A more personal reaction is registered below.

Jim Clark—an admittedly bitter man whose family has been plagued with medical problems and whose yard is littered with signs like one reading "Welcome to Chemical City"—is one resident who feels there's need for scientific studies.

"My kidney just solidified and quit functioning," he said.

"My four kids all display hyperactivity. We have three members of the family now who have skin problems. My one son quit growing at 12, developed an ulcer at 15, and he's an acute diabetic. My wife has cardiovascular problems and just everybody feels generally rotten." (*Palouse Empire News* [May 19, 1979] p. 2)

On August 2, 1978, New York State Health Commissioner Robert J. Whalen declared an emergency and on August 7, President Jimmy Carter declared it a limited disaster area and sent Federal Disaster Administrator William H. Wilcox to investigate. Subsequently, the state evacuated 239 families and purchased their homes for about $12 million.

Despite finding traces of chemicals after taking 5,000 soil samples, health investigators admit that they can find no pattern to the chemical traces nor a direct indication that they are flowing from the dump.

RESPONSIBILITY

"We take moral responsibility, not legal liability," declared Bruce Davis, executive vice president of Hooker's industrial chemical group. "What do you expect us to do—put up signs and tell people not to buy houses here?" Elsewhere he is quoted as saying, "We've had no control of that property for 25 years." He also claimed that Hooker did not want to sell the land to the school board but did so only when the Board of Education threatened to condemn the land. Hooker included a clause in the deed to the Board noting the past use of the land and required that the board assume risk of liability for any future claims that might result from the buried chemicals.

At the time the dumping occurred there were no federal or state statutes that controlled the dumping of waste materials. However, the dangers of the dumping did not become evident for the first time in 1978. In 1958 several children suffered chemical burns from playing near the closed dump. Hooker sent investigators who found chemical residues exposed apparently from material excavated to put a road through the site. The school was notified by Hooker but no further action was taken.

According to *The New York Times* (January 21, 1979)[2]:

In 1971, when almost every lot had a house on it, rainwater leaked into the canal bed, stirring up chemicals. Drums broke open on the surface, creating three-foot pools of pesticide. Dogs and cats lost their fur and died. Children burned their feet. Five infants with birth defects were born at the southern end of the canal. The miscarriage rate went up.

RELATED ACTIVITIES

1972 (New York): At Hyde Park, also in Niagara Falls, where Hooker operated another chemical waste dump, the manager of an adjacent plant wrote to Hooker complaining of "an extremely dangerous condition affecting our plant and employees . . . our midnight shift workers have (sic) complained of coughing and sore throats from the obnoxious and corrosive permeating fumes from the disposal site."

1976 (New York): Mirex, which causes cancer in laboratory animals, was being discharged illegally by Hooker's Niagara Falls plant at a rate of one pound per day. In September, 1976, the New York Department of Environmental Conservation banned consumption of seven species of fish from Lake Ontario, warning they were contaminated with Mirex. In March 1977 Hooker released a study that reported a failure to find Mirex in twelve species of Lake Ontario fish; however the Department of Environmental Conservation was not satisfied with the study.

[2] © 1979 by The New York Times Company. Reprinted by permission.

1976/1977 (Virginia): Suits of more than $100 million were filed by employees of Life Science who were exposed to Kepone dust. Symptoms ranged from severe trembling to sterility. Hooker was named as defendant since it supplied certain raw materials used in the manufacturing process. In January 1977 the suit was settled out of court. The terms of the settlement were not disclosed. A spokesman for Occidental Petroleum (who acquired Hooker in 1968) said that the settlement would have negligible impact on the earnings of Hooker.

1977 (Michigan): Hooker was ordered to pay $176,000 for discharging HCCPD, a building block for Mirex and Kepone pesticides, in a lake.

1979 (Michigan): Michigan officials sued Hooker for air, water, and land pollution around its plant in Montague. State Attorney General Frank Kelly calls Montague "an environmental time bomb." More than thirty chemicals have been identified on the site.

1979 (New York): In January the New York State Health Department surveyed residents near Hyde Park. In February, the town of Niagara Falls filed a $26 million suit against Hooker regarding its Hyde Park landfill dump.

Questions

1. Relate this case to the material presented in Part One of the textbook.

2. Discuss the ethical, legal, and managerial issues raised by this case.

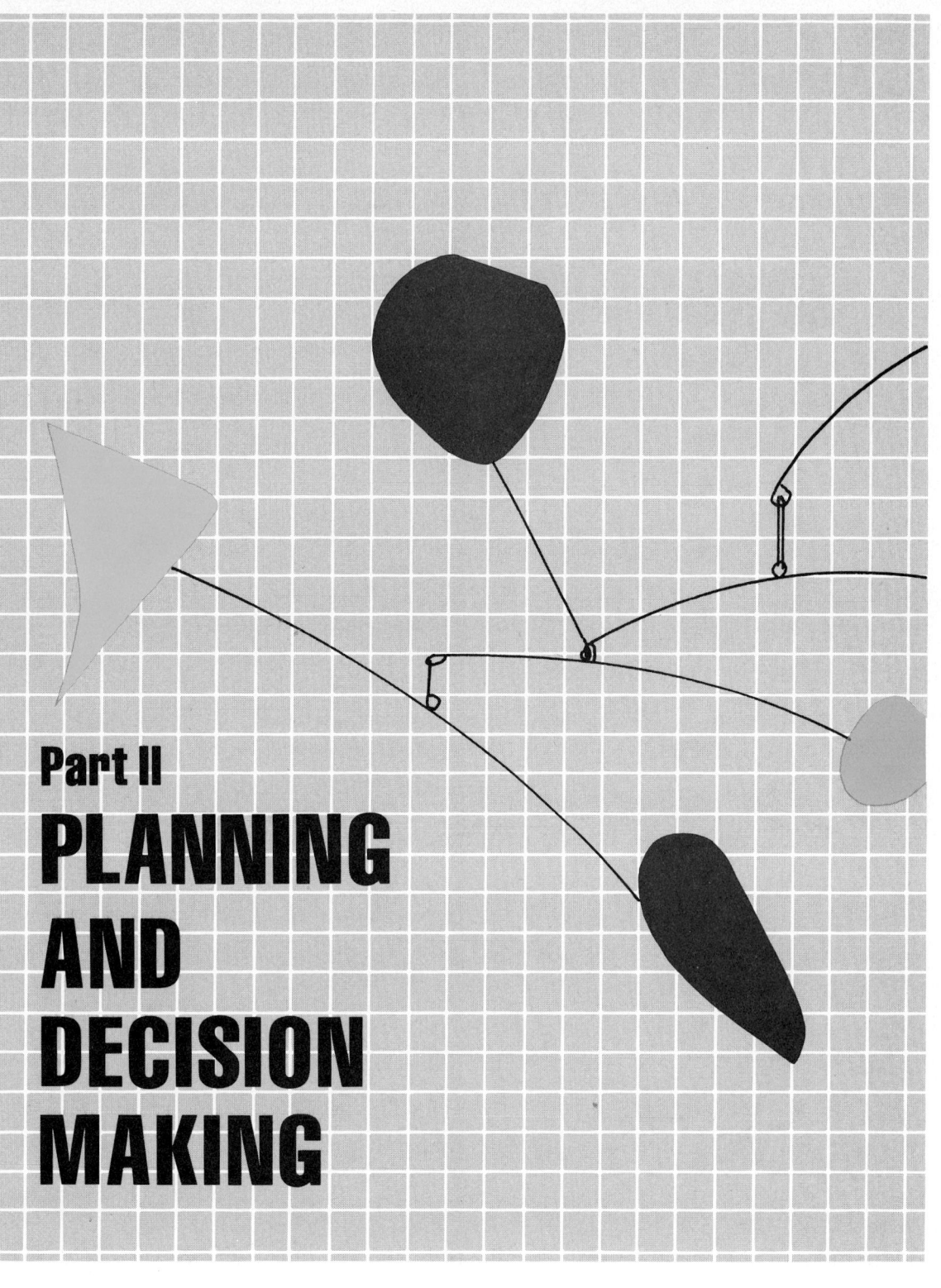

Part II
PLANNING
AND
DECISION
MAKING

4. Objectives

Learning Objectives

AFTER STUDYING THIS CHAPTER YOU SHOULD BE ABLE TO

1. Identify three major benefits provided by objectives in improving organizational effectiveness.
2. Distinguish between external and internal objectives.
3. Identify six characteristics of soundly developed goals.
4. List the steps involved in the management by objectives (MBO) process.
5. Explain the chief benefits of an MBO program.
6. Identify common problems encountered in installing an MBO program.

Key Terms

objectives

goals

short-range objectives

long-range objectives

external objectives

internal objectives

social objectives

management by objectives

Fixing your objective is like identifying the North Star—you sight your compass on it and then use it as the means of getting back on the track when you tend to stray.

MARSHALL E. DIMOCK

If someone has to be the winningest coach, it might as well be me.

PAUL W. "BEAR" BRYANT

For almost fifty years, Curt Carlson has been setting goals for himself. Goal setting began in a small way in 1937 when he began selling soap for Procter & Gamble to grocery stores for $85 a month. He noticed that some stores were generating considerable increases in sales by offering trading stamps and decided there was room for another trading-stamp company that concentrated on the grocery field. His company, the Gold Bond Stamp Company, was started with $50 in borrowed funds in Minneapolis. Carlson recorded his goals for the company on a piece of paper and put it in his wallet.

Soon the company had grown to the point where Carlson could quit the job at P&G and expand beyond his native Minneapolis. Having reached his first goal, he replaced the paper in his wallet with another one. In 1952 Carlson signed up Super Valu, his first large grocery chain. Others followed in the next few years, and he soon earned his first million. By this time he had replaced the paper-in-the-wallet technique with a giant wall chart in his company headquarters, but accomplished goals were replaced by new ones.

When trading stamps began to lose favor in the mid-1960s, Carlson diversified by acquiring the Radisson Hotel in Minneapolis and building it into a twenty-five unit "collection." Today, his privately owned Carlson Companies generates $2 billion in sales in a diverse range of businesses that include catalog showrooms, restaurants, sales incentive and motivational groups, property development, leasing, manufacturing, travel agencies, and construction.

Carlson Companies employs more than 27,000 people and ranks in the top 15 of privately owned businesses in the United States. The firm's wall chart of goals, which lays out company goals by years, occupies a prominent location at headquarters and is updated on a regular basis. At the top of the chart is the current goal: "4 billion by '87."[1]

---

[1] See Maurice Barnfather, "Capital Formation," *Forbes* (March 29, 1982), pp. 94–95; William Souder, "Executive of the Year: Curtis L. Carlson," *Corporate Report Minnesota* (January 1982), pp. 51–57; and Ted Anderson, "Is Entrepreneur a Clean Word?" *Twin Cities* (March 1982), pp. 42–47ff.

Objectives Guide the Organization

In Chapter 1 management was defined as the use of people and other resources to accomplish organizational objectives. Determination of objectives is a primary management responsibility. Objectives become guideposts in defining standards of what the organization should accomplish in such areas as customer service, profitability, and social responsibility. Without clearly stated objectives, no means exist to make these evaluations. As the Cheshire Cat told Alice in Lewis Carroll's *Alice in Wonderland*, "If you don't know where you are going, any road will get you there."

Goals Versus Objectives

Objectives are the desired outcomes that management hopes to attain.

GoALS – meANS to ACComplish oBJeCtives

Although goals and objectives are often used to mean the same, there is a difference. *Objectives* represent the desired outcome that management hopes to attain eventually. *Goals* are more concrete aims of the organization. They are more specific than objectives and often include a time schedule for completion. Goals are the specific means by which the ultimate objectives of the organization are achieved. Table 4-1 illustrates the difference between objectives and goals for four major American corporations. While one of Alcoa's objectives is profitability, the specific goal for the organization is a 20 percent return on investment before taxes.

In some organizations, notably the military and the church, the term *mission* is substituted for *objective*. The commander of a United Nations peacekeeping task force may be assigned the mission of preventing further fighting between

Table 4-1 OBJECTIVES AND GOALS OF SELECTED FIRMS	COMPANY	OBJECTIVE	GOAL
	Alcoa	Earn acceptable profits	20% return on investment (before taxes); higher on new products
	General Electric	Provide fair return on investment	20% on investment (after taxes); 7% on sales (after taxes)
	Johns-Manville	Maintain market share and increase return on investment	Market share not greater than 20%; return on investment greater than last 15-year average (about 15% after taxes)
	Sears, Roebuck	Increase market share Provide fair return on investment	Attain market share of 8–10%; realize traditional return on investment of 10–15% (after taxes)

SOURCE: Goals of these firms are listed in Robert F. Lanzillotti, "Pricing Objectives in Large Companies," *American Economic Review* (December 1958), pp. 921–940.

combatants. A minister's mission might include an increase in church membership or improved standards of living for neighborhood families through providing day-care facilities.

Objectives Improve Organizational Effectiveness

Objectives are the starting point for managerial decision making. Plans are developed to achieve organizational objectives. Policies, procedures, and performance standards all result from objectives. Control methods are based upon comparisons of performance with expectations.

Objectives improve the effectiveness of an organization by producing three major benefits:

1. *Objectives provide direction.* Clearly defined objectives specify an end goal for the organization. In the same way that the beacon of a lighthouse guides ship captains to safety, objectives direct the efforts of managers into certain channels in the pursuit of these objectives.

2. *Objectives serve as standards.* A temperature of 70° Fahrenheit reflects the homeowner's definition of a comfortable setting. In a similar manner, objectives serve as standards for the manager. Accomplishments can be measured against

"Mr. Fine, the management will thank you
to omit 'Money Is the Root of All Evil'
from your repertoire."

PROFITS—AN IMPORTANT COMPANY OBJECTIVE

SOURCE: *The New Yorker* (September 7, 1981), p. 33. Drawing by Bernard Schoenbaum; © 1981 The New Yorker Magazine, Inc.

For years the name Peter Drucker has been synonymous with objectives, goal setting, and planning—basic concepts of effective management. A consultant sought after by corporate concerns of all types, Drucker uses the great breadth of his training and experience to help his clients synthesize a successful approach to management. The Viennese-born management expert's early career in Germany included experience as an economist, financial analyst, teacher of law, and newspaper editor. After immigrating to the United States in 1937, he took on teaching assignments at Sarah Lawrence College and, later, in politics and philosophy at Bennington College.

It was a consulting assignment at General Motors, however, that changed the focus of Drucker's career. His eighteen-month study of GM's top management and structure led him to the unshakable conviction that the large corporation is the representative social institution of the American way of life. Through his insights into the nature of corporations, he hopes to help American society roll smoothly into the future. The spokes in his wheels of progress are all the aspects of a people-shaped environment—government, politics, history, economics, philosophy. The hub, of course, is management.

Drucker uses a Socratic approach in helping his clients define their organization's mission, forcing them with careful questioning to arrive at a statement of their goals and objectives. He views the lack of a well-defined mission as one of the three major causes of a company's worst mistakes. (The other two are a misunderstanding of what the company is really good at and an inability to make personnel decisions, particularly at top management levels.)

Now in his seventies, Drucker likes to characterize himself as a writer. Indeed,

these standards and performances can be evaluated. Without clearly defined objectives to serve as standards, managers possess no tools for evaluating performance; no means of deciding whether work is satisfactory or unacceptable.

3. _Objectives serve as motivators._ In addition to serving as standards and providing direction, objectives perform a role in encouraging workers to put forth their best efforts to achieve the end goals.[2] Employees who understand the objective of profitability and their role in generating profits may be motivated to work harder or more efficiently under a bonus or other profit-sharing program. Professor Edwin A. Locke argues that, so long as people view objectives as instrumental in achieving their own personal needs, they serve as powerful motivators.[3]

[2] Gary P. Latham and Gary P. Yukl, "A Review of Research on the Application of Goal Setting in Organizations," _Academy of Management Journal_ (December 1975), pp. 824–825. See also John M. Ivancevich and J. Timothy McMahon, "The Effects of Goal Setting, External Feedback, and Self-Generated Feedback on Outcome Variables: A Field Experiment," _Academy of Management Journal_ (June 1982), pp. 359–372.

[3] Edwin A. Locke, "The Ubiquity of the Technique of Goal Setting in Theories and Approaches to Employee Motivation," _Academy of Management Review_ (July 1978), pp. 594–601. See also Gary P. Latham and Edwin A. Locke, "Goal Setting—A Motivational Technique," _Organizational Dynamics_ (Autumn 1979), pp. 68–80.

his books, including *Concept of the Corporation, The Practice of Management,* and *Management: Tasks, Responsibilities, Practices,* have sold millions of copies worldwide. Although some academicians criticize his writings as "unscientific generalizations," he counters that the purely mechanistic and static methods of contemporary research are inadequate for absorbing and anticipating change. What is needed, he believes, is a science that examines events in terms of their direction rather than their causes. "It's tough for managers to realize that one's work is not defined by what one did yesterday but by what one intends to do tomorrow. For . . . the oil business, [for example] that may mean getting into other forms of energy, because petroleum in the year 2000 is going to be just another of many sources of energy that will be required to sustain the world's economy."

Management must concern itself with the future, and the future will require heavy investment in good management, Drucker believes. He argues that, with the world moving into a state of total economic integration, the most valuable development of the twentieth century, and clearly the business institution of the future, is the multinational firm. But not the conglomerate or the multinational conglomerate. The former, he claims, is virtually unmanageable; the latter, absolutely unmanageable.

The proliferation and expansion of service institutions such as hospitals, colleges, and government will also offer a great challenge to management, according to Drucker. These institutions, often typified by inefficient and ineffectual management, must be better run if they are to fulfill the only justification of any profit or nonprofit organization in his eyes: "to liberate and make productive human strength."

Sources

"Peter Drucker: A New Compendium for Management," *Business Week* (February 9, 1974), pp. 49–51.

Ronald G. Greenwood, "Management by Objectives: As Developed by Peter Drucker, Assisted by Harold Smiddy," *Academy of Management Review* (April 1981), pp. 225–230.

"Inside Peter Drucker," *Nation's Business* (March 1974), pp. 61–65.

Patricia Korenvaes, "Peter Drucker: Troubleshooter at the Top," *Dun's Review* (July 1964), pp. 43, 78–79.

Downs Matthews, "Businessmen Must Manage for the World of Tomorrow," *EXXON USA* (Third Quarter 1978), pp. 28–31.

How Many Objectives?

"What are the objectives of business?" Ask ten people this question and the most typical answer is *"profits."* The success stories of such firms as Twentieth Century-Fox and IBM are typically summarized in sales and profit figures.

But profits are not the only objective of an organization—even a business organization. Peter Drucker argues that profits are not even a major objective.

> There is only one valid definition of business purpose: to create a customer. . . . What the business thinks it produces is not of first importance—especially not to the future of the business and to its success. What the customer thinks he is buying, what he considers "value" is decisive—it determines what a business is, what it produces, and whether it will prosper.[4]

Henry Ford was even more adamant that profits are merely a means to an end. He had formed Ford Motor Company with a simple—but specific—objective in mind: to provide the American public with inexpensive transportation. According to Ford, "If one does this, one can hardly get away from profits."

[4] Peter F. Drucker, *The Practice of Management* (New York: Harper & Row, 1954), p. 37.

Profits are obviously necessary for the survival of a business firm. But profitability may also be viewed as a measure of the firm's ability to serve its customers by providing desired goods and services. Customer service is of equal importance in the nonprofit organization.

SHORT-RANGE AND LONG-RANGE OBJECTIVES

Short-range objectives refer to a period of one year or less.

Some of the firm's objectives may be labeled *short-range*, since they refer to a time period of one year or less. Intermedics, Inc., has achieved rapid growth since it introduced the first small lithium-battery pacemaker in 1976, increasing the life of heart-regulating implants from two years to six or more. Its 1984 corporate objective is a sales increase of 30 to 40 percent over 1983 sales. However, its long-term objective is to capture the number one position in the medical implants industry by surpassing the leader, Johnson & Johnson's Iolab, Inc., in sales. Since Intermedics' top management feels that achieving this aim will take more than a single year, this represents a *long-range* objective.[5]

Long-range objectives refer to a period longer than one year.

EXTERNAL AND INTERNAL OBJECTIVES

External objectives refer to service to customers and to society as a whole.

Objectives may also be divided into external and internal aims. *External* objectives are service objectives. They include service to customers and to society as a whole. Every socially responsible organization is operating in a manner designed to attain these external objectives. Failure to consider such responsibilities often results in adverse publicity, passage of restrictive legislation, establishment of consumer and environmental protection agencies, and impaired sales and profitability.

Internal objectives are designed to satisfy groups within the organization.

Internal objectives are those aims designed to satisfy groups within the organization. These objectives include such areas as sales, profitability, growth, and market standing. These areas affect such groups as managers, operative employees, and stockholders. Other internal objectives may be directed toward employees in such forms as safe working conditions, equitable wages, and attractive fringe benefit programs.

Even though objectives may be classified as internal and external, they are not totally independent. In a very real sense in the business world of the 1980s, organizations must recognize their responsibilities to both customers and to society as a whole if they are to accomplish their internal objectives.

Social objectives are objectives designed with the larger interests of society in mind.

Firms increasingly recognize a number of *social objectives*. These may include such areas as providing job opportunities for all qualified workers, paying fair wages, making factories and offices safe places to work, offering job training to handicapped workers and the hard-core unemployed, and being a good corporate citizen of the community.

Figure 4-1 describes the objectives of Ralston Purina Co., the diversified St.

[5] "Intermedics: Out to Be No. 1 in the Medical Implants Market," *Business Week* (January 18, 1982), pp. 58, 60.

CORPORATE OBJECTIVES

Our primary objective is to optimize use of our resources . . . to produce short- and long-term growth consistent with the balanced best interest of customers, shareholders, employees, suppliers, and society at large. To achieve these results, we must perform effectively in the following key result areas:

Customer satisfaction . . . Management development and performance . . . Employee attitude and performance . . . Social responsibility . . . Productivity . . . Innovation.

1

We recognize that the primary purpose of our business is to perform a necessary economic service by creating, stimulating, and satisfying customers. We must be a market-oriented company dedicated to the principle that, in order to supply the right product or service at the right time and in the right way, we need first to establish what the customer wants, where, when, how, and at what price.

2

Building on our base of protein and nutrition, we will remain diversified in our operations, multinational in organization, and global in outlook.

3

We dedicate ourselves to the principle of continuous self-renewal so that individuals, organization structure, products, facilities, and systems do not stagnate. We recognize that:

People are the ultimate source of renewal. We will bring to the corporation a steady flow of able and highly motivated individuals and then provide positive constructive programs of management development.

Organizational structure must be flexible. We will evolve subject only to the yardstick of what is most successful and meets our requirements.

We will continue to ask the question What next? We must recognize and manage the accelerating rate of change.

We will analyze assets and functions in which potential is diminishing in terms of contribution to earnings, cash flow, and tie-in value to other units in order to develop a course of action which may include disinvestment.

We must maintain an environment which fosters individual effort, rewards initiative and encourages the free and open exchange of ideas; self-criticism, and constant restudy are vital to the present health of the enterprise and are essential elements to future growth—we welcome challenging positions and opinions.

We will maintain effective and simple systems and procedures to implement organizational structure, and we will evaluate them at regular intervals.

Since the dynamics of an organization are related to motivation, conviction and morale, we will endeavor to make every employee know that his optimum efforts make a difference.

We must be results-oriented, measured and held responsible.

We must create a climate of technology, special knowledges, and services which induce in our customers a desire to buy our products and/or our services.

4

We will consistently and systematically strive to delegate decision-making authority intelligently to the proper lowest level without abrogating management responsibilities. We will measure qualitative and quantitative results through a simple and sensitive control system.

Louis-based manufacturer. Ralston Purina's statement reflects corporate awareness of numerous objectives, both internal and external, domestic and international.

Rather than develop a single list of objectives for all of its diverse subsidiaries, top management at the General Electric Company singled out eight "key result areas" that are considered essential to the continued vitality of the corporation. The areas are

1. Profitability—defined in terms of both percentage of sales and return on invested funds MOST IMPORTANT
2. Market position
3. Productivity
4. Leadership in technological research
5. Personnel development

Figure 4-1 CORPORATE OBJECTIVES OF RALSTON PURINA COMPANY

SOURCE: Ralston Purina Company. Reprinted by permission.

6. Employee attitudes and relations
7. Public attitudes and responsibility
8. Balance between short-range and long-range plans

Once these areas were defined, managers were given the responsibility for establishing specific objectives in each area, developing plans for their accomplishment, and implementing those plans.

In an attempt to determine the actual objectives of business, Y. K. Shetty surveyed a group of managers of large American business organizations and asked them to indicate specific organizational objectives.[6] Figure 4-2 shows the results of this study and compares them with the results of a similar survey conducted twelve years earlier by George W. England.

Profitability and growth were the objectives most often mentioned by the respondents of both studies. However, the two studies differ greatly in the emphasis placed on the objectives of social responsibility, resource conservation, and multinational expansion. The listing of these objectives by the respondents in the more recent study is evidence of the impact of the environment upon the organization and its objectives. Such objectives were rare in the 1950s and 1960s, and many managers argued that the attainment of objectives related to

[6] Y. K. Shetty, "New Look at Corporate Goals," *California Management Review* (Winter 1979), pp. 71–79.

Figure 4-2
THE OBJECTIVES OF BUSINESS: A COMPARISON OF THE ENGLAND AND SHETTY STUDIES

SOURCES: The Shetty data are adapted from Y. K. Shetty, "New Look at Corporate Goals," *California Management Review*, 22, no. 2, p. 73, © 1979 by the Regents of the University of California. It is adapted by permission of the Regents. The England data are from George W. England, "Organizational Goals and Expected Behavior of American Managers," *Academy of Management Journal* (June 1967), p. 108.

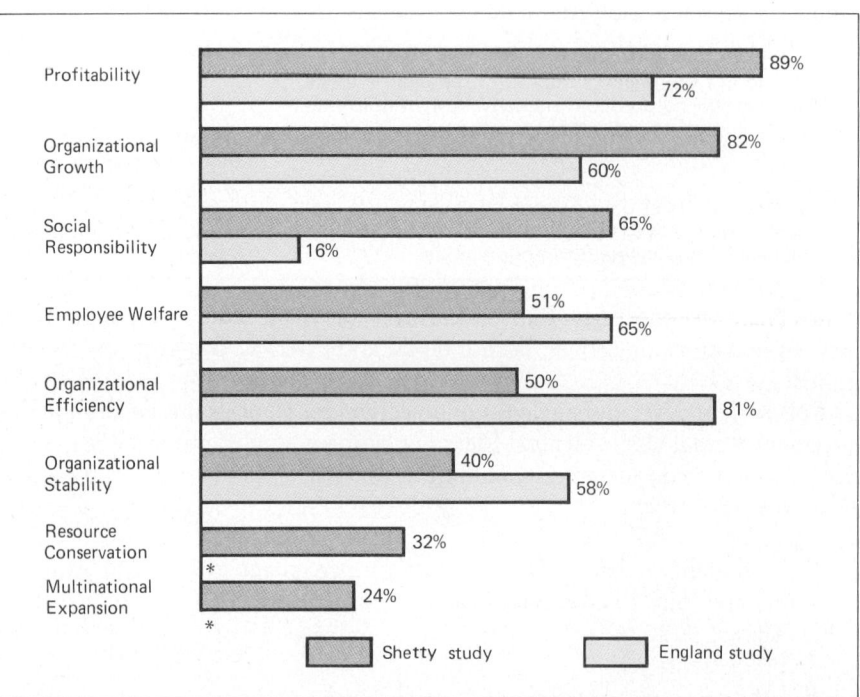

*Not mentioned as a separate category in the England study.

efficiency, productivity, and profitability were prerequisites to accomplishing social and employee objectives.[7] While many managers continue to hold this
viewpoint, the typical statement of organizational objectives in the 1980s includes these social and employee aims as explicit objectives of the firm. In addition, the more consumer-oriented environment of the past decade and the
increased international competition for resources and markets influenced one
respondent in four to specify multinational expansion as an organizational objective in the recent survey.

Hierarchy of Objectives

Not only do most organizations have a number of objectives, but these objectives typically exist in a hierarchy. At the top are the overall objectives of the entire organization.[8] The broader aims of service, market share, sales, profitability,
and return on investment are then broken down into objectives for each division,
operating facility, department, work group, and individual employee. Once this
is accomplished, each member of the organization can relate his or her contribution to the overall organizational objectives.

The number of levels in the hierarchy depends upon the size and complexity
of the organization. Large, multiproduct firms generally have more levels of objectives than do smaller organizations. Figure 4-3 illustrates the hierarchy of objectives for a typical firm.

Characteristics of Sound Goals

Goals are derived from the general objectives of profitability, market position,
customer service, human resource development, growth, public attitudes, and
aims related to the general public and the environment. Soundly conceived goals
have the following characteristics:

Goals are the concrete aims of the organization. They are more specific than objectives.

1. *Goals should be specific.* Perhaps the most common weakness of organizational goals is that they are stated in too general terms. While some flexibility is
desirable, goals that are too general become little more than platitudes. An organizational objective of growth must be reflected in specific goals specifying
what is meant by growth. Specific growth goals could then specify adequate sales
growth ("Five percent sales increase over last year"), market position ("Attain a
15 percent share of the market by 1986") and profitability ("10 percent increase
in profits over last year"). Specific high-level goals also simplify the process of
goal setting at lower levels in the organization.

[7] George W. England, "Organizational Goals and Expected Behavior of American Managers,"
Academy of Management Journal (June 1967), pp. 107–117. See also Kamal M. Abouzeid and
Charles N. Weaver, "Social Responsibility in the Corporate Goal Hierarchy," *Business Horizons*
(June 1978), pp. 29–35.
[8] See Charles H. Granger, "The Hierarchy of Objectives," *Harvard Business Review* (May–June
1964), p. 63ff.

Figure 4-3
THE HIERARCHY OF
OBJECTIVES—FROM
CORPORATE LEVEL
TO INDIVIDUAL
WORKER

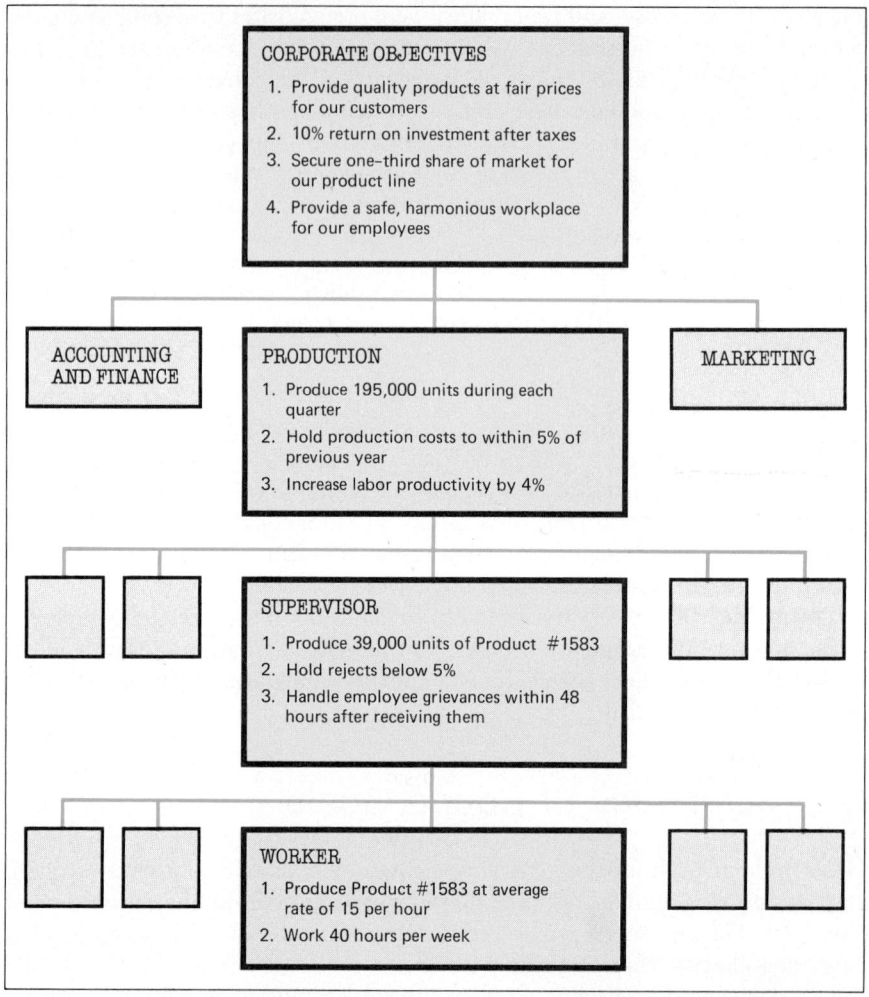

CORPORATE OBJECTIVES

1. Provide quality products at fair prices for our customers
2. 10% return on investment after taxes
3. Secure one–third share of market for our product line
4. Provide a safe, harmonious workplace for our employees

ACCOUNTING AND FINANCE

PRODUCTION

1. Produce 195,000 units during each quarter
2. Hold production costs to within 5% of previous year
3. Increase labor productivity by 4%

MARKETING

SUPERVISOR

1. Produce 39,000 units of Product #1583
2. Hold rejects below 5%
3. Handle employee grievances within 48 hours after receiving them

WORKER

1. Produce Product #1583 at average rate of 15 per hour
2. Work 40 hours per week

2. *Goals should be measurable.* Goals that are measurable have built-in performance indicators. A goal of increasing market share by 5 percent during the next fiscal year allows each manager to measure progress during the year and to compare performance with expectations. It also implies specific actions for all of those persons involved in activities affecting the accomplishment of the goal. In contrast, a goal of increased market share is of little value since its meaning will differ with different people. Both a 1 percent increase and a 40 percent increase in market share would meet the general goal. The measurable goals provide mutual understanding and a definite basis for comparing actual performance with expectations.

Some goals are more difficult to measure than others. How can a manager make such goals as improved employee morale, good corporate citizenship, and provision of a safe workplace measurable? Although it is more difficult to trans-

The bumblebee is probably most often associated with former heavyweight boxing champion Muhammad (''Float like a butterfly, sting like a bee'') Ali. But in the corporate world, it has been chosen to reflect the goals of Dallas-based Mary Kay Cosmetics.

The firm's founder, Mary Kay Ash, is a renowned saleswoman, boasting a direct sales career with such companies as Stanley Home Products and World Gifts and enshrinement in the Direct Selling Hall of Fame. She retired to write a book on sales for women; then in 1963 she changed her mind and founded Mary Kay Cosmetics, Inc. Her cosmetics lines were based originally upon a formula for softening animal hides. Ash began with a $5,000 investment and a team of ten saleswomen. And she developed several goals. The symbol she chose to reflect these goals was the bumblebee. As any aerodynamics engineer will explain, the bumblebee can't fly—its wings are too small to lift its body. But since none of the engineers bothered to tell the bumblebee, it flies anyway.

Today Mary Kay Cosmetics is also soaring. Its annual sales exceeded $235 million in 1981 and its team of 150,000 beauty consultants cover the United States, Canada, and Australia.

SOURCE: The Mary Kay Cosmetics success story is described in Howard Rudnitsky, ''The Flight of the Bumblebee,'' *Forbes* (June 22, 1981), pp. 104–106.

late these goals into measurable terms than sales and profit goals, it is certainly not impossible. Employee safety might be translated into a goal of reducing employee workdays lost as a result of accidents by 5 percent over the previous year. Employee morale may be reflected in terms of absenteeism or turnover, and specific goals may be developed to apply to these areas. Corporate citizenship may be reflected in the number of hours employees devote to civic roles, reduction of pollution by a stated amount, or the hiring of hard-core unemployed. Once measurements are determined, management can establish control procedures to determine whether performance is acceptable in each area.

3. *Goals should be time-specific.* Goals should have time frames within which they will be accomplished. In addition to being measurable, goals should indicate the period in which they are to be attained. Within the organization, goals may be set on a daily, weekly, monthly, and annual basis.

4. *Goals should focus on results, not activities.* Activities are the means by which goals are accomplished. Additional training for production workers may facilitate the accomplishment of the firm's goal of improving employee productivity by 5 percent over 1984. However, the goal continues to be the productivity increase.

5. *Goals should be challenging but realistic.* Goals that are unrealistically high are ineffective as soon as employees realize they are unattainable. On the other hand, those goals that call for the best efforts of all employees for their accomplishment provide a sense of accomplishment and are effective means for motivating people.

6. *Goals should be set by the people responsible for accomplishing them, whenever possible.* It is much easier to obtain commitment to goals when those

THE PERILS OF NONPARTICIPATIVE GOAL-SETTING

Richard Beeson quickly discovered just how uncomfortable specific goals could be when they are handed down from top management instead of agreed to by subordinates and superiors. Beeson, president of Canada Dry, a subsidiary of Norton Simon, Inc., describes his experiences in working with Norton Simon chief executive David J. Mahoney, in the following interview:

"I had been on the job only a couple of weeks," Beeson says, "when we had a Canada Dry board meeting. I said to Mahoney, 'Dave, we're a little bit below budget now, and I think we can hold that for the rest of the year. It won't get any worse.'

"Dave looked at me, smiled, and said: 'Be on budget by the six-month mark; be on by the year.'

" 'But Dave,' I said, 'there isn't enough time to get on by the *half*. I inherited this situation, after all.'

"Still smiling, Dave looked at me and said, 'Do I pay you a lot of money? Do I argue with you over what you want to spend? Do I bother you? Then don't tell me what the goals should be. Be on by the half; be on by the end of the year.'

" 'What if I can't, Dave?' I asked.

" 'Then clean out your desk and go home.' "

Beeson . . . began running through the reasons why he could not meet the goals, but Mahoney said: "Not interested. My board and my stockholders want me to make my numbers. The way I make my numbers is for you guys to make *your* numbers. Make your numbers."

SOURCE: " 'The Way I Make My Numbers Is for You Guys to Make Your Numbers,' " *Forbes* (February 15, 1982), p. 26.

persons responsible for their accomplishment have played a role in developing them.

Management must ensure that goals are communicated to all members of the organization. Each employee should understand how his or her individual work goals relate to the overall organizational goals. Goals should not be so numerous or complex that they confuse rather than direct members of the organization. And management must be prepared periodically to refine—or even replace—goals with new ones. As the organization and the environment in which it operates change, goals may require adjustments to reflect these changes.

Management by Objectives

What do General Motors, Du Pont, RCA, General Foods, 3M Company, Honeywell, the Air Force Logistics Command, Paul Revere Life Insurance, and the City of Tulsa Parks Department have in common? All of these organizations have successful management by objectives (MBO) programs in operation.

Few management techniques have received more publicity in the past two decades than management by objectives. Although MBO was being employed by a few firms since the 1930s, it was first popularized by Peter Drucker, who described it this way:

The objectives of the district manager's job should be clearly defined by the contribution he and his district sales force have to make to the sales department, the objectives of the project engineer's job by the contributions he, his engineers and draftsmen make to the engineering department. . . . This requires each manager to develop and set the objectives of his unit himself. Higher management must, of course, reserve the power to approve or disapprove his objectives. But their development is part of a manager's responsibility; indeed, it is his first responsibility.[9]

Management by objectives often carries different labels: *managing for results, management by results, goals management,* and *management by commitment.* While *management by goals* is probably a more appropriate title, the technique has been popularized by the MBO name. MBO may be defined as a process whereby the superior and subordinate managers of an organization identify goals common to each, define areas of responsibility in terms of expected results, and use these measures as guides for operating the unit and assessing the contribution of each member of the organization.[10] MBO programs are designed to improve employees' motivation through their participation in setting their individual goals and knowing in advance precisely how they will be evaluated.

STEPS INVOLVED IN AN MBO PROGRAM

Most MBO programs follow this sequence:

1. The subordinate develops a description of his or her job and discusses the description with the superior.
2. Short-term performance goals are established.
3. During the period in which the MBO program is operating, the subordinate meets regularly with the superior to discuss progress toward the goals.
4. Specific intermediate checkpoints are established to measure progress toward meeting the goals.
5. At the end of the defined period, subordinate and superior meet to evaluate the results of the subordinate's efforts. New goals for the following period are established.

Figure 4-4 illustrates the MBO system used by ALCOA.

BENEFITS OF AN MBO PROGRAM

The major benefit of any MBO program is the linking of the objective setting with individual motivation. Since the individual employee participates in setting

[9] Drucker, *The Practice of Management,* pp. 128–129.

[10] George Odiorne, *Management by Objectives: A System of Managerial Leadership* (New York: Pitman, 1965), p. 55. Three other major contributions to the MBO literature are Stephen J. Carroll, Jr., and Henry L. Tosi, Jr., *Management by Objectives: Applications and Research* (New York: Macmillan, 1973); Douglas M. McGregor, "An Uneasy Look at Performance Evaluation," *Harvard Business Review* (May–June 1957), pp. 89–94; and George S. Odiorne, *MBO II: A System of Managerial Leadership for the 80s* (Belmont, Calif.: Fearon Pitman, 1979).

Figure 4-4
THE MANAGEMENT BY OBJECTIVES SEQUENCE AT ALCOA

SOURCE: The Alcoa MBO program is described in Walter S. Wikstrom, *Managing by-and-with Objectives,* Studies in Personnel Policy, No. 212 (New York: Conference Board, 1968), p. 3.

STEP 1
Individual lists major performance objectives for coming period with target dates for accomplishing them.

STEP 2
Goals are submitted to superior for review. Discussions between superior and subordinate result in agreed-upon set of goals.

STEP 4
At the end of the year individual prepares "accomplishment report" which lists major accomplishments and comments on the variances between expected and actual performance.

STEP 3
Superior and subordinate meet on a quarterly basis to review progress and make revisions or update goals as needed.

STEP 5
Self-appraisal is discussed with superior. Reasons for goals not being met are explored.

STEP 6
New set of goals is established for the next year.

his or her own goals, there is a commitment to them. Workers know both the tasks to be accomplished and how they will be evaluated. Improved morale may also result from regular face-to-face communications between employees and their superiors.

MBO AT EVERY LEVEL IN THE ORGANIZATION?

MBO is a particularly flexible management technique that may be implemented for a single department or for the entire organization. It is generally agreed that an MBO program should begin with the chief executive officer of the organization setting specific goals in consultation with the board of directors. The process should then extend throughout the organization.

MBO FOR EVERY ORGANIZATION?

Although early applications of MBO were limited to business organizations, it has since spread to such diverse organizations as the Department of Defense, educational agencies, local government bodies, and charitable organizations. MBO has considerable merits in settings where performance measures are vague or lacking.[11]

PROBLEMS WITH MBO

Experience with MBO programs indicates that they can make significant contributions to the organization if used with judgment and a great deal of planning. However, one study of the top 500 manufacturing firms in the United States revealed that only 10 percent of the industrial giants were totally satisfied with their MBO programs.[12]

When MBO programs fail or do not measure up to management expectations, one or more of the following problem areas are likely to exist:

1. Lack of support and involvement by top management
2. Lack of commitment
3. Objectives handed to subordinate rather than the result of joint agreement
4. Poor implementation methods
5. Little coaching and assistance
6. Overemphasis on appraisal
7. Overemphasis on paperwork[13]

MBO programs are doomed without the total support of top management. All too often, top management begins an MBO program as "the latest fad" and delegates its implementation to subordinates. In some instances, top management specifies organizational goals and leaves no flexibility for subordinates. In other cases, organizations rush into implementation of an MBO program without sufficient preparation or understanding. Hollman and Tansik quote one

[11] Dale D. McConkey, *MBO for Nonprofit Organizations* (New York: AMACOM, 1975); Mark A. Covaleski and Mark W. Dirsmith, "MBO and Goal Directedness in a Hospital Context," *Academy of Management Review* (July 1981), pp. 409–418.

[12] Fred E. Schuster and Alva F. Kindall, "Management by Objectives: Where We Stand—A Survey of the Fortune 500," *Human Resources Management* (Spring 1974), pp. 8–11. For a survey of empirical research on MBO effectiveness, see Jack N. Kondrasuk, "Studies in MBO Effectiveness," *Academy of Management Review* (July 1981), pp. 419–430.

[13] Adapted from W. J. Reddin, *Effective Management by Objectives* (New York: McGraw-Hill, 1970), p. 122

manager in a public sector organization who expresses the confusion that often results from a hurried, inadequately planned implementation:

> First we heard all about MBO. We took a 3-day workshop and were told how to go about doing MBO in a city government. Then somebody in Personnel began pushing a Management by Results (MBR) seminar. Right now we don't know what we're *supposed* to be doing. I do know what we are doing though—just what we've always done. We'll react when their intentions are clear.[14]

Some MBO programs suffer from managers' unwillingness to devote time to the regular face-to-face meetings required in MBO programs. Still others fail as a result of a mechanical approach relying on volumes of paperwork for both superior and subordinate.[15]

MBO programs have a greater probability of success when they are implemented by top management in an orderly, unhurried fashion and all participants receive training prior to its implementation. Other programs in similar organizations may be studied. Limited testing and debugging of the proposed program may prove extremely beneficial. The normal time for implementing a successful MBO program on an organization-wide basis may be three years or more.[16]

[14] Robert W. Hollman and David A. Tansik, "A Life Cycle Approach to Management by Objectives," *Academy of Management Review* (October 1977), p. 682. See also George S. Odiorne, "The Politics of Implementing MBO," *Business Horizons* (December 1974), pp. 13–21.

[15] See Bruce D. Jamieson, "Behavioral Problems with Management by Objectives," *Academy of Management Review* (September 1973), pp. 496–505; and Charles H. Ford, "MBO: An Idea Whose Time Has Gone," *Business Horizons* (December 1979), pp. 48–55. Ivancevich has conducted two small-scale studies that suggest that the positive effects of MBO may wear off over time. See John M. Ivancevich, "A Longitudinal Assessment of Management by Objectives," *Administrative Science Quarterly* (March 1972), p. 126; and John M. Ivancevich, "Different Goal Setting Treatments and Their Effects on Performance and Job Satisfaction," *Academy of Management Journal* (September 1977), p. 406.

[16] Glenn H. Varney, *Management by Objectives* (Chicago: Dartnell Corporation, 1971), pp. 39–40.

Summary

Objectives are the starting point for any organization. They guide the members of the firm in their planning, policy and procedures development, and controlling. In addition to providing direction for the organization, they also serve as standards by which actual performance can be compared with expectations. Finally, they serve as motivators for organizational members who are given clear aims for which to strive.

All organizations recognize a number of objectives. These include such aims as survival and growth, profits, and organizational efficiency. Social objectives also

exist and are recognized by enlightened management. Objectives may be classified as short range and long range, external and internal. Short-range objectives are those referring to a time period of one year or less. Long-range aims cover a time period in excess of one year. External objectives are service objectives, including service to customers and to society as a whole. Internal objectives are those aims designed to satisfy such groups within the organization as management, employees, and stockholders.

Although the terms are often used as if they were

synonymous, it is useful to distinguish between goals and objectives. *Objectives* is a broader term referring to the desired outcome that management hopes to attain eventually. *Goals* are more specific, concrete aims of the organization and typically include a time schedule for completion. Both goals and objectives exist in a hierarchy ranging from the overall aims of the organization to the specific goals and objectives of each individual worker.

Soundly conceived goals possess the following characteristics:

1. They should be specific.
2. They should be measurable.
3. They should be time-specific.
4. They should focus on results, not activities.
5. They should be challenging but realistic.
6. They should be set by the people responsible for accomplishing them, whenever possible.

Management by objectives is a widely used program that focuses on employee participation in setting individual work goals. Manager and subordinates agree on goals, and each participates in evaluating the worker's success in achieving these goals. Each member of the organization knows in advance what is expected and the basis of evaluation.

Many MBO program failures have occurred because of lack of top management support; hurried, inadequately planned implementation; lack of regular contacts and mutual agreement to match the leadership styles of individual managers; excessive paperwork; and a variety of other problems. Successful implementation requires the support of top management and typically starts with the chief executive of the firm. Careful planning, complete understanding of MBO by all members of the organization, and sufficient time for implementation should increase the likelihood of success.

REVIEW EXERCISES

1. Define the following terms: (a) objectives (b) goals (c) short-range objectives (d) long-range objectives (e) external objectives (f) internal objectives (g) social objectives (h) hierarchy of objectives (i) management by objectives.

2. Identify the three major benefits provided by objectives in improving organizational effectiveness.

3. Distinguish between internal and external objectives.

4. What were the major findings of the Shetty and England studies of organizational objectives?

5. Distinguish between goals and objectives. Include an example in your answer.

6. What determines the number of levels in a hierarchy of objectives?

7. Identify and briefly explain six characteristics of soundly conceived goals.

8. What are the steps involved in a typical management by objectives program?

9. Describe the primary benefits of an MBO program.

10. What are the common problems encountered in installing an MBO program?

ASSIGNMENTS/PROBLEMS/ DISCUSSION QUESTIONS

1. What two objectives do you feel are likely to be ranked highest by the following:

    a. Manager of the local travelers' aid office
    b. Supervisor of the quality control department at Olympia Brewing Co.
    c. Executive director of the Boston Pops symphony
    d. Head of the business office at your college or university

2. Identify the objectives of your college or university. Then give examples of how each objective might be translated into specific goals.

3. Make a list of your personal goals for the next twelve months. Compare this list with the characteristics of sound goals described in the chapter.

4. Design an MBO program for an organization of which you are a current member.

5. As the text indicates, a number of problems are often encountered in the installation of an MBO program. Suggest methods by which these problems may be reduced.

A MANAGERIAL INCIDENT

Objectives of the Arizona Public Service Company

Below is a listing of the objectives of a large public utility that serves individual, business, and government customers throughout the state of Arizona.

The eight categories of objectives recognized by Arizona Public Service Company reflect corporate awareness of numerous objectives, both internal and external, short-range and long-range.

CUSTOMER SERVICE AND PRODUCT QUALITY

To supply gas and electric service for the home, the community, commerce, agriculture, industry, and government

- at the lowest possible cost
- in the quantities customers demand
- with constantly improved quality
- with increasing beneficial uses of our service.

PROFITABILITY

To earn an adequate profit so that

- investors' risk and replacement and obsolescence of capital assets can be provided for
- earnings can be reinvested and new capital can be attracted and retained
- the company's total efforts and net effectiveness will be financially sound.

EMPLOYEE ATTITUDES AND INCENTIVES

To attain skillful, safe performance, loyalty and teamwork of individual employees by

- establishing good wages, benefits, and working conditions
- maintaining security of employment
- preserving individual human values and human dignity
- assuring opportunity for self-improvement, advancement, and self-realization.

MANAGERIAL PERFORMANCE AND DEVELOPMENT

To provide for a continuity of managerial leadership and company progress by

- stimulating continuous moral and technical self-development of managerial personnel
- soundly designing a dynamic organization structure
- clearly defining objectives, policies and standards of managerial performance
- assuring opportunity and authority to perform within the bounds of capacities, objectives, and job functions
- establishing incentives proportionate to responsibilities, risks, and results.

PHYSICAL AND FINANCIAL RESOURCES

To provide for the future financial and physical needs of the company by planning and providing for

- continuing sources of adequate fuel and power
- adequate office facilities, tools, and equipment
- capital supply requirements.

PRODUCTIVITY

To attain constantly improving productive performance of all employees through

- effective and balanced utilization of human and material resources
- development and adoption of new tools, equipment, and methods, and through refinements of proven methods of work
- feasible but challenging standards of performance for individual employees and each segment of the organization.

INNOVATION AND RESEARCH

To engage in research and study in all fields and areas of work relating to business and the utility industry by

- contributing to, developing, and utilizing technological advances
- developing sensitivity to changing conditions—economic, technological, and scientific
- developing new, better, and more efficient methods of rendering service to customers
- keeping up with advances in knowledge and skills in all major areas of activity.

PUBLIC RESPONSIBILITY

To recognize the company's public responsibility and earn public confidence by

- leading in efforts to bring about community and industrial growth, development, and betterment
- opposing efforts to destroy individual initiative and the private business system
- maintaining constructive and forthright relationships with governmental bodies
- contributing to the development and strength of the utility and allied industries, sharing our advances and benefiting from experience and ideas.

SOURCE: Arizona Public Service Company.

Questions and Problems

1. A statement of objectives should produce three benefits aimed at improving organizational effectiveness. Identify each benefit and relate it to the Arizona Public Service Company corporate objectives.

2. Classify the objectives of Arizona Public Service Company on the following bases:

   a. Short range and long range
   b. Internal and external

3. Give an example of specific goals that might be related to each objective of Arizona Public Service Company.

5. Planning

Learning Objectives

AFTER STUDYING THIS CHAPTER YOU SHOULD BE ABLE TO

1. Identify the steps in the planning process.
2. Explain the relationship between planning and decision making.
3. List the major benefits of planning.
4. Categorize plans on the bases of time, usage, and scope or depth.
5. Identify the factors that determine how an organization will structure its planning activities.
6. Explain the relationship between time management and planning.

Key Terms

planning

plan

commitment principle

single-use plan

program

project

budget

standing plan

policy

procedure

rule

strategic planning

tactical planning

staff planning group

Plans are nothing; planning is everything.

DWIGHT D. EISENHOWER

No amount of sophistication is going to
allay the fact that all your knowledge is
about the past and all your decisions
are about the future.

IAN E. WILSON

The firm was renowned throughout the world for its luxury cars. The models—Silver Shadow, Phaeton, Corniche—were regarded as the ulti-mate in elegance as well as price. Company executives claimed with pride that of all the automobiles it had manufactured since 1905, at least half were still on the road.

Although the general public closely identified the Rolls-Royce name with motor cars, 95 percent of corporate sales resulted from the design and manufac-ture of aircraft engines. And it was this part of the firm's business that would ultimately lead to disaster.

In 1968 Rolls-Royce startled the aircraft industry by underbidding its U.S. competitors and receiving a $489 million contract to build the RB-211 engine that would power the new Lockheed L-1011 plane. The engineer salesperson who secured the contract was knighted for his efforts. Rolls-Royce was so confi-dent that its skilled teams of engineers and technicians would be able to cut costs by achieving technological breakthroughs in developing a carbon-fiber ma-terial for the engine turbine blades that it agreed to a $120 million penalty should it be unable to deliver the engines in 1971.

The Rolls-Royce plan called for an expenditure of $156 million in develop-ment costs with the objective of achieving the technological improvements nec-essary to sell the engines to Lockheed at $840,000 per unit and earn a profit. But events were not progressing according to plan. The technological breakthroughs never occurred, and development costs soared above $400 million. By 1970 it had become apparent that the production cost of each engine would exceed the sales price by at least $264,000 and that the late delivery penalties would be lev-ied.

In late 1970 the British government agreed to bail out the company with a $100 million loan. But three months later, Rolls-Royce requested that the loan be increased to $360 million. At this point the British government refused, and

the once-proud firm went into voluntary liquidation. The government national-
ized the firm's aircraft engine business, forming a new, state-owned corporation
called Rolls-Royce (1971) Ltd. The prestigious automobile business was sold
through a public offering of shares—and a new company called Rolls-Royce Materials (Holdings) Ltd. was formed in 1973.[1]

Planning—A Crucial Function in Every Organization

Don Shula, head coach of the Miami Dolphins, tells his listeners that planning
is the key to his organization's success and that many of his team's victories can
be attributed to careful pregame planning. The director of the local United
Fund organization echoes Shula's statements concerning the necessity of careful
planning in order to achieve yearly goals. Most organizations—profit and nonprofit—develop plans and then work closely within the framework of these plans
in order to accomplish objectives.

Managers engaged in the ongoing process of planning count on at least one
constant in the fast-paced world of the 1980s: *change*. U.S. computer manufacturers are affected by government policies restricting sales to the Soviet Union.
Cable television companies expecting to offer subscribers new programs provided through additional communications satellites are required to adjust their
plans when the satellites malfunction, or when the Federal Communications
Commission modifies its transmission rules. Plans for a new production facility
may have to be changed should zoning changes required for construction fail to
be approved by the local zoning authority.

Although unexpected developments are not always negative, they can often
devastate the ill-prepared. Engaging in planning forces managers to anticipate
change and to prepare to cope with it. Change can often result in new opportunities, new markets, a chance for growth—*if* plans have been made to capitalize
upon such change.

The ability to develop effective plans and the need for planning are not limited to large organizations. Although larger organizations often have the added
resources, specialized talent, and time to allow them to develop detailed plans,
effective planning may be even more important to the smaller organizations. In
many cases the small organization possesses limited resources and cannot afford
the luxury of trial and error or of failure.

The planning process and its resultant plans have become increasingly sophisticated as organizations recognize that no managerial function is more important than planning. Quantitative techniques and computers are frequently
employed. Yet all plans utilize one crucial component: *human resources*. People
engage in planning, develop plans, are part of them, and are directly affected by
them. Their understanding, motivation, and productivity must be major factors
in any planning activities.

[1] The Rolls-Royce events are documented in "Rolls-Royce's Woes," *Newsweek* (August 17, 1970),
p. 74; "The Bankrupt Bonanza," *Dun's Review* (March 1975), pp. 76–77; and C. Northcote
Parkinson, *Big Business* (Boston: Little, Brown, 1974), pp. 161–165.

What Is Planning?

"Should we open a new branch bank in the Skyline Plaza to capitalize on the city's growth in that direction?"

"Will our concert audience be offended if we add a Pops series to the Philharmonic's offerings this season, or will this new series enable us to increase the number of season ticketholders?"

"If we commit $1.9 million to battery capacity research, what if the market for battery-driven autos grows by only a 3 percent rate between now and 1990?"

Questions such as these are posed frequently in small firms as well as in very large organizations. Managers must anticipate future environmental changes that may affect operations. Such changes might consist of changes in the inflation rate, technological innovations by competitors, raw material shortages, or political disturbances in a country where the firm has production facilities. While these changes are beyond the control of managers, effective planning aids in reducing risk and preparing the firm to withstand the roller coaster ride of future uncertainty.

Planning can be defined as the process by which managers set objectives, assess the future, and develop courses of action designed to accomplish these objectives. As the definition states, the planning process actually includes the determination of appropriate goals and objectives and the optimum timetable for achieving them. Effective planning often means the difference between success, mediocrity, and failure. It is a continuous function that directs the organization through a change-oriented environment in the pursuit of established objectives. It also specifies the actions needed to reach these objectives.

As Figure 5-1 indicates, organizations are recognizing the importance of the planning function by actively seeking individuals who exhibit skill in this vital area. The positions described are typical of those found in the classified section of any major newspaper.

Planning is the process by which managers set objectives, assess the future, and develop courses of action to accomplish these objectives.

PLAN VERSUS PLANNING

As the formal definition states, the planning process involves the continual re-evaluation, analysis, and adjustment of organizational activities toward defined and agreed-upon objectives. One writer stated that successful planning must be based on a searching look within, a broad look around, and a long look ahead.[2] The *look within* involves thorough reviews of organizational assets, including human resources, facilities and equipment, location, and patents and trademarks. The *broad look around* is relations-oriented, focusing upon such factors as the organization's relations with suppliers, lenders, customers, and the community. The *long look ahead* combines these factors with forecasts that relate the present to the future. The alternative to planning is random behavior.

[2] Ewing W. Reilley, "Planning the Strategy of the Business," *Advanced Management* (December 1955), pp. 8–12.

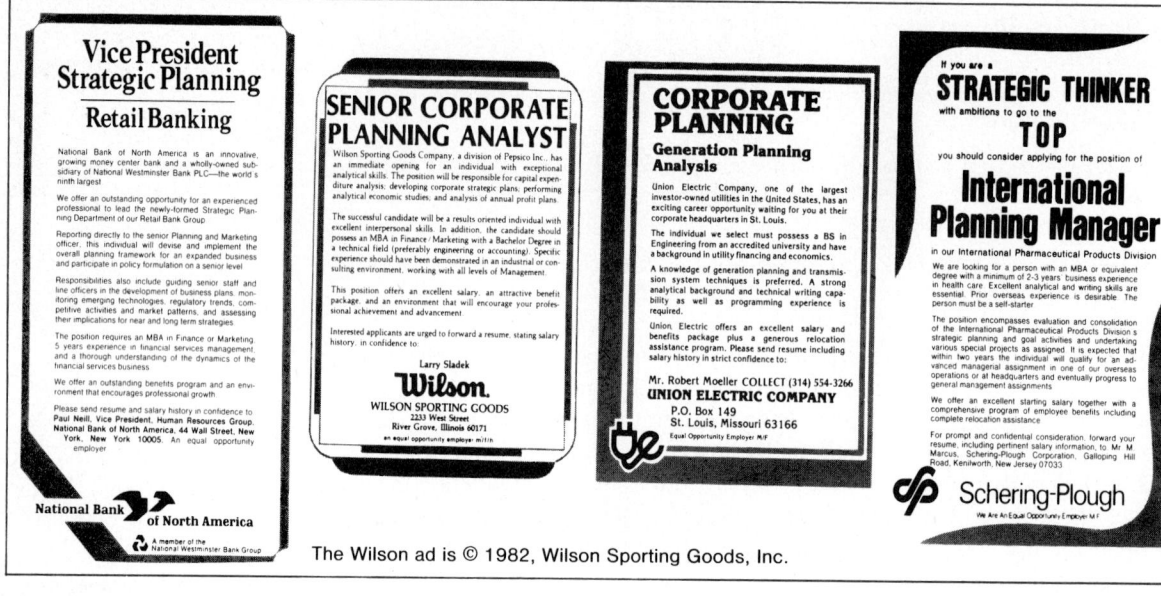

**Figure 5-1
CLASSIFIED
ADVERTISEMENTS
FOR QUALIFIED
PLANNERS**

SOURCE: *National Business Employment Weekly* (published by *The Wall Street Journal*) (June 6, 1982), pp. 18, 22, 29, 45. The ads are reprinted by permission of the companies.

Plans are detailed expressions of actions necessary to accomplish stated organizational objectives.

Plans are natural outgrowths of the planning process. They are detailed expressions of actions necessary to accomplish stated organizational objectives. Once plans are formulated and implemented, they are periodically evaluated to determine their success in moving the organization in the direction of its stated goals.

THREE STEPS IN PLANNING

The planning process consists of three phases:

1. *Setting organizational objectives.* Organizational objectives, the subject of Chapter 4, are part of the planning process. They may be considered *ends* since they serve as the focal point for organizational decisions and activities.

The importance of establishing organizational objectives is made clear by the following example. ROLM Corp. decided to accomplish its growth and profitability objectives by challenging American Telephone & Telegraph, the communications giant, as a supplier of telecommunications systems to corporations. ROLM's introduction in 1975 of a 400-line computerized branch exchange (CBX) with sophisticated switching gear proved quite successful in serving smaller organizations, but the corporate giants required greater line capacity. Following careful analysis of such factors as cost, market potential, and competitive offerings, ROLM introduced two larger versions: a 1,500-phone CBX and a very large 4,000-line CBX. As a result ROLM sales grew at a 60 percent rate annually, and recent sales have passed the $400 million mark. All twenty of America's largest corporations have installed ROLM equipment. Clearly, ROLM has successfully met the objectives it set for itself.[3]

---

[3] *The Successful Strategist.* Copyright 1979 by Alexander-Norton Publishers, Inc., 100 Fifth Avenue, New York, New York 10011. All rights reserved.

**PLANS ARE THE
RESULT OF THE
PLANNING PROCESS**

SOURCE: Cartoon by Reg
Hider. Reprinted from *The
Wall Street Journal* by per-
mission of Cartoon Features
Syndicate.

*"Things must be going badly—he keeps
referring to it as my plan."*

2. *Developing planning premises.* Premises are assumptions about the environment in which the organization exists. Changing environmental factors
continually influence an organization's activities, forcing adaptations of current
operations and reviews. Skilled managers employ every available information
source to anticipate and plan methods of coping with such contingencies. These
factors may develop outside the organization (declines in sales of recreational
vehicles as a result of increased gasoline prices); in one or more parts of the organization (reduced production costs as a result of using less expensive raw materials); or within the manager's own immediate scope of authority (reduced
productivity among new employees). Forecasts often aid the manager in developing alternative plans to serve as the *means* by which organizational ends are
reached.

3. *Developing methods to control the operation of the plan.* Although the
evaluation and control process is discussed in detail in Chapters 16–18, it is
closely related to the planning process. Controlling involves the continual analysis and measurement of actual operations to the established standards developed
during the planning process. Failure to provide the follow-up control mechanisms is similar to enacting a new law without bothering to develop methods to
enforce it. Control is the safeguard that ensures plans are properly carried out.

THE RELATIONSHIP BETWEEN PLANNING
AND DECISION MAKING

Decision making occurs at all managerial levels. It involves identifying options
and choosing those courses of action necessary to perform a given task. Such decisions trigger actions designed to keep plans in motion. Decision making is

He spent a lifetime in industry, observing and applying management practices, and ultimately developed a philosophy and theory of management. They were expressed in his great book *Administration générale et industrielle*, first published in 1916 and translated into English in 1929. In his book Henri Fayol wrote that the art of administration involves five major activities: planning, organizing, commanding, coordinating, and controlling. Planning, he emphasized, is indispensable, for it serves to integrate and give meaning to all the other activities. Fayol was one of the first management theorists to recognize that a strategic plan is essential to effective management.

Born of French parents in 1841 in Istanbul, Fayol was trained as an engineer at the Ecole des mines de Saint-Etienne. At nineteen he joined a large mining company and during the next twenty-eight years he distinguished himself as a scientist and engineer. In 1888 he became the managing director of the company, which at that time was near financial ruin. Intrigued by the problems of management, Fayol reorganized the company and made it prosper.

Fayol insisted that the "administrative function" of an organization be viewed as distinct from all other functions—technical, commercial, financial, security, and accounting. He quickly pointed out that this function was not the sole responsibility of the chief executive officer, but was part of the responsibilities of subor-

closely related to planning, since all planning involves making decisions. However, not all decision making is planning.

Planning, as an area of decision making, involves three special characteristics:

1. *Anticipatory decision making.* Managers must decide what to do and how *before* action is required.

2. *A system of decisions.* Managers should recognize the interconnections between one decision or set of decisions and others. As a result, an entire network of decisions is present, and each impending decision should be considered not only in isolation, but also in terms of how it will affect every related decision.

3. *Creation of desired future states.* Managers engage in decision making concerning the objectives for their organization. This important decision vitally affects all other decisions and organizational activities by focusing decisions and activities upon the attainment of agreed-upon objectives.[4]

The Importance of Planning

While planning does not automatically guarantee success in accomplishing organizational objectives, it is rare for an organization to succeed solely by luck or

[4] Russell Ackoff, *A Concept of Corporate Planning* (New York: Wiley/Interscience, 1970), pp. 2–4.

dinate managers and supervisors. Fayol felt that the proportion of time the individual manager devoted to the administrative function was positively correlated with that individual's position in the firm; the higher the level of the position, the greater the administrative responsibility.

Fayol knew all too well that no formal training was available for the study of management, and he spoke out strongly in behalf of developing formal education programs in management. All organizations, he insisted, from departments of government to small or large private firms, require effective management. Acting on these convictions, he founded the Center of Administrative Studies in France—the first institution of its kind.

Fayol's greatest work was published in France in the midst of World War I and was not translated for another thirteen years. As a result it received very little attention in Europe until the 1920s. In the United States, management study focused on the scientific approach of Frederick Taylor to effective shop management, and Fayol's methodology for top management was almost unknown. Nearly two decades passed after the death of Fayol in 1925 before U.S. management theorists became familiar with his work. It is today acknowledged that Taylorism and Fayolism were complementary rather than competitive approaches to management.

Sources

Peter Chambers, "Europe's Greatest Management Pioneer," *International Management* (June 1974), pp. 49–51.

"Famous Firsts: Discoveries from Looking Inward," *Business Week* (June 6, 1964), p. 152ff.

Grande Larousse, Encyclopedique en six volumes, s.v. "Fayol."

Hano Johannsen and G. Terry Page, *International Dictionary of Management: A Practical Guide,* s.v. "Fayol, Henri."

Norman M. Pearson, "Fayolism as the Necessary Complement of Taylorism," *American Political Science Review* (February 1945), pp. 68–80.

circumstance. Careful planning should result in the development of a *blueprint* describing the means to accomplish objectives. Such a blueprint will typically include checkpoints where actual operations can be compared with expectations to determine whether these activities are moving the organization toward its objectives. There are several reasons why planning is considered to be a vital function for every manager.

PLANNING IS RELATED TO PERFORMANCE

A number of empirical studies provide evidence concerning the importance of planning in organizational success. An investigation of thirty-six firms in the machinery, drug, food, steel, oil, and chemical industries revealed that companies that engaged in formal planning consistently outperformed those firms with no formal planning.[5] A follow-up study by David M. Herald showed that the performance superiority (measured by such factors as return on equity and invested capital, sales, and growth in earnings per share) of firms engaged in formal planning had increased since the original study.[6] Similar

[5] Stanley S. Thune and Robert J. House, "Where Long-Range Planning Pays Off," *Business Horizons* (August 1970), pp. 81–87.

[6] David M. Herald, "Long-Range Planning and Organizational Performance: A Validation Study," *Academy of Management Journal* (March 1972), pp. 91–102.

results were obtained by Wood and LaForge, Stagner, and Eastlack and McDonald.[7]

PLANS FOCUS ATTENTION ON OBJECTIVES

Once organizational objectives are defined, the planning process involves the development of methods for achieving them. Plans continually reinforce the importance of these objectives by focusing upon them. Every decision is measured in terms of its contribution to the achievement of organizational objectives. The presence of plans that focus upon these objectives aids in preventing overinvolvement of managers in less important decisions and activities.

PLANS HELP OFFSET UNCERTAINTIES AND ANTICIPATE PROBLEMS

A significant aspect of any planning process is the collection of information for use in forecasting the future. The three "alternative futures" considered by RCA in the box on the next page illustrate the development of contingency plans based upon possible future events. These alternatives are called *scenarios*. By developing plans for alternative future contingencies, decision makers are better prepared to take actions with minimal interruptions when one of these scenarios occurs. Forecasting is discussed in detail in the following chapter.

PLANS PROVIDE GUIDELINES FOR DECISION MAKING

Since plans specify the actions necessary to accomplish organizational objectives, they serve as the bases for decisions about future activities. Managers have standards and their decisions must be consistent with them. Johnson Products Co.'s success as the leading manufacturer of cosmetics for blacks was based largely on a single product: a hair straightener for blacks who wanted to imitate the hair styles of whites. But the tremendous popularity of the natural hair styles resulted in decisions to manufacture a broad line of cosmetics for blacks.

PLANS ARE NECESSARY TO FACILITATE CONTROL

The controlling process serves management by determining whether plans are being implemented correctly and whether organizational objectives are being achieved. Well-developed plans can aid this process in the following ways:
   1. *Establish advance warnings of possible plan deviations.* Once the possible

[7] D. Robley Wood, Jr., and R. Lawrence LaForge, "The Impact of Comprehensive Planning on Financial Performance," *Academy of Management Journal* (September 1979), pp. 516–526; Ross Stagner, "Corporate Decision Making," *Journal of Applied Psychology* (February 1979), pp. 1–13; Joseph Eastlack, Jr., and Philip McDonald, "CEO's Role in Corporate Growth," *Harvard Business Review* (May–June 1970), pp. 150–163.

The technology of the 1970s and 1980s created numerous opportunities for business firms throughout the world. In the consumer electronics field, innovations made it possible for consumers to purchase machines that would allow them to play prerecorded entertainment and educational programs on their television receivers—at their convenience. Radio Corporation of America, long a pioneer in consumer electronics and entertainment, was actively involved. But at least three alternatives were available: videocassette recorders capable of recording television programs for replay as well as playing prerecorded programs; laser-disc videodisc players capable of very high visual quality programs but incapable of recording new programs; and less expensive diamond stylus videodiscs whose quality was poorer than that of the laser-disc models but considerably better than that of the videocassettes.

RCA planners recognized several possible "futures":

1. Acceptance of the diamond stylus videodisc player would be poor due to its inability to record.
2. The lower price (initially $599, but later reduced to $299 less retailer discounts) of the videodisc player would more than compensate for the added features of the videocassettes. In addition, the higher price of the laser-disc player would force consumers to settle for the diamond stylus videodisc.
3. Although the laser-disc player would be priced higher than its other competitors, their greater capacity (the entire Encyclopedia Britannica can be stored on a few discs) and quality picture would offset the higher prices, especially to industrial users and government purchasers.

RCA chose the second scenario and introduced SelectaVision in 1982, following expenditures of over $200 million in development. Although expected sales for the first year were 200,000 units, the firm sold only 65,000—even after a last-minute $22 million advertising campaign for the Christmas season.

SOURCE: The introduction of SelectaVision is discussed in Laura Landro, "RCA Blaming Excessive Optimism for Slow Sales of Videodisc Player," *The Wall Street Journal* (January 26, 1982), p. 25; and A. F. Ehbar, "Splitting Up RCA," *Fortune* (March 22, 1982), p. 63.

VIDEOCASSETTE? VIDEODISC? OR SELECTAVISION?

contingencies have been identified during the initial planning process, management may establish a schedule of review dates or warning signals to alert it to deviations. These review systems may take the form of monthly operating statements or even daily reports of deviations from specified production, sales, or even profit levels. Such deviations can then be investigated and remedial action may be considered.

2. *Provide concrete data.* In addition to establishing methods of determining deviations from expectations, plans may also specify quantitative data for use in making comparisons of actual performance. Such data may be internally developed data concerning production or sales, competitive information purchased from private research groups, industry statistics, or market forecasts.

Types of Plans

Since organizations may be involved with thousands of plans of widely varying degrees of importance, a method of classifying plans must be developed. Plans can be classified on three bases: *time, use,* and *scope* or *breadth.*

THE TIME DIMENSION IN PLANNING

Of all the ingredients in the planning process, time is one of the most critical, most elusive, and most often abused. The time available to conduct a major research and development effort, correct a safety hazard, react to a business downturn, or acquire another firm varies widely. Certain types of plans take years to complete. Fifteen years elapsed between the initial development of the Xerox electrostatic copier and its full-scale introduction.

A voter once pointed to the legs of six-foot, four-inch candidate Abraham Lincoln and asked him how long he thought a man's legs should be. "Long enough to reach the ground," Lincoln replied. Planning should be considered in the same manner. Plans should reach far enough into the future to cover the subject under consideration.

The planning horizon for Georgia-Pacific Corp. reaches into the twenty-first century. Georgia-Pacific managers know that it takes ninety-nine years to grow Douglas firs in the Northwest. Only by planting seedlings today is it possible to guarantee pulp supplies in ninety-nine years. As Figure 5-2 indicates, similar plans are being implemented at Potlatch Corp.

THE COMMITMENT PRINCIPLE DETERMINES
LENGTH OF PLANNING PERIOD

The period of time covered by organizational planning should be related to the commitments of the organization. Honda Motors' decision to open an automobile assembly plant in Columbus, Ohio, required long-range commitments in facilities, raw materials, and component parts, and commitments to the 2,000 American workers it employs. Honda's long-range planning reaches into the 1990s as it attempts to capture an increased share of the nearly 3 million imported automobiles purchased annually in the United States. Sears, Roebuck, and Co. commits itself for a period of six months when it distributes millions of semiannual catalogs to its mail-order customers. The *commitment principle* states that an organization should plan for a period of time in the future sufficient to fulfill the commitments resulting from current decisions.[8]

Planning must encompass a sufficiently long time frame to meet the commitments of current decisions. A long-range plan is built upon the foundations of short- and intermediate-range plans, all attainable within a specified time frame.

The commitment principle states that an organization should plan in the future for a period of time sufficient to fulfill the commitments resulting from current decisions.

[8] The commitment principle was first proposed by Harold Koontz and Cyril O'Donnell. See their *Principles of Management* (New York: McGraw-Hill, 1955), p. 442.

Figure 5-2 LONG-RANGE PLANNING AT POTLATCH CORPORATION

SOURCE: Potlatch Corp. Used with permission.

SHORT-RANGE, INTERMEDIATE-RANGE, AND LONG-RANGE PLANNING

The following time frames are typically used by managers in describing planning periods:

Short range: One year or less

Intermediate range: Between one and five years

Long range: Five years or more

Table 5-1 lists several examples of planning activities for each of the different planning periods.

The planning activities for each of the different time horizons may vary among organizations. General Motors Corp., for example, has invested more than ten years in research activities aimed at developing an improved capacity battery storage system for electric cars. A utility company such as Consolidated Edison may view five years as a relatively short planning period in planning major expenditures for new generating facilities. On the other hand, a sportswear firm such as Ocean Pacific may view six months as a relatively long planning period.

Table 5-1 SHORT-RANGE, INTERMEDIATE-RANGE, AND LONG-RANGE PLANNING	TIME HORIZON	EXAMPLES

	Short-range planning	Annual plan
		    Sales/Revenue
		    Production
		    Materials requirements
		    Operating expenses budget

	Intermediate-range planning	Development of new products Modernization of facilities
	Long-range planning	Long-term leases on production or warehouse facilities Construction of Alaska Pipeline

THE USE DIMENSION IN PLANNING

Plans may be divided into two major categories on the basis of their usage: single-use plans and standing plans. *Single-use plans* are predetermined courses of action developed for relatively unique, nonrepetitive situations. The decision of a corporation such as American Airlines to move its home office from New York to Dallas required numerous one-time plans. The three basic types of single-use plans are programs, projects, and budgets.

A *program* is a large-scale, single-use plan involving numerous interrelated activities. The program will typically specify the objectives, major steps necessary to achieve these objectives, individuals or departments responsible for each step, the order of the various steps, and resources to be employed. Programs are often major undertakings such as the joint British and French program to develop the Concorde supersonic airplane or the U.S. program that resulted in landing astronauts on the moon. On a smaller scale, programs may be developed for reducing absenteeism and improving employee morale in an organization. Still other programs may be developed by a school superintendent to improve mathematics test scores of high school graduates.

Single-use plans are predetermined courses of action developed for nonrepetitive situations.

Program is a large-scale, single-use plan involving numerous interrelated activities.

A *project* is a single-use plan that is a component of a program or that is on a smaller scale than a program. The Concorde program was originally divided into numerous specific subprograms. The subprograms were then divided into specific projects. Each project was then assigned to a government contractor for completion. These projects resembled small-scale programs, since each contractor's assignment contained the same steps present in a program. Other examples of projects include the conversion of police vehicle engines from gasoline fuel to gasohol, the installation of new machinery in a manufacturing facility, or a plan to enlarge the seating capacity of the Rose Bowl.

A *budget* is simply a financial plan listing in detail the resources or funds assigned to a particular program, project, product, or division. Budgets are discussed in detail in Chapter 17 as important devices for controlling organizational activities. In addition, they are important components of both programs and projects. However, budgets are also considered as single-use plans since the process of developing budgets is clearly planning and since it takes objectives into account in deciding in advance how to allocate resources among alternative activities. Many organizations utilize the budget as the basis for planning and coordinating other activities.

Standing plans are predetermined courses of action developed for repetitive situations. Such plans speed the decision-making process and allow the managers to handle similar situations in a consistent manner. Standing plans are developed for situations as diverse as the Sears policy of promoting employees from within the organization whenever possible, a local supermarket's check-cashing policy requiring customers to complete an application and have a checking account at a local bank, or a rule prohibiting smoking in the company dining room.

Managers at Scott Paper Co.'s Mobile, Alabama, manufacturing facility had become increasingly concerned with tardiness and absenteeism. The rate of absenteeism had risen to 7 percent by the early 1970s, and a plan was developed to deal with the problem. The plan, which calls for a five-step system of oral and written warnings and suspensions, was incorporated into the firm's labor agreement. As a result, tardiness has lessened, absenteeism has dropped to 4.4 percent, and almost seventy employees have been dismissed in the past five years.

Standing plans may be categorized as policies, procedures, or rules on the basis of their scope. *Policies* are general guidelines for decision making. Many organizations provide parameters within which decisions must be made. Human resources policies may focus upon hiring from within; purchasing department policies may prohibit gifts from suppliers; pricing policies may permit district sales managers to meet the lowest prices of competitors.[9]

Procedures are guides to action that specify in detail the manner in which activities are to be performed. They tend to be narrower in scope than policies and are often intended to be used in implementing policies. Scott Paper Co.'s policies regarding tardiness are implemented by a set of written procedures.

Project is a single-use plan that is a component of a program or that is on a smaller scale than a program.

Budget is a financial plan listing the resources or funds assigned to a particular program, project, product, or division.

Standing plans are predetermined courses of action developed for repetitive situations.

Policies are general guidelines for decision making.

Procedures are guides to action which specify in detail the manner in which activities are to be performed.

[9] Some writers confuse the different types of standing plans. For a discussion of this problem, see Milton Leontiades, "The Confusing Words of Business Policy," *Academy of Management Review* (January 1982), pp. 25–34.

**ROADBLOCKS FOR
THE A-10 PROGRAM**

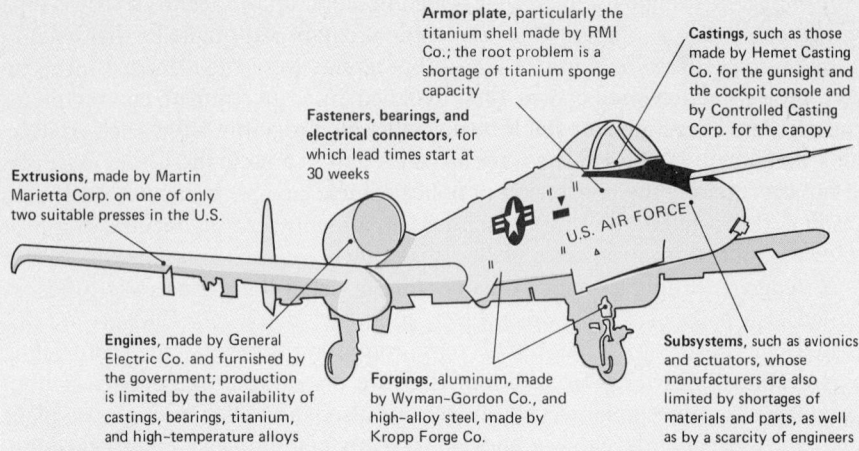

Armor plate, particularly the titanium shell made by RMI Co.; the root problem is a shortage of titanium sponge capacity

Castings, such as those made by Hemet Casting Co. for the gunsight and the cockpit console and by Controlled Casting Corp. for the canopy

Fasteners, bearings, and electrical connectors, for which lead times start at 30 weeks

Extrusions, made by Martin Marietta Corp. on one of only two suitable presses in the U.S.

Engines, made by General Electric Co. and furnished by the government; production is limited by the availability of castings, bearings, titanium, and high-temperature alloys

Forgings, aluminum, made by Wyman-Gordon Co., and high-alloy steel, made by Kropp Forge Co.

Subsystems, such as avionics and actuators, whose manufacturers are also limited by shortages of materials and parts, as well as by a scarcity of engineers

When the United States Air Force decided to acquire the A-10 attack plane to provide close air support for ground troops, it turned to Fairchild Republic Co. to develop the program. The Air Force placed orders for 733 of the attack

Rules are statements of actions that must be taken or not taken in a given situation.

Rules are the simplest type of standing plan. They are statements of actions that must be taken or not taken in a given situation. Rules serve as guides to behavior. Most organizations utilize a great variety of rules. Certain rules may require employees to wear protective head coverings and safety shoes in construction sites. Other rules may prohibit food and drinks in a retail store. Although procedures may incorporate rules, rules do not incorporate procedures. Rules, unlike procedures, do not specify a time sequence. They permit no deviation from a stated course of action, and the manager's discretion is limited to deciding whether or not to apply a rule in a given situation.

THE SCOPE OR BREADTH
DIMENSION IN PLANNING

The third method of categorizing plans is by scope or breadth. Some plans are very broad and long range, focusing upon key organizational objectives. Other types of plans specify how the organization will mobilize to achieve these objectives. The two basic types are strategic plans and tactical plans.

Strategic planning is the process of determining the major objectives of an organization and the adoption of courses of action and the allocation of resources necessary to achieve those objectives.

Strategic planning is the process of determining the major objectives of an organization and then adopting the courses of action and allocating the resources necessary to achieve those objectives.[10] Such planning provides the organization with overall long-range direction and leads to the development of more specific plans, budgets, and policies. It formed the basis of such fundamental management decisions as

Levi Strauss & Company's product line expansion from men's blue denim

[10] Alfred D. Chandler, Jr., *Strategy and Structure* (Cambridge, Mass.: MIT Press, 1962), p. 13.

planes equipped with 30-mm rapid-fire, antitank guns and an arsenal of bombs and missiles. Fairchild Republic divided the program into numerous projects. Some of the projects were assigned to the firm's plants in Farmingdale, New York, and Hagerstown, Maryland. Others were assigned to subcontractors. As the figure on the left shows, a large number of subcontractors play major roles in the program.

Fairchild Republic had agreed to supply the planes at a rate of twelve per month, but the Air Force requested that the production rate be accelerated in the face of increased global tension in the early 1980s. But a program is only as effective as its underlying projects. The forgings project proved to be a key problem. The big forgings that make up the A-10's main frame have to be ordered 114 weeks in advance from Wyman-Gordon, one of only three U.S. forging manufacturers with sufficiently large presses. Materials shortages provide headaches for contractors assigned the armor shield projects. The titanium armor must be ordered 92 weeks ahead.

SOURCE: "Why the U.S. Can't Rearm Fast," *Business Week* (February 4, 1980), pp. 80–86. Illustration by Bob Conrad. Reprinted from the February 4, 1980 issue of *Business Week* by special permission. © 1980 by McGraw-Hill, Inc.

work pants to women's and children's clothing, fashion-oriented clothing, shoes, and automobile seatcovers.

Motorola's decision to abandon the consumer-goods market and concentrate on industrial products.

Du Pont's decision to acquire Conoco Oil Company.

Although strategic planning focuses upon *what the organization will be* in the future, tactical planning emphasizes *how* this will be accomplished. *Tactical planning* refers to the implementation of activities and the allocation of resources necessary in the achievement of the organization's objectives. In some instances strategic planning is short term, as in the case of the Du Pont-Conoco merger. In most cases, however, it is associated with longer-term planning. Tactical planning, on the other hand, typically focuses upon short-term implementation of activities and resource allocations.

Tactical planning focuses on short-term implementation of current activities and the allocation of resources for those activities.

Strategic planning is the critical ingredient in the long-term success of the organization. It is discussed in detail in Chapter 6.

Table 5-2 shows the three bases for classifying planning.

Organizing the Planning Function

Planning is a major responsibility of every manager. As a result managers at every level in the organizational hierarchy spend part of their workdays engaged in planning activities. Top management of most organizations spends greater proportions of its time engaged in planning than do middle- and supervisory-level managers, whose plans tend to be derivative. In addition, top management typically focuses its planning activities in the development of longer-range stra-

Table 5-2 THREE CLASSIFICATION BASES FOR PLANNING	

FACTOR	TYPES
Time	Short range (one year or less)
	Intermediate range (between one and five years)
	Long range (five years or more)
Use	Single-use plans
	Programs
	Projects
	Budgets
	Standing plans
	Policies
	Procedures
	Rules
Breadth or scope	Strategic plans
	Tactical plans

tegic plans while middle-level managers generally concentrate on planning for their divisions, and supervisory management focuses its planning activities on developing action programs to meet the goals of its divisions. Figure 5-3 shows how managers at various levels might allocate their planning activities in a typical organization.

STRUCTURING PLANNING ACTIVITIES

A number of factors affect the method used in an organization to structure its planning activities. These factors include

1. *Size of the organization.* The larger the organization, the greater the number of people and planning specialists available to plan. Smaller organizations may be forced to rely on one—or a few—managers to perform any planning activities. Large organizations can afford to utilize planning specialists and may be in a better position to free their managers for the time required to engage in planning.

2. *Degree of decentralization.* Planning in a multiproduct, decentralized organization is likely to be more diffused than in a centralized organization. Each division or production facility in a decentralized operation is likely to play a major role in developing major plans. Although such plans may be coordinated with a planning authority located at the headquarters office, managers of a decentralized organization are likely to have more responsibility for planning than their counterparts in highly centralized operations. (The centralization-decentralization issue is discussed in detail in Chapter 9.)

3. *The personality of top management.* Some top managers prefer to work with a specialized planning staff. Others desire participation from middle and supervisory level managers and require them to assume the major responsibility for planning.[11]

4. *Nature of the product.* Multiproduct companies may be characterized by

[11] Jacob Naor, "How to Motivate Corporate Executives to Implement Long-Range Plans," *MSU Business Topics* (Summer 1977), pp. 41–49.

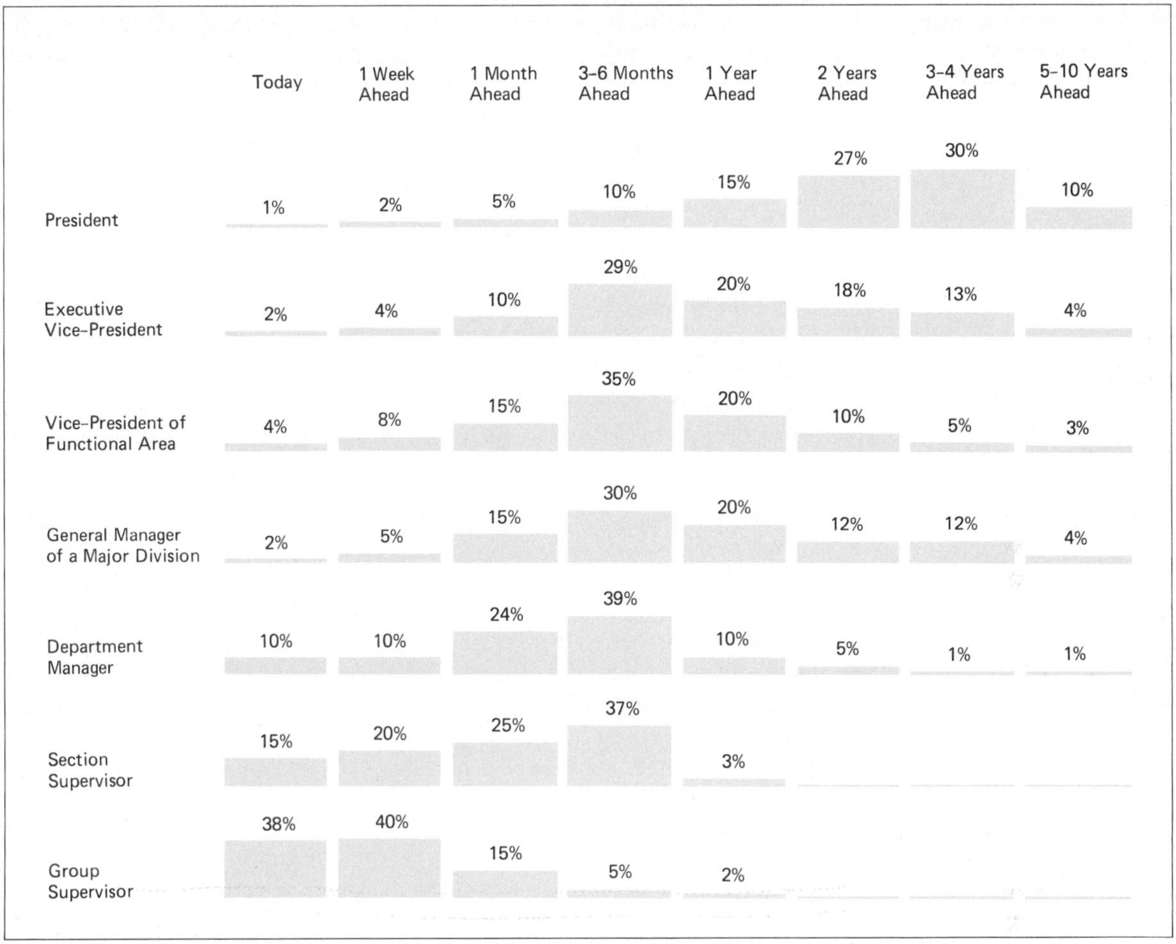

	Today	1 Week Ahead	1 Month Ahead	3-6 Months Ahead	1 Year Ahead	2 Years Ahead	3-4 Years Ahead	5-10 Years Ahead
President	1%	2%	5%	10%	15%	27%	30%	10%
Executive Vice-President	2%	4%	10%	29%	20%	18%	13%	4%
Vice-President of Functional Area	4%	8%	15%	35%	20%	10%	5%	3%
General Manager of a Major Division	2%	5%	15%	30%	20%	12%	12%	4%
Department Manager	10%	10%	24%	39%	10%	5%	1%	1%
Section Supervisor	15%	20%	25%	37%	3%			
Group Supervisor	38%	40%	15%	5%	2%			

planning responsibilities assigned at relatively low organizational levels. This may be particularly true in organizations such as department stores where fashions and customer tastes change rapidly and where single products do not represent major portions of total sales. In the automobile industry, by contrast, planning and decision making take place at numerous levels within the organization. Such diverse subjects as design, marketing, and government regulations must be coordinated at the highest levels. Such planning arrangements as General Motors Corporation's "management by committee" approach results from this need to oversee and coordinate the inputs of numerous departments.[12]

THE USE OF STAFF PLANNING GROUPS

The growth in the size of organizations and the recognition of the importance of planning in achieving organizational objectives have led to the development of

Figure 5-3
THE PLANNING PROCESS FROM A TIME-SPAN PERSPECTIVE FOR MANAGERS AT DIFFERENT LEVELS IN THE ORGANIZATION

SOURCE: George A. Steiner, *Top Management Planning* (New York: Macmillan, 1969), p. 26. Copyright © 1969 by The Trustees of Columbia University in the City of New York.

[12] See Michael E. Porter, "How Competitive Forces Shape Strategy," *Harvard Business Review* (March–April 1979), pp. 137–145.

Staff planning groups assist managers by developing a planning system, helping to develop corporate and divisional plans and gathering and evaluating information.

specialized *staff planning groups* within the organization. Such groups assist the managers by developing a planning system, guiding and assisting managers in developing corporate and divisional plans, and gathering and evaluating needed information. Such specialized groups combine many talents and can devote the time necessary in planning major, long-term activities. They can also provide an important service in coordinating the overall planning efforts of the organization and can insure that the more specific plans at the middle- and supervisory-management levels are consistent with the broader plans developed by top management.

The advent of specialized staff planning groups is a relatively recent phenomenon. Du Pont has been in existence since 1802, but it did not establish a corporate planning staff until 1975. Although the danger always exists that some managers will accept the planning group's recommendation as a substitute for their own decisions, the use of such groups is widespread among large enterprises.[13]

Time Management—Ensuring That Managers Have Time to Plan

An all-too-frequent barrier to effective planning is finding time to engage in planning activities. Lack of sufficient time to devote to planning is a common complaint of managers and a frequently expressed explanation for planning deficiencies. Busy managers have two alternatives in finding a way to save time: do less or work faster. A considerable portion of most managers' daily activities could be performed by subordinates. Executives who assign tasks to subordinates may use a format such as that illustrated in Table 5-3 to identify the amount of authority being granted to subordinates and the freedom of action granted to them.

The second method of saving time is to perform at a faster rate. Some research studies have shown that the average manager wastes two hours or more every day and that managers spend as much as 80 percent of their time on rel-

[13] Shea Smith III and John Walsh, Jr., *Strategies in Business* (New York: Wiley/Interscience, 1978), p. 220. See also Kenneth R. Andrews, "Corporate Strategy as a Vital Function of the Board," *Harvard Business Review* (November–December 1981), pp. 174–176ff.

Table 5-3 LEVELS OF AUTHORITY AND INITIATIVE GRANTED TO SUBORDINATES

LEVEL OF INITIATIVE GRANTED TO SUBORDINATES	DEGREE OF AUTHORITY GRANTED TO SUBORDINATES
LEVEL 1. Take action. Notify superior routinely.	Most authority
LEVEL 2. Take action. Notify superior immediately.	Some authority
LEVEL 3. Recommend. Take no action without our prior approval.	Little authority

SOURCE: Adapted from Thomas V. Bonoma and Dennis P. Slevin, "In Pursuit of Time Management," *Managing*, #Two 79, p. 6. Reprinted with permission of the publisher, University of Pittsburgh Graduate School of Business.

atively unimportant matters that produce only 20 percent of the results.[14]

In order to improve the effectiveness of time on the job, managers should analyze how they are currently using their time. Such analysis might take the form of a logbook recording a manager's actions at fifteen- or thirty-minute intervals throughout the day. Analysis of the logbook data may prove quite revealing, especially the first time such data are collected.

The manager should then critically assess his or her use of time by asking such questions as

"Should I perform this task or assign it to a subordinate?"
"Can I perform this task at a faster rate?"
"How much of my time is wasted, and how can I reduce this waste?"
"How can I reduce the amount of time I spend on the telephone?"

ESTABLISHING PRIORITIES

Analysis of actual time usage should be followed by the establishment of priorities. Many hard-working, enthusiastic managers are ineffective due to a lack of priorities to guide their use of time. Such priorities should aid in preventing the following problems:

The division executive who reads and deals with all of her own mail but doesn't get around to writing the working paper on the division's strategic direction.

The production manager who spends half of every day fighting fires on the shop floor but doesn't have time to work with his staff on production planning and scheduling systems.

The quality control director who wades through the detailed results of every quality trial but can't find the time to organize much-needed quality improvement projects.[15]

Table 5-4 shows a typical approach to developing priorities.

---

[14] "Ways to Stop Wasting Time on the Job," *U.S. News & World Report* (March 5, 1979), p. 60.
[15] Reprinted by permission of the Harvard Business Review. Excerpt from Ronald N. Askenas and Robert H. Schaffer, "Managers Can Avoid Wasting Time," *Harvard Business Review* (May–June 1982), p. 99. Copyright © 1982 by the President and Fellows of Harvard College; all rights reserved.

ANNUALLY	**Table 5-4**
Set global objectives. Divide them into routine, problem solving, and personal objectives.	**ESTABLISHING PRIORITIES: ANNUALLY, MONTHLY, AND DAILY**
MONTHLY	
Evaluate the progress on these global objectives and revise them if appropriate.	
DAILY	
Set priorities on a "do" list, preferably the night before.	

SOURCE: Thomas V. Bonoma and Dennis P. Slevin, "In Pursuit of Time Management," *Managing,* #Two 79, p. 7. Reprinted with permission of the publisher, University of Pittsburgh Graduate School of Business.

	CATEGORY	REQUIRED ACTION
Table 5-5 SYSTEM FOR HANDLING PAPER FLOWS	1. Action: immediate	Read and take appropriate immediate action to dispense with the piece of paper.
	2. Action: pending	If you can't take action immediately, you may place the paper in a pending file, but only after initiating action on the matter.
	3. Read and distribute or discard	These are items read for information purposes. Distribute only those items that you are confident will benefit the individuals to whom you send them. (Be considerate of their time, also.) If the item is of no value, discard it.

SOURCE; Thomas V. Bonoma and Dennis P. Slevin, "In Pursuit of Time Management," *Managing*, #Two 79, p. 7. Reprinted with permission of the publisher, University of Pittsburgh Graduate School of Business.

MANAGING TIME EFFECTIVELY

Managers who succeed in solving the problem of too little time typically utilize time budgets for working hours. They set aside the necessary time to devote to major tasks and assign less important activities to subordinates. By separating the essential from the nonessential, they ensure that larger amounts of time are devoted to priority areas.

Two major sources of interruption are the telephone and paper flows.[16] Filtering systems should be established to protect the manager from most telephone calls while retaining access in case of emergencies. Most calls can be grouped together and returned in the late afternoon.

One time management specialist recommended that a manager should handle each piece of paper only once. Secretaries or assistants may be used to sort incoming mail and other paper flows into one of the three categories shown in Table 5-5. Such screening of paper flows and other interruptions should result in time savings and improved performance.[17]

[16] Michael LeBeouf, "Managing Time Means Managing Yourself," *Business Horizons* (February 1980), p. 42.
[17] See Alan Lakein, *How to Get Control of Your Time and Your Life* (New York: Wyden, 1973); and Joseph Cooper, *How to Get More Done in Less Time* (New York: Doubleday, 1962).

Summary

Planning is a critical function of management and a continuing responsibility of every manager. It consists of setting objectives, assessing the future by developing planning premises, and developing courses of action designed to accomplish these objectives. Plans, the natural outgrowths of the planning process, should contain methods for controlling the operation of the plan.

Planning is important for a number of reasons:

1. Many research investigations report a positive relationship between the presence of formal planning and organizational performance.

2. Plans focus attention on objectives.
3. Plans help offset uncertainties and anticipate problems.
4. Plans provide guidelines for decision making.
5. Plans facilitate control by specifying concrete data for use in comparing actual and planned performance and by establishing early warning systems of possible plan deviations.

The numerous types of plans in any organization may be categorized on three bases: time, use, and scope or breadth. Classifying plans on a *time* dimension involves three categories: short range (one year or less), intermediate range (between one and five years), and long range (five years or more). A classification scheme based upon *use* divides plans into single-use and standing plans. Programs, projects, and budgets are all one-time, single-use plans. Standing plans are predetermined courses of action developed for repetitive situations; they include organizational policies, standard procedures, and rules. The third classification method is based upon *scope* or *breadth* and includes two types: strategic planning and tactical planning. Strategic planning focuses upon what the organization will do in the future and involves the determining of objectives and adoption of courses of action and allocation of resources necessary to achieve these objectives. Tactical planning is much narrower in scope; its primary focus is upon how the activities specified by strategic plans are to be accomplished.

Although managers at every level in the organization engage in planning, top management tends to devote relatively more time to planning and is more likely to focus on the development of longer-range strategic plans. Middle managers and supervisory managers tend to be involved in derivative plans for their divisions and in developing action programs to meet division goals. Planning activities in an organization are affected by the following factors:

1. Size of the organization
2. Degree of decentralization
3. Personality of top management
4. Nature of the product

Specialized planning groups or departments are frequently found in larger organizations. Although such groups are advisory in nature, they can assist the managers by developing planning systems, coordinating planning activities at the various levels of the organization, and gathering and evaluating needed information.

Effective planning requires a precious commodity: time. Managers must develop plans for utilizing their valuable time if they are to have sufficient time to engage in planning. Time management results from a critical assessment of how the manager's time is being utilized and the establishment of a priority system for activities. In some cases time management results in assigning activities that were previously performed by the managers to others in the organization. It also involves a separation of essential from nonessential activities and the development of a system of focusing upon priority items and minimizing such interruptions as telephone calls and distracting, nonessential personal contacts. The result of a time management system should be the generation of sufficient time to engage in the vital process of planning.

REVIEW EXERCISES

1. Define the following terms: (a) planning (b) plan (c) commitment principle (d) single-use plan (e) program (f) project (g) budget (h) standing plan (i) policy (j) procedure (k) rule (l) strategic planning (m) tactical planning (n) staff planning group.

2. Identify and briefly explain each of the steps in the planning process.

3. What are the chief benefits of planning?

4. Explain the use of scenarios in planning.

5. Identify and explain the three methods for classifying plans.

6. Distinguish between short-range, intermediate-range, and long-range plans. Include an example of each type.

7. Categorize the following plans on the basis of usage: (a) rule (b) program (c) project (d) procedure (e) budget.

8. Distinguish between strategy and tactics.

9. Identify the factors that collectively determine how an organization will structure its planning activities.

10. Relate the concept of time management to planning.

ASSIGNMENTS/ PROBLEMS/ DISCUSSION QUESTIONS

1. "I keep six honest serving men
   They taught me all I knew:
   Their names are What and Why and When
   and How and Where and Who."

   Rudyard Kipling*

Refer to the questions in Kipling's poem. Provide a one- or two-sentence answer to each question by relating the questions to the appropriate part of Chapter 5.

2. Confusion is possible concerning the meaning of the following terms:

   a. plans and planning
   b. planning and decision making

Explain how to avoid confusion by contrasting each term. Include examples to emphasize the difference in the terms.

3. Several factors were discussed in the chapter as affecting the planning activities of an organization and the approaches that might be utilized. Briefly explain each factor and provide an example

* "The Elephant's Child," from *Just So Stories* by Rudyard Kipling. Reprinted by permission of the National Trust and Doubleday & Company, Inc.

from your own experiences of how these factors affect organizational planning.

4. Give an example of a strategic plan, tactical plan, policy, procedure, rule, program, project, and budget that might be appropriate for each of the following:

   a. Atari Division of Warner Communications
   b. The Boeing Company
   c. Kenney Shoes retail outlet
   d. Baltimore Museum of Art

5. Prepare a logbook of your activities for a single day. Utilize your logbook analysis to explain how you could apply time management concepts to your activities.

A MANAGERIAL INCIDENT

Safeway Stores

The year 1973 was a landmark year for Oakland, California-based Safeway Stores. That year it surpassed A&P in sales and moved into first place in the U.S. food retailing industry. Continued growth allowed Safeway's 2,500 retail outlets to ring up $18 billion in sales by 1982. But problems had arisen.

Safeway's market share had actually decreased in nine of its fourteen major markets—Portland,

Los Angeles, San Diego, Dallas, Denver, Kansas City, Des Moines, Salt Lake City, and Washington, D.C.—during the previous five years. Continued financial losses and poor growth prospects resulted in a decision to close all stores in its Omaha and Memphis divisions. A costly 1981 price war in Washington, D.C., between Safeway and its competitor, Giant Food, Inc., cost the firm an estimated $50 million. In Los Angeles, Safeway saw its market share drop 50 percent in a single five-year period.

In 1980 Safeway named a new chairman and chief executive officer, 37-year-old Peter A. Magowan. Magowan, one of the youngest chief executive officers ever for so large an organization, had started with Safeway bagging groceries as a teenager. His first weeks at the helm were spent assessing the current situation, its causes, and Safeway's options.

One major culprit appeared to be an overly influential legal department that fostered a strict interpretation of laws and regulations. Safeway had thus become overcautious. Price discounts were used sparingly lest Safeway be accused of monopolistic practices. Health-food departments were opposed by the lawyers because of the myriad regulations. The result was that Safeway had become a follower instead of a leader.

Since taking the reins, Magowan has made a number of major moves. The authority of the legal department was reduced; additional authority was placed in the hands of the managers of Safeway divisions. Several hundred smaller stores have been replaced with larger 40,000- to 60,000-square foot "super stores." Health food and pharmacy departments have been added to many of the Safeway supermarkets. Since Safeway cashes one million checks a day for its four million customers, Magowan is even considering the possibility of adding some financial services. But major changes take time. As one competitor states, "Safeway is not driving a PT boat, but a battleship; and you just can't move that fast."

SOURCE: Safeway's recent plans and activities are described in Jeff Blyskal, "A&P West?" Forbes (April 12, 1982), pp. 62–64; and "Safeway Stores: Back to Price Wars for a Company That Played It Too Safe," Business Week (April 5, 1982), pp. 108–109. The quotation is from p. 109 of the Business Week article.

Questions and Problems

1. A number of benefits that result from planning are discussed in the chapter. List these benefits and indicate how Safeway's actions can be related to each.

2. Explain how the decisions made by Magowan are likely to affect Safeway's future performance. What potential dangers are present?

3. Make additional recommendations that Safeway should consider in its attempts to maintain and improve its competitive position.

6.
Strategic Planning

Business is like war in one respect. If its grand strategy is correct, any number of tactical errors can be made and yet the enterprise proves successful.

GEN. ROBERT E. WOOD
Former president,
Sears, Roebuck & Co.

No plan can prevent a stupid person from doing the wrong thing in the wrong place at the wrong time—but a good plan should keep a concentration from forming.

CHARLES E. WILSON
Former president,
General Motors Corp.

Halfway through its five-year strategic planning cycle designed to move the organization into second place in the low-density polyethylene film market, Gulf Oil Corp. received an unexpected bit of news. A major Gulf competitor, Union Carbide Corp., announced that it had developed a new process to produce the film at a cost 20 percent less than the conventional methods used by Gulf.

Gulf's strategic plan had been developed in the mid-1970s for each of its seven business units. Its priorities were specified as follows: invest heavily in domestic oil production, make refining and marketing viable businesses, expand Gulf's chemical business, and increase investments in Gulf's coal and uranium operations.

The Gulf chemical unit felt the goal of attaining the number two position in the market for low-density polyethylene film was realistic. Management had thoroughly assessed the industry's growth potential, the firm's current market position, its competitors, and any inherent risks, as well as the funds required to reach its goals. But, as Figure 6-1 shows, plans are only as good as the assumptions underlying them.

Since demand was forecasted to increase at an annual rate of 10 percent, Gulf planners built into the strategic plan the cost of constructing a new plant in 1979. The Gulf research staff concluded that technological breakthroughs in the production of polyethylene were highly unlikely, so financial commitments to research and development were minimal.

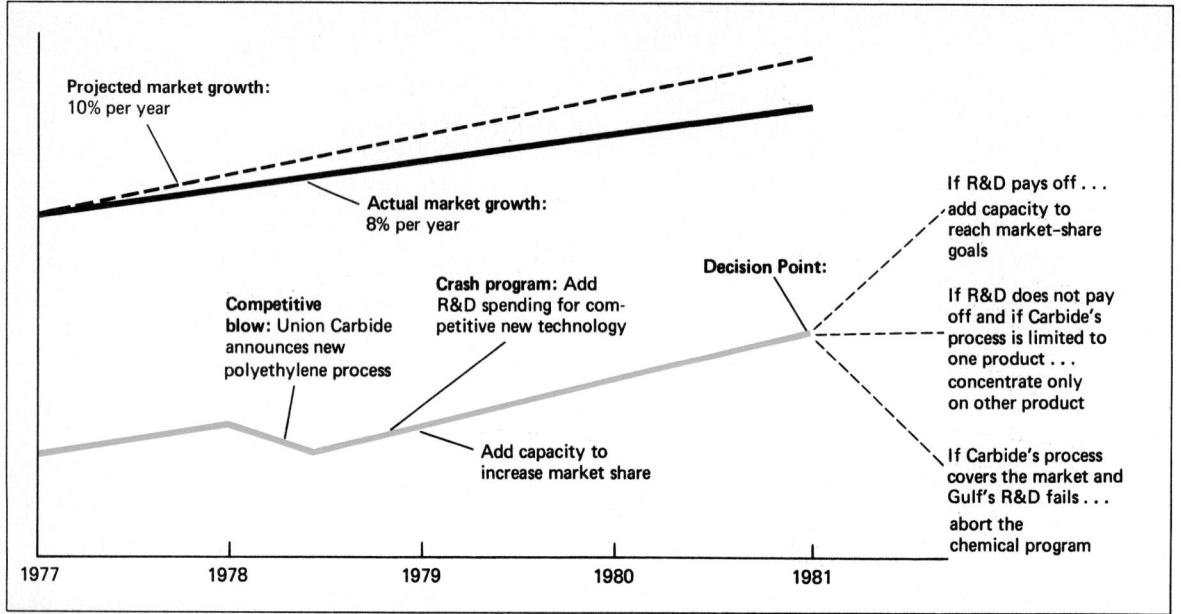

Projected market growth:
10% per year

Actual market growth:
8% per year

Competitive
blow: Union Carbide
announces new
polyethylene process

Crash program: Add
R&D spending for com-
petitive new technology

Decision Point:

If R&D pays off . . .
add capacity to
reach market–share
goals

If R&D does not pay
off and if Carbide's
process is limited to
one product . . .
concentrate only
on other product

Add capacity to
increase market share

If Carbide's process
covers the market and
Gulf's R&D fails . . .
abort the
chemical program

1977   1978   1979   1980   1981

Figure 6-1
HOW GULF'S
STRATEGIC PLAN
FOR CHEMICALS
EVOLVED

SOURCE: Reprinted from the
December 18, 1978 issue
of *Business Week* by
special permission. © 1978
by McGraw-Hill, Inc.

But deviations from the plan occurred and adjustments had to be made by Gulf managers. Market growth was only 8 percent annually, so the decision to add capacity was delayed for two years. Union Carbide's announcement of the new production technology presented Gulf two alternatives: license the technology or intensify its own research spending and attempt to develop a similar or superior process.

The first alternative was dismissed when Gulf executives learned the high cost of licensing the new technology. As a result management conducted a comprehensive reexamination of its strategic plans in the chemical divisions as well as other divisions. The polyethylene research was given top priority since it affected the entire strategic plan. A monitoring program was also established to determine the extent of the Union Carbide breakthrough and whether it applied to both the high-clarity film used for food wrap and the low-clarity film used in trash bags. If the new process affected only one segment, Gulf would shift its concentration to the other.

The responses of other competing firms to the Union Carbide innovation were also monitored. This move resulted in the development of a third alternative for Gulf. Faced with competitive problems similar to those of Gulf, several other firms had developed a means of adapting their current machinery and methods to produce a product similar to Union Carbide's. Gulf planners could consider licensing these technologies.[1]

---

[1] The Gulf strategic planning process is described in "The New Planning," *Business Week* (December 18, 1978), pp. 62–68. Updated information courtesy of Gulf Oil Corp.

What Is Strategic Planning?

In Chapter 5 *strategic planning* was defined as the process of determining the major objectives of an organization and then adopting the courses of action and allocating the resources necessary to achieve those objectives.[2] The word *strategy* is derived from the Greek word *strategos,* meaning "the art of the general." Strategic plans provide the organization with long-range direction. They focus on relatively uncontrollable environmental factors that affect the achievement of organizational objectives. Although strategic planning is generally associated with long-range planning, it is also involved in such short- and intermediate-range questions as whether to merge with another organization or to broaden activities from a domestic to an international market.[3]

Strategic Planning Versus Tactical Planning

The outcome of strategic planning is to provide the organization with an overall context for the development of more specific plans, policies, forecasts, and budgets. While strategic planning focuses upon what the organization will be doing in the future, *tactical planning* places emphasis on how these activities will be accomplished. Tactical planning is concerned with current and pending activities, focusing upon the effective allocation of resources to assure their implementation. While wars are guided by strategic planning, single battles may be won (or lost) due to tactical planning.

Although strategic and tactical planning are different, both should be integrated into an overall system designed to accomplish organizational objectives. Strategic plans form the basis for the development of tactics. American Hospital Supply Co. managers incorporate both types of planning into an overall corporate plan. A five-year strategic plan is established, and tactical plans for the next twelve months are then developed. Because of rapid environmental changes, the assumptions of the five-year plan are reviewed annually, and the plan is reworked. By reviewing and adjusting plans annually, American Hospital Supply Co. decision makers can keep both strategic and tactical plans sufficiently flexible, permitting their adjustment to changing environmental factors while maintaining their focus upon organizational objectives.[4]

[2] Alfred D. Chandler, Jr., *Strategy and Structure: Chapters in the History of the Industrial Enterprise* (Cambridge, Mass.: MIT Press, 1962), p. 13. See also Donald W. Beard and Gregory G. Dess, "Corporate-Level Strategy, Business-Level Strategy, and Firm Performance," *Academy of Management Journal* (December 1981), pp. 663–668; Peter M. Ginter and Donald D. White, "A Social Learning Approach to Strategic Management: Toward a Theoretical Foundation," *Academy of Management Review* (April 1982), pp. 253–261.

[3] See Dan E. Schendel and Charles W. Hofer (eds.), *Strategic Management: A New View of Business Policy and Planning* (Boston: Little, Brown, 1979).

[4] See Thomas P. Hustad and Ted J. Mitchell, "Creative Market Planning in a Partisan Environment," *Business Horizons* (March–April 1982), pp. 58–65.

Few individuals have made greater contributions to the evolution of strategic planning in business, government, and the university business classroom than George A. Steiner. Steiner, Kunin Professor of Business and Society and professor of Management and Public Policy at UCLA, has been a major influence in the emergence of strategic planning, a task he has accomplished through dozens of seminal writings and through his leadership roles in business, government, and academe.

Steiner was born May 1, 1912, in Norristown, Pennsylvania, and attended Temple University as an undergraduate. He earned an M.A. from the Wharton School of the University of Pennsylvania in 1934 and a Ph.D. from the University of Illinois in 1937. His teaching career in finance at Indiana University was interrupted in 1942 by World War II. Following a four-year stint in the U.S. Navy, he returned to Illinois, where he taught for a decade prior to moving to UCLA.

His academic career was again interrupted during the Korean War, when he assumed the dual posts of director of policy development in both the Defense Production Administration and the Office of Defense Mobilization in the Executive Office of the President of the United States. Steiner's experiences as senior economist with Lockheed Aircraft Corp. during 1953–1955 and his membership on the boards of directors of a number of corporations provided added insights for his writings and teaching.

Steiner's more than thirty books and pamphlets include *Top Management Planning* (New York: Macmillan, 1969), which received the Academy of Management award as the best management book published that year and is still considered a standard in the field. In one of his most recent books—*Strategic Planning: What Every Manager Must Know* (New York: The Free Press, 1979)—he continues his attempts to disseminate the central features of a first-rate strategic planning system and to explain what are currently the major pitfalls to the management community.

Included on his list of major pitfalls are

Failure to encourage managers to engage in strategic planning in firms in which performance appraisal and rewards are based solely on short-range performance measures

THE NEED FOR FLEXIBILITY

Although the Gulf strategic plan depicted in Figure 6-1 combines precise goals with methods for attainment, it is sufficiently flexible to adapt to major environmental developments. Whenever possible, plans should contain built-in means of changing direction in response to unexpected developments. Such flexibility is particularly valuable in long-range strategic planning, for unexpected future events may disrupt operations. The ability to shift direction is built into the strategic plans at Westinghouse Electric. The firm's strategic plans contain built-in "milestones," at which point adjustments can be made in response to changes in environmental factors. Publilius Syrus noted the importance of flexibility two thousand years ago: "It is a bad plan that admits of no modification."[5]

[5] See V. K. Narayanan and Liam Fahey, "The Micro-Politics of Strategy Formulation," *Academy of Management Review* (January 1982), pp. 25–34.

Failure to tailor and design the strategic planning system to the unique characteristics of the company and its management

Tendency of top management to become so engrossed in current problems that they spend insufficient time on the strategic planning process

Failure to modify the strategy planning system as conditions within the company change

Steiner, who celebrated his seventieth birthday with the 1982 publication of the second edition of *Management Policy and Strategy* (written with John B. Miner and Edmund Gray), recently offered his own prognostication for the future of strategic planning:

There is no doubt whatever in my mind that the strategic planning function will increase in importance in the management of organizations and will become an ever-more powerful process in managerial decision making. I base this prediction on many forces. Environmental forces will continue to be complex, turbulent, unpredictable, and dangerous. At the same time, extraordinary opportunities will develop in the environment. The strategic planning process is designed to identify opportunities and threats in the environment, in a systematic way. This, in turn, helps managers to identify strategies to exploit opportunities and avoid threats.

At the same time, substantial research is going on in both the academic and business world to improve the strategic planning process, from strategy formulation to implementation. This involves new insights into preferred strategies in given situations, the development of new powerful analytical tools, and better understanding about how to implement strategies. This certainly strengthens the strategic planning process.

Finally, experience with strategic planning is making clear those principles and practices which are essential for effective strategic planning. In more and more companies these lessons of experience are being applied to the design and operation of the strategic planning process. This, too, serves to make the process more effective and useful to managers.

Source:

Personal correspondence and telephone interview.

FLEXIBILITY—AN IMPORTANT PLANNING INGREDIENT

SOURCE: "Crock" by Rechin, Wilder & Parker (September 23, 1980). © 1980 Field Enterprises, Inc. Courtesy of Field Newspaper Syndicate.

WHAT STRATEGIC PLANNING IS NOT

In discussing the importance of strategic planning in the accomplishment of organizational objectives, it is equally important to understand what is *not* strategic planning. According to Peter Drucker:

1. Strategic planning is *not* applying quantitative techniques to business decisions. It is analytical thinking and a commitment of resources to action.
2. It is *not* forecasting. Drucker stresses that strategic planning is necessary *because* of the difficulty of forecasting beyond a relatively short time period with any degree of precision. Forecasts are regularly upset by entrepreneurs who develop innovations that, by definition, alter the course of economic, political, and social events.
3. Strategic planning does *not* eliminate risk. It aids managers in weighing the risks they must take.

SOURCE: Peter F. Drucker, *Management: Tasks, Responsibilities, Practices* (New York: Harper & Row, 1974), pp. 123–125. Used with permission.

Steps in the Strategic Planning Process

Mission is the unique and fundamental purpose that sets a firm apart from other firms of its type and that identifies the scope of its operations in product and market terms. The mission is a general, enduring statement of company intent.

Strategic planning involves both the development of organizational objectives and specifications for how they will be accomplished. Development of strategic plans forces managers to broaden their concerns from an exclusive focus on short-range matters to an examination of broad organizational issues.

The strategic planning process consists of six steps:

1. *Determine the basic areas of emphasis for the organization.* In order to determine the objectives and more specific goals, the firm must assess its mission. "The *mission* of a business is the fundamental, unique purpose that sets it apart from other firms of its type and that identifies the scope

THREE EXAMPLES OF COMPANY MISSION

Prudential Insurance Co.: "To provide security against an ever-increasing range of risks and hazards that threaten the financial welfare of individuals, families, groups, and businesses at every economic level that can be served by the private sector."

Northwestern Mutual Life Insurance Co.: "To provide the best value in individual life insurance and disability income contracts—highest quality products at lowest net cost."

Sea-Land Industries, Inc.: "To continue to build a profitable, competitively strong, financially sound containerized sea and land transportation system."

SOURCE: Reprinted from Louis A. Allen, *Making Managerial Planning More Effective* (New York: McGraw-Hill, 1982), p. 144.

of its operations in product and market terms. The mission is a general, enduring statement of company intent."[6] Each enterprise expresses its mission in its own unique way, but the tendency is to express what it is and why it exists. The statements of company mission by Prudential Insurance Co., Northwestern Mutual Life Insurance Co., and Sea-Land Industries, Inc., are examples.

2. *Develop long-range goals.* The establishment of specific goals for the organization results from the determination of the organizational mission.
3. *Forecast normal growth expectancy.* Forecasting, a critical ingredient in planning, is discussed later in the chapter.
4. *Develop a long-range strategic plan.* The comprehensive plan of major actions by which a firm intends to achieve its long-term goals is the long-range plan.
5. *Develop annual plans.* More specific, shorter-term plans result from the long-range strategic plan.
6. *Revise long-range strategic plan to reflect current conditions.* The final stage indicates the need to adapt plans to changed conditions.

Figure 6-2 shows the steps in the strategic planning process. The process is illustrated by examination of the Allstate Insurance strategic planning sequence. Allstate engages in a systematic process, integrating short- and long-range planning into an overall plan. Each major step is included on the left-hand page, while the right-hand page indicates the decision process for each step.

The strategic planning process develops answers to three questions:

1. Where are we now?
2. Where do we want to be at a specified future date?
3. How will we get there?

Answers to the first question are developed from data on current operations. Information concerning the organization's financial status, current market share, and relative strengths and weaknesses (human, financial, material) is utilized in an overall assessment of the firm's present position in relation to organizational objectives. This assessment is important in answering the second question and developing premises related to these objectives. Forecasts of market growth, economic conditions, political and legal changes, and technological developments are invaluable in the development of strategic plans.

Answers to the third question involve a determination of the activities necessary to achieve established goals. It requires an identification of resources necessary to implement the plan as well as the establishment of a monitoring system to review actual performance and inform management of possible adjustments that should be made in the plan.

---

[6] John A. Pearce II, "An Executive-Level Perspective on the Strategic Management Process," *California Management Review* (Fall 1981), p. 40.

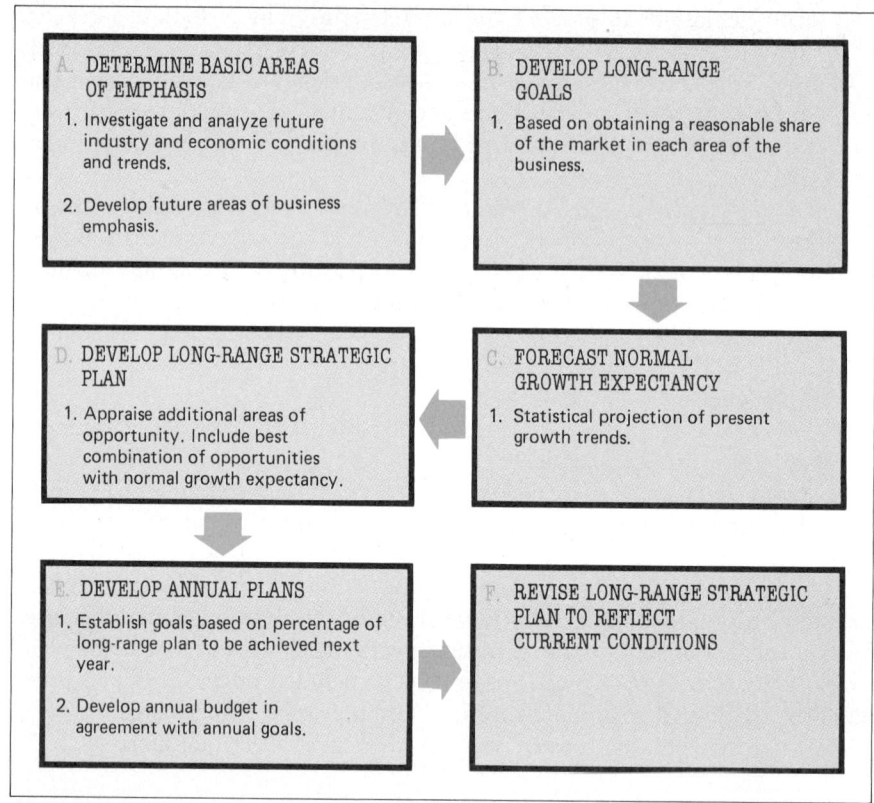

Figure 6-2
**STEPS IN THE STRATEGIC PLANNING PROCESS AT ALLSTATE
INSURANCE CO.**

SOURCE: Adapted by permission from George A. Steiner, *Managerial Long-Range
Planning* (New York: McGraw-Hill, 1963).

USING THE SBU CONCEPT IN STRATEGIC PLANNING

**Strategic business
units (SBUs) are
divisions composed of
key businesses within
multiproduct companies
with specific managers,
resources, objectives,
and competitors. SBUs
may encompass a
division, a product line,
or a single product.**

Strategic business units (SBUs) are divisions composed of key businesses within
multiproduct companies with specific managers, resources, objectives, and competitors. SBUs may encompass a division, a product line, or a single product.
The SBU concept began in 1971 at General Electric, the world's most diversified company. GE executives decided to base their strategic planning on viewing
their organization as a "portfolio" of businesses. GE's nine product groups and
forty-eight divisions were reorganized into forty-three SBUs. Food preparation
appliances that previously had been located in three separate divisions were
merged into a single SBU serving the "housewares" market. The concept was
quickly adopted by numerous diversified organizations, including General
Foods, Union Carbide, International Paper, and Boise Cascade. An estimated

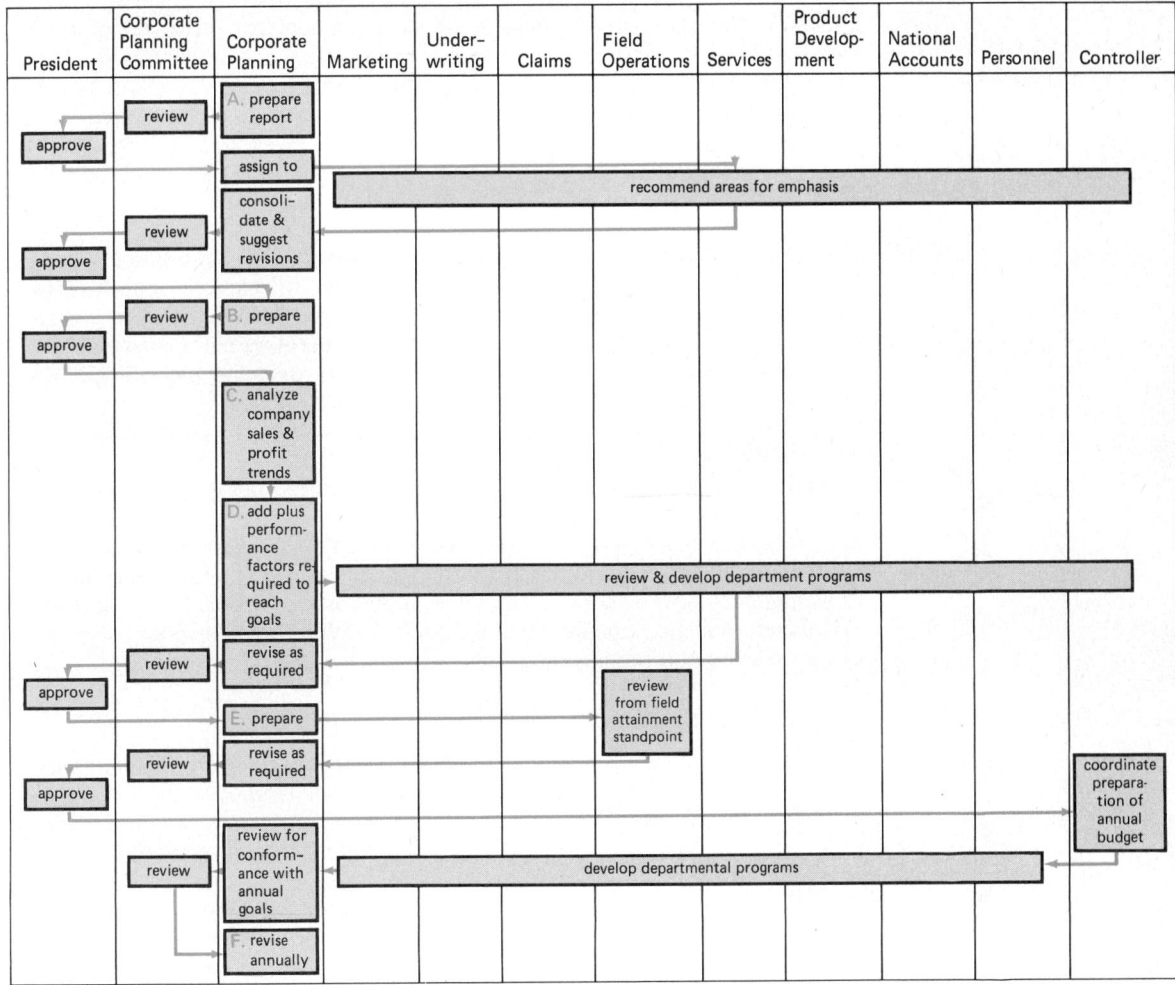

President	Corporate Planning Committee	Corporate Planning	Marketing	Under-writing	Claims	Field Operations	Services	Product Develop-ment	National Accounts	Personnel	Controller
	review	A. prepare report									
approve		assign to									
		consolidate & suggest revisions	recommend areas for emphasis								
approve	review										
	review	B. prepare									
approve											
		C. analyze company sales & profit trends									
		D. add plus performance factors required to reach goals	review & develop department programs								
approve	review	revise as required									
		E. prepare				review from field attainment standpoint					
approve	review	revise as required									coordinate preparation of annual budget
	review	review for conformance with annual goals	develop departmental programs								
		F. revise annually									

45 percent of the 500 largest corporations in the United States are currently using the SBU concept.[7]

A conceptual matrix is utilized that relates SBUs to competitors and assesses the long-term product-market attractiveness. General Electric planners use such dimensions as segment size and SBU growth rate, market share, profitability, margins, technology position, strengths or weaknesses, image, environmental impact, and management. Figure 6-3 shows a typical matrix with labels for each cell developed by the Boston Consulting Group, a consulting firm that has pioneered many of the conceptual developments in the matrix approach to strategic planning.

[7] Philippe Haspeslagh, "Portfolio Planning: Uses and Limits," *Harvard Business Review* (January–February 1982), p. 58.

THE EVANS PRODUCTS CO. STRATEGIC PLAN

Evans Products Co. actively utilizes the strategic business unit concept in its strategic planning activities. The following description is a summary of the firm's strategic plan, including the identification of key trends affecting the retail group, custom-built homes group, shelter products group, and forest-fiber products group.

STRATEGIC PLAN 1981–1985

The primary objectives of Evans' long-term strategic planning are to (1) identify and anticipate trends in our major businesses, (2) explore opportunities within the expected market environment, and (3) evaluate alternative investments. Some of the key trends, strategies and operating plans developed in 1980 to achieve profitable and consistent growth over the plan period are summarized here.

Key Trends

More homes are being fixed up these days than are being built. There are several good reasons why this is happening. High new home prices and mortgage rates are making remodeling existing homes the more attractive financial alternative . . . Turnover in the nation's 87 million housing units is spurring improvements by new owners . . . Rising energy costs are continuing to prompt installation of energy conservation products . . . Old homes in inner cities are being restored at a record rate.

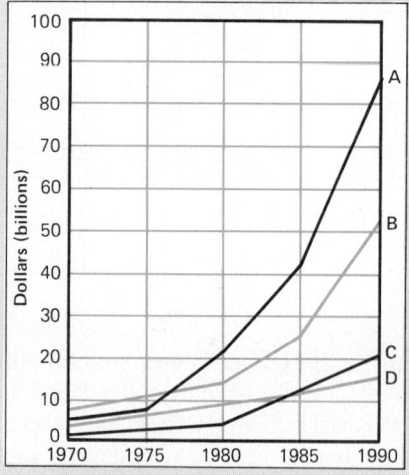

Home improvement product sales by types of retailers:
A *Home centers ("Do-It-Your-selfer" sales exceed 80% of total sales.)*
B *Contractor-oriented lumber & building materials (L&BM) dealers ("Do-It-Yourselfer" sales are less than 30% of total sales.)*
C *Consumer-oriented L&BM dealers ("Do-It-Yourselfer" sales are between 50% and 80% of total sales.)*
D *Hardware stores*

Source: National Home Center News *and Frost & Sullivan*

Basic Strategy

Emphasize marketing directly to the consumer through retail building materials stores and the sale of affordable, custom-built homes. Focus manufacturing activities on specialty products and products used by the growing remodeling market.

Operating Plans

RETAIL STORES:

By 1985 our *Retail Group* anticipates operating 450 stores and a near doubling of revenues.

The percentage of sales to the growing "Do-It-Yourself" market should increase due to:

1. The above-average growth rate inherent in the market.
2. Emphasizing cash-and-carry stores in the new store program.
3. Enlarging and remodeling dual yards, which serve both the consumer and contractor, to accommodate increased consumer sales. Dual yards will continue to be operated where substantial contractor business is available.

We plan to expand our market penetration in the 20 states we now serve, and to expand into additional states.

Existing stores will be continually evaluated in terms of the need to remodel, relocate or remerchandise. The primary goal is to improve our return on investment.

We will strive to maintain our strong consumer image as the "building materials specialist" by stocking ranges of merchandise which allow the customer to choose quality products at a variety of price levels. Equally important is customer assistance from free literature and knowledgeable sales personnel.

Personnel training programs will be intensified to enhance customer service, as well as to provide management for our increasing number of stores.

CUSTOM-BUILT HOMES:

Through increased penetration of existing markets and entering into new market areas, our *Homes Group's* output is expected to approach its current rated capacity by 1985.

Evans Financial Corp. will continue to develop innovative loan programs that are responsive to home loan market conditions and to maintain reliable external investment sources to fund such programs.

MANUFACTURING:

Our *Shelter Products Group* plans to increase the portion of its building product sales to the remodeling market. The Group plans to enter new market areas, as well as to serve existing sales areas more efficiently by opening additional plants for the manufacture of aluminum doors and windows and kitchen cabinets.

Our *Forest-Fiber Products Group* anticipates improved profitability from its wood products activities as higher operating rates and improved efficiencies are attained in more favorable markets. Additional offshore markets will be developed.

The Group's battery separator business is expected to strengthen its market position primarily by capitalizing on technological advances as its markets expand.

SOURCE: Evans Products Co. 1980 Annual Report. Reprinted by permission.

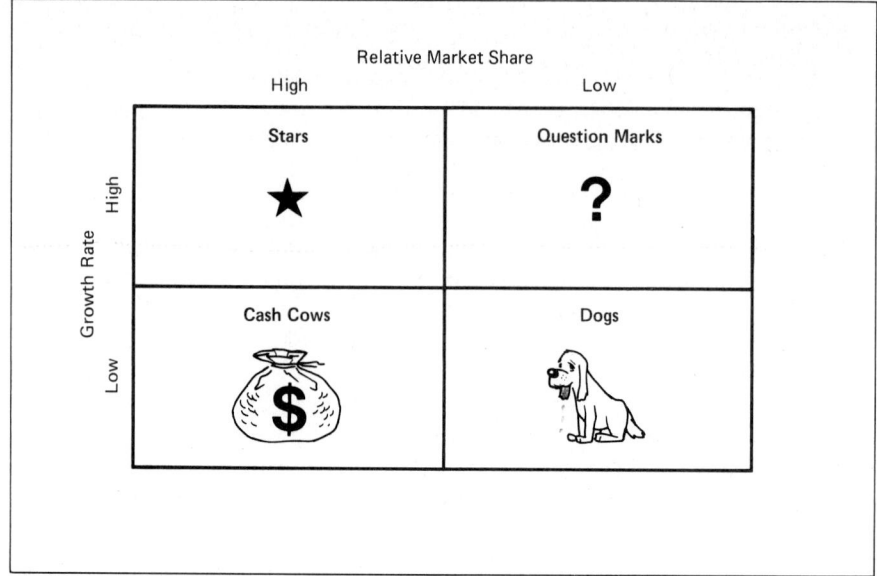

Stars are products or businesses that are high-growth market leaders. Although they generate considerable funds, the funds are more than offset by the funds needed to finance the additional investments they require and the working capital needed to finance their continuing growth. Because of their current competitive position and future potential, stars represent desirable investments for the firm.

Cash cows are products or businesses with high market share but low growth prospects. As a result they generate considerable inflows of funds for the firm.

Dogs are products or businesses with both low market shares and poor growth prospects. Although they may generate some funds for the firm, their future prospects are poor, and most organizations attempt to withdraw from these businesses or product lines as quickly as possible.

Question marks are products or businesses with low market shares in a high growth market. Due to the growth nature of the market, question marks typically require more cash than they are able to generate. Such situations require the manager to make a basic go/no go decision. Unless the question marks can be converted to stars, the firm should pursue other alternatives.

Although the labels attached to each cell may vary among the different organizations employing the SBU approach, the approach is quite similar from organization to organization. In developing strategic plans for handling the portfolio of SBUs, most proponents of this approach recommend the following:

Dogs and cash cows are managed for short-term cash flow. Over the long run, dogs are divested or eliminated, while cash cows ultimately become dogs as their competitive position declines.

Question marks must either get into the star category or get out of the portfolio. In the first case, they should make the move with carefully developed strategic plans so that major risk elements are identified and contained.

Stars are short-run cash consumers and are managed for long-term position. Over the long run, as their segment attractiveness ultimately declines, they will become cash cows, generating cash to support the next round of stars.[8]

Critics of the matrix approach typically focus upon the tendency of some managers to employ it too mechanically. While it permits managers of a multi-product company to array on one graph all of the firm's businesses based upon common measures, it can be used as a prescriptive measure without considering available means for converting low-ranking SBUs to larger market shares or to faster market growth rates. As one manager remarked, "A lot of dogs have been liquidated that could have been turned around."[9]

Another criticism of the matrix approach and its emphasis on market growth and share of that market focuses upon environmental factors. In recent years a number of industries have declined from "go-go" to "no-grow." Stars and question marks were more difficult to locate. As the chief planner at Norton Simon, Inc., stated, "If your portfolio has no businesses that have significant growth, you'd better forget about the matrix and learn to manage for efficiency and return."[10] The advantages of the matrix approach must be balanced against its potential shortcomings by each organization.

Forecasting—Critical Planning Ingredient

Forecasts are estimates or predictions of future events or outcomes for a specified future period. While most firms focus upon sales or production forecasts, planners may attempt to predict technological breakthroughs, economic changes, or variations in the legal or societal environments. Such forecasts play critical roles in the planning process and their accuracy is reflected in the accuracy of plans that are developed.

The forecasting process is a difficult undertaking for most organizations. One management writer has pointed out that there are only three certainties about the future:

Forecasts are estimates or predictions of future events or outcomes for a specified future period.

---

[8] William K. Hall, "SBUs: Hot New Topic in the Management of Diversification," *Business Horizons* (February 1978), p. 21. See also Yoram Wind and Vijay Mahajan, "Designing Product and Business Portfolios," *Harvard Business Review* (January–February 1981), pp. 155–165.

[9] Walter Kiechel III, "Playing by the Rules of the Corporate Strategy Game," *Fortune* (September 24, 1979), p. 114.

[10] Walter Kiechel III, "Oh Where, Oh Where Has My Little Dog Gone? Or My Cash Cow? Or My Star?" *Fortune* (November 2, 1982), p. 149.

1. The future will not be like the past.
2. The future will not be what we think it's going to be.
3. The rate of change will be faster than ever before.[11]

Even though such predictions involve uncertainty, forecasts are the foundation for all organizational production, financial, personnel, and marketing planning. They also provide the basis for the establishment of performance standards. Actual performance is then compared with these standards. Without such standards, comparisons would not be possible since inadequate performance cannot be recognized without some definition of *adequate* performance.

Forecasts may be short run or long run. Long-run forecasts attempt to predict such variables as company sales for five, ten, or even twenty or more years in advance. Such forecasts are quite general and typically are not used to predict the sales of specific products. Short-term forecasts attempt to predict sales, production, or other variables for one year or less, often by specific territories, product lines, or divisions. Such forecasts are used to regulate production, materials purchases, and inventory. They also aid in planning cash requirements and establishing sales quotas.

Any forecast attempts to include both facts and executive judgment. Most forecasting techniques attempt either to limit the areas in which judgment must be totally relied upon or to improve the quality of judgment by reinforcing it with concrete data.[12]

mathematical

Quantitative forecasting provides estimates or predictions of future events or outcomes based upon such statistical techniques as trend extensions, statistical correlation, computer simulations, econometrics, and/or mathematical programming.

existing in ones mind

FORECASTING METHODS

Forecasting methods may be divided into two broad categories: qualitative (or subjective) and quantitative. *Quantitative methods* are based upon statistical techniques and produce numerical forecasts. They include such techniques as statistical trend extensions based upon past data, statistical correlation, computer stimulations (which are treated in detail in Chapter 8), econometrics, and mathematical programming.[13]

Qualitative methods may produce numerical forecasts, but they rely heavily upon the subjective predictions of key executives; estimates by the field sales force; surveys of customer attitudes, opinions, and intentions; and the expectations of experts in the industry who might participate in attempts to predict future events.

Qualitative forecasting provides subjective estimates or predictions of future events or outcomes based upon such inputs as customer surveys, sales force estimates, predictions of key executives, and/or expectations of other industry experts.

[11] Robert M. Randolph, *Planagement—Moving Concept into Reality* (New York: AMACOM, 1975), p. 5.

[12] See Robert S. Sobek, "A Manager's Primer on Forecasting," *Harvard Business Review* (May–June 1973), p. 6ff.

[13] For a description of the use in simulation in a major firm, see Terry W. Rothermel, "Forecasting Resurrected," *Harvard Business Review* (March–April 1982), pp. 139–147.

One of the newest methods of forecasting is called _Delphi forecasting_. It was developed at the Rand Corp. and has been used for a variety of studies during the past decade. The Delphi method is based on two premises: (1) those who are most knowledgeable in a given field will make the best forecasts, and (2) the combined knowledge of several persons is better than that of one person. However, the method does not use a committee of experts as the premises imply but instead uses a panel of experts acting individually with provisions for anonymous interaction among all of the experts.

To use the technique, several experts in one field of interest are invited to participate. At first they may be asked to list the major developments or areas of concern in their field of knowledge. From these initial inputs, a group of questions is formulated about when certain things are expected to happen (or when they will happen with a fifty-fifty chance). The experts answer the questions individually, and their answers are compiled and sent to all panel members. A second round of answers to the same questions is requested, and the panelists are urged to include statements that challenge or support predictions that fall outside of the central range of answers. The process is repeated until answers stabilize. The consensus answer is indicated by the central tendency of panel predictions for each question.

Delphi has been used by some industries and government agencies to predict scientific breakthroughs. Such forecasts provide useful guides for market studies of potential new products, research and development planning, product and defense system evaluations and improvements, and resource allocations. In the last few years, forecasts of social changes have also been made that have had and will continue to have great significance for the planners and top managers in all types of social institutions. Economic forecasts have been made by panels of experts that compare favorably with those made by the most sophisticated mathematical models, and some efforts have been made to predict political and natural environmental changes.

SOURCES: Adapted from Harold W. Henry, "Delphi Forecasting," _Tennessee Survey of Business_ (October 1972), p. 12. See also E. Bruce Peters, "Technological Forecasting: An Investment Analysis Aid," _Managerial Planning_ (July–August 1978), p. 5.

DELPHI FORECASTING

Each method contains advantages in assessing an uncertain future. It is, therefore, not surprising that most organizations utilize a combination of methods in their attempts to produce more accurate predictions of future events.[14]

While managers are not expected to be experts in every forecasting technique, they should be thoroughly familiar with the strengths and weaknesses of each and sufficiently knowledgeable to determine situations in which one group of techniques is superior to another. In most instances the choice of forecasting method will depend upon its purpose and the way in which it will be utilized. Table 6-1 shows appropriate techniques at each stage in a product's life cycle.

[14] See Don Lebell and O. J. Krasner, "Selecting Environmental Forecasting Techniques for Business Planning Requirements," _Academy of Management Review_ (July 1977), pp. 373–383.

Table 6-1 FORECASTING TECHNIQUES FOR EACH STAGE IN THE PRODUCT LIFE CYCLE	Product life cycle stage			
	PRODUCT DEVELOPMENT	INTRODUCTORY STAGE	GROWTH STAGE	MATURITY STAGE
	Delphi method	Consumer surveys	Tracking & warning systems	Time series analysis & projection
FORECASTING TECHNIQUES	Historical analysis of comparable (substitute) products	Test market data	Market surveys	Market surveys

SOURCE: Reprinted by permission of the Harvard Business Review. Adapted from "How to Choose the Right Forecasting Technique" by John C. Chambers, Satinder K. Mullick, and Donald D. Smith (July–August 1971). Copyright © 1971 by the President and Fellows of Harvard College; all rights reserved.

Summary

Strategic planning is designed to provide a blueprint for the entire organization, providing it with a perspective for the development of more specific plans, forecasts, budgets, and procedures. It focuses upon what the organization will do in the future. It involves determining the organization's objectives and then adopting the courses of action and allocating the resources necessary to achieve these objectives. Tactical planning, on the other hand, is much narrower in scope; it focuses primarily upon how the activities specified by the strategic plans are to be accomplished. Flexibility is an important ingredient for both strategic and tactical planning.

The strategic planning process consists of six steps:

1. Determine the basic areas of emphasis for the organization
2. Develop long-range goals
3. Forecast normal growth expectancy
4. Develop a long-range strategic plan
5. Develop annual plans
6. Revise the long-range strategic plan to reflect current conditions

A growing number of diversified, multiproduct organizations employ the strategic business unit (SBU) concept in strategic planning, viewing their organizations as a "portfolio" of businesses. SBUs are then assessed through comparisons with competitors and the evaluation of long-term product–market attractiveness. Although the concept is potentially dangerous because it can be utilized mechanically in developing plans, it allows managers to focus upon all aspects of the organization in a balanced fashion, utilizing common measures.

Forecasts are estimates or predictions of future events or outcomes for a specified future period. Forecasting is vital in establishing planning premises. The forecasting period is typically tailored to the needs of the organization, and many firms develop both short- and long-term forecasts. Forecasting methods can be divided into quantitative methods, which utilize statistical techniques to produce numerical forecasts, and qualitative methods, which rely more heavily upon subjective predictions of executives, sales personnel, customers, and industry experts. Since forecasting typically involves the combination of facts and executive judgments, both methods play important roles in the final forecast.

REVIEW EXERCISES

1. Define the following terms: (a) strategic planning (b) tactical planning (c) mission (d) strategic business unit (e) stars (f) cash cows (g) dogs (h) question marks (i) forecasts (j) quantitative methods (k) qualitative methods (l) Delphi forecasting.

2. Distinguish between strategic planning and tactical planning.

3. Why is flexibility an important characteristic of effective planning?

4. Identify the steps in the strategic planning process.

5. Relate the concept of company mission to goal setting and strategic planning.

6. Explain the role of the strategic business unit (SBU) concept in strategic planning.

7. List the names and characteristics of products and businesses in each cell of the SBU matrix.

8. Explain the major problems in applying the SBU concept.

9. Identify the two categories of forecasting methods and give two examples of each.

10. Suggest methods for applying Delphi forecasting technique to business situations.

ASSIGNMENTS/PROBLEMS/ DISCUSSION QUESTIONS

1. Relate the discussion of Gulf Oil's strategic planning to the steps in the strategic planning process shown in Figure 6-2. Make any necessary assumptions.

2. Suggest methods of adding flexibility to the plans of the following organizations:

    a. Attendance plan for a United Football League franchise
    b. Registration plan at your university
    c. Expansion plan by a local bank
    d. Evacuation plan of a local hospital

3. Identify two products that fit the following profiles:

    a. Star
    b. Dog
    c. Cash cow
    d. Question mark

Suggest actions that should be considered by management in each case.

4. Review the criticisms of the strategic business unit approach in strategic planning. Suggest methods by which these criticisms may be addressed.

5. The corporate planning division at AT&T includes eight humanities-oriented persons who work jointly with forty economists and statisticians on such projects as regulatory trends. Prepare a brief proposal showing how AT&T might implement a Delphi forecasting method. Explain both the potential benefits and pitfalls of this approach to forecasting.

A MANAGERIAL INCIDENT

Olin Corporation

A few years ago, Olin Corporation was awash in aggressive marketing plans for goose-down sleeping bags, propane stoves, tents, and other camping products. At the same time, Olin was pushing industrial mainstays such as polyester film and polyvinyl chloride. But profits were still lackluster at best. Today, however, the $1.5 billion Stamford, Connecticut, conglomerate has jettisoned all these products and is putting its capital into such areas as brass sheeting and hydrazine chemicals —products that fit in much better with its established corporate expertise. Reason: Olin has turned to a planning method that stresses overall corporate goals above individual product potentials.

The concept, known variously as strategy planning or strategic management, enables a company to spot—and capitalize on—its strengths in certain markets, and to sacrifice those market areas where growth is marginal. Although its cutthroat nature can make individual product managers unhappy at times, "it shows you how to drop your dogs and pick up stars," explains one veteran corporate planner.

Olin, which introduces fresh thinking to its units' strategy planning sessions by having an "outsider'' sit in, claims the system, among other things, has helped it weed out such ailing businesses as a polyester film plant in Greenville, South Carolina, sold in 1974 for $22 million; this was followed by the sale of its Statesville, North Carolina, tent business to National Canvas Products Corporation of Toledo, its Seattle Quilt Company to Raven Industries, Inc., in Sioux Falls, South Dakota, and its Turner Company (propane camping appliances) to Cleanweld Company in Los Angeles—all for a total of $9 million.

At the same time, the system has helped pinpoint the need for investments: more than $100 million to build a chlorine-caustic soda plant in McIntosh, Alabama, which will boost the line's production 60 percent; $75 million to $80 million to expand its polyols, hydrazine, and swimming-pool chemical operations; and $80 million to boost growth in its copper-based alloy markets.

The key to Olin's system is the process in which plans are formulated. In a traditional planning approach, managers of a business unit would sit down by themselves once a year to hammer out a five-year plan. But at Olin, managers from each of thirty-odd strategic planning units (components for which the company can define specific goals) meet with two or three managers from other areas of the company who generally know very little about that unit's operation. Such outside managers are called ''profilers,'' and it is their job to lend perspective and to help the planning unit's managers communicate better. ''We act as a catalyst to stimulate discussion,'' explains Joseph R. Rindler, a profiler whose main job is director of financial analysis. ''We're there to offer planning unit managers enlightened objectivity.''

Profilers, who number about 35 to 40, come from both staff and line jobs that range from per-

sonnel executive to product manager. But because they are not professional planners—they spend only 3 percent to 5 percent of their time in the profiler role—each must go through a brief training program to prepare for the annual planning sessions, which last one or two days. The planning sessions focus on reaching a consensus on the business unit's optimum strategy. The resulting profile is outlined in a standard two-page format and, in turn, is passed up the line to top management.

From this profile, management prepares a yearly ''action document'' for each of Olin's groups—a kind of nonfinancial budget of actions that should be taken to meet long-range goals. Actions prescribed involve moving into new geographic markets or phasing out of existing ones, seeking acquisitions, or unloading properties.

SOURCE: ''Olin's Shift to Strategy Planning,'' *Business Week* (March 27, 1978), p. 102. Reprinted from the March 27, 1978 issue of *Business Week* by special permission. © 1980 by McGraw-Hill, Inc.

Questions and Problems

1. Prepare a list of the benefits that might result from developing and utilizing an approach to strategic planning similar to the one used by Olin Corp.

2. Identify the potential problems of such an approach and make recommendations for reducing the likelihood that such problems would occur.

7.

The Decision-Making Process

Learning Objectives

AFTER STUDYING THIS CHAPTER YOU SHOULD BE ABLE TO

1. Explain the major types of decisions.
2. Compare the economic man concept with the description of the satisficing modern manager.
3. Identify the steps in the decision-making process.
4. Explain the benefits of a written problem statement.
5. Compare the strengths and weaknesses of group decision making.
6. Explain the Vroom-Yetton model of decision making.

Key Terms

decision making

technical decisions

managerial decisions

institutional decisions

programmed decisions

nonprogrammed decisions

satisficing

bounded rationality

problem

performance gap

synectics

brainstorming

efficiency

effectiveness

feedback

It is only in our decisions that we are important.

JEAN-PAUL SARTRE

To be conscious that you are ignorant of the facts is a great step to knowledge.

BENJAMIN DISRAELI

The magazine industry scoffed at Walter H. Annenberg's pint-sized new entry. The five-by-seven-and-a-half-inch weekly was comprised primarily of television program listings and carried an appropriate name: *TV Guide.* But how could such an unlikely magazine compete with such entrenched giants as *Life, Look,* and the *Saturday Evening Post?*

But compete it did, and by 1983 more than 17 million *TV Guides* were sold every week of the year. Not only is it the nation's best-selling magazine, but it accounts for one out of every five magazine copies sold in the United States. As one executive at company headquarters remarked: "More copies of our magazine fall off the back of delivery trucks than even *Time* sells."

To find out how a pint-sized magazine has attained such prominence, it is necessary to go back to the early 1950s when Mr. Annenberg became interested in adding a magazine on the fledgling television industry to his string of publications, which then included the Philadelphia *Inquirer* and the Philadelphia *Daily News,* as well as the magazines *Racing Form* and *Seventeen.* He also owned a chain of TV and radio stations.

Mr. Annenberg was particularly attracted by the success of the small television magazines that had been started a few years earlier in New York, Chicago, and Philadelphia. He began questioning buyers of the magazines to find out why they were willing to pay extra for program information carried by most newspapers. He found that viewers liked the magazines because of their accuracy, their articles on television personalities, and their compactness. "I came away convinced," he says.

In 1953 he paid $2.3 million for a New York magazine called *TeleVision Guide* that had been started in 1948 by two men, one a book salesman, the other a lawyer. In the same year he paid over $1 million for *TV Digest,* a Philadelphia magazine, and about $1 million for a Chicago magazine, *TV Forecast.*[1]

The first edition of the new magazine was published April 3, 1953. Today its advertising revenues exceed $239 million for 108 regional editions, and it employs a staff of 1,400 in 33 field offices, including the 820 employees in the Radnor, Pennsylvania, headquarters. A Univac 1180 computer ties local shows together with the network programming and stores more than 250,000 movie and television show synopses. When a local station schedules the showing of, say, episode 272 of "I Love Lucy," the computer will produce a description such as "Lucy tries out some ill-acquired Spanish when Ricky's mother comes to visit."

Annenberg's decision has clearly paid off.

What Is Decision Making?

The decisions made by *TV Guide*'s founder had a vital effect on the success of his organization. Other decisions are much less significant. Each day of our lives we make hundreds of decisions: what to wear, what to eat, where to go, and what to do are all decisions that must be made. But decision making is more than just attending to the details of everyday life. It is a vital and unique kind of activity, for it is through decision making that people define the boundaries of their lives.

Management is also a uniquely human activity. *Homo sapiens* is a species that plans, that organizes, that controls, that "manages" its own future. It should come as no surprise, therefore, that many management writers feel that management *is* decision making. They argue that it is only by making decisions (about planning, organizing, and controlling) that people manage to do anything.

Decision making involves making a choice among alternative courses of action.

Decision making can be defined as making a choice among alternative courses of action. This definition implies that managers are faced with a problem or opportunity, alternative courses of action are proposed and analyzed, and a choice is made that is likely to move the organization in the direction of its goals.

Types of Decisions

There have been many attempts to categorize and classify the types of decisions that organizations commonly face. One widely accepted model divides all organizational decisions into three categories based upon the subject involved. The three categories are technical, managerial, and institutional decisions.[2] Accord-

---

[1] John E. Cooney, "Pint-Sized *TV Guide* Attains Giant Profits, Circulation in 25 Years," *Wall Street Journal* (November 6, 1978), p. 1. Reprinted by permission of the *Wall Street Journal,* © Dow Jones & Company, Inc., 1978. All rights reserved.

[2] See Talcott Parsons, *Structure and Process in Modern Organizations* (New York: The Free Press, 1960); James D. Thompson, *Organizations in Action* (New York: McGraw-Hill, 1967); and George P. Huber, *Managerial Decision Making* (Glenview, Ill.: Scott, Foresman, 1980).

ing to the model, not only are these decisions different in kind, but they are also typically made by different individuals within the organization.

TECHNICAL DECISIONS

In every organization decisions must be made about *core* activities—those activities relating directly to the "work" of the organization. The core activities of Exxon would include exploration, drilling, refining, and distribution. Decisions concerning these activities are technical in nature. The information required to solve problems related to these activities is most likely concerned with the operational aspects of the technology involved. It is important that the term *technology* be considered in its broadest sense.

> By technology is meant the action that an individual performs upon an object, with or without the aid of tools or mechanical devices, in order to make some change in that object. The object, or "raw material," may be a living being, human or otherwise, a symbol or an inanimate object. People are raw materials in people-changing or people-processing organizations; symbols are raw materials in banks, advertising agencies and some research organizations; the interactions of people are raw materials to be manipulated by administrators in organizations.[3]

Technical decisions concern the process by which inputs are changed into outputs by the organization. Such inputs may be people, information, or products.

> **Technical decisions concern the process whereby inputs are changed into outputs.**

MANAGERIAL DECISIONS

The second category of decisions includes those related to issues of coordination and support of the core activities of the organization. Since all organizations tend to become differentiated or specialized over time, a need arises for the *integration* or coordination of the differentiated parts. Decisions about the process are the primary focus of *managerial decisions*.

Managerial decision making is also concerned with regulating the relationship between the organization and its immediate environment. In order to produce maximum efficiency of its core activities, management must insure that these activities are not disturbed by short-term changes in the environment. For this reason, many organizations will stockpile raw materials and finished goods in inventory. Maintenance and control of these inventories and forecasting of short-term changes in supply-and-demand conditions are all part of managerial decision making.

> **Managerial decisions are related to the coordination and support of the core activities of the organization.**

INSTITUTIONAL DECISIONS

Institutional decisions involve long-term planning and policy formulation. They concern such issues as diversification of activities, large-scale capital expansion,

> **Institutional decisions involve long-term planning and policy formulation with the aim of assuring the organization's survival as a productive part of the economy and society.**

[3] Charles Perrow, "A Framework for the Comparative Analysis of Organizations," *American Sociological Review* (April 1967), pp. 194–208.

mergers, shifts in research and development activities, and other critical organizational choices. If an organization is to survive over a long period of time, it must occupy a useful, productive place in the economy and society as a whole. As society and the economy change, organizations must also change or cease to exist. Although forecasters have predicted the demise of the internal combustion engine for the past thirty years, it continues to be the primary power source for automobile transportation. But General Motors Corp. has made the decision to enter the urban mass transit system market. Faced with the increasing scarcity of fossil fuels, GM's institutional decision makers chose to diversify the organization's activities in order to take advantage of this fact.

The three types of decision making—technical, managerial, and institutional—are encountered by every organization. Figure 7-1 illustrates each type for three different organizations: one profit-seeking firm (an oil company) and two nonprofit organizations (a hospital and the National Aeronautics and Space Administration [NASA]).

DECISION MAKING AT DIFFERENT LEVELS IN THE ORGANIZATION

An analysis of the three categories of decisions indicates that they are not evenly spread throughout the organization. As Figure 7-2 indicates, institutional deci-

Figure 7-1 THREE ORGANIZATIONS AND THREE KINDS OF DECISIONS

	Institutional Decisions	Managerial Decisions	Technical Decisions
For an oil company	Should we bid on an offshore drilling lease or diversify into coal or uranium?	What land/sea leases should we choose?	Where should we drill the well? Dig the mine?
	How should we react to the president's new energy program?	How much should we spend on public relations versus lobbying?	Which members of Congress should we concentrate on?
For a hospital	Should we add a radiation therapy unit to the facilities?	How will we staff the unit? Where will it go?	What should the treatment schedule for this patient be?
	Should we develop an outreach capability beyond our present emergency room facilities?	How do we integrate present personnel into the new program?	Should health education be carried out in the clinic?
For NASA	Should we ask Congress to fund a manned Mars mission before the Space Shuttle program is completed?	What subcontractors should be used? On what schedule? How much cost overrun should we expect?	How do we build a self-contained biosphere? What orbit do we use?
	Should most of our efforts be spent on more basic research or on the industrial utilization of "near earth space"?	What percentage of the Space Shuttle flights over the next five years should be reserved for private industry?	What kind of experiments will be most effective in establishing the industrial potential of near space?

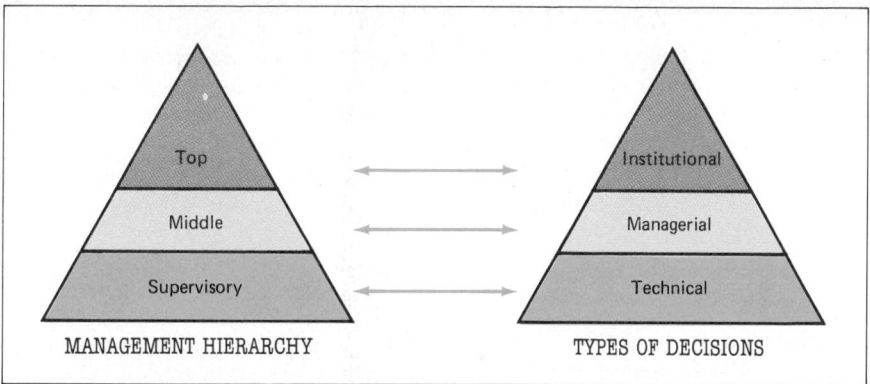

Figure 7-2
THE RELATIONSHIP
BETWEEN TYPES OF
DECISIONS AND THE
MANAGEMENT
HIERARCHY

sions are most often made at the top management level of the organization, while technical decisions are more predominant at the supervisory level.

While the figure provides an indication of the relative number of each type of decision made at each level in the organization, the categories are by no means exclusive. The production vice-president of a heavy equipment manufacturer might be engaged primarily in technical decisions, while a member of the legal staff might be involved solely in institutional matters.

PROGRAMMED AND NONPROGRAMMED DECISIONS

Decisions differ not only in their content but also in terms of their relative uniqueness. By *relative uniqueness* we mean the degree to which a problem or decision (1) has been seen before; (2) occurs frequently and on a regular basis; and (3) has been solved or resolved in a satisfactory manner. *Programmed decisions* are those involving simple, common, frequently occurring problems that have well-established and understood solutions. *Nonprogrammed decisions* are those that deal with unusual or novel problems.[4]

Managers regularly have a series of recurring decisions to make. As a result the organization develops decision rules, programs, policies, and procedures to use. Salary scales are utilized to determine starting pay for a new security officer. Reordering of raw materials occurs when inventory on hand reaches a stated minimum. Routing of the organization's fleet of trucks is determined by specially designed quantitative models. Programmed decisions can be made quickly, consistently, and inexpensively since the procedures, rules, and regulations eliminate the time-consuming process of identifying and evaluating alternatives and making a new choice each time a decision is required. While programmed decisions limit the flexibility of managers, they take little time and free the decision maker to devote his or her efforts to unique, nonprogrammed decisions.

In situations in which nonprogrammed decisions are the rule, the creation of alternatives and the selection and implementation of the most appropriate one

Programmed decisions are those involving simple, common, frequently occurring problems that have well-established and understood solutions.

Nonprogrammed decisions are those that deal with unusual or novel problems.

[4] Herbert A. Simon, *The New Science of Management Decisions* (New York: Harper & Row, 1960), pp. 5–6.

A single-minded devotion to business characterized the career of Alfred Pritchard Sloan, Jr., whose twenty-year career at the helm of General Motors transformed the auto firm into one of the industrial giants of the world. His prowess in corporate decision making led him and the companies he shepherded along a straight path to financial success. The principles of operation he espoused called for a direct approach to management problems and decision making: "Get the facts. Recognize the equities of all concerned. Realize the necessity of doing a better job every day. Keep an open mind and work hard. The last is most important of all. There is no short cut."

Sloan, born May 23, 1875, in New Haven, Connecticut, soon exhibited a talent for scientific disciplines. He passed the entrance examination for MIT, but he was too young to gain admission. When he was finally permitted to enter that institution, he completed the four-year curriculum in three years, obtaining his B.S. in electrical engineering at the age of twenty.

Sloan's first job after college was at the Hyatt Roller Bearing Company as a drafter. Six years later he had advanced to the company presidency.

Curiously, the firm's major product at the time Sloan came to work there was billiard balls. But Sloan could foresee the tremendous expansion that was about to take place in the automobile industry and he began to redirect the company in the task of perfecting steel roller bearings to be marketed to the auto manufacturers. Sloan not only perfected the new product; he dedicated himself to the task of selling it. As Hyatt's chief traveling salesperson, he became intimately ac-

become the critical tasks. By definition a nonprogrammed problem is one that has not been encountered before. Managers earn their salaries by making nonprogrammed decisions. They are often evaluated on their ability to apply creativity and judgment to the solution of problems and to make decisions in a logical, step-by-step manner. The description of the decision-making process in this chapter is related primarily to nonprogrammed decisions.

Converting Nonprogrammed Decisions to Programmed Decisions

Although managers are judged on their effectiveness in making nonprogrammed decisions, they should strive to convert nonprogrammed decisions into programmed ones. Many organizations treat routine decisions—inventory control, supplier selection, individual salary decisions—as special decisions requiring unique solutions. Converting such decision areas into programmed decisions frees the manager to devote more time and effort to making truly nonprogrammed decisions.

How Good Should the Decision Be?

For more than 200 years, many economists have accepted the description of a decision maker—the so-called *economic man*—proposed by Adam Smith. This decision maker obtained information concerning all possible alternatives and quainted with all aspects of automobile production as well as all the important personalities in the industry. Under Sloan's leadership Hyatt's profits soared.

Fearful that the great auto manufacturers might decide to produce their own steel roller bearings, Sloan negotiated the merger of his firm with United Motors, an organization established by General Motors in 1916. Two years later the two firms merged, and Sloan became a vice-president and member of GM's executive committee. He assumed the GM presidency in 1923, and by 1936 he was the highest paid executive in the United States. The following year he was named chairman of GM's board of directors.

General Motors' seemingly perpetual prosperity under Sloan's guidance has been attributed to his management style, which underlined the importance of individual executives exercising their own initiative. Sloan emphasized this fact in his statement that "the organization of which I am now president would be impossible without the principle of individual initiative." To eliminate the possibility that a decentralized management philosophy might lead to divisions operating at cross-purposes, Sloan instituted a set of "standard procedures" and a committee system, both of which functioned to keep information circulating in an orderly fashion.

Alfred P. Sloan retired in 1956 after a sixty-year career in business. Business was his life—both his work and his hobby. He had no other significant interests. He died in 1966 at the age of ninety-one.

Sources

"Businessmen in the News," *Fortune* (May 1956), p. 55.

Current Biography: Who's News and Why (1940), s.v., "Sloan, Alfred Pritchard, Jr."

Current Biography Yearbook (1966), Obituaries, s.v., "Sloan, Alfred Pritchard, Jr.," p. 471.

chose the best solution designed to achieve a particular goal. The chosen alternative was that choice which would maximize profit or some other value.

Nobel Prize laureate Herbert Simon conducted extensive investigations of managerial behavior and concluded that modern managers were not accurately described by the economic man concept. In too many instances they are forced to make decisions with incomplete information. They rarely consider all possible alternatives to the solution of a problem but instead examine a few alternatives that appear to be likely solutions. Most nonprogrammed decisions involve too many variables for a thorough examination of each. Instead of attempting to maximize, the modern manager *satisfices*, according to Simon. He or she examines the five or six most likely alternatives and makes a choice from among them, rather than investing the time necessary to examine thoroughly all possible alternatives. A decision concerning a new plant location in the United States could involve the analysis of literally hundreds or thousands of possible sites. The manager may choose to focus instead on the three locales that appear most feasible and conduct a careful analysis of each alternative prior to making the final selection.

Today's manager is acting within what Simon calls *bounded rationality*.[5] This concept refers to boundaries or limits that exist in any problem situation that necessarily restrict the manager's picture of the world. Such boundaries include

[5] James G. March and Herbert A. Simon, *Organizations* (New York: Wiley, 1958), p. 170.

Satisficing is the term Herbert Simon has used to describe the way modern managers must, necessarily, make decisions with incomplete information, by choosing from among a minimum of likely alternatives.

Bounded rationality is Herbert Simon's term for boundaries or limits that exist in any problem situation that necessarily restrict the manager's picture of the world and so his or her ability to make decisions.

GERBER: RESPONDING TO A DECLINING BIRTHRATE

The firm's mission had always been summed up in its motto: "Babies are our business . . . our *only* business." But the 1970s saw the baby boom turn into a birth dearth as more and more couples decided to limit the size of their families, marriage and childbearing were postponed, and zero population growth became at least temporarily a reality. And top management at Gerber Products Co., the nation's largest baby-food maker, was worried.

Reaction to the dip in births and fertility rates were drastic at other companies. Lane Bryant, Inc., which had pioneered maternity fashions at the turn of the century, began dropping its maternity departments in its newer suburban stores. Johnson & Johnson started to stress the use of its shampoo, baby powder, and baby oil for adults.

Although the term *bounded rationality* probably never entered the discussions at Gerber's Fremont, Michigan, headquarters, the concept was obviously at work. First, the slogan had to go, since it limited the firm's flexibility to react to changing conditions. Gerber began to diversify, establishing a chain of day-care centers and a mail-order life insurance company offering policies to young parents. A line of single-serving adult foods called "Singles" was also developed in an attempt to reach the growing number of smaller-sized households. But management discovered that the Gerber name was a handicap in developing a food for adults. "No matter what we labeled it," recalls one Gerber executive, "we discovered that people still thought of it as baby food, or something for adults who couldn't eat real food."*

Research data emphasized that parents had a positive image of Gerber products, and company executives decided to exploit this strength by developing additional entries in the juvenile products business. Four hundred products have been introduced, including toiletries, bottles, clothing, and toys. In addition, the birth rate, which had sunk to all-time lows in the mid-1970s, began to climb during the 1980s as the increasing number of women at or near the age of thirty decided to start families. But Gerber's new strategy is aimed at catering to parents who had bought Gerber baby food for their infants and are willing to purchase other products as their children grow older. Although baby food still accounts for four-fifths of company sales, other baby and children's products are being sold. And the firm's objective reflects the new decision: "Selling more to the same mothers is our objective now."

* "Gerber: Selling More to the Same Mothers Is Our Objective Now," *Business Week* (October 16, 1978), p. 192.

individual limits to any manager's knowledge of all alternatives as well as such elements as policies, costs, and technology that cannot be changed by the decision maker. As a result the manager seldom seeks the optimum solution but realistically attempts to reach a *satisfactory* solution to the problem at hand.

Simon's view of the modern manager presents a realistic picture of a decision maker subject to both internal and external constraints. *Internal* constraints include the individual's intellectual ability, training and experience, personality, attitudes, and motivation. *External* constraints refer to the influence exerted by members of the organization and groups outside it. While this view does not mean that managers do not attempt to make effective decisions, it does recognize that often the decision maker will decide that the quality of a decision must be balanced with the time and money costs of making it.

Steps in Decision Making

All decisions, ranging from size of the employee parking lot to determination of the number of factories to produce a product line, involve a definite series of steps that lead to a particular result. Some decisions are made in minutes as the manager mentally proceeds through each step in the process. Others take months or even years. Decisions may be poorly made in a hurried manner, or they may be the result of much deliberation and careful consideration of alternatives. But all decisions go through these steps. Figure 7-3 illustrates the steps in the decision process.[6]

PERCEPTION OF THE ENVIRONMENT

Before any decision is possible, the individual decision maker must become aware of and be sensitive to the decision environment. This sensitivity results from two inputs:

1. Specific information of relevance to the decision maker (quality control reports, quarterly sales reports, data on supplier bid forms)
2. More general, impressionistic information about conditions and operations (the manager's "feel" for the situation)

It is important to note the difference between the environment as an objective entity and the manager's *perception* of the environment. All individuals filter the information they receive; that is, they pay more attention to *some* information than to *other* information. This filtering of information sometimes proves disastrous to both individuals and organizations.

A primary task of management is to monitor the environment for potential change. Built into every management information system is an *early warning signal* system of reporting various environmental developments—new or adapted products by competitors; changes in consumer sentiments; improved production methods—to alert decision makers. If the organization is to remain healthy over a long period of time, it must be ready to adapt and evolve in response to such changes. The development of such systems is treated in detail in Chapter 18.

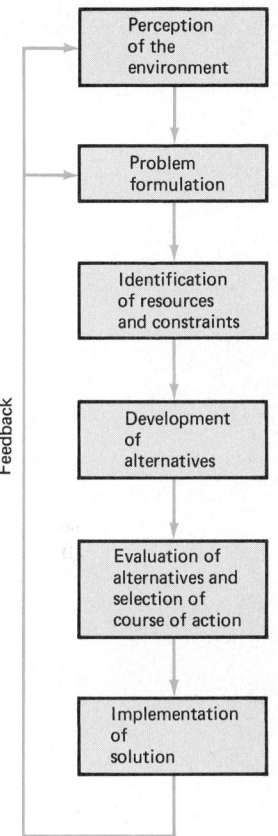

**Figure 7-3
THE DECISION-
MAKING PROCESS**

---

[6] The systematic approach to decision making has been treated by a number of writers. See John Dewey, *How We Think* (New York: Heath, 1910), pp. 101–105; Peter F. Drucker, *The Practice of Management* (New York: Harper & Row, 1954), pp. 354–365; Charles H. Kepner and Benjamin B. Tregoe, *The Rational Manager* (New York: McGraw-Hill, 1965); and "How to Make a Business Decision: An Analysis of Theory and Practice," *Management Review* (February 1980), pp. 43–47.

OVERCOMING THE "ROSE-COLORED GLASSES" SYNDROME

All organizations filter the information they receive—they pay attention to some of it and ignore the rest. In particular, distressing or threatening information tends to be ignored until it finally forces its way into consciousness. United Technologies Corp., manufacturers of products as diversified as Pratt & Whitney aircraft jet engines, Jenn-Air kitchen ranges, Carrier air conditioning systems, Sikorsky helicopters, and Otis elevators, has long recognized the need for sensitivity to the decision environment. This need is well documented in the following advertisement that appeared in the *Wall Street Journal*:

Where Do You Get Your Information?

When's the last time
you sat in the
bleachers?
When's the last time
you heard a
Jefferson Starship record?
(More than a million
were sold last year.)
Did you see
Superman II?
(It did $14 million
its first weekend.)
Do you read
Reader's Digest?
(The circulation is
31 million worldwide.)
Have you seen the top
10 TV shows?
When's the last time
you took a trip on
a Greyhound bus?
How many times
each month do you
shop in a supermarket?
Have you seen
evangelists on TV?
(Viewers send them
millions of dollars.)
Have you browsed through
a card shop?
(Hallmark sells one billion
cards a year.)
Have you stood on an
assembly line?
Gone down into a
coal mine?
Spent time on
a farm?
If you don't know
what's happening in other
people's worlds,
you can't make good decisions
in the business world.

SOURCE: © United Technologies Corp., 1982.

PROBLEM FORMULATION

Problems are barriers to the achievement of organizational goals. They are obstacles to be overcome by the decision makers. When an organization fails to achieve its goals, there is a *performance gap.* This gap is the difference between the predicted or expected level of performance and the actual level. The existence of such a gap is an important part of the decision environment since it provides considerable motivation for problem solving and innovation.

How Performance Gaps Occur

There are two distinct ways in which a gap can occur. First, goals can remain constant while performance slips. These conditions usually indicate the existence of a "problem"—some malfunction or miscalculation on the part of management. Second, performance can remain constant while goals change. Under the circumstances it can be said that either a problem or an opportunity exists. The fact that goals may change over time should not be neglected as a source of performance gaps, for only under these conditions can organizations change and innovate.

Goals change in response to one or more of three occurrences. First, aspiration levels tend to rise if present goals have been met for a period of time. A manufacturing facility that meets its goal of a 5 percent rejection rate for six months in a row may no longer be satisfied with that level of performance and may establish a new goal of 3 percent. Second, there may be changes in the internal environment of the organization. New people may join the organization with new ideas; new ways of doing things may be discovered; power shifts within the management structure may occur. Finally, the external environment of the organization may change. For Chrysler Corp., such changes might include the establishment of new federal emission control and mileage standards for 1986 model automobiles.

Problem Formulation: The Neglected Step in the Decision-Making Process

Problem formulation is perhaps the most neglected aspect of the decision-making process. Too often it is simply *assumed* that the nature of a managerial problem is obvious to all concerned. An employee "isn't motivated"; there exists a "personality conflict"; "What we have here is a failure to communicate." Why is problem formulation so difficult?

A major problem is that it is psychologically uncomfortable to think about problems. The manager becomes anxious and worried, and often his or her response becomes, "Don't just sit there; do something!" Such a tendency is reinforced by the fact that many academic programs spend considerable amounts of time teaching problem solving, not problem formulation. Finally, time pressures are a very real part of the managerial work. Often, managers simply do not allow themselves sufficient time to consider the situation and do an effective job of problem formulation.

Preparing a Written Problem Statement

The development of a written problem statement is a relatively straightforward task. However, the importance of such a document should not be underrated.

Problems are barriers to the achievement of organizational goals.

Performance gap refers to the difference between the predicted or expected level of performance and the actual level.

Stating a problem in a written form has three distinct benefits. First and most important, it forces decision makers to clarify their thinking. This exercise provides a natural check on the tendency to spend insufficient time "finding" the problem. Second, a well-written problem statement acts as a foundation upon which joint problem solving can be based. Much problem solving in modern organizations is a multiperson activity, and it is extremely important that everyone be working to *solve the same problem*. A written problem formulation is an excellent communications device to ensure this.

Finally, a written statement provides historical documentation of the decision-making process. Just as communication between different people is important, so also is communication between different stages in the decision-making process. In a certain sense, a written problem statement works to keep the decision maker honest. In the manager's world there are great pressures—for success, for efficiency, for getting the job done *now*. And there is occasionally the temptation to redefine the problem in the process of solving it. In other words the decision maker might unconsciously change the problem from a difficult one to an easier one by simply ignoring or forgetting about the unpleasant aspects. The written statement provides a tangible check for preventing such an occurrence.

There are four basic guidelines in preparing a written problem statement:

1. The problem should be stated explicitly. Avoid general statements about vague feelings of concern.
2. A working diagnosis should be included. This contains a description of the symptoms observed, the nature of the suspected problem, and what the underlying causes are thought to be.
3. The problem should be stated in specific behavioral terms. Individuals are generally unable to change general conditions, but they can alter specific behavior. Telling subordinates that they lack motivation leaves them to interpret what is meant by *motivation*. Telling them that they report to work late too often does not.
4. The problem statement should specify how this problem relates to the organization as a whole and to its various parts. Although the *primary* responsibility for a particular problem may be found in one department, other departments may also play a role. While the marketing department may bear the primary responsibility for low sales, improper quality control by the production department might be an important contributing factor.[7]

IDENTIFICATION OF RESOURCES AND CONSTRAINTS

Problem solving does not occur in a vacuum. It is embedded in the fabric of the organization and its environment. It is also true that organizations generally face

---

[7] Alvar Elbing, *Behavioral Decisions in Organizations* (Glenview, Ill.: Scott, Foresman, 1978), p. 110. Copyright © 1978 by Scott, Foresman and Company. Reprinted by permission.

Sherlock Holmes once remarked that it is a capital mistake to theorize in advance of the fact. He might also have said that it was an even more grievous error to mistake the "obvious" facts one has assembled for the true underlying nature of the problem. In virtually every Holmes story, Inspector Lestrade or Dr. Watson offers a common-sense, obvious explanation for a mystery. And the explanation proves to be totally wrong. Yet all too often, managers find themselves playing Lestrade by not digging deeply enough and considering only the most visible symptoms of the problem—rather than its causes.

To be an effective problem solver, the manager must understand the relationship among symptoms, problems, and causes. *Symptoms* are those visible indicators that tell the decision maker that something is wrong. The *problem* is whatever gave rise to the symptoms, and the *causes* of the problem are those factors that allow it to exist.

A physician who discovers anemia, severe stomach cramps, and weakness in a patient is observing symptoms. By adding data that the patient is a child who lives in an old tenement building, the doctor might conclude that the problem is lead poisoning and treat it accordingly. If the symptoms are relieved, has the problem been solved? If the causes still exist, the child will be back again shortly with the same symptoms, or worse. Only when the source of the lead is discovered and eliminated will the problem be solved. Managers, too, should work to change or eliminate causes rather than attempting to suppress symptoms.

**PROBLEMS,
SYMPTOMS,
CAUSES**

more than one problem at the same time. These problems compete for the manager's attention and for the scarce resources of the organization.

By definition anything that can be used to help in solving a problem is a resource. Resources include time, money, personnel, expertise, equipment, raw materials, and information. These resources are referred to in Figure 7-4 as *The Five Ms of Management.*[8]

Constraints are factors that impede problem solution or limit managers in their efforts to solve a problem. Lack of adequate resources might prove to be a significant constraint. Other elements such as worker attitudes or government programs may prove to be a resource, a constraint, or both.

The decision maker should develop a brief but explicit listing of the major resources and constraints relevant to a given problem. Such a listing of resources allows the decision maker to budget organizational assets in order to maximize their usefulness. The listing of constraints alerts the decision maker to the important stumbling blocks affecting a solution so that they can be avoided. In addition organizations sometimes encounter situations in which the absence of a specific resource or the existence of a particular constraint is a significant problem itself. Pizza Hut is the world's largest pizza maker, for outdistancing such

---

[8] The "Five Ms" concept was first suggested by L. T. White. See U.S. Small Business Administration, *Strengthening Small Business Management: Collections from the Pages of L. T. White,* edited by Joseph C. Schabacker (Washington, D.C.: U.S. Government Printing Office, 1971), p. 21.

**Figure 7-4
THE FIVE Ms OF
MANAGEMENT—BASIC
RESOURCES OF THE
ORGANIZATION**

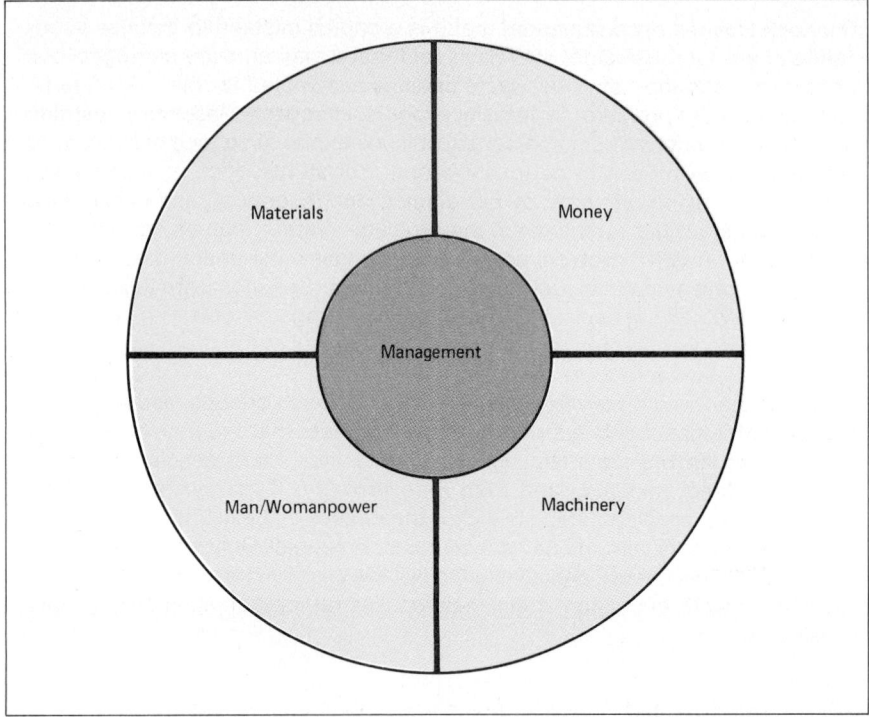

competitors as Godfather's, Pizza Inn, Noble Roman, Shakey's, and combination pizza maker–video game emporiums Chuckie Cheese and Showtime Pizza. A major cost factor in pizza manufacturing is mozzarella cheese, whose price has exceeded $1.00 per pound in recent years. If Pizza Hut should attempt to increase sales by 40 percent in a single year through the expansion of the number of outlets, the reduction of prices to stimulate additional sales, or by other means, its management might find that both the price and the limited supply of mozzarella would make its goal impossible to attain, regardless of the alternative chosen. This barrier would then form the basis of a subsidiary problem whose goal would be to obtain needed raw material resources. In this manner the overall problem situation is broken down into smaller, more easily handled subproblems.

DEVELOPMENT OF ALTERNATIVES

The generation of a number of possible alternatives is essential for the decision maker. In too many instances managers quickly identify one or two alternatives and choose from among them. This short-cut approach often results in more effective alternatives never being considered. Creativity is needed at this step in developing a variety of alternatives for consideration.

OVERCOMING CONSTRAINTS WITH LITTLE ORPHAN ANNIE

For decades the production of sheets was a simple matter of turning out white cotton rectangular bed covers. The industry grew with increases in population and counted on repeat business since the sheets would last only a year or two due to the washing, bleaching, and ironing. Then cotton prices rose and decision makers at such textile mills as Spring Mills and J .P. Stevens decided to produce sheets from a mixture of cotton and polyester. But these sheets lasted twice as long as the cotton variety (a constraint) and excess inventory rapidly built up, creating a problem in the $850-million-a-year industry.

A careful analysis of the problem led sheet-making firms to begin the production of decorated bedsheets. And the decision paid off. Children's sheets now carry the likeness of Little Orphan Annie, Conan the Barbarian, or Darth Vader. Adults' beds are adorned with sheets depicting a Monet painting, a Chinese landscape, or the designs of Bill Blass, Calvin Klein, or Oscar de la Renta. A survey reported that 35 to 40 percent of shoppers were using sheets for home decoration, and a small percentage were even making clothes from them. Creative decisions appear to have overcome the problem affecting the growth of the bedsheet industry.

SOURCE: Based on Ann-Byrd Platt, "Sleeping with Darth and Annie Is Stirring a Drowsy Business," *Wall Street Journal*, July 3, 1978, p. 1. Reprinted by permission of the Wall Street Journal. © Dow Jones & Co., Inc., 1978. All rights reserved.

The Use of Creativity in Developing Alternatives

A widely used technique for the generation of alternative solutions is the synectics approach.[9] The term *synectics* is derived from two Greek words that mean the joining together of different and apparently irrelevant elements. One writer describes the synectics approach as follows:

> Synectics in operation depends heavily on two mechanisms: making the strange familiar, and making the familiar strange. The first of these is the search for similarity; confronted with a new problem, we ask ourselves whether it is not an old problem, had we but the wit to see it. Seeing even partial resemblances may lead to the application of familiar methods in solving the new problem. Making the familiar strange is a way of shedding preconceptions and perceptual habits. Innocence of vision, a certain naivete, and ingeniousness characterize the creative individual; if these qualities can be cultivated the novelty of invention and problem solution should be increased.[10]

Synectics approach is the technique widely used to generate alternative solutions; by synectics, the manager examines analogous methods and perceptions of other fields in order to gain insight into management problems.

Analogy is the primary mechanism to make the strange familiar and the familiar strange. Often, it takes the form of borrowing from nature. Alexander Graham Bell is said to have gotten the basic idea for the telephone from studying the construction of the human ear. Leonardo da Vinci's idea for a helicopter

[9] See W. J. J. Gordon, *Synectics* (New York: Harper, 1961).
[10] Frank Barron, *Creative Person and Creative Process* (New York: Holt, Rinehart and Winston, 1968), p. 133.

analogy - comparison of an unfamiliar thing to a more familiar one.

came from watching leaves twirl in the wind. Although the famous story of Newton discovering gravity by having an apple fall on his head has no basis in fact, it is still popular because it is a credible example of the use of analogy.

Often, analogy becomes an exercise in pure imagination. It might be visual rather than verbal and equate to a mental juggling of concepts and ideas until an "attractive" formation occurs. The decision maker who uses this form of analogy is attempting to associate an event in two different frames of reference. What occurs is applied make-believe, the art of "what if?" Table 7-1 summarizes and illustrates the use of analogy in developing alternatives.

Synectics and the use of analogy point to an important psychological aspect of problem solving. Often, it is far more effective and efficient to "think around" the problem than to attack it directly. Every decision maker encounters an occasional mental block. Creative techniques such as synectics are proven methods of removing such blocks, or at least of getting around them.

Other creative techniques use the "more is better" approach.[11] This approach is based on the assumption that concentration on a few alternatives to the exclusion of other, less likely ones may blind the decision maker to many opportunities. *Brainstorming* is the chief technique of this approach. Brainstorming involves sessions of several persons who toss out ideas to each other. Each idea is recorded for later evaluation. There are four rules in brainstorming:

Brainstorming is a technique used to bring forth many alternative solutions; it involves a group of people brought together with the purpose of exchanging ideas.

1. There is *no* evaluation of any suggestion during the brainstorming session. In fact, even discussion should be kept to an absolute minimum.
2. Quantity is desired. Participants are cautioned to forget about quality at

[11] See F. D. Barrett, "Creativity Techniques: Yesterday, Today, and Tomorrow," *Advanced Management* (Winter 1978), pp. 25–35.

Table 7-1 USE OF ANALOGY IN THE CREATIVE PROCESS	ALTERNATIVES	EXAMPLES
	1. Decision makers imagine themselves to be an actual, physical part of the problem under consideration.	Superintendent of gem mine plays role in which he or she is one of the miners in an attempt to determine methods of employee theft and its prevention.
	2. Decision makers develop alternatives by studying similar situations in other industries, geographical areas, or subjects.	Du Pont decision makers adapt a heat resistant material named Teflon to a variety of uses ranging from cookware to disc brakes.
	3. Decision makers use imagination to develop a series of answers to a series of "what if?" questions.	Managers of new-product development at Campbell Soup Co. develop new types of soup by considering such blends as meat with vegetables; fruit with vegetables; milk with fruit; and so forth.

Problem Background   The head of engineering of a national sporting goods company describes his problem as follows: "Years ago my president asked me to design a fish lure with hooks that would hook a fish's mouth but would not snag weeds or sunken logs. (See 1.) I have tried all kinds of solutions. For instance, I bought a commercially made lure that has a protective spring inside the sharp end of the hook. (See 2.) The theory is that in its excitement a fish will push back the spring and impale itself on the hook that lies right behind it. However, I've found that most water plants will push back the spring as well. When I strengthened the spring, I found that a fish's mouth couldn't push it out of the way. I'd get bites, but no fish."

1. 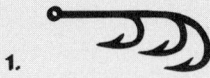   **2.** spring

Problem Description   Considering all the approaches I've tried, it appears that to the degree that a lure is made so that it won't snag on weeds, it won't hook fish either—and vice versa.

Hypothetical Creative Process

Thought 1   The better the hook is for catching fish, the fewer fish are caught because that hook snags more easily.

Thought 2   Like a con artist, the more obvious his "hook," the less the suckers will bite.

Thought 3   He hides the "hook" contained in his crooked deal behind his inviting soft sell.

Thought 4   An inviting soft lure would hide the fishhook.

New Idea   Make the lure out of something soft and put the hook inside it. A weed does not "bite" the way a fish does. Thus the lure would slide off weeds, but a fish would bite down hard enough to be caught by the hook.

SOURCE: Arthur G. Bedeian and William F. Glueck, *Management* (Hinsdale, Ill.: Dryden Press, 1983), p. 257. The problem is adapted from William J. J. Gordon and Tony Poze, *The New Art of the Possible: The Basic Course in Synectics* (Cambridge, Mass.: Porpoise Books, 1980), pp. 58–63, and is reprinted by permission.

this stage. If something occurs to a participant he or she should state it.
3. Freewheeling is encouraged. The stranger the idea the better.
4. Tag-on ideas and the modification or combination of existing ideas are desired.[12]

These rules are based on two insights into the psychology of creativity. First, it is difficult if not impossible to be both creative and judgmental at the same time. It is as if the decision maker possessed two sets of mental "gears"; trying to use them at the same time may strip them both. As a result any form of criticism or evaluation is absolutely forbidden. Second, creativity can be both an individual and a group process. In the same way that the splitting of one atom of U^{235} in the core of a nuclear reactor sets off other atoms, so do ideas generated in a brainstorming session touch off other ideas, and a chain reaction results.

A number of studies of the effectiveness of the brainstorming approach have been conducted. Findings generally support the effectiveness of this approach in producing large numbers of novel solutions.[13] Most effective use of the technique occurs when

1. Group members know of the problem in advance and spend some time "brainstorming" on their own;
2. The group works together on a more or less regular basis; and
3. Individual members of the group again work on the problem on their own after the meeting.

How Much Time Should Be Invested in Developing Alternatives?

The ultimate scarce resource of the manager is time. And since there are always additional alternatives waiting to be discovered, the alternative generation process could conceivably go on forever.

Three factors should be considered in determining the appropriate amount of time to spend generating alternatives. First, *how important is this problem or opportunity?* The more important the decision, the greater the value of marginal improvements in the solution. A 2 percent improvement in the solution of a $10 million problem produces a further profit or savings of $200,000. The same percentage improvement for a $10,000 problem produces less impressive results. Improvements in a solution typically occur when a relatively large number of alternatives are considered. As a result, decision makers who face major problems should invest as much time as is necessary to create a variety of alternatives.

Second, *how able is the decision maker to differentiate accurately among alternatives?* If the decision maker cannot, in advance, tell the difference between two alternatives and cannot accurately rank them according to their likely effec-

[12] Alex Osborn, *Applied Imagination* (New York: Scribner's, 1958).
[13] See S. J. Parnes and H. F. Harding, *A Source Book of Creative Thinking* (New York: Scribner's, 1962).

tiveness, then nothing is gained. Two factors affect the decision maker's ability to differentiate among alternatives: the amount of data available and the cost of performing the evaluation/ranking. The difficulty of distinguishing among alternatives and determining their relative effectiveness decreases with increases in the amount of available data. Under conditions of high uncertainty (little data), decision makers should not devote large amounts of time to generating alternatives. Similarly, the more the cost of distinguishing among alternatives, the more likely the decision maker is to prefer relatively few alternatives. Consider again the $10 million problem with a potential 2 percent improvement in solution. If the cost of evaluating an additional alternative is $250,000, the evaluation costs $50,000 more than the possible savings ($250,000 cost less $200,000 possible improvement). The marginal increase in the improvement of a solution should always be more than the marginal cost of performing the additional evaluation.

Third, *the greater the number of people a problem concerns, the more likely that a large number of alternatives will be sought.* When dealing with complex problems affecting numerous people, it is often necessary to compromise on some points. But compromises by their very nature require participants to sacrifice some of their interests. This can lead to considerable dissatisfaction or frustration. These "human costs" are often considerable, even though they are difficult to measure in dollars and cents.

EVALUATION OF ALTERNATIVES AND SELECTION OF A COURSE OF ACTION

The evaluation of alternatives and the choosing of the most appropriate action are at the very heart of the decision-making process. Up until this point, all of the activities of the decision maker have been preparatory. It is at this step that he or she finally *decides what to do.*[14] This crucial stage has three distinct phases:

1. Determine which alternatives are feasible
2. Evaluate alternatives
3. Choose the most appropriate alternative

Determining Feasible Alternatives

In cases where a large number of alternatives have been generated, it is likely that many of them will not be feasible. Either the resources necessary to implement the alternative are unavailable or there are prohibitive constraints. If judgment was suspended during the creative generation of alternatives in the previous step, most of the alternatives generated would fall into the infeasible category. Separating the feasible alternatives from the infeasible ones saves time,

[14] See Douglas R. Emery and Francis D. Tuggle, "On the Evaluation of Decisions," *MSU Business Topics* (Spring 1976), pp. 42–48.

since the decision maker can then evaluate only those alternatives that are likely to be chosen.

Evaluation of Alternatives

The formal evaluation of alternatives is an extremely complex subject. In fact, many of the management science techniques developed during the past half-century are methods of determining the relative efficiency of various alternatives. The major techniques are discussed in detail in Chapter 8.

One writer has proposed the following rules for evaluating alternatives:

1. A solution should be of a *quality* satisfactory to meet organizational goals.
2. A solution must be *acceptable* to those affected by it and to those who must implement it.
3. A solution should be evaluated in terms of the *anticipated responses* to it.
4. The *risks* of each alternative should be considered.
5. The choice of solution should focus on *present* alternatives, not past possibilities.[15]

Is Quality Consistent with Goals?

Efficiency in decision making is a comparison of the costs involved in generating an expected return or other stated objective.

The quality of a solution has two dimensions: effectiveness and efficiency. *Efficiency is simply the ratio of outputs to inputs (O/I)*. It is therefore the forerunner of benefit/cost analysis, breakeven analysis, and numerous other techniques that compare expected return with projected investment. *Effectiveness, by contrast, is a measure of the extent to which an alternative meets the stated objective (regardless of the cost)*. Before attempting to evaluate the quality of any alternative, the decision maker must first establish the extent to which each of these criteria will be used.

Effectiveness is a measure of the extent to which a decision alternative meets the stated objective regardless of the costs involved.

A good example of the impact of these two criteria—effectiveness and efficiency—can be seen in the health care industry. In the United States, this industry has traditionally stressed effectiveness over efficiency—no cost was too great to care for the sick or prolong human life. Recently, this "policy" has been called into question by a number of well-publicized instances in which severely brain-damaged persons were kept breathing for extended periods by means of life support equipment. The astronomical costs of health care (particularly in the high-technology areas such as complete life support procedures, where prognosis is often highly unfavorable) have caused industry decision makers to consider efficiency as well as effectiveness. This is not to say the efficiency should be the major concern; only that it should be taken into account along with effectiveness.

Are Solutions Acceptable to Affected Personnel?

The chosen alternative must be acceptable and preferably liked by those who must implement it and by those who must live with the consequences of the de-

[15] Elbing, *Behavioral Decisions in Organizations.*

cision. Failure to meet this condition is the *single most likely reason for failure* of the decision-making process to solve problems.

Questions about the acceptability and efficiency/effectiveness of a proposed solution can only be answered by considering the anticipated responses to it. *Anticipated response refers to the reactions of the organization and its individual members to a chosen alternative.* This should be of critical concern to the manager/decision maker since even a technically mediocre solution may prove effective if it is implemented with enthusiasm and dedication. On the other hand, the technically correct alternative may fail to succeed if implementation is half-hearted and haphazard. For this reason many writers stress the importance of including as many organization members as feasible in the decision-making process. Participation in problem solving by organization members should increase their receptiveness to the chosen alternative.

The risks associated with each alternative must be considered. Specific techniques of risk assessment will be discussed in Chapter 8. It should be noted at this point that different risks are involved for different individuals and groups in the organization. As pointed out above, the differences among those who make decisions, those who implement them, and those who must live with them should not be minimized. In a political election, for example, the voters make the decision by casting their ballots; the election commission implements the decision by counting the votes and certifying the results; and the candidates are the primary persons who must live with the decision. Voters realize some small risk; the election commission experiences virtually no risk; and the candidates view the decision as an all-or-nothing proposition. How are their responses to a proposed change in election laws likely to vary?

LIFE BOAT STATION

*"Since there are no women or children on board,
Mr. Aaron here has suggested that we go
in alphabetical order."*

THE CHOSEN ALTERNATIVE MUST BE ACCEPTABLE TO AFFECTED PERSONNEL

SOURCE: *The Saturday Evening Post* (May–June 1982), p. 48. Reprinted with permission from The Saturday Evening Post Society, a division of BFL & MS, Inc. © 1982.

IMPLEMENTATION OF SOLUTION

Earlier in the chapter, decision making was defined as making a choice from several alternatives. Most formal approaches to decision making emphasize methods of selecting the most appropriate alternative—and devote little consideration to questions of implementation. Implementing a chosen alternative is often assumed to be a straightforward and trouble-free process. Unfortunately, while this assumption may be true of strictly technical decision making, most managerial problems are intimately concerned with the human element in the organization. Implementation, therefore, is typically anything but simple.

While no generalized rules have been developed that deal with managing the implementation phase, three questions must be answered.

First, *what should the internal structure of implementation be?* In other words what should be done when by whom? Since the solution of most managerial problems requires the combined effort of many organizational members, each should understand what role he or she is to play during each phase of the implementation process.

Second, *how can the manager reward organization members for participating in the implementation of the proposed solution?* Managers may make the decisions, but it is typically the responsibility of other organization members to carry them out. Care should be taken to ensure that those individuals responsible for implementation have some stake—financial or otherwise—in the success of the solution.

Third, *have provisions for evaluation and modification of the chosen solution during the implementation process been made?* As implementation proceeds, members of the organization should be able to modify the solution based on what they learn during implementation. But unless some specific provision for modification has been made, the chosen alternative may be treated as a "sacred cow" and implemented without any thought of possible modification—even in instances where minor adjustments would produce better solutions.

FEEDBACK

Feedback is information transmitted by a receiver back to the original sender of a message.

Feedback is a necessary component of the decision process, providing the decision maker with a means for determining the effectiveness of the chosen alternatives in solving the problem or taking advantage of the opportunity and moving the organization closer to the attainment of its goals. Three items are necessary in such an evaluation of the effectiveness of a decision.

First, *a set of standards must exist against which to compare performance.* For this reason the importance of quantifiable, measurable goals was stressed in Chapter 4. If such goals are in use, they become the necessary standards. If the firm's sales goal for the next three months is $2 million more than the current quarter, the relevant standard is present sales plus $2 million. If the firm adopts a zero-defects program, a zero rejection rate for output becomes the relevant standard.

Second, *performance data must be available so that the comparison to standards may be made.* The design of management information systems is the chief approach to formalizing the data collection process; it is the subject of Chapter 18.

Finally, *a data analysis strategy must be developed*. Such a strategy includes a formal plan outlining how the data will be used. One unfortunate characteristic of most data collection is that large amounts of data are never used. Managers who know exactly how the data are to be analyzed will be able to specify the types of data they need, the most perferred format, and the time sequence in which they are needed. Such advance specifications should aid in reducing the amount of useless data that are collected.

Group Decision Making and the Use of Committees

Although discussion of the steps involved in the decision-making process focused primarily on the individual decision maker, many of the decisions in large, complex organizations are made by *groups*. The shared power, bargaining activities, and need for compromise present in most group decisions further complicate the decision-making process.

Group decision making is the norm in Japanese organizations. The typical decision-making process in Japan begins with supervisory managers meeting as a group to analyze a problem or opportunity and develop alternative solutions. Two or three of the most likely alternatives are then presented to top management, where the final decision is made. Use of lower-level managers in the preliminary stages of the decision process provides them with a sense of responsibility in the decision, while simultaneously reducing the amount of time top management must devote to the process.

American managers often criticize the committee approach to decision making as a waste of time and a certain method of obtaining only compromise solutions. The definition of a camel as "a horse designed by a committee" illustrates the sentiments of many managers. But the increased complexity of the world in which the organization operates makes it increasingly difficult for a single manager to make complex decisions independently. Task forces, conferences, committees, and staff meetings are increasingly used in making important decisions.

GROUP DECISION-MAKING STRENGTHS

Evidence indicates that groups tend to make more accurate decisions than individuals.[16] This is particularly true in cases involving complex problems where no one member is an expert in the problem area. The "two heads are better than one" philosophy means that more information can be processed by the various group members. The presence of several group members also means that more

---

[16] See James H. Davis, *Group Performance* (Reading, Mass.: Addison-Wesley, 1969); and L. Richard Hoffman, *The Group Problem Solving Process: Studies of a Valence Model* (New York: Praeger, 1979).

alternative solutions may be proposed; individuals can "piggyback" ideas presented with other proposed alternatives; and a greater number of proposed solutions can be analyzed. Participation in decision making should increase the managers' acceptance of the final choice. Individual members of the groups can also more easily communicate the decision—and its rationale—to the members of their own departments or units. A major strength of group decision making is the relative ease of *implementing* decisions that have been made. But there are also a number of weaknesses involved with group decision making.[17]

GROUP DECISION-MAKING WEAKNESSES

The major disadvantage of group decision making is *time*. Decisions made by groups take longer—as much as 50 percent longer than individual decisions, according to one study.[18] In addition, group decisions are often compromises resulting from differing points of view of individual members—rather than the most appropriate choice for solving the problem. There is often pressure to accept the decision favored by most group members. Groupthink—a phenomenon in which the desire for group cohesiveness and consensus becomes stronger than the desire for the best possible decision—may occur.[19] Some groups experience more indecisiveness than individual decision makers since the pressure to reach a decision is diffused among the group members. In situations in which clear lines of authority and responsibility for making a decision have not been drawn, members of the group may engage in *buckpassing*—blaming one another for a poorly made compromise decision or the lack of a decision. The buckpassing phenomenon can be prevented if the leader accepts the ultimate responsibility for decision making. Often, one person or a few individuals will dominate the

[17] Herbert and Estes propose a method of retaining many of the benefits of group decision making by managers who make individual decisions. See Theodore T. Herbert and Ralph W. Estes, "Improving Executive Decisions by Formalizing Dissent: The Corporate Devil's Advocate," *Academy of Management Review* (October 1977), pp. 662–667.

[18] Irving Lorge, David Fox, Joel Dantz, and Marlin Brenner, "A Survey of Studies Contrasting the Quality of Group Performance and Individual Performance: 1920–1957," *Psychological Bulletin* (November 1958), 337–372.

[19] Irving Janis, *Victims of Groupthink* (Boston: Houghton Mifflin, 1972).

GUIDELINES FOR GROUP DECISION MAKING	1. Clearly explain the goals of the group. 2. Keep higher status group members from dominating the decision-making process. 3. Encourage contributions from all participants. 4. Include in the group specialists from all areas affected by the decision. 5. Develop an agenda, but make it flexible enough to adapt to developments at the meeting of the group. 6. Ask the chairperson and other group members to refrain from expressing their preferred alternative during the discussion of alternatives. 7. Continue discussions until a consensus decision is reached.

STRENGTHS	WEAKNESSES	Table 7-2 STRENGTHS AND WEAKNESSES OF GROUP DECISION MAKING
Group decisions may be more accurate than individual decisions.	Group decisions are slower than individual decisions—and the cost is multiplied, due to the number of personnel involved.	
More information can be processed by the group than by an individual decision maker.	Group decisions are often compromise decisions—rather than the selection of the most appropriate alternative.	
More alternatives can be proposed and the brainstorming of ideas can be conducted.	Indecisiveness and buckpassing are sometimes characteristic of groups.	
Managers' acceptance of solution is increased through their participation.	Groups are occasionally dominated by one or a few individuals; this is particularly common when individuals who rank higher in status in the organization are present.	
Managers can communicate decisions and reasons for them to their own work group.		

group because of differences in status or rank from the other members or through force of personality.[20] Table 7-2 summarizes the strengths and weaknesses of group decision making.

An Applied Approach to Decision Making

Two researchers, Victor Vroom and Philip Yetton, have recently developed a normative model of decision making.[21] It is normative in the sense of specifying the manner in which managers *should* make decisions. They identify five styles of decision making based on the degree of participation by subordinates in choosing an alternative. The five styles are as follows:

1. Managers make the decision themselves, using the information available at the time.
2. Managers obtain information from subordinates, then make the decision themselves.

[20] An excellent summary of the strengths and weaknesses of group decisions is included in Norman R. F. Maier, "Assets and Liabilities in Group Problem Solving," *Psychological Review* (July 1967), pp. 239–249.

[21] Victor H. Vroom and Philip W. Yetton, *Leadership and Decision Making* (Pittsburgh: University of Pittsburgh Press, 1973). See also Victor H. Vroom, "A New Look at Managerial Decision Making," *Organizational Dynamics* (Spring 1973), pp. 66–80.

3. Managers discuss the problem with subordinates as a group, but make the decision themselves.
4. Managers discuss the problem with subordinates on an individual basis, but make the decision themselves.
5. Managers share the problem with subordinates as a group. Alternatives are generated and evaluated jointly by managers and subordinates and the decision is made by consensus. Managers accept and implement any solution that has the support of the group.

Vroom and Yetton propose a list of seven "Yes-No" questions dealing with the amount of available information, the type of decision required, and the involvement of subordinates. By answering these questions, the manager determines the most appropriate style of decision making to use. The seven questions are

A. Is there a quality requirement such that one solution is likely to be more rational than another?
B. Does the manager have sufficient information to make a high-quality decision?
C. Is the problem structured? In other words can the manager identify the required information for the decision and how to obtain it?
D. Is acceptance of the decision by subordinates critical to its successful implementation?
E. If the manager makes the decision without consulting subordinates, is the decision likely to be accepted by them?
F. Do subordinates share the organizational goals to be obtained in solving this problem?
G. Is conflict among subordinates likely to occur if the preferred solution is made?

The authors develop a decision model by matching the decision styles to the situation as determined by answers to the seven questions. By answering these questions, the preferred management decision style for each type of problem is identified. Figure 7-5 shows how the Vroom-Yetton model works. The flow chart provides the manager with a step-by-step approach to determining the most appropriate style of decision making under a given set of circumstances. To see how the model works, take the example of the manager facing a decision situation in which quality differences in alternative solutions are not likely to be great and where subordinates' acceptance of the decision is not crucial to its effective implementation.

In this instance the manager can utilize style 1, where the decision is made in an autocratic fashion without consulting subordinates. On the other hand, consider the following situation: (1) additional information is needed to solve the problem; (2) the manager can identify the needed information and its location; and (3) acceptance of the decision by subordinates is not critical to its successful

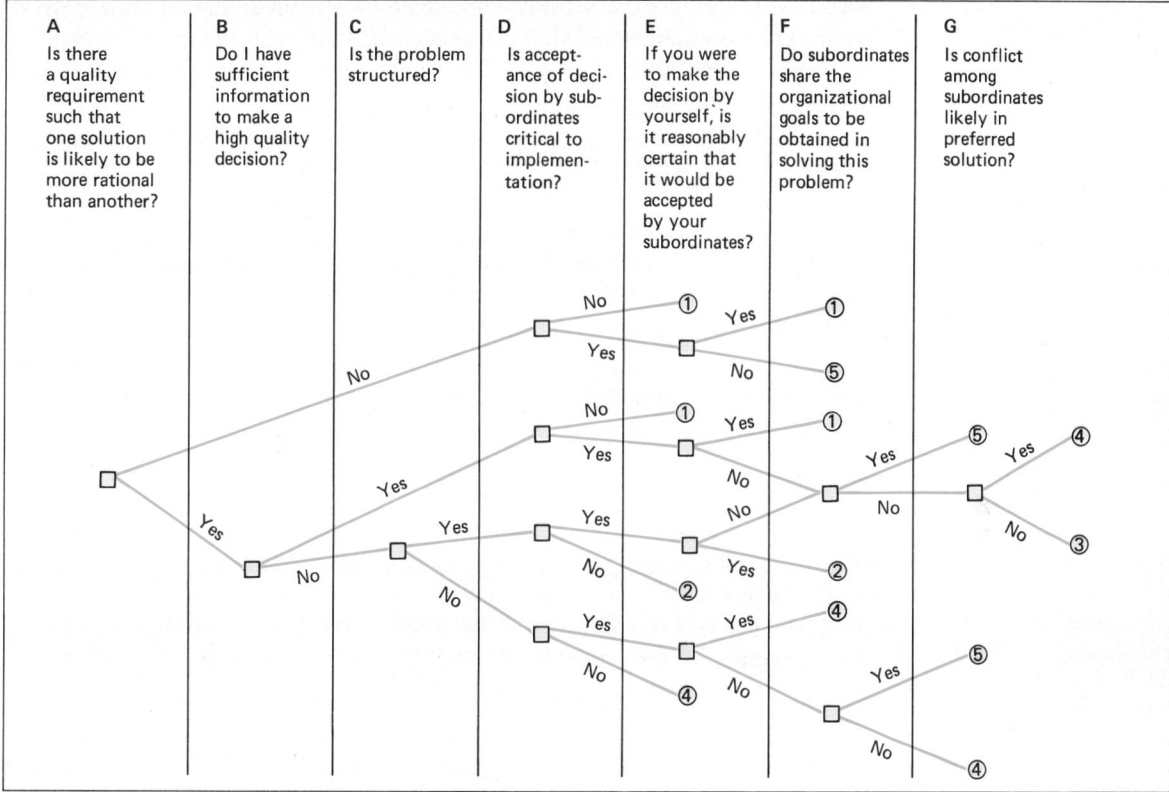

A	B	C	D	E	F	G
Is there a quality requirement such that one solution is likely to be more rational than another?	Do I have sufficient information to make a high quality decision?	Is the problem structured?	Is acceptance of decision by subordinates critical to implementation?	If you were to make the decision by yourself, is it reasonably certain that it would be accepted by your subordinates?	Do subordinates share the organizational goals to be obtained in solving this problem?	Is conflict among subordinates likely in preferred solution?

■ "Yes-No" questions listed at the top of the model.
● Preferred decision-making style for a particular problem situation.

Figure 7-5
FLOWCHART OF THE DECISION PROCESS

SOURCE: Reprinted from Victor H. Vroom and Philip W. Yetton, *Leadership and Decision-Making*, by permission of the University of Pittsburgh Press. © 1973 by the University of Pittsburgh Press.

implementation. The most appropriate decision style in this case is style 2, in which the managers obtain information from subordinates but do not involve them in making the decision. A variety of other decision situations are matched to the most appropriate decision-making styles by the model.

In some instances the model identifies decisions in which more than one management style may be used. For example, a manufacturing facility has decided to convert to twenty-four-hour production days and has developed three shifts: 7:00 A.M. to 3:00 P.M.; 3:00 P.M. to 11:00 P.M.; and 11:00 P.M. to 7:00 A.M. A decision must be made concerning whether employees will be permanently assigned to one of the three shifts or whether all employees should rotate through the shifts on a regular basis. In such a situation group suggestions and acceptance are important, a consultative style is effective, and the manager may choose to meet with subordinates on an individual basis (style 3) or as a group (style 4). Vroom recommends that the manager choose the style that is least costly in terms of time or money.

The Vroom–Yetton model is relatively new and its applications to date have been limited. Some early research conducted by Vroom and other management scientists has demonstrated that decisions consistent with the model have been successful.[22] The model appears to have great potential to aid the manager who must make important nonprogrammed decisions.

[22] Promising results have been obtained in early attempts to test the model's validity. See Victor H. Vroom and Arthur G. Jago, "On the Validity of the Vroom–Yetton Model," *Journal of Applied Psychology* (April 1978), pp. 151–162; C. Margerison and R. Glube, "Leadership Decision-Making: An Empirical Test of the Vroom and Yetton Model," *Journal of Management Studies* 16 (1979), pp. 45–55; and Arthur G. Jago and Victor H. Vroom, "An Evaluation of Two Alternatives to the Vroom–Yetton Normative Model," *Academy of Management Journal* (June 1980), pp. 347–355.

Summary

Decision making concerns the manager's role of solving problems and taking advantage of opportunities. Many management authorities feel that it is at the core of all management activity. Organizational decision making can be divided into three categories: (1) *Technical* decisions concern the process by which inputs are changed into outputs by the organization. Most of these decisions are made at the supervisory level. (2) *Managerial* decisions relate to the issues of coordination and support of the core activities of the organization. Middle management is typically involved in these matters. (3) *Institutional* decisions involve long-term planning and policy information. Top management makes most institutional decisions.

Decisions can also be classified by their relative uniqueness. Programmed decisions involve simple, common, frequently occurring problems that have well-established and understood solutions. Nonprogrammed decisions deal with unusual or novel problems. Managers should strive to convert as many decisions as possible to the programmed category, thereby freeing their time for definitely unique problem situations.

The work of Herbert Simon has contributed to the understanding of managerial decision making. Simon discounts the traditional profit maximization objective by arguing that managers really *satisfice* rather than maximize. They examine only the most likely alternatives, rather than investing the cost and time required to identify and evaluate all possibilities. Simon feels that managers are constrained by *bounded rationality*.

In other words there are limits to a manager's knowledge and understanding in any problem situation. As a result the decision maker seeks a satisfactory solution, not necessarily the optimal one, according to Simon.

Decisions are made in a sequential order:

1. Perception of the environment
2. Problem formulation
3. Identification of resources and constraints
4. Development of alternatives
5. Evaluation of alternatives and selection of course of action
6. Implementation of solution
7. Feedback

Management must monitor the decision-making environment with the aid of some type of early warning signal designed to identify developments requiring executive attention. Problems are barriers to the achievement of organizational goals. Problem formulation is an important—but often neglected—step in decision making. A written problem statement should be developed by the decision maker. Managers should also realize that problem solving occurs within a given set of resources and constraints. These resources—"The Five Ms of Management"—include time, human resources, expertise, and equipment.

The generation of alternatives is aided by the creativity of the persons involved in the decision. Synectics and brainstorming are commonly used creativity techniques.

The fifth step in the decision-making sequence—evaluation of alternatives and selection of course of action—involves three separate phases: (1) determining which alternatives are feasible; (2) evaluating alternatives; and (3) choosing the most appropriate alternative. A number of factors should be considered in the first two phases: efficiency (the ratio of outputs to inputs); effectiveness (the extent to which an alternative meets the stated objective); acceptability of the decision to affected individuals and groups; the risks involved; and the viability of implementing the alternative under consideration. The eventual choice is dependent upon both objective and emotional components. The decision maker's own value system is a key ingredient in the actual solution of the problem.

Implementation of the solution requires a plan spelling out what should be done when by whom. It should also specify methods by which the manager can reward organizational members for participating in the implementation of the proposed solution and provide the necessary flexibility for modification based upon what is learned during implementation.

Feedback is the final component in decision making. Three items are necessary in the evaluation of the effectiveness of a decision:

1. A set of standards must exist against which to compare performance.

2. Performance data must be available in order to compare results with standards.
3. A data analysis strategy outlining how the collected data will be used must be developed.

Not all decisions are made by individuals. Many organizations prefer group involvement in decision making, and most firms involve a number of persons in making major decisions. The major strengths of group decisions are greater accuracy; processing of more information; generation of more alternatives; increased acceptance of the solution through participation; and better communication of decisions to affected parties. Its chief weaknesses include slower decisions; compromise decisions; indecisiveness and buckpassing; and the possibility of dominance by one or a few members.

The Vroom–Yetton model is a normative model of the decision-making process, suggesting how managers should make decisions. Five decision-making styles are identified, based upon the degree of participation by subordinates in the selection of alternatives. Seven "Yes–No" questions are used to determine the most appropriate decision-making style. The amount of available information, type of decision required, and subordinate involvement are considered. The Vroom–Yetton model is a potentially invaluable aid to nonprogrammed decision making.

REVIEW EXERCISES

1. Define the following terms: (a) decision making (b) technical decisions (c) managerial decisions (d) institutional decisions (e) programmed decisions (f) nonprogrammed decisions (g) satisficing (h) bounded rationality (i) problem (j) performance gap (k) synectics (l) brainstorming (m) efficiency (n) effectiveness (o) feedback.

2. Differentiate among the three major types of decisions.

3. A manufacturer's computer automatically prints purchase orders for new supplies once their stock reaches a designated level. The orders are forwarded to the director of purchasing for approval. Is this director's action a programmed or nonprogrammed decision?

4. Explain Herbert Simon's contribution to the study of decision making.

5. Outline the model of the decision-making process.

6. What are the major benefits of a written problem statement?

7. Identify the steps involved in the selection of an alternative.

8. Relate decision making to the concepts of effectiveness and efficiency.

9. What are the strengths and weaknesses of group decision making?

10. Briefly explain the Vroom–Yetton model.

ASSIGNMENTS/PROBLEMS/ DISCUSSION QUESTIONS

1. Relate one of your most recent decisions to the model shown in Figure 7-3.

2. Select a firm in your city or state. After carefully researching the company, identify the daily decisions that will face its management in the future.

3. Prepare a written problem statement for a problem that you face.

4. Southland Corp.'s decision to locate some of its 7,000 7-Eleven stores in urban locations appears to have paid off. Although rent and utility expenses are higher than in suburban locations, the heavy traffic generated in urban locations assisted 7-Eleven in experiencing a 150 percent sales increase to $5 billion in a four-year period ending in 1982.

Conduct a brainstorming session on 7-Eleven's future techniques for generating additional sales growth. This will require the participants to research the company extensively prior to the session.

5. Apply the Vroom–Yetton model to the following decisions:

a. A decision to convert a factory's power plant from oil to coal because of cost and supply factors
b. The dismissal of a key vice-president because of ineffective performance
c. The introduction of a new product on a trial basis in four cities

A MANAGERIAL INCIDENT

Winnebago Industries

When gasoline prices shot up in the wake of the fall of the Shah of Iran in early 1979, no industry suffered more than motor homes. From a high of 293,600 in 1978, motor-home shipments plunged to 172,600 in 1979 and to 99,900 in 1980. Half of the country's motor-home dealers went out of business, and manufacturers laid off thousands of workers.

Industry giant Winnebago was no exception. The firm saw its shipments fall from 17,836 in

1978 to only 5,303 in 1980, while sales slid from $229 million to only $92 million. "All of a sudden, there was no spring," recalls company spokesman Frank Rotta.

Enter John K. Hanson. The chairman, now 68, had led the firm during the boom years of the 1960s and was called out of retirement by the board of directors in 1979 to get Winnebago out of its crisis.

John K., as he is called around town, set to work on a number of changes: Vehicles were designed to run on lower-cost propane fuel; lighter-weight models were developed; top management was shaken up; inventory was cut in half; inefficient plants were closed or sold, and operating costs were trimmed drastically. "We had to drive down our expenses," says Hanson. "We looked under every stone."

The strategy seems to have worked. Sales in the three months that ended May 30, 1981, were $41.1 million, up from only $15.7 million in 1980. Earnings totaled $1.8 million, compared with a loss of $5.4 million in 1980.

The company also is looking ahead to new uses for its products. It recently won a $9 million contract to build trams for Universal Studios. In addition, the firm hopes to establish leasing arrangements with airlines and other travel operations. The firm also has signed a contract to license the Winnebago name for apparel and camping equipment.

Winnebago officials explain that with prices that average $20,000, motor homes are out of the reach of most consumers but that recreational vehicles still hold great appeal. Observes Fred Emmert, marketing vice-president: "Companies that get involved in rental and leasing will be the ones that are going to survive."

SOURCE: Reprinted by permission from "We Had to Drive Down Our Expenses," *U.S. News & World Report* (July 20, 1981), p. 72. Copyright, 1981, U.S. News & World Report, Inc.

Questions and Problems

1. Relate the decision process of Winnebago's chairman John K. Hanson to the model shown in Figure 7-3. Make any assumptions necessary.
2. In what areas is Winnebago potentially vulnerable? Suggest methods by which its executives can obtain feedback and adjust their decisions.

8.
Quantitative Techniques for Planning and Problem Solving

Learning Objectives

AFTER STUDYING THIS CHAPTER YOU SHOULD BE ABLE TO

1. Compare the chief advantages and limitations of quantitative techniques in solving organizational problems.
2. Explain the value of models to planning and decision making.
3. Identify the major categories of models.
4. Explain the steps involved in the quantitative approach to problems and their solution.
5. Identify the major quantitative techniques and problem areas where they may be used.

Key Terms

operations research

scientific method

model

iconic model

analog model

symbolic, or mathematical, model

probability

linear programming

simulation

queuing model

game theory

decision tree

174

Exact scientific knowledge and
methods are everywhere, sooner or
later, sure to replace rule-of-thumb.

FREDERICK W. TAYLOR

It isn't that they can't see the solution.
It is that they can't see the problem.

G. K. CHESTERTON

The world fuel crisis is producing an enormous effect on almost every industry. But the airline industry has already experienced these effects—during the first shortage in the mid-1970s—and learned from this experience. In a single five-month period during 1974 fuel prices increased by 57 percent, and the U.S. government established monthly allocations for each air carrier based on the previous year's usage.

But even with the allocation system, fuel suppliers in some cities were unable to meet the air carriers' needs. The problem was compounded by the changes in flight schedules that had been made during the previous year—changes that had not been taken into account when the fuel allocations were made. The need to plan fuel purchases for a week to a month in advance became crucial, and management at many airlines found themselves unable to prepare such plans. As a result some carriers found their monthly supply depleted by the middle of the month, producing canceled flights, exorbitant prices paid for spot purchases, and record increases in operating costs. Fuel became the largest single cost item for the airlines.

Pan American Airlines attacked this critical problem by developing a sophisticated mathematical model. The model's objective was to minimize the effect of price increases and fluctuating allocation levels and to maintain a planned flight schedule. The model enabled Pan Am to reduce its total fuel cost significantly.

The difficult task of constructing the model began with Pan Am's flight schedule, or rotation. The rotation is actually a chain of flights, or "legs," that each aircraft follows. For example, Pan Am's Flight 36 flies from Los Angeles to Fort Lauderdale with stops in Tampa and Miami. The same plane departs Fort Lauderdale as Flight 144, flies to New York, and then returns to Fort Lauderdale. It then continues as Flight 11 to Miami, Houston, and Los Angeles, where it becomes Flight 36 once again. Fuel for any of these flights may be purchased at the departure city or any of the cities serviced by the flight.

Industrial engineer Frank B. Gilbreth demanded precision and accuracy in everything he did. He had the kind of mind that saw waste and inefficiency in even the most routine tasks, and he had the creative spark to devise new solutions to old problems. He applied his special genius in the home he shared with his wife Lillian and their twelve children and in industry, where he became known as a pioneer in the field of industrial efficiency and the father of motion study.

Gilbreth's talents became obvious early in his career. Born in Fairfield, Maine, in 1868, he received his early education in Andover and Boston, Massachusetts, and passed the entrance examination for the Massachusetts Institute of Technology. Gilbreth attended MIT at night and worked for a Boston construction engineering firm during the day.

It was at this job that he mastered the skills of many different construction trades and observed the waste and inefficiency that were part of factory and plant life. In 1895 Gilbreth went into business for himself as a general contractor; he subsequently built factories, mills, power plants, dams, canals, and offices throughout the United States and Europe. He also invented such labor-saving devices and construction method improvements as an improved scaffold for bricklayers, which enabled workers to use their time more efficiently with the least amount of fatigue. During this period Gilbreth's motion studies increased the hourly output of bricklayers from 120 to 350 bricks.

As his business grew and expanded to New York, San Francisco, and London, Gilbreth instituted a method of taking "progress" pictures in order to keep

In order to obtain the lowest total fuel cost, the model had to consider such factors as price and availability at each location, the maximum and minimum quantity of fuel that the airplane could carry, and the maximum landing weight allowed at a station. Although low fuel prices at a given supply station might encourage the airline to make maximum purchases and "tanker" the fuel for later flights, the added weight produces increased consumption per mile flown. As a result the model must take into consideration the entire flight schedule in order to determine the best possible fuel purchase patterns.

Pan Am's fuel management and allocation model contains some 800 constraints and 2,400 variables for a flight schedule of 350 segments, 50 station/vendor combinations, and the different types of aircraft flown. By considering the factors of prices, availability, fuel burn, flight data, and cost of tankerage, it specifies the most appropriate fueling station and vendor for each flight. The model has saved Pan Am millions in fuel costs and provided the organization with a means of minimizing the effect of future price increases throughout the system and of continuing normal schedule operations even when faced with erratic supply changes.[1]

[1] Adapted by permission from D. Wayne Darnell and Carolyn Loflin, "National Airlines Fuel Management and Allocation Model," *Interfaces* (February 1977), pp. 1–16. Copyright 1977 The Institute of Management Sciences. The authors have updated their investigation in "Fuel Management and Allocation Model," *Interfaces* (February 1979), pp. 64–65.

abreast of the status of each project. Working with his wife Lillian, he also devised such management tools as the cost-plus contract, the process chart, flow diagrams, and a merit-rating system for employees. In addition the Gilbreths set up laboratory studies to determine how environmental factors, including the choice of equipment, affected worker performance; and they established methods to determine the skill levels and ambitions of workers and to devise systems for worker selection and training.

In 1911 Frank gave up his construction business to devote all his time to efficiency engineering. He formed Frank B. Gilbreth, Inc., consulting industrial engineers, and worked with managers in busines and industry to improve worker performance. With the goal of increasing an entire organization's awareness of motion efficiency, Gilbreth helped managers analyze all phases of business operations from the initial product selection and design to production, sale, and final use.

Frank Gilbreth was considered a pioneer in the science of motion study. His life's work was based on the philosophy that it is possible for workers to express themselves in creative, effective ways while conserving time and energy. His methods for recording motions, developing efficient skills, and minimizing fatigue served to provide quantitative tools for operating managers. They also became the cornerstones of motion study, and even today they continue to benefit professionals in the fields of engineering, education, and personnel administration.

Frank Bunker Gilbreth died in 1925.

Source

National Cyclopaedia of American Biography, Vol. 26, s.v. "Gilbreth, Frank Bunker."

Operations Research—Quantitative Techniques for Management Decisions

Managers spend a considerable amount of time making decisions about and within systems in order to achieve organizational objectives. Decision making is the process managers use to bring unity where there is disunity, simplicity where there is complexity, meaning where there is uncertainty, and effective purpose where there is aimlessness. Making a decision can be an exhilarating as well as a frustrating experience; it can be a rewarding as well as an unrewarding experience.

Decisions for individuals—as well as individual managers—vary in terms of importance. Most decisions would not be labeled as crucial; in fact, many of them are based on personal taste. How much salt on an omelet, how wide the parking spaces, how high the stereo volume—these are examples of such decisions. But other decisions are far more critical—and managers frequently are under pressure to make major decisions with incomplete information and little time. Determining the "correct" or optimal course of action as opposed to the "wrong" or less optimal course is extremely important when it might lead to a monetary loss or wasted opportunity for the decision maker's firm.

Since incorrect or nonoptimal decisions can have serious implications, it is important that the most appropriate decision-making tools be used to generate the best possible information base upon which to make a decision. Although managers have always made some use of quantitative data in making decisions, never have the quantities of available data and the methods for analysis been so available. In fact, a new field called operations research, or management science, has developed to assist managers in developing and applying mathematical techniques to decision making.

Operations research is an umbrella term describing the application of mathematical techniques to managerial planning, decision making, and problem solving. It involves the use of models to describe and provide an understanding of a problem and its alternative solutions.[2] An operations research problem may be as specific as how much JP4 aviation fuel American Airlines Flight 164 should tanker from one leg of a flight to an intermediate destination because of price differences, or as broad as the establishment of a long-range corporate strategy.

Operations research is an interdisciplinary field utilizing concepts from such areas as mathematics, computer science, systems analysis, economics, and engineering. Although advances in the scientific approach to management problems can be traced to Frederick W. Taylor, Henry L. Gantt, Frank Gilbreth, and other early scientific management writers and even to such eighteenth- and early nineteenth-century luminaries as Adam Smith and Charles Babbage,

Operations research is the application of mathematical techniques to managerial planning, decision making, and problem solving.

[2] James B. Dilworth, *Production and Operations Management* (New York: Random House, 1983), p. 26.

COOLING OVERHEATED JET ENGINES WITH THE SCIENTIFIC METHOD

Operations research professor Arthur C. Laufer used a problem encountered by several airlines that purchased a new passenger aircraft to illustrate the steps involved in the scientific method. The following steps are employed by airline personnel in attempting to solve the serious problem of engine overheating.

PROBLEM RECOGNITION
Gauges indicate engine overheating in simulated tests in test flights.

PROBLEM STATEMENT
Aircraft engines are overheating to a danger point, resulting in delayed or canceled flights as well as costly maintenance.

HYPOTHESIS
Improper design of engine fan blades is causing the overheating.

EXPERIMENTAL DESIGN
Fan blades will be redesigned by the engine manufacturer, and laboratory and field tests of engines with the new design will be carried out. Records of actual performance data will be maintained. Engines of both designs will be operated for various periods of time and under a variety of operating conditions normally encountered while in actual flight.

DATA COLLECTION AND ANALYSIS
Data will be collected and recorded. The data will be subjected to a series of statistical tests of difference to determine the relative merit of the new design.

operations research began to emerge as a recognized discipline during World War II. The British military establishment assembled a team of specialists to tackle such vital problems as effective use of radar, civilian defense, antisubmarine warfare, and the optimal deployment of convoy vessels to accompany supply ships. The United States followed Great Britain's lead in assembling "operations analysis" groups to conduct mathematical analyses of military data. Soon after the war these analytical methods were applied to problems of government and industry, with favorable results. By 1980 operations research departments were firmly established in most large- and medium-sized organizations.

Usually included under the broad label of operations research are management science, decision sciences, information sciences, and some aspects of systems analysis.[3] While there are subtle distinctions among these terms, all of them employ the scientific method in dealing with their activities.

What Is the Scientific Method?

The *scientific method* is essentially a way of thinking about problem situations. It is a systematic and logical approach to the identification and solution of prob-

The scientific method is a systematic and logical approach to the identification and solution of problems facing the decision maker.

[3] David R. Anderson, Dennis J. Sweeney, and Thomas R. Williams, *Essentials of Management Science: Applications to Decision-Making* (St. Paul, Minn.: West Publishing Co., 1978), p. 1.

INTERPRETATION
The results of these statistical tests will be examined to determine what inferences can be drawn and what interpretations can be made from the data analysis.

CONCLUSIONS
Statements regarding the operations of the jet engine with the newly designed part as compared with the previous operations results can now be made. Depending on the outcome of the above steps, this statement might indicate that the new design is satisfactory; that it is unsatisfactory; or it might include a new hypothesis that suggests other required changes in the engine design.

RECOMMENDATIONS
Recommendations could be made to rebuild or replace all engines with the new fan if the results indicate this course of action. Other possible recommendations include further research or further tests of the new design.

IMPLEMENTATION
If the recommendation to rebuild or replace the engines is made, instructions would be issued to put into effect the actions required to carry out such recommendations.

SOURCE: Adapted from Arthur C. Laufer, *Operations Management* (Cincinnati: South-Western, 1975), p. 18.

QUANTITATIVE TECHNIQUES CAN ASSIST THE MANAGER IN MAKING DIFFICULT DECISIONS

lems facing the decision maker. Objectivity is at a premium whether the problem involves the physical or biological sciences or exists in a business setting. The basic premise is that the greater the degree of objectivity, the greater the probability that other observers will reach the same decision. In order to gain objectivity, precise observation, careful recording of data, analysis, and interpretation of findings are approached in a logical, step-by-step manner.

Since the scientific method is more a way of thinking about problems than a precise guide, the specific number of steps in the process can vary widely. The critical issue is that the problem solver consider all aspects of the problem in a comprehensive and logical way.

Quantitative Analysis: Advantages and Limitations

Since most business problems and opportunities involve complex situations with varying degrees of uncertainty and risks associated with them, operations research techniques can make major contributions in analysis and identification of the optimal solution. It is, however, a mistake for managers to use these analytical tools as "security blankets," since they are not substitutes for executive judgment. The capabilities and limitations of operations research must be kept in clear perspective so the manager will use it as an aid to decision making rather than as a crutch for indecision. Table 8-1 presents a summary of the advantages and limitations of operations research techniques.

ADVANTAGES OF QUANTITATIVE TECHNIQUES IN DECISION MAKING

The use of quantitative methods in making organizational decisions is clearly increasing.[4] Perhaps their most important benefit is the *systematic focus* they

[4] W. N. Ledbetter and J. F. Cox, "Are OR Techniques Being Used?" *Industrial Engineering* (February 1977), pp. 19–21; and Colin Eden, "Problem Construction and the Influence of OR," *Interfaces* (April 1982), pp. 50–60.

ADVANTAGES	LIMITATIONS	**Table 8-1 QUANTITATIVE APPROACH TRADE-OFFS**
1. Rational approach to problems is encouraged by providing systematic focus for manager.	1. There is often a lack of "meeting of the minds" between operations research specialists and line managers.	
2. Development of large data base of factual information about problem situation, and thus a more accurate and thorough analysis, is necessary.	2. Short lead time for decision making may preclude development and use of models.	
3. By breaking complex problem issues into smaller parts, such techniques allow manager to better solve complex problems.	3. Managers may resist use of new approaches if they do not understand methods used or view them as threats.	
4. Models provide methods of risk evaluation for alternative solutions.	4. Models developed with misleading or incorrect information misrepresent reality and produce poor solutions.	
5. Model permits consideration of numerous alternatives by manipulating data inputs.	5. Models tend to concentrate on quantifiable data and may ignore human factors that are difficult to measure.	
	6. Use of sophisticated techniques is often expensive.	

provide for the manager. The quantitative approach encourages rational thinking. Clear, precise objectives must be established, relationships must be defined explicitly, and risk must be assessed in order to develop the appropriate analytical model. The underlying assumptions that support the analysis must be identified. The systematic thinking demanded by quantitative techniques improves the likelihood of effective decisions.

A second benefit of the use of operations research techniques is the development of a large *data base*. Large amounts of pertinent data are required to utilize analytical tools. The data base allows decision makers to refine and alter decisions as new data become available. Such a data base forms the foundation of an organization's management information system; it is discussed in detail in Chapter 18.

A third advantage of quantitative techniques is their ability to break complex problem issues into smaller, more manageable parts. This *simplifying of a problem situation* allows the manager to better diagnose and understand the thousands of possible elements of a particular issue.

A final benefit of quantitative analysis is that these analytical techniques *aid the manager in comparing and contrasting possible alternatives*. The decision maker is made more aware of the risks, benefits, and difficulties of each alternative. This increased awareness increases the likelihood of an improved decision.

LIMITATIONS OF QUANTITATIVE TECHNIQUES
IN DECISION MAKING

Perhaps the most serious problem facing integration of analytical tools in the decision-making process is the *lack of understanding between line managers and the operations research specialists.* Managers are typically action-oriented with little patience, understanding, and appreciation of quantitative analysis. Operations research specialists may exhibit more interest in the method than in the solution, failing to recognize the need for quick decisions. The specialists may seek the optimum solution regardless of the time involved, while the manager may be interested in satisficing—finding a quick, satisfactory course of action. There is still a gap between personnel trained in mathematics and computer applications and the line manager, who has final responsibility for decision making.

Misrepresentation of reality is another potential problem in utilizing quantitative tools. The very nature of such tools makes possible the introduction of misleading or incorrect assumptions and inputs. "GIGO"—garbage in, garbage out—summarizes the results of a quantitative technique with incorrect data inputs. Such techniques are effective only when the underlying assumptions and variables included in the technique are also present in the real-world environment.

The *short lead time* for decisions often precludes the use of sophisticated and time-consuming quantitative techniques. Input data required to use such techniques are often difficult to assimilate in short periods of time.

Resistance to change by line managers may prove a major hurdle in the utilization of operations research tools. Managers have already developed their own approaches to decision making and may resist new methods, especially if the new approach is technically oriented and is accompanied with a complete new glossary of abstract terms. It has been said that many managers would rather live with a problem that they cannot solve than use a solution that they do not understand.[5] In addition, managers may resist providing all of the information necessary to use the quantitative tools, due to vested interests or basic distrust of the new approach.

Oversimplification is another potential danger in employing analytical techniques in problem situations. This possible limitation is similar to the problem of misrepresenting reality in a mathematical model, but it refers to the difficulty of determining all of the complex relationships operating in a problem situation and reducing them to a mathematical representation. Often such very real organizational situations as morale, consequences of strikes, or internal power struggles are so difficult to quantify that they are ignored in the model used. As a result the solution proposed by the model may not be best for the organization.

A final limitation of quantitative problem-solving approaches is *cost.* The combination of specialized personnel, computer capability, and time often discourages widespread use of quantitative techniques. This is particularly true of the more sophisticated techniques requiring considerable financial investment in model development and computer capability.

[5] William J. Kearney and Desmond D. Martin, "Quantitative Methods in Management Development," *Business Horizons* (August 1974), p. 52.

NEED FOR UNDERSTANDING AND COOPERATION

A very real need exists for operations research specialists and line managers to work more closely together in order to understand both the strengths and weaknesses of the specialists' quantitative tool kit and the areas in which specific techniques are most appropriate. Cooperation between the specialists and the line managers will assist in implementing the correct technique and in generating improved solutions to organizational problems.[6]

The Role of Models in Operations Research

A crucial element in operations research is the development and implementation of models. A *model* is a representation, or abstraction, of a real object, situation, or system. It is used to capture the key elements, but not the detail, of the entity it represents. Many different disciplines use models on a regular basis. Aeronautical engineers test scale-model airplanes in wind tunnels; the U.S. Army Corps of Engineers has constructed a ten-acre model of the Mississippi River near Vicksburg to test the impact of varying rainfalls in different parts of the United States on the Mississippi and its tributaries. Economists employ ab-

Model is a representation, or abstraction, of a real object, situation, or system.

[6] The need for operations research specialists and line managers to work together in implementation and integration of quantitative techniques in decision making is discussed in John C. Anderson and Thomas R. Hoffman, "A Perspective on the Implementation of Management Science," *Academy of Management Review* (July 1978), pp. 563–571. See also Richard Richels, "Building Good Models Is Not Enough," *Interfaces* (August 1981), pp. 48–54; and Richard H. McClure, "Educating the Future Users of O.R.," *Interfaces* (October 1981), pp. 108–112.

MODELS VERSUS REALITY

Andrew Vazsonyi provides two anecdotes to illustrate the problems involved when models are mistakenly assumed to reflect reality totally. His first example involves two of Mark Twain's most beloved characters. His second describes the woes of a traveler.

Huckleberry Finn was quite indignant when Tom Sawyer tried to convince him on their trip in the balloon that they were flying over the state of Illinois. Huck said: "Teacher showed me the map, and Illinois was red." The discussion that followed finally pushed Huck to a conclusion: "The map maker was a liar."

A man drove late into the night on a country road, hit a rut and broke the axle of his car. So he got mad and tore up his map. That same man would probably throw away a quantitative model because the behavioral aspects of the situation were not included in the mathematics.

MORAL: The model user must not confuse a *map* with a *territory*, a *word* with the *thing*, a *model* with *reality*.

SOURCE: Adapted by permission from Andrew Vazsonyi, "Semantic Pollution in Information Systems," *Interfaces* (August 1973), p. 45. Copyright 1973 The Institute of Management Sciences.

stract models to predict future economic activity and ecologists use them to estimate potential effects of mining, refining, or other production activities on the environment.[7]

Experimenting with models generally requires less time, money, and human resources than experimenting with the actual object or situation. Judgments and inferences can then be made about the effect of these variables on the phenomenon represented by the model.

TYPES OF MODELS

Three general categories of models are used in analyzing and understanding real-world situations: iconic, analog, and symbolic, or mathematical, models.

An *iconic model* is a physical replica or a scale representation that actually looks like the object it represents. A ship model or a small-scale model of a railroad or bridge is an iconic model; so also are schematic representations of the actual item such as a picture or a photograph.

An *analog model* is a physical representation of a real object or situation that does not have the same physical appearance of the object being modeled. Gasoline gauges, speedometers, and thermometers are analogies of volume, speed, and temperature.[8] Flow charts are analog models in computer programming.

The third general category, *symbolic, or mathematical, models,* is of primary interest to the quantitative decision maker. Such models use equations or groups of equations to express the relationship among factors in a given process or system being modeled. Although this type of model is the least familiar to most persons, it can provide a high degree of abstraction and aid significantly in analyzing the complex problem situations. The equation $A = B + C$ is a mathematical model stating that the object symbolized by A is the simple sum of the object labeled B and the second object labeled C.[9]

OTHER MODEL CLASSIFICATIONS

Although all models may be categorized as either iconic, analog, or symbolic, other classifications have been developed in order to compare different types of models on such bases as purpose of the model, type of elements included, methodologies used, and the effect of time on the situation being analyzed. The decision maker must recognize that the choice of the appropriate model is determined by its ability to reflect reality. Different problem situations may call for different types of models and for different operations research techniques.

1. *Normative versus descriptive models.* This method of classification is based on what the model attempts to do. A model designed to prescribe what ought to be done is considered a *normative model.* Such a model attempts to identify specific methods for accomplishing specific objectives and attempts to identify the

An iconic model is a physical replica or a scale representation that looks like the object it represents.

An analog model is a physical representation of a real object or situation that does not have the same appearance of that which it represents.

Symbolic, or mathematical, model uses equations or groups of equations to express the relationship among factors in a given process or system being modeled.

---

[7] Thomas M. Cook and Robert A. Russell, *Introduction to Management Science* (Englewood Cliffs, N.J.: Prentice-Hall, 1977), p. 11.

[8] Anderson, Sweeney, and Williams, *Essentials of Management Science*, p. 6.

[9] Dilworth, *Production and Operations Management*, p. 36.

Although almost anything imaginable can be—and has been—used to represent reality, all models can be divided into three general categories: iconic, analog, and symbolic. A number of models are shown below. Identify each type and place the appropriate letter in the box. (Answers are printed upside-down below.)

CAN YOU IDENTIFY THE MODEL?

1.   □

2. $E = mc^2$ □

3.
   Exam Processing → Compute Exam Percent → Accumulate Totals → Write Detail Line → Read Exam Card — at End — Move 'Yes' to Cards-at-End → Exit   □

4.   □

5.   □

6. $Y_c = a + bx + cx^2$ □

ANSWERS: (1) iconic, (2) symbolic; (3) analog; (4) iconic; (5) analog; (6) symbolic.

best or optimum solution. The Vroom–Yetton model discussed in the previous chapter is an example of a normative model.

A *descriptive model* is designed to present occurrences, situations, or circumstances as they are. Such a model will not provide specific solutions to problems, but it will identify what will happen when problem variables are changed. Management of Sea Ray Boats may want to know the effect of the energy shortage on production schedules. This would justify the development of a descriptive model to provide a summary of relevant factors affected by the shortage. A simulation model described later in the chapter is an example of a descriptive model.

2. *Deterministic versus probabilistic models.* A second method of classifying models is by the types of elements they include. If the elements or variables of a

model can be quantified precisely, the model is classifed as *deterministic*. In such a model, chance or probability plays no part. Linear programming and economic order quantity models are examples of deterministic models.

If certain variables of the model situation are subject to probabilities or chance, the model is called *probabilistic*, or *stochastic*. Problems involving uncertainty and risk require probabilistic models for analysis. Input data and solutions are expressed as probabilities rather than as certainties. Consumer response to advertising and the resultant product demand are very uncertain; consequently, models developed by such firms as Lever Brothers or Colgate Palmolive to make advertising decisions would generally be probabilistic. Since risk and uncertainty are characteristic of much business activity, the mathematics of statistics and probability has been widely used in model building for business decisions. Decision-tree methods and expected value concepts—two quantitative techniques discussed later in the chapter—are examples of probabilistic methods.

3. *Empirical versus theoretical models.* A third method of classifying models is by the methodology they use. A *theoretical model* applies or assigns probabilities of the occurrence of events solely on the basis of accepted assumptions regarding the mechanism that generates the outcomes. The theoretical probability of an event in a given test is obtained under the following conditions: (1) the total number of ways an event can occur can be counted; (2) the number of possible occurrences is known; and (3) each occurrence is assumed to be equally likely. For example, the probability that one throw of a six-sided die will display a 3 can be calculated theoretically, based on the following information. The die is assumed to be balanced and, therefore, each of the six sides has an equal chance of appearing after a throw. Six occurrences are possible (1, 2, 3, 4, 5, or 6). There is only one way a 3 can be displayed after a throw. The theoretical probability is calculated as follows:

$$\text{Probability (3)} = \frac{\text{number of ways 3 can occur}}{\text{number of possible occurrences}} = \frac{1}{6} = .16667$$

The theoretical method calculates the probability of a 3 appearing on the throw of a single die at .16667.

In contrast, the *empirical model* assigns probabilities of the occurrence of events solely on the basis of statistical data recorded from previous experiences or experiments. In other words the probabilities are assigned *ex post*. The empirical probability of an event must be determined when it cannot be assumed that all the possible occurrences are equally likely to happen. Such a condition frequently exists in business situations, and construction of a model must be based on experiences or experiments of what has occurred on similar occasions in the past. Business decision makers often develop empirical models by estimating their own subjective probabilities of the occurrence of an event when encountering problem situations.

4. *Static versus dynamic models.* The final major method of classifying models is by the effect time has on the situation being analyzed. A *static model*

is involved with problems in which no time element is present. Static models are typically developed when no requirement for continuing analysis is present.[10]

Dynamic models deal not only with random variations but also with changes that occur over time. The time-dependent element in many problems requires a model that will allow the decision maker to determine the impact of variables that change over time.

Quantitative Approaches to Decision Making

The systematic, step-by-step approach of the scientific method is employed by managers in making organizational decisions and solving problems. Models are used in complex situations in order to determine the optimum solution. The steps involved include the following:

1. Formulate the problem.
2. Construct a mathematical model that represents the system being studied.
3. Derive a solution from the model.
4. Test the model and the solution derived from it.
5. Establish control over the situation.
6. Implement the solution.

These steps generally reflect the procedures of the scientific method. The emphasis here is on development, testing, and use of the most appropriate mathematical model in solving the problem under consideration.

PROBLEM FORMULATION

A dominant theme of the quantitative approach to decision making is problem formulation—especially those problem situations that thwart normal courses of activity and do not have an obvious solution. In order to utilize the tools of operations research effectively, a clear and concise definition of the specific problem confronting the manager is an essential first step.

Most problem definitions begin as broadly stated general descriptions of the problem area—and often focus on symptoms rather than causes. Declining profit margins for a product line of industrial cleaning supplies may be blamed on increased production costs. But production costs are the result of numerous factors, and effort and imagination are required to transform a general description of the problem are into a specifically defined problem. Specific objectives and constraints must be identified and both controllable and uncontrollable variables defined. As the problem is gradually formulated, its elements that can be corrected by management decisions must also be identified.

Once the problem's elements are identified, objectives and constraints defined, and problem variables constructed, the essence of the problem is formulated. The next step is to construct a mathematical model that can represent the system being studied.

---

[10] Gilbert Gordon and Israel Pressman, *Quantitative Decision-Making for Business* (Englewood Cliffs, N.J.: Prentice-Hall, 1978), p. 340.

MODEL DEVELOPMENT

The construction of a model to represent the system in which the problem exists allows the testing of the problem under investigation. Many problems cannot be tested in a real-world environment without considerable cost and disruption of normal working conditions. Development of a mathematical model that represents the system being studied allows the decision maker to manipulate the problem's variables in an economical manner while not interfering with the work of the system or organization.

DERIVING A SOLUTION

The third step is to derive a solution to the problem based upon analysis of the data generated by the model. All uncontrollable inputs (or data) must be specified before a solution can be derived from the model. Uncontrollable inputs for the manager of the local Nissan Motors dealership might include size of the lot, any franchise agreement specifying a ratio for the assortment of models that must be ordered, and the amount of space each type of vehicle occupies. The preparation of such data for the model is an important step; the solution derived from the model is no better than the data inputs. And the time required to collect the necessary data is often substantial. A moderate-sized model with about 50 decision variables and 25 constraints will generate more than 1,300 data elements.[11]

Once the values of the uncontrollable variables are specified and allocated as inputs to the model, the values of the controllable variables will change. The manager of the Nissan dealership would consider as controllable variables such decisions as the number of various sedan models, trucks, and its 280-ZX sports cars to order during the next sixty days. The results of the changes in the values of the controllable variables will then be analyzed to determine a condition that most closely meets the manager's objectives. The values that create the most favorable condition represent the solution to the problem.

Figure 8-1 shows how the mathematical model could be used to determine the best "mix" of automobile and truck models for the Nissan dealer. The model would consider changes in the controllable variables and ultimately identify the "best" solution to optimize the dealership's profits and space subject to the constraints that are present.

TESTING THE MODEL AND THE SOLUTION(S) DERIVED FROM IT

Once a solution or group of alternative solutions is identified, it can be tested in the model. The various types of models and the tools of operations research used to test the hypotheses are discussed in the next section. The aim of this step in

---

[11] Anderson, Sweeney, and Williams, *Essentials of Management Science*, p. 11.

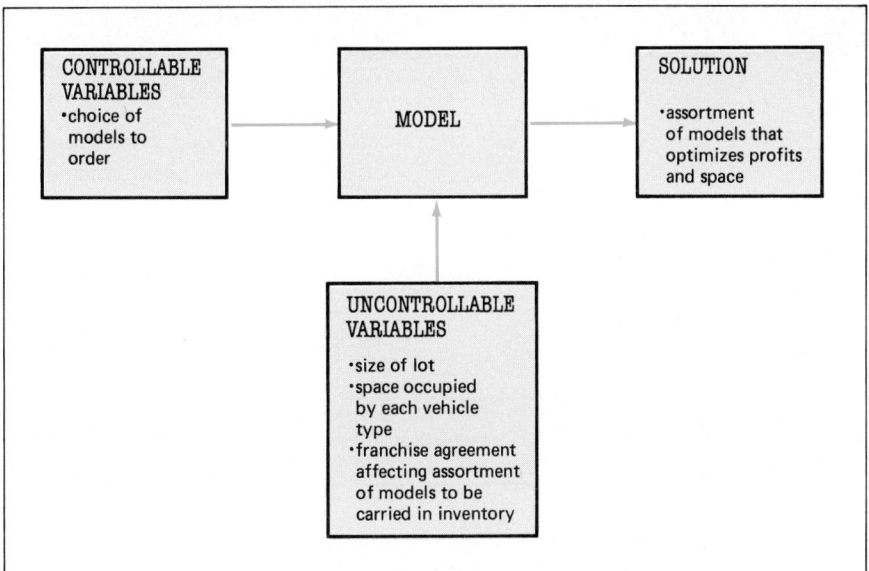

Figure 8-1
SIMPLIFIED MODEL FOR DETERMINING OPTIMAL INVENTORY ASSORTMENTS

the problem-solving process is to ensure that the solution is both economically effective and practical.

ESTABLISHING FEEDBACK CONTROLS

It is important to devise feedback and control mechanisms for each step of the decision process. In general, control involves the development of criteria for use in measuring the effectiveness of the system. The essence of control is the evaluation and interpretation of information regarding the actual operation of the system, the comparison of this information with the effectiveness measure, and the implementation of any corrective action needed to generate the system output at the desired state.[12]

Feedback is an essential part of establishing control of the scientific decision-making process. Feedback, discussed in chapters dealing with systems analysis and design, objective-setting, and planning, is essentially a diagnostic tool for the manager. It is the ongoing mechanism by which the decision maker collects and evaluates information concerning the procedures in operation at each stage of the decision process. This constant refining of information is matched against the control criteria and used to direct and control the performance of the decision procedures. Similar to the guidance system of a heat-seeking missile, feedback is a self-regulating device. As Figure 8-2 shows, the feedback mechanism should operate at each stage of the decision process, allowing the design of accurate models that can provide realistic and workable solutions to problems.

[12] Arthur C. Laufer, *Operations Management* (Cincinnati: South-Western, 1975), p. 27.

**Figure 8-2
ESTABLISHMENT OF
FEEDBACK
CONTROLS IN THE
OPERATIONS
RESEARCH
DECISION-MAKING
PROCESS**

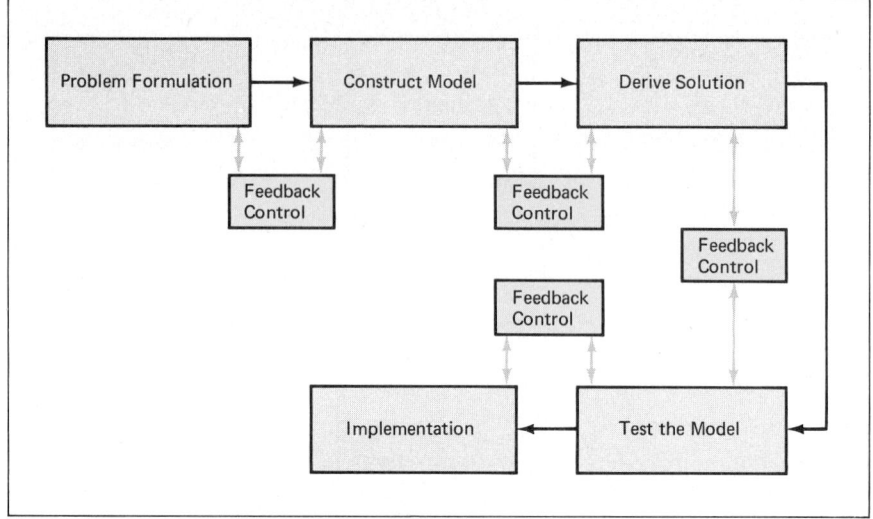

IMPLEMENTATION

The development, testing, and utilization of sophisticated models are merely an intellectual exercise of questionable value unless the solution is implemented. The steps involved in the decision process shown in Figure 8-2 lead to a tested solution, but it is the manager who must apply the findings. In many instances the step of converting the model's proposed solution into a course of action by the manager is a major one. Implementation is made easier when managers facing problems to be solved by an operations research department are involved from the very beginning of the process. Such involvement encourages close cooperation between the staff specialists and the line management. Research has indicated that operations research projects that have included the line manager as a participant in the problem formulation stage are twice as likely to be implemented as those projects in which the manager does not participate in problem definition.[13]

Quantitative Tools for Decision Making

A growing number of quantitative techniques are available for use in decision making. Such techniques must be selected carefully and often can be adapted to solve the right type of problem. A skilled golfer will choose the proper club for the shot under consideration. Just as the golfer recognizes the inappropriateness of a driver for a ball in a sand trap or a wedge for a putt, managers must be aware that unsatisfactory results will occur if the wrong analytical tool is chosen. While most managers will never become experts in the development and use of all op-

[13] Lars Lonnstedt, "Factors Related to the Implementation of Operations Research Solutions," *Interfaces* (February 1975), p. 24.

erations research techniques, they should be thoroughly familiar with their strengths and their limitations. The techniques described are linear programming; simulation; queuing, or waiting-line, models; game theory; and decision trees. Before the techniques are described, it is important to have a basic understanding of probability theory.

PROBABILITY THEORY

Probability theory forms the foundation of many of the quantitative techniques used in decision making. *Probability* is the likelihood of occurrence of some uncertain event or condition. Uncertainty surrounds most organizations and their activities. Such uncertainty should not be ignored in decision making; the models used should acknowledge its presence and, whenever possible, incorporate it as an estimatable degree of risk. Probability theory makes this incorporation possible.

Expected value concepts are useful in many managerial decisions. The expected value of any event is equal to the income it would produce should the event occur multiplied by the likelihood of the event's occurrence. By summing the expected value of all possible events in a decision situation, it is possible to calculate an average expected value for numerous types of problems.

For example, an investment being considered has the potential of providing cash returns of either $300, $500, or $750 per year for the next decade. The returns will be determined by the state of the economy. Management places a 50 percent probability of normal economic conditions and a 30 pecent likelihood of a recession and feels there is a 20 percent chance for markedly improved conditions. Based upon this information, the expected value of the cash flow of the investment can be calculated as follows:

Cash Flow		Economic Condition		
$300	×	.3 (Recession)	=	$ 90
500	×	.5 (Normal)	=	250
750	×	.2 (Boom)	=	150
		Expected Value =		$490

Based on the assumption of potential cash flow and the estimated likelihood of various levels of economic growth, $490 is the "best" estimate of the annual cash flow that will be generated by the investment. This return can now be compared with alternative investments in order to determine the investment that generates the highest expected returns, given the risks management is willing to assume.

Financial decision makers use expected value concepts in capital budgeting. This technique is a method of evaluating various projects that require current investment which will generate future cash flow benefits by either increasing profits or decreasing costs.

Cafeteria managers may use probability theory concepts in determining the number of meals to be prepared. The number of items needed in inventory to satisfy consumer demand for a given period; the number of life insurance policyholders in a certain age category expected to die during the next year; the num-

QUANTITATIVE ANALYSIS STRIKES OUT AT THE PRICE COMMISSION

C. Jackson Grayson, Jr., former dean of the business school at Southern Methodist University, accepted the position as head of the Federal Price Commission in 1971. Grayson was extremely knowledgeable about sophisticated quantitative techniques; and here was his opportunity to put these tools to work on major problem areas. But it didn't turn out that way.

At the Price Commission we operated, I think fairly successfully, without getting the data we "should" have had, without using any explicit decision tools, without once formally consulting a management scientist, and without building models of our decision-making processes.

I am not especially proud of these facts; I am a member and an intellectually loyal member, of ORSA, TIMS, and AIDS (Operations Research Society of America, the Institute for Management Science, and American Institute for Decision Sciences). I believe in the general direction in which these organizations want to go. But I also have a personal dedication to action, a sense of the urgency and immediacy of real problems, and a genuine responsiveness of management science models to my managerial needs.

I have asked myself the question whether we might have done better by using some management science models, and my honest answer is no. . . .

Consider the severity of the demands that were made. Establishment of the Price Commission required fulfillment of seemingly impossible tasks and directives:

ber of persons to overbook on an airline flight; and how many defective parts an assembly line will produce can all be solved by using probability theory.

LINEAR PROGRAMMING

Organizational efficiency has long been a prime objective of management. In decision after decision, a manager attempts to meet specified goals under the restriction of limited resources. How do managers use their available resources in such a manner as to maximize profits or minimize costs? Linear programming has proven extremely useful in solving such problems. *Linear programming* is a mathematical technique that is used to find the best solution to a given problem from a set of feasible solutions.[14] The essence of linear programmming is optimizing the allocation of scarce resources. The adjective *linear* means that the relationships among variables can be expressed as directly proportional functions. The term *programming* refers to a specific type of mathematical model designed to optimize outputs when resources are scarce. Linear programming is commonly used to determine the most advantageous product mix for a firm, to allocate advertising budgets, and to allocate resources such as machinery and per-

Linear programming is a mathematical technique that is used to find the best solution to a given problem from a set of feasible solutions; linear programming employs a model designed to optimize outputs when resources are scarce.

[14] Stephen P. Shao, *Mathematics and Quantitative Method for Business and Economics* (Cincinnati: South-Western, 1976), p. 148.

☐ Create and staff a fully competent organization.

☐ Work out regulations worthy to bear the force of law.

☐ Keep the program consistent with policies established in Phase I and the current state of the economy.

☐ Work in conjunction with the Pay Board, the Internal Revenue Service, and the Cost of Living Council.

☐ Control the prices of hundreds of millions of articles and commodities in the world's largest economy.

☐ Do not inhibit the recovery of the economy.

☐ Do not create a postcontrol bubble.

☐ Do all of this with a regulatory staff of 600.

☐ Have the entire operation functioning in 16 days.*

Grayson points out several well-known problems in the failure to utilize operations research techniques at the Price Commission. Chief problems were the tremendous time constraints in decision making and the inaccessibility of relevant data.

* Reprinted by permission of the Harvard Business Review. Excerpt from "Management Science and Business Practice" by C. Jackson Grayson, Jr. (July–August 1973). Copyright © 1973 by the President and Fellows of Harvard College; all rights reserved.

sonnel. A survey of U.S. firms indicated that linear programming was most commonly used in production problems. Almost three of every five respondent firms reported using linear programming in the production management area. Table 8-2 summarizes the findings of the survey.

AREA	PERCENT OF FIRMS USING LINEAR PROGRAMMING IN THIS AREA
Production Management	59
Financial and Investment Planning (Capital Budgeting)	11
Marketing	10
Cost and Profit Analysis	10
Transportation Scheduling	5
Inventory Control	4
Pollution Control	1
Energy Allocation	1
Risk Analysis	1

**Table 8-2
APPLICATIONS OF LINEAR PROGRAMMING BY RESPONDENT COMPANIES**

SOURCE: Reprinted by permission from Frank J. Fabozzi and Joseph Valente, "Mathematical Programming in American Companies: A Sample Survey," *Interfaces* (November 1976). p. 97. Copyright 1976 The Institute of Management Sciences.

Major Requirements of the Linear Programming Model

Linear programming is the appropriate quantitative tool for problem solving when the following conditions are present:

1. The manager is attempting to achieve a specific objective (such as maximizing profits or minimizing costs).
2. Alternative courses of action are present.
3. Resources are scarce.
4. The firm's objective and resource limitations can be expressed as a linear mathematical equation or inequality.[15]

Consider again the case of the Nissan automobile dealer. The inventory is divided between sedans and sports cars. Assume that consumer demand is sufficiently great to purchase any combination of these high-fuel economy models and that the sedans contribute $650 per unit to profits after costs have been paid and the sports cars contribute $950. The conditions listed above are as follows:

Objective: to maximize profits
Alternative: dealer can stock any combination of sedans and sports cars
Resource limitations: limited storage/display space limits the dealer to an upper limit of 15 sedans or 10 sports cars (since sports cars require 50 percent more display space than sedans)
Mathematical equation: P = Total profit
A = Number of sedans ordered
B = Number of sports cars ordered
P = $650A + $950B

This equation represents the objective function for the dealership. The manager must select the values of A and B that will maximize profits for the organization. Profit is a linear function of A, B, and the contribution factor of both. A and B are the decision variables of the problem. In other words the values of A and B are the variables over which the dealer has control in the attempt to maximize profits. The manager does not, however, have absolute control, due to the storage and display space limitations. This basic constraint can be translated into mathematical language. Total capacity is 15 sedans or 10 sports cars (15 As or 10 Bs). A sedan takes up 1 unit of space as compared with 1.5 units for a sports car, if units of space are defined in terms of sedans with an upper limit of 15. An equation that will require solution with respect to the space limitation constraint is

$$A + 1.5B \leq 15$$

[15] Richard I. Levin and Charles A. Kirkpatrick, *Quantitative Approaches to Management* (New York: McGraw-Hill, 1978), p. 261. Used with permission.

This equation is an inequality that takes into consideration all the combinations of A and B that do not exceed the space limitation. An inequality is a statement indicating that one algebraic expression is greater than (>) or less than (<) another expression. The symbol ≤ means equal to or less than.

The franchise agreement requires that each dealer must carry both sports cars and sedans in inventory. This can be expressed by

$$A, B \geq 1$$

The problem facing the manager of the dealership can be summarized in the following manner:

Maximize: P = $650A + $950B
Subject to: A + 1.5B ≤ 1.5
A, B, ≥ 1

The problem can be solved by listing the results of the only feasible solutions. Table 8-3 lists the solutions that satisfy the constraints and are eligible for consideration in choosing the optimal solution. The optimal solution subject to the franchise and storage/display constraints is an inventory composed of 12 sedans and 2 sports cars. This solution gives the dealer a profit contribution of $9,700, the highest of all possible combinations of sedans and sports models.[16]

Most linear programming problems are more complex than the dealership example and require formal procedures to solve them. Linear programming is a powerful and frequently used quantitative tool and numerous books are available to explain the various methods that may be used in the solution of manage-

[16] Ira Horowitz, *An Introduction to Quantitative Business Analysis* (New York: McGraw-Hill, 1972), p. 7.

SEDANS A ($650)	SPORTS CARS B ($950)	SPACE UNITS 15	PROFITS
1	9	14.5	1 (650) + 9 (950) = $9,200
2	8	14	2 (650) + 8 (950) = 8,900
3	8	15	3 (650) + 8 (950) = 9,550
4	7	14.5	4 (650) + 7 (950) = 9,250
5	6	14	5 (650) + 6 (950) = 8,950
6	6	15	6 (650) + 6 (950) = 9,600
7	5	14.5	7 (650) + 5 (950) = 9,300
8	4	14	8 (650) + 4 (950) = 9,000
9	4	15	9 (650) + 4 (950) = 9,650
10	3	14.5	10 (650) + 3 (950) = 9,350
11	2	14	11 (650) + 2 (950) = 9,050
12	2	15	12 (650) + 2 (950) = 9,700
13	1	14.5	13 (650) + 1 (950) = 9,400

Table 8-3 THE EFFECT OF ALTERNATIVE INVENTORY COMBINATIONS OF SEDANS AND SPORTS CARS ON DEALERSHIP PROFITS

ment problems involving the choice of optimum combinations or allocations of limited resources to obtain a desired objective.[17]

SIMULATION MODELS

Simulation is a process for replicating the major aspects of an existing system or process that is too complex to be expressed in mathematical terms; elements are described by probability distributions, then combined in various ways so their effect on the model can be studied.

Simulation is a process for replicating the major aspects of an existing system or process that is too complex to express all of the elements and their interrelationships in mathematical terms. In developing a simulation model, the behavior of as many elements as possible is described by probability distributions. Various tests are then conducted by varying different combinations of factors and analyzing their effect on the model. Such tests might be considered as experiments being conducted on the model. Through a trial-and-error process, the interaction of any number of variables can be promptly observed. Such an experiment in the real-world environment would prove both costly and time consuming.

Simulation models can be used to solve problems and train personnel in situations as diverse as the use of wind tunnels in testing aircraft design, simulation trainers for pilots, or simulated moon-landing exercises for astronauts. Inland Steel Company operations research specialists have developed a simulation model of the steel-making process. When an equipment failure occurs, an Inland Steel manager defines the new conditions resulting from the failure and enters them in the model. Less than two hours later, the model provides a manager with the necessary data for estimating new costs and for preparing a revised profit projection.[18]

Gulf Oil Corp. uses its sophisticated U.S. energy model in analyzing synthetic fuels strategy. The model covers all major energy forms, conversion technologies, transportation modes, and demand. It also projects investment, resource depletion, and financing to the year 2025 and computes price based upon supply-and-demand variations.[19]

Although simulation models require sizable computer capability, they hold great promise for management decision makers. In fact, the conditions required for the use of simulation describe many management decision situations. These conditions are

1. A mathematical solution is not possible.
2. Observation of the actual environment is not possible or is expensive.
3. Time is not available to observe the actual environment.
4. Actual operation and observation of the environment may be too disruptive of other operations.[20]

[17] Two excellent basic linear programming books are R. Stansbury Stockton, *Introduction to Linear Programming* (Homewood, Ill.: Irwin, 1971); and Saul Gass, *Illustrated Guide to Linear Programming* (New York: McGraw-Hill, 1970).
[18] James B. Boulden and Elwood S. Buffa, "Corporate Models: On-Line, Real-Time Systems," *Harvard Business Review* (July–August 1970), p. 65.
[19] *Business Week* (April 28, 1975).
[20] Levin and Kirkpatrick, *Quantitative Approaches to Management*, p. 429.

Simulation has already become one of the most commonly used quantitative tools in major corporations, and its use is expected to increase during this decade.[21]

QUEUING, OR WAITING-LINE, MODELS

Most commerical organizations have one or more functions that generate waiting lines. Customers at a bookstore checkout or gasoline station, parts waiting to be labeled, machines in need of servicing, automobile drivers at a stop light intersection, and units waiting to be painted are all examples of queuing requirements. *Queuing,* or *waiting-line, models* attempt to solve problems caused by waiting lines by determining the appropriate balance between the cost of providing the extra service (such as additional service personnel or new checkout lines to eliminate the cost of waiting) and the cost of having people, machines, or materials wait. The costs are depicted in Figure 8-3.

   Excessive waiting lines cost money in terms of idle employee or machine time, lost revenues, and dissatisfied customers. In addition, the demand for service is likely to vary. Queuing models assist in predicting the outcomes of different combinations of service facilities and aid in developing a system to minimize total expected cost.[22]

Queuing models attempt to solve problems caused by waiting lines by determining the appropriate balance between the cost of providing extra service and the cost of having people, machines, or materials wait.

GAME THEORY

Game theory is a technique for determining the strategy that is likely to produce maximum profits in a competitive situation. It allows the manager to test such possible strategies as the introduction of a new product, a price increase, or the launching of a new advertising campaign by considering the likely reactions of competitors. Since the manager cannot predict with certainty the responses of

Game theory is a technique for determining the strategy that is likely to produce maximum profits in a competitive situation.

[21] Ledbetter and Cox, "Are OR Techniques Being Used?" p. 19. See also Fred C. Weston, "Operations Research Techniques Relevant to Corporate Planning Practices: An Investigative Look," *Operations Research Bulletin* (Spring 1971).

[22] See Jack Byrd, Jr., "The Value of Queuing Theory," *Interfaces* (May 1978), pp. 22–26.

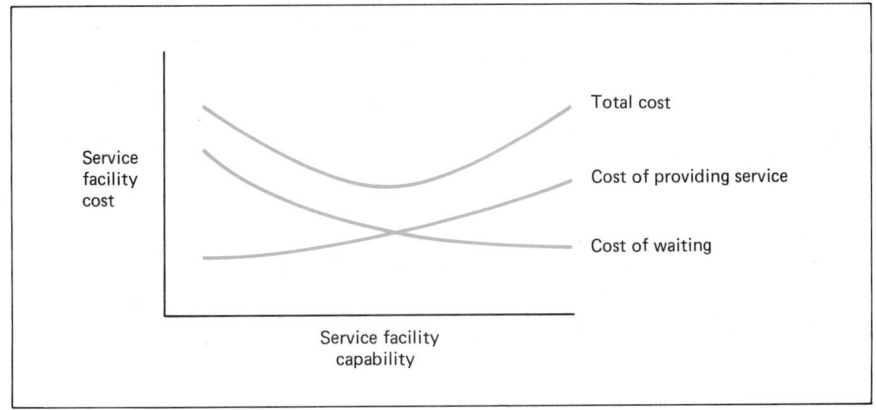

**Figure 8-3
COSTS IN THE
QUEUING MODEL**

competitors, this technique uses probability theory to test the effects on profits or market share of various possible competitive moves.

Game theory has been utilized extensively by military planners in training and decision making. It is used less frequently in business organizations, due to the complexity of most business situations and the large number of competitors. One investigation of the use of seven operations research models in major corporations revealed that game theory was the least frequently used quantitative tool.[23] Although the mathematics has not been developed to deal with more complex decision-making situations, game theory may assist the manager in predicting how a rational person would react in a competitive situation.

DECISION TREES

The decision tree is a branched model helpful in identifying alternative courses of action.

Another useful quantitative technique is the *decision tree*. This is a graphic method for identifying alternative courses of action, assigning probability estimates for the payoffs associated with each alternative, and indicating the course of action with the highest payoff. The decision maker is required to assign financial results to various courses of action and to estimate the likelihood of occurrence of each alternative.

To solve a problem by the decision-tree method, the following procedures are used:

1. Illustrate the problem by developing a decision-tree diagram. A separate branch is drawn for each course of action, producing a structure that looks like a tree laid on its side.
2. Determine and assign probabilities to each outcome.
3. Determine the financial result of each outcome.
4. Use the above steps to determine which alternative will yield the highest expected value or financial result.[24]

How Decision Trees Work

The following decision illustrates the decision-tree methodology. Public Service Company-Midwest has decided to construct a new power-generating facility. Initial research indicated the two most favorable choices: (1) build a conventional plant using coal as the energy source; or (2) construct a nuclear facility. The larger nuclear plant is estimated to cost $13.2 million to build and put into operation, as compared with $6.2 million for the smaller, conventional plant. Public Service forecasters developed the following energy demand estimates for the next twenty years:

High demand:	Probability = .6
Moderate demand:	Probability = .3
Low demand:	Probability = .1

[23] Ledbetter and Cox, "Are OR Techniques Being Used?" p. 19.
[24] Barry Shore, *Quantitative Methods for Business Decisions: Text and Cases* (New York: McGraw-Hill, 1978), pp. 118–119.

Additional extensive research has been conducted to determine the expected profitability of the alternative generating plant types based upon different energy demand estimates. These findings are as follows:

ALTERNATIVE A: LARGE NUCLEAR-POWERED PLANT

1. High-demand environment will yield profits of $2 million per year.
2. Moderate-demand environment will yield annual profits of $1.2 million.
3. Low-demand environment will yield annual profits of $0.3 million.

ALTERNATIVE B: SMALLER CONVENTIONALLY POWERED PLANT

1. High-demand environment will yield annual profits of $0.7 million.
2. Moderate-demand environment will yield annual profits $0.9 million.
3. Low-demand environment will yield annual profits of $1.5 million.

Figure 8-4 provides a graphic illustration of the alternatives. The net expected value of profits generated by the nuclear-powered generating facility is $18.6 million over the next twenty years, a $10 million advantage over the conventionally powered facility. The larger nuclear-powered plant appears to be the appropriate decision based upon the information analyzed. But the Public Service

**Figure 8-4
DECISION
TREE—EXPECTED
PAYOFF FROM
NUCLEAR PLANT AS
COMPARED WITH
CONVENTIONAL
PLANT**

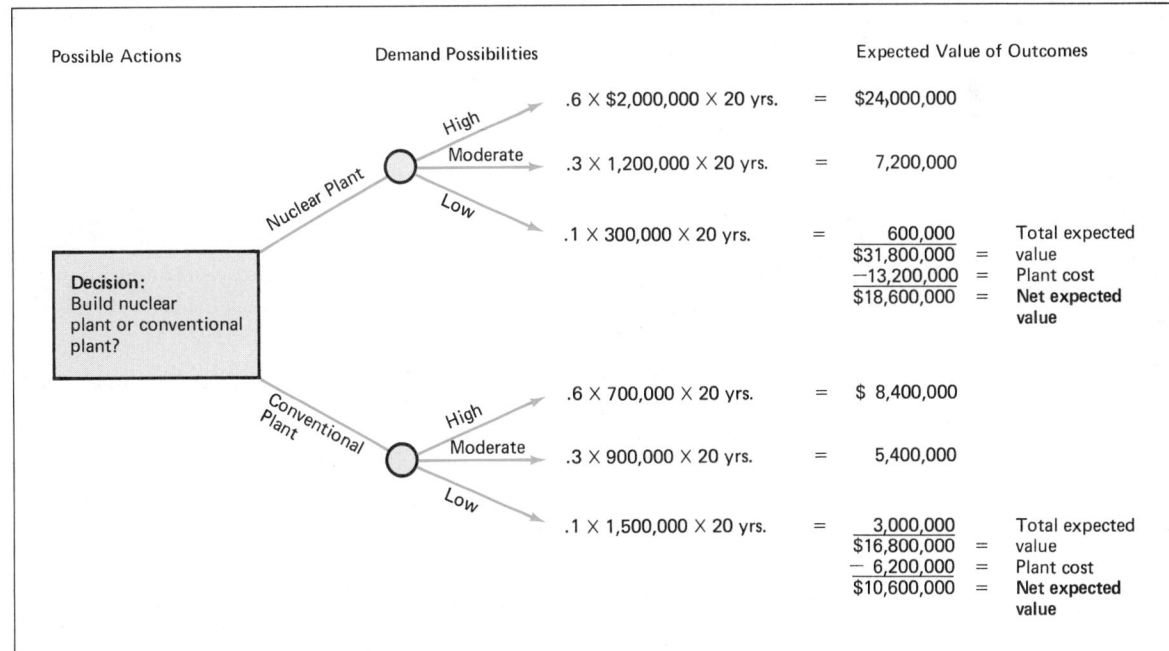

decision makers must also give careful consideration to other important factors that may ultimately alter their choice:

1. Political and ecological considerations are critical elements. The danger of accidents such as the 1979 crisis at the Three Mile Island, Pennsylvania, nuclear generating facility may outweigh other considerations.
2. The demand probabilities for energy may not be constant.
3. The time value of money must be considered. Since funds received several years from today are worth less than funds received today (since they cannot immediately be put to use in generating new funds), these future streams of funds should be discounted in order to compare them with present values.

Decision trees can be used in marketing, investment, equipment purchases, pricing, new venture analysis, and a variety of other decisions. They provide a means for formalizing the risk assessment and planning required to make successful decisions.[25]

Applying Quantitative Techniques

The use of quantitative techniques has increased as the tools have been refined for business problems and as line managers have become more familiar with their capabilities. Important problems of inventory control, allocation of scarce resources, equipment replacement decisions, scheduling and sequencing work flows, and waiting-line regulation are frequently solved with the aid of operations research tools.

INVENTORY CONTROL DECISIONS

Inventory control involves the balancing of the costs of ordering inventory with the costs of holding inventory. Ordering costs include the cost of placing orders, of shipping and handling, and of not receiving quantity discounts offered by suppliers. Such costs decline as the average amount of inventory on hand increases. Carrying costs include the costs of funds invested in accumulated inventory, storage costs, insurance, and depreciation. Such costs increase as the average level of inventory held increases. As a result inventory planning involves the balancing of conflicting objectives. In large organizations with complex production processes, the shortage of an important part could result in missed production deadlines and lost customers. On the other hand, large amounts of inventory on hand to eliminate any possible shortage may prove prohibitively expensive. A balance is required to optimize the situation by minimizing the combined order

---

[25] An excellent discussion of decision-tree analysis is contained in Jacob W. Ulvila and Rex V. Brown, "Decision Analysis Comes of Age," *Harvard Business Review* (September–October 1982), pp. 130–141.

and carrying costs. Such quantitative techniques as economic order quantity models, linear programming, and, in some complex situations, simulation may be used to solve inventory control problems.

RESOURCE ALLOCATION AND EQUIPMENT REPLACEMENT

Linear programming is an effective tool in determining the optimum allocation of scarce organizational resources and the determination of the timing and most efficient method of replacing capital equipment. In situations in which a certain combination of resources can be used in different ways to perform a task, linear programming can determine the optimum way to minimize cost or maximize profits. By balancing the increasing cost of operating older, less effective equipment and the cost of its replacement, linear programming can also determine the most appropriate time for making such replacements.

SCHEDULING AND SEQUENCING WORK FLOWS

A common production problem is to determine the most appropriate sequencing of a product through a series of work stations. Although the various work activities required to produce a finished product may be performed in different orders, some sequences are more efficient than others. Simulation can be used to solve sequencing problems.

Scheduling problems deal with *when* is the best time for a job to be performed as well as *in what order* (sequence). Linear programming, queuing models, and simulation can be applied to complex routing problems.

WAITING-LINE REGULATION

One motto of today's society appears to be "Hurry up and wait!" Waiting in line is a common occurrence of persons, products, processes, and parts. Waiting-line models deal with creating facilities to meet the needs for service. Loading platforms, vehicle servicing, drive-in bank facilities, and aircraft inspections are additional examples of such problems. Queuing models are particularly appropriate in finding solutions.

QUANTITATIVE METHODS AID—BUT DO NOT REPLACE—THE DECISION MAKER

As mentioned throughout the chapter, quantitative methods can provide major assistance to line managers in solving many types of complex organizational problems. But quantitative analysis has limitations and cannot replace the experience, judgment, and intuitive wisdom of the manager. The effective manager recognizes that the ultimate decision rests with him or her, but relies on the contributions of quantitative techniques for guidance and direction.

Summary

Quantitative techniques can assist managers in making improved decisions. Operations research, or management science, is a relatively new field that has evolved to assist managers in developing and applying mathematical techniques to problems of organizations. Such techniques offer the important advantages of a systematic focus on the problem and its alternative solutions. They promote a more accurate and thorough analysis of problems through the development of a required data base of factual information of the problem situation; and they assist in solving complex problems by breaking them down into smaller, more manageable parts. Limitations of such techniques include the potential for failure of a "meeting of the minds" between the operations research specialists and the line manager; the short lead time often associated with decision making; resistance to change on the part of decision makers; expense involved with the development and use of sophisticated analytical techniques; and overconcentration on quantifiable data and failure to incorporate ill-defined but important human factors.

Models—or representations of real objects, situations, or systems—are crucial elements in operations research. Three general categories of models exist. An iconic model is a physical replica or a scale representation that actually looks like the object it represents. An analog model is also a physical representation of a real object or situation, but it does not have the same physical appearance as the object being modeled. Symbolic, or mathematical, models use equations to express relationships among factors in a process or system being modeled. Other model classifications include descriptive and normative; deterministic and probabilistic; empirical and theoretical; and static and dynamic.

Six steps are involved in the quantitative approach to problem solving:

1. Formulate the problem.
2. Construct a mathematical model that represents the system being studied.
3. Derive a solution from the model.
4. Test the model and the solution derived from it.
5. Establish control over the situation.
6. Implement the solution.

The major quantitative techniques used in organizational decision making are linear programming; simulation; queuing, or waiting-line, theory; game theory; and decision-tree analysis. Linear programming is a mathematical technique to optimize the allocation of scarce resources in order to find the best solution to a given problem. Simulation is a process for replicating the major aspects of an existing system or process and conducting numerous tests by varying different combinations of factors and analyzing their effect on the model. Queuing models attempt to solve problems caused by waiting lines by determining the appropriate balance between the cost of additional service facilities and the cost of having people, machines, or materials wait. Game theory is a technique for determining the strategy most likely to produce maximum profits in a competitive situation. The final technique, decision-tree analysis, is a graphic method for identifying alternative courses of action, assigning probability estimates for the payoffs associated with each alternative and indicating the course of action with the highest payoff.

Although managers must recognize the limitations of quantitative techniques and combine their use with experience and judgment, such techniques can play major roles in decision areas like inventory control problems, resource allocation and equipment replacement, scheduling and sequencing work flows, and waiting-line regulation.

REVIEW EXERCISES

1. Define the following terms: (a) operations research (b) scientific method (c) model (d) iconic model (e) analog model (f) symbolic, or mathematical, model (g) probability (h) linear programming (i) simulation (j) queuing, or waiting-line, model (k) game theory (l) decision tree.

2. Explain the major advantages of quantitative techniques in planning and problem solving. What are their chief limitations?

3. Explain how the use of models can aid managers.

4. Identify and give an example of each of the three general categories of models.

5. Distinguish between the following: (a) normative and descriptive models (b) deterministic and probabilistic models (c) empirical and theoretical models (d) static and dynamic models.

6. List the steps in the quantitative approach to problems and their solutions.

7. Identify each of the major quantitative techniques.

Suggest specific problem areas in which each technique might be used.

8. What costs are balanced through the use of queuing models?

9. Discuss the problems of applying game theory to business decisions.

10. Outline the basic procedures of decision-tree analysis.

Applications

1. Refer to the discussion of the Pan American Airlines fuel management model found at the beginning of the chapter. What quantitative technique did Pan Am Airlines use in developing its model? Defend your answer.

2. Suggest the most appropriate quantitative technique for the following problems:

  a. General Motors Corporation is attempting to determine the impact of increased retail prices and gasoline shortages on demand for its X line of subcompacts.
  b. The Cleveland Sanitation Department is attempting to develop trash routes for its trucks.
  c. International Paper Co. is trying to decide whether to modernize its existing West Coast paper manufacturing plant or construct an entirely new facility.
  d. Chase Manhattan Bank is in the process of determining the appropriate number of automatic tellers at its new drive-in facility.

  e. Texas Instruments is attempting to assess the competitive impact of its new digital home thermometer.

3. Develop a step-by-step proposal for implementation of operations research techniques in a large manufacturing firm.

4. The owner of a local sporting goods store was offered a special discount price of $10 per football if the order were placed before July 1. Orders placed after July 1 would receive the regular rate of $12 each. The balls could only be purchased in quantities of even dozens. Retail prices are $18 per football and the estimated level of demand is the following:

Demand (in dozens)	Probability
2	.25
3	.30
4	.30
5	.15

Draw the decision tree based on the above information and determine the appropriate number of footballs to order.

A MANAGERIAL INCIDENT

Emergency Medical Service

During the 1960s the New York City Emergency Medical Service served the city's inhabitants by stationing its ambulances at forty-nine hospitals. Each hospital represented a separate district and dispatched its ambulances only to respond to requests from within its district. The average response time was 13.5 minutes, and managers of the service were seeking methods of reducing it.

One proposal for improving the ambulance service was to locate at least some ambulances at satellite garages in demand centers within the established hospital districts. A second proposal involved assigning each of the 135 ambulances to a nine-square block area and then incorporating the Emergency Medical Service into the city-wide 911 emergency telephone system. Persons requiring ambulances would dial 911 and the call would immediately be transferred to the Emergency Medical Service's computerized communications center. From there the dispatcher would route the call to the closest available ambulances.

In order to determine the best method for reducing average response time, some method of comparing the two proposals with the existing system was needed. Such a method would have to consider such factors as the number of ambulances for each district, location of hospitals, satellite garage locations, as well as the geographic distribution and the frequency of calls within each district. *

SOURCE: E. S. Savas, "Simulation and Cost-Effectiveness Analysis of New York's Emergency Ambulance Service," *Management Science* (August 1969), pp. 608–627. 1983 data provided by New York City Emergency Medical Service.

* The latter alternative was ultimately chosen. Each of the city's 135 ambulances are kept on the city streets between 7 A.M. and 1 A.M. (Fewer ambulances operate during the late-night hours.) Each ambulance is assigned a specific geographic area to facilitate rapid response to emergency calls.

Questions and Problems

1. Suggest a method by which managers of the Emergency Medical Service can evaluate the proposed changes in ambulance service.
2. What other government services could utilize similar quantitative techniques?

Case II-1

THE DEVELOPMENT OF CORPORATE PLANNING
AT BORG-WARNER: A CASE HISTORY

Formal corporate long-range planning is a relatively new phenomenon. Very few American corporations practiced formal planning prior to 1950. As late as 1957, there were only approximately 200 large corporations with formal planning departments.[1] But by that time planning was beginning to become fashionable and a decade later over 1,000 corporations had formal planning departments.[2]

Chicago-based Borg-Warner was one of the pioneer planning firms. Prior to 1950 Borg-Warner's growth was directed by an informal planning system. But after 1950 Borg-Warner introduced a formal system. Borg-Warner's planning approach evolved in a manner that provides students of management with fascinating insights into both the history of planning and the nature of the planning process.

The case that follows describes some of the highlights of the history of corporate planning at Borg-Warner.

THE INFORMAL PLANNING PERIOD:
1928–1950

The formation of Borg-Warner represented an attempt by five automobile industry suppliers to offset the growing bargaining power of their major customers, Ford Motor Co., General Motors, and other automobile companies. After extensive discussions four of the five companies merged to form the Borg-Warner Corp. in 1928. The fifth company, the Ingersoll Steel and Disc Co., joined Borg-Warner in 1929.

This case was prepared by Professors Richard E. Hattwick of Western Illinois University and William C. Scott of Indiana State University as a basis for class discussion rather than to illustrate either effective or ineffective handling of an administrative situation. Adapted and reprinted by permission of the authors.

[1] C. W. Roney, "How to Accomplish the Two Purposes of Business Planning," *Managerial Planning* 25, no. 4 (January–February 1977), p. 1.
[2] *Ibid.*

In the early years of its history, Borg-Warner was organized into five highly autonomous divisions, one division for each of the predecessor companies. This arrangement was designed to make it possible for the leaders of each of the founding companies to continue to run their companies much as they had before the merger that created Borg-Warner. Each of the leaders had a place on the board of directors, and together they made corporate policy while running their own divisions. Coordinating their efforts was President Charles Davis.

The experiences of the Ingersoll Steel and Disc Division illustrate the nature of informal planning during this period. Major new strategies at the division usually resulted from the occurrence of "motivational situations" rather than long-range planning. The reactions of division president Roy Ingersoll to the situations that arose represented the planning process. Five such "motivational situations" deserve brief discussion.

INNOVATION MOTIVATED BY THE DESIRE TO GAIN MARKET SHARE

The first motivational situation that prompted major change at Ingersoll's division was the desire to increase market share. The primary example of this phenomenon at work actually occurred several years prior to the Borg-Warner merger. Ingersoll's business was the manufacture and sale of steel discs for use in agricultural implements. Between 1910 and 1921, Roy Ingersoll directed the company through a 1,300 percent increase in sales, yet by 1921 Ingersoll's share of the market was still quite small. Feeling somewhat stymied in his quest for market share, Ingersoll hit upon the idea of product innovation as a way of gaining ground. In the case of his disc product, the most promising innovation was to develop a disc with greater durability than that offered by the competitors. Therefore, Ingersoll initiated a laborious research project that culminated in the development of a production process that produced discs of substantially greater durability. The new product was a success in the marketplace and Ingersoll greatly increased his market share.

INNOVATION MOTIVATED BY THE DESIRE TO SURVIVE

The second motivational situation prompting major change occurred in the late 1920s. The onset of the Great Depression in 1929 caused Ingersoll's disc business to drop 85 percent. Faced with the prospect of bankruptcy, Ingersoll searched long and hard for alternative uses for his discs. He finally decided to make discs for truck wheels. But there was a problem. Most of America's truck wheels were being produced by the Budd Wheel Co. under a patent from a French firm. To get into the business, Ingersoll would have to come up with a different process to get around the patent. Ingersoll devoted months of experimentation to the problem and finally developed an alternative process, which he patented. He then sold his product to the Kelsey-Hayes Wheel Co.

INVESTING IN "TURN-AROUND SITUATIONS"

A third motivational situation causing Ingersoll to make major improvements was the periodic appearance of "turn-around situations." In 1910 Ray Ingersoll had temporarily taken over management of a bankrupt steel mill that had been supplying Ingersoll with a specialty steel needed for his discs. Ingersoll took the job strictly as a method of maintaining a flow of steel for his discs. But once in the management position, Ingersoll discovered that he had a talent for turning a seemingly hopeless case into a profitable operation. He was able to "turn the financial situation at the steel mill around."

Having discovered his ability, Ingersoll subsequently looked for other steel facilities that he could acquire and make profitable. In 1930 he persuaded the Borg-Warner Board of Directors to acquire the Chicago Rolling Mill Co., and Ingersoll found methods of making that facility profitable. In 1935 the scenario was repeated when Borg-Warner purchased the financially troubled Calumet Steel Rolling Mill. And in 1937 Borg-Warner purchased a run-down steel plant in Kalamazoo,

Michigan, and gave Ingersoll the job of making the operation profitable.

OPPORTUNITIES CREATED BY WAR

A fourth motivational situation was the outbreak of World War II, which created a huge demand for products related to the war effort. In the case of the Ingersoll Steel Division at Borg-Warner, the war created an opportunity to enter the business of manufacturing amphibious landing vehicles. The Kalamazoo facility was transformed into a plant to manufacture the product. An effective vehicle was produced, and the division received numerous commendations for its contributions to the war effort.

OPPORTUNITIES CREATED BY ORGANIZED RESEARCH AND DEVELOPMENT

Prior to World War II, Borg-Warner's research programs were conducted by the individual divisions. Shortly after the war ended, the Board of Directors took the first step in the direction of formalized long-range planning by establishing a corporate-level research unit. The primary purpose of the unit was to develop an automatic transmission. That research goal was achieved, and Borg-Warner signed a major contract to supply the transmission to the Ford Motor Co. Once the transmission product was completed, the corporate-level approach to research was continued and became a source of new product ideas for the entire corporation.

FORMAL PLANNING: 1950–1975

Conditions Leading to the Adoption of Formal Long-Range Planning

The successful automatic transmission project created a new problem for Borg-Warner. The contract with Ford gave Ford the right to manufacture all of its own transmissions under Borg-Warner license after the 1958 model year. It seemed likely to many at Borg-Warner that Ford would exercise that option. Hence, Borg-Warner would have to make plans to offset the loss of the Ford business in 1958.

In 1950 Roy Ingersoll was elected president of Borg-Warner. Ingersoll was concerned about the potential loss of the Ford business. He was also convinced that most other Borg-Warner products would eventually have to be replaced in order for the corporation to grow. Ingersoll therefore led the company in the adoption of a system of long-range planning. The system had many of the features of what later came to be called *strategic planning*. Each Borg-Warner Division was asked to actively search for new product areas where the company's strengths would enable it to compete successfully. Each division was asked to develop plans for replacement of existing products and expansion in markets currently occupied. Ingersoll himself concentrated his efforts on a program of acquisitions to fill the gap left by the expected loss of the Ford business.

The planning system introduced by Ingersoll was made possible by the fact that Borg-Warner already had a decentralized organizational structure. Many firms that were later to become leaders in the area of planning were not prepared to employ strategic planning in the early 1950s because they did not yet possess a decentralized structure. A prime example of such a firm is General Electric, a company whose name became synonymous with planning excellence in later decades.

Nature of Ingersoll's Planning Process

The planning system required each of Borg-Warner's divisions to prepare and submit for review a detailed plan for five years into the future. Included in the information to be submitted were

1. Long-range goals dealing with business functions, industries to be served, products or services, market share, sales, profits.
2. Five-year sales forecasts by product and market share plus information on marketing plans and major competitors.
3. Research and development programs dealing with present and new products including expenses and five-year budget data.
4. Manufacturing facilities, including needs for both existing and new products.
5. Financial requirements for five years, in-

cluding capital for replacement, expansion, working capital, profit margins, and return on investment estimates.
6. Human resources requirements for five years for personnel in management, technical areas, sales, finance, and factory positions.

Each of the twenty-eight divisions submitted its plan to one of the committees created specifically to review the plans. Known as *supervisory boards*, the committees represented and included members of top management.

Evolution of the Planning Process

During the 1950s Roy Ingersoll devoted his efforts to the task of convincing the management at lower levels to take planning seriously and of completing the acquisitions needed for growth. The acquisitions program was successful in offsetting the loss of the Ford business. However, some of the acquisitions did not live up to their promise, and by 1960 Borg-Warner faced the need to divest itself of the unsuccessful parts of the business.

In 1961 Robert Ingersoll succeeded his father, Roy, as chairperson of Borg-Warner. (Robert Ingersoll became president and CEO in 1958.) Bob Ingersoll faced the task of consolidating the progress achieved during the 1950s. This involved analyzing all of Borg-Warner's business in the light of the new environment of the 1960s and 1970s. In order to do this effectively, it was also necessary for Borg-Warner to analyze its corporate purpose. The process of rethinking Borg-Warner's corporate purpose and then arranging the divestiture of parts of the business that did not fit consumed much of top management's energies during the 1960s. In 1971 Borg-Warner announced a new five-year plan that included a new statement of goals and a new planning structure. The new structure provided for greater involvement in the planning process by corporate officers. As explained in the 1971 Annual Report:

. . . management has embarked on a new long-range planning system. Last November, a new five-year plan (for 1971–1975) was developed under this system. Line and staff people throughout the company worked on the plan, the most comprehensive in Borg-Warner history.

The major difference in the new planning approach and the previous method is the greater involvement of corporate and group officers in deploying Borg-Warner's assets.

The goal of the new plan was to increase earnings to $4.00 per share in 1975. The goal represented 2.4 times the 1970 earnings of $1.65 per share. The plan also contained a sales growth of 8 percent per year and a capital investment goal of at least $330 million over the five-year period, while keeping the debt to equity ratio at .35 or lower.

After operating under the new planning system for one year, new president James Bere described the system as follows:

Very briefly, the divisions prepare five-year business plans which first are consolidated by the group officers to their standards and then are submitted to our new formed Policy and Planning Committee, made up of five senior executive officers.

Here we hammer out an overall corporate plan to meet the objectives we seek, and then communicate the plan throughout the organization. We have set standards to measure the performance of each operating unit and we intend to be diligent in our follow-up of the results.[3]

STRATEGIC PLANNING: 1975–

Progress under the five-year plan of 1971 was brought to a halt by the nationwide recession of 1974–1975. As related by Borg-Warner's top planner, Dr. D. W. Collier,[4]

The . . . recession brought on severe declines in a number of our major markets . . .

and a cold examination of our position in the industries in which we competed pointed out clearly to a history of cyclical, below average return. . . .

It became clear to Borg-Warner's top management that a new planning approach was needed and the Boston Consulting Group's concepts of strategic planning were selected. Collier explained this choice as follows:[5]

Strategic planning was appropriate to the times because it asked *First: Do we want to be in that business at all?* Before asking . . . *How do we do it better?* In addition, strategic planning began to focus management's attention on markets . . . their growth and our share in them, rather than on product, which had been our traditional focus.

In 1975 Borg-Warner's top management worked with the basic concepts developed by the Boston Consulting Group. This included the use of the "business matrix." As originally developed by the Boston Consulting Group, this tool required management to rate each of its "businesses" in terms of high or low market share and high or low market growth. Thus, each "business" could be placed in one of four cells of a two by two matrix. (See Exhibit 1.) By 1976, however, management decided to adopt a more realistic approach to the business matrix, in recognition of the fact that ". . . the outlook for a business was based on more than market share and market growth."[6] Consequently, Borg-Warner adopted a nine-cell matrix and expanded the concepts of market growth and market share. Market growth was expanded into a concept called *market attractiveness,* which included such factors as "cyclicality . . . competitive intensity . . . (and) availability of raw materials."[7] Market share was expanded into a concept called *business strengths,* which included product quality, product differentiation,

[3] Borg-Warner 1972 Annual Report.
[4] Speech by Dr. D. W. Collier at the Strategic Planning Conference, New York, October 4–5, 1978. (Sponsored by *Business Week.*)

[5] *Ibid.*
[6] *Ibid.*
[7] *Ibid.*

Exhibit 1
BORG-WARNER—1975 VERSION OF THE
BUSINESS MATRIX

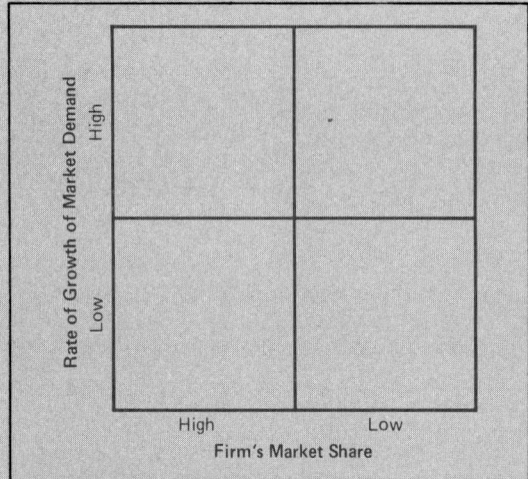

Exhibit 2
BORG-WARNER—1976 VERSION OF THE
BUSINESS MATRIX

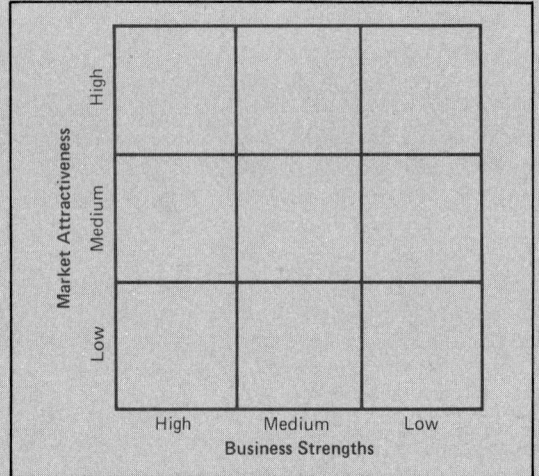

management depth, and other factors.[8] The resultant matrix is shown in Exhibit 2.

Closely related to the decision to use a nine-cell matrix in 1976 was the decision to "move to a *Strategic Business Unit* approach in order to facilitate a more sophisticated analysis of business attractiveness ... and to provide ... an organization and plan to which resources could be allocated and portfolio management concepts applied."[9] In 1975 capital allocations had been made on a group basis. In 1976 the group basis was still used, but the attractiveness of strategic business units within each group partially determined how much capital the corporation allocated to each group. In 1977 capital allocations were made directly to each strategic business unit.[10]

The strategic planning concepts were used to establish a new five-year plan for the period 1975–1979. This plan placed the emphasis on establishing an optimum business mix in order to maximize return on investment. Higher profit margins were given top priority and were to be supported by allocating capital to strategic business units that promised the highest margins. Also em-

phasized were (1) a search for new businesses that could be developed either through research and development or through acquisitions[11] and (2) a careful analysis of existing businesses to determine whether or not Borg-Warner should keep them.

Borg-Warner's 1976 Annual Report proudly announced a new planning system with a front cover picture featuring strategic planning and a lengthy inside article explaining the new system. The 1976 Annual Report also summarized the company's goals and methods with the pithy statement that management was ... "determined to beat the median rate on equity for Fortune 500 companies before 1980, essentially by two steps":[12]

—sharpening the efficiency of our present operations;
—changing our business mix, by preferentially growing the more profitable segments of present businesses and by acquisitions in areas of greater promise.

The 1976 Annual Report explained that top

[8] *Ibid.*
[9] *Ibid.*
[10] *Ibid.*

[11] Borg-Warner 1975 Annual Report and Borg-Warner 1976 Annual Report.
[12] Borg-Warner 1976 Annual Report, p. 10.

management had identified a limited number of major issues, called *strategic issues,* which senior management would address. And the report hinted at the fact that sophisticated financial modeling was being used to analyze the company's options.

During the next two years further improvements were made in Borg-Warner's planning system. The data available from the PIMS program[13] was integrated into the planning process and used to help develop strategic business unit plans, and in 1978 a procedure was developed to define the ''invest-

[13] PIMS is a research program originally started by Harvard University and designed to identify the variables that determine profits in a wide variety of markets. Participating corporations provide data and can then ''tap into the data base'' to evaluate their market prospects.

ment in technology'' needed by each strategic business unit.[14] Strategic planning, in short, was an evolving concept at Borg-Warner. But it was firmly established as the corporation's basic approach to planning.

[14] Speech by D. W. Collier, *op. cit.*

Questions

1. Assess the evolution and current status of corporate planning at Borg-Warner.

2. What else could management do to ensure that corporate planning is effective at Borg-Warner?

Case II-2
CHARLESBANK INDUSTRIES: HARRISON TWEED AND BEN HAGEN

Charlesbank Industries, in its third decade now, had come a long way since its beginnings in a pair of rented barns. William Charles, the founder and chief executive, steered the company through good times and bad. When he surrendered operating control of the company, he found an able successor in his son William Charles, Jr. The company continued to prosper under all types of conditions; prospects still looked promising.

The company was now a national corporation. The executive staff included Harrison Tweed, vice-president of Administration and Planning; Ben Hagen, vice-president of the Basic Commodities Group; Al Hyde, vice-president of the Chemical Group; and Al Meier, vice-president of the Industrial Group. The executive staff reported to Charles; divisional managers reported to the executive vice-president.

HARRISON TWEED

Harrison Tweed had joined the company at the invitation of William Charles, Jr. As a condition of

This case was prepared by Professors Hugh M. O'Neill and George S. Odiorne of the University of Massachusetts. Reproduced by permission of the authors, 1983.

accepting the position of company president, Charles had insisted that he be allowed to add some of his own choices to the executive staff. Tweed was his first addition. Tweed and Charles first met in college, where Tweed (an honors student) tutored Charles in some of his most difficult subjects. They parted ways after college when Charles went to work and Tweed pursued an Ivy League law degree. They met again when Tweed's law firm was engaged to handle a labor relations matter for Charles' employer, American Medical Products.

Tweed's keen mind and sharp wit served him well. He earned a national reputation in labor relations. He was an active member of several political groups. He was on the Board of Directors of several major corporations. Charles found that Tweed still served as an excellent tutor; while negotiating for American Medical, Tweed helped Charles solve several major problems. Their shared interest in tennis kept them in contact after Tweed finished his work for American Medical.

Charles scheduled an executive meeting in early April. The agenda for the meeting listed strategic planning as the major topic. A week before the meeting, Hagen called Harrison Tweed. ''Harry, I see we have a meeting scheduled to consider our strategic plans. What do you think I should have ready for this meeting? Our divisions have always thrived on their independence, and I want to keep that independence. Does strategic planning mean I must sacrifice freedom?''

BEN HAGEN

Hagen's career with Charlesbank began when they were both young. He was one of the first specialists to join the company; his training was in agricultural science. In his early years with the company, his educational background triggered resentment among several company officials, but his ideas always helped the company. He recognized the potential for diversifying into other agricultural products; this diversification helped provide stability for the company. Hagen lacked some production and marketing skills, but he was a true technician in the commodities market. He spent much of his time dealing in commodity futures and buying commodities for his division. He left most other operational decisions to his general managers.

Tweed's answer to Hagen's question was a vague one. ''Well, good planning always allows flexibility. Good planning also requires honest communications from the divisional level. So, in that respect, you will still have freedom. However, we can't have one division undercutting the territory of another division. There are many areas that require divisional cooperation. The purpose of this planning is to assure that cooperation. You might spend some time before the meeting analyzing your strengths and weaknesses. You should also prepare some long-range production and sales forecasts.'' Hagen thanked Tweed for his help.

Hagen did not have the time, nor the desire, to prepare for the strategic planning session. The Chicago commodity product markets were about to enter their busiest season, and Hagen was anxious to enter the wheeling and dealing contests. He always suspected that other vice-presidents resented his success at trading; his success had led to attractive bonuses annually. He suspected that Tweed had instigated the planning meeting to improve his own standing in the company. Hagen resented Tweed's smooth style. Like others who had been with Charlesbank for a long time, Hagen

felt that Tweed did not understand the unique history of Charlesbank.

STRATEGIC PLANNING WITHIN HAGEN'S DIVISIONS

Regardless of his suspicions, Hagen was not about to ignore a request that originated in the chief executive's office. He decided to ask his general managers in the three top divisions to prepare the strategic plan.

The general managers of the soybean, flour products, and animal feeds divisions arrived in Minneapolis the next morning. Joan Pittman, Arthur Oates, and Jack Fowler were Hagen's most successful general managers. They had worked as a team before. They possessed the production and marketing skills that Hagen lacked.

They had little trouble preparing sales forecasts for their own divisions. Their divisions in past years had increased sales by an average of 10 percent; they predicted an increase of another 10 percent in each of the coming years. The past performance of other divisions did not match their own. After calling the general managers of these divisions, they forecast increases ranging from 2 to 5 percent for them.

The analysis of strengths and weaknesses was not so easy. They each insisted that there were no important weaknesses in their own divisions. ''We have kept costs down, we have increased sales, and we have developed new products in the soybean division,'' Pittman said. ''I cannot see any weaknesses in that.''' Oates and Fowler echoed these sentiments regarding their own divisions. After some discussion of these issues, Fowler suggested that they list their own divisions (and one or two others) as the strengths of the corporate group, and the poor performing divisions as the corporate weaknesses. Oates agreed: ''Let's get some facts and figures to back this up; then we can get back to our real work.''

Hagen reviewed their report the night before the executive meeting. The facts, figures, and charts that the team put together were impressive. Hagen memorized the most important details and went to sleep confident.

THE STRATEGIC PLANNING MEETING

Charles briefly addressed the executives before the meeting. He thanked them for coming and hinted that he hoped their preparation was adequate. He indicated that he would not take an active part in the meeting. He asked Tweed to chair the meeting.

Tweed turned to Hagen, and asked for his presentation. Hagen posted his charts and began with the sales forecasts. Before he finished, Tweed interrupted him. "What are these forecasts based on?" "Past performance," Hagen replied. "You mean you expect your poor divisions to replicate their bad performance? What will you do to bring them up to par?" Tweed retorted. Hagen began to shape a reply, but Tweed continued. "Didn't some of your good divisions benefit from foreign sales that are not likely to continue? Didn't some of these divisions recently expand to national markets, which supplied their growth? How can you expect these trends to continue?" Hagen shouted, "You asked for forecasts; these are forecasts. No forecast is perfect. Let me finish!" Tweed seemed nonplused and shocked at the outburst, and the others were still and obviously shocked at the display of anger. Tweed attempted to soothe things over. "After all, I just asked questions; I didn't criticize." "Questions hell, you are giving me the third degree like a lawyer grilling a witness. I am not a defendant here, and this isn't a courtroom."

At this point Charles spoke out, "Harry, why not let Hagen finish his presentation, then we can all question him."

Hagen continued with his analysis of strengths and weaknesses. He talked of the successes of his best general managers. He mentioned several new general managers he had hired in the past two years who had gone elsewhere in the corporation and who might turn their divisions around. Although his notes did not mention his successful commodities trading, he gave a quick summary of his past outstanding record.

As he finished, Tweed spoke, "I believe that I can now ask questions. What is your manpower planning? If divisions are increasing sales, should you be adding workers? Should you be cutting back in other areas? What are your union problems? You know the affirmative action laws are

getting tougher. Why is it I have never noticed minorities in your divisions? What are you doing to recruit them? And what about OSHA? You know there has been a lot of press about the dangers of grain dust. Have you been inspected? Will you be? Do your divisions meet OSHA standards? What about developing new plans and markets? Do you expect to succeed by standing still? How come all the other divisions develop more new products than yours?"

Hagen was torn between embarrassment and anger. Anger won out. "Who the hell do you think you're talking to? You were barely out of diapers when I was developing the new products for this company. Your position would not even exist if I didn't out-hustle every trader in Chicago to get us new raw materials. My division built Charlesbank; its record stands for itself. I won't stand here and listen to your abuse."

Tweed responded quickly. He was obviously rattled by the counterattack and dropped his previous interrogatory style. "I won't argue with past history. But past history won't pay tomorrow's dividends. Good traders are a dime a dozen today. What we need are good vice-presidents. How could you prepare a strategic plan when you were off on a junket to Chicago? If you have the nerve to waste my time with this type of speculative nonsense, I'll talk to you any way I want."

Charles again interrupted. "Let's take a few minutes to review Hagen's facts and figures. Meanwhile, we can get some coffee and cool down."

Hagen left the room, followed by Hyde, another senior vice-president. They encountered each other in the executive lounge. "You know, I have not liked Tweed since he got here. Who needs a Philadelphia lawyer? He knows nothing about business. Why should I put up with that type of cross-examination? Who is he to check up on me and criticize where I've been? Old man Charles was a terror, but only when things went bad. You could handle old man Charles. This guy is impossible."

Hyde agreed. "I'm with you. I think Charles, Jr., is using Tweed as his hatchet man. I suspect that he resents all the old-timers. But the ball is in his court. We have to play his game now. And you don't have much time to get ready. Perhaps you should take your licking and be prepared the next time.''

"I don't know what I'll do. If they are ready to get started, stall for a few minutes. I need time to calm down and think. I'm tempted to call Charles, Sr., and invite him to this meeting. I think he would like to know what's going on. I'll see you in a few minutes.''

Questions

1. How should Hagen respond to Tweed when the meeting continues?

2. What role should William Charles, Jr., play in this discussion?

3. Discuss the implementation of strategic planning at Charlesbank Industries.

Part III
ORGANIZING

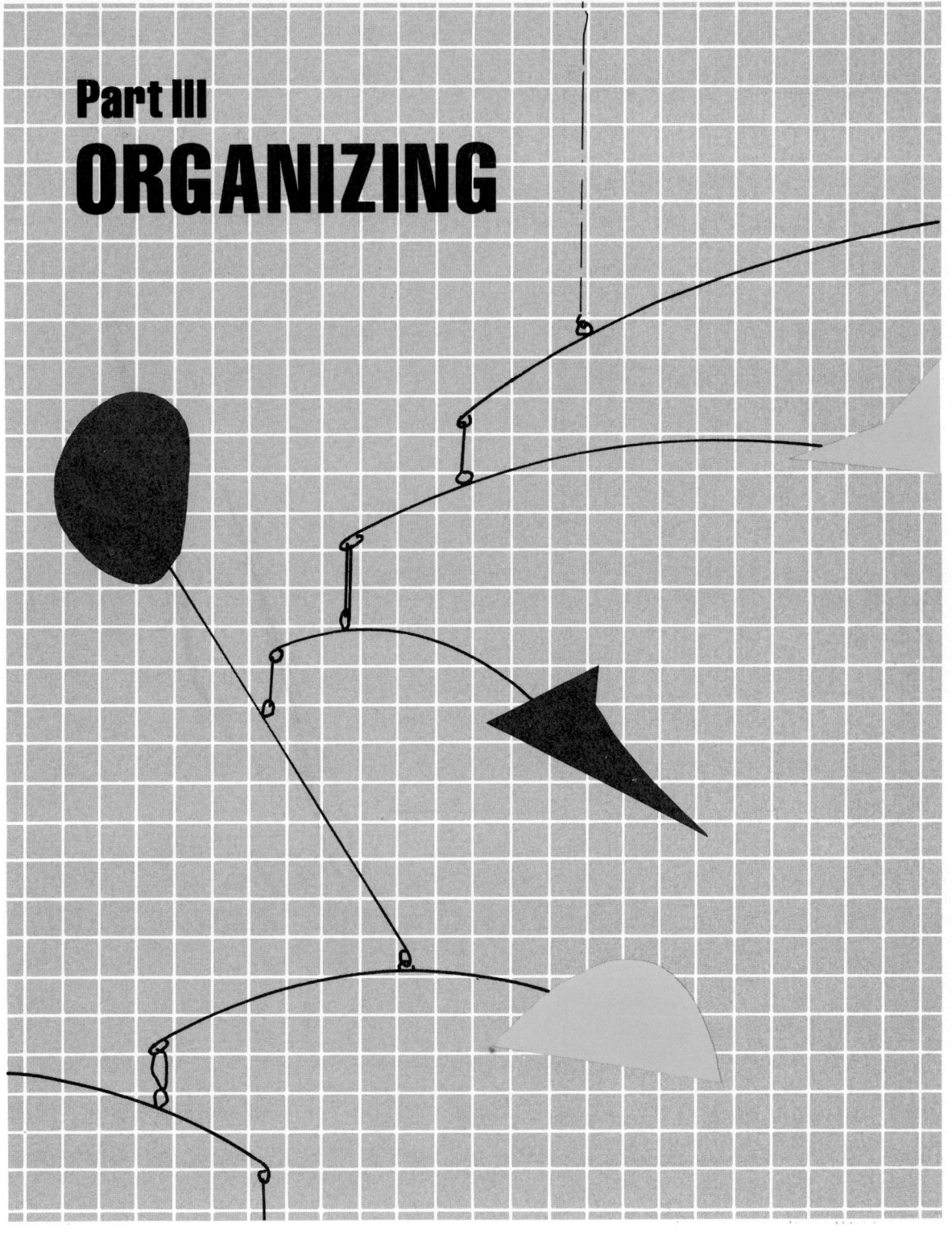

9. The Organizing Process

Learning Objectives

AFTER STUDYING THIS CHAPTER YOU SHOULD BE ABLE TO

1. Describe the five bases for departmentalization within an organization.
2. List the factors involved in determining the optimum span of management.
3. Differentiate between tall and flat organizational structures.
4. Explain the advantages and disadvantages of decentralization.
5. Identify and explain the three types of authority that exist within an organization.
6. List the three historical periods of organizational design and the contributions of each.
7. Explain the matrix approach to organization.

Key Terms

organizing

specialization

departmentalization

unity-of-command concept

span-of-management concept

organization chart

exception principle

authority

responsibility

delegation

accountability

scalar principle

office of the chief executive

matrix organization

flexitime

compressed work week

job sharing

The executive's chief business is to organize, deputize, and supervise.

GEORGE RIPLEY

Everyone's responsibility is no one's responsibility.

ANONYMOUS

I have built my organization upon fear.

AL CAPONE

t is easily the most massive building ever built on earth. Its height equals one and one-half football fields, while its square base covers more than thirteen acres. The most incredible fact about the Great Pyramid is that it was built more than 4,600 years ago by men who had neither machinery nor iron tools. The two million stone blocks that made up the planned resting place of the pharaoh whom the Greeks called Cheops sometimes weighed more than fifty tons each. Some were moved from nearby quarries; others were transported by boat from southern quarries down the Nile. The stones, cut with copper chisels and saws, were so finely cut that the joints measured less than one-fiftieth of an inch in thickness.[1] The building's outer casing of white polished limestone was laid so smoothly that the Great Pyramid appeared to have been cut from a single stone. Not surprisingly, some observers have speculated that such a marvel of architectural perfection must have been constructed by extraterrestrial beings.

Construction of the Great Pyramid required immense organizational skills. Several thousand skilled workers were employed for more than twenty years on the project. Unskilled workers added their services when Nile floods made farming impossible. Numerous specialties were required: surveyors, quarry workers, toolmakers, overseers, priests, engineers, and scribes. Teams of peasants dragged the stones from the quarries or boats to the building site. Ramps were used to drag the stones to the next layer. Some men specialized in pouring milk under the sledges to lubricate the runners and move the stones upward. The rewards for service to the organization were wages paid in bread, onions, meat, salt, and beer. The pride of the workers is reflected in the graffiti found on many of the pyramid blocks. The names of the work gangs are proudly listed: Boat Gang, Enduring Gang, Sceptre Gang.[2] The results of this effort of organizing human and other resources—one of humanity's most spectacular achievements—are

[1] Peter Lemesurier, *The Great Pyramid Decoded* (New York: St. Martin's Press, 1977), pp. 3–5.
[2] Rafael Steinberg, *Man and the Organization* (New York: Time-Life Books, 1975), pp. 13–14.

even more impressive when one remembers that the construction dates from the very edges of prehistory.

Managers and the Organization

All managers make decisions on matters involving their department, division, section, team, plant, or whatever their units are called. In a sense each manager is head of his or her own organization. In many cases people in these departments behave as if they were existing in a completely autonomous organization—in their own world. But the manager is ever aware of the larger structure of which his or her unit is a part.

Since each unit affects and is affected by the total organization, each manager should recognize the major impact of the organization on decisions; these decisions are judged not only by their immediate results in the department but also by the effect on the larger organization.

A manager whose decision-making style is to make most decisions and rely upon subordinates to implement them may cause numerous problems in an organization characterized by heavy involvement of employees in the decision-making process. The organization may encounter difficulty in transferring or promoting subordinates from this department due to their lack of decision-making experience.

FROM STRATEGY TO STRUCTURE

Chapters 4–8 focused upon the crucial process of organizational planning. Planning involves the establishment of objectives and determination of the methods needed to accomplish them. These strategies for achieving goals are the starting point in creating the necessary organizational structure. Investigations of such major firms as Du Pont, Sears, General Motors, and Standard Oil Company of New Jersey have confirmed that strategy is a prerequisite for structure.[3] Knowledge of organizational objectives and strategies serves as the basis for blending human and other resources.

What Is Organizing?

Organizing is the second fundamental function of management. It can be defined as the act of planning and implementing organization structure. It is the process of arranging people and physical resources to carry out plans and accomplish organizational objectives.

The organizing process (the verb) results in the creation of a formal organization structure (the noun). The organization is characterized by explicit objectives, an elaborate system of rules and regulations, and a formal status structure

[3] Alfred D. Chandler, Jr., *Strategy and Structure* (New York: Doubleday, 1966).

with clearly marked lines of communication and authority.[4] All of these characteristics assist—and restrain—managers in handling their organizational units.

Division of Work

Organizational activities for small businesses are relatively simple. The owner–manager of a small print shop employs a few workers to operate the presses and copiers, make deliveries, perform routine maintenance, and meet customers who require printing services. Although accounting and tax services are typically provided by an independent accountant, the owner is usually directly involved in making work assignments, placing orders for paper and chemicals, and directing the operation of the business.

As the size of the organization grows, the need for structuring activities increases. The print shop may have one person responsible for typesetting and operating the presses; a giant printing operation such as Kingsport Press may employ dozens of specialists for three separate work shifts.

Increased organization size and a larger number of employees permit *specialization* or *division of labor:* concentration on one or on a small number of activities. By concentrating on a specific activity, people can become more efficient by learning how best to perform that activity and by developing their skills to the utmost.

> **Specialization** is the concentration on one or on a small number of activities in order to increase efficiency.

The benefits of specialization can be found throughout recorded history. Plato summarized the benefits of specialization or the division of labor in *The Republic:*

> Which would be better—that each should ply several trades, or that he should confine himself to his own? He should confine himself to his own. More is done, and done better and more easily when one man does one thing according to his capacity and at the right moment. We must not be surprised to find that articles are made better in big cities than in small. In small cities the same workman makes a bed, a door, a plough, a table, and often he builds a house too. . . . Now it is impossible that a workman who does so many things should be equally successful in all. In the big cities, on the other hand . . . a man can live by a single trade. One makes men's shoes, another women's, one lives entirely by the stitching of the shoe, another by cutting the leather. . . . A man whose work is confined to such a limited task must necessarily excel at it.[5]

DEPARTMENTALIZATION

Departmentalization is the subdividing of activities and responsibility areas into units within the organization. This process permits the organization to realize

> **Departmentalization** is the subdividing of activities and responsibility areas into units within the organization.

[4] See Peter M. Blau and W. Richard Scott, *Formal Organizations* (San Francisco: Chandler, 1962), pp. 5, 14.
[5] Francis Cornford, *The Republic of Plato* (New York: Oxford University Press, 1959), pp. 165–167.

the benefits of specialization and to coordinate the activites of the component parts. Profit-seeking firms may be broadly divided into production, marketing, and finance units. Major service responsibility areas include legal, personnel, and electronic data processing. Further subdividing of an area such as marketing may produce departments responsible for advertising, marketing research, customer relations, and sales.

BASES FOR DEPARTMENTALIZATION

Five primary bases for departmentalization exist: function, geography, product, customer, and process. *Function* refers to the various responsibility areas of an organizational component. The human resources department typically handles recruitment, management development and training, compensation, employee benefits, health and safety, and industrial relations. *Geographic* departmentalization is an organizational division based upon location. Such major firms as Ford Motor Co., H. J. Heinz, and IBM have both domestic and international divisions. The Bell Telephone System also utilizes this basis for departmentalization.

Departmentalization on the basis of *product* is common in large multiproduct organizations. The basic structure of General Motors Corp. consists of the Chevrolet, Oldsmobile, Buick, Pontiac, Cadillac, and GMC Truck & Coach divisions. IBM Corp. has an office products division and a data processing division. The office products division is responsible for IBM's line of typewriters, supplies, and other office equipment; the data processing division is responsible for sales and service of the firm's computer-related products.

A fourth basis for departmentalization is *customer.* A large publisher such as Random House contains a college division, a juvenile division, and a trade division. Banks often have specialized departments handling commercial accounts. A food service firm such as the International Multifoods may have different divisions for college and university food service, airlines, and hospitals.

A final major basis for departmentalization is *process.* A cabinet-making operation may involve cutting wood, heat-treating it, painting it, and installing hinges and handles. Each step in the process of converting the wood, paint, and other materials into a finished cabinet may be assigned to a group of specialists.

As the above discussion illustrates, the choice of the most appropriate basis for departmentalization depends upon the specific characteristics of the organization. In fact a number of different bases are often utilized in the same organization. Figure 9-1 is an example of how several bases may be efficiently utilized.

THE UNITY-OF-COMMAND CONCEPT

The **unity-of-command concept** states that each organizational member should report to only one supervisor for any single function.

Figure 9-1 illustrates a classical concept of organization: *unity of command.* This principle states that each organizational member should report to only one supervisor for any single function. It is based upon the truism that employees work most efficiently when they receive orders, advice, and recommendations from a single boss. When several persons are giving orders, the potential for

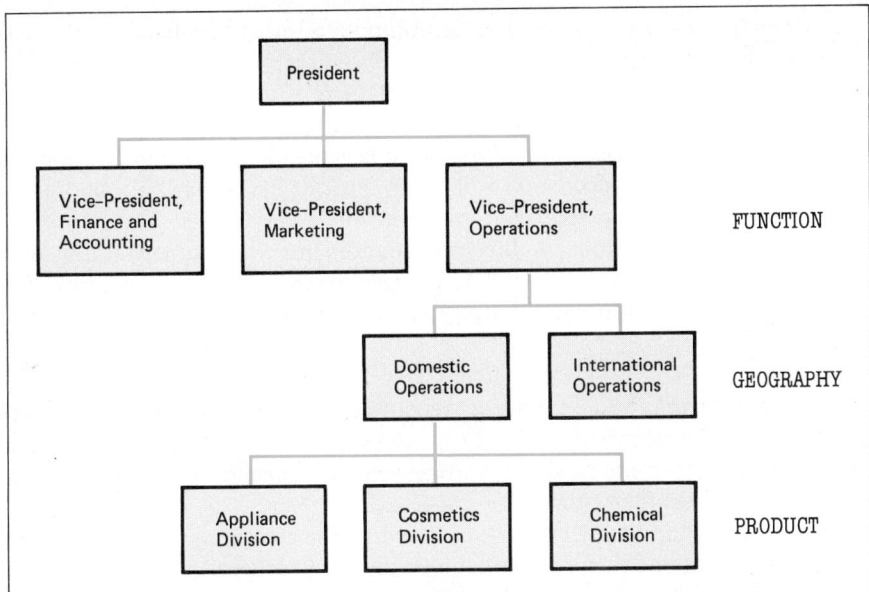

**Figure 9-1
AN ORGANIZATION
USING SEVERAL
BASES FOR
DEPARTMENTALIZA-
TION**

conflict, divided loyalties, and confusion exists. Adherents of this organizational principle compare its violation to the dilemma of a driver receiving instructions from one passenger to turn right at the next intersection while the second passenger insists upon a left turn.

Although the unity-of-command principle is a widely accepted management axiom, it is frequently violated in complex organizations where personnel specialists, safety engineers, quality control personnel, and the immediate superior are all interested in aspects of the individual's performance. A critical problem in organizational design is the recognition of situations in which this principle *must* be violated. In such instances it is critical to ensure that conflict does not arise due to instructions issued by several sources for the same function. Organizational designers must tackle the problem of coordination by reducing the likelihood of possible conflicts in such instances. In general the closer an organizational structure follows the principle of unity of command, the less likely are instances of such conflict.

THE SPAN-OF-MANAGEMENT CONCEPT

"No man can command more than five distinct bodies in the same theatre of war." This was Napoleon's conclusion in regard to the organizational question that management writers later labeled the *span of management*.[6] The span of

---

[6] Quoted in David D. Van Fleet and Arthur G. Bedeian, "A History of the Span of Management," *Academy of Management Review* (July 1977), p. 358. The term "span of management" was coined by Harold Koontz and Cyril O'Donnell in their book *Principles of Management* (New York: McGraw-Hill, 1964).

Span-of-management concept refers to the optimum number of subordinates a person can effectively manage.

management (or span of control) is the optimum number of subordinates a person can effectively manage.

Although there is general agreement that there is a limit to the number of subordinates a superior can effectively supervise, manage, or control, no agreement exists on the precise number. In fact it is generally recognized that the optimum span of management will vary greatly, even within the same organization. While top managers may directly supervise only three to eight persons, supervisory managers directing subordinates who are performing relatively routine activities may be able to manage much larger numbers efficiently.

The critical factors in determining the appropriate span of management include the following:

1. *Type of work.* Simple, routine, repetitive work activities permit a greater span of management.
2. *Ability of the manager.* Some managers are capable of managing more subordinates than others.
3. *Degree of interdependence among units.* The greater the need for coordination of interdependent work units, the smaller the span of management.
4. *Training of subordinates.* Highly trained workers require less direction and control. Experienced subordinate managers are capable of performing their functions with less continued direction and advice than less experienced persons. In such cases a greater span of management is possible.

THE ORGANIZATION CHART

An organization chart is a blueprint of the organization, indicating lines of authority within it.

A common method of documenting organizational relationships is in the form of an *organization chart.* This document is a blueprint of the organization, indicating lines of authority within it. It is a simplified representation of the various positions in the organization, identifying their basic functions and the person or department to which each individual reports. The organization chart for General Motors Corp. is shown in Figure 9-2. GM's organization is noteworthy for several reasons. First, it depicts authority–responsibility relationships of one of the largest organizations in the entire world. Second, it reflects the strong use of committees at top management levels. Finally, it reveals the use of several bases of departmentalization by the auto giant. Both geographic and product departmentalization are extensively used at different levels in the GM organization.

TALL VERSUS FLAT ORGANIZATIONAL STRUCTURES

The General Motors organization chart indicates a number of different levels in the organization. This results from the size and complexity of this industrial giant. Span of management is another important factor in determining the number of required organizational levels. Structures characterized by narrow spans tend to have a greater number of different levels than those with broader spans.

A landmark analysis of the impact of design on performance and morale was conducted by James Worthy at Sears, Roebuck & Co. Sears executives decided to "flatten" their organizational structure by eliminating a layer of managers be-

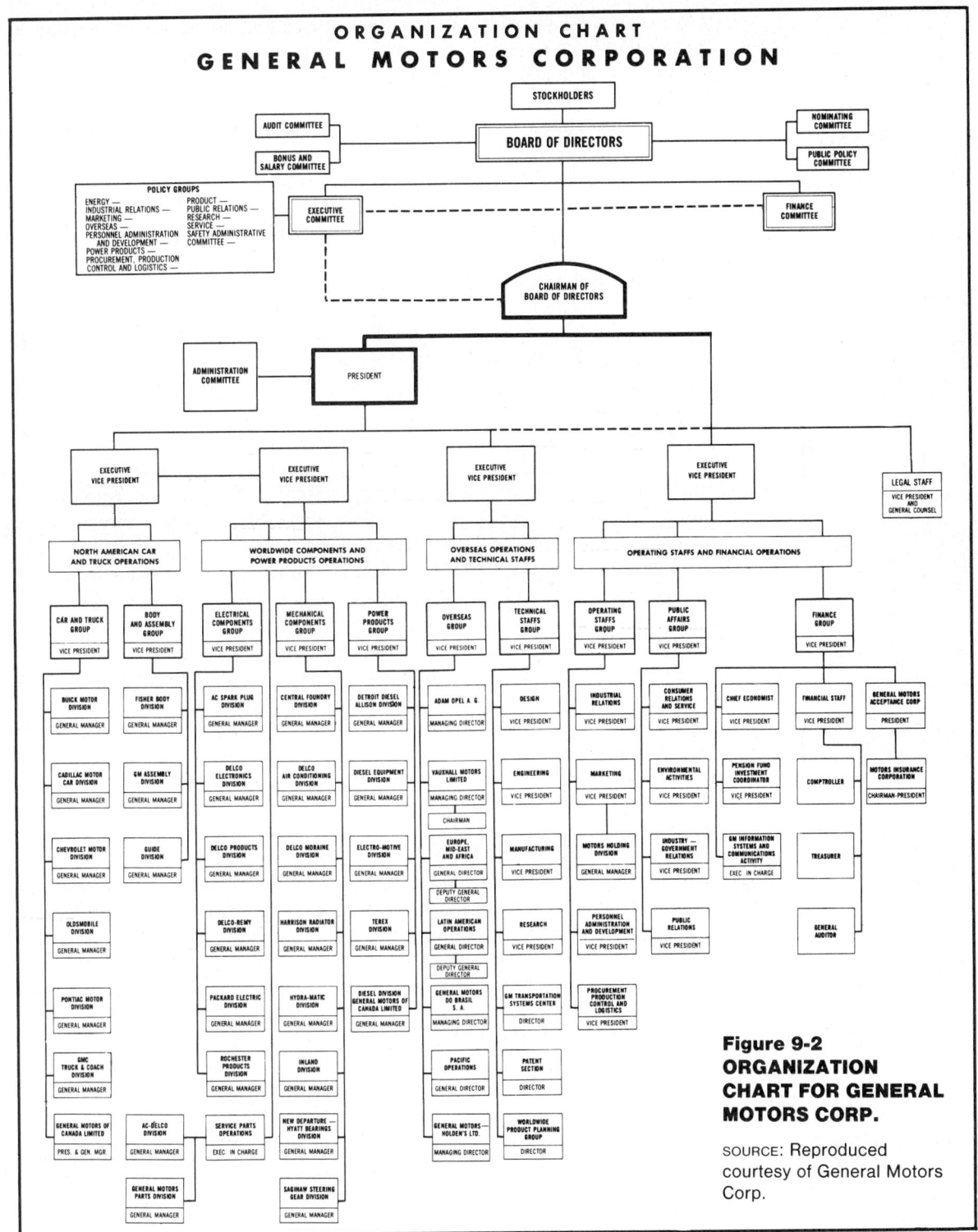

Figure 9-2
ORGANIZATION CHART FOR GENERAL MOTORS CORP.

SOURCE: Reproduced courtesy of General Motors Corp.

tween each store manager and the various department managers in the store. Although problems were expected to occur as a result of increasing the span of management in many areas, the new design proved superior—in terms of profit, sales volume, morale, and improved communications. Store managers gave each department manager more authority; subordinates were forced to handle more managerial tasks and both morale and performance improved; subordinates were both hired and trained more selectively due to their increased importance; and paperwork was streamlined to save time.[7]

Subsequent investigations have also reported that people are more satisfied in flat organizations since such structures tend to produce greater autonomy, responsibility, and initiative.[8]

Concepts of Coordination

The previous section stressed the benefits of specialization. The focus on departmentalization and the discussion of optimum spans of management were designed to permit the organization to be structured at maximum efficiency. However, departmentalization also creates potential conflicts since formal structuring of work units may reduce the number of physical contacts between group members and coordination may become a major problem.

Managers possess a number of techniques for improving coordination among the individuals and departments within the organization. Management by objectives programs, discussed in Chapter 4, are frequently utilized to improve coordination in addition to the other purposes discussed earlier. Since the program involves the establishment of goals by managers, each superior is involved in this process with his or her subordinates. The effect is to align individual and departmental goals with overall organizational goals. Individual activities must fit like puzzle parts into accomplishing larger projects. Day-to-day activities should mesh—not clash—with month-to-month and yearly programs.

THE LINKING PIN THEORY

Rensis Likert proposed the linking pin theory as an explanation of how departments are connected in the organization.[9] He views managers as links between the groups they manage and the higher group to which they report. As Figure 9-3 shows, this view of the groups as overlapping as a result of the manager being a link between more than one group should reduce tendencies of the individual department to develop autonomously, since its manager is simultaneously a link to the department at the next level.

---

[7] James C. Worthy, "Organization Structure and Employee Morale," *American Sociological Review* (April 1950), pp. 169–179.

[8] See Edwin E. Ghiselli and Jacob Siegel, "Leadership and Managerial Success in Tall and Flat Organization Structures," *Personnel Psychology* (Winter 1972), pp. 617–624; and Lyman Porter and Edward Lawler, "The Effects of Flat and Tall Organization Structures on Managerial Job Satisfaction," *Personnel Psychology* 17 (1964), pp. 135–148.

[9] See Rensis Likert, *New Patterns of Management* (New York: McGraw-Hill, 1961).

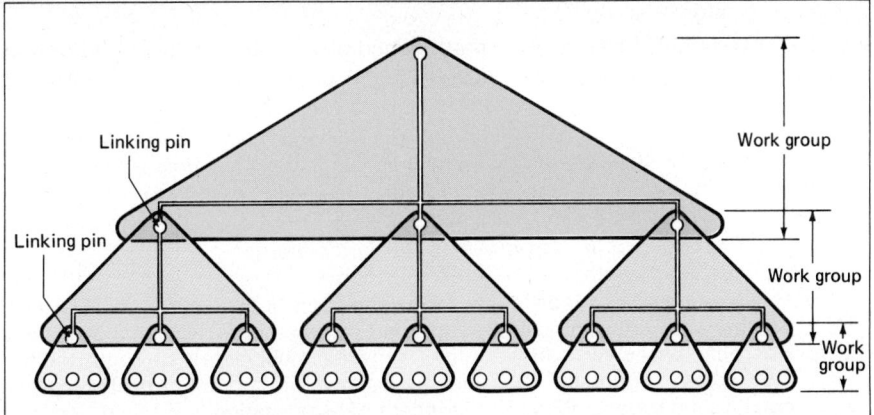

Linking pin

Linking pin

Work group

Work group

Work group

Figure 9-3
THE LINKING PIN
CONCEPT

SOURCE: Rensis Likert, *New Patterns of Management* (New York: McGraw-Hill, 1961), p. 104. Used with permission of McGraw-Hill Book Co.

Managers with overlapping group memberships link their groups to the total organization. By fulfilling this role, they are able to integrate the efforts of the two groups.

Authority Relationships

Top management at Trans-World Airlines were directly affected by a recent earnings deficit. In fact the deficit caused TWA president Ed Meyer to suffer a $32,250 salary cut. Meyer ordered salary reductions of 10 to 25 percent for 800 TWA managers earning more than $35,000 and included his own salary in the order. Although he vowed to restore the executive salaries to their former levels and to return the amounts withheld when specified performance standards were attained, this drastic measure was effective in communicating the importance of managers in the organization's success—or failure. And the pay cuts represented a painful indication of their responsibility in the firm's financial fate.[10] As Harry Truman was fond of saying, "The buck stops here."

Critical to the success of the organization is the development, coordination, and communication of the authority relationships that exist at each level. These relationships are determined by such concepts as the exception principle, delegation of authority, the scalar principle, and consideration of centralization versus decentralization.

THE EXCEPTION PRINCIPLE

Closely related to the concept of specialization is the *exception principle*. This principle states that managers should permit their subordinates to make routine recurring decisions and that only unusual or highly important problems and decisions should be referred to higher levels in the organization. As emphasized in

Exception principle states that managers should permit their subordinates to make routine, recurring decisions, and that only unusual or highly important problems should be referred to higher levels in the organization.

[10] William M. Carley, "TWA Will Slash Salaries of Management Up to 25% of Amounts Exceeding $35,000," *Wall Street Journal* (February 1, 1980), p. 8.

Early in his career, Chester I. Barnard gained a reputation in the world of management for his great organizational abilities. A pragmatist as well as a theorist, Barnard expounded his management philosophy in two books: *The Functions of the Executive* (1938) and *Organization and Management* (1948). In the latter book, Barnard discusses his basic conception of an organization—a conception he claimed was useful not only for theoretical analysis but also for practical application. The focus is on the organization as a *group of coordinated activities* rather than as a *group of individuals.* In Barnard's words:

> The relationship of individuals to organization is frequently so ephemeral that they are not conveniently regarded as "members" of an organization, whereas in my view, certain of their activities must clearly be regarded as a part of the "organized" activities associated with and, as I prefer to think, constituting organization. This concept of organization is a "field" concept in which activities take place in and are governed by a field of "forces," some human and social, some physical.

Born in Malden, Massachusetts, in 1886, Barnard began to work at an early age. By working as a school janitor, he paid his own way at Mt. Hermon Preparatory School, an institution combining its academic curriculum with a daily work program. He won a scholarship to Harvard and earned extra money as a piano tuner and leader of a dance band. An excellent as well as an independent student, Barnard attended Harvard for three years but failed to earn a degree because of his refusal to take a required laboratory science course. He had passed the lecture session with honors and argued unsuccessfully against the university rules.

After leaving Harvard he went to work with American Telephone and Telegraph (AT&T) as a foreign language translator in the Boston office. A European assignment to study telephone company organization led to exhaustive analyses that won him recognition as an expert on telephone commercial practice and the economics of rate structures. Barnard's talents were soon recognized and he rose quickly through the Bell System ranks. In 1927, at the age of 40, he became

---

Authority is the legitimate power a manager possesses to act and make decisions in carrying out responsibilities.

Responsibility is the obligation of the manager to carry out assigned duties.

Delegation is the assignment of authority and responsibility to subordinates.

the discussion of time management in Chapter 5, managers should devote their limited time to handling more difficult or fundamental issues and rely upon subordinates for more routine matters.

THE DELEGATION OF AUTHORITY

Authority can be defined as the legitimate power a manager possesses to act and make decisions in carrying out responsibilities. *Responsibility* is the obligation of the manager to carry out assigned duties. Lower-level managers possess authority through the process of *delegation*—the assignment of authority and responsibility to subordinates. The manager who delegates specific assignments to subordinates must also provide the necessary authority to accomplish them.

The third basic concept is *accountability:* the act of holding the subordinate liable for performing those activities for which he or she has been delegated the

president of the newly formed New Jersey Bell Telephone Company, a position he held until his retirement in 1952.

It was not within the context of the AT&T organization, however, that Barnard met what he called "the most difficult single organization and management in my experience." His years at the helm of the United Service for National Defense Organization (USO) provided that challenge. As USO president from 1942 to 1945, he was confronted with the problem of developing and managing USO units around the world. He applied his organizational theories with overwhelming success, expanding the number of units from just under 700 to almost 3,000. In addition, he established the National USO Council, regional offices, and a centralized accounting system in order to provide better coordination of the massive organization.

Barnard's classic *The Functions of the Executive* was published in 1938. In his book he viewed organization as a "system of cooperation" in which authority was accepted by subordinates on the basis of choice rather than an imposition placed on them by executives. As a result communication becomes a critical ingredient for management.

> The coordination of efforts essential to a system of cooperation requires an organized system of communication. Such a system of communication implies centers or points of interconnection and can only operate as these centers are occupied by persons who are called executives. It might be said that the function of executives is to serve as channels of communications.
>
> A person can and will accept a communication as authoritative only when four conditions simultaneously obtain: (a) he can and does understand the communication; (b) *at the time of his decision,* he believes that it is not inconsistent with the purpose of the organization; (c) *at the time of his decision,* he believes it to be compatible with his personal interest as a whole; and (d) he is able mentally and physically to comply with it.

Barnard died in 1961, leaving behind an incredible record of professional and humanitarian accomplishments.

Sources

Chester I. Barnard, *The Functions of the Executive* (Cambridge, Mass.: Harvard University Press, 1938).

Chester I. Barnard, *Organization and Management* (Cambridge, Mass.: Harvard University Press, 1948).

Current Biography: Who's News and Why, s.v. "Barnard, Chester I(rving)."

The National Cyclopaedia of American Biography, Vol. 46, s.v. "Barnard, Chester Irving."

necessary authority and responsibility. It is the process by which the manager justifies the use of resources for which he or she was responsible in carrying out delegated activities.

THE SCALAR PRINCIPLE

Effective delegation is effected by a fundamental organizational principle known as the *scalar principle.* This concept states that authority and responsibility should flow in a clear, unbroken line from top management to supervisory levels. Lines of authority should be clearly defined. In order to develop clear linkings to the chief executive officer, General Electric has created several sector executive positions. These top managers are responsible for a group of GE operations with a specific industry identity. Sector executives delegate the necessary authority and responsibility to subordinates in their areas and are accountable to the office

Accountability is the act of holding the subordinate liable for performing those activities for which he or she has been delegated the necessary authority and responsibility.

Scalar principle states that authority and responsibility should flow in a clear, unbroken line from top management to supervisory levels.

of the chief executive. Other large multiproduct firms such as American Can and W. R. Grace have adopted this concept.[11]

CENTRALIZATION VERSUS DECENTRALIZATION

Delegation of authority is an individual process between a superior and a subordinate. It is a way of sharing power. But the collective effect of all these individual practices can have a dramatic overall organizational impact. If managers in a firm tend to delegate considerable authority and responsibility, more decisions are shifted to lower levels in the organization. Supervisory and middle managers in such firms possess considerable influence in making major decisions. In these cases where managers disperse considerable amounts of authority to subordinates, the organization is considered to follow a managerial philosophy of *decentralization.*

On the other hand, some managers retain most of the authority, depending upon subordinates to implement assignments. This practice of dispersing little authority is referred to as *centralization.* Such managers feel that they can maintain maximum control and coordination by retaining most of the authority.

The centralization–decentralization issue is a fundamental organizational decision. It is not a simple choice, since both alternatives possess advantages and disadvantages.

Decentralization tends to encourage innovation and experimentation. General Motors Corp. grants considerable authority to each of its divisions on the theory that independent approaches may result in ideas that can then be shared by other divisions. The decision by Alfred P. Sloan to decentralize GM in 1921 is considered to be the first large-scale use of this approach.[12]

Firms utilizing decentralization provide middle and supervisory level managers with more decision-making experience than their counterparts in firms with a centralized management philosophy. This experience means that a talent pool is being created for later promotions. Of course these fledgling managers often make mistakes, a price centralized companies do not have to pay.

As in many decisions, the centralization–decentralization issue depends upon the interplay of many factors in each organization. Lawrence and Lorsch discovered that successful companies in stable industries, such as cardboard container manufacturing, typically utilize centralized authority. But in more dynamic industries, such as plastics, decentralization has proved more profitable.[13]

[11] "GE's New Billion-Dollar Small Businesses," *Business Week* (December 19, 1977), pp. 25–26. For a discussion of the current use of delegation, see Bonnie J. Gray and Robert K. Landrum, "Are You Ready for Tomorrow's Management Style?" *Business* (November–December 1979), pp. 32–38.

[12] The evolution of the decentralization issue is explained in Ernest Dale's classic article, "Centralization Versus Decentralization," *Advanced Management* (June 1955), pp. 11–16.

[13] Paul R. Lawrence and Jay W. Lorsch, *Organization and Environment* (Boston: Harvard University, Graduate School of Business Administration, 1967), p. 143.

HOW NOT TO
ORGANIZE THE
WHITE HOUSE

Former President Jimmy Carter was determined that the White House would be organized differently than it had been by his predecessors. Presidents Ford and Nixon had organized the executive branch under a chief of staff who directed and controlled its assorted personnel. The White House chief of staff was in a position to literally control what matters were considered in the Oval Office. H. R. Haldeman was the best known of these aides. Carter, elected as a "Washington outsider," was determined to avoid this organizational arrangement.

The new president opted for what he called a *spokes-of-the-wheel* approach, in which all senior level staff members had direct access to him. Carter felt this concept would "open up" the executive branch by exposing the president to new ideas and differing viewpoints. Instead, he quickly found mountains of details piling up on his desk because of the lack of screening. Some of the president's early decisions concerned issues such as approving all major trips by his staff; identifying which staff personnel could use the White House tennis courts and swimming pool; and shipment of the presidential limousine by truck rather than by air at a saving of $1,000.

Carter's concern for detail led to indecision on the part of some staff, who continued to flood the Oval Office with new memos generated in accordance with the spokes-of-the-wheel approach. Finally, in 1979, Carter had had enough and appointed Hamilton Jordan as White House chief of staff.

Carter's successor, Ronald Reagan, also chose the chief of staff approach.

CHIEF EXECUTIVE OFFICERS—TOP OF THE ORGANIZATIONAL STRUCTURE

The chief executive officer (CEO) bears the ultimate accountability for his or her organization's performance. Although the CEO does little of the "work" of the firm, his or her performance may be evaluated in terms of how well others perform.

Chief executive officers represent the top management level in the organization. They typically report to a board of directors made up of organizational officials (including themselves) and persons outside the organization. They direct a number of subordinates who generally hold the position of vice-president. Middle management includes plant managers and department heads who are more involved in specific operations within the organization. Supervisory management, the third level in the management hierarchy, includes the supervisors who are in direct and continuing contact with operative employees in carrying out the plans and assignments developed by middle and top management.

A study by Porter and Ghiselli reported that top managers of business organizations view themselves as the drivers of the organization, whereas middle managers view themselves as the "backbone" of the firm. Top managers tend to view themselves as risk-takers who must make hard decisions when the facts are incomplete or unknown. Middle managers pride themselves on their ability to analyze the data they possess. Middle managers also view themselves as taking action only after cautious deliberation. Top managers see themselves as confident, action-oriented leaders.[14]

It is evident from this study that top managers differ from a middle managers in action and thought. However, they must coordinate the activities of these subordinates. They encourage cooperation by setting the tone of the organization. Much of the CEO's job is to communicate to subordinates the fact that they work for the entire organization and that each subordinate manager has an obligation to cooperate and work for the benefit of all.

THE OFFICE OF THE CHIEF EXECUTIVE

Office of the chief executive is an approach to top management that involves the use of several executives who share the responsibilities for directing the firm.

One of the latest authority relationships to be established in a number of organizations is the *office of the chief executive*. This organizational concept involves the utilization of several executives who share the responsibilities involved in directing a firm. Such a format has been used by such diverse firms as Ford, RCA, Bendix, TWA, and Aetna.

Although this unorthodox approach to filling the office of the chief executive is a clear violation of the unity-of-command principle, it does offer several advantages. A multiple-executive arrangement may be useful in producing a broadened knowledge base and assuring continuity while simultaneously alleviating the pressures of the office and developing a better performance climate.

But as Figure 9-4 shows, the traditional single-executive format produces better accountability, less ambiguity, greater motivation, and more timeliness. Fac-

---

[14] Lyman W. Porter and Edwin E. Ghiselli, "The Self-Perceptions of Top and Middle Management Personnel," *Personnel Psychology* (Winter 1957), pp. 397–406.

**Figure 9-4
COMPARING
MULTIPLE AND
SINGLE TOP
EXECUTIVE
ORGANIZATIONAL
ARRANGEMENTS**

SOURCE: Adapted from Anthony F. Jurkus, "The Multiple Executive Office: Panacea or Selective Cure?" *University of Michigan Business Review* (July 1978), p. 18.

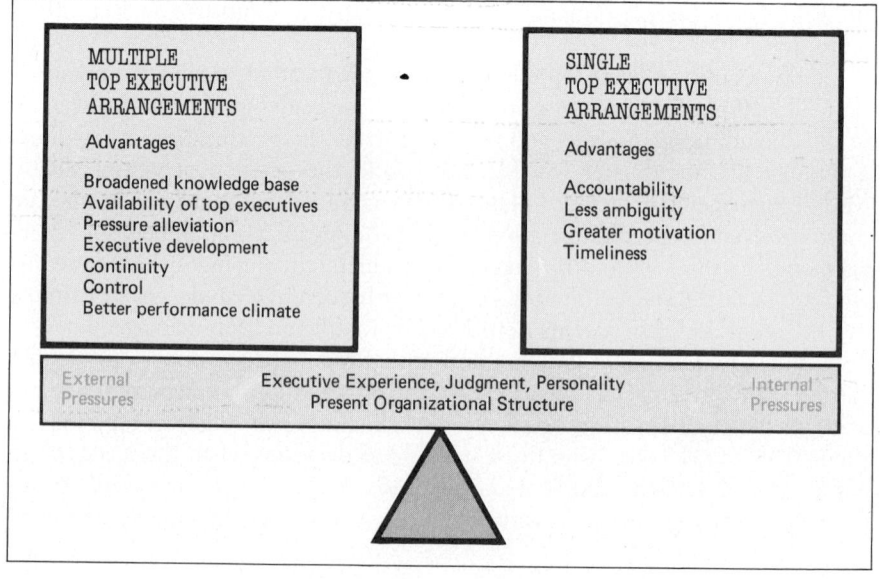

tors affecting choice of the most appropriate arrangement include executive experience, judgment, personality, and present organizational structure. At Ford Motor Co., the office of the chief executive was originally composed of Henry Ford II, Philip Caldwell, and Lee A. Iacocca. The concept was eventually abandoned because of a personality conflict between Ford and Iacocca.[15]

Line and Staff Relationships

Three types of authority exist in the organization:

1. *Line authority* is the relationship existing between a superior and a subordinate in an organization. The head of the purchasing department possesses the legitimate power of his or her office to direct the actions of subordinates in the department. Line authority flows are simple and direct. They relate specifically to the unity-of-command principle and the scalar principle.

2. *Staff authority* is advisory in nature. Managers possessing staff authority may conduct investigations and make recommendations to the line manager, but they do not possess the necessary authority to implement these recommendations. Staff authority is possessed by managers in such departments as personnel, legal, accounting, and data processing. Staff departments serve the line by providing advice and specialized service such as forecasts or special studies and by monitoring the activities of the line department.

3. *Functional authority* is the power to direct or require certain procedures, policies, or specific practices in other departments not under the direct supervision of the person or department possessing this authority. A staff department such as personnel may possess the necessary functional authority to require line departments to pay certain salaries for different employees or to follow safety regulations developed from conferences between personnel officials and government agencies. The head of the data processing department may require data to be provided in specific formats at specific times.

The three types of authority are shown in the organization chart in Figure 9-5.

The term *staff* is typically used to refer to those individuals or departments assisting managers in the performance of their basic production, marketing, or

THE CHIEF EXECUTIVE IS ULTIMATELY RESPONSIBLE FOR MAINTAINING AN EFFECTIVELY FUNCTIONING ORGANIZATION

SOURCE: © 1966 United Feature Syndicate. Used by permission.

---

[15] See Anthony F. Jurkus, "The Multiple Executive Office: Panacea or Selective Cure?" *University of Michigan Business Review* (July 1978), pp. 15–19.

**Figure 9-5
THREE TYPES OF
AUTHORITY**

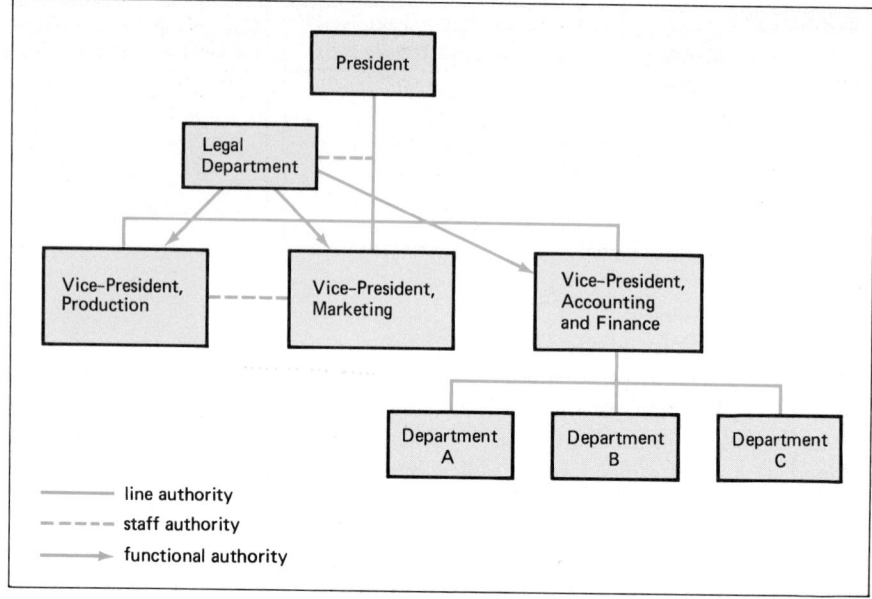

financial functions. The latter managers are called *line* because they form a part of the main line of authority (or chain of command) that flows throughout the organization. Staff personnel might include an economist who assists in forecasting future environmental conditions or an operations research team that assists in determining optimal warehouse locations.[16]

While these personnel are often considered to be staff, it is actually their relationship to line managers—not their activities—that defines them as staff. A research and development department may be considered staff in a manufacturing firm since it assists the production departments in solving problems of product and machine technology. But in a firm involved in developing product and process technology for sale to other companies, research and development is a line activity.

While these staff departments perform staff functions, they exercise line authority in their own departments. The staff-authority relationship exists *between* departments.

WHY STAFF DEPARTMENTS EMERGE

Two common motives for the formation of staff individuals and departments are expertise and economy. *Advisory staff* offer the managers the advantage of expert, objective opinion. Managers cannot be expert in all aspects of their jobs, and they rely upon specialists to provide expertise in certain areas. The staff advice may come from an engineer, the legal department, a scientist, an economist, or a human resources specialist, among others.

[16] See Neil B. Holbert, "The Life of Staff," *Business Horizons* (June 1978), pp. 79–82.

In cases in which economy is the motive for formation of staff positions, these persons are termed *service staff.* They are involved in such activities as computer programming, maintenance activities, preparing financial calculations, filing reports, or typing letters. It is generally less expensive to perform such functions by using separate service groups such as secretarial pools, data processing units, and maintenance departments than to rely upon line managers to arrange for their accomplishment.[17]

Organizational Design

Organizational design can be viewed historically in terms of three periods: classical, neoclassical, and modern. Each period built upon the contributions of the previous period in its attempts to treat the developments and problems of its own era.[18]

Classical organization theorists focused their attention on formal organization structure and the use of authority. The scalar, unity-of-command, and specialization principles are all examples of subject matter of the classical writers. The classical writings began in the late 1800s and early 1900s and paralleled the development of the first truly large-scale organizations in such basic industries as transportation, mining, and mass manufacturing. They filled a need to literally describe, chart, and define a whole new way of managing, such as that experienced on the early automobile assembly lines.

The *neoclassical* period extended from the 1930s into the 1950s. These writers and researchers focused on the new problems of their age, particularly those involving management–employee relations. Neoclassical theory brought behaviorism to the management sciences and an investigation of "informal" organizations existing outside the formal organizational structure. It raised questions about the effect of division of labor on worker morale and productivity. It focused on questions of leadership and motivation, and its contributions continue to be significant in the 1980s. A number of neoclassical contributions to management and organizational thought are discussed in detail in Chapter 11.

Neoclassical scholars also reflected the environment of their times. Major organizations were emerging in such new fields as electronics and communications. Industrial unions were relatively new and powerful, and employees had learned to expect more from their work than a paycheck.

Since the 1950s organization theory has grown in complexity, much as organizations have. *Modern* scholars attempt to view organizations as open to a wide variety of external variables—many more than the primarily economic ones considered by the classical and neoclassical writers. Included are such concerns as

[17] For a discussion of possible line–staff conflicts and their resolution, see Vivian Nossiter, "A New Approach Toward Resolving the Line and Staff Dilemma," *Academy of Management Review* (January 1979), pp. 103–106.

[18] The development of theories of organizational design is discussed at length in William G. Scott, *Organization Theory: A Behavioral Analysis for Management* (Homewood, Ill.: Irwin, 1967), Chapters 1 and 2.

the impact on organization design of technology, culture, government, social change, and political structure. They seek methods for determining how organizations should adjust to changes in these variables.

THE MATRIX ORGANIZATION

The matrix approach attempts to integrate the activities of several specialists from different departments in the organization for specific projects.

A relatively recent development in adjusting organizational structures to changing requirements is the *matrix approach*. This approach, which developed in the 1960s in the aerospace industry, attempts to integrate the activities of several specialists from different departments in the organization. Matrix organizations have been established in such diverse organizations as Dow Chemical, General Electric, Citibank, Shell Oil, and Texas Instruments.[19]

The identifying feature of a matrix organization is that some managers report to two superiors instead of to the traditional single boss. Organizations tend to utilize matrix forms in the following instances:

1. When it is essential that they be highly responsive to two sectors simultaneously, such as markets and technology;
2. When they face uncertainties that generate very high information processing requirements; and
3. When they must deal with strong constraints on financial and/or human resources.[20]

The matrix organization is built around specific projects or problems. Once these projects or problems are identified, a team is selected based upon the specific needs of the project and the individual abilities of the members. A team may consist of representatives from research and development, finance, marketing, design, and electronic data processing. The head of the matrix organization is granted the necessary authority to complete the project. While the members of the team report to two bosses—their superior in the department from which they were recruited and the major member of the team—the project manager typically is granted the authority to make salary increase recommendations, promotions, and other personnel actions during the length of time the individuals are assigned to the matrix team. Once the project is completed, the team members return to their original departments or are assigned to other matrix teams. Figure 9-6 shows a typical matrix organization.

Although the flexibility of the matrix organization and the ability to focus strongly on specific major problems or unique technical issues have led to its increasing use by a large number of major organizations, it is not without limitations. Team members must be comfortable working for more than one boss.

[19] Harvey F. Kolodny, "Evolution to a Matrix Organization," *Academy of Management Review* (October 1979), pp. 543–544. See also H. R. Smith, "A Socio-Biological Look at Matrix," *Academy of Management Review* (October 1978), pp. 922–926.

[20] Stanley M. Davis and Paul R. Lawrence, "Problems of Matrix Organizations," *Harvard Business Review* (May–June 1978), p. 134.

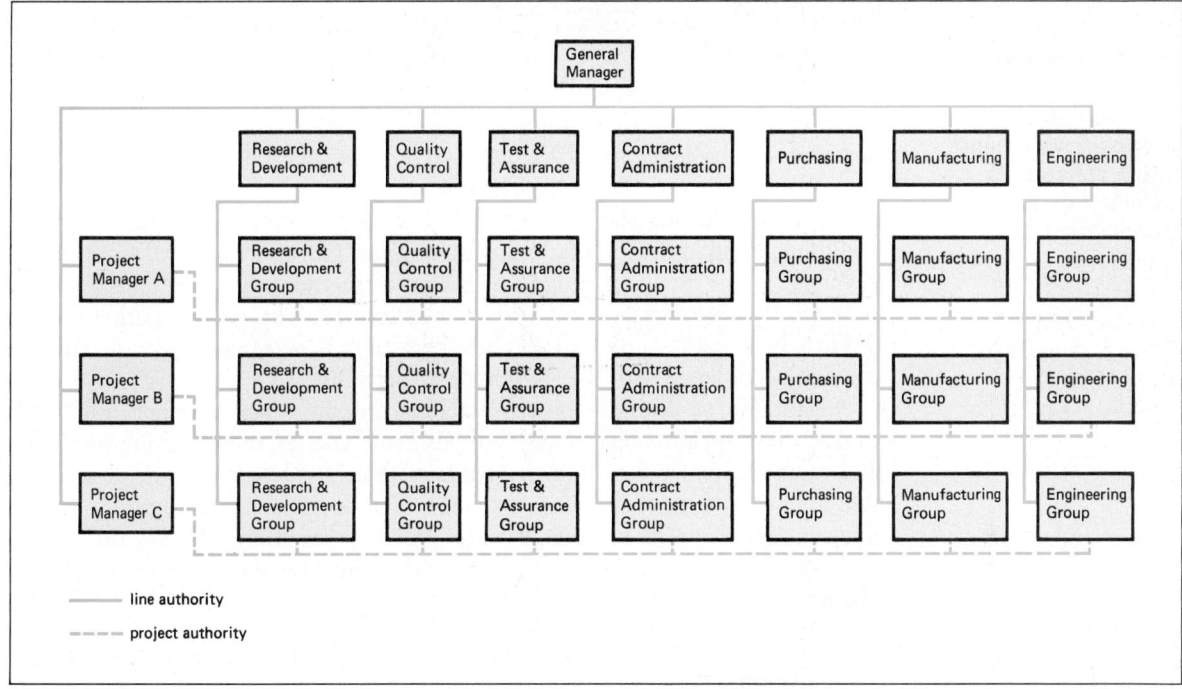

Cooperation may be a problem as the matrix team manager attempts to coordinate a diverse group of individuals from numerous parts of the organization. Its strengths are considerable, however, as is evidenced by its emergence as a critical organizational format for many companies.

The Impact of Work Schedules on the Organization

Organizations are often faced with the need to adapt to new trends in working and employee expectations. The work force at Los Angeles–based Occidental Life Insurance Co. begins work at varying times between 6:00 A.M. and 9:00 A.M. Meanwhile, personnel at United Services Automobile Association, a San Antonio insurance firm, work a Monday-through-Thursday week. And in Des Moines, two women share a third-grade teaching position.[21] These situations reflect three of the latest trends in work scheduling: flexitime, compressed work weeks, and job sharing.

Figure 9-6
MATRIX
ORGANIZATION

SOURCE: From *Management: Theory, Process and Practice*, Second Edition, by Richard M. Hodgetts. Copyright © 1979 by W. B. Saunders Company. Copyright 1975 by W. B. Saunders Company. Reprinted by permission of Holt, Rinehart and Winston, CBS College Publishing.

[21] These examples are quoted in "The Swelling Ranks of Workers Who Set Their Own Hours," *U.S. News & World Report* (August 1, 1977), p. 62; Joann S. Lublin, "Employee Lives Change as More Firms Adopt New Work Schedules," *Wall Street Journal* (February 16, 1977); "Two People, One Job—How Teachers Do It," *U.S. News & World Report* (April 4, 1977), p. 80.

FLEXITIME

Flexitime is a work scheduling system that allows employees to set their own work hours within constraints specified by the organization.

Flexitime is a work scheduling system that allows employees to set their own work hours within constraints specified by the organization. The concept developed from the efforts of a Munich company to reduce traffic congestion on an access road during the late 1960s.[22] Twelve percent of the U.S. nonfarm labor force is currently on a flexitime schedule.[23]

The typical flexitime format is to allow workers to start work within a specified time period in the morning, such as between 7:00 and 9:00 A.M. All employees must be on the job during a set period of the day when meetings and the bulk of other interpersonal activities are performed. This period, perhaps from 9:00 to 3:00, is called *core time*. Once core time is over, employees are free to leave in accordance with the morning starting time.

Advantages of flexitime systems include employee convenience, improved morale, reduced absenteeism and tardiness, cost savings, improved productivity, and more efficient use of transportation modes. Disadvantages include its limited applicability in such jobs as assembly line operations and continuous production operations, higher energy usage, problems resulting when key people are not available at crucial times, and the opportunity for some people to "shortchange" the system.[24]

COMPRESSED WORK WEEKS

A *compressed work week* is one in which workers spend fewer days on the job but work approximately the same number of hours. The best-known format is the "four-day/forty-hour week."[25] However, a report by the University of Michigan and the Society of Manufacturing Engineers predicts a four-day/thirty-two-hour week in most industries by 1990.[26]

Advantages of the compressed work week include more time for personal pursuits, energy savings, improved employee morale, better productivity, and reduced absenteeism. Disadvantages include increased moonlighting, physical exhaustion, and lethargy during long workdays. It is estimated that some 1.9

[22] "Flexitime a Success," *Administrative Management* (January 1978), p. 14.

[23] U.S. Department of Labor, Bureau of Labor Statistics (Washington, D.C.: Government Printing Office, 1981).

[24] These advantages and disadvantages are suggested in Robert J. Kuhne and Courtney O. Blair, "Flexitime," *Business Horizons* (April 1978), pp. 42–44. See also Jay S. Kim and Anthony F. Campagna, "Effects of Flexitime on Employee Attendance and Performance: A Field Experiment," *Academy of Management Journal* (December 1981), pp. 729–741; and George Bohlander, William B. Werther, and Marshall N. Wolfe, "Non-Standard Work Schedules: A Survey of Practices," *Arizona Business* (January 1979), pp. 3–10.

[25] The December 1977 issue of *Academy of Management Journal* contained two excellent articles: Randall B. Dunham and Donald L. Hawk, "The Four-Day/Forty-Hour Week: Who Wants It?" pp. 644–655; and Myron D. Fottler, "Employee Acceptance of a Four-Day Workweek," pp. 656–668.

[26] "Workweek of 4 Days Expected in 12 Years for Many Industries," *Wall Street Journal* (July 7, 1978), p. 14.

million people, or 2.7 percent of the U.S. labor force, are now on a four-day work week, twice as many as in 1973.[27]

JOB SHARING

Job sharing refers to the division of one job assignment among two or more persons. Although the concept is still relatively limited in most industrial settings, it has become a noticeable trend in such areas as teaching. Proponents of job sharing point out that it allows employers to secure the best efforts of two people, rather than of a single worker. Increased productivity is the result in such cases. Critics, on the other hand, point out that job sharing is limited to areas where job assignments can be easily divided and where limited training is required. They also argue that job sharing basically involves the regular use of part-time personnel. The most frequent use of the concept in industry has been in clerical functions and retailing.

[27] U.S. Department of Labor, Bureau of Labor Statistics (Washington, D.C.: Government Printing Office, February 24, 1981).

Summary

Organizing is the act of planning and implementing organizational structure. People and other resources are organized so as to accomplish the objectives of the enterprise. The division of work activities is called *departmentalization*. The five bases for departmentalization are function, geography, product, customer, and process.

Unity of command is a basic concept in organizational structures. This principle holds that each organizational member should report to only one superior for any single function. The span of management—the optimal number of subordinates a person can effectively manage—is another key organizational concept. Organization charts are typically used to depict the organizational relationships.

Coordination is an important need in any organization, particularly large, complex ones. Rensis Likert argues that managers serve as linking pins between the groups they manage and the higher-level groups to which they report. These overlapping managers can play important roles in achieving coordinative efforts of different departments.

Authority is the legitimate power a manager possesses to act and make decisions. Responsibility is the obligation of the manager to carry out assigned duties. Authority and responsibility are often delegated, or assigned, to subordinates who are then held accountable for their performance. Effective delegation should be based on the scalar principle, which holds that authority and responsibility should flow in a clear, unbroken line from top management to supervisory levels. An organization where extensive delegation is commonplace is considered to be decentralized. If little authority is assigned to subordinates, the organization is termed centralized. At the top of the organizational structure is the chief executive officer, the person with the ultimate accountability for organizational performance. A multiple-chief executive office—usually called the office of the chief executive—is a recent trend in organizational structures.

Line and staff relationships are also important in organizations. There are three types of authority: (1) line authority, the relationship between a superior and a subordinate; (2) staff authority, which is advisory in nature; and (3) functional authority, the power to direct or require certain procedures, policies, or specific practices in other departments not under the direct supervision of the person or department possessing this authority.

There have been three distinct periods in organizational design: (1) classical, with its emphasis on formal organizational structure and the use of authority; (2)

neoclassical, with its particular concern for management–employee relations; and (3) modern, characterized by the use of such techniques as the matrix approach. The matrix organization sets up teams of specialists from various functional areas to deal with specific organizational projects or problems. Members of these teams report to both their functional superiors and to their project managers.

Chapter 9 concludes with a discussion of the impact of work scheduling on the organization. The concepts of flexitime, compressed work weeks, and job sharing are explored.

REVIEW EXERCISES

1. Define the following terms: (a) organizing (b) specialization (c) departmentalization (d) unity-of-command concept (e) span-of-management concept (f) organization chart (g) exception principle (h) authority (i) responsibility (j) delegation (k) accountability (l) scalar principle (m) office of the chief executive (n) matrix organization (o) flexitime (p) compressed work week (q) job sharing.

2. Describe the five bases for departmentalization within an organization.

3. What are the factors involved in determining the optimum span of management?

4. Differentiate between tall and flat organizational structures.

5. Explain Likert's linking pin concept.

6. Discuss the centralization–decentralization issue.

7. Identify and explain the three types of authority in an organization.

8. Outline the three historical periods of organizational design.

9. Describe the matrix approach to organization.

10. What conditions are conducive to the use of matrix organizations?

ASSIGNMENTS/PROBLEMS/DISCUSSION QUESTIONS

1. Draw a chart showing the organizational structure of your college or university.

2. Napoleon Bonaparte once remarked: "Do you know what amazes me more than anything else? The importance of force to organize anything." Relate his observation to the material presented in Chapter 9.

3. Determine the various spans of management within an organization with which you are familiar. Do you regard these spans of management as appropriate for the particular management levels involved?

4. Analyze the organization of a local nonprofit enterprise. Is the current structure appropriate for the organization's mission?

5. Prepare a report on the organization of the nearest professional sports franchise. How does the organization compare with those of other business firms?

A MANAGERIAL INCIDENT

The Organizational Style of J.C. Penney

Top management at J.C. Penney is heavily dependent upon consensus in planning and decision making. Penney has abandoned the unity-of-command concept in favor of the team approach. From the office of the chairman (comprised of Penney's vice-president of merchandising operations, the chief financial officer, chief executive officer Donald V. Seibert, and vice-chairman Walter J. Neppel) to ad hoc task forces focusing upon specific problems, committees are in control at the headquarters of the retail giant. A fourteen-member management committee is responsible for strategic decisions in the areas of human resources management, merchandising, and public affairs among others. Even though only four members of

the management committee have seats on Penney's board of directors, all regularly attend board meetings as a means of familiarizing younger officers with all aspects of the corporation's activities and assuring continuity.

While the disadvantages of decisions by committee are present in the Penney organizational set-up, so also are the advantages. As *Business Week* described the situation:

For example, the economic affairs subcommittee tackled the thorny issue of allocating corporate costs to divisions. The controller's office wanted subsidiaries such as Thrift Drug Co. and the insurance operations to base their share of corporate personnel, legal, and auditing costs on their revenues. The subsidiaries contended that they maintained their own personnel and legal departments, and should be assessed for less.

How was the issue resolved? Robert B. Gill, Penney's head of corporate personnel and corporate planning, explained:

[T]he subcommittee addressed the issue by asking the corporate departments to approximate the time costs involved in servicing the subsidiaries. The final allocation plan, based on these studies, cost the divisions less than they were initially assessed but more than they wanted to pay. Nonetheless, the plan was implemented easily.

SOURCE: "Teamwork Pays Off at Penney's," *Business Week* (April 12, 1982), p. 107.

Questions and Problems

1. Identify the strengths and weaknesses of J.C. Penney's *team approach* as compared with the traditional *single top executive* arrangement.

2. Suggest modifications that Penney might consider in its current consensus management approach to minimize its major shortcomings.

10. Human Resources Management

Learning Objectives

AFTER STUDYING THIS CHAPTER YOU SHOULD BE ABLE TO

1. Identify and briefly explain the major federal laws affecting human resources management.
2. List the steps in the recruitment and selection process.
3. Compare and contrast the different types of on-the-job and off-the-job training and management development programs.
4. Identify the basic types of compensation programs.
5. Explain the major types of separation.

Key Terms

human resources management

job analysis

job description

job specification

equal employment opportunity

affirmative action program

on-the-job training

apprenticeship training

vestibule training

job rotation

coaching

job evaluation

wage

salary

fringe benefit

promotion

transfer

separation

You can dream, create, design and
build the most wonderful place in the
world, but it requires people to make
the dream a reality.

WALT DISNEY

A company is known by the people it
keeps.

ANONYMOUS

Until three years ago, the personnel department at Standard Brands,
Inc., was virtually indistinguishable from those that have existed since
the dawn of the corporate era. Composed of a director of labor relations and a
director of benefits—each with a salary in the $30,000 range—and a staff of
about twenty, the department routinely administered hiring and firing procedures, handled labor negotiations, maintained employee records, administered
benefits, and saw to it that paychecks went out on time. Its decisions could vitally affect individual employees but had little impact on the direction of the
corporation, and the department was buried well below finance, marketing, and
planning in the corporate bureaucracy.

The old personnel staff is still performing many of the same functions at
Standard Brands today, but now it is part of a new human resources department,
four times the size of the original personnel department, and headed up by a corporate vice-president, Madelyn P. Jennings, whose salary and responsibilities
easily double those of the two directors combined. Part of that growth is the result of a flood of new government regulations that have increased the importance and the complexity of traditional personnel administration tasks. Since
joining the company in 1976, Jennings has instituted a national compensation
program, overhauled benefits, and developed an employee appraisal system.

But much of the stunning growth of Jennings' department is the result of a
brand-new role that has been assigned to personnel administration at Standard
Brands: the development and implementation of the company's first manpower
planning system, one that is directly tied to carrying out corporate strategies.
This new personnel function at Standard Brands is typical of changes taking
place in most other large corporations. These changes promise to lift top personnel administrators, who increasingly are adopting the human resources desig-

For most of her early working life, Mary Parker Follett devoted herself to serving the poor and underprivileged in Boston's Roxbury section. After graduating summa cum laude from Radcliffe College in 1898, Follett organized evening centers in the hope of getting young people off the streets and finding them jobs. She soon became a national figure in the community center movement and was elected vice-president of the National Community Center Association.

From this unlikely beginning as a social worker, Mary Parker Follett became a modern management pioneer who advised businesspeople on personnel problems and made important contributions to the field of human resources management. Even though she never set foot in a factory except as an observer or participated in the management of a company, Follett understood the critical role managers played in bringing about the kind of constructive change that enables businesses to function.

Attracted to the practical approach of business managers and their need to translate theories into changes that produced results, Follett applied what she had first observed in her community center activities to the management of business. She focused on the cross-fertilization of thinking that occurs when people operate in groups. She observed that the ideas that come out of group thinking could not be duplicated by any individual working alone and that all group participants undergo important changes in thinking simply because of their participation in the group. Moreover, Follett believed that when group members take part in a discussion, they begin to think in a more compatible, harmonious way. It is the role of the manager to cultivate this group interaction so that it produces the optimal results.

Central to Follett's theory is the concept of *integration*—the harmonious blending of the differences of group members to produce a solution acceptable

nation, into prominence as powerful officers in the corporate hierarchy. Already, experts estimate, such human resources executives—whether they carry the title or not—now hold manpower planning responsibilities in almost all of the nation's 500 largest industrial companies, compared with only a handful of companies five years ago.

While their staffs still handle such mundane chores as allocating spaces in the company parking lot, they are also expected to work closely with senior operating managers to create staffing plans that are designed to meet corporate goals and to satisfy the growing demands by employees for clear career paths they can follow. "Management realizes that its important assets are not simply financial resources but having the people on hand at the right time and in the right place to make a thing go," observes Thomas C. Stevens, who in 1974 filled a new post as corporate director of human resources at J. I. Case Co., the construction and farm equipment subsidiary of Tenneco, Inc.[1]

[1] "Personnel Widens Its Franchise," *Business Week* (February 26, 1979), p. 116. Reprinted from the February 26, 1979 issue of *Business Week* by special permission. © 1980 by McGraw-Hill, Inc.

to all. This solution is usually short-lived, for new differences are always arising. However, Follett believed that new solutions are always contained within the differences themselves and that it is the function of the manager to preside over the process of reintegration. Managers who try to dominate the group for the purpose of bringing about a preconceived goal usually fail, for the process of talking and ironing out differences is ever-changing. Managers have little advance notions of the most appropriate solution when conflicts first appear. Follett advises them to use the goals of the evolving situation as a guide to their own behavior as long as they are willing to change these goals as new differences and new possible integrations arise.

Follett likened this process to planting an unfamiliar seed and cultivating it without knowing whether to expect a flower or a fruit, a tree or a bush. Only after the results appear does the manager know what he or she has been working toward all along.

Although Mary Parker Follett was born in 1868 into an old New England family and died in 1933, her views on human resources management are as important today as they were then. Underlying her work is a respect for industry and for the process of management. She described her feelings in this way:

> Industry is the most important field of human activity, and management is the fundamental element in industry. It is now generally recognized that not bankers, not stockholders, but management is the pivot of business success. It is good management that draws credit, that draws workers, that draws customers. Moreover, whatever changes should come . . . they will always have to be managed. Management is a permanent function of business.

Source

Elliot M. Fox and Lyndall Urwick (eds.), *Dynamic Administration: The Collected Papers of Mary Parker Follett* (London: Pitman Publishing, 1973). The quotation is from pp. xvii–xviii.

The Importance of Human Resources Management

Although the typical organization is made up of a number of different resources, none is more important than people. While the machinery, inventory, financial resources, and information may be invaluable, the organization can do nothing if it lacks sufficiently competent employees to operate the machinery, make decisions based upon analysis of the information, sell the firm's output, handle the correspondence, and supervise the myriad operations. Since the value of effective human resources is obvious, it would appear equally obvious that all organizations would practice effective human resources management. But as news sources continue to reveal, many organizations fail to manage their human resources properly.

U.S. Industries had four presidents in less than a year. The chairman and chief executive officer of First Wisconsin Mortgage Co. resigned "for personal reasons" after three weeks on the job. Burlington Industries lost two long-time employees who were vice-presidents and directors after a new president was cho-

HUMAN RESOURCES MANAGEMENT ON THE GRIDIRON

PROFESSIONAL FOOTBALL PLACE KICKER NEEDED

Minimum 4 yrs. college & 2 yrs. professional football expr. Annual Salary from $20,000. Contact your nearest Texas Employment Commission Office. Job Order No. 1465638. Ad paid for by Equal Opportunity Employer.

The organization had always prided itself on its enlightened approach to human resources management. Huge quantities of data on the qualifications of virtually every potential job candidate in the country were fed into the computer for analysis each year before making job offers. The successful applicant received significant employee benefits: a salary averaging over $50,000 in the industry and a twenty-six week annual vacation. The organization was the Dallas Cowboys Football Club. It was willing to provide these employee benefits, due to management's recognition of the importance of a skilled place kicker in maintaining the team's competitive position.

Rafael Septien, the Mexican national who had performed admirably in the position the previous year, informed the Cowboys of his intention to apply for a permanent visa. The club's personnel officials recognized that a number of steps would have to be taken in order to comply with Texas state employment regulations before Septien could be employed for the next season. The regulations in question dealt with the importation of alien workers and required the Cowboys to show that Septien would not be taking the job away from a U.S. citizen. So the club's personnel officials turned to orthodox approaches by listing the position with the Texas Employment Commission, running the classified advertisement shown above in the *Dallas Morning News*, and interviewing all applicants during a thirty-day period.

The advertisement reawakened dreams of ex-football players throughout the Southwest and produced a number of applications from would-be professionals. However, none of the applicants possessed both of the qualifications: a minimum of four years of college and two years of professional football experience. Personnel's recommendation was accepted by the Cowboy's top management and the position was once again filled by Rafael Septien.

SOURCE: Advertisement reproduced courtesy of the Dallas Cowboys Football Club.

sen. The employee turnover rate in the fast food industry often approaches 200 percent. Sun Oil Co. and its subsidiaries agreed to pay $250,000 to 250 women employees who accused the firm of sex discrimination. An additional $105,000 was awarded to two other plaintiffs and their attorneys.

The growth in the size of the typical organization and the increasing number of regulations affecting employment practices have resulted in the need for specialists in human resources management. Although more than 50 percent of all workers were self-employed in 1850, less than 10 percent of today's work force work for themselves. Major business organizations such as General Motors,

Westinghouse, International Telephone and Telegraph, Ford, and General Electric employ more than 200,000 workers *each*.

Such organizations have a continuing need for new personnel to replace people who change jobs, receive promotions, or retire. Effective training is vital in producing efficient, competent employees. Compensation programs must be developed and managed; health and safety programs must be administered; and benefit programs and performance evaluations must be given expert attention.

WHAT IS HUMAN RESOURCES MANAGEMENT?

Although most organizations recognize the importance of human resources management, the specific title of the person or department having primary responsibility varies considerably. Some organizations use the term *personnel management*, while others label the function *employee relations*. Still others term the function simply *staffing*. Increasingly, however, the term *human resources management* is being adopted as more and more organizations recognize a greatly expanded role for the traditional personnel functions.[2]

Human resources management may be defined as the organizational function of planning for human resource needs, recruitment, selection, development, compensation, and evaluation. These responsibilities are great and call for an enlightened approach to the management of the organization's human resources.

Responsibilities for the human resources department include

1. Planning employee needs and recruiting job candidates
2. Interviewing job candidates
3. Selecting job candidates
4. Orienting and training new employees
5. Wage and salary management (compensating employees)
6. Providing incentives and benefits
7. Appraising performance
8. Face-to-face communicating (providing feedback, counseling, disciplining)
9. Developing managers
10. Equal opportunity and affirmative action
11. Employee health and safety
12. Handling grievances and labor relations[3]

THE HUMAN RESOURCES DEPARTMENT— A STAFF DEPARTMENT

Although the manager of human resources is given major responsibilities for the performance of these functions, he or she is a *staff* manager with the primary du-

Human resources management is the organizational function of planning for human resources needs, recruitment, selection, development, compensation, and evaluation.

---

[2] Although human resources departments have made great progress in recent years, much remains to be done. See Wickham Skinner, "Big Hat, No Cattle: Managing Human Resources," *Harvard Business Review* (September–October 1981), pp. 106–114.

[3] Gary Dessler, *Personnel Management* (Reston, Va.: Reston Publishing Co., 1978), pp. 2–3. Reprinted by permission of Reston Publishing Co., Inc., a Prentice-Hall Company.

ties of assisting and advising line managers. The ultimate authority for making staffing and other human resources decisions rests with the line managers, who rely upon the expertise of the personnel department to provide major assistance in recruiting, testing, conducting screening interviews, training, facilitating the performance appraisal process, and proposing solutions to grievances and disciplinary problems.

ORGANIZATION OF THE HUMAN RESOURCES DEPARTMENT

The human resources department varies considerably in size and authority among different organizations, ranging from one-person departments to major operations of dozens of specialized members. Determinants of a department's size include rate of employee turnover, level and variety of required skills, overall organizational size, types of fringe benefits, and complexity of wage payment plans. The average U.S. business firm has one personnel department employee for every 100 employees on the payroll. A recent study revealed that the average salary—excluding bonuses—of senior human resources executives in large companies is $69,300.[4]

Figure 10-1 illustrates an organization chart for a human resources department in a large firm with more than 1,000 employees.

Human Resources Planning

Like all the other divisions of an organization, the human resources department must plan for the future. The basic planning process is built around two fundamental questions:

[4] *ASPA-BNA Survey No. 41: Personnel Activities, Budgets, and Staffs: 1980–1981* (Washington, D.C.: U.S. Government Printing Office, Bureau of National Affairs, May 21, 1981), p. 7.

**Figure 10-1
ORGANIZATION OF A
TYPICAL HUMAN
RESOURCES
DEPARTMENT**

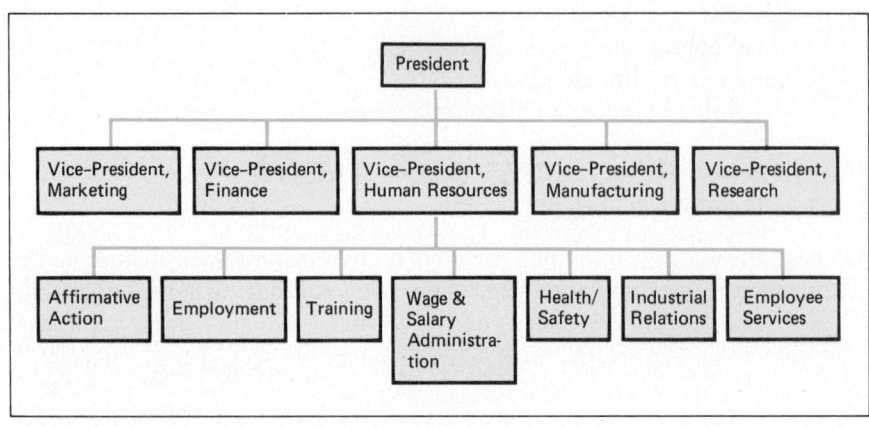

1. What type of employees does the organization need? (*quality*)
2. How many of each type are needed? (*quantity*)

Answers to both questions require a forecast of the organization's personnel needs. This involves an estimate of the number of people and the different types of skills required in the future to perform the work of the organization. Considerable information on future needs is available from employee records of promotion, turnover, and retirement. Such information can be helpful in development of projections of employee needs. Information on organizational plans for expansion or contraction in various areas is also utilized in development of forecasts of future personnel requirements. Job analysis, job descriptions, and job specifications are invaluable in the planning process.

JOB ANALYSIS

In order to recruit and hire the appropriate persons for specific vacancies, it is necessary to know what the job itself requires. Job analysis enables the manager to specify the duties and responsibilities of each job and the skills that are required of the person who fills it. It is the starting point for human resources planning.

Job analysis may be formally defined as a systematic detailed study of jobs, consisting of identifying and examining the requirements of the person assigned to the job and the elements and characteristics of the job. The analysis is often conducted by the use of a questionnaire completed by persons currently holding the job and by their immediate supervisors. The analysis focuses upon answering the following questions:

Job analysis is the systematic study of jobs, consisting of identifying the requirements of the person assigned to the job and the elements and characteristics of the job.

Who does the work?

What is done?

When is it done?

Where is it done?

How is it done?

Why is it done?

Job analysis is the basis for both job descriptions and job specifications.

JOB DESCRIPTION

The *job description* is a written statement describing the objectives of a job, the work to be performed, the skills needed, the responsibilities involved, the relationship of the job to other jobs, and its working conditions. The description is utilized for a number of important personnel functions. It is used in the selection of new employees, in orientation and training, and in the appraisal process.

Job description is a written statement describing the objectives of a job, the work to be performed, the skills needed, the responsibilities involved, the relationship of the job to other jobs, and its working conditions.

**Figure 10-2
STANDARD
FACTORY JOB
DESCRIPTION, THE
BOEING COMPANY**

Code: C3408
Grade: 8
Job Title: Inspector Fabrication A

DETERMINING DUTIES AND RESPONSIBILITIES
Lead, work with, check, and coordinate the work of a group of lower grade employees (up to twenty-five) engaged in inspecting fabricated parts, materials, and assemblies. Supplement the instruction and training of lower grade employees regarding inspection procedures, use of equipment, interpretation of standards and functions of the inspection department.

and/or

Lead, work with, check, and coordinate the work of a group of employees of lower classification engaged in quick-fix work in the Tooling Unit's quick-fix shop. Coordinate with customer, engineering, shop representatives, and other personnel outside the Quality Control organization on rejections, corrective action to be taken, and other problems relative to inspection of quick-fix work. Supplement the training of employees of lower classification regarding procedures, use of equipment, interpretation of standards, and functions of the Quality Control Department.

ASSOCIATED DUTIES AND RESPONSIBILITIES
1. Use precision measuring instruments, inspection devices and equipment, shop mathematics, including trigonometry, handbook formulas, various documents, inspection books, etc., to accomplish work assignments.
2. Plan and arrange sequence of own work and inspection assignments of lower grade inspectors.
3. Pass on pertinent information to succeeding shift inspector regarding own work assignment. Write tie-ins in inspection book.
4. Contact other departments within the company and the customer in order to coordinate the inspection activities and accomplish work assignments.
5. Perform required rework investigation and make recommendations as to possible salvage subject to supervisor's approval.
6. Arrange work within own group to promote an efficient operation, expedite special jobs, to keep current with production schedules.
7. Within own group see that records and procedures are properly and uniformly executed.
8. Make decisions as to usability of materials, workmanship and processes.
9. Use blueprints, drawings, standards manuals and catalogs, documents, etc., to identify parts and assemblies and to obtain dimensions and specifications.
10. Establish and maintain all necessary records.
11. Refer questionable cases, discrepancies, suggested improvements or changes to supervisor.

Figure 10-2 is a job description for an inspector in a manufacturing firm. The job description contains three basic elements:

1. *Job identification.* The title of the job, department, pay grade, and code specified by the U.S. Department of Labor's *Dictionary of Occupational Titles* (D.O.T.).

2. *Job summary.* Short description giving the essence of what the job contains.

3. *Job duties.* The list of job duties and responsibilities, typically listed in order of their importance.

JOB SPECIFICATION

A key companion to the job description is the *job specification.* This is a written document describing the special qualifications required of a person who fills a particular job. It lists skills, education, and previous experience needs. While the job description concentrates on the job, the job specification focuses upon the person performing the job. A combined job description and job specification for a juvenile probation officer is shown in Figure 10-3.

Figure 10-3 is a valuable document since it specifies the performance expected of the individual and the conditions under which the job is to be performed and sets standards for minimally acceptable performance of each of the

Job specification is a written description of the special qualifications required of a person who fills a particular job, including skills, education, and previous experience.

JUVENILE PROBATION OFFICER

Tasks	Conditions	Standards
Meets with probationers weekly to assess their current behavior	Caseload of not more than 60 appointments scheduled by receptionist; supervisor will help with difficult cases; use procedures stated in rules and regulations	All probationers must be seen weekly; those showing evidence of continued criminal activity or lack of a job will be reported to supervisor
Prepares pre-sentence reports on clients	When requested by the judge; average of 5 per week, per instructions issued by judge; supervisor will review and approve	Your reports will be complete and accurate as determined by judge; he/she will accept 75 percent of presentence recommendations

Skills, Knowledge, and Abilities Required:
• Knowledge of the factors contributing to criminal behavior
• Ability to counsel probationers
• Ability to write clear and concise probation reports
• Knowledge of judge's sentencing habits for particular types of offenders and offenses
• Knowledge of law concerning probation

Minimum Qualifications:
• High school degree or equivalent; plus four years' experience working with juvenile offenders, or a B.S. degree in criminal justice, or psychology, or counseling
• Ability to pass a multiple choice test on relevant probation law
• Possess a valid driver's license

Figure 10-3 COMBINED JOB DESCRIPTION AND JOB SPECIFICATIONS FOR A JUVENILE PROBATION OFFICER

SOURCE: Donald E. Klingner, "When the Traditional Job Description Is Not Enough." Reprinted with permission of *Personnel Journal.* Copyright April 1979.

duties of the job. Managers can utilize it in orienting new employees to expected performance levels, setting MBO goals, and objectively evaluating actual performance. The employee is provided with a clear statement of performance expectations and the minimum qualifications for promotion or reassignment.

Legal Considerations in Human Resources Management

One important factor in the growing role of human resources departments is the numerous laws and specific regulations from all levels of government spelling out how organizations must treat current and prospective employees. Such laws range from the Equal Pay Act of 1963 to state and federal safety standards. The number of statutes enforced by the United States Department of Labor increased from 40 in 1960 to 130 in 1980. Compliance with these numerous laws can be expensive. Peabody Coal Co.'s human resources department spent $500,-000 to simulate the various mining conditions in order to train its 15,000 miners to comply with the Mining Safety and Health Act.[5] Although interpretation of the myriad regulations requires considerable expertise, it is important to be familiar with the major statutes affecting human resources management. The major laws are described briefly in Table 10-1.

PROVIDING FOR EQUAL EMPLOYMENT OPPORTUNITIES

Equal employment opportunity is the right of all persons to work and to advance on the basis of merit, ability, and potential without any form of discrimination because of race, color, religion, sex, or national origin.

Equal employment opportunity may be defined as the right of all persons to work and to advance on the basis of merit, ability and potential without any form of discrimination because of race, color, religion, sex, or national origin. The primary legal base for equal employment opportunity actions is Title VII of the Civil Rights Act of 1964 as amended by the Equal Employment Opportunity Act of 1972. Supporting legal acts are the Equal Pay Act of 1963, the Age Discrimination in Employment Act of 1967 and its 1978 amendments, the Vocational Rehabilitation Act of 1973, state laws, and presidential executive orders.

The provisions of these acts currently apply to private employers of fifteen or more, state and local governments, public and private employment agencies, and labor unions with fifteen or more members.

Affirmative action programs are designed to increase opportunities for females and minorities through recruitment, training, and promotion so they are fairly represented in the work force.

The Equal Employment Opportunity Commission (EEOC) is an agency of the executive branch of the federal government that was created in 1972 to administer the various acts related to providing equal opportunity in hiring and employment. The EEOC provides assistance to employers in establishing "affirmative action" programs and in halting discriminatory hiring and employment practices.

Affirmative action programs are designed to increase opportunities for females

[5] "Personnel Widens Its Franchise," *Business Week* (February 26, 1979), p. 116.

A. LEGISLATION PROVIDING FOR EQUAL EMPLOYMENT OPPORTUNITIES

1. Equal Pay Act of 1963. This act requires "equal pay for equal work" and states that members of one sex may not be compensated at a rate lower than that paid to employees of the opposite sex who are performing equivalent work.
2. Title VII of the Civil Rights Act of 1964 as amended by the Equal Employment Opportunity Act of 1972. This is the most sweeping federal law dealing with job bias, prohibiting discriminatory actions based on race, color, religion, sex, or national origin. The Equal Employment Opportunity Commission (EEOC) was established to enforce this law.
3. Age Discrimination in Employment Act of 1967. This act was amended in 1978 to prohibit job discrimination based upon age for persons between 40 and 70.
4. Vocational Rehabilitation Act of 1973. This act requires affirmative action programs for the handicapped in businesses with federal contracts or subcontracts.

B. LEGISLATION DEALING WITH HEALTH AND SAFETY OF EMPLOYEES

1. Occupational Safety and Health Act of 1970. This act is designed to assure safe and healthful working conditions for the American labor force by requiring employers to develop and implement health and safety plans. Such plans must include inspection of work facilities, removal of all hazards, promotion of job safety, and preparation of reports for submission to the federal enforcement body, the Occupational Safety and Health Administration (OSHA).

C. LEGISLATION AFFECTING COMPANY–UNION RELATIONS

1. National Labor Relations Act of 1935 (Wagner Act.) This act legalized collective bargaining and required employers to bargain with the elected officials of their employees.
2. Fair Labor Standards Act of 1938. This act outlawed the use of child labor and set a minimum wage and maximum basic hours of work for employees of firms engaged in interstate commerce. The first minimum wage was twenty-five cents per hour. The current minimum wage is $3.35.
3. Taft-Hartley Act of 1947. This act was designed to balance the power of unions and management by prohibiting a number of unfair union practices, including the so-called closed shop in which management is prohibited from employing nonunion workers.
4. Landrum-Griffin Act of 1959. This act requires regularly scheduled elections of union officers by secret ballot. It also regulates the handling of union funds.

and minorities through recruiting, training, and promoting minorities and women so that they will ultimately be represented in the employer's work force in percentages similar to their percentage in the labor market from which the employer draws workers. Such programs include analysis of present work force and establishment of specific hiring and promotion goals with target dates in areas that currently underutilize minorities and/or females. Action plans should also include an active search for minorities and females to be placed into upward mobility positions within the organization. Federal contractors and organizations receiving federal financial assistance must also develop affirmative action programs for handicapped workers, disabled veterans, and veterans of the Vietnam War era.[6] Figure 10-4 outlines the typical contents of an affirmative action plan and shows the EEOC report form used.[7]

A number of financial penalties have been levied against organizations for violating equal employment opportunity laws. One notable case involved a consent decree signed by American Telephone and Telegraph whereby the utility giant agreed to pay approximately $15 million in back wages to employees who had suffered due to discriminatory practices and committed another $50 million in annual payments for promotion and wage adjustments to women and minorities.[8]

The most widely reported case of reverse discrimination was that of Allan Bakke, who charged the University of California with discriminating against him on the basis of race. Bakke proved that the university had admitted less qualified (based upon entrance tests and grades) minorities to its medical school, and the U.S. Supreme Court ruling ordered the university to admit him. The Court did rule that race could be *one* of several factors used in determining admissions. However, it stated that the university's affirmative action admissions program was "unjustifiably biased against white applicants" since a specific number of positions were reserved for minority applicants.

The Recruitment and Selection Process

The recruitment and selection process is a systematic attempt to implement the human resources plan by recruiting, evaluating, and selecting qualified managers and operative employees. The job analysis, job descriptions, and job specifications are important tools in the selection process. Figure 10-5 lists the steps in the recruitment and selection process, the qualifications considered at each step, and the rationale for possible rejection of applicants at each step.

RECRUITMENT

A number of sources for potential employees exist. The first place that most managers look when attempting to fill a position is within the organization. Policies of promotion from within are widely used since they aid in employee morale

---

[6] See Sara M. Freedman and Robert T. Keller, "The Handicapped in the Workforce," *Academy of Management Review* (July 1981), pp. 449–458.

[7] See Daniel Seligman, "Affirmative Action Is Here to Stay," *Fortune* (April 19, 1982), pp. 143–162; *Affirmative Action & Equal Employment: A Guide Book for Employers* (Washington, D.C.: U.S. Equal Employment Opportunity Commission, 1974); and Alice G. Sargent, *Beyond Sex Roles* (St. Paul, Minn.: West Publishing Co., 1977).

[8] Carol J. Loomis, "AT&T in the Throes of 'Equal Employment,'" *Fortune* (January 15, 1979), pp. 44–48ff.

SOME REQUIRED CONTENTS OF
AFFIRMATIVE ACTION PROGRAMS

Utilization analysis
"Underutilization" is having fewer minorities
or women in a job classification than would
reasonably be expected by their availability.

Establishment of goals and timetables
Employer should consider the results which
could reasonably be expected from putting
forth every good faith effort.

Development of an equal employment opportunity policy in all personnel actions.

Formal internal and external dissemination of the equal employment opportunity policy.

Establishment of responsibility for implementation of the affirmative action program.

Active support of community action programs designed to improve employment opportunities of women and minorities.

Implementation of an internal audit and reporting system to measure the effectiveness of the total program.

Figure 10-4
SOME REQUIRED CONTENTS OF AFFIRMATIVE ACTION PROGRAMS AND SECTIONS OF THE EQUAL EMPLOYMENT OPPORTUNITY FORM

SOURCE: U.S. Department of Labor, Office of Federal Contract Compliance, Title 41—Public Contracts and Property Management, Chapter 60, Part 60-2.

Section D — EMPLOYMENT DATA

Employment at this establishment--Report all permanent, temporary, or part-time employees including apprentices and on-the-job trainees unless specifically excluded as set forth in the instructions. Enter the appropriate figures on all lines and in all columns. Blank spaces will be considered as zeros

JOB CATEGORIES	OVERALL TOTALS (SUM OF COL B THRU K)	MALE					FEMALE				
		WHITE (NOT OF HISPANIC ORIGIN)	BLACK (NOT OF HISPANIC ORIGIN)	HISPANIC	ASIAN OR PACIFIC ISLANDER	AMERICAN INDIAN OR ALASKAN NATIVE	WHITE (NOT OF HISPANIC ORIGIN)	BLACK (NOT OF HISPANIC ORIGIN)	HISPANIC	ASIAN OR PACIFIC ISLANDER	AMERICAN INDIAN OR ALASKAN NATIVE
	A	B	C	D	E	F	G	H	I	J	K
Officials and Managers											
Professionals											
Technicians											
Sales Workers											
Office and Clerical											
Craft Workers (Skilled)											
Operatives (Semi-Skilled)											
Laborers (Unskilled)											
Service Workers											
TOTAL											
Total employment reported in previous EEO-1 report											

(The trainees below should also be included in the figures for the appropriate occupational categories above)

Formal On-the-job trainees	White collar										
	Production										

1. NOTE: On consolidated report, skip questions 2-5 and Section E.
2. How was information as to race or ethnic group in Section D obtained?
   1 ☐ Visual Survey   3 ☐ Other — Specify ....
   2 ☐ Employment Record   ....
3. Dates of payroll period used —

4. Pay period of last report submitted for this establishment

5. Does this establishment employ apprentices?
   This year? 1 ☐ Yes 2 ☐ No
   Last year? 1 ☐ Yes 2 ☐ No

Section E — ESTABLISHMENT INFORMATION

1. Is the location of the establishment the same as that reported last year?
   1 ☐ Yes 2 ☐ No 3 ☐ Did not report last year 4 ☐ Reported on combined basis

2. Is the major business activity at this establishment the same as that reported last year?
   1 ☐ Yes 2 ☐ No 3 ☐ No report last year 4 ☐ Reported on combined basis

OFFICE USE ONLY

3. What is the major activity of this establishment? (Be specific, i.e. manufacturing steel castings, retail grocer, wholesale plumbing supplies, title insurance, etc. Include the specific type of product or type of service provided, as well as the principal business or industrial activity)

e.

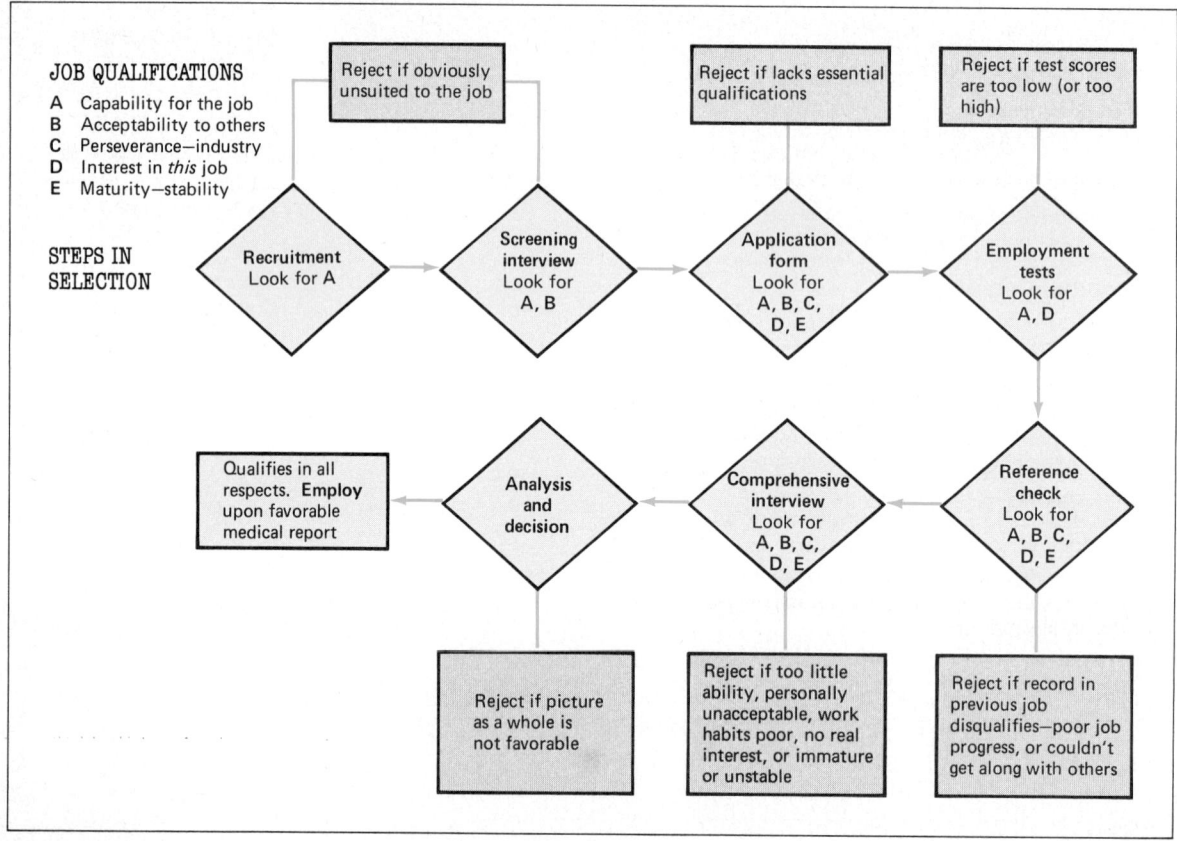

JOB QUALIFICATIONS

A   Capability for the job
B   Acceptability to others
C   Perseverance—industry
D   Interest in *this* job
E   Maturity—stability

STEPS IN
SELECTION

Reject if obviously
unsuited to the job

Reject if lacks essential
qualifications

Reject if test scores
are too low (or too
high)

Recruitment
Look for A

Screening
interview
Look for
A, B

Application
form
Look for
A, B, C,
D, E

Employment
tests
Look for
A, D

Qualifies in all
respects. **Employ**
upon favorable
medical report

Analysis
and
decision

Comprehensive
interview
Look for
A, B, C,
D, E

Reference
check
Look for
A, B, C,
D, E

Reject if picture
as a whole is
not favorable

Reject if too little
ability, personally
unacceptable, work
habits poor, no real
interest, or immature
or unstable

Reject if record in
previous job
disqualifies—poor job
progress, or couldn't
get along with others

**Figure 10-5
STEPS IN THE
SELECTION PROCESS**

SOURCE: Adapted by permission of the publisher from *The Employment Interview,* AMA Research Study #47, by Milton Mandel, © 1961 by American Management Association, Inc. All rights reserved.

while reducing recruiting, hiring, and training costs. Most organizations give strong preference to internal sources of employees. Others—such as Sears and Delta Airlines—promote *only* from within.

External sources of potential employees are utilized in instances in which periods of rapid growth or the need for specialized skills require that qualified applicants be obtained outside the organization. Some of the most frequently used external sources include private employment agencies, educational institutions, professional and trade journals, newspaper and radio advertisements, public employment agencies, union hiring halls, and recommendations of present employees.

SCREENING INTERVIEWS

Once a group of applicants has been secured through recruiting, the *screening process* focuses upon determining which candidates are best suited for the job. The process is basically the same for operative, technical, or managerial employees. The applicant is asked to complete an application form containing biographical information—name and address, previous experience, education, type of work desired. This form is analyzed to determine whether the applicant pos-

**EMPLOYEE
SELECTION: CRITICAL
PROCESS IN HUMAN
RESOURCES
MANAGEMENT**

SOURCE: *The New Yorker*
(June 14, 1982), p. 37.
Drawing by Chas. Addams;
© 1982 The New Yorker
Magazine, Inc.

sesses the necessary qualifications and provides the basic information used in beginning the interview.

The one selection instrument that is universally employed is the interview. Interviews are typically included in the selection process due to the desire of managers to make a personal determination of whether the new employee will "fit" into the department or division. One study of 2,500 U.S. companies reported that 64 percent of the respondents considered the interview to be the single most important criterion in employment decisions. Previous experience was second at 32 percent, and all other factors were mentioned by only 4 percent of the respondents.[9] While questions dealing with work experience, education, and military experience may be asked, the interviewer must avoid irrelevant and potentially discriminatory questions about age, race or color, national origin, religion or creed, or marital status.[10]

A series of interviews may be conducted with potential applicants both by members of the human resources department and by the line manager for whom the prospective employee will work. Interviewers may use directed or nondirected interviews. *Directed* interviews are based upon a list of questions developed prior to the interview. *Nondirected* interviews utilize open-ended questions designed to stimulate the prospective employee to do most of the talking. Regardless of the type of interview employed, the interviewer should understand the specific objectives of the interview and know as much as practical about the applicant prior to it. The interview should be conducted in a location in which the conversation cannot be overheard and in which the applicant will be comfortable and more willing to speak openly.

[9] *Personnel Management: Policies and Practices, Report #22* (Englewood Cliffs, N.J.: Prentice-Hall, 1975).
[10] "Questions a Job Interviewer Shouldn't Ask You," *Changing Times* (August 1979), pp. 19–22.

WOULD YOU HIRE THE FOLLOWING APPLICANTS?

Selecting a future manager is a difficult task. Some individuals perform beyond a manager's wildest hopes; others are total failures. The personal sketches below contain more information than is often available when a hiring decision is to be made. Decide whether or not you would hire each of the following four people. The actual name of each person is revealed on the facing page.

A   UPI

Applicant A: He dreamed of being an inventor, but he had had only three months of formal schooling—he was expelled because the schoolmaster considered him "retarded." In early life his biggest joy was planning pranks designed to anger his father, who once beat the boy in public in the village square. He was fired from his first job for accidentally starting a fire. In his thirties, he paid little attention to his family, neglected his dress, chewed tobacco, was rejected by "polite society," and was ridiculed by theoretical scientists as an "anti-intellectual." He was egotistical and, to fellow workers, both a tyrant and their most entertaining companion.

B   UPI

Applicant B: At the age of 21, he was of medium height and thin. He wore glasses, had an unpleasant toothy grin and affected flashy clothes. He spoke indistinctly, stumbled, hesitated, appearing to have almost a speech impediment. His companions thought he was odd and eccentric, and his seniors were irritated by him. He was a particular nuisance in class—bumptious, cocky, boyishly positive, know-it-all. He was earnest, outspoken, and tactless. His hot temper, nervousness, and childish manner made an unfavorable impression. He was a good student, making Phi Beta Kappa in his senior year in college. He had an array of interests, and for some time after college graduation he was unable to decide what he wanted to do in life.

REFERENCE CHECKS

Many organizations use reference checks to verify certain information provided by applicants. Work histories are common subjects for such checks. Much verification is conducted by telephone rather than by the slower—and possibly less accurate—use of letters to references supplied by the applicant.

C   UPI

Applicant C: He was born in a middle-class residential section of a large midwestern city. His father was a stern, religious, scrupulously honest man. He was a bright youngster with a piercing goal to become rich and famous. He had a prodigious mechanical aptitude and manual dexterity. According to his first boss, he was "very fast and accurate . . . sober, honest, and very industrious." He was very popular with young people in the local church. He was fond of baseball, and he spent some time in the U.S. Navy.

D   UPI

Applicant D: He was red-haired, sturdy, and not handsome. He had a distinct speech impediment, which was a combination of a stammer and lisp. He was uncommonly self-assured, obstinate, bumptious, and arrogant. He was foolhardy, often taking unnecessary chances with his life. He hated school and refused to absorb anything that didn't interest him. When students were listed according to scholastic achievement, he was always at the bottom. In the army, he was a wild and careless soldier, but he did receive several decorations for bravery. He was thrown out of politics shortly after undertaking it as a career.

ANSWERS   *Applicant* A: Thomas A. Edison, B: Theodore Roosevelt, C: John Dillinger, D: Winston Churchill

SOURCE: Slightly adapted from William Rudelius, W. Bruce Erickson, and William J. Bakula, Jr., *An Introduction to Contemporary Business* (New York: Harcourt Brace Jovanovich, 1976), p. 113. Reprinted by permission of the publisher. Much of the material was provided by Judith Furrer of Inver Hills Community College.

PHYSICAL EXAMINATIONS

Although many organizations do not require physical examinations for applicants, they continue to be widely used in the case of jobs involving physical activity. The purpose of the examination is to determine whether the applicant has the capability to perform the duties required in the job description and to deter-

HOW NOT TO TURN DOWN JOB APPLICANTS

The selection process is a systematic attempt to identify and employ those applicants best suited for the position. Many applicants may be rejected at each stage. The student body of the American Graduate School of International Management assembled the following collection of letters from companies turning down the job applications of some of those about to be graduated. The following excerpts were extracted from those letters:

After most careful consideration of your qualifications and background, we are unable to identify anything you can do for us . . .

We're certain you could be more useful some place else . . .

You write you'll visit our headquarters in Los Angeles and I thought before you spent too much time trying to find it, we'd tell you our headquarters are in Portland, Oregon . . .

. . . but we're sure you will find something you can do.

My conscience doesn't allow me to encourage you.

Unfortunately, we have to be selective . . .

I am sorry, but because of the nature of our work we have to be more careful than others in our hiring . . .

SOURCE: Malcolm S. Forbes, "How Not to Turn Down Job Applicants," *Forbes* (June 15, 1977), p. 22. Reprinted by permission.

mine whether the individual has a physical problem that might be used as a basis for subsequent workers' compensation claims.

TESTING

Testing is employed to gain a more objective picture of the qualifications of prospective employees than the self-described credentials on the application form. Testing is a controversial issue in the 1980s, due to the questions of whether tests actually predict job success and whether they are culturally biased. The EEOC requires that all tests must be closely job-related and both reliable and valid. *Reliability* means that the test results are consistent (a person who takes a test three or four times should achieve similar scores). *Validity* means that the test measures what it is intended to measure. (A typing speed test is an invalid predictor of intelligence, but it may be entirely valid in evaluating the skills of a potential typist.)

ORIENTATION OF THE NEWLY HIRED WORKER

The end result of the selection process is the hiring of the most qualified candidate for the position. Most medium- and large-sized organizations utilize a formal orientation program to introduce the new member to colleagues and procedures. Orientation is typically the joint responsibility of the human resources department and the department in which the new employee will work.

An effective orientation program should provide the individual with a basic understanding of the organization and its philosophy, objectives, policies, and organizational structure. The compensation, appraisal, and benefits programs are typically explained in detail during the orientation program.

Training and Development

Although organizations often attempt to employ fully qualified individuals who require little or no training, training is usually essential for new organizational members as well as for seasoned managers, who require improved skills in order to advance in the organization. Employees at all levels—operative, technical, and managerial—will require some training at one or more points in their careers. Although the methods, objectives, and course or program contents often differ, the basic principles of teaching/learning are the same.

TRAINING VERSUS MANAGEMENT DEVELOPMENT

Differences are present between training and management development programs, although the distinctions are not always clearcut. In fact educational programs generally have elements of both development and training. Training differs from development in that it relies more heavily upon the instructor; development, on the other hand, relies more upon the student's initiative in asking questions to bring out important points and their relevance. Development is, in fact, self-development. Table 10-2 shows how programs change as the content and the hierarchical level of the students change.

EMPLOYEE TRAINING PROGRAMS

Training is a systematic process by which the individual learns skills, abilities, knowledge, or attitudes to further organizational and personal goals. Several basic approaches to training are commonly used. The approaches may be divided into two categories: on-the-job training and off-the-job training.

An estimated 90 percent of all training is performed *on the job.* The underlying belief is that the individual can best learn the specifics of the job—how to operate a machine, conduct an interview, or sell the firm's products—through training in the actual work environment. This method is often used when the job to be learned is relatively simple, and special classes or instructors are unnecessary. Typically, the immediate supervisor or another experienced worker handles the training.

One of the oldest types of training is *apprenticeship training.* This technique is widely used in such highly skilled crafts as plumbing, printing, construction, welding, and barbering. Apprentice training is regulated by the U.S. Department of Labor, which determines the lengths of apprenticeships and the mini-

On-the-job training consists of learning the specifics of a job in the actual work environment.

Apprenticeship training is a combination of on-the-job training and off-the-job instruction.

**Table 10-2
GENERAL
MODEL OF
TRAINING AND
DEVELOPMENT**

PURE TRAINING		PURE DEVELOPMENT
CHARACTERISTICS		
Lecture	→	Variety of techniques
Spoon-feeding	→	Students must seek answers
Highly descriptive	→	Abstract
Basic facts	→	Conceptual
Little "homework"	→	Much "outside" study
Passivity	→	Participation
Emphasis on teaching	→	Emphasis on learning
Narrow scope material	→	Broad topical coverage
Related to day-to-day problems	→	Related to long-term problems
Problem correction	→	Prevention of problems

LEVEL

Shop or Clerical Programs

    First Line Supervisory Training Programs

        Top Supervisory or Lower Executive Development Programs

           Mid-Management Development Programs

               Top Management Development Programs

LOCATION

On-Site Classrooms or On-the-Job ————→ Off-Site (often at resort areas)

SOURCE: Adapted from Edgar T. Busch, "Industrial Education," Working Paper, Western Kentucky University, 1980. Used with permission.

mum requirements for classroom instruction. A typical apprenticeship lasts three to five years and represents a major time and expense commitment by both trainees and the firm.

Apprentice programs are a combination of both on-the-job and off-the-job training. The on-the-job portion consists of instructions from an experienced employee called a *journeyman.* It is common for labor unions to be heavily involved in off-the-job classroom or theory instruction, which may be conducted at a local union hall. In other instances such off-the-job training may be obtained from an approved school.

Off-the-job training is any form of training conducted away from the individual's work area. This approach is utilized in instances in which the participation of the new worker would slow production and/or be potentially dangerous. In such instances the organization can construct a training area equipped with similar machines and processes as those found on the job. This approach, called *vestibule training,* is designed to build skills by allowing the individual to perform the work under the supervision of a trainer before being assigned to the actual work area.

Vestibule training is designed to build skills by allowing the individual to perform the work in a training area under the supervision of a trainer before being assigned to the actual work area.

Off-the-job training also is typically used when the employee must gain a considerable body of knowledge and theory before beginning the job. Classroom training programs utilize traditional techniques of lectures, programmed instruction materials, conferences, films, and other audio-visual aids, as well as special machines to develop the necessary skills before the individual is assigned to the work area. Technical companies, such as IBM, Motorola, Xerox, and AT & T, conduct extensive classroom training programs for their sales and service personnel.

MANAGEMENT DEVELOPMENT PROGRAMS

Although the concept of job training has been applied for thousands of years, the special focus upon the training and development of present and potential managers is a twentieth-century phenomenon. One of the earliest development programs was developed in 1901 by the retailing pioneer James Cash Penney. Penney developed a system whereby the manager-partner of each drygoods store in the chain would select and train one prospective manager, who would then be sent out to found another store.[11]

Since every organization has a continuous need for effective managers at every level, management development programs have spread rapidly. One survey of U.S. firms employing 1,000 or more employees revealed that almost three-fourths of the respondents have formal management development programs.[12]

Management development programs can also be categorized as on-the-job and off-the-job. One commonly used on-the-job development technique is *job rotation*, whereby managers are assigned to different departments to familiarize them with the various operations of the organization and the contributions of each. *Coaching* of junior executives by having them work closely with a senior manager (the person's *mentor* or *sponsor*) is another widely used technique. At the Jewel Cos. a sponsor is formally assigned to each management trainee. In a national survey of 1,250 executives, nearly two-thirds of the respondents reported having had a mentor or sponsor.[13]

Off-the-job management development may include regular university courses (leading, perhaps, to a graduate degree), special in-house management programs conducted by professional organizations or consultants, or formal courses conducted off the company premises in special institutes established by the firm. Such major firms as Texaco, McDonald's, and General Motors offer such programs at company institutes which resemble colleges.

Management development programs may also be classified on the basis of levels of managers. As Table 10-2 indicates, as the management levels change from supervisory to middle to top management, the emphasis shifts from training to development.

Job rotation is a management development technique in which managers are assigned to different departments to familiarize them with various operations of the organization.

Coaching is a management development technique in which junior executives work closely with a senior manager, called a mentor or sponsor.

[11] Gerard R. Roche, "Much Ado About Mentors," *Harvard Business Review* (January–February 1979), p. 24.
[12] Desmond D. Martin and William J. Kearney, "The Behavioral Sciences in Management Development Programs," *Journal of Business* (May 1978), p. 28.
[13] Roche, "Much Ado About Mentors," p. 14.

Supervisory programs typically focus upon assisting supervisors in fulfilling their responsibilities. Although the programs vary considerably, such topics as processing union grievances, seniority policies, nondiscrimination requirements, safety procedures, and discipline are usually covered. It is also common for such programs to include tours of other areas of the organization and explanations of job evaluations and merit ratings in order to provide the first-line manager with a broader perspective of the total organization, rather than a total focus on his or her department.

Middle management programs utilize such techniques as on-the-job coaching, job rotation, and special committee assignments as part of a long-range plan to increase the breadth of the manager as he or she progresses in the organization. Off-the-job development programs are also frequently employed. Figure 10-6 shows a two-week middle management program offered by the University of Denver.

Development programs for top management are clearly self-developmental in nature. Managers at or near the top of the organization may have to determine for themselves their needs for expanded knowledge. Seminars, special courses, and other on-the-job assignments are as useful for these executives as for middle-level managers.

**Figure 10-6
TWO-WEEK
DEVELOPMENT
PROGRAM FOR
MIDDLE MANAGERS**

SOURCE: Center for Management Development, University of Denver. Used with permission.

FIRST SESSION JUNE 3–JUNE 7

Monday June 3	Tuesday June 4	Wednesday June 5	Thursday June 6	Friday June 7
8:30–11:45 ECONOMICS Inflation/Unemployment—the classic dilemma	8:30–11:45 FINANCE The nature of capital markets	8:30–11:45 MARKETING Marketing management and government regulation	8:30–11:45 ACCOUNTING Financial disclosure: The right to know (external)	8:30–11:45 MANAGEMENT Executive development: Its advantages and disadvantages
Lunch				
1:30–4:45 INTERNATIONAL MARKETS Natural resources	1:30–4:45 MONETARY POLICY Its meaning to the individual firm	1:30–4:45 MARKETING RESEARCH Applications of research to marketing management	1:30–4:45 FINANCIAL DISCLOSURE The right to know (internal)	1:30–4:45 BOARDS OF DIRECTORS The obligations and responsibilities

SECOND SESSION JUNE 10–JUNE 14

Monday June 10	Tuesday June 11	Wednesday June 12	Thursday June 13	Friday June 14
8:30–11:45 ENERGY RESOURCES Alternatives and risks re: The energy crisis	8:30–11:45 CIVIL RIGHTS Equal Employment Opportunity: What's on the horizon?	8:30–11:45 LEGAL PROBLEMS Current problems: Consumerism and legislation	8:30–11:45 SOCIETAL ISSUES Social change and its significance to the firm	8:30–11:45 A PLEA FOR ETHICS A society of ambivalence
Lunch				
1:30–4:45 TRANSPORTATION A new perspective: What are the options?	1:30–4:45 POLLUTION Who pays the bill?	1:30–4:45 CORPORATE POWER Is it used wisely?	1:30–4:45 BUSINESS AND SOCIETY Current issues and challenges	1:30–4:45 SUMMARY AND CONCLUSIONS

It is important to stress the fact that development comes from within. No one can develop another person; he or she can only aid that person in reaching his or her potential. The second point to realize about development is that it is directed toward broadening the individual manager. In many cases promotion channels lead the manager to a series of positions of increased authority and responsibility within a specialized functional area. Development programs must broaden potential top executives by exposing them to other functional areas if they are to become general managers, presidents, or chief executive officers. In addition candidates for top management positions need experience with such external organizations as trade associations, community-wide organizations, governments, and, possibly, other nations. Although top managers possess specialized knowledge, they must operate as *generalists.* Effective management development programs can make major contributions in achieving these results.[14]

Performance Appraisal

The performance of every employee is continually evaluated by that person's superior. If no formal appraisal system exists, that appraisal is likely to produce all of the disadvantages and none of the advantages of appraisal. Informal systems too often result in supervisors emphasizing personal traits such as appearance, sincerity, and loyalty rather than such factors as quantity of work and the quality of that work. In cases where there is no formally organized system, supervisors may not be consistent in evaluating all workers in a department. Worker A might be rewarded for often coming to work early while Worker B receives no recognition for a perfect record of being prompt—but not early. Without a formal system, few checks and balances exist.[15]

Formal systems of performance appraisal were begun to bring order to the appraisal process and thereby reduce worker complaints about favoritism, inequity, and lack of fairness. Current methods attempt to ensure that all employees in each department are consistently evaluated on fair criteria. Fairness is important since performance appraisals are often significant factors in determining pay increases and promotion opportunities. To achieve equal treatment, a number of appraisal formats exist. Graphic rating scales, forced distribution, and management by objectives (MBO) forms are three widely used examples.

Graphic rating scales are performance appraisal forms listing a number of factors, with a continuum for each factor ranging from poor or unacceptable to superior. The rater checks the appropriate degree of merit on each factor being evaluated. Since each degree of merit typically has been assigned a point value, total scores can be determined for the purpose of allocating merit pay increases or other rewards. A rating scale used by the U.S. Air Force in evaluating company grade officer effectiveness is shown in Figure 10-7.

[14] See Jeremy Main, "The Executive Yearn to Learn," *Fortune* (May 3, 1982), pp. 234–248.

[15] Douglas Cederblom, "The Performance Appraisal Interview: A Review, Implications, and Suggestions," *Academy of Management Review* (April 1982), pp. 219–227.

**Figure 10-7
UNITED STATES AIR
FORCE COMPANY
GRADE OFFICER
RATING FORM**

I.	RATEE IDENTIFICATION DATA *(Read AFR 36–10 carefully before filling in any item)*		
1. NAME *(Last, First, Middle Initial)*	2. SSAN *(Include Suffix)*	3. GRADE	4. DAFSC
5. ORGANIZATION, COMMAND, LOCATION			6. PAS CODE
7. PERIOD OF REPORT FROM: THRU:	8. NO. DAYS OF SUPERVISION	9. REASON FOR REPORT	

II. JOB DESCRIPTION 1. DUTY TITLE:
2. KEY DUTIES, TASKS AND RESPONSIBILITIES:

III. PERFORMANCE FACTORS
¹Specific example of performance required

	NOT OBSERVED OR NOT RELEVANT	FAR¹ BELOW STANDARD	BELOW¹ STANDARD	MEETS STANDARD	ABOVE¹ STANDARD	WELL¹ ABOVE STANDARD
1. JOB KNOWLEDGE *(Depth, currency, breadth)*	O					
2. JUDGMENT AND DECISIONS *(Consistent, accurate, effective)*	O					
3. PLAN AND ORGANIZE WORK *(Timely, creative)*	O					
4. MANAGEMENT OF RESOURCES *(Manpower and material)*	O					
5. LEADERSHIP *(Initiative, accept responsibility)*	O					
6. ADAPTABILITY TO STRESS *(Stable, flexible, dependable)*	O					
7. ORAL COMMUNICATION *(Clear, concise, confident)*	O					
8. WRITTEN COMMUNICATION *(Clear, concise, organized)*	O					
9. PROFESSIONAL QUALITIES *(Attitude, dress, cooperation, bearing)*	O					
10. HUMAN RELATIONS *(Equal opportunity participation, sensitivity)*						

AF FORM NOV 79 707   PREVIOUS EDITIONS ARE OBSOLETE   OFFICER EFFECTIVENESS REPORT

Forced distribution scales require evaluators to place a predetermined percentage of persons being evaluated into four or five categories. For example, a scale might require the appraiser to assign 10 percent to the poor category, 20 percent as below average, 40 percent as average, 20 percent as above average, and the top 10 percent as excellent. The advantage of the forced distribution format over the traditional graphic rating scale is that it forces the rater to differentiate among subordinates by prohibiting the common characteristic of categorizing persons as average or above average. Such a format would have prohibited one U.S. Navy unit from rating 95 percent of its graduates in the top 5 percent of its class.

Management by objectives is another widely used evaluation technique. As described in Chapter 4, the MBO procedure involves agreement by both superior and subordinate on the subordinate's objectives for the forthcoming period. At the end of the period, the subordinate is evaluated on how well he or she performed in meeting the agreed-upon objectives. An MBO form is shown in Figure 10-8.

It is common practice for superiors to discuss the formal appraisal results with the subordinate during an appraisal interview. Such an interview provides an opportunity for both the evaluator and the subordinate to discuss differences of opinion concerning performance and the causes of and possible solutions for unsatisfactory performance.[16]

Compensation and Employee Benefits

Ronald Reagan, Mike Schmidt, and William Agee have at least one thing in common: Each earned more than $200,000 in 1983. Schmidt's salary was one of four major league baseball salaries—along with Dave Winfield of the New York Yankees, Gary Carter of the Montreal Expos, and George Foster of the New York Mets—that exceeded $1.5 million. Agee, former chief executive officer of Bendix Corp., failed to even make the top twenty in industrial salaries with a recent total compensation estimated at just under $1 million.[17] At the opposite extreme, the worker receiving the minimum wage earns a gross salary of $134 weekly.

A sound compensation program will assist in attracting employees and in retaining them. Since the compensation administration program affects every member of the organization, it is one of the most important and time-consuming tasks of the human resources department.

JOB EVALUATIONS—DETERMINING COMPENSATION LEVELS FOR DIFFERENT JOBS

All employees—operative workers, technical employees, and managers—want to feel that they are paid fairly compared to other jobholders. To assure that positions requiring the least skill, responsibility, and effort are paid at the lowest levels and those jobs requiring high levels of effort, skill, and responsibility are rewarded accordingly, many firms conduct *job evaluations*. This is a method for

Job evaluation is a comparison of different jobs on such bases as responsibilities and education, skill, and physical requirements to determine the relative worth of a job.

---

[16] See H. John Bernardin and M. Ronald Buckley, "Strategies in Rater Training," *Academy of Management Review* (April 1981), pp. 205–212.

[17] "Executives' Pay Goes Up, Up and Away," *U.S. News & World Report* (May 24, 1982), pp. 59–61.

GENERAL APPRAISAL OF EMPLOYEE PERFORMANCE	TO BE COMPLETED BY EMPLOYEE			TO BE COMPLETED BY SUPERVISOR			
Complete items 1 through 8 for all employees and items 9 and 10 when applicable. Differences between ratings by employee and by supervisor must be discussed.	EXCEEDS EXPECTATIONS	MEETS EXPECTATIONS	NEEDS IMPROVEMENT	EXCEEDS EXPECTATIONS	MEETS EXPECTATIONS	NEEDS IMPROVEMENT	INSUFFICIENT OPPORTUNITY TO OBSERVE
1. JOB KNOWLEDGE: Consider overall knowledge of duties and responsibilities as required for current job or position	☐	☐	☐	☐	☐	☐	☐
2. PRODUCTIVITY: Evaluate amount of work generated and completed successfully as compared to amount of work expected for this job or position	☐	☐	☐	☐	☐	☐	☐
3. QUALITY: Rate correctness, completeness, accuracy and economy of work—overall quality	☐	☐	☐	☐	☐	☐	☐
4. INITIATIVE: Self motivation—consider amount of direction required—seeks improved methods and techniques—consistence in trying to do better	☐	☐	☐	☐	☐	☐	☐

**Figure 10-8
MANAGEMENT BY
OBJECTIVES FORM**

SOURCE: State of Illinois, Department of Personnel.

Wage refers to a method of payment based on a calculation of the number of hours worked or the number of units produced by an employee.

Salary refers to compensation for white-collar workers based on a unit of time.

determining wage levels for different jobs by comparing different jobs on such bases as responsibilities, education, skill requirements, and physical requirements.[18] This comparison process is used in determining the relative worth of a job. Jobs whose relative worths are similar are included in the same pay grade, labor grade, or job class. A pay scale is then determined for each pay grade. The U.S. Civil Service has placed its jobs into eighteen classes. The pay range for each of the classes is shown in Table 10-3.

Should the organization decide to utilize a *pay range* for each grade or class instead of a single fixed rate, it must also have a plan for determining the bases for employee movement within the range. Some organizations permit step pay increases solely on the basis of time on the job (seniority), while others use the results of performance appraisals to determine whether a person merits a move to a higher step (merit).

Although the terms *wage* and *salary* are often used interchangeably, *wage* refers to a method of payment based on a calculation of the number of hours worked or the number of units produced by an employee. *Salary* refers to compensation for white-collar workers such as clerks, office workers, and managers based upon a unit of time. Managers—unlike workers receiving wages and non-

[18] See Elliott Jaques, "Taking Time Seriously in Evaluating Jobs," *Harvard Business Review* (September–October 1979), pp. 39–42.

5. USE OF TIME:	Uses available time wisely—is punctual reporting to work—absenteeism—accomplishes required work on or ahead of schedule	☐	☐	☐	☐	☐	☐	☐
6. PLANNING:	Sets realistic objectives—anticipates and prepares for future requirements—establishes logical priorities	☐	☐	☐	☐	☐	☐	☐
7. FOLLOW-UP:	Maintains control of workloads—allocates resources economically—insures that assignments are completed accurately and timely	☐	☐	☐	☐	☐	☐	☐
8. HUMAN RELATIONS:	Establishes and maintains cordial work climate—promotes harmony and enthusiasm—displays sincere interest in assisting other employees	☐	☐	☐	☐	☐	☐	☐
9. LEADERSHIP:	Sets high standards—provides good managerial example—encourages subordinates to perform efficiently—communicates effectively	☐	☐	☐	☐	☐	☐	☐
10. SUBORDINATE DEVELOPMENT:	Helps subordinates plan career development—grooms potential replacements—gives guidance and counsel	☐	☐	☐	☐	☐	☐	☐

Table 10-3   FEDERAL PAY SCALE

PAY STEP	1	2	3	4	5	6	7	8	9	10
GS-1	$ 8,342	$ 8,620	$ 8,898	$ 9,175	$ 9,453	$ 9,615	$ 9,890	$10,165	$10,178	$10,439
GS-2	9,381	9,603	9,913	10,178	10,292	10,595	10,898	11,201	11,504	11,807
GS-3	10,235	10,576	10,917	11,258	11,599	11,940	12,281	12,622	12,963	13,304
GS-4	11,490	11,873	12,256	12,639	13,022	13,405	13,788	14,171	14,554	14,937
GS-5	12,854	13,282	13,710	14,138	14,566	14,994	15,422	15,850	16,278	16,706
GS-6	14,328	14,806	15,284	15,762	16,240	16,718	17,196	17,674	18,152	18,630
GS-7	15,922	16,453	16,984	17,515	18,046	18,577	19,108	19,639	20,170	20,701
GS-8	17,634	18,222	18,810	19,398	19,986	20,574	21,162	21,750	22,338	22,926
GS-9	19,477	20,126	20,775	21,424	22,073	22,722	23,371	24,020	24,669	25,318
GS-10	21,449	22,164	22,879	23,594	24,309	25,024	25,739	26,454	27,169	27,884
GS-11	23,566	24,352	25,138	25,924	26,710	27,496	28,282	29,068	29,854	30,640
GS-12	28,245	29,187	30,129	31,071	32,013	32,955	33,897	34,839	35,781	36,723
GS-13	33,586	34,706	35,826	36,946	38,066	39,186	40,306	41,426	42,546	43,666
GS-14	39,689	41,012	42,335	43,658	44,981	46,304	47,627	48,950	50,273	51,596
GS-15	46,685	48,241	49,797	51,353	52,909	54,465	56,021	57,577*	59,133*	60,689*
GS-16	54,755	56,580	58,405*	60,230*	62,055*	63,880*	65,705*	67,530*	69,355*	
GS-17	64,142*	66,280*	68,418*	70,556*	72,694*					
GS-18	75,177*									

* The rate of basic pay payable to employees at these rates is limited to $57,500.00, the rate payable for level V of the executive schedule. Prior to January 1, 1982, the maximum was limited to $50,112.50.

managerial salaried employees—typically do not receive extra compensation for the extra hours they sometimes work.

In addition to base wages or salaries, organizations occasionally develop *incentive* compensation programs designed to reward employees for superior performance. Bonuses and profit-sharing plans are common methods for rewarding employees for above-average output and/or profitability.

FRINGE BENEFITS—NONMONETARY BENEFITS

Fringe benefits are nonmonetary benefits such as insurance, retirement plans, paid vacations, holidays, and the like.

The total benefits package includes more than the contents of the worker's take-home pay. *Fringe benefits* are such nonmonetary benefits as health and life insurance, retirement benefits, paid vacations and holidays, sick-leave pay, credit unions, recreational programs, and health and safety programs. Such benefits currently cost the organization an additional thirty-five cents for each dollar in direct wages or salaries. Increasingly common fringe benefits for operative employees are dental insurance, employee counseling, legal advice, and prescription drug insurance. Managers may receive such benefits as relocation allowances, stock options, low-interest loans, financial counseling, and liberal expense accounts.[19] Salaried employees at Anheuser-Busch are given two cases of beer each month to take home.

Many organizations attempt to inform their employees of the benefits received and their cost to the firm. Often this information is conveyed by means of a quarterly or annual statement of benefits. An example of such a statement is shown in Figure 10-9.

Promotion, Transfers, and Separations

A promotion is movement to a position with higher pay, more responsibility, and added status.

It is probable that most persons will experience promotions, transfers, and separations during their working lives. A *promotion* is movement to a position with higher pay, more responsibility, and added status. Although promotions are occasionally based upon friendship or family connections, they normally are based upon more objective criteria. Promotions for both managerial and nonmanagerial positions typically result from three primary factors: (1) merit—appraisal of current and past performance; (2) seniority—length of service; and (3) ability—perceived capacity to perform higher-level work.

Transfer is a lateral movement to another position which usually does not include a pay increase or added responsibilities.

Transfers are lateral movements to other positions that ordinarily do not include pay increases or added responsibilities. Transfers occur for a number of reasons: to gain broader work experience and avoid overspecialization; to meet changing demands for work skills among departments or work shifts; to accommodate personal needs of the employee; and to correct a mismatch of worker and job.

A separation refers to a resignation, a layoff, a dismissal, or a retirement.

The term *separation* includes resignations, layoffs, dismissals, and retire-

[19] J. H. Foegen, "The Creative Flowering of Employee Benefits," *Business Horizons* (May–June 1982), pp. 9–13.

Benefit Statement 1981

As of   12-31-81

Based on your annual salary of $14,628

Birth Date   OCTOBER 1953

For: DOE, JOHN
Soc. Sec. No.:   123-45-6789
Agency No.:   129-COMM-001
          PERSONNEL & TRAINING

VSRS RECORD

Membership Date	Service Credit Years	Service Credit Months	Total Contributions	Total Interest	Account Balance
05-80	01	08	$1,083.42	$3.82	$1,087.24

Service credit assumes continuous service under VSRS since membership date. Your actual service credit may be less than reported here if you had a break in service.

SERVICE RETIREMENT ESTIMATE

Estimated Monthly Benefit
$421 State Retirement Plan
$512 Social Security
$933 Total

Estimate Assumes	State Plan	Soc. Sec.
Retirement Age	65-00	65-00
Retirement Date	10-01-2018	10-01-2018
Years of Contributions	38-05	43-00
Average Final Salary	$13,001	

Total Benefits Received Over Average Retiree Life Span

	State Plan	Soc. Sec.
	$90,968	$110,592

Your dependent spouse may receive at age 65 a Social Security benefit that is half of your benefit.

DISABILITY RETIREMENT ESTIMATE

Estimated Monthly Benefit
$0 State Retirement Plan
$569 Social Security for you
$285 Additional Social Security
    for dependent family

Estimate Assumes	State Plan	Soc. Sec.
Disability Age	28-02	28-02
Disability Date	12-31-1981	12-31-1981
Years of Contributions	01-08	06-03
Average Final Salary	$13,001	

YOU ARE NOT ELIGIBLE FOR A VSRS BENEFIT UNTIL YOU HAVE 5 YEARS OF SERVICE CREDIT UNLESS YOUR DISABILITY IS WORK RELATED.

AFTER YOU RETIRE

Annual cost of living increases may be payable to you. If you have at least five years of service, your life insurance continues in reduced amounts.

IF YOU DIE WHILE EMPLOYED

LUMP SUM PAYMENTS

Group Life Insurance

$30,000 Natural Death Benefit
$30,000 Additional Accidental
          Death Benefit

$1,087.24 Refund of VSRS Account

ESTIMATED MONTHLY BENEFIT TO SURVIVORS

Social Security Payment Ranging From:

$407 Minimum (Spouse at least 60 years old)
          up to
$997 Maximum (Spouse and at least 2 dependent
          children under 18 years old)

Estimate Assumes	Soc. Sec.
Age at Death	28-02
Date of Death	12-31-81
Years of Contributions	06-03

Your state retirement benefit is administered by VSRS on behalf of the Commonwealth of Virginia. It is not guaranteed by VSRS. These projections assume continuing participation in the plan by you and the Commonwealth.

HEALTH CARE BENEFITS

YOU HAVE COVERAGE FOR YOURSELF ONLY.

Your Coverage Is With
BLUE CROSS AND BLUE SHIELD

DEFERRED COMPENSATION PLAN

Balance as of 12/31/81

Fixed Income Fund	$0.00
Equity Fund	$0.00
Savings Fund	$0.00
Total	$0.00

IF THERE IS A MISTAKE IN YOUR BIRTH DATE OR ANY VSRS OR LIFE INSURANCE IN-FORMATION, CONTACT VSRS, MCA RESEARCH ANALYSIS SECTION, P.O. BOX 3-X RICH-MOND, VA. 23207, (804) 786-3831, EXT. 282. IF THERE IS ANY OTHER ERROR, CONTACT YOUR PERSONNEL OFFICE OF THE DEPARTMENT OF PERSONNEL AND TRAINING, 101 N. FOURTEENTH ST., RICHMOND, VA. 23219, (804) 225-2132.

VSRS   DEPARTMENT OF PERSONNEL AND TRAINING

NOTES

VSRS

Service Credit -- The service credit figure assumes you have had continuous VSRS service since your membership date. If you ever had a break in your VSRS service, your actual service credit might be less than reported here. Your service credit includes purchased credit and credit under all VSRS employer plans.

Contributions -- The member contribution rate is 5 percent of annual salary.

Interest -- Four percent interest is added to your account on June 30 of each year, based on the balance in your member contribution account on the previous June 30.

Service Retirement Benefit --The Basic Benefit payment is reported here. It is based on your highest 36 consecutive months of salary out of the last 42 months. If you did not have 36 months of service credit, it is based on your average salary over that period.   For a more accurate projection of your benefits, you may contact a retirement advisor at VSRS.

When you retire, you may choose the Basic Benefit or an optional benefit.

If you have no service credit before April 1, 1980, your state retirement benefit plus one-half of your primary Social Security benefit cannot be more than 62.5 percent of your average final compensation. If this ceiling applies to you, the state retirement benefit reported here has taken the ceiling into ac-count.

Disability Retirement Benefits -- You are eligible to apply for regular disability retirement after you have five years of service. Work-related disability retirement does not have a service credit requirement. You must be permanently disabled to receive the state retirement benefit.

Beneficiaries -- Keep VSRS informed of your beneficiary changes.

SOCIAL SECURITY

Assumptions -- Your Social Security estimates assume you have made contributions to Social Security since age 22 or since 1951, whichever is later. If your VSRS membership date was before age 22, the estimates assume you have made contributions since your membership date or since 1951, whichever is later.

The estimates are based on your annual salary as listed here and they assume that your salary level relative to the national average salary has remained the same since your contributions began. Only Social Security can establish eligibility and amount of benefits. Because your Social Security salary history is not available to the state, the amounts shown here are only estimates. If there is anything unusual in your salary history, such as years with little or no earnings covered by Social Security, your actual benefit will vary from the estimates in this statement. Check with your local Social Security of-fice before making a retirement decision.

Disability Retirement -- You must be totally disabled and the disability must be expected to last at least 12 months or end in death to receive Social Security disability benefits. Benefits are not available until you have been disabled for five months.

GROUP LIFE INSURANCE

Dismemberment -- Your Group Life Insurance also covers you for accidental dismemberment and loss of sight.

Insurance After Service Retirement -- If you have at least five years of VSRS service credit when you retire, your natural death benefit will continue in reduced amounts. It will reduce by 2 percent per month until it reaches one-fourth of its value. The accidental death and dismemberment benefits end when you retire.

Insurance After Disability Retirement -- The continuation of insurance is the same as for service re-tirement, except the natural death benefit does not begin to reduce until you reach age 65.

Beneficiaries -- Keep VSRS informed of your beneficiary changes.

HEALTH CARE PLAN

Type of Membership -- Information on your type of membership is taken from payroll information on the "as of" date shown on the reverse side. If the type of membership reported here is not what you thought you had, contact your agency for assistance.

DEFERRED COMPENSATION PLAN

Balances -- Your balances reflect year-end adjustments, including expense adjustments. The deferred com-pensation plan is a voluntary retirement savings plan. If no amounts are shown, you did not choose to join the plan.

Consult your benefits handbooks and brochures for further details. The availability and amounts of all benefits are governed by the legal documents pertaining to them.

Figure 10-9
STATEMENT OF EMPLOYEE BENEFITS

Reprinted by permission of VSRS.

ments. Employees voluntarily leave the organization for a variety of reasons—desire to live in another part of the country, job transfers of spouses, competitive job offers at increased salary, or more challenging work. Layoffs are temporary separations resulting from business slowdowns due to reduced sales, plant conversions, or physical relocation of facilities. Dismissals are separations initiated by the organization, generally as a result of poor performance or flagrant and repeated violations of rules. Dismissals occasionally result from staff reductions and from corporate mergers that result in elimination of duplicate functions.

A major cause of separation is retirement. This type of separation has traditionally been fairly predictable, since most workers retire after a certain number of years on the job or at age sixty-five. However, two factors are contributing to difficulties in predicting the number of retirements: high rates of inflation, which may lead workers to work longer because of a fear that they will be unable to live on their private pensions plus social security benefits,[20] and changes in federal laws prohibiting mandatory retirement at age sixty-five.

The amendment to the Age Discrimination in Employment Act of 1967 prohibiting discrimination against workers between forty and seventy is concrete recognition that the work force of the 1980s are living longer than previous generations of workers and are usually able to perform satisfactory work beyond their sixty-fifth year. While 700,000 workers reach age sixty-five in an average year, less than 10 percent of them will choose to continue working. Although the current trend is toward early rather than postponed retirement, continued inflation could change this trend in the future.

[20] See James B. Shaw and Lisa L. Grubbs, "The Process of Retiring: Organizational Entry in Reverse," *Academy of Management Review* (January 1981), pp. 41–47. See also Allen C. Bluedorn, "Managing Turnover Strategically," *Business Horizons* (March–April 1982), pp. 6–12.

Summary

No organizational resource is more important than people. Organizations recognize the importance of effective human resources by developing human resources (or personnel) departments staffed by specialists in such areas as recruiting, training and management development, wage and salary administration, employee health and safety, industrial relations, and employee services.

The human resources department performs a staff function. It advises and serves the line organization in developing forecasts of employee needs; recruiting and interviewing job candidates; hiring and training; administering wage and salary programs, benefits, and health and safety programs; and evaluating employee performance.

Most firms attempt to fill positions by promotion from within. Only when special skills are needed that are not possessed by the organization's employees will outside sources of employees be considered. External sources include private and pubic employment agencies, educational institutions, professional and trade journals, newspaper and radio advertisements, union hiring halls, and recommendations of present employees.

The selection process includes an initial screening, a detailed application, and final interviews. In some instances testing, reference checks, and physical examinations are utilized. The orientation program of newly hired workers is at least partially a responsibility of the human resources department.

Organizations utilize two types of training programs: on-the-job and off-the-job training. Relatively simple jobs may be learned directly on the job; more complex jobs may be taught through special vestibule schools or through a formal classroom program. Management development programs may take the form of job rotation, use of experienced managers as coaches or mentors, and special programs and classroom seminars.

Although performance appraisals are the responsibility of each employee's immediate superior, formal systems are often administered by the human resources department. Such systems are designed to provide consistent, objective measurement criteria. Such appraisal formats as graphic rating scales, forced distribution scales, and management by objectives forms are often used.

Compensation is an important factor in every organization. Direct monetary compensation may be in the form of wages, salaries, bonuses, or profit sharing. Indirect forms of compensation—commonly called *fringe benefits*—include retirement plans, health and life insurance programs, and paid holidays, vacation, and sick leave, among others. These benefit programs are typically administered by the human resources department.

REVIEW EXERCISES

1. Define the following terms: (a) human resources management (b) job analysis (c) job description (d) job specification (e) equal employment opportunity (f) affirmative action program (g) on-the-job training (h) apprenticeship training (i) vestibule training (j) job rotation (k) coaching (l) job evaluation (m) wage (n) salary (o) fringe benefit (p) promotion (q) transfer (r) separation.

2. Why is the human resources (or personnel) department categorized as staff?

3. Relate the job analysis to job descriptions and job specifications. How does it affect job evaluations?

4. Identify and briefly describe the major federal laws affecting human resources management.

5. List the steps in the recruitment and selection process.

6. Distinguish between training programs and management development programs.

7. Compare and contrast on-the-job and off-the-job training. Under what circumstances should each be used?

8. What is the major advantage of forced distribution scales in a performance appraisal?

9. Under what circumstances should incentive compensation programs be used?

10. Identify and briefly explain the major forms of separation.

ASSIGNMENTS/ PROBLEMS/ DISCUSSION QUESTIONS

1. Critically evaluate the various sources of potential job candidates mentioned in the chapter. Recommend a system for generating applicants for technical positions for a Du Pont research facility based upon your analysis.

2. "Job quotas should exist for women and minorities." Do you agree? Defend your answer.

3. Recommend a compensation plan for each of the following positions. Justify your recommendations.

   a. Assembly line worker at Volkswagen's New Stanton, Pennsylvania, manufacturing facility
   b. Industrial salesperson who calls on clients in a two-state area
   c. Center for San Antonio Spurs professional basketball team
   d. Chief executive officer at Hallmark Cards
   e. Manager of the data processing department at a medium-sized company

4. In previous years a number of organizations retained older workers on the payroll because of the mandatory retirement policies in force in their firms even though their work was marginal. In what ways will the Age Discrimination in Employment Act affect policies of the organization's human resources department and practices in the older worker's division or department?

5. Make suggestions for tailoring a fringe benefit program for employees of the following organizations:

   a. Bank of America
   b. Amtrak Passenger Rail System
   c. AT & T
   d. Sears, Roebuck, & Co.

A MANAGERIAL INCIDENT

The Pregnant Manager

The growing ranks of female managers have produced a new human resources issue at firm after firm: How to accommodate the special needs of mothers who are also managers or risk the danger of losing them. The issue has become especially acute due to the increased tendency of households to postpone having children. In the past eight years, the number of women over thirty having a child has almost doubled; for highly educated women over thirty who reside in metropolitan areas, the number is even higher. Barbara Boyle Sullivan, president of a New York management-consulting firm specializing in women managers, states: "This is a part of the changing work force of the 1980s. Women now want to have the satisfaction of having a family along with having a good, challenging job. In the past, they chose one or the other. Women who have postponed having children now are finding that their biological clock is running out of time."

The decision to postpone having children means that many of the new mothers have already had a chance to move up the corporate ladder to positions of increased responsibility. Their departure—whether for a few weeks or several months—often is a major disruption for the firm. In addition motherhood can have a serious effect on their own careers.

A growing number of firms are initiating procedures for reducing the disruptions—both for the individual and for the company. One of the major strengths of the move to flexitime, discussed in the previous chapter, is the flexibility it provides for the manager who is also a mother. As *Business Week* describes the practice:

> Although managers return to work full or part-time shortly after childbirth, some prefer to stay home with the baby for several months—a choice that gives management less trouble than it had expected. Replacing a mother temporarily is no different from replacing a manager who is out for several months because of illness, companies have found. Mothers of children past the infant stage seem to find flexitime a particular boon because it fits in smoothly with the occasional teacher's conference or Little League game.

In many instances, availability of the flexible arrangement means the difference between retaining a valuable employee or losing her to another, more accommodating firm. At Chicago's Continental Illinois National Bank & Trust Co., flexible working hours were necessary to entice Elizabeth M. Carlson, the firm's former manager of personnel systems and research, to return. As *Business Week* explains:

> Carlson, a Phi Beta Kappa and MBA with three children, quit Continental in 1976 because the bank would not be flexible about hours. She joined Bell & Howell Co., which was willing to make adjustments in her schedule, and returned to the bank only after it had changed policy. "When good people like Mrs. Carlson begin to leave because your hours are not compatible with theirs, you get the message—and we did in 1979," says Owen C. Johnson, Jr., Continental Bank's vice-president for corporate personnel services.

Some firms—such as Aetna Life & Casualty—extend special arrangements to fathers as well as mothers.

SOURCE: Sullivan quotation from Earl C. Gottschalk, Jr., "Firms Are Disrupted By Wave of Pregnancy at the Manager Level," *Wall Street Journal* (July 20, 1981), p. 1. The *Business Week* quotations are from "Working Around Motherhood," *Business Week* (May 14, 1982), p. 188.

Questions and Problems

1. Suggest a human resources program designed to deal with the issues raised in this case. Consider both the individual manager and the corporation in the program.

2. Identify methods by which female managers might deal with the impact of childbearing and motherhood on their careers.

11.

Management of Change and Organization Development

The most distinguished hallmark of the
American society is and always has
been change.

> ERIC SEVAREID

You must be in tune with the times and
prepared to break with tradition.

> WILLIAM M. AGEE
> *Former president*
> *of Allied Corp. and chairman*
> *of Bendix Corp.*

Minnesota Mining & Manufacturing Co. (3M) is proud of its accomplishments in developing new products. In fact 3M now offers 45,000 different products. Some of these products were discovered by accident. Scotchgard resulted from research chemist Patsy Sherman's spilling a 3M chemical on her tennis shoes. The chemical could not be washed off and kept the shoes from soiling. But most 3M products were developed by extending and modifying existing product lines. These items were then produced and marketed by forty separate product groups, up from twenty a decade earlier.

Minnesota Mining & Manufacturing is a successful company with some $6.5 billion in sales. It is particularly strong in foreign growth markets. About 34 percent of 3M sales come from overseas. Yet board chairman and chief executive officer, Lewis Lehr, was worried that the company's organizational structure slowed its movement into profitable new markets. The diversified 3M product line and organization worked against overall corporate goals. Vincent Ruane, who heads 3M's electronics division, put it this way: "Each division took its own little slice of the future. We were becoming too fragmented."

Lehr's solution was to reorganize 3M into four market groups: electronics and information technologies; graphics; industrial and consumer services; and life sciences and health care products and services. Lehr's purpose was to stop 3M's decline in some traditional markets like office copiers. The changes were communicated within the organization through a series of meetings in which Lehr commented: ". . . we are changing to remain manageable for the future."

The board chairman then convened a meeting of directors and top management at a Minnesota lodge. The group continued plotting the company's future development. An improved product research program was necessary. Concern was expressed over the fact that 3M was weak in computers and communications. Since the meeting 3M has made some acquisitions in the communications field.[1]

Clearly, Lewis Lehr is facing squarely the problem of organizational change.

All organizations—profit or nonprofit—must change if they are to remain viable. The problems of organizational change and development are among the most important aspects of the organizing function.

Change is an inherent aspect of management. A manager performs the functions of planning, organizing, directing, and controlling in order to accomplish goals. The management job is to move a department or division from point A to point B—to cause change. In fact one might argue that this whole book is about change.

Change is now so important that experts are struggling to define it, model it, categorize it, and study it just as a zoologist examines animal life or a botanist examines plant life. Entire books are now devoted to the subject of change. Probably the volume that has most alerted the public to the forces of change around them is Alvin Toffler's *Future Shock.* Toffler argues:

> The acceleration of change in our time is, itself, an elemental force. This accelerative thrust has personal and psychological, as well as sociological, consequences . . . unless man quickly learns to control the rate of change in his personal affairs as well as in society at large, we are doomed to a massive adaptational breakdown.[2]

This chapter will focus on the changes managers face that affect the whole organization, work groups, and individual employees. The emphasis is on identifying resistance to change, the techniques to overcome this resistance, the success of these techniques, and some of the precautions a manager should take in dealing with such matters. Resistance to change is normal and should be expected in any organization. Absence of resistance to change can suggest a problem. The role of organization development is also considered in this overall process.

Resistance to Change

While it is easier to consider the limitless change processes now occurring, it is important to recognize that change has always been a challenge for virtually every organization. Imagine the changes faced by a colonial merchant, a Civil War era manufacturer, or a firm trying to survive the Great Depression. Change has always been a part of the managerial environment. And the most common characteristic of the change process has been *people's resistance to it.* There is a natural human tendency to resist change because it forces individuals to adopt new ways of doing something. Psychological discomfort is often associated with having to learn a new method, technique, environment, or strategy.

[1] This section is based on and quotes from Maurice Barnfather, "Can 3M Find Happiness in the 1980s?" *Forbes* (March 1, 1982), pp. 112–116.
[2] Alvin Toffler, *Future Shock* (New York: Random House, 1970), pp. 3–4.

The following list of reasons has been suggested for why people resist change.[3]

1. *Lack of clarity:* Uncertainty resulting from changes that persons do not understand leads to resistance by those affected.
2. *Distortion of information:* Workers may sometimes incorrectly estimate the relative importance of information concerning proposed changes or otherwise distort it.
3. *Countervailing forces and reward structures:* In some cases employees may perceive that the reasons or forces for change are balanced by reasons *not* to change. In other words the benefits of change are offset by those associated with maintaining the status quo.
4. *Levels of participation:* Minimal participation in the decisions surrounding the change usually means greater resistance to change.
5. *Pace of change:* Rapid change may also create greater resistance by those involved than would a more gradual change.

A number of studies have investigated the problems of resistance to change. A few of the best-known ones are cited here.

[3] Randall S. Schuler, "Organizational and Individual Change," *Bulletin of Business Research* (November 1977), pp. 6–7.

RESISTANCE TO CHANGE IS COMMONPLACE IN THE ORGANIZATION

SOURCE: © 1982 by NEA, Inc.

THE BANK WIRING ROOM EXPERIMENT

The Hawthorne research, which will be discussed in detail in Chapter 13, recognized that technology was changing the workplace.[4] In the bank wiring room of Western Electric's Hawthorne plant, experimenters found that workers appeared to behave irrationally. A departmental piece-rate pay system was utilized under the assumption that workers would produce more if they were rewarded by increased pay. But this did not occur.

Instead, the workers operated as a group to enforce a stable daily output. Anyone who worked harder than this was disciplined by the rest of the group. The same held true for those who did not work fast enough. From an economic standpoint, this seemed irrational.

Resistance to change appears to have been the explanation for this phenomenon. The technology of the jobs held by these Western Electric employees had been changing rapidly. These changes required the workers to learn new tasks and often disrupted the arrangement of the group. The researchers concluded that the informal group's action in opposition to the piece-rate pay system was an attempt to resist or control change. By enforcing its norms, the group could maintain the network of friendships developed over a long period of time. It was also possible to sustain a work routine with which the members were familiar and comfortable, reducing their anxieties about the technological changes.

THE COCH AND FRENCH STUDY

Lester Coch and John R. P. French, Jr., published a classic study on resistance to change more than three decades ago.[5] The research dealt with a pajama factory in rural Virginia. The firm used a piece-rate incentive plan that included a compensating bonus to protect a worker against a loss in earnings if a transfer was necessary. Labor relations within the plant were good.

Competitive conditions required that the plant make certain production method changes. The Coch and French research was conducted during the introduction of these changes. Employees being transferred to new jobs were formed into four groups. The groups were closely matched on such factors as efficiency, extensiveness of the change to which they were exposed, and group cohesiveness.

The first set of employees was the control group. Management explained the job changes and new piece rates at a group meeting. The group was told that competitive conditions had necessitated the change. Time was allocated for employee questions. The second group also had a meeting. The situation—and the

---

[4] The bank wiring room research is described in F. J. Roethlisberger and William J. Dickson (with Harold A. Wright), *Management and the Worker* (New York: Wiley, 1964), pp. 379–548. Another perspective on the Hawthorne studies is contained in H. McIlvaine Parsons, "What Caused the Hawthorne Effect? A Scientific Detective Story," *Administration and Society* (November 1978), pp. 259–283.

[5] Lester Coch and John R. P. French, Jr., "Overcoming Resistance to Change," *Human Relations* (August 1948), pp. 512–532.

need for cutting costs—was explained with a dramatic demonstration of product quality and price. Then a group of special operators was designated to assist with the development of the details involved in the change. Later, the new methods and piece rates were introduced at a second group meeting. The special operators then went on to become trainers for the other employees. The third and fourth groups were smaller than the second group. Again, the competitive conditions were explained. But this time all of the employees participated in developing the new work situation.

The results were startling. The efficiency ratings of the control group remained essentially the same. Seventeen percent quit within forty days; hostility toward management was noted; and a grievance was filed about the new piece rate. In the second group—the one with representative participation—the employees achieved the plant's standard efficiency rating (the rate at which employees are expected to produce) within fourteen days. No one quit his or her job, and the change was characterized by cooperation. The performance of the special operators was no different from that of the others in the group. The third and fourth groups—those with total participation—exceeded even the record of the limited participation group. No one quit. The workers were cooperative, and their efficiency eventually went to 14 percent over what it was prior to the changes.

When the control group showed no progress thirty-two days after the change, the remaining individuals were reassigned within the plant. A second experiment was conducted two and a half months later involving the remaining thirteen members of the control group. The individual transfers were then operating at slightly above standard efficiency in their new jobs. Again, a new job was introduced. But this time the total participation method was used. The group went on to exceed the standard efficiency rating. An employee concern over seniority was quickly resolved. The changeover was considered harmonious, and no one left during the first nineteen-day period.

The Coch and French research demonstrated the importance of participation in overcoming resistance to change within an organization. Favorable productivity, minimal turnover, and good employee relations resulted from increased levels of participation in decision making surrounding a job change. While considerable research has been done since, the Coch and French study remains a classic in this aspect of management.[6]

OTHER SMALL GROUP RESEARCH

Chapter 15 discusses additional research related to this topic. The studies of groups arranged into circle, chain, Y, and wheel configurations found that the decentralized circle configuration was better at solving complicated, uncertain problems (such as arithmetical tasks) than were the other, more centralized net-

---

[6] An excellent discussion of participative management appears in William E. Hallal and Bob S. Brown, "Participative Management: Myth and Reality," *California Management Review* (Summer 1981), pp. 20–32.

works.[7] (See Figure 15-3.) The same was true for most other tasks. The centralized networks excelled only on the simpler, more stable problems.

The reason for the circle's advantage under conditions of uncertainty is the flexibility of its response. The wheel is awkward and tends to respond in only one way, but the circle is flexible, bending with the *changing* requirements of the job. More people have a better chance to give their viewpoint more quickly in the circle than in the wheel.

The Process of Change

Change may be viewed as a process in that several steps are involved. Changes are not instantaneous, although the process may be relatively quick. The process of change may also be studied for both individuals and an organization. Change agents and interventions are vital components of the change process.[8]

CHANGE AGENTS AND INTERVENTIONS

A change agent is the person who initiates a change within an organization.

All changes involve a *change agent*, the person who initiates the change.[9] In many cases this can be an outside person such as a consultant, auditor, or outside director. In still other cases, new management can be the change agent. For example, Lewis Lehr's role at 3M was that of a change agent.

One of the best examples of management acting as a change agent is Henry Ford II's assumption of the presidency of Ford Motor Co. in 1945. He was only twenty-eight at the time. Ford's grandfather pioneered assembly line production of automobiles, and his company was the dominant U.S. producer for many years. But General Motors surpassed Ford in the 1920s. Ford continued to slip, and by the mid-1940s the company was in dire circumstances. Ford was not expected to be a significant factor in the post–World War II marketplace. But within four years of Henry Ford II's assumption of leadership, the company was again a profitable entity.[10]

An intervention refers to the changes that are introduced to either individuals or the organization.

An *intervention* refers to the changes that are introduced to either individuals or the organization. Implementation of a consultant's proposal for new work rules would be an example of an intervention. Henry Ford II's development of

[7] See Harold J. Leavitt, "Some Effects of Certain Communication Patterns on Group Performance," *Journal of Abnormal and Social Psychology* (January 1951), pp. 38–50; M. E. Shaw, "Some Effects of Problem Complexity upon Problem Solution Efficiency in Different Communication Nets," *Journal of Experimental Psychology* XLVII (1954), pp. 211–217; and Harold J. Leavitt, *Managerial Psychology*, 2nd ed. (Chicago: University of Chicago Press, 1964).

[8] An interesting article is Danny Miller and Peter H. Friesen, "Structural Change and Performance: Quantum Versus Piecemeal-Incremental Approaches," *Academy of Management Journal* (December 1982), pp. 867–892.

[9] Change agents are discussed in Richard N. Ottoway and Gary L. Cooper, "Moving Toward a Taxonomy of Change Agents," *International Studies of Management and Organization* (Spring–Summer 1978), pp. 7–21.

[10] Ted Kade, "Ford Firm Still 'Runs' at Age 75," *Detroit News* (July 14, 1978), pp. 1-A, 4-A.

new products and initiation of financing controls were the interventions that
helped return Ford to profitability.

THE LEWIN MODEL OF INDIVIDUAL CHANGE

Kurt Lewin produced a generally accepted description of the way individual
change occurs.[11] According to Lewin individuals must go through three basic
steps in the process of making a successful change:

1. Unfreeze
2. Move
3. Refreeze

**". . . THE CHINESE
SYMBOL FOR
CRISES SIGNIFIES
BOTH DANGER AND
OPPORTUNITY."**

SOURCE: Reprinted from
Jeffrey D. Ford, "The
Management of
Organizational Crises,"
Business Horizons
(May–June 1981), p. 16.

First, an individual has to unfreeze the current situation—say, an existing idea
or level of performance. Complacent behavior must often be shocked into
change. The unfreezing stage involves people's natural resistance to change.

Second, the individuals have to move to some new behavior or performance
level. The change should be seen as desirable from the perspective of the people
undergoing change.

Third, the new behavior or level of performance must become the accepted
behavior or level of performance. This is Lewin's refreezing stage. The new pattern has to replace the former completely for successful change to take place.

Examples of how Lewin's model might work in contemporary society are suggested in the highly publicized instances of brainwashing reported in the past.
Kidnap victims, hostages of terrorists, and prisoners of war have sometimes undergone such profound shock that their normal behavior patterns have been un-
frozen, and they have eventually been moved to alternative behavior patterns.
Their new behavior is then refrozen to become what the person then views as
the norm. While readjustment can be traumatic for these individuals, they can
return to their original behavior patterns by again starting the unfreezing–moving–refreezing process. Another illustration is the widely discussed and controversial deprogramming of some former cultists.

THE GREINER MODEL OF ORGANIZATIONAL CHANGE[12]

Larry E. Greiner examined eighteen separate studies dealing with organizational
change. His research considered the similarities and differences among instances
of successful and unsuccessful change. Greiner's overall observations are as follows:

1. Successful change requires a redistribution of power within the existing

[11] Kurt Lewin, "Frontiers in Group Dynamics: Concept, Method, and Reality in Social Science,"
Human Relations (June 1947), pp. 34–35.
[12] This section is based on Larry E. Greiner, "Patterns of Organization Change," *Harvard Business
Review* (May–June 1967), pp. 119–122, 125–130.

structure. Greiner noted that successful change was characterized by a greater degree of shared power within the organizational hierarchy.

2. This redistribution of power occurs as a result of a "developmental process of change." In other words it is a sequential process rather than a sudden shift.

THE STAGES OF SUCCESSFUL ORGANIZATIONAL CHANGE

Greiner identified six separate phases common to successful change. The stages of successful organizational change are shown in Figure 11-1. The following list summarizes the activities in each phase of the total developmental process.

Phase 1: Pressure and Arousal. Successful organizational change usually begins with significant pressure from either (1) an environmental factor such as falling sales volume or the announcement of a major new competitive product, or (2) an internal event like a strike or cost problem. The need for change is more readily apparent if there are multiple pressures that do not offset each other. Greiner reported that strong pressure was not as noticeable in the cases of unsuccessful change.

Phase 2: Intervention and Reorientation. Since management may rationalize the pressures of Phase 1, an outsider is required for effective change to occur.

**Figure 11-1
GREINER'S STAGES
OF SUCCESSFUL
ORGANIZATIONAL
CHANGE**

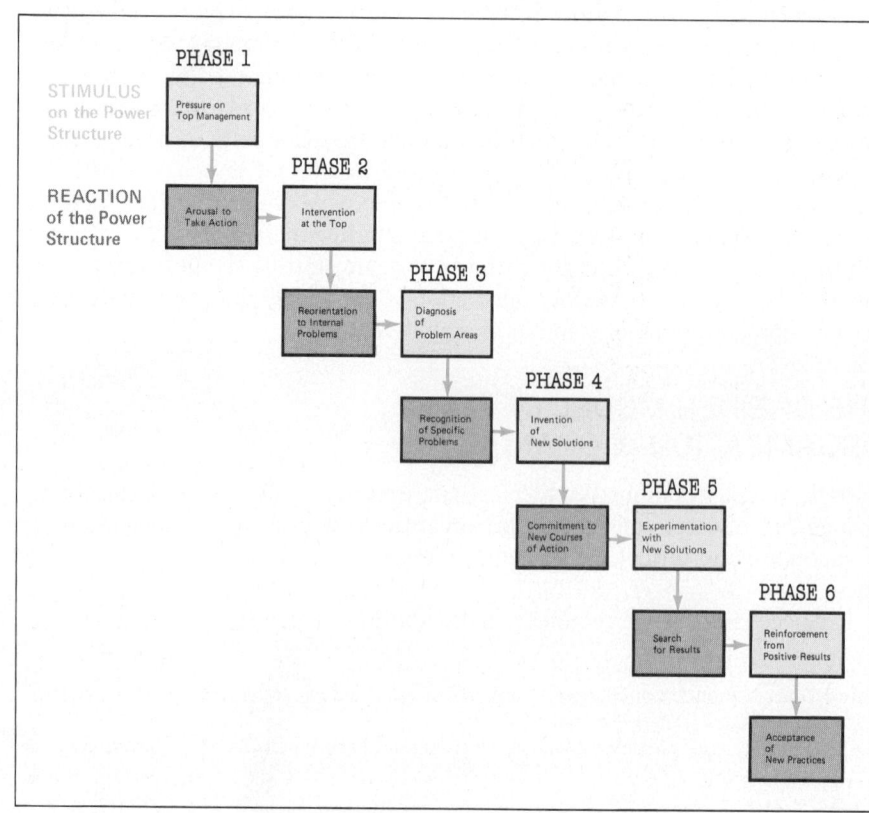

This person should be respected and enter at the top of the organizational hierarchy. Top management is encouraged to review the situation, thereby reorienting management to its internal problems. Management no longer assumes that it knows all of the problems within the organization.

Phase 3: Diagnosis and Recognition. In the third phase of successful change, the entire organization becomes involved in seeking out problems and their causes. A shared approach between superiors and subordinates is common in this stage. The decision-making process has been broadened as management shows its willingness to recognize tough problems and to change. Greiner noted that this step was always avoided in the studies dealing with unsuccessful change.

Phase 4: Invention and Commitment. With the active assistance of the outsider, the firm moves toward creative solutions to the problems that have been identified. The shared approach again predominates in this phase. Once solutions are developed, commitment to the new course of action is obtained. Greiner notes that none of the unsuccessful changes ever reached this stage in the developmental process.

Phase 5: Experimental Search. Greiner refers to this stage as a *reality testing phase* where various minor decisions are implemented throughout the organization. It is a stage in which tentative decisions and the shared power concept used in their development are tested before major changes are installed.

Phase 6: Reinforcement and Acceptance. The positive reports coming from the experiments in Phase 5 add reinforcement to the change process. More problems are being resolved by more people. And the shared power concept becomes a standard part of the organization. There has been a general reorientation in the decision-making structure of the entity undergoing change.

The Impact of Change on the Organizational Structure and Decision Making

Change has a varying impact on the organizing function. In some cases the impact is significant. In others it is minimal.

THE LAWRENCE AND LORSCH STUDY

Paul Lawrence and Jay Lorsch conducted a wide-ranging study dealing with organizational change in a number of different industries. The researchers compared firms in the dynamic plastics market; the food market, which has an intermediate amount of change; and the stable container market.[13] They found that successful firms in the rapidly changing plastics market were more highly differentiated than those in the food market, which were in turn more differentiated than the container firms. A *highly differentiated firm* has more specializa-

---

[13] Paul R. Lawrence and Jay W. Lorsch, *Organization and Environment: Managing Differentiation and Integration* (Boston: Division of Research, Graduate School of Business Administration, Harvard University, 1967).

tion than a firm with less differentiation. Departments are more specialized and rigidly defined in such firms. People in the various departments of a highly differentiated firm tend to think quite differently about their jobs; in less differentiated firms, people in different departments tend to hold similar viewpoints.

Lawrence and Lorsch concluded that the environment dictates how much a firm must differentiate or departmentalize. In order to cope successfully with all the changing aspects of their market, the plastics firms had to have highly specialized departments. At the other extreme, the container firms faced little change and could be successful with less specialized departments.

Problems with Differentiation

Differentiation is not without its problems. When a firm splits people into departments, it must find a way to coordinate or integrate their work in order to get the joint task done. The more the departments are different, the more difficult it is to coordinate their work. The Lawrence and Lorsch study found that the management of plastics firms had to devise numerous techniques to coordinate their departments' work. In addition to the usual system of paperwork and the managerial hierarchy, these firms had to set up permanent task or project forces as well as coordinating departments.

At the other extreme, the container industry had few differences that resulted in conflict between departments. As a result the usual paperwork system and management hierarchy provided adequate coordination. The food industry fell in the middle of the extremes. These firms had to use temporary project teams and individual liaison officers to integrate effectively.

Other Conclusions of the Study

Another Lawrence and Lorsch finding concerned whether decision making should be centralized or decentralized. Successful firms in these three industries showed distinct differences. In the dynamic plastics firms, success came as a result of decentralizing authority. This is probably true because it is important that lower-level managers be able to react quickly to changes.

In the container industry, the lack of numerous abrupt changes meant that the immediate response by lower-level management was less critical. These firms could be successful by centralizing most decision-making power with a few top managers. The food industry again placed in the middle.

The Lawrence and Lorsch study dramatically reveals that firms facing complex changes must employ similarly complex techniques to deal with them. The differences between a successful firm and an unsuccessful one might be based upon factors as simple as whether staff coordinating officers have backgrounds that make them acceptable to the departments with which they must deal.

Organization Development

Organization development is a crucial subject in every organization. It is a logical outcome of attempts to manage change and the resistance to it. Organization development involves a comprehensive and continuing management program to improve the organization.[14]

ORGANIZATION DEVELOPMENT: DEFINITION AND GOALS[15]

Organization development (OD) has been defined as "an effort (1) planned, (2) organization-wide, and (3) managed from the top, to (4) increase organization effectiveness and health through (5) planned interventions in the organization's 'processes,' using behavioral-science knowledge."

Development and maintenance of an effective, healthy organization require that specific operational goals be met:

1. Move toward an organizational structure based on the tasks to be performed rather than vice-versa.
2. Build feedback procedures into the organization.
3. Reduce dysfunctional competition between separate units of the organization.
4. Bring organizational conflicts into the open so they can be resolved.
5. Base decision making on the best source of information rather than on organizational role and its related authority.

Organization development (OD) is an effort by management to increase organization effectiveness by planned intervention in the organization's processes.

Precedents for Organization Development

Organization development as it is known today is the result of an evolutionary process that began in the 1940s. The three major precedents for OD were

1. Laboratory training
2. Survey research and feedback
3. Kurt Lewin's work[16]

---

[14] An interesting discussion of organization development appears in Anthony T. Cobb and Newton Marguliee, "Organization Development: A Political Perspective," *Academy of Management Review* (January 1981), pp. 49–59; L. J. Bourgeois and Manual Boltvinik, "OD In Cross-Cultural Setting: Latin America," *California Management Review* (Spring 1981), pp. 75–81; and John M. Nicholas, "The Comparative Impact of Organization Development Interventions on Hard Criteria Measures," *Academy of Management Review* (October 1982), pp. 531–542.

[15] This section is based on and quotes from Richard Beckhard, *Organization Development: Strategies and Models* (Reading, Mass.: Addison-Wesley, 1969), pp. 9–14.

[16] These sources are suggested in Wendell French and Cecil Bell, "A Brief History of Organization Development," *Journal of Contemporary Business* (Summer 1972), pp. 1–4. This paper is based on French and Bell's book, *Organization Development: Behavioral Science Interventions for Organization Improvements* (Englewood Cliffs, N.J.: Prentice-Hall, 1973), pp. 21–26. A similar discussion appears in Wendell French and Cecil Bell, *Organization Development: Behavioral Science Interventions for Organization Improvements*, 2nd. ed. (Englewood Cliffs, N.J.: 1978), pp. 20–24.

LABORATORY TRAINING

Laboratory training refers to the use of unstructured small group discussions to induce interactions that will produce behavior change in the participants.

T-groups consist of those executives undergoing a laboratory training experience.

Sensitivity training is a process of group dynamics that influences a T-group participant's behavior.

Laboratory training refers to the use of unstructured, small group discussions to induce interactions that will produce behavior change in the participants. The concept is usually dated from a 1946 workshop held in New Britain, Connecticut, in which Kurt Lewin and others were involved.[17]

These initial efforts later developed into T-groups and sensitivity training.[18] *T-groups* are those executives undergoing a laboratory training experience. *Sensitivity training* refers to a process of group dynamics that influences a T-group participant's behavior.

Sensitivity training's purpose is to make a manager sensitive to the effect his or her behavior has on subordinates. This is done by placing the manager in a group of strangers in some off-the-job, relaxed place, such as a lodge. The open, honest criticism of the individual by other members of the group is expected to unfreeze the manager's old attitudes, change them, and refreeze them into more sensitive ones. The manager should then be able to go back to the job to use open communication and participatory techniques with his or her employees.

The laboratory approach has been criticized for lack of results. It may change attitudes temporarily, but once back on the job managers tend to slide into previous behavior patterns. Some blame this tendency on not learning on the job and the lack of reinforcement from others in the firm who have not had the training. Regardless of its mixed record in actual application, laboratory training was an important step toward modern organization development.

SURVEY RESEARCH AND FEEDBACK

Survey research and feedback refers to action research involving attitude surveys and the resulting feedback to employees.

Survey research and feedback refers to action research involving attitude surveys and the resulting feedback to employees. A workshop format is commonly used in the feedback phase. This technique was developed at MIT's Research Center for Group Dynamics. Kurt Lewin had organized the center in 1945. After his death in 1947, it was moved to the University of Michigan, where it became part of what is now the Institute for Social Research.[19]

KURT LEWIN'S WORK

Lewin's work in applying behavioral science to management problems was an important aspect in the evolution of organization development. He made major contributions to both its laboratory training and survey research and feedback precedents.[20]

---

[17] *Ibid.*

[18] An interesting discussion of T-groups and sensitivity training appears in Robert A. Luke, Jr., "Matching the Individual and the Organization," *Harvard Business Review* (May–June 1975), pp. 17–18, 20, 24, 28, 30, 32, 34, 165.

[19] See note 16.

[20] *Ibid.*

The Emergence of OD Concept

Union Carbide and Esso were the first firms to launch organization development programs in the late 1950s.[21] Union Carbide, with the assistance of Douglas McGregor, formed an internal consulting group that counseled other managers. Esso (now Exxon) also began conducting rudimentary OD activities with the assistance of Robert Blake, who with Jane Mouton had begun work at the University of Texas on what was to become known as the Managerial Grid, one of contemporary organization development's most successful techniques (see the section on the Managerial Grid that follows). John Paul Jones, Birny Mason, Jr., and Herbert Shepard were the executives at the two pioneering firms who were most closely identified with this work.

French and Bell describe the emergence of organization development in the following paragraph:

> Shepard, Blake, McGregor, and others clearly were trying to build on the insights and learnings of laboratory training toward more linkage with and impact on the problems and dynamics of ongoing organizations . . . in the history of OD, we see both external consultants and internal staff departments departing from traditional roles and collaborating in quite a new approach to organization improvement.

Contemporary Approaches to Organization Development

Many of the current OD techniques are offshoots of the earlier work cited here. A partial list of these approaches includes the Managerial Grid, MBO, job enrichment/job enlargement, and team building. Although several of the approaches will be discussed in chapters dealing with such subjects as objective setting, motivation, and leadership, they are also important topics in organization development.

THE MANAGERIAL GRID®

The Managerial Grid® was developed by Robert R. Blake and Jane S. Mouton and has become one of the most popular concepts in modern organization development.[22] The Managerial Grid® has been used as the approach to a firm's

---

[21] This section is based on and quotes from French and Bell, "A Brief History of Organization Development," pp. 2–3. See also French and Bell, *Organization Development: Behavioral Science Interventions* (1973), pp. 22–25. A similar discussion appears in French and Bell, *Organization Development: Behavioral Science Interventions for Organization Improvements* 2nd. ed., pp. 20–24.

[22] See Robert R. Blake, Jane S. Mouton, Louis B. Barnes, and Larry E. Greiner, "Breakthrough in Organization Development," *Harvard Business Review* (November–December 1964), pp. 133–155.

comprehensive organization development program. It has also been presented in a book suitable for self-study.[23]

Blake and Mouton argue that managerial behavior is a function of two variables: concern for people and concern for production. The relative degree of concern, rather than the real outcomes of such orientations, is the important factor. The concern for people is shown on the vertical axis and the concern for production on the horizontal axis of Figure 11–2. A 1 to 9 scale is noted for each axis, with the higher numbers indicating greater concern for that specific variable. The Managerial Grid® that is developed has five management styles. The least desirable is a 1, 1 style that exhibits a minimal concern for both people and production. The 9, 1 manager is very production-oriented but has minimal concern for people. The reverse is true of the 1, 9 style. The 5, 5 manager has a "middle-of-the-road" style. The most desirable leadership style is 9, 9 where there is a maximum concern for both people and production.

[23] Robert R. Blake and Jane S. Mouton, *The Managerial Grid* (Houston: Gulf Publishing Company, 1964).

Figure 11-2
THE MANAGERIAL GRID®

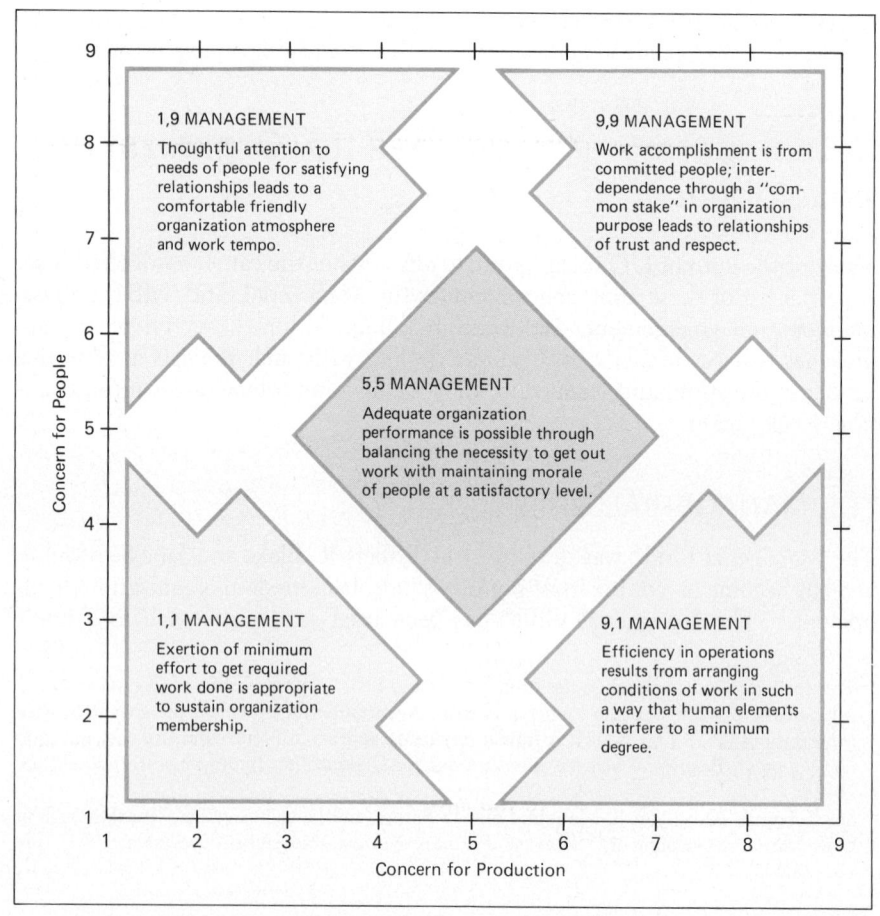

1,9 MANAGEMENT
Thoughtful attention to needs of people for satisfying relationships leads to a comfortable friendly organization atmosphere and work tempo.

9,9 MANAGEMENT
Work accomplishment is from committed people; interdependence through a "common stake" in organization purpose leads to relationships of trust and respect.

5,5 MANAGEMENT
Adequate organization performance is possible through balancing the necessity to get out work with maintaining morale of people at a satisfactory level.

1,1 MANAGEMENT
Exertion of minimum effort to get required work done is appropriate to sustain organization membership.

9,1 MANAGEMENT
Efficiency in operations results from arranging conditions of work in such a way that human elements interfere to a minimum degree.

Concern for People

Concern for Production

The objective of the Managerial Grid® is to move the organizational climate and the people involved toward a 9, 9 style. Blake and Mouton have developed a six-phase program that can be implemented within an organization. It includes laboratory seminar training, team development, intergroup development, organizational goal setting, goal attainment, and stabilization. Managers are first required to identify their current style, then work toward a 9, 9 approach. Managers begin by working on simulated problems. Later, they work on actual problems in their departments and eventually with people from other departments. The emphasis is on getting the manager to change to new styles, work on organizational rather than personal problems (as is often the case with sensitivity training), and gain the support of others throughout the firm who are undergoing similar development.

MBO PROGRAMS

A management by objectives (MBO) program is usually thought of as a planning and evaluative technique (see Chapter 4). But it can also be important to organization development. For instance, MBO can be an extremely useful device for getting executives to move toward a more participatory management style.

A management by objectives program is organization-wide. Top managers are supposed to set their operating objectives, to be followed by meetings with the second level of managers in order to set their goals. These managers are then to meet with their subordinates to help set their goals, and so on down the line to the lowest level. In this way every level is linked with every other level. Short-run objectives should mesh with long-run objectives; broad organizational objectives should mesh with departmental goals, which should mesh with individual goals. The chances are increased that the organization will work as a coordinated whole, even in the face of change.

JOB ENRICHMENT/JOB ENLARGEMENT

Many managers find that jobs which were acceptable to employees just a few years ago are no longer satisfactory. Boredom on the job, sometimes called the *blue-collar blues*, is a type of change affecting all kinds of workers. Once their basic needs are satisfied, experienced workers begin to expect more out of their jobs. As noted elsewhere they want their jobs to be more challenging, expressive, and fulfilling.

Managers often find that newer employees are younger, better educated, more inquisitive, and less financially dependent. This not only makes them more demanding but puts them in a strong bargaining position. From the manager's viewpoint, this is a dramatic change from the attitude of previous employees.

What can a manager do about this kind of change? One solution is simply not to put people into jobs that are too simple for them. Employees who are unhappy with dull, repetitive jobs may increase the costs of labor by absenteeism, poor productivity, turnover, or substance abuse problems. This is one of the major reasons firms have sought ways to automate many such jobs.

Throughout his long career as an academic and consultant to business, Chris Argyris, James B. Conant Professor of Education and Organizational Behavior at Harvard University, has focused on the individual within the organization. He has dealt with such difficult questions as, How do organizational development theory and practice differ? How is professional competence acquired? How is leadership effectiveness linked to the nature of learning?

Although Argyris perceives a deep-seated problem of organizational management, he also provides hope that change is possible. In *Theory in Practice: Increasing Professional Effectiveness,* Argyris and his co-author Donald A. Schon state:

> Our theory of action can enhance human activity, responsibility, self-actualization, learning, and effectiveness and make it likely that organizations will begin to decrease the movement toward entropy and increase the forces toward learning and health. We present a view of man actively seeking to master himself and his environment in a way that makes organizations effective. If we are to accomplish these objectives, we must become aware of both espoused theories and tacit theories that govern behavior. *

Argyris believes that most organizations are guided by unilateral defensive strategies that pit one worker against another. These "Model I" organizations are predicated on four overriding values: Define your purpose, then achieve it; do everything you can to win; restrain all negative emotions; and above all, be rational. When these values are put into action, workers are motivated by the desire to manipulate others and to protect themselves from others. There is little opportunity for risk-taking or new learning.

Argyris believes that organizations can break out of this self-defeating model

* Chris Argyris and Donald A. Schon, *Theory in Practice: Increasing Professional Effectiveness* (San Francisco: Jossey-Bass Publishers, 1974), p. xi.

Enlarging the Job

Another approach to solving this problem of high expectations is just the opposite of automation. Basically, if a job is too simple, why not make it more complicated—as it might have been years ago?

Suppose that an assembly line worker merely fastens the seats onto the frames of ten-speed bicycles. One worker assembles the handlebars and the next person down the line connects the gearshift mechanism. Each of them does this same job over and over again. One way to complicate their work would be to let each do all three operations. In other words each worker would walk along the line

by adopting procedures that enable them to learn from their mistakes and keep up with the changing demands of society. These "Model II" organizations are governed by a very different set of values: Give workers access to information so that they can make free and informed choices; allow them to design their own work settings, contribute original thoughts to a project, express feelings about it, and ultimately take responsibility for their contributions along with others involved; and set up a sophisticated system for monitoring the results of workers' decisions. Workers in a Model II environment, says Argyris, are less manipulative and more willing to learn and to take risks.

The cornerstone of Argyris' Model II organization is his theory of "double-loop learning," the process in which one's underlying values and assumptions are changed in the face of complex problems. Double-loop learning enables managers to break out of the cycle of ineffective behavior by asking the right questions; creating an effective problem-solving network; and effectively channeling the energy and commitment of workers to produce the solution.

Model II behavior is something most organizations embrace yet few actually put into practice. Argyris has spent much time and effort analyzing the reasons for this failure and, more importantly, initiating his Model II theory at actual companies.

The ultimate goal of Argyris' organizational development efforts are best summarized in his book *Management and Organizational Development: The Path from XA to YB*:

> The challenge of organizational development is close to . . . the very foundation for the design of a new quality of life that looks upon man's potentiality as . . . something . . . to be continually actualized in systems that respect and require human dignity and organizational health.†

† Chris Argyris, *Management and Organizational Development: The Path from XA to YB* (New York: McGraw-Hill, 1971).

Sources

Donald C. King, "Model I: A Model-T Approach to Effective Professional Behavior," *Contemporary Psychology* 20, no. 9 (1975), pp. 710–711. (A review of *Theory in Practice: Increasing Professional Effectiveness* by Chris Argyris and Donald A. Schon.)

Review of *Management and Organizational Development* by Chris Argyris, *Personnel Journal*, November 1972, pp. 848–849.

Veronica F. Nieva, "Perspectives on Improving Leadership," a review of *Increasing Leadership Effectiveness* by Chris Argyris, *Contemporary Psychology* 22, no. 12 (1970), pp. 874–876.

Review of *Theory in Practice: Increasing Professional Effectiveness* by Chris Argyris and Donald A. Schon, *Journal of Higher Education* XLVII, no. 1 (January–February, 1976), pp. 113–115.

Peter B. Vaill, "Learning to Learn to Learn to . . .," a review of *Organizational Learning: A Theory of Action Perspective* by Chris Argyris and Donald A. Schon, *Contemporary Psychology* 24, no. 6 (1979), pp. 514–515.

fastening the seat, assembling the handlebars, and connecting the gearshifts. Rearranging jobs to increase their complexity is known as *job enlargement*.

Enriching the Job

Jobs can also be rearranged by a process called *job enrichment*, whereby the employee is involved in some job-related decisions.[24] Take the job of fastening the

Job enlargement is the rearranging of jobs to increase their complexity.

Job enrichment is a rearrangement of jobs in order to get employee involvement in job-oriented decisions.

[24] An interesting discussion appears in Antone F. Alber, "The Real Cost of Job Enrichment," *Business Horizons* (February 1979), pp. 60–72.

seat to the ten-speed bicycle frame. When this job was designed, all kinds of decisions were made about the color and style of seats to be put on, as well as the types of tools and work methods to be used in assembly. The assembly worker simply does what others have decided. Job enrichment would occur if he or she were involved in making some of these choices as part of the job.

Both job enlargement and job enrichment are attempts to add variety and challenge to jobs—bringing them into line with employees' expectations. Both have been used in a wide range of occupations from assembly line work to management. In effect, increasing workers' involvement in decision making through participatory leadership practices is job enrichment. In many cases these improvements lead to increased motivation and decreased costs due to dissatisfaction.

Limiting Factors

There are important limitations to rearranging jobs. For example, the costs of altering assembly line operations can exceed the savings resulting from more satisfied workers.

Another limitation has to do with the nature of workers. Take the example of the ten-speed bicycles again. How long would it be before the workers found doing even all three operations boring? Could the job be enlarged again? College professors, doctors, lawyers, and others have been known to find their jobs boring, often quitting to go into new careers. There may be no amount of job enlargement or enrichment that can provide lasting satisfaction.

TEAM BUILDING[25]

The most popular OD approach in contemporary management is team building. The basic assumption is that various types of teams exist within any organization and that such teams are the vehicles for task accomplishment. Improving the team means better performance by the organization.

Team building is "a process of diagnosing and improving the effectiveness of a work group with particular attention to work procedures and interpersonal relationships within it, especially the role of the leader in relation to other group members." Task performance and human processes are both considered important in a team-building effort.

Different types of teams exist within organizations. These may include family teams, cousin teams, project teams, and startup teams. Organizations have *family teams,* or functional work groups like a design department. *Cousin teams* are groups of peers such as all of the district sales managers. *Project teams* put together people from several different departments to accomplish some specific task. *Startup teams* are groups that are charged with introducing some new entity or activity.

Team building is a process designed to improve the effectiveness of a work group with emphasis on work procedures and interpersonal relationships.

[25] This section is based on and quotes from Michael E. McGill, *Organization Development for Operating Managers* (New York: AMACOM, 1977), pp. 77–79. See also Thomas H. Patten, Jr., "Team Building. Part I. Designing the Intervention," *Personnel* (January–February 1979), pp. 11–21.

General Electric is big! Its $28 billion in annual sales accounts for nearly 1 percent of the nation's gross national product. General Electric is involved in some 250 different businesses. A recent poll of chief executives rated General Electric the best managed industrial company in the United States. And John F. Welch intends to keep it that way.

The GE board chairman is trying to keep the huge corporation an innovator by moving decision-making responsibility back to its 250 individual business units. Welch also abandoned his predecessors' policy of transferring personnel among the business groups to give them experience. He prefers to build effective management teams in each unit and to give them the appropriate degree of authority and responsibility. Welch has a simple requirement of these managers: Build their business into the Number 1 or Number 2 competitor in their business. Alternatively, his subordinates can develop superior technology that results in a marketplace advantage. It is estimated that about 70 percent of GE's businesses are ranked either first or second in their industry sectors.

Welch explains his views toward organization development this way: "Managements that hang on to weaknesses for whatever reason—tradition, sentiment, their own management weaknesses—won't be around in 1990." It is clear that John F. Welch expects General Electric to be as strong as ever in 1990.

SOURCE: This section is based on and quoted from Ann M. Morrison, "Trying to Bring GE to Life," *Fortune* (January 25, 1982), pp. 50–53, 56, 58.

JOHN F. WELCH'S OLD 1–2

The typical pattern for team building is for an OD consultant to interview group members about issues they perceive as blocking team goal accomplishment. Then an offsite meeting is held, usually lasting three to five days. The meeting is devoted to considering the issues emanating from the interviews on a priority order basis. The OD consultant provides the framework for a frank discussion of all issues that might hinder team performance. The group's leader must be involved in these sessions. Finally, action steps are agreed upon and assigned to a group member. Usually, a follow-up procedure is also established.

THE CURRENT STATUS OF ORGANIZATION DEVELOPMENT

Organization development programs have been increasingly accepted in American industry.[26] A wide variety of firms have or are currently initiating such pro-

[26] See, for example, Howard C. Carlson, "Organization Research and Organization Change: GM's Approach," *Personnel* (July–August 1977), pp. 11–22; and two articles in the *Atlanta Economic Review* by Carl A. Bramlette, Jr., Donald D. Jewell, and Michael H. Mescon. See also "Designing for Organizational Effectiveness: A Better Way" (September–October 1977, pp. 35–41) and "Designing for Organizational Effectiveness. How It Works" (November–December 1977, pp. 10–15).

**ORGANIZATION
DEVELOPMENT AT
SHERWIN-WILLIAMS**

Sherwin-Williams has been active in organization development for several years. Gerhard Friedrich, a Sherwin-Williams consultant, developed a model illustrating the organization development process at the firm. As shown below the process is an interactive system where a change in one part has an effect on other segments of the model. Goal setting and achievement are the core of organization development at Sherwin-Williams, just like they are in other organizations.

A MODEL FOR SHERWIN-WILLIAMS ORGANIZATION DEVELOPMENT PROCESS

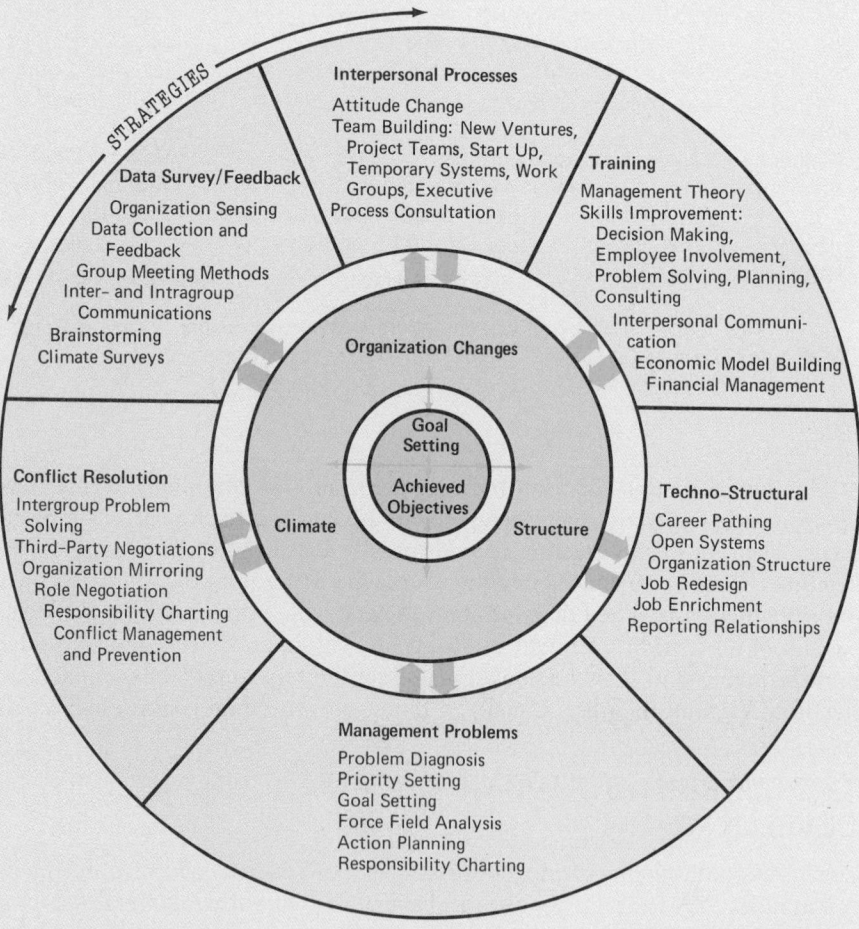

SOURCE: Reprinted by permission of the publisher from Ernest C. Miller, "Consensus: Organization Development: A Dynamic New Force?" *Personnel* (November–December 1977), p. 7. © 1977 by AMACOM, a division of American Management Associations. All rights reserved.

grams. As more and more managers become aware of the value of organization development, it appears likely that this effort will expand and become further refined in the future. The description of the way OD is envisioned at Sherwin-Williams, noted on page 294, is illustrative of this movement.

Summary

Change is an inherent part of any organization. And the contemporary environment is one of the most challenging that has ever faced management. Understanding change is an important part of the organizing function.

Resistance to change is commonplace. One authority suggested five reasons why people resist change: (1) lack of clarity, (2) distortion of information, (3) countervailing forces and reward structures, (4) levels of participation, and (5) pace of change. The classic Coch and French study concluded that participation is a valuable tool in overcoming resistance to change.

A change agent is a person who initiates a change; an intervention refers to the changes that are introduced to either individuals or organizations. Lewin's concept of the three basic steps to the individual change process—unfreeze, move, refreeze—is a widely accepted model of this type of change. By contrast, Greiner's model of organizational change is based on the premises that successful change requires increased shared power within an organization and that it occurs in a sequential process. In this chapter we also consider the impact of change on the organizational structure and decision making.

Organization development has been defined as "an effort (1) planned, (2) organization-wide, and (3) managed from the top, to (4) increase organization effectiveness and health through (5) planned interventions in the organization's 'processes,' using behavioral-science knowledge." Three precedents to organization development have been identified: laboratory training, survey research and feedback, and Kurt Lewin's work. Contemporary approaches to organization development include the Managerial Grid, MBO, job enrichment/job enlargement, and team building.

REVIEW EXERCISES

1. Define the following terms: (a) change agent (b) intervention (c) organization development (d) laboratory testing (e) T-groups (f) sensitivity training (g) survey research and feedback (h) job enlargement (i) job enrichment (j) team building.

2. Why do people resist change?

3. Summarize the findings of the Coch and French study.

4. Describe the Kurt Lewin model of change.

5. Explain the Greiner model of organizational change.

6. Identify the precedents to organization development.

7. Describe the Managerial Grid.

8. Differentiate between job enrichment and job enlargement.

9. What is meant by team building?

10. Discuss the model for organizational development developed at Sherwin-Williams.

ASSIGNMENTS/PROBLEMS/DISCUSSION QUESTIONS

1. What is the current status of organizational change at Minnesota Mining & Manufacturing?

2. Recall the last time you changed your opinion about some matter, idea, or person. Relate this experience to the Lewin model of individual change.

3. Identify a firm that has undertaken an organization development program. Examples are sometimes reported in the business press, such as *Business Week, Forbes, Fortune,* or *Dun's Review.* Interview some of the individuals involved and prepare a paper on this experience.

4. Stora Kopparbergs Bergslags AB of Falun, Sweden, may be the oldest company in the world. The firm, which began with a copper mine and is now into paper, pulp, and power, is believed to have begun sometime near the year 1000. However, Stora Kopparbergs admits that its records only go back to 1288.

Outline the major problems an organization development consultant might expect to encounter at Stora Kopparbergs Bergslags AB.

5. Choose an organization or work group to which you belong. Identify the organization development needs that you see existing in this entity. How would you approach these issues?

A MANAGERIAL INCIDENT

Guidelines for Change at Volvo

Pehr G. Gyllenhammar, Volvo's president, has offered these guidelines based on the experiences of the Swedish auto maker.

VOLVO'S GUIDELINES

Our experiences with change in our various plants have produced a few rules of thumb that may be helpful to others:

Each unit should be free to develop individually, without detailed control or interference from headquarters

An active and positive top management attitude toward change is a prerequisite for positive results. However, when this attitude turns into a drive from above to install programs, projects, and plans, management tends to fail.

Headquarters is most effective when its role is sanctioning investments for new approaches and challenging local managers to take more radical initiatives and risks.

Our positive achievements seem related to the extent our managers understand that the change process will sooner or later affect several organizational levels regardless of where it started.

We encounter problems if we formalize change and request targets, minutes, and figures too early. Change requires time and freedom of action. When people view it as a continuing search-and-learning process of their own, the chances of lasting effects are increased.

The initiative for change should be a line responsibility, with specialists as supporters rather than initiators. Changes specialists initiate seldom have lasting effects. They can, however, act as sounding boards and catalysts, carrying know-how from one place to another.

Steering committee members should be the strongest possible people, sharing commitment to change.

The fastest way to get ideas flowing seems to be to set up discussion groups in each working area. A working area in this sense (and in a group-working sense) should probably contain fewer than twenty-five people.

Groups that have money to spend on their own facilities and a mandate to list their own problems seem to achieve cohesion and cooperation most rapidly. It need not cost the corporation more money to apportion facilities or safety budgets to the groups themselves than to experts.

A new plant, a new product, or a new machine is an opportunity to think about new working patterns.

An investment in one new facility or one group area often results in spontaneous changes in related facilities or groups. These can be encouraged by alert managers.

Most factories have a number of tasks that need not be done as assembly lines. Once a few have been found and changed, others will reveal themselves.

So that the change suggestions will emerge from inside, changes of work organization must be integrated with a structure of employee consultation.

Progress seems to be fastest when a factory or company starts by forming a joint management and union steering committee to look at its own problems.

Some of the most effective changes in work organization at Volvo have taken place naturally, without projects, without scientific sophistication, without being reported to anybody. Those changes occur simply because people are keen and interested. Finding ways to encourage such changes is management's challenge.

SOURCE: Reprinted from Pehr G. Gyllenhammar, *People at Work* (Reading, Mass.: Addison-Wesley, 1977), pp. 124–126. Copyright © 1977, Addison-Wesley Publishing Company, Inc. Reprinted with permission.

Questions and Problems

1. Would the Volvo guidelines be applicable in United States industry?

2. Relate Gyllenhammar's suggestions to the material in this chapter.

Case III-1

NATIONAL INSURANCE CO.:
A PROBLEM OF ORGANIZATIONAL CHANGE

For nearly thirty years, the National Insurance Co. had operated their Investment Division as shown in the organizational chart in Exhibit 1.

Aaron Jackson, executive vice-president for investments, was responsible for all company investments, including mortgage loans, securities, and the small amount of company-owned real estate. In the preceding ten years, National had significantly increased its sales of large group insurance policies and was administering several large trust funds, such as state teachers' retirement funds. This increase had resulted in inflows of great sums of money, which had to be invested, in accordance with various legal and fiduciary restrictions, in treasury bills, bonds, other securities, and real estate. Also, top management had decided to decrease its involvement with residential mortgages because of their relatively low yields in relation to the costs of processing and servicing them. It now appeared that the commercial loans and real estate were more promising investment alternatives.

THE NEED FOR CHANGE

Two major problems had developed with the exist-

This case was prepared by Professors Thomas R. Miller and James M. Todd, Memphis State University. The case is disguised.

ing organization given the changing needs of the Investment Division. Mr. Jackson was concerned that he had too many people reporting directly to him. His day-to-day involvement with the Securities Department was rather extensive, as he had formerly headed up this department and had maintained a close association with it in his current position. He felt that he could not "keep up" with the operations under him. Furthermore, with the deemphasis on residential loans, there were now too many employees in the Residential Loan Department with not enough work to do, both at the headquarters level in Chicago and at the field-level offices in the smaller cities.

THE NEW ORGANIZATIONAL STRUCTURE

In an effort to deal with the changing demands on the Investment Division, Mr. Jackson appointed a committee to conduct a study of the current organization and submit its findings and recommendations to him for submission to the Board of Directors. Six months later the organization plan in Exhibit 2 was recommended to and then later approved by the board for implementation early in the following year.

Under the reorganization plan, there was to be a change from three vice-presidents reporting on mortgage loans to one senior vice-president in

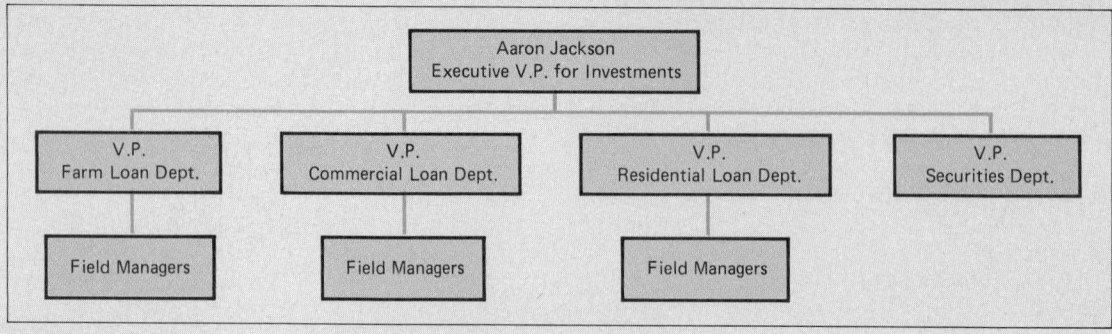

Exhibit 1
NATIONAL INSURANCE CO.—ORGANIZATIONAL CHART

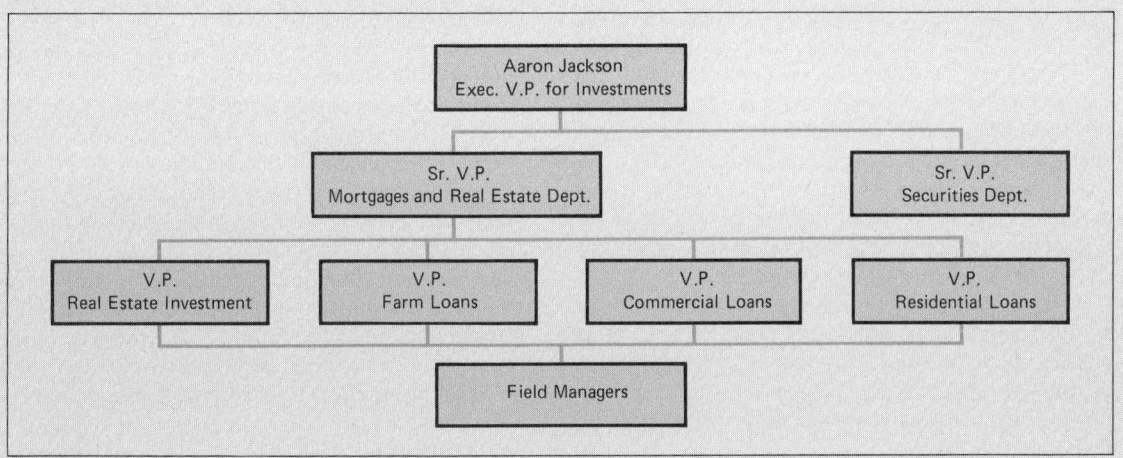

Exhibit 2
NATIONAL INSURANCE CO.—REVISED ORGANIZATIONAL CHART

charge of all mortgages. This made it necessary to consolidate the three mortgage departments into one. With the increased activity in real estate investment, a new real estate section was to be placed under the senior vice-president.

Early in January the management team of the Investment Division, including the field managers, were called to a meeting in Chicago. This had been billed as the announcement of the reorganization of the Investment Division. In presenting the restructure, the executive vice-president for investments stated that there were two major reasons for the organizational change: (1) There had been too many people reporting directly to him, and (2) the investment market today made it necessary to have an organization that was fluid enough to shift its efforts to the most desirable investment opportunities. He explained that the reorganization would require training and recycling of some employees in order for them to meet their new responsibilities effectively. However, in accordance with established company policy, no employees would lose their jobs nor would anyone receive a cut in pay. (In fact, many of the employees affected actually received increases in pay, due partly to inflation and partly because it was thought that this would promote their acceptance of the new organization). Mr. Jackson announced the appointments of the two senior vice-presidents

and the four vice-presidents of Real Estate Investment, Farm Loans, Commercial Loans, and Residential Loans, who were charged to commence implementation of the necessary changes in their units immediately, and wished them well in their new positions.

THE RESTRUCTURED ORGANIZATION CREATES SOME PROBLEMS

Although everything was worked out "on paper," soon problems began to emerge in the mortgage loan units. The three vice-presidents who had formerly been department heads were now only vice-presidents reporting to a department head. They did not relish their reduced status. At the level of the field organization, there were also subsequent changes. Where before there had been a field manager for each of the Farm, Commercial, and Residential Loan units, there was now only one field manager for all mortgage loans. Thus, where there had been three field offices in each major city, there was now one office per city for all mortgage loans. Some former field managers were now only field representatives reporting to a field manager. As the field offices were consolidated, there were also shifts among the administrative and clerical employees. With the change to one field office, there was a need for just one office manager, not three, and this was not well accepted by the people who were no longer managers. In several instances employees who had worked together as peers for many years were now cast into the roles of superior and subordinates because of restructured jobs and reporting relationships.

For some employees the restructuring seemed to offer expanded opportunities, and they were eager to "get the show on the road." However, others felt that they were not getting their "share of the grapes" and were somewhat resistant and even uncooperative. Although earnest efforts were made to convince the personnel that the new organization would ultimately provide greater opportunities, for various reasons they were not all convinced.

Some of the managers affected by the reorganization had spent many years with National and were approaching retirement age. They felt that they had "paid their dues" in service to the firm over many years. Some of them had spent fifteen to twenty years doing the same job and doing it very well. They had become comfortable with the status quo and wanted everything to stay as it was. Gradually, some discontented workers adjusted and continued to make excellent employees with their new assignments. Others withstood their dissatisfaction until they could retire, while a few younger managers left the organization.

RESISTANCE TO CHANGE

Specific forms of resistance to the reorganization were varied. One senior appraiser who had previously worked in a small field office did not like the fact that his new office didn't open into the reception area. Certain long-time residential appraisers felt it "beneath their dignity" when now called upon to appraise farm property. A farm appraiser left the company because he felt farm loans would eventually be cut out altogether.

As certain key positions were filled with people from Commercial Loans, it was rumored, "This is not a reorganization but a Commercial Loan Department takeover." One of the reasons for the reorganization was to make better use of the large Residential Loan workforce by transferring them to Commercial Loan units, which were now understaffed. The rumor then started that the same thing would happen to the Farm Loan employees unless they worked together and produced a high volume of farm mortgages. This proved to be unsettling to the Farm group.

In retrospect, one thing that National apparently overemphasized was the belief that existing personnel could be retrained to assume all positions in the new structure. While some employees were successfully retrained, such as residential appraisers who became competent to do commercial appraisal work, it was found that outside specialists had to be brought in to fill certain key positions, particularly in the Commercial Loan and Real Estate Investment units.

Questions

1. Relate the National Insurance case to the discussion of organization change that appears in the textbook.

2. Did National's management handle the situation effectively. Why or why not?

3. What can management do to improve the situation as it now exists?

Case III-2

RAWLINS ELECTRIC CO.

It finally happened! As was widely expected in the company, on June 18, 1981, Dave Hawky was selected by the board of directors to be the next president of Rawlins Electric. He would take over a year from that date, June 18, 1982.

Rawlins Electric of Cleveland, Ohio, was established in 1919 by Richard Rawlins. Mr. Rawlins, who came to the United States from England in 1884, had worked at various trades and finally became an electrician in about 1914. Then he established his own enterprise in 1919, doing mostly electrical wiring. In the 1920s Rawlins' business shifted toward commercial wiring—wiring office buildings and small factories.

In 1947 Mr. Rawlins suffered a heart attack and was not capable of running the business anymore, so his two sons—Harry, who had a degree in business, and John, who had a degree in electrical engineering—joined forces to run the company. They each owned 50 percent of the stock. In 1967 Harry sold his share to John and left the company. John Rawlins became sole owner and the president of Rawlins Electric. Since then, the company has found business growing by leaps and bounds, and in 1981 it was the second largest electrical contractor in the state of Ohio, with a stable pool of 140 electricians providing services to the Cleveland metropolitan area. The company's major competitive advantage is its excellent image for high quality service. Exhibit 1 shows its sales for 1980–1983.

THE INDUSTRY

Electrical contracting is a very competitive industry. It consists of national and local firms. The new national contractors usually bid only on very large projects throughout the United States while local companies typically work on contracts in only one state or city.

This case was prepared by Professor Mansour Javidan of the University of Alberta, Canada. Adapted and reprinted by permission of the author.

| | Years Ended February 28 | | | |
	1983	1982	1981	1980
Sales				
Completed Contracts	$11,215,145.00	$ 9,786,564.60	$8,706,727.20	$8,522,637.00
Jobbing and Other	1,316,306.50	1,041,252.00	861,396.00	755,123.00
Total Sales	$12,531,451.50	$10,827,816.60	$9,568,123.20	$9,277,760.00
Operating Expenses	11,927,299.00	10,398,686.00	9,326,522.00	9,099,472.00
Operating Earnings	$ 604,152.50	$ 429,130.60	$ 241,601.20	$ 178,288.00
Other Income (Expenses)	1,592.40	25,343.00	55,727.00	14,000.00
Earnings before Income Taxes	$ 605,744.90	$ 454,473.60	$ 297,328.20	$ 192,288.00
Provision for Income Taxes	299,377.90	224,510.00	145,689.80	94,221.10
Earnings for the Year	$ 306,367.00	$ 229,963.60	$ 151,639.40	$ 98,067.90
Retained Earnings—Beginning of Year	1,154,402.90	924,439.30	772,800.60	674,733.70
Retained Earnings—End of Year	$ 1,460,769.90	$ 1,154,402.90	$ 924,439.00	$ 722,800.60
EARNINGS PER COMMON SHARE	$ 329.30	$ 276.94	$ 115.31	$ 98.10

Exhibit 1
RAWLINS ELECTRIC CO.——STATEMENT OF EARNINGS AND RETAINED EARNINGS

Business is usually in one of two forms, either "time and material" or "contract." The T&M work is priced on a stated hourly rate basis, plus materials, plus a percentage for overhead and profit. The contract type of work is obtained through competitive bidding. *Dodge Bulletin,* a special weekly publication, lists all the construction projects in the area along with the approximate size of the electrical work in each of them. Electrical contractors make their bids based on this information. Usually, there are two types of contracts; some construction companies provide their own design while others require both design and electrical work. In any case the bids should be low enough to win and at the same time high enough to be profitable.

Another important aspect of this industry is that generally the contractor is required to have bonding coverage. This is compulsory for government projects. The bonding company guarantees performance and will be responsible in case of default.

ORGANIZATION

Exhibit 2 shows the organization chart for Rawlins Electric. The Jobbing Department is responsible for small projects, which are mainly maintenance or minor additions or modifications. Estimators do the bidding for contractors. In cooperation with the purchasing and warehouse manager and the accountant, they have to determine the costs and decide on a reasonable profit margin. Once they

win the contract, they are responsible for that project and contact the superintendents to allocate the required manpower.

The Design and Engineering Department works on bids that require design and electrical work. The Outside Construction Department bids on such projects as street lighting and traffic lights. All of these departments report to Dave Hawky, who has been with the company for eighteen years. Bill Burton, purchasing and warehouse manager, has been with the company for four years. Jack Davis has been in charge of accounting for six years. They both provide valuable information to the estimators who are bidding on contracts.

MANAGEMENT PHILOSOPHY

Management philosophy at Rawlins Electric is in fact shaped according to John Rawlins' personal beliefs. He is a strong supporter of delegation and group decision making: "You should be nice, open, and as fair as possible to your people. Teamwork will produce good salable products." Based on this philosophy, he offered to sell some of his stock to high-level employees. In 1980 all the members of the top management and a few estimators owned stock in the company and found it a very profitable investment.

Although an engineer by education, Mr. Rawlins never liked engineering; therefore, he delegated a great deal of responsibility and authority to his

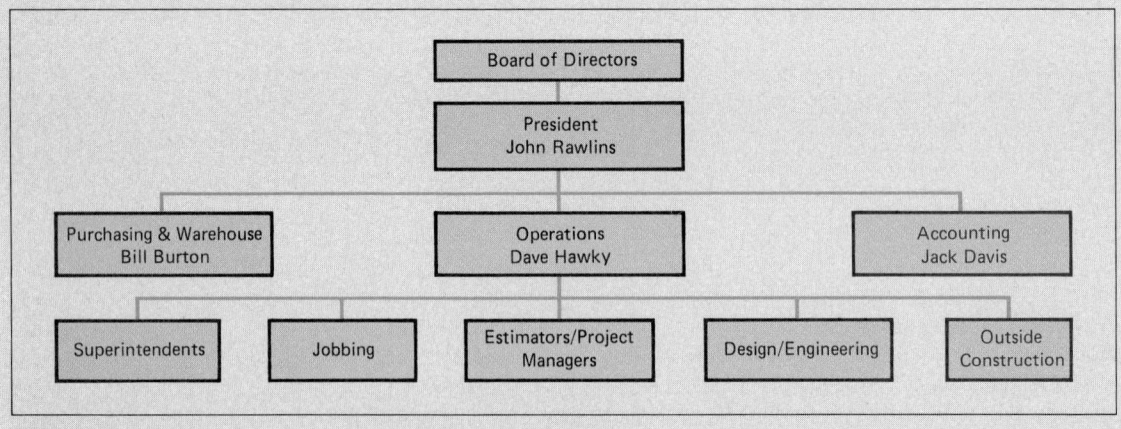

Exhibit 2
RAWLINS ELECTRIC CO.——ORGANIZATION CHART

subordinates. In the past few years in particular, he was primarily involved in the external contacts of the company.

With regard to his employees, he believed that "we have very good people with the best tools available and enjoy an excellent image." The company's expenses for new equipment, reconditioning of existing equipment, and maintenance of its fleet of vans and automobiles were higher than those of any other competitor of comparable size.

Mr. Rawlins' view toward the company's social responsibility was that "we shouldn't profit at the expense of others. We get more enjoyment by performing professionally and producing a good product." Rawlins Electric is among the few small companies in the 5 Percent Club, contributing 5 percent of its profits before taxes to civic projects.

THE NEW PRESIDENT

For the past few years, Mr. Rawlins has been thinking about leaving the company and living in Florida. He had implicitly designated Dave Hawky as the next president and his successor but formally announced his intentions of retiring in 1983, when he asked the Board of Directors to name Dave as the next president as of 1984. The board—consisting of Rawlins, Hawky, Burton, Davis, and two other employees in the Operations Department—approved.

The news of Dave Hawky's forthcoming promotion was no surprise. He had more experience with the company than anyone else in top management. He had attended a vocational school and had very high credentials. Starting as an assistant estimator, he had progressed very rapidly because of his capabilities and expertise. In twelve years, at the age of thirty, he had become the vice-president of operations. He was very ambitious and always wanted to be at the top. He expected others to perform at the highest level of quality and would be furious if they didn't, even if they were not working under him. In one instance, when it became clear that the manager of the Jobbing Department was devoting excess time to his own vending machine business at the expense of Rawlins, Dave, who was an estimator at the time, was the major force in making Mr. Rawlins aware of the situation and firing the manager. He always wanted to know as

many details as possible, and as vice-president for operations reviewed all the estimators' bids and would usually cut the costs estimated in the bid to make it more competitive. In some cases this disturbed the estimators, who used to have autonomy in making their bids. Two of them had even complained to Mr. Rawlins, but without much success.

Dave's demanding personality had even made a few suppliers hesitant in calling him. He was very aggressive and sometimes let others know his feeling of superiority. In the past two years in particular, he had gained a great deal of power and had even ignored Mr. Rawlins' directives in many cases.

Despite the fact that as a practical matter he had been running the company for the past few years, Dave was extremely delighted at the news of the official promotion and planned a large party, inviting all his neighbors and friends outside the company. His next move was to ask for a 37 percent salary increase for his new position.

THEN . . . AN ANNOUNCEMENT THAT SHOCKED THE COMPANY

On June 10, 1984, just eight days before becoming the new president of Rawlins Electric, Dave Hawky was fired! The announcement that morning shocked the staff. It was unbelievable. The next day, in a meeting with all the administrative personnel, Mr. Rawlins explained: "I fired Dave because I finally decided that he wouldn't be suitable for the job. He was trying to win a contract that would require bonding coverage much beyond our regular bonding capacity. His ambitious and unrealistic expansion plans worried our bonding company. His outrageous salary demand, which was 30 percent more than what I receive, was the last straw. His expense account for the past two years was much higher than the accounts of the other members of the management team combined; and finally, without my knowledge, he was searching for a new office building. As you know, I own the present one."

The general mood in the company was shock and disbelief, but a few days later, three key employees told Mr. Rawlins that they would have left the company if Dave had become president. During the next few days, Mr. Rawlins mentioned

Dave's lack of a strong educational background as another reason for this decision.

On June 18, 1984, Mr. Rawlins kept his promise of retiring. Since then a three-member committee consisting of the accountant, the manager of purchasing, and the new vice-president for operations has been very successful in running the company. They have grown very rapidly and have been able to arrange bonding coverage well beyond their normal official limit.

Questions

1. Describe the current top management organization at Rawlins.

2. Why do you think Dave Hawky was fired?

3. Discuss the organizational issues raised in this case.

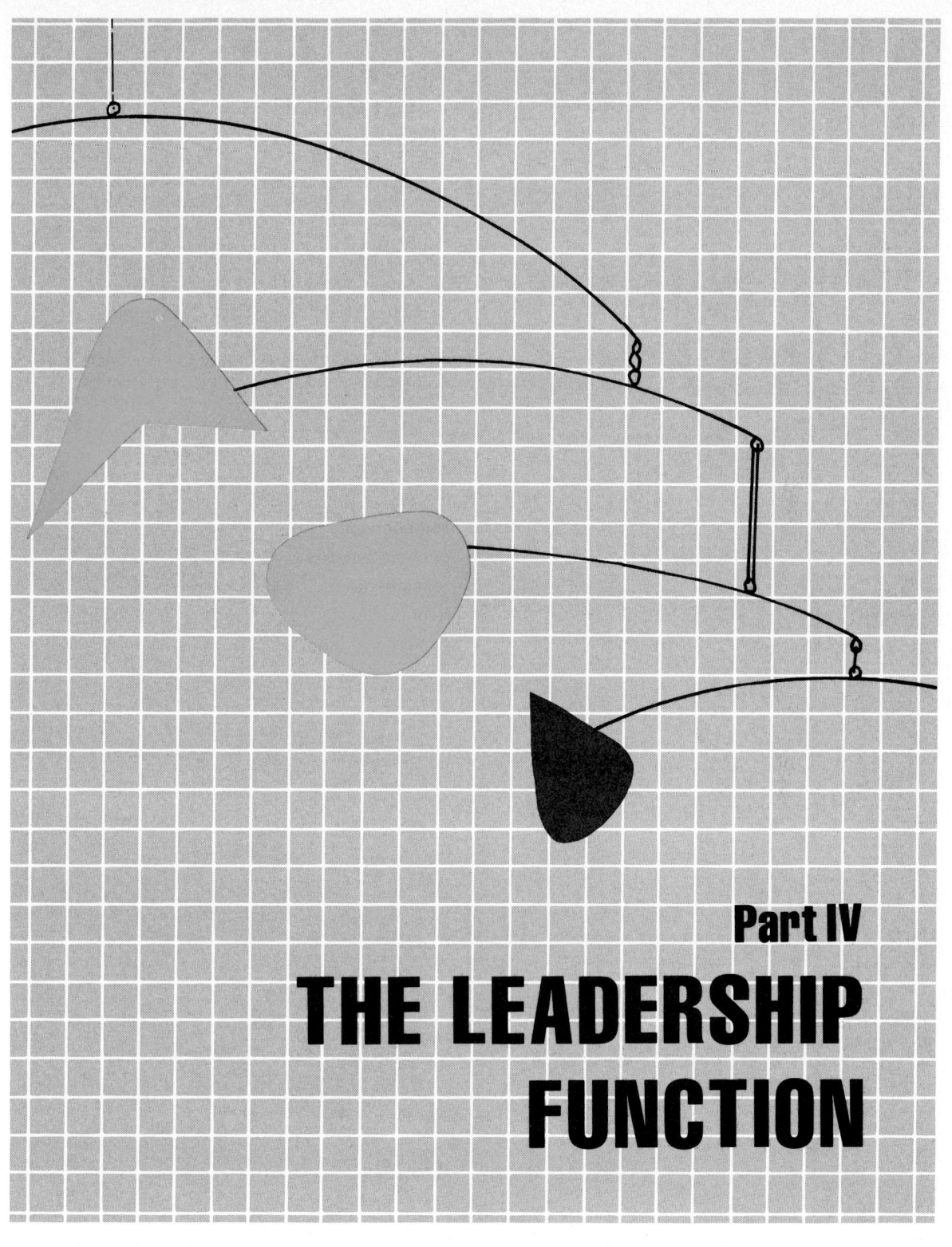

Part IV
THE LEADERSHIP FUNCTION

12.
Motivation: Individual Behavior

Learning Objectives

AFTER STUDYING THIS CHAPTER YOU SHOULD BE ABLE TO

1. Explain the concept of motivation.
2. Outline Maslow's hierarchy of needs.
3. Explain McClelland's contributions to motivation theory.
4. Discuss Herzberg's two-factor theory of motivation.
5. Explain Skinner's contribution to motivation theory.
6. Relate expectancy theory to motivation.
7. Discuss the concept of locus of control.

Key Terms

motivation

self-concept

operant behavior

reflex behavior

reinforcement

expectancy theory

locus of control

Nothing in the world can take the place of persistence. Talent will not; nothing is more common than unsuccessful men with talent. Genius will not; the world is full of educated derelicts. Persistence and determination alone are important. The slogan "press on" has solved and always will solve the problems of the human race.

CALVIN COOLIDGE

I've had smarter people around me all my life, but I haven't run into one yet that can outwork me. And if they can't outwork you, then smarts aren't going to do them much good. That's just the way it is. And if you believe that and live by it, you'd be surprised at how much fun you can have.

WOODY HAYES

Alexis was having a tough day in the lacquer department of the furniture factory. Fumes filled the air, and he was experiencing considerable frustration with his job. But fortunately he had already booked a stint in the plant's balcony "relaxing room." Alexis could spend eight to ten minutes sitting in a soft rocking chair in the air-conditioned and soundproofed room that can serve twelve workers at once. Bird calls signal a restful interlude that includes a female voice singing: "This day is very happy. We shouldn't be sad. It will always be like this. There will always be summer." Meanwhile, the lights have been dimmed, and a photographic presentation is offered on one wall. The scenes include sailboating, forests, brooks, and the Kremlin!

Alexis works at the Vilnius (Lithuania), USSR, furniture plant. Similar psychological rest breaks are enjoyed each day by about 150 of the factory's 2,400 employees. The Vilnius relaxing room is part of a Russian experiment to increase worker productivity. A medical researcher writing in *Pravda*, the Communist Party newspaper, predicted a 10 percent productivity increase from such motivational efforts. While the relaxing room at Vilnius is popular, no one has as yet attempted to measure the results exactly.[1]

Motivation is one of the most important management functions in contemporary organizations—be they in the United States or the Soviet Union. In this chapter various concepts in motivation and behavior will be considered.

[1] Based on "Some Red Music for Blue Workers," *Detroit News* (February 16, 1979), pp. 1-A, 2-A (Los Angeles Times News Service).

The Concept of Motivation

Motivation is a commonplace aspect of everyone's life, yet it is a difficult concept to define—let alone apply—within an organizational perspective. *Motivation* refers to the forces leading to behavior directed toward the satisfaction of some need. Hunger and the desire for financial security are needs, or motives. Behavior designed to satisfy these needs is motivated behavior, or motivation.[2]

Not all behavior is motivated; some behavior is habitual, or reflexive. But managers must deal with motivated behavior. As noted above motivated behavior can be subdivided into individual and group behavior. Effective management requires a working knowledge of both aspects of behavior. Successful managers must also understand the causes of behavior patterns. Psychologist Kurt Lewin's field theory offered such an explanation. Lewin believed that people were influenced by a variety of factors and that this established their behavior patterns. Lewin labeled his conceptualization of behavior as field theory and suggested the following formula:[3]

$$B = f(P,E)$$

Lewin's equation states that behavior (B) is a function of factors (f) related to the person (P), as well as the environmental factors (E) that affect the individual. The recognition of both personal and environmental influences was an important contribution to management's understanding of behavior and motivation.

Chapter 12 approaches motivation from the individual and group viewpoints. Various theories of individual behavior are advanced, with particular attention given to the major contributors in this area. Chapter 13 will examine motivation from a group perspective. Classic studies such as the Hawthorne research and the work done by Miles, Whyte, Seashore, Bales, Kahn, and Likert will be explored. Chapter 13 concludes with a section on the problems and constraints in applying motivation theory.

Theories of Individual Behavior

Motivation is a critical subject for management, and a number of theories have been developed in an attempt to explain motivated behavior. Maslow, McClelland, Herzberg, Skinner, Vroom, and Rotter are some of the names associated with the various theories that have been advanced to explain why people behave as they do. Each of these viewpoints offers an important perspective or insight related to the study of motivation.

[2] An excellent recent article on motivation is Terence R. Mitchell, "Motivation: New Directions for Theory, Research, and Practice," *Academy of Management Review* (January 1982), pp. 80–88.
[3] Kurt Lewin, *Field Theory in Social Science* (New York: Harper & Row, 1951), p. 62.

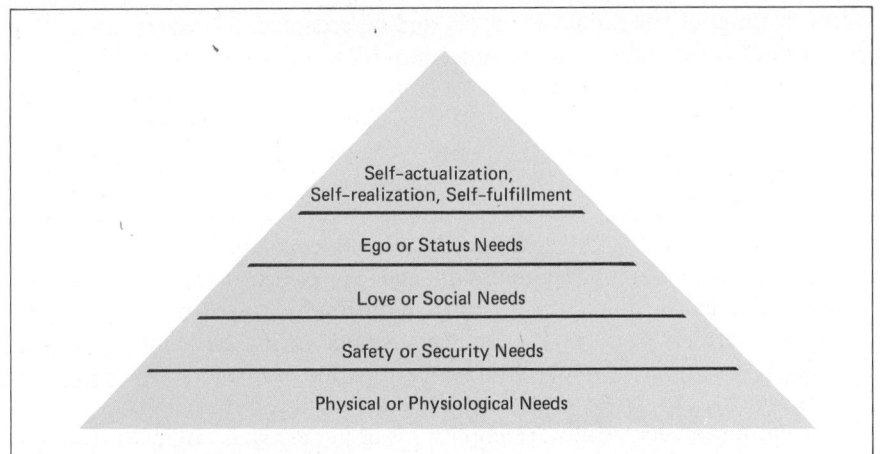

Figure 12-1
MASLOW'S
HIERARCHY OF
NEEDS

SOURCE: Based on Abraham
H. Maslow, "A Theory of
Human Motivation," *Psy-
chological Review* (July
1943), pp. 370–396.

Maslow's Hierarchy of Needs

One of the best-known explanations of individual motivation is a proposition formulated by psychologist Abraham Maslow. In 1943 Maslow identified several needs in people and arranged them in a hierarchical order (see Figure 12-1).[4] Maslow's theory was later popularized when it was put into managerial terms in Douglas McGregor's book *The Human Side of Enterprise*, published in 1960.

MASLOW'S CLASSIFICATION SYSTEM

Maslow theorized that people are driven by several needs, not just one. These can be categorized as physical or physiological needs, safety or security needs, love or social needs, ego or status needs, and self-actualization needs (also called *self-realization* or *self-fulfillment needs*).

Physical needs are those related to food, clothing, and shelter. The manager can motivate people through these needs by offering adequate wages and salary. Other factors relating to physical needs that might be under the manager's control are working hours and aspects of the physical environment, such as rest rooms, temperature, lighting, and noise level.

It is one thing to have food in the stomach and a roof over the head for one day; it is something else again to have these things day after day. The need to ensure against deprivation is the *security need*. Again, there are many ways managers can appeal to this need. Insurance, retirement benefits, and unemployment compensation are common security need satisfiers. Others include consistent supervisory treatment, grievance procedures, and job continuity.

The *social needs* include the need to talk to others, to associate with others, to

[4] A. H. Maslow, "A Theory of Human Motivation," *Psychological Review* (July 1943), pp. 370–396.

express feelings of friendship, to accept and be accepted. Managers satisfy this type of need by providing opportunities for employees to interact. This can be done by arranging the physical layout of the plant or office to allow people to interact, by allowing coffee breaks, providing lunch facilities, and offering recreational activities.

The *ego needs* involve the esteem one has for oneself as well as the esteem one has in the eyes of others. A manager can give a deserving employee many symbols of status that fulfill these ego needs: job titles, privileged parking, private secretaries, spacious offices, promotions, and pay packages that include stock options, a company car, and merit awards. Contributing to the self-esteem of an employee, while more difficult to achieve, is still within the manager's reach. The assignment of a meaningful project within the employee's capability will provide a chance for considerable self-esteem. Providing adequate training will help an employee successfully accomplish his or her work and enjoy the fruits of that labor.

The highest of Maslow's needs is *self-actualization*. Of all the needs listed, this is the vaguest and perhaps most controversial. Maslow described self-actualization this way: "What a man can be he must be."[5] This is clarified somewhat by his description of a self-actualized person: good perception of reality, spontaneous, accepting of self and others, problem centering, creative, independent. Most management experts feel that an employee's drive to self-actualize can be tapped by giving the person freedom of expression. This might be accomplished by allowing employees to participate in decision making and giving them the power to shape their own jobs.

As the model in Figure 12-1 indicates, a person's first concerns are with meeting his or her immediate physical needs. Once these have been satisfied, the person's concerns focus on other matters; namely, securing the basic needs over the long run. When one feels secure, new needs will emerge—the social needs. Once physical, safety, and social needs have been at least partially met, the person will next be concerned with ego needs. And once ego needs have been satisfied, the individual will move on to the endless task of self-actualization.

According to Maslow people move from one need level to the next, in building-block fashion. This seems to be a fairly accurate picture of the way most individuals behave, and so Maslow's hierarchy has become widely accepted in the field of management. The model's powers of description can be highlighted by looking at the hierarchy in reverse. Consider, for instance, the successful executive—confident, accomplished, and widely admired. Suddenly, the person's life is shattered by the loss of the spouse. The person's love needs are removed. The person's work suffers and he or she loses a sense of direction. Finding meaningful relationships with people is now more important than power and prestige. Only when the individual's social needs are satisfied do status and achievement once again have real meaning.

An even more drastic example of the hierarchy operating in reverse is to consider the disruptions created by a major crisis such as a natural disaster or a food

---

[5] *Ibid.*, p. 383.

shortage. Even the most civilized people have been known to forget their desires for friends and status in the scramble to survive. The higher needs do seem to have meaning only when resting upon the satisfaction of lower ones.

Maslow noted that the needs hierarchy is only a general model. He thought that while most people behaved this way, the hierarchy was not perfectly accurate. There is overlap where several needs may be acting at once, although one probably predominates. Also, the amount of need satisfaction varies from person to person. The dedicated artist may move rapidly through meager lower-level need satisfaction in order to reach a point of self-expression.

Maslow also recognized that some people fixate at one need level and seem never to move on to another. One possible cause is a severe denial of that need level earlier in life. An example could be the retreat of some young people who are well prepared to succeed in modern enterprise into communes, where there is an overwhelming emphasis on love and human relationships. If these individuals came from homes where parents had little time to devote to their children, it could be that later in life these offspring fixated at the social need level.

MASLOW'S CRITICS

Many people take exception to Maslow's claim of a valid general model of behavior. Maslow, in his original writings, was quite clear in saying that the total, fully functioning human being is a self-actualized one. Anyone at less than this level is basically not satisfied; in his words, a person deprived of higher need satisfaction "is as surely sick as if he had suddenly developed a strong salt hunger or calcium hunger."[6] The criticism expressed widely in the management literature is that since few people ever have the opportunity to reach the level of self-actualization, most people are doomed to a restless state of dissatisfaction. It would seem to critics that too many people functioning at lower need levels are relatively satisfied for Maslow's observation to be true. Maslow's critics argue that his overall theory may be descriptive of many people, but that it is doubtful that it is true of most people.

Carl Rogers and others have discussed the *self-concept*, the image a person has of who he is or she is.[7] The self-concept is shaped over long periods by many outside forces such as parents, teachers, friends, and work associates, among others.

This viewpoint would suggest that one's self-concept can influence the impact the needs hierarchy has on individual motivations. For example, a person can learn as he or she matures and goes through life that he or she is good at relating to other people. The person's self-concept is that of a social person. If this becomes a stable pattern, such a person would not feel unfulfilled at never experiencing other motives such as ego or self-actualization, to use Maslow's terms. In the same way, a stable self-concept could form around some other

The self-concept is the image a person has of who he or she is; it is shaped over a long period of time by many outside forces.

[6] *Ibid.*, p. 396.
[7] See, for example, Saul W. Gellerman, *Motivation and Productivity* (New York: American Management Association, 1963), pp. 185–199.

When Leon Festinger first introduced his theory of cognitive dissonance in 1957, he stimulated a great deal of thought in the academic community. Over twenty-five years later, his theory remains a landmark in psychology. Its lasting impact is due in part to its relevance to many different areas of human behavior, including the day-to-day decision making of managers.

Cognitive dissonance is a psychological state that results when a person's ideas conflict with one another or with that person's behavior. Experiencing discomfort because of this lack of harmony (which Festinger termed *dissonance*), the individual tries to restore balance and consistency by changing his or her attitudes or behavior or even distorting perceptions. Cognitive dissonance is a "motivating state of affairs," says Festinger, "just as hunger impels a person to eat, so does dissonance impel a person to change his opinions or his behavior." *

Individuals must often weigh equally attractive alternatives and decide that one is better than the other. As soon as a choice is made, the individual tries to reduce the dissonance he or she feels concerning the attractive features of the rejected alternative and the unattractive features of the chosen alternative. The person decides that what looked good about the other choice is less attractive on second thought and the drawbacks of the chosen course are really not drawbacks at all.

* Leon Festinger, "Cognitive Dissonance," *Scientific American* (October 1962), p. 93.

need or combination of needs. People may not feel an inevitable drive to climb the needs hierarchy, as Maslow depicts it.

MASLOW'S CONTRIBUTION TO MANAGEMENT'S UNDERSTANDING OF MOTIVATION

Maslow's model has been of considerable value to the practice of management.[8] Perhaps its most important contribution is that it has encouraged managers to use a wide variety of motivational tools to appeal to several motives, rather than depend on one or a few.

A second contribution of Maslow to practicing managers was his insistence that satisfied needs are not motivators. Enlightened managers must attempt to locate the optimal point in each effort to motivate subordinates. Once a need has been satisfied, it loses its motivational importance and is replaced by a different need. Employees may insist on economic security to the point that they will strike to get it. But once they have comprehensive insurance coverage, their concerns will shift. Next they might be concerned with the "humanization" of their workplace, such as having access to some place where they can meet and mingle with other people. The manager who continues offering insurance policies to employees who have moved on to social needs will obtain little motivational payoff while incurring additional economic costs.

[8] An interesting male–female comparison of higher-level needs is offered in Ross Reck and Suzanne H. Cook, "Self-Esteem and Its Implications for Men and Women Managers," *Arizona Business* (November 1978), pp. 16–22.

Thus, when a manager decides to build a new manufacturing plant adjacent to a major state highway instead of a railroad link, he or she may cope with dissonance by downplaying the future of the country's rail system ("If we build next to the railroad, we may find ourselves with no transportation link in ten years.") and by reconsidering doubts about the price of diesel fuel ("Fuel prices have started to fall already. Within five years, they will probably be a bargain."). Unaware that this unconscious process of dissonance reduction is taking place, the manager only knows that the right decision has been made.

Cognitive dissonance is at one and the same time a beneficial and dangerous tool. It enables individuals to feel comfortable about their decisions but it also blinds them to the decision's negative effects. Festinger summed up the importance of his theory of cognitive dissonance when he said it carries "useful lessons for everyone concerned with understanding human behavior in a world where everything is not black and white."† This is especially true in the world of management.

Leon Festinger's contribution to the study of human behavior was recognized in 1959 when the American Psychological Association awarded him its Distinguished Scientific Contribution Award.

Source

Leon Festinger, "Cognitive Dissonance," *Scientific American* (October 1962), pp. 93–102.

† *Ibid.*, p. 102.

McClelland's Achievement, Affiliation, and Power Needs Theory

David C. McClelland, professor of psychology at Harvard University, is also credited with extensive contributions to motivation theory.[9] McClelland identifies three needs:

1. *Need for achievement.* The desire to accomplish some goal or task more effectively than has been the case in the past.
2. *Need for affiliation.* The desire to have close, amenable relations with other people.
3. *Need for power.* The desire to be influential and to have impact on a group.

McClelland and his associates have conducted numerous workshops at which participants are asked to write narrative comments about a series of work-related pictures. These stories are then analyzed and scored according to the person's relative concern for achievement, affiliation, and power. A comparison to na-

[9] Except for the citation in note 10 below, this section is based on David C. McClelland and David H. Burnham, "Power Is the Great Motivator," *Harvard Business Review* (March–April 1976), pp. 100–110. The McClelland–Burnham article notes that the three needs are from David C. McClelland's *The Achieving Society* (Princeton, N.J.: Van Nostrand, 1961), and *Power: The Inner Experience* (New York: Irvington, 1975).

tionwide norms is also part of the process. McClelland also studies the degree of self-control or inhibition that the individuals exhibit in their stories.

Much of McClelland's early work suggested that the need for achievement was important to business people, scientists, and professional persons.[10] A later report restricted to managers concluded that the need for power was most important to management. McClelland identifies three types of managers:

1. *Affiliative managers* (affiliation greater than power, high inhibition).
2. *Personal power managers* (power greater than affiliation, low inhibition).
3. *Institutional managers* (power greater than affiliation, high inhibition).

He concluded that the institutional managers who were high in the need for power and self-control, but low in the need for affiliation, were typically the most successful leaders.

McClelland believes that the workshop technique can accurately assess people's achievement, affiliation, and power motivations. More important, he believes that people can be taught to adopt a more appropriate approach to their job.

Herzberg's Two-Factor Theory of Motivation

Frederick Herzberg's research on motivation led to the development of his two-factor theory, which considered both job satisfaction and job dissatisfaction.[11] Herzberg, Distinguished Professor of Management at the University of Utah, asked 200 accountants and engineers what was satisfying about their work; that is, what were they willing to work harder to get. The accountants and engineers gave these answers: the opportunity to achieve through their work; some recognition by others for their work; the opportunity for promotion; the chance to grow, learn, and take on new responsibilities. Herzberg called these factors *motivators*.

Herzberg also asked his sample what factors dissatisfied them, making them unwilling to produce. Surprisingly, a whole new set of factors was mentioned. People complained when their supervision was poor, when they didn't get a chance to mingle with other people on the job, when physical working conditions were uncomfortable, when their pay and benefits were too low, and when they thought they might lose their jobs. These were called *hygienic* factors by Herzberg.

Herzberg's original study was replicated several times by other researchers. Figure 12-2 shows the factors affecting job attitudes based on twelve such stud-

[10] See Herbert G. Hicks and C. Ray Gullett, *Organization: Theory and Behavior* (New York: McGraw-Hill, 1975), p. 282.
[11] Frederick Herzberg, Bernard Mausner, and Barbara Block Snyderman, *The Motivation to Work* (New York: Wiley, 1959), pp. 113–119.

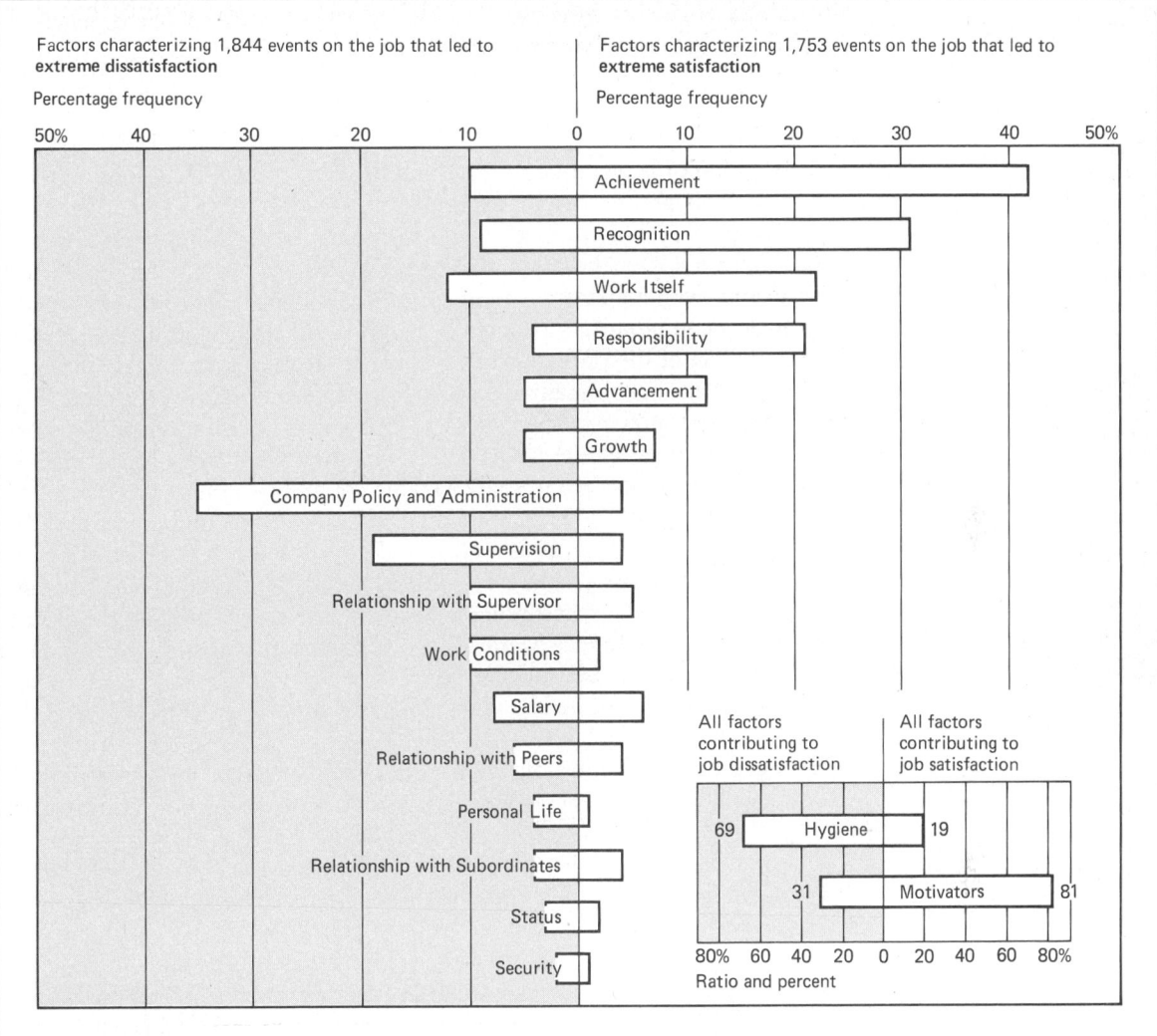

Figure 12-2
FACTORS AFFECTING JOB ATTITUDE, AS REPORTED IN TWELVE INVESTIGATIONS

SOURCE: Reprinted by permission of the Harvard Business Review. Exhibit from "One More Time: How Do You Motivate Employees?" by Frederick Herzberg (January–February 1968). Copyright © 1968 by the President and Fellows of Harvard College; all rights reserved.

ies. Respondents included lower-level supervisors, professional women, agricultural administrators, men about to retire from management positions, hospital maintenance personnel, manufacturing supervisors, nurses, food handlers, military officers, engineers, scientists, housekeepers, teachers, technicians, female assemblers, accountants, Finnish foremen, and Hungarian engineers.[12]

IMPLICATIONS FOR MANAGEMENT

The resolution of hygienic problems prevents employees from being dissatisfied and keeps their productivity at expected levels. Consider the special efforts of Eaton Corp. and Nabisco. Eaton Corp. has created an aura of mutual respect in its factories built over the past fifteen years. With no history of mutual distrust to overcome, both management and employees of Eaton's newest fifteen plants have made some important changes in traditional factory conditions, including the elimination of the probationary employment period, time clocks, and buzzers. Benefits have been equalized for factory and office workers at the same salary level. Supervisors now hold periodic departmental meetings, often with a subordinate as discussion leader.[13] Nabisco's Houston plant now has a management–employee committee to study working conditions. A remodeled cafeteria, improved security, and additional training programs have resulted from this undertaking.[14]

The extra effort from employees—doing more than normal—comes from providing the motivators, according to Herzberg's theory. Note that the motivators are roughly the same as Maslow's ego and self-actualization needs, whereas the hygienic factors are basically the physical, security, and social needs. In fact, Herzberg's research is viewed by some writers as concrete proof of Maslow's theory.

Herzberg's research illustrates that innate feelings about motivation can be misleading. The opposite of satisfaction may not be dissatisfaction, and eliminating dissatisfaction may not make people satisfied.

The implications for management are further complicated by the inconsistency of the research findings. Herzberg's conclusions have been confirmed by other studies, but they have been challenged by still others. Some studies have found that certain people apparently reverse the motivators and hygienic factors.[15] These people are motivated by the same factors that Herzberg's theory considered to be hygienic, and they are dissatisfied by what he labeled as motivators. While the results of such investigations may vary, Herzberg's recognition of two-factor theory job satisfaction and job dissatisfaction is a widely discussed

[12] Frederick Herzberg, "One More Time: How Do You Motivate Employees?" *Harvard Business Review* (January–February 1968), pp. 57–58.

[13] Donald N. Scobel, "Doing Away with the Factory Blues," *Harvard Business Review* (November–December 1975), pp. 132–142.

[14] "How to Promote Productivity," *Business Week* (July 24, 1978), p. 146.

[15] Michael R. Malinovsky and John R. Barry, "Determinants of Work Attitudes," *Journal of Applied Psychology* (December 1965), pp. 446–451; Richard Centers and Daphne E. Burgental, "Intrinsic and Extrinsic Job Motivations Among Different Segments of the Working Population," *Journal of Applied Psychology* (June 1966), pp. 193–197; and Donald C. Ott "The Generality of Herzberg's Two-Factor Theory of Motivation," unpublished doctoral dissertation, Ohio University, Athens, Ohio, *Dissertation Abstracts*, Vol. 26, No. 3 (1965), pp. 1767–1768.

A survey of NFL head coaches indicated that motivation theories popular in management also play a role in professional football. The researchers asked the coaches to indicate their relative agreement or disagreement with twenty-five statements concerning the motivation and handling of their team members. The questions were phrased in football terminology, but each was designed to solicit the viewpoints of the coaches toward a specific motivational theory and its importance in professional football. For example, one item said: "The player's present salary is his number one motivator for the present season," and was intended to obtain the person's view of Herzberg's two-factor theory.

The researchers concluded that NFL coaches generally support the various motivational theories used by business management. The coaches' tendency is to emphasize psychological motivation such as ego building or the rejection of being benched, rather than to rely on motivations such as money or tougher practice sessions. The researchers observed that the successful coaches specifically noted that individual motivations varied among players and that these differences had to be recognized and dealt with effectively.

SOURCE: Charles N. Waldo and Kelly Kerin, "NFL Coaches and Motivation Theory," *MSU Business Topics*, Autumn 1978, pp. 15–18. Reprinted by permission of the publisher, Division of Research, Graduate School of Business Administration, Michigan State University.

MOTIVATION THEORY IN THE NATIONAL FOOTBALL LEAGUE

contribution to the literature of motivation—both by academicians and by practicing managers.

B. F. Skinner—Modifying Operant Behavior

B. F. Skinner, a noted psychologist, has offered some important contributions to the study of motivation. While Skinner's work has been criticized on many counts, it remains a strong theoretical underpinning to much of applied motivational theory in management.

Skinner distinguishes between *operant behavior* (that which is voluntary) and *reflex behavior* (that which is involuntary).[16] He advocates the premise that operant behavior can be modified through the process of reinforcment. *Reinforcement* refers to the confirmation of outcomes of behavior. It can be either positive or negative. Skinner described the difference this way:

Operant behavior is voluntary behavior.

Reflex behavior is involuntary behavior.

Reinforcement is the process by which behavior is modified by either positive or negative factors.

> A positive reinforcer strengthens any behavior that produces it: a glass of water is positively reinforcing when we are thirsty, and if we then draw and drink a glass of water, we are more likely to do so again on similar occasions. A negative reinforcer strengthens any behavior that reduces or terminates it; when we take off a shoe that is pinching, the reduction in pressure is negatively reinforcing, and we are more likely to do so again when a shoe pinches.[17]

[16] B. F. Skinner, *About Behaviorism* (New York: Knopf, 1974), p. 40.
[17] *Ibid.*, p. 46.

YURI ANDROPOV HAS A PLAN FOR MODIFYING OPERANT BEHAVIOR

One of the first things that Yuri Andropov did after succeeding Soviet leader Leonid Brezhnev was to announce a crackdown on corruption and waste in order to improve productivity. Part of his campaign concentrated on reducing absenteeism in Russian industry. The scarcity of consumer services and products and the limited hours of Soviet shops caused many workers to skip part of their workday to attend to personal chores. Andropov asked shops to provide more flexible hours, but he also cracked down on workers who engaged in such practices. Police demanded the papers of daytime bar patrons. Communist Party workers searched barber shops, stores, restaurants, and the like. Television news camera crews were even stationed outside plant gates.

Party leader Andropov commented: "Apparently the strength of inertia and adherence to old ways are still at work. Moreover, some people, perhaps, just do not know how to set about doing the job."

SOURCE: Steven R. Hurst, "Soviets Track Down Absent Workers to Raise Productivity," *Journal-American* (January 10, 1983), p. 6-B (AP Story).

Many management experts believe that reinforcement theory[18] can be applied successfully within an organizational perspective. Management should reinforce positive behavior and not reinforce negative behavior. Certainly, the terminology used in the Skinner analysis of behavior has become widely prescriptive of many current management practices.

Expectancy Theory

Expectancy theory is another important viewpoint in the study of motivation. Victor Vroom, professor of administrative sciences and psychology at Yale University, has described the concept of *expectancy* as "a momentary belief concerning the likelihood that a particular act will be followed by a particular outcome."[19] Vroom believes that the force to perform any act is a function of (1) the expectancy and (2) the perceived value of the outcome. He termed this second variable *valence*.[20]

Consider the case of a sales representative participating in an employer-sponsored sales contest. The salesperson getting the most orders for a new product line will win a vacation trip to Mexico. The representative's perception of the trip's value is the valence. The expectancy factor is the probability of the individual actually winning the trip. If the firm has a sales force of 150 people, the representative may rate his or her expectancy as relatively low.

Lawler and Porter and others have described expectancy theory as a path-goal concept. The basic premise is that people take actions that are likely to result in

---

[18] A brief review of the background of reinforcement theory appears in Larry E. Pate, "Cognitive Versus Reinforcement Views of Intrinsic Motivation," *Academy of Management Review* (July 1978), pp. 506–507.

[19] Victor H. Vroom, *Work and Motivation* (New York: Wiley, 1964), p. 17.

[20] *Ibid.*, pp. 15–19.

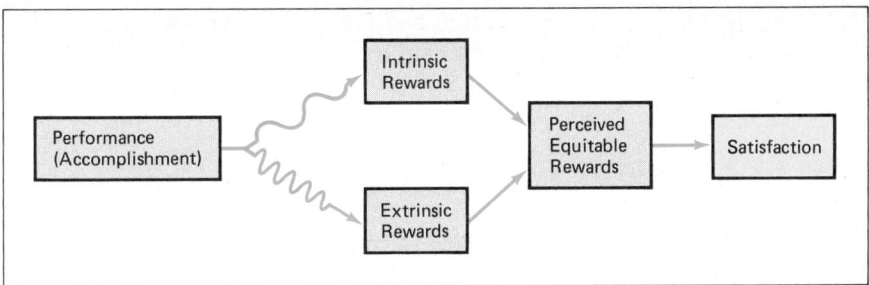

**Figure 12-3
THE
LAWLER–PORTER
MODEL**

SOURCE: Edward E. Lawler III and Lyman W. Porter, "The Effect of Performance on Job Satisfaction," *Industrial Relations* (October 1967), p. 23. Used with permission.

rewards that are considered worthwhile.[21] A generalized definition might be: *Expectancy theory* refers to motivated behavior designed to achieve highly probable and valued rewards, which, in turn, lead to job satisfaction if the rewards are deemed fair.

Lawler and Porter have offered a theoretical model of this process (see Figure 12-3). According to the model, performance or accomplishment produces rewards. *Extrinsic rewards* are those offered by the organization such as pay, promotions, and job security. The wavy, connecting line suggests the imperfect linkage between performance and such rewards. By contrast, the semiwavy line to intrinsic rewards suggests that these are subject to less disruption. *Intrinsic rewards* are those that the individual gains internally. Self-actualization is an intrinsic reward.

There is no direct link between the rewards and job satisfaction because the rewards must be perceived as equitable in relationship to the level of job performance. The individual has to view the rewards as in fair balance with the ef-

Expectancy theory refers to motivated behavior designed to achieve rewards which are likely to lead to job satisfaction.

---

[21] The remainder of this section follows Edward E. Lawler III and Lyman W. Porter, "The Effect of Performance on Job Satisfaction," *Industrial Relations* (October 1967), pp. 20–28.

"It's still considered income, Mr. Harris, whether you had it spent before you saw it or not."

EXPECTANCY THEORY OR NOT . . . THE IRS STILL WANTS ITS DUE

SOURCE: *The Wall Street Journal* (May 3, 1982), p. 28. Permission–Cartoon Features Syndicate.

fort he or she exerts on the job. Lawler and Porter have empirically tested the model, and their findings suggest that it is a valid description of motivation.[22]

The Locus of Control Concept[23]

Locus of control refers to a person's perception of the controlling factors in their own destiny.

Julian B. Rotter's discussion of the locus of control is also a major contribution to the literature of motivation theory.[24] _Locus of control refers to a person's perception of the controlling factors in their own destiny._ Individuals who believe that what they do affects their lives are said to have _internal control._ In other words a person who thinks that extra effort on the job will result in a future promotion can be classified as someone with internal control. By contrast, _external control_ describes a situation in which individuals perceive outside variables as the determining factors in their own destinies. Someone who believes that luck, environmental factors, or others are the causal factors in their personal situation can be classified as an adherent to external control. The terms _internal_ and _external_ are often used to identify these differing viewpoints in locus of control.

Most research conducted since Rotter's original proposal has generally supported the locus of control concept. This work has significant implications for management. A review by Gavin and Fleenor suggests that if a work force consisted largely of internals, management would be well advised to consider participative management techniques. If externals dominate the work force, management should ". . . provide relatively structured tasks with responsibilities clearly delineated so as to provide a surfeit of clues to help employees ascribe responsibility for success or failure to their own actions."[25]

Like the other theories of individual behavior reported here, locus of control is an important aspect of understanding what motivates people. Chapter 13 will examine another perspective of motivation, group behavior.

---

[22] Another interesting article on expectancy theory is Hugh J. Arnold, "A Test of the Validity of the Multiplicative Hypothesis of Expectancy-Valence Theories of Work Motivation," _Academy of Management Journal_ (March 1981), pp. 128–141.

[23] This section is based on an unpublished paper by William B. Gavin and C. Patrick Fleenor, "The Relationship of the Locus of Control Construct in an Industrial Environment to the Expectancy-Valence Model of Behavior." Other interesting discussions appear in Dan R. Dalton and William D. Tudor, "Union Steward Locus of Control, Job, Union Involvement, and Grievance Behavior," _Journal of Business Research_ (March 1982), pp. 85–101; and Danny Miller, Manfred F. R. Kets De Vries, and Jean-Marie Toulous, "Top Executive Locus of Control and Its Relationship to Strategy-Making, Structure, and Environment," _Academy of Management Journal_ (June 1982), pp. 237–253.

[24] See Julian B. Rotter, _Social Learning and Clinical Psychology_ (Englewood Cliffs, N.J.: Prentice-Hall, 1954); and "Generalized Expectancies for Internal Versus External Control of Reinforcement: Psychological Monographs," _General and Applied_, 80, no. 1 (1966), 1–28. Also see Rotter and R. C. Muhry, "Internal Versus External Control of Reinforcement and Decision Time," _Journal of Personality and Social Psychology_, 2, no. 4 (1965), pp. 598–604.

[25] Gavin and Fleenor, "The Relationship of the Locus of Control Construct in an Industrial Environment to the Expectancy-Valence Model of Behavior."

Summary

Motivation refers to behavior directed toward the satisfaction of some need. Motivated behavior can be divided into individual and group behavior. Effective management requires a working knowledge of both aspects of behavior.

Kurt Lewin offers a generalized concept of behavior in his formula

$$B = f(P,E)$$

where behavior is viewed as a function of factors related to the person and the environmental factors that affect him or her. A variety of other theories of individual behavior have been offered.

A. H. Maslow's classification of needs identifies five basic needs: physical or physiological; safety or security; love or social; ego or status; and self-actualization needs. According to Maslow these needs can be put into a hierarchical arrangement. David C. McClelland suggests three needs: the need for achievement, the need for affiliation, and the need for power. Frederick Herzberg's two-factor theory considers both job satisfaction and job dissatisfaction, which are often unrelated to each other. B. F. Skinner discusses the importance of reinforcement (the confirmation of outcomes of behavior) on operant (voluntary) behavior. Victor Vroom, Edward Lawler, and Lyman Porter are associated with expectancy theory, a concept that refers to motivated behavior designed to achieve highly probable and valued rewards, which in turn lead to job satisfaction if the rewards are deemed fair.

Locus of control, a concept proposed by Julian B. Rotter, refers to a person's perception of what influences his destiny. People who have an internal locus of control believe that they can largely determine their own destiny. People who have an external locus of control perceive outside factors as controlling what happens to them. The locus of control concept impacts the effectiveness of management practices.

REVIEW EXERCISES

1. Define the following terms: (a) motivation (b) self-concept (c) operant behavior (d) reflex behavior (e) reinforcement (f) expectancy theory (g) locus of control.

2. Discuss the basic points made in the profile for Chapter 12.

3. Explain the concept of motivation.

4. Discuss Kurt Lewin's field theory.

5. Describe Maslow's classification of needs.

6. Outline McClelland's achievement, affiliation, and power needs theory.

7. Explain Herzberg's two-factor theory of motivation.

8. Describe B. F. Skinner's contribution to motivation theory.

9. What is expectancy theory?

10. Discuss the locus of control concept.

ASSIGNMENTS/PROBLEMS/ DISCUSSION QUESTIONS

1. Consider the remarks of two former presidents.*

I found that the men and women who get to the top were those who did the jobs that they had in hand, with everything they had of energy and enthusiasm and hard work.

Harry S. Truman

Some people think you're finished when you lose. You are finished only when you quit. Never quit. Never, Never, Never.

Richard M. Nixon

Compare and contrast these viewpoints. Relate the remarks about motivation to the career paths of these men.

2. Atlanta Envelope Co. achieved some impressive results with a program to improve employee attendance. Absenteeism was cut 50 percent and productivity hiked 15 percent when the firm offered a two-hours-of-pay bonus to any- one who did not miss a day during a month. Six months' perfect attendance led to an eight hours' bonus, and a year to an extra week's pay.† Evaluate this program in terms of the concepts presented in this chapter.

3. Relate your own behavior to Maslow's needs hierarchy.

4. ROLM Corp. faces a tough job market in Santa Clara, California. As a result the company goes to elaborate lengths to attract and retain good personnel. The company offers flexible work schedules, subsidized meals in an outdoor cafe, discounted trips to Europe, sailing and aerobic dance lessons, and a complete gym and swimming pool facility. Six-year employees qualify for a paid twelve-month leave, or a six month leave with double pay.** Relate ROLM's unique fringe benefit package to the material contained in Chapter 12.

5. James Buchanan Duke, the tobacco industry pioneer, was quoted as saying:

* The Truman quote is from "Thoughts on the Business of Life," *Forbes* (February 5, 1979), p. 118. The Nixon quote is from "Well, Hello Richard," *Newsweek* (December 18, 1978), p. 38.

† *Staff* (May 1978), p. 2. © 1978 Business Research Publications, a division of Man & Manager, Inc., 799 Broadway, New York, N.Y. 10003.
** Reported in Carol Pucci, "Some of the 'Workers' Paradise May Spill Over Here," *The Seattle Times,* (May 18, 1982), p. 1-E.

I have succeeded in business, not because I have more natural ability than many people who have not succeeded, but because I have applied myself harder and stuck to it longer. I know plenty of people who have failed to succeed in anything who have more brains than I had, but they lacked application and determination.‡

Do you agree with Duke's observations? Do you think Duke would have agreed with the Truman and Nixon comments above? Discuss.

‡ Quoted in B. C. Forbes, *Men Who Made America Great*, p. 68. This is a reprint from a 1917 work originally entitled *Men Who Are Making America Great*. Reprinted by Hamilton Press, Box 583, Brookfield, Wis. 53005.

A MANAGERIAL INCIDENT

Lincoln Electric Co.

Cleveland-based Lincoln Electric Co. is the market leader in arc-welding equipment with annual sales of $542 million. It is also a very innovative company when it comes to motivating employees. Lincoln has used a piece-work system since 1914, and its production workers average $44,000 an-nually. A piece-rate system is used as the base compensation plan. It is supplemented by an annual bonus that doubles the workers' yearly earnings. Employees are also guaranteed thirty hours of work each week, and no one has been laid off since 1951.

Lincoln's incentive management program has created a stable, highly motivated, and very productive work force. In fact, Lincoln has even driven giant General Electric out of the arc-welding equipment industry. There are no seniority rights at Lincoln, and everyone must be willing to be switched to another job. Lincoln's management tries to even out production so it can live up to its employment guarantee. Lincoln workers are very satisfied with the firm's unique compensation plan. In fact, they once voted down a dental plan because it might have reduced year-end bonuses.

Source: William Baldwin, "This Is the Answer," *Forbes* (July 5, 1982), pp. 50, 52.

Questions and Problems

1. Relate the Lincoln Electric incentive system to the material presented in Chapter 12.

2. Pick a firm with which you are familiar. Would a motivation program similar to the one at Lincoln Electric work in this firm? Why or why not?

13.
Motivation: Group Behavior

Work is for man and not man for work.

POPE JOHN PAUL II

I have yet to find the man, however ex-
alted his station, who did not do better
work and put forth greater effort under
a spirit of approval, than under a spirit
of criticism.

CHARLES SCHWAB

ntel is now a $900 million electronics firm in Santa Clara, California. It was started by three scientists who split off from Fairchild Semiconductors. The company earns a 20 percent pretax margin, doubling that of the competition. Intel can attribute a substantial part of its success to effective motivational practices.

The founders run Intel from a three-person executive office that is dedicated to keeping bureaucratic practices out of the company. Intel makes extensive use of councils that make decisions and monitor programs in given areas. The newly hired and executives alike participate as equals in these councils.

There are no closed offices, dress codes, executive dining rooms, reserved parking, or limousines at Intel. The company's participative management practices are communicated in a variety of training sessions. The Intel philosophy is explained this way by President Andrew S. Grove:

> It isn't symbolism. . . . It's a necessity . . . I can't pretend to know the shape of the next generation of silicon or computer technology anymore. That's why people like me need the knowledge from the people closest to the technology. That's why we can't have the hierarchical barriers to our exchange of ideas and information that you have at so many corporations.[1]

Intel is an excellent illustration of the importance of group behavior. Chapter 13 examines a range of research and theories of group behavior. The Hawthorne studies, human relations school, human resources model, the contributions of William F. Whyte and Stanley Seashore, equity theory, and reference groups are described here. Chapter 13 also looks at informal group leaders, morale and productivity, money as a motivator, and the problems and constraints of applying motivation theory.

[1] Steve Lohr, "Overhauling America's Business Management," *The New York Times Magazine* (January 4, 1981), pp. 44–45.

The discoveries made by Professor of Industrial Research Elton Mayo in the course of his experiments on motivation among industrial workers were revolutionary. Not only did they cause Mayo to reverse his own thinking, they pointed new ways for management to increase productivity through the study and improvement of personnel relations.

Born in Adelaide, Australia, in 1880, Mayo graduated and received his Master of Arts degree (1917) from the University of Adelaide and his Ph.D. from Queensland University (1919). In 1923 he was hired as a research associate at the University of Pennsylvania, and from 1926 on he was a member of the Harvard faculty.

When he began the first phase of his famous Hawthorne experiments, Mayo firmly believed that every social problem was "ultimately individual." At the Hawthorne Works of the Western Electric Co. in Chicago, where he and his assistants did their study, however, Mayo soon found that group rather than individual psychology was the key factor in production performance of the workers.

Based on the premise that fatigue was the main factor affecting output, Mayo's study had three phases. The first phase was a day-by-day statistical evaluation of the output of five female telephone assemblers who were segregated in a controlled work environment. The analysis of their work performance was carefully related to changes in their working conditions that were periodically introduced, as well as to the characteristics of their work environment (temperature and humidity, for example) and variations in their personal routines (for example, different meals, few or many hours of sleep). Mayo and his team were puzzled to find *no* correlations of any significance. Though the output of the women rose as coffee breaks were added and hours shortened, it did not decline when the group was once again required to work under the original, control conditions. These findings revealed that the determining factors were the significance the experiment had for the workers and their desire to cooperate with the researchers and facilitate their work.

Theories of Group Behavior

Groups play a major role in overall behavior patterns. A simple experiment has shown the dramatic effect other people can have on an individual.[2] Three unequal lines were shown to a group of people. They were then given a fourth line and asked to match it visually with the line of the same length in the original cluster of three lines. People in the group could accomplish this task with very few mistakes over many matching trials.

But then the experiment was varied. In another group doing the same task, all but one person were told to lie about which lines matched. This person, who was unaware of the change, was found to match the wrong lines in about half the trials, usually making the same "mistake" as the others had been told to make. Even though the person knew the correct answer, he or she often changed an opinion just to fit into the group. In other words the individual was conforming.

[2] S. E. Asch, "Effects of Group Pressure upon the Modification and Distortion of Judgments," in Dorwin Cartwright and Alvin Zander (eds.), *Group Dynamics: Research and Theory,* 2nd ed. (Evanston, Ill.: Row, Peterson, 1960), pp. 193–194.

This discovery launched the second phase of the Hawthorne study: interviews, somewhat psychoanalytic in nature, of thousands of workers to determine the meaning they ascribed to their work and personal relationships within the factory. Eventually Mayo developed the revolutionary hypothesis that "the working group as a whole actually determined the output of individual workers by reference to a standard, predetermined but never clearly stated, that represented the group conception of a fair day's work." His research also indicated that "this standard was rarely, if ever, in accord with the standards of efficiency engineers."

The final phase of Mayo's investigation consisted of the observation of a group of workers and served to verify his hypothesis that the group, not the individual worker, plays the crucial role in setting standards for output. He further concluded that even economic needs and interests of the individual are subordinated to the group's standards. "Management," Mayo wrote in his *Social Problems of an Industrial Organization* (1945), "in any continuously successful plant, is not related to single workers but always to working groups. In every department that continues to operate, the workers have—whether aware of it or not—formed themselves into a group with appropriate customs, duties, routines, even rituals; and management succeeds (or fails) in proportion as it is accepted without reservation by the group as authority and leader."

A man of many interests, Mayo did not confine his studies to industrial relations but examined as well the problems of individuals and society in coping with the rapid rate of change characteristic of an industrial civilization (*The Human Problems of an Industrial Civilization*, 1933). Upon his death in 1949 he was widely recognized for his contributions to the study of humanity, both within his own discipline and beyond it, through his talent for synthesizing the social sciences.

Sources

Stuart Chase, "Calling All Social Scientists," *Nation* (May 4, 1946), pp. 538–540.

P. Sargant Florence, "Professor Elton Mayo" (Obituary), *Nature* (October 15, 1949), p. 646.

"The Fruitful Errors of Elton Mayo," *Fortune* 34 (November 1946), pp. 180–183, 238, 241–242, 244, 247–249.

John W. McConnell, "George Elton Mayo, 1880–1949" (Obituary), *Industrial and Labor Relations Review* 3 (January 1950), pp. 305–306.

Conformity is probably the most distinctive part of an individual's behavior in a group. In the following discussion, several studies will be cited. Note how conformity, or the lack of it, is important to motivation.

The Hawthorne Studies and the Human Relations School

Probably the most famous studies of work group behavior are the Hawthorne studies, performed during the six-year period, 1927 to 1933, at the Hawthorne plant of the Western Electric Co. in Chicago. A total of 20,000 employees were included in this research.[3]

The Hawthorne studies looked into the effects of physical working conditions and pay schemes on worker output. The researchers expected to prove how

Hawthorne studies were a series of investigations that revealed money anf job security are not the only sources of employee motivation. They led to the development of the human relations approach to employee motivation.

[3] See F. J. Roethlisberger and William J. Dickson (with Harold A. Wright), *Management and the Worker* (New York: Wiley, 1964). A new perspective on the Hawthorne studies is contained in H. McIlvaine Parsons, "What Caused the Hawthorne Effect? A Scientific Detective Story," *Administration and Society* (November 1978), pp. 259–283.

GROUP BEHAVIOR—THE DATA TERMINAL SYSTEMS CASE

Massachusetts-based Data Terminal Systems had experienced rapid growth since its founding in 1970. The firm builds electronic cash registers and checkout scanning systems. While Data Terminal had experienced an average annual growth rate of 95 percent, its president, Robert Collings, feared that the firm was becoming too departmentalized and that an overall orientation to company goals was lacking.

So Collings decided to offer an expenses-paid one-week vacation to either London or Disney World for all employees if they doubled sales and profits. The following year Collings offered a trip to Rome if the figures were again doubled. Employees were paid full salary for the week off. The company paid most expenses and gave everyone $100 spending money. Guests and family members paid their own way. Workers who decided to stay home got a week's paid vacation plus $100. Currently, outstanding employees are also eligible for expenses-paid cruises and super weekender award trips.

By most accounts the motivational program was immensely effective. Data Terminal's president believes that peer pressure was responsible for the firm's achieving its goals. As Collings put it: "They didn't want anyone to screw up their vacation."

SOURCE: Stephen Soloman, "How a Whole Company Earned Itself a Roman Vacation," *Fortune* (January 15, 1979), pp. 80–83. Material based on the original article which appeared in the January 15, 1979 issue of *Fortune* Magazine and reprinted by special permission; © 1979 Time Inc. The 1982 update was provided by Data Terminal Systems, Inc.

much improving work and pay conditions would increase output. The results were a surprise that has had a far-reaching impact on management.

One set of experiments in the Relay Assembly Test Room involved setting aside a special group of female assemblers, improving such factors as lighting and temperature and measuring the effect on productivity. As the factors improved, output went up. To verify the conclusion, the researchers reversed the conditions (by dimming the lights, for instance) and again measured output. To their astonishment output continued to climb; the worse things got, the higher the productivity rose.

In studying the situation closely, the researchers found that the women were responding to changes other than the experimental ones. The women felt special

AS THE SIX WOMEN INVOLVED IN THE FAMOUS HAWTHORE STUDIES PROVED, MORALE OFTEN HAS A GREATER EFFECT ON PRODUCTIVITY THAN DO BETTER WORK AND PAY CONDITIONS.

SOURCE: Courtesy of Western Electric Co.

because they had been picked for the experiment. Also, the arrangement was more informal than the assemblers were accustomed to. They could talk, help each other when someone was not feeling well, and get extra help from the supervisor. Work became more of a social event that even included birthday parties. These unexpected results have been labeled the *Hawthorne effect*.

BIRTH OF THE HUMAN RELATIONS SCHOOL

The morale of the group had improved and production rose. As a result of these findings, a movement in management practice began that continued well into the 1950s. It was called the *human relations approach to management aims*. The human relations school of management was based on the belief that better treatment of subordinates would make them more productive. The accepted viewpoint was that contented employees would work harder.

Human relations management has been praised and condemned, and today few managers accept its tenets without major reservations. The problem was that too many generalizations were drawn from the Relay Assembly Test Room experiments. Many times managers worked hard at human relations only to find that workers ended up disliking them. The employees were unhappy and unproductive. Ironically, the Hawthorne studies themselves could have been used to foresee this, if only more attention had been paid to the Bank Wiring Observation Room experiments.

THE BANK WIRING OBSERVATION ROOM STUDY

In the Bank Wiring Observation Room study, workers were paid on an incentive pay plan wherein their pay increased as their output increased. It was expected that worker output would rise over time; instead, it stayed at a fairly constant level. Further research was required to discover the cause of this situation.

The researchers found a complicated "informal" social life among the workers. It seemed that they had their own idea of what was "a fair day's work" and enforced it themselves. Most of them, the *regulars*, ignored the incentive plan and voluntarily conformed to the group's standard output, called a *group norm*. Those who did not conform, the *deviants*, were disciplined by the group. Employees working too fast were called "ratebusters" or "speed kings" and sometimes were physically threatened to bring them into line. Those working too slow were ridiculed as "chiselers." Anybody complaining to management was a "squealer" and was likely to end up as an *isolate*, totally ignored by the group.

As a group morale was high in the Bank Wiring Room, and yet productivity did not increase. In a sense high morale was working against management, but these results unfortunately were not remembered as well as the Relay Assembly Test Room results.

BASIC LESSONS FOR THE MANAGER

The Hawthorne studies illustrated that employees' social needs could be a very important part of their motivation. These needs appear in the context of an in-

Hawthorne effect refers to the positive impact on employee motivation of factors other than money and job security, as revealed by the Hawthorne studies.

The **human relations approach** to management aims to improve and increase employees' production by boosting their morale.

formal organization that works along with the formal organization and can help
or hinder management. From the viewpoint of a supervisor, an informal group
can be a positive situation because workers discipline each other and they keep
production going at an acceptable pace.

The Human Resources Model

Douglas McGregor, Rensis Likert, Mason Haire, and Raymond E. Miles,
among others, have suggested a major adaptation to the human relations

Table 13-1 COMPARISON OF THE HUMAN RELATIONS AND HUMAN RESOURCES MODELS	HUMAN RELATIONS	HUMAN RESOURCES
	Attitudes Toward People	
	1. People in our culture share a common set of needs—to belong, to be liked, to be respected.	1. In addition to sharing common needs for belonging and respect, most people in our culture desire to contribute effectively and creatively to the accomplishment of worthwhile objectives.
	2. They desire individual recognition but, more than this, they want to feel a useful part of the company and their own work group or department.	2. The majority of our work force is capable of exercising far more initiative, responsibility, and creativity than their present jobs require or allow.
	3. They will tend to cooperate willingly and comply with organizational goals if these important needs are fulfilled.	3. These capabilities represent untapped resources which are presently being wasted.
	Kind and Amount of Participation	
	1. The manager's basic task is to make each worker believe that he or she is a useful and important part of the department "team."	1. The manager's basic task is to create an environment in which his or her subordinates can contribute their full range of talents to the accomplishment of organizational goals. He or she must attempt to uncover and tap the creative resources of the subordinates.
	2. The manager should be willing to explain his or her decisions and to discuss subordinates' objections to his or her plans. On routine matters he or she should encourage subordinates to par-	2. The manager should allow, and encourage, subordinates to participate not only in routine decisions but in important matters as well. In fact, the more important a decision is to the manager's de-

school.[4] They argue that the *human relations school*, as it has been popularized in management literature and practice, is really only a modest alteration of the autocratic model that prevailed before the Hawthorne studies. By contrast, they argue that a comprehensive human resources model should be employed in motivational efforts.

The *human resources model* suggests that management should be responsible for establishing an environment that can employ all the human resources of the work group with the goal of improved decision making and performance. The basic differences between the human relations and human resources models are outlined in Table 13-1.

[4] This section is based on Raymond E. Miles, "Human Relations or Human Resources?" *Harvard Business Review* (July–August 1965), pp. 148, 152, 154, 156, 158, 160, 163.

> **The human resources model suggests that management should be responsible for establishing an environment that best utilizes all the human resources for improved decision making and performance.**

HUMAN RELATIONS	HUMAN RESOURCES
ticipate in planning and choosing among alternative solutions to problems.	partment, the greater should be his or her effort to tap the department's resources.
3. Within narrow limits, the work group or individual suborordinates should be allowed to exercise self-direction and self-control in carrying out plans.	3. The manager should attempt to continually expand the areas over which subordinates exercise self-direction and self-control as they develop and demonstrate greater insight and ability.
Expectations	
1. Sharing information with subordinates and involving them in departmental decision making will help satisfy their basic needs for belonging and for individual recognition.	1. The overall quality of decision making and performance will improve as the manager makes use of the full range of experience, insight, and creative ability in his or her department.
2. Satisfying these needs will improve subordinate morale and reduce resistance to formal authority.	2. Subordinates will exercise responsible self-direction and self-control in the accomplishment of worthwhile objectives that they understand and have helped establish.
3. High employee morale and reduced resistance to formal authority may lead to improved departmental performance. It should at least reduce intradepartment friction and thus make the manager's job easier.	3. Subordinate satisfaction will increase as a by-product of improved performance and the opportunity to contribute creatively to this improvement.

SOURCE: Reprinted by permission of the Harvard Business Review. Exhibit from "Human Relations or Human Resources?" by Raymond E. Miles (July-August 1965). Copyright © 1965 by the President and Fellows of Harvard College; all rights reserved.

Miles points out that research indicates that managers have adopted a two-sided view of motivation. He says that managers have widely accepted the tenets of the human relations school and believe it is appropriate for their own subordinates. But when it comes to their own relationships with superiors, managers support the human resources model as the best approach.

Whyte's Contributions to the Study of Group Behavior

William F. Whyte, in a study of factory workers, found that regulars and rate-busters tend to have different backgrounds.[5] The conforming regulars were joiners even outside the workplace, where they were members of various social groups and community organizations. They also tended to spend rather than save their earnings and came from the cities.

On the other hand, ratebusters were loners at work and at home. They usually came from rural backgrounds and were thrifty with their money. Whyte found that the ratebusters, who he said behave in accordance with the *Protestant ethic*, were the only workers responding to the piece-rate incentive pay plan. Those who restricted their output to the group norm acted in accordance with what Whyte called the *social ethic*.

The Research by Seashore

Stanley Seashore, professor of psychology at the University of Michigan, conducted extensive research on group behavior, involving a total of 228 factory work groups.[6] Seashore concluded that there was substantial evidence suggesting that these workers actually controlled production.

The group pressure toward conformity was called *cohesiveness* by Seashore. Groups with high cohesiveness were found to make their members feel more secure and were more likely to have uniformly enforced production norms than were groups with low cohesiveness.

Of the many groups studied by Seashore, some were found to have high productivity and others low productivity. Comparing these groups, Seashore observed that the difference was in the amount of company supportiveness felt by each group. If a group felt confident in management, it would enforce a high production level. If it had a poor opinion of management, its production was uniformly low. Interestingly, group morale was high in either case.

[5] William Foote Whyte, *Money and Motivation* (New York: Harper & Row, 1955).
[6] Stanley F. Seashore, *Group Cohesiveness in the Industrial Work Group* (Ann Arbor: Survey Research Center, University of Michigan, 1954).

The U.S. Army recently announced an innovative new organizational plan that applies many of the theories of group behavior discussed here. COHORT—Cohesion Operational Readiness Training—is the first significant change of its type since World War II. Instead of transferring soldiers in and out of a company on an individual basis, COHORT keeps the same 180 people together all the way through their three-year enlistment. The army believes that group cohesiveness and behavior will improve the combat effectiveness of the designated units.

SOURCE: "Army to Organize Along Buddy Lines," *The Seattle Times* (December 18, 1982), p. 3-A (UPI story).

COHORT—APPLYING MOTIVATION THEORY TO THE U.S. ARMY

The Role of Equity Theory and Reference Groups

People usually possess a sense of equity or fairness, which they judge by comparing themselves with some other group. *Equity theory* refers to the human tendency to try to balance work efforts or inputs with the rewards received. People innately try to reach what they consider to be a fair balance by either reducing or increasing their input in accordance with their perception of the relative rewards of their effort.[7] Reference groups play a key role in such evaluations.

The concept of a reference orientation among workers is the product of studies of group behavior. *Reference groups* are those sets or categories of people with which a person identifies. This identity is often with some group other than the one to which the person belongs, and sometimes it is with people outside the firm. Behavior patterns are often predicated on what an individual perceives to be happening with his or her reference group.

Many supervisors have been dismayed when suddenly, for no apparent reason, the amount or quality of their workers' production drops off. Studies have found that the explanation is often a change in some other department or group of employees that has upset the workers' sense of equity.[8] For instance, if another department got a pay raise for basically the same work, it could set off this kind of reaction: "If they got a raise and aren't working any harder for it, then relatively speaking we are worse off. But if we work less for our pay, then things will balance out."

Conversely, other supervisors have been surprised to see production rise even

Equity theory has been offered to explain the human tendency to balance work efforts or inputs with the rewards received.

Reference groups are those sets or categories of people with which a person identifies.

[7] Equity theory is discussed in Michael R. Carrell and John E. Dittrich, "Equity Theory: The Recent Literature, Methodological Considerations, and New Directions," *Academy of Management Review* (April 1978), pp. 202–210; and Sam Gould, "An Equity-Exchange Model of Organizational Involvement," *Academy of Management Review* (January 1979), pp. 53–62.

[8] Martin Patchen, "A Conceptual Framework and Some Empirical Data Regarding Comparison of Social Rewards," in Herbert H. Hyman and Eleanor Singer (eds.), *Readings in Reference Group Theory and Research* (New York: Free Press, 1960), pp. 169–184.

when no changes were made in their departments. The explanation: A change was made in some other department, such as a less desirable work schedule that made other workers feel that they were better off. Feeling a sense of guilt, they instinctively worked harder to make things right again.

Reference orientation has been found to be especially important among professional workers.[9] A college professor who identifies with his or her college or an engineer who identifies with his or her firm are said to have a *bureaucratic* or *local* orientation. Those who identify with groups outside their organization, such as with trade or professional associations or colleagues employed elsewhere, are said to have a *professional* or *cosmopolitan* orientation. Locals are much more likely to be loyal to their employer and seldom switch jobs. Cosmopolitans are more likely to make frequent job changes.

Informal Group Leaders

Informal group leader is a leader in a group who functions as a social–emotional task leader.

Robert F. Bales performed some interesting experiments with small task groups.[10] One of his goals was to find what would cause a person to be identified as group leader by the members. This was done by having the group work at a task and then asking the members anonymously to identify the leader when they were finished. Bales consistently found that the person who had the best ideas and offered the group the most guidance toward doing its task was identified as the leader.

Then Bales asked the group members to identify the person they liked the most. The groups tended to pick someone other than the leader as most popular. Bales concluded that the groups naturally tended to have two leaders. He called one the *task leader* (formal leader) and the one best liked the *social–emotional leader* (informal leader). Further study by Bales found that the social–emotional leader performed certain functions in the group different than those of the task leader. This leader typically helped the others, laughed, exhibited understanding toward others, and supported their ideas. He or she helped the group relax by means of democratic techniques. Meanwhile, the task leader was creating tension by pushing the group toward its goal with more autocratic techniques.

Some formal leaders feel threatened by informal leaders so they attempt to undermine or eliminate their power. But this may prove to be a mistake. The job and the employee may have differing leadership needs. The existence of both a task leader and a social–emotional leader may be very desirable under such circumstances.

[9] L. B. Barnes, *Organizational Systems and Engineering Groups: A Comparative Study of Two Technical Groups in Industry* (Boston: Division of Research, Harvard Business School, Harvard University, 1960); Alvin W. Gouldner, "Cosmopolitans and Locals: Toward an Analysis of Latent Social Roles—I," *Administrative Science Quarterly* (March 1958), pp. 444–480; and Peter M. Blau and W. Richard Scott, *Formal Organizations: A Comparative Approach* (San Francisco: Chandler, 1962), pp. 73–74.

[10] See Talcott Parsons, Robert F. Bales, and Edward A. Shils, *Working Papers in the Theory of Action* (New York: Free Press, 1953).

Morale and Productivity

Most people believe that a satisfied group is a productive group and, as noted earlier, this thinking propelled the human relations movement. Yet research has shown that this is not always true, and so the relationship of morale to productivity deserves special attention. In an extensive summary of research conducted by the University of Michigan's Survey Research Center, Robert L. Kahn concluded that there is no reliable relationship between satisfaction and productivity.[11] These studies covered workers as varied as life insurance clerks, railroad gangs, and factory workers and employed numerous measures of satisfaction. In addition, another comprehensive review of the literature found little relationship between job satisfaction and measures of performance.[12]

Many persons simply find work to be an irritant—the more they do, the more dissatisfied they are. Many employees look upon their job as something they must do. Their real satisfaction, however, lies with friends, family, or colleagues off the job. Efforts to satisfy such people may not translate into increased productivity. Morale and productivity may rise only if the inducement is made conditional upon increasing production. It should be noted that, for a great number of people, the desire to produce is at odds with their need to fit in with their work group.

It would seem that the strongest relationship between satisfaction and productivity exists when someone derives fulfillment from his or her work. The more the person works, the happier he or she is. If the factors like working conditions are poor, then such a worker may express dissatisfaction; yet as long as the individual can work, production will remain high.

The manager should try to create work groups that are satisfied and produce at high levels. If this is not possible, the manager may have to choose between satisfied, low-producing groups or dissatisfied, high-producing employees. Managers typically opt for the dissatisfied, high-output combination because of the pressure to produce results.

Rensis Likert has argued that this is the wrong choice, at least in the long run.[13] In the short run, having high-producing, dissatisfied employees may get the job done, but in many cases dissatisfaction causes costs that must be offset against the short-run productivity gains. These costs include employee tardiness, absenteeism, turnover, and even sabotage. Likert argues that sustained dissatisfaction causes a depletion of the human asset. The problem may be com-

---

[11] Robert L. Kahn, "Productivity and Job Satisfaction," *Personnel Psychology* (Autumn 1960), pp. 275–287.

[12] Victor H. Vroom, *Work and Motivation* (New York: Wiley, 1964), pp. 181–186.

[13] Rensis Likert, *New Patterns of Management* (New York: McGraw-Hill, 1961); and Likert, *The Human Organization* (New York: McGraw-Hill, 1967). A recent article of interest is Rabi S. Bhagat, "Conditions Under Which Stronger Job Performance–Job Satisfaction Relationships May Be Observed: A Closer Look at Two Situational Contingencies," *Academy of Management Journal* (December 1982), pp. 772–789.

pounded by the fact that most firms do not periodically assess their employees' attitudes.[14] Likert recommends that firms keep track of their human assets just as carefully as they do their financial assets through what he calls *human asset accounting,* or systematic employee attitude surveys.

The situation described by Likert exists in many firms. Large assembly operations with strong unions are particularly vulnerable to the indirect costs of prolonged dissatisfaction. It behooves management to try to eliminate these costs. But this may be impossible because of technological and economic constraints. It may also be beyond management's power to cure dissatisfaction. Furthermore, dissatisfaction does not always lead to absenteeism, tardiness, turnover, and the like. For example, even dissatisfied workers tend to stay on the job during periods of high unemployment.

Money as a Motivator

Probably the most powerful motivational tool that a manager has is money. As an exchange medium, a worker may use money to buy practically any type of need satisfaction. A person can buy food, a house, insurance, investments, entertainment, and a status automobile and achieve fulfillment by paying tuition for college courses. A person can achieve much of Maslow's hierarchy with the purchasing power of money alone.

Money also has an important symbolic value. On the job a worker's status may be determined by the extra ten cents per hour he or she gets for doing one job rather than another. The word *bonus* often implies that a manager is in a high-status job. And accumulated wealth is sometimes used by people as a measure of level of accomplishment in life.

Despite money's power it is worth noting that it sometimes does not exert the effect a manager expects. As Herzberg points out, money can be a hygienic factor for some people, preventing dissatisfaction but not motivating them to do more work than the minimum required to keep their jobs.

But the most dramatic effect of money as a motivator comes from the work group. The Bank Wiring Room experiments at Hawthorne and the studies of factory workers by Whyte suggest that the need of a worker to be accepted by his or her peers can be a more important motivator than money.[15] In both studies only a small minority—about 10 percent in Whyte's study—actually responded to a monetary incentive. And Whyte found that his deviants planned to use the money to educate and train themselves so they could get a better job somewhere else.

[14] Interesting discussions of work values appear in M. R. Cooper, B. S. Morgan, P. M. Foley, and L. B. Kaplan, "Changing Employee Values: Deepening Discontent?" *Harvard Business Review* (January–February, 1979), pp. 117–125; and David Glenn Bowers and Jerome L. Franklin, "American Work Values and Preferences," *University of Michigan Business Review* (March 1977), pp. 14–22.

[15] See earlier references to these studies.

GUY ODOM RELIES ON FINANCIAL MOTIVATION AT U.S. HOME

Guy Odom—chairman of the U.S. Home Corp., the biggest homebuilder in the United States—is an avid reader. Odom has been known to read three books a week. One of his favorites is Alfred P. Sloan, Jr.'s, *My Years with General Motors*. Odom has patterned his own organization after what he learned from this extensive reading program.

U.S. Home Corp. is a highly disciplined firm under Odom, but one that inspires considerable entrepreneurship among its executives. Odom believes in assigning profit responsibility to the lowest possible level in the organization. Rewards are commensurate with relative success. There are forty-three homebuilding divisions at U.S. Home, and the division presidents make most operational decisions. The divisions actively compete against each other. Ten divisions, for example, compete in the Houston marketplace. The division presidents—with a median age of thirty-five—are highly motivated managers. In fact, Odom has never been the firm's highest paid executive. The top division president for 1981 earned $77,125 more than Mr. Odom. In 1980 Odom was the company's sixth highest paid executive. A classic, textbook-style company, U.S. Home Corp. clearly realizes the value of financial motivation.

SOURCE: Alexander Stuart, "U.S. Home's Management Religion," *Fortune* (December 4, 1978), pp. 66–68, 72, 76, 78. Material based on the original article, which appeared in the December 4, 1978, issue of *Fortune* Magazine and reprinted by special permission; © 1978 Time, Inc. The 1982 update was provided by U.S. Home Corp.

Equity theory showed money to be a relative thing. Of course, employees are concerned with the absolute amount of their wages, but whether they are satisfied depends in part on how well they compare to other groups with whom they refer. Employees of one group may be quite satisfied with their wages until they find out that some other group or union received a larger pay hike. Suddenly

"*Money may not be worth as much these days but I still love it.*"

MONEY IS APPARENTLY NOT A HYGIENIC FACTOR FOR THIS EXECUTIVE

SOURCE: *The Wall Street Journal* (March 3, 1982), p. 23. Permission–Cartoon Features Syndicate.

they feel dissatisfied, clamor for more money, and adjust the quality or amount of their work.

Problems and Constraints in Applying Motivation Theory

Motivation theory is obviously an imperfect science. Perhaps the most important lesson that one can learn from studying modern motivation theories is the extent of management's incomplete knowledge of individual and group behavior. Due care must be taken in attempting to apply such a rudimentary knowledge.

What are the practical limitations of motivating an employee? The biggest problem is simply finding out what it is that motivates a particular person. How does the manager know, for instance, if an employee considers security to be a motivator or a hygienic factor? How does the manager know at which level the person is in Maslow's hierarchy?

One crude way is to check whether the employee fits the descriptions of the research samples. So, if the person is an accountant, he or she may behave the same as Herzberg's sample.

Another way would be simply to ask employees what they consider important, either directly or through a survey, as in Likert's human asset accounting. But sometimes the employee's declared attitude is different from his or her real attitude. Many respondents will tell a questioner what they think they are expected to say. Even trained researchers find it difficult to get at people's real attitudes. Then there is the question of whether attitudes will be translated into behavior.

As a result of these problems and constraints management must rely on trial-and-error application of motivation theories. The manager might try to motivate employees with more money, and if that is not effective, other motivational techniques may be tried. Motivation theory and research can help management make educated guesses about employees' needs, but the application stage must involve a trial-and-error approach.

While much of motivation theory emphasizes the individual, and the need for management to individualize its dealings with people, there is considerable pressure to do exactly the opposite. Unions, fearing arbitrary management decisions, battle for uniform work rules that assure equal treatment of workers. Our legal framework also works against individual motivation of subordinates. Even minute aspects like physical working conditions can be mandated to meet certain standards, as with the Occupational Safety and Health Act.

Overall, modern managers face many constraints in treating people as individuals. Still, compared to their predecessors, they have greater knowledge available to help them in efficiently and effectively motivating subordinates—as either group or individuals.

Summary

Group behavior is an important aspect of the study of motivation. The best-known research in this area are the Hawthorne studies, conducted over fifty years ago. The researchers expected to prove that better work and pay conditions would increase output. Instead, their studies suggested a link between morale and productivity. The so-called human relations school was largely based on these findings.

The human resources model implies that executives should create an environment that uses all the available human resources so as to improve both performance and decision making. McGregor, Likert, Haire, and Miles among others are associated with this viewpoint.

Further research by Whyte and Seashore found that certain workers often restricted or controlled output in accordance with what they viewed as group norms. Another aspect of group behavior is equity theory, which states the human tendency to balance work efforts or inputs with the rewards received. People compare their relative inputs and rewards with those of reference groups, those categories of persons with which individuals identify.

Robert F. Bales concluded that all groups have a task leader and a social–emotional leader. The task leader tends to be the individual with the best ideas for guiding the group toward the completion of its task. The social–emotional leader is the person best liked by the group.

Chapter 13 also points out that morale is not always linked to productivity. In addition, the use of money sometimes produces unexpected results. Examples of such situations are reported in the discussions of the Hawthorne experiments, research by Herzberg and Whyte, and equity theory. The chapter concludes with a brief description of the problems and constraints involved in applying motivation theory.

REVIEW EXERCISES

1. Define the following terms: (a) Hawthorne studies (b) Hawthorne effect (c) human relations school (d) human resources model (e) equity theory (f) reference group (g) informal group leader.

2. Discuss the basic points made in the management profile for Chapter 13.

3. Discuss the Hawthorne studies and the development of human relations school.

4. How does the human resources model differ from the human relations school?

5. Explain William F. Whyte's contribution to the study of group behavior.

6. Discuss the research conducted by Stanley Seashore.

7. Outline the contributions of equity theory and reference groups to the study of group behavior.

8. Describe Robert F. Bales' research on informal group leaders.

9. Relate the concept of morale to productivity.

10. Explain the role of money as a motivator.

Applications

ASSIGNMENTS/ PROBLEMS/ DISCUSSION QUESTIONS

1. General Motors was considering closing its Clark, New Jersey bearings plant in 1981. Some 2,000 jobs were on the line. So the plant's employees bought the factory and formed Hyatt-Clark Industries. The work force dropped, wages and benefits were cut, but the plant survived and is now profitable. Nationwide, there are about 4,000–5,000 employee-owned companies.* Assess the concepts of group behavior and motivation as they might apply to a firm like Hyatt-Clark Industries.

2. Prepare a brief, critical review of a study on motivation that has been published in the last five years in the *Academy of Management Journal*. Compare the study to what you learned in this chapter.

3. The National Football League Players Association originally asked for 55 percent of the league's gross revenue during 1982 negotiations.† How

* Alan Fram, ''A Worker-Owned Experiment That Is Succeeding,'' *Journal-American* (June 20, 1982), p. B 2.
† Peter McAlevey, ''55–45 or Fight,'' *Forbes* (March 1, 1982).

might the implementation of such a plan affect group behavior on an NFL team?

4. Prepare a paper on one of the major contributors to the study of group behavior.

5. Relate the concepts presented in Chapter 13 to a work or social group to which you belong.

A MANAGERIAL INCIDENT

Romac Industries

The sign on the bulletin board at Seattle's Romac Industries, a pipe-fitting manufacturer, stood out from the usual mimeographed ads of cars for sale. It was welder Tim Baker's appeal for a 45¢ hourly raise. ''I'm requesting this increase because of inflation,'' he wrote alongside a color photo of himself busy welding a stainless-steel clamp. ''The cost of living keeps going up, and the pay's the same. I work hard—just ask me. P.S.: Girls cost more to take out too.''

Baker was not pitching to management, but to his 55 fellow employees, who would decide whether or not to grant his raise. In a secret ballot five days later, they voted overwhelmingly to boost his pay from $5.55 an hour to $6.

Romac began letting its employees decide their own wages in 1974, after a second attempt by the Teamsters to unionize the plant was only narrowly defeated. The management began posting on the bulletin board both monthly production figures and the wages of all workers up to plant supervisor. The idea was that employees could see the output trends, figure how much the company could afford and decide who deserved the most. Says President Manford McNeil, whose salary of "more than $25,000" is set by the board of directors: "The workers are bound to have a better idea of how hard-working or reliable an employee is than I have. If it were up to me, I'd probably give the wrong guy a raise."

The company generally hires unskilled workers and starts them out at $4.50 an hour. After six months new employees may request raises by filling out a form; an applicant lists the size of his last raise, if any, his current pay, the amount of the requested raise and the reasons for it. Each worker sets an election date at least five days after so that other employees will have time to observe him on the job. The majority rules.

In all, 95% of the requests are granted. John Heins, who works in the rubber department, got two raises in two months for a total 80¢-an-hour increase (to $6.50), and plans to request another. . . . Pay requests have been so reasonable, . . . that management has never exercised its veto right.

. . . So far at Romac, productivity has surged, and last year the company had record sales of $3 million. By all accounts, workers like the chance to have their peers acknowledge a job well done. Says John Heins: "The system makes this a pretty good place to work."

SOURCE: Adapted from "Voting for Pay," *Time* (February 26, 1979), p. 69. Reprinted by permission of *Time*, The Weekly Newsmagazine; Copyright Time Inc. 1979.

Questions and Problems

1. Assess the Romac compensation plan. What are the benefits and pitfalls of such an effort?

2. Discuss the Romac illustration in terms of the concepts outlined in this chapter.

14. Leadership

I haven't changed my style in 20 years
. . . and that style is to get mad when
things go wrong.

ALEXANDER HAIG

The question, "Who ought to be
boss?" is like asking "Who ought to be
the tenor in the quartet?" (Obviously,
the man who can sing tenor.)

HENRY FORD

A leader is a dealer in hope.

NAPOLEON

The admiral was known to be a tough interviewer when it came to candidates for his nuclear submarine program. Hyman G. Rickover, the builder of today's nuclear navy, would create stressful situations to test the reactions of program candidates. He looked for quick responses, even if they were a bit antagonistic.

Elmo Zumwalt, who later became an admiral himself and chief of naval operations, recalls his interview with Admiral Rickover:

Rickover: "Everyone who interviewed you tells me you are extremely conservative and have no imagination. What do you have to say about that?"

Zumwalt: "I need a few minutes to reflect on that, Admiral. It is the first time I have received a charge like that about me."

Rickover then exploded and ordered Zumwalt out of the room to wait until he was ready to continue the interview. The admiral told Zumwalt: ". . . When you come back in here, you better be able to maintain proper respect."

Admiral Zumwalt was not the only naval officer to be tested by Rickover. Another, Dick Laning, commented: "Those interviews were a very effective way or method of leadership. Once someone had been through the stress of an interview, he never forgot who the boss was."[1]

---

[1] Copyright 1981 by Norman Polmar and Thomas B. Allen. From *Rickover*, by Norman Polmar and Thomas B. Allen. Distributed by the *Los Angeles Times* Syndicate. Excerpted in Norman Polmar and Thomas B. Allen, "Rickover Held Bruising Sessions with Nuclear Hopefuls," *The Seattle Times* (November 26, 1981), pp. 24-A, 25-A, 26-A.

By contrast, look at the way Hunter Simpson runs Physio Control (now part of Eli Lilly), an $80 million–$90 million a year maker of electronic medical devices. The company is growing at the rate of 30 percent a year. There are *no* employees at Physio Control's Redmond, Washington facility. People who work at Physio Control are known as *team members.* Simpson has a personal management style. His office door is always open and he answers his own telephone. Team members call him by his first name. But there are some unique aspects of Simpson's managerial style.

Physio Control provides free tea and coffee throughout the day.

Most team members work only four days a week. But others who want to go to school work a three-day, thirty-six-hour weekend. The company covers their tuition and books.

Team members meet quarterly to go over goals and the latest quarterly results.

Physio Control has a profit-sharing plan that typically pays a bonus equivalent to 5 to 6 weeks of salary.

Hunter Simpson attributes 50 percent of Physio Control's success to the company's products. "The other half is the spirit of the team" he explains.[2]

What do Hyman Rickover and Hunter Simpson have in common despite the differences in their organizations and personal styles? They are both leaders. They are both performing the most noticeable part of the manager's job. Managers set objectives, plan, organize, staff, and control, but most of these activities go unnoticed by the general public. Most people tend to think of management as someone leading a group of people. A drill sergeant marching the troops, a conductor directing an orchestra, a coach calling the plays for a football team, a supervisor bossing a road crew, a minister preaching divine guidance to parishioners, or a movie director shouting, "Lights, camera, action!" These examples of leadership are typical of what the public considers management.

Leadership is the most visible aspect of management. It is the function by which a manager unleashes the available resources in order to get the organization to carry out plans to accomplish objectives. *Leadership* is defined as the act of motivating or causing people to perform certain tasks intended to achieve specified objectives. Leadership is the act of making things happen.

Even though leadership is the most visible part of the manager's job, it is still one of the least understood and agreed upon—no doubt because it deals so much with people. A variety of names have been used for what this text terms *leadership.* Some writers call it *actuating,* others call it *initiating.* Then there are *directing, guiding, commanding,* and *inspiring.* But they all mean about the same thing, and since *leading* is the most popular term it will be used here.

Leadership is the act of motivating people to perform certain tasks intended to achieve specified objectives.

[2] Richard Buck, "Disaster Plot Turns Out to Be Formula for Success," *The Seattle Times* (April 6, 1982), pp 1-B, 5-B.

The Concept of Power

No matter what leadership is called, it involves the use of power.[3] *Power* is simply the ability of one person to influence the behavior of another. There are several sources of power available to the leader. Some leaders may use only one or two of these types of power while other leaders may draw upon all of them.

In one classification of power five sources are identified.[4] The first is *reward* power. This is the ability of a leader to give followers things they want. In the case of a manager these things may be pay, bonuses, vacations, insurance, a desirable job assignment, and so on. According to this scheme, *not* giving someone something he or she *does not* want has a psychological effect similar to positive reward. For example, consider the relief of a student when an instructor grants a week's extension on a term paper that has not been finished by the original due date.

A second type of power is *coercive* power, just the opposite of reward power. Here the leader essentially punishes or threatens to punish a subordinate by giving him or her things that are not sought or withholding things that are. One common form of discipline is to give an employee an undesirable job such as assignment to some remote branch of the company. Docking a person's pay is another common example of coercive power that will influence an employee not to repeat a mistake.[5]

Expert power is another source of influence that some leaders possess. People often follow the advice of someone with considerable knowledge of a particular subject. People will often blindly do what they are told by doctors or lawyers. Similarly, a supervisor who was once a superior tool and die maker may be respected by the subordinate tool and die makers in the department.

A fourth type of power is *referent* power. This is a subtle source of power based on a leader's charisma and an employee's desire to be like his or her leader. Many children emulate sports superstars like Larry Holmes, Wayne Gretzky, Magic Johnson, Chris Evert Lloyd, Steve Garvey, and Walter Payton. Similarly, an employee who aspires to a management position may be most eager to please his or her superior.

Finally, there is *legitimate* power, or *authority*. This is the power the manager has because he or she is the manager. It is power that is sanctioned by an organization, by law, by custom, or simply by common sense. A person will accept spiritual guidance from a priest because the priest has the blessing of the

Power is the ability of one person to influence the behavior of another.

---

[3] The importance of power is discussed in John P. Kotter, "Power, Dependence, and Effective Management," *Harvard Business Review* (July–August 1977), pp. 125–136. Another interesting article is Richard S. Blackburn, "Lower Participant Power: Toward A Conceptual Integration," *Academy of Management Review* (January 1981), pp. 127–131.

[4] John R. P. French, Jr., and Bertram Raven, "The Bases of Social Power," in Dorwin Cartwright and Alvin Zander (eds.), *Group Dynamics: Research and Theory*, 2nd ed. (Evanston, Ill.: Row, Peterson, 1960), pp. 607–623.

[5] Both positive and punitive rewards are discussed in Robert T. Keller and Andrew D. Szilagyi, "Employer Reactions to Leader Reward Behavior," *Academy of Management Journal* (December 1976), pp. 619–627.

Church. Upon request a person might stay out of a neighbor's yard because it is private property and the neighbor is backed up by the law. A worker may correct defects on a product at the quality control manager's request simply because he or she knows that someone has to be in charge of checking the product.

In organizations such as business firms, the five sources of power in the above scheme may derive from a person, a position, or both.[6] Someone whose power derives only from his or her position—mostly reward, coercive, and legitimate power—can be termed an *official.* The opposite number is the person who wields power but has no position, the so-called *informal leader.* (See the discussion in Chapter 13.) Such leaders rely on expert, referent, and symbolic forms of reward and coercive power. Finally, people who combine positional and personal power might be called *formal leaders.* A formal leader could be a persuasive department head, whereas an informal leader could be just a persuasive person, and an official could be simply a department head.

While all leadership involves the use of power, it is also dependent upon the selection of a way in which to lead others to accomplish goals. The concept of leadership style is vital to effective management.

Leadership Styles

The example of Hyman Rickover and Hunter Simpson was chosen to show the common basis for leadership. Both these leaders would fit into the notion of the formal leader discussed above. But this example also shows the differences in leading. They are both doing, or did, the same thing—making things happen—but not in the same manner. Rickover was the tough disciplinarian. By contrast, Hunter Simpson relies on positive motivation and team building to accomplish his objectives.

Leadership style is the way a person uses available power in order to lead others.

The selection of a way to lead and how to use available power is known as *leadership style.* People have been leading people as long as there have been people. Surely at one time or another every possible way of leading has been tried, from screaming and threatening to pleading and begging to bribing and promising.

But social scientists have studied leadership for only a few decades. At first, the hope was for some simple theory that was easy to understand, teach, learn, and practice. For a long time people clung to the theory that "leaders are born, not made." Finding someone with the right traits was the key. Then there was "leaders are made, not born." With this theory, anyone could be thrown into a situation and become a leader.

These simple theories are giving way to the realization that leadership style is a complicated matter. Research has shown that numerous factors affect a manager's choice of the proper leadership style. This selection process is often represented by the following equation:

$$\text{Leadership Style} = f \text{ (the leader, subordinates, situation)}$$

[6] Amitai Etzioni, *Modern Organizations* (Englewood Cliffs, N.J.: Prentice-Hall, 1964), pp. 59–61.

Sandy McDonnell, the chairman and chief executive officer of the St. Louis–based McDonnell Douglas Corp., likes to tell a story about his uncle, the late James S. McDonnell, when he was the firm's board chairman. James S. McDonnell, or "Mr. Mac," as he was called, was known for setting a conservative, frugal, and technically oriented leadership style for the firm he founded about forty years ago.

Sandy McDonnell recalls that soon after becoming chief executive at McDonnell Douglas, he clashed with his uncle. Mr. Mac refused to concede the point, so the new chief executive reminded his uncle, ". . . you and the board made me president last year, and you've just made me chief executive officer."

"That's right, you're the CEO, and I'm the boss," Mr. Mac shot back. It seems quite apparent that James S. McDonnell understood the role of power in leadership behavior.

SOURCE: "Where Management Style Sets the Strategy," *Business Week* (October 23, 1978), pp. 88–92, 94, 99. Reprinted from the October 23, 1978 issue of *Business Week* by special permission. © 1978 by McGraw-Hill, Inc.

MR. MAC UNDERSTOOD THE CONCEPT OF POWER

Leaders themselves, subordinates, and the situation confronting the manager are the determinants involved. As stated above leadership style is a function of all three of these variables. All are discussed in detail later in the chapter.

Not enough is known yet to be able to teach everyone to be a great leader, but enough is known to give a new manager a head start over those who are not knowledgeable in this aspect of management theory.

Types of Leadership and Related Management Assumptions

The three factors involved in choosing a leadership style indicate that there is a multiplicity of leadership styles available to a manager. One of the most important variables is the manager's assumptions about the nature of those being led. This assumption will have a direct impact on the leadership style selected. Douglas McGregor offers two basic assumptions called Theory X and Theory Y.[7]

THEORY X

A leader espousing a *Theory X* orientation believes that subordinates require an autocratic leadership style. Theory X leaders believe their subordinates prefer to escape work and responsibility. Employees are seen as lacking ambition and

Theory X proposes that subordinates dislike work and require an autocratic style of leadership.

[7] Douglas McGregor, *The Human Side of Enterprise* (New York: McGraw-Hill, 1960), pp. 33–34, 47–48.

seeking the security of a leader-directed environment. Management must therefore use its reward, coercive, legitimate power (authority) to get subordinates to accomplish organizational objectives. Theory X managers view their role as supervisory and as evaluating the work activities of uninspired subordinates.

THEORY Y

Theory Y advocates a democratic style of leadership in which employees are encouraged to participate in the decision-making process.

At the other end of the leadership scale are the democratic leaders, called *Theory Y* managers by McGregor. These managers use a people-centered or employee-oriented style of leadership. Theory Y leaders view work as a rewarding experience for all employees. People are seen as reaching out to management for increased responsibility and productivity.

Democratic leaders encourage their employees to participate in the decision-making process. Emphasis is shifted from punishment to reward. Communications flow openly both from leader to follower and from follower to leader. This type of leader tries to create a favorable environment for employees so that they can achieve the goals of the particular work unit.

These extremes of leadership style are generally thought to be incomplete explanations. More comprehensive models have been offered by Rensis Likert and by Robert Tannenbaum and Warren Schmidt.

THE LIKERT MODEL

Rensis Likert developed a comprehensive leadership model[8] with four basic leadership systems. Each system represents a different leadership style, as shown in Figure 14-1. System 1 is an exploitative authoritative style. This represents dictatorial leadership behavior, with all decisions made by the managers. There is little employee participation, and a general attitude of distrust exists between the parties.

System 2 is a benevolent authoritative style; the leader, while autocratic, tries to be paternalistically supportive of subordinates. Distrust between managers and employees is still commonplace.

System 3 reflects consultative leadership behavior. Mutual regard is enhanced because the manager solicits advice from those in subordinate roles, while retaining the right to make the final decision.

System 4 is a participative leadership style. Subordinates are actively involved

[8] Likert's concepts are outlined in *New Patterns of Management* (1961) and *The Human Organization* (1967), both published by McGraw-Hill.

Figure 14-1
THE LIKERT MODEL

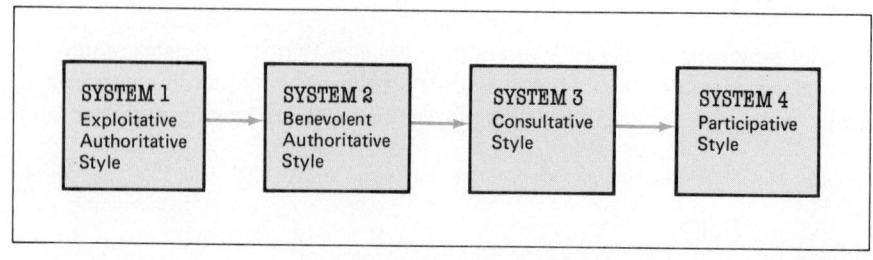

in the decision-making process. Consensus management as practiced by Japanese firms is an example.

Research by Likert and others concluded that high productivity was associated with systems 3 and 4 leadership, while systems 1 and 2 were characterized by lower output.

TANNENBAUM AND SCHMIDT'S CONTINUUM OF LEADERSHIP BEHAVIOR

Robert Tannenbaum and Warren Schmidt also noted that a democratic/authoritarian dichotomy was inadequate. They proposed a continuum of leadership behavior specifying a full range of leadership styles.[9] Their model is shown in Figure 14-2.

Some managers use their authority to make all decisions. These decisions are then accepted by subordinates. The opposite situation is where managers and nonmanagers made decisions jointly within prescribed limits. Tannenbaum and

[9] This section is based on Robert Tannenbaum and Warren Schmidt's original article, "How to Choose a Leadership Pattern," *Harvard Business Review* (March–April 1958), pp. 95–101; and the "Retrospective Commentary" that appeared fifteen years later. See *Harvard Business Review* (May–June 1973), pp. 166–168.

Figure 14-2
CONTINUUM OF MANAGER–NONMANAGER BEHAVIOR

SOURCE: Adapted by permission of the Harvard Business Review. Exhibit from "How to Choose a Leadership Pattern" by Robert Tannenbaum and Warren Schmidt (May–June 1973). Copyright © 1973 by the President and Fellows of Harvard College; all rights reserved.

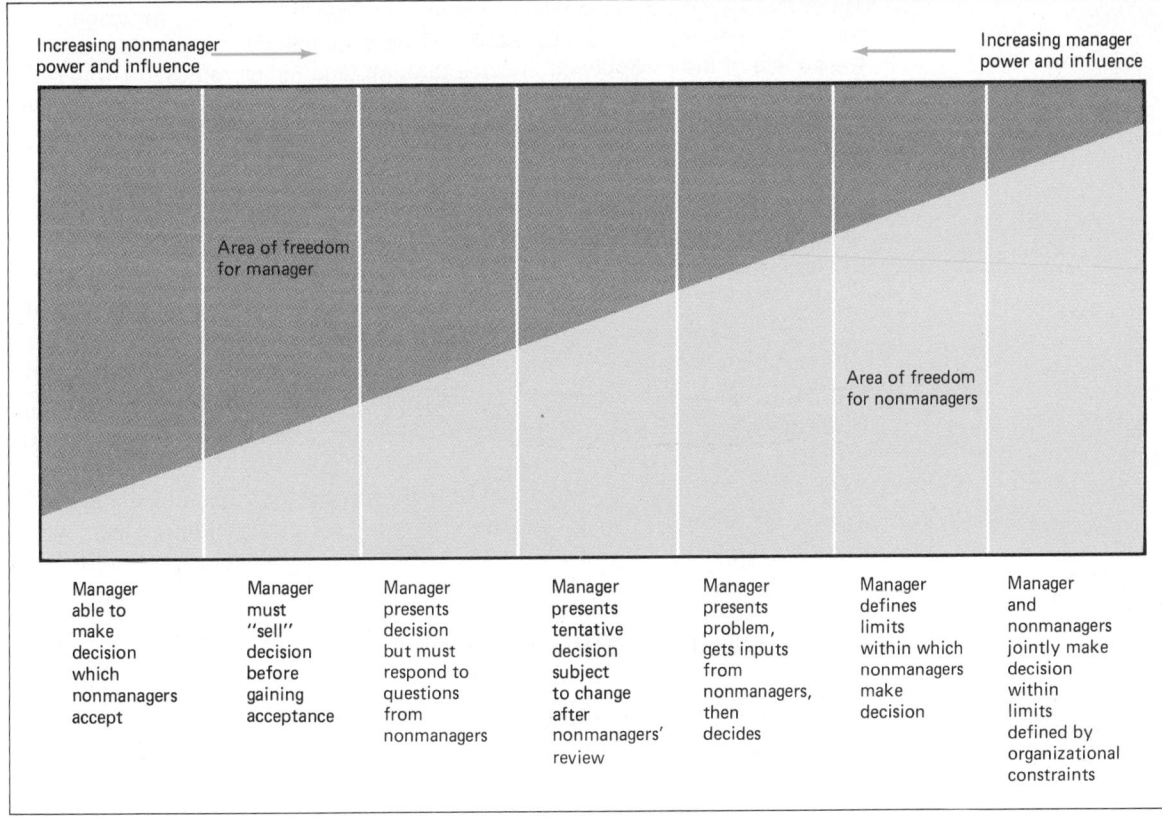

Increasing nonmanager power and influence

Increasing manager power and influence

Area of freedom for manager

Area of freedom for nonmanagers

| Manager able to make decision which nonmanagers accept | Manager must "sell" decision before gaining acceptance | Manager presents decision but must respond to questions from nonmanagers | Manager presents tentative decision subject to change after nonmanagers' review | Manager presents problem, gets inputs from nonmanagers, then decides | Manager defines limits within which nonmanagers make decision | Manager and nonmanagers jointly make decision within limits defined by organizational constraints |

Douglas MacArthur was an avid student of military leadership. If he had explored the various leadership theories discussed in this chapter, he would likely have been a proponent of the "Great Man" Theory. MacArthur was born into a family headed by a Civil War hero who had been awarded the Congressional Medal of Honor. Raised on frontier army posts, MacArthur, it was said, could ride and shoot before he could read and write. But he graduated from West Point in 1903 at the top of his class. His scholastic average was the highest since Robert E. Lee's and the third highest in the history of the academy.

In 1904 MacArthur joined his father's staff in Japan and was soon convinced that his destiny lay in Asia. He was appointed to the General Staff in 1913. In 1917 MacArthur was made chief of staff of the Rainbow Division with the World War I American Expeditionary Forces (AEF) in France. Dubbed the "Beau Brummell of the AEF" because of his flamboyant dress—a vivid turtleneck beneath his jacket and a flowing muffler—he also soon became known for his excellence as a combat officer.

After the war MacArthur served as superintendent of West Point, then did a stint as commanding general of the Philippine Division. He returned to the United States to become Army Chief of Staff in 1930.

At the end of his term in that office, in 1935, he went back to the Philippines. There he addressed himself with typical optimism to the formidable task of making the islands defensible against military attack. When the Japanese invasion in 1941 forced Filipino and American forces to retreat to the Bataan peninsula, MacArthur was given command of American forces in Australia. Arriving in Australia after a daring trip from Bataan by PT boat, he made his dramatic promise to the people of the Philippines: "I came through, and I shall return."

The general's reputation as an adroit leader grew as his forces carried out highly successful amphibious operations throughout the Pacific. By mid-1944 he

Schmidt specifically noted that neither end of the continuum is absolute since some limitations are always applicable.

Three major factors in deciding on a leadership style are suggested by the model. These include forces in the *manager* (such as his or her value system and confidence in subordinates), the *subordinates* (such as their expectations of management behavior), and the *situation* (such as the values and traditions of the organization). In other words, Tannenbaum and Schmidt suggested the now classic equation noted earlier: Leadership Style = f (the leader, subordinates, situation).

The amount of power and influence that both the manager and the nonmanager have is influenced by the organizational and societal environments in which they operate.

Early Leadership Theories

Leadership theory can be divided into two distinct groupings: the early, traditional theories and the more contemporary, situational viewpoints. Both will be explored in this chapter.

was able to use his persuasive powers and his prestige—carefully nurtured by his own politicking and his public relations staff—to gain President Roosevelt's approval for the liberation of the Philippines. On Leyte beach as the invasion progressed, he proclaimed over a microphone: "People of the Philippines: I have returned. . . . Rally to me. . . . The guidance of Divide God points the way." MacArthur always seemed to know what people expected in a leader, and he tried to provide it.

The confidence MacArthur exuded explains in part his success as Supreme Commander for the Allied Powers (SCAP) in rebuilding war-shattered Japan. He combined aggressive leadership with the hope of the demoralized Japanese people to bring about profound social and economic change. He was instrumental in producing such changes as the introduction of democratic institutions, land reform, religious freedom, and women's suffrage.

His battlefield successes, his leadership role in the reconstruction of Japan, his calculated politicking, and his flair for timing and eloquence in speech making boosted the general to a pinnacle of popularity with the American public in 1951. This was the year that President Truman removed him from his post as SCAP in order to end his popular but divisive criticism of American foreign policy in Korea. MacArthur was welcomed back to New York by masses of frenzied and adoring supporters—while Truman was burned in effigy. Indeed, the general's address to a joint session of Congress was hailed by Missouri Representative Dewey Short as "the voice of God."

His military career over, MacArthur looked to new leadership challenges. At age seventy-two he became chairman of the board of Remington Rand, now Sperry Rand. Gen. Douglas MacArthur died in 1964, a legend in effective leadership.

Sources

William Manchester, *American Caesar* (Boston: Little, Brown, 1978).

Lawrence S. Wittner, ed., *MacArthur* (Englewood Cliffs, N.J.: Prentice-Hall, 1971).

Leadership theory originally concentrated on who the leader was and the personal characteristics or traits of the identified leader. These approaches are often termed the *Great Man* and *trait* theories of leadership. Later, the emphasis switched to a more situational view of leadership.

GREAT MAN THEORY

Most early writings on leadership stressed the emergence of a single person, the so-called Great Man, as the cause of any action. Significant political, economic, or social change may have been attributed to a great ruler ascending a throne or to a powerful pope or finance minister. Accounts of the American Revolution and the resulting United States Constitution often stress the contributions of such important people as George Washington, Benjamin Franklin, and Thomas Jefferson. Many history books arrange historical events by reigns of kings and queens or presidential administrations.

The *Great Man Theory* assumed that such people were remarkably different from others and that only they were capable of playing prominent leadership roles. The theoretical emphasis was on identifying the leader's characteristics

The **Great Man Theory** states that only an exceptional person is capable of playing a prominent leadership role.

351

rather than explaining the actions that he or she took.[10] Early students of leadership concentrated on the traits or personal characteristics of identified leaders. Some of the supposed leadership attributes were personality factors like aggressiveness; others concerned habits like work behavior; and still others dealt with physical features like height.

The research and resulting lists were often contradictory. Some "great men" possessed characteristics diametrically opposed to the traits of other widely accepted leaders. According to one offshoot of the Great Man Theory, Gerald Ford should have beaten Jimmy Carter in the 1976 presidential election. Leadership folklore has taller people always winning elections over shorter opponents since voters allegedly view height as a leadership trait.

The Great Man Theory was obviously an incomplete explanation of the leadership phenomenon. The study of leadership traits was subsequently expanded and intensified in an attempt to develop a comprehensive model of leadership behavior.

TRAIT THEORY

Trait theory concerns the identification and measurement of traits or attitudes that are associated with a leader's behavior.

Trait theory concerns the identification and measurement of traits or attitudes that are associated with leadership behavior. It may be thought of as a natural extension of the early investigations of the Great Man Theory. Essentially, the objective was the same: to distinguish between leaders and nonleaders.

Edwin Ghiselli's work is perhaps the best-known work in the field of trait theory.[11] Ghiselli has studied leadership for over twenty years, and his research keeps trait theory alive in an era dominated by situationalists.

Ghiselli has developed "The Ghiselli Self-Descriptive Inventory" to measure leadership traits. The inventory consists of sixty-four adjective pairs. Testing time averages fifteen minutes, with the subjects checking the adjectives that best describe themselves for half the pairs and indicating the least descriptive word in the other thirty-two pairs.

[10] See Jeffrey C. Barrow, "The Variables of Leadership: A Review and Conceptual Framework," *Academy of Management Review* (April 1977), p. 232.

[11] This discussion of Ghiselli's work is based on James F. Gavin, "A Test of Ghiselli's Theory of Managerial Traits," *Journal of Business Research* (February 1976), pp. 45–52. See also E. E. Ghiselli, *Explorations in Managerial Talent* (Pacific Palisades, Calif.: Goodyear, 1971).

SILENT CAL'S CONTRIBUTION TO TRAIT THEORY

President Calvin Coolidge did not say much, but what he did say is often cited even today. "Silent Cal," as the president was known, once told Ethel Barrymore: "I think the American people want a solemn ass as a president . . . and I think I will go along with them."

SOURCE: Hoyt Gimlin (Editorial Research Reports), "Niche of Silent Cal Undisturbed," *Journal-American* (January 9, 1983), p. 5-D.

	IMPORTANCE VALUE*	Table 14-1 GHISELLI'S MANAGERIAL TRAITS
Supervisory ability (A)	100	
Occupational achievement (M)	76	
Intelligence (A)	64	
Self-actualization (M)	63	
Self-assurance (P)	62	
Decisiveness (P)	61	
Lack of need for security (M)	54	
Working class affinity (P)	47	
Initiative (A)	34	
Lack of need for high financial reward (M)	20	
Need for power (M)	10	
Maturity (P)	5	
Masculinity-femininity (P)	0	

* Importance value: 100 = very important; 0 = plays no part in managerial talent.
NOTE: A = ability trait; P = personality trait; M = motivational trait.

SOURCE: James F. Gavin, "A Test of Ghiselli's Theory of Managerial Traits," *Journal of Business Research* (February 1976), p. 46, as adapted from E. E. Ghiselli, *Explorations in Managerial Talent* (Pacific Palisades, Calif.; Goodyear Publishing Company, 1971). Used by permission of the *Journal of Business Research* and Goodyear Publishing Company.

Thirteen traits have been studied by Ghiselli, and each has been ranked according to its value in identifying managerial talent. These rankings are indicated in Table 14-1.

Factors Affecting Leadership Style

John D. deButts, the retired chief executive officer of American Telephone and Telegraph, once attributed his own leadership style to a blending of the styles of his predecessors.

> The first [CEO] was very definitely the authoritarian type. He issued instructions. The CEO who followed him came up through the personnel department and spent a great deal more time on the human side of business—kind of pulled the group together. The next CEO was a hard, two-fisted line guy who came up through the plant department on the operating side of the business. He was demanding and yet he was extremely understanding. Under my leadership, if you will, we attempt to use a combination of what we call cooperation and what I would call natural competitiveness in any business.[12]

The deButts remarks suggest the variety of factors contributing to or influencing one's leadership style. One set of factors is the people who are being

[12] Quoted in Steven H. Appelbaum, "Management by Cooperation: The Views of Seven Chief Executive Officers," *University of Michigan Business Review* (November 1977), p. 20.

led. Since these people are doing some kind of work, another set of factors is the nature of the job itself. Then there is the factor of the management support the leader gets from those higher up in the organization. And another important set of factors has to do with the manager's own personal characteristics. All may be considered categories of the variables mentioned earlier in the leadership style equation.

PEOPLE

Leadership behavior is closely tied to the performance levels and expectations of both managers and their subordinates.[13] Research studies have determined that there is typically a close relationship between these variables. One study of a naval air research and development command considered the interactions of seniors (supervisors) and juniors (subordinates). The study concluded:

> The findings of this study tend to support the hypothesis of reciprocal influence. The behavior of seniors is to some extent related to the expectations of juniors, but the behavior of juniors is also related to the behavior and expectations of seniors.[14]

Chapter 12 suggested that different people can develop different motivations. Some people, often those who have been deprived, are concerned mostly with basic security needs such as a minimum standard of living. Anything that will give them a sense of security will be welcome. These motives are suitable to a work-centered style of leadership.

The autocratic leader structures the world for such an employee, which is exactly what the employee seeks. This type of employee actually is satisfied with close supervision. Work is not a means of self-expression for such a person. He or she prefers to associate with friends, family, and the community outside the company, so interest in the workplace will be correspondingly low. Some research on blue-collar and lower-level white-collar workers suggests that autocratic leadership not only is satisfying to them but makes them productive.[15]

On the other hand, many employees are motivated by their work. These people like to be involved and take pride in their accomplishments. They want to earn the respect of other people on the job. Such employees respond well to a people-centered style of leadership.

---

[13] Interesting articles include Burt K. Scanlon, "Creating a Climate for Achievement," *Business Horizons* (March–April 1981), pp. 5–9; James M. McFillen, "Supervisory Power as an Influence in Supervisor–Subordinates Relations," *Academy of Management Journal* (September 1978), pp. 419–433; and David M. Herold, "Two-Way Influence Processes in Leader-Follower Dyads," *Academy of Management Journal* (June 1977), pp. 224–237.

[14] Ralph M. Stogdill, Ellis L. Scott, and William E. Jaynes, *Leadership and Role Expectations* (Columbus: Bureau of Business Research, Ohio State University, 1956), p. 132.

[15] William Foote Whyte and Lawrence K. Williams, "Supervisory Leadership: An International Comparison," in *Proceedings, CIOS XIII International Management Congress* (New York: Council for International Progress in Management, 1963), p. 485.

The democratic leader asks for the opinions of employees, who in this case are anxious to give them. This type of leader allows some room on the job for such an employee to innovate and express his or her originality. The democratic leader allows these employees to work more on their own, giving achievement-oriented individuals a measure of self-respect. Research has shown that democratic leadership leads to high productivity and satisfaction for many blue-collar, white-collar, and professional workers.[16] General Motors, for instance, has recently freed its units to develop their own unique divisional images. Pontiac quickly improved its use of materials and product quality.[17]

Subordinates' motivations are not the only people factors that affect the choice of leadership style. The number of subordinates has a strong influence, no matter what type of employees are being managed. A manager of two or three persons has a much greater chance to develop friendly, open relationships than does a manager of twenty or thirty people. Research has consistently shown that increasing the number of people decreases the sense of closeness among the group members and increases the threatening social nature of the group for each member.[18] A small group makes it easier to use a democratic style of leadership,

---

[16] Robert Kahn and Daniel Katz, "Leadership Practices in Relation to Productivity and Morale," in Dorwin Cartwright and Alvin Zander (eds.), *Group Dynamics: Research and Theory*, 2nd ed. (Evanston, Ill.: Row, Peterson, 1960), pp. 554–570; and Frederick Herzberg, Bernard Mausner, and Barbara Block Snyderman, *The Motivation to Work* (New York: Wiley, 1959).

[17] "Answer to Ailing Industry: Overhaul at the Very Top," *U.S. News & World Report* (January 17, 1983), p. 39.

[18] A. Paul Hare, *Handbook of Small Group Research* (New York: Free Press, 1962), p. 231.

*"The other employes hate your guts, Mervin.
Keep it up."*

**SUBORDINATES ARE
A FACTOR IN
LEADERSHIP STYLE**

SOURCE: *The Wall Street Journal* (February 2, 1982). Permission–Cartoon Features Syndicate.

while a large group pushes the leader toward the autocratic end of the scale.

Note the apparent reversal here of cause and effect between leadership style and the criterion of satisfaction. Many democratic leaders like to think that it is their leadership style that causes a group to be satisfied. However, if the group is small, it may be satisfied just because of its size. In this case the satisfaction of the group may be enabling the leader to use a democratic style. In leadership research there are many instances where cause and effect are unclear.

THE JOB

The job's time frame may also affect the choice of leadership style. If a task must be completed in a short period of time, the autocrat may be more effective. The autocrat simply tells people when, where, and how to do the job. When time-delaying mistakes are made, he or she quickly takes remedial action.

Democratic leaders call for subordinates to participate in deciding when, where, and how to do the job. Employees must be familiarized with the problem and given time to think and respond. When they make mistakes, the employee-centered manager helps them find the reason so they can correct it themselves. Such a style is too slow and awkward for the platoon leader to use when an enemy ambush is anticipated or for the supervisor to use when cars are relentlessly marching past workers on the assembly line. Yet it may be suited to the marketing director and his or her staff preparing next season's advertising strategy or to the research director whose scientists are seeking new chemical formulations.

Research has uncovered another job-related factor that affects leadership style. When a manager's job requires analysis for solution, such as finding out why a machine has broken down, then an open, participatory style may be best because it elicits more ideas from more people than an autocratic style.[19] But when a job involves coordination, such as scheduling the movement of goods from the loading dock to the warehouse to the shipper to the customer, a directive style of leadership may be best. In this case the important factor is that people and other resources are where they are supposed to be when they are supposed to be there.

Another important job factor is uncertainty. Studies have shown that people-oriented styles are better in "uncertain" jobs than are work-centered styles, and vice versa for "certain" jobs.[20] Basically, a democratic leader has more inputs from subordinates than an autocratic leader. In an uncertain situation characterized by rapid change, the democratic leader has an increased advantage over the autocratic leader in being able to spot the change and to determine what to do about it. For example, consumers' tastes are always changing, and the wise mar-

---

[19] M. E. Shaw, "Some Effects of Problem Complexity upon Problem Solution Efficiency in Different Communication Nets," *Journal of Experimental Psychology* (January 1954), pp. 211–217.

[20] Paul R. Lawrence and Jay W. Lorsch, *Organization and Environment* (Boston: Graduate School of Business Administration, Harvard University, 1967), pp. 31–36.

keting manager listens closely to his or her salespeople. A marketing manager who sets a marketing strategy without sales force input is taking a needless risk.

On the other hand, the foundry business is slow to change. The production manager who solicits opinions about this job from employees is not likely to learn much and may waste time that could be spent casting metal. While the morale benefits of this approach may be worth the time and effort invested, it is easy to understand why an autocratic style is more often used in such a case.

MANAGEMENT SUPPORT

Managers do not work in a vacuum. They have superiors who manage them, and this can have a direct influence on the choice of leadership style.

The reward system set up for managers is a management support factor. Supervisors often complain that their pay and bonuses depend on short-run criteria such as the amount of daily output or the number of delinquent customer accounts. This forces them to put pressure on their employees, resulting in authoritarian leadership. However, this situation may be changing. For instance, Koppers Co. now bases its management incentive program on the results of a three-year period. Phillips Petroleum uses a five-year period.[21] On the contrary some managements put great emphasis on employee morale. The supervisor judged on this basis is more likely to use a democratic, people-oriented style.

The people-oriented leader faces another problem. As he or she tries to respond to the individual needs of employees, the approval and support of higher management will be needed. For instance, these leaders may want greater flexibility in scheduling vacation days or additional money to alter jobs to fit the employees' capabilities.

Research has found that such supervisors tend to satisfy their employees only when they actually deliver on their promises.[22] This means that they must have a good relationship with their superiors. Supervisors without this upward influence, regardless of their good intentions, create dissatisfied, unproductive employees.

The lack of upward influence may reduce the ability of a manager to use a people-oriented leadership style. But the autocratic leader may run into problems this way, too. An employee may be told, for example, that one more case of tardiness will result in a three-day layoff. But the manager's credibility will be damaged if high-level executives refuse to support such an action. On the contrary the supervisor who can win executive backing will be seen as that much more authoritative by employees. Part of the art of autocratic leadership is knowing when to issue ultimatums and knowing how to make them stick.

---

[21] "Answer to Ailing Industry: Overhaul at the Very Top," p. 39.
[22] Donald C. Pelz, "Influence: A Key to Effective Leadership in the First-line Supervisor," *Personnel* (December 1952), pp. 209–217.

PERSONAL CHARACTERISTICS

Many of the personal characteristics of the leader have a powerful effect on his or her ability to select and use the proper leadership style.[23] Some of these characteristics are his or her sincerity, knowledge, and need to be accepted.

Managers have faults, strengths, and complicated motives, just like their employees. A manager is as likely to have developed a fairly stable self-concept as a subordinate. Part of this self-concept may be a tendency to deal with people in a structured, authoritarian way or in an open, supportive way.

The person with authoritarian tendencies will find it quite natural to use an autocratic leadership style, just as the person with supportive tendencies will find a democratic style natural. The difficulty comes when either of these two types tries to switch roles. Role inconsistency can create superior–subordinate problems. Employees have been found to be very sensitive to insincerity in a leader.[24] Employees who feel that they are being manipulated will be dissatisfied with their manager and are not likely to perform well. Being friendly with employees can be an effective approach in some instances, but it must be genuine, not forced.

Another personal characteristic of the leader that affects his or her leadership style is knowledge of the job. New managers and supervisors often ask, "Do I have to be better than my employees at their jobs?" Sometimes this is an impossible expectation, especially when skilled people are being managed. A highly skilled manager might also discourage an employee from performing the task. Small group research has shown that leaders gain acceptance if they are simply good at whatever their employees do.[25] Mutual respect permits the leader to use a directive approach with his or her subordinates based on expert power.

But in some cases a manager cannot do the work performed by his or her subordinates. This situation is especially true in high-technology industries. A people-oriented approach can work well in such cases. The leader simply tells the subordinates that he or she is dependent on their expertise in their jobs. The leader will rely on their ideas as to how best to get the job done. The best leader in these instances is really a good follower.

Such a leader will coordinate the group's efforts and ensure that management provides the resources that the group needs. Upward influence is imperative in these circumstances. Even though workers and leader are expert in different areas, their mutual regard can serve as an effective basis for productive effort.

A leader's need to be accepted by his or her employees is yet another factor affecting the style used. Many managers complain about the loneliness of leader-

---

[23] Personal needs and characteristics are examined in articles such as Douglas E. Durand and Walter R. Nord, "Perceived Leader Behavior as a Function of Personality Characteristics of Superiors and Subordinates," *Academy of Management Journal* (September 1976), pp. 427–438; and Donald L. Helmich and Paul F. Erzen, "Leadership Style and Leader Needs," *Academy of Management Journal* (June 1975), pp. 397–402.

[24] Peter M. Blau and W. Richard Scott, *Formal Organizations: A Comparative Approach* (San Francisco: Chandler, 1962), p. 159.

[25] Hare, *Handbook of Small Group Research*, p. 292.

ship. This refers to the fact that leaders often have to make hard decisions for which they may not be liked. This is especially true of autocratic leaders. They may be admired and have referent power over their followers, but they may also be isolated. Some people resist this sense of alienation and use a democratic style, whether the situation calls for it or not. A collegiate example of this is a professor who is not honest with students when their performance is poor.

better to be respected than liked

The Development of Contingency Leadership Theory

A new leadership theory has emerged. It is called *contingency theory*. Simply stated this theory says that effective leadership style is contingent upon the situation. In some situations one style is best, and in others another style is best.[26] As noted in the contributions of Likert and of Tannenbaum and Schmidt, there is no one best way to lead.

Like most theoretical constructs, contingency theory has a historical derivation in earlier research literature. Many of today's concepts might be traced back to research done in the post–World War II period.

Contingency theory states that effective leadership style is contingent upon the situation: Different styles of leadership are best for different situations.

THE OHIO STATE STUDIES

Researchers at Ohio State University began some important leadership studies in the late 1940s, establishing an ongoing program in this area.[27] Names like Stogdill, Coons, Halpin, Winer, Kerr, Schriesheim, and Murphy are associated with this work.

The Ohio State studies originally dealt with military leadership questions such as commander–crew relations in B-52 bombers. The research was later extended to combat situations in Korea and industrial settings.

The researchers sought to identify the important leadership behavior dimensions. As the studies were extended and the questionnaires refined, two primary leadership behavior factors were uncovered: consideration and initiation of structure. Initiation of structure concerned the leader's efforts to organize the work effort or activity, instruct his or her subordinates, and clarify the superior–subordinate relationship. In other words initiation of structure referred to the task-oriented aspects (such as a bombing sortie) of leadership behavior. Consideration, or a subordinate orientation, was the second factor. It involved the leader's concern for the welfare of his or her subordinates as exhibited through friendliness, respect, and so forth.

---

[26] An interesting discussion appears in Wickham Skinner and W. Earl Sasser, "Manager with Impact: Versatile and Important," *Harvard Business Review* (November–December 1977), pp. 140–148.

[27] This section is based on Chester A. Schriesheim, James M. Tolliver, and Orlando C. Behling, "Leadership Theory: Some Implications for Managers," *MSU Business Topics* (Summer 1978), pp. 35–36; and Barrow, "The Variables of Leadership," p. 232.

Later studies related these leadership dimensions to subordinate satisfaction and productivity. High consideration–high structure leadership behavior was usually found to be the most desirable. While contradicting results were also reported in some cases, it is clear that the Ohio State studies were major contributions to the leadership literature.

THE UNIVERSITY OF MICHIGAN STUDIES

Other significant studies were being conducted by researchers at the University of Michigan's Survey Research Center.[28] The Michigan studies, employing interviews, reached essentially similar conclusions to those derived at Ohio State. The Michigan studies identified employee orientation and production orientation as the two primary ingredients of leadership style. The similarity of the Michigan results to Ohio State's consideration and initiation of structure seems quite evident.

THE MANAGERIAL GRID® AND REDDIN'S TRI-DIMENSIONAL MODEL OF LEADERSHIP EFFECTIVENESS[29]

Robert Blake and Jane Mouton's work in developing a Managerial Grid® should be noted as a contemporary application of some of the basic research cited above.[30] The Managerial Grid®, discussed in detail in Chapter 11, conceptualized two dimensions to leadership style: task-oriented and relations-oriented. Five behaviors are possible, according to Blake and Mouton:

Low-task and low-relations leadership style

Low-task and high-relations leadership style

High-task and low-relations leadership style

Medium-task and medium-relations leadership style

High-task and high-relations leadership style

In most cases, high-task and high-relations behavior is the most desirable.

Reddin's Tri-Dimensional Model of Leadership Effectiveness is an extension of the Managerial Grid.®[31] It considers effectiveness as a model variable and allows a determination of the leadership behavior most appropriate in a specified

---

[28] This section is based on Schriesheim, Tolliver, and Behling, "Leadership Theory," p. 36; and Barrow, "The Variables of Leadership," pp. 232–233.

[29] This section is based on Barrow, "The Variables of Leadership," pp. 235–236.

[30] See Robert R. Blake and Jane S. Mouton, *The Managerial Grid* (Houston: Gulf Publishing Co., 1964); and Robert R. Blake, Jane S. Mouton, Louis B. Barnes, and Larry Greiner, "Breakthrough in Organization Development," *Harvard Business Review* (November–December 1964), pp. 133–155.

[31] See William J. Reddin, "The 3-D Management Style Theory," *Training and Development Journal* (April 1967), pp. 8–17; and William J. Reddin, *Managerial Effectiveness* (New York: McGraw-Hill, 1970).

situation. Reddin's model permits an evaluation of the relative effectiveness of various behaviors under a given set of circumstances.

Actually, much of the earlier discussion of Theory X and Theory Y assumptions and the work of Tannenbaum and Schmidt was an introduction to the basics of contingency theory, even though the term was not used. The discussion was made possible by grouping scattered research items into a contingency format and defining the situation to include the four sets of factors affecting leadership style. Research on the contingency concept itself was not included.

FIEDLER'S CONTRIBUTION TO CONTINGENCY THEORY

Fred Fiedler, professor of psychology and management at the University of Washington, has conducted the research that led to the conceptual development of contingency theory. Fiedler sought to evaluate the leadership success relationship between leadership style and situational favorableness.[32] He measured leadership style by asking leaders to rate their least preferred co-worker (LPC score). Situational favorableness consists of leader–member relations, degree of task structure, and leader's power. Leaders with high LPC scores viewed their least preferred co-workers more favorably than did those with low LPC scores. High LPC leaders were considered people-centered, while low LPC scores implied a task-centered leadership style.

Fiedler found that task-centered leadership is best when the situation is either very favorable or very unfavorable. People-centered styles are best in the in-between situations.[33] Figure 14-3 illustrates the concept.

While Fiedler's work has been criticized by some management writers, it is clear that the contingency approach is now an accepted part of leadership theory. Certainly, it offers some valuable insights for the practicing manager. Not all the factors affecting leadership style are in harmony with each other in real-life situations. Some factors in a situation may favor people-oriented style and others a task-oriented style. Contingency thinking can help the manager find systematic ways to handle even the most complicated situations.

The emphasis in contingency thinking is on determining precisely what the leader faces, what he or she can or cannot change, and then finding the opti-

[32] Fiedler's model is summarized in Barrow, "The Variables of Leadership," p. 234. Some of this discussion follows this summary.

[33] Fred E. Fiedler and Martin M. Chemers, *Leadership and Effective Management* (Glenview, Ill.: Scott, Foresman, 1974), p. 87.

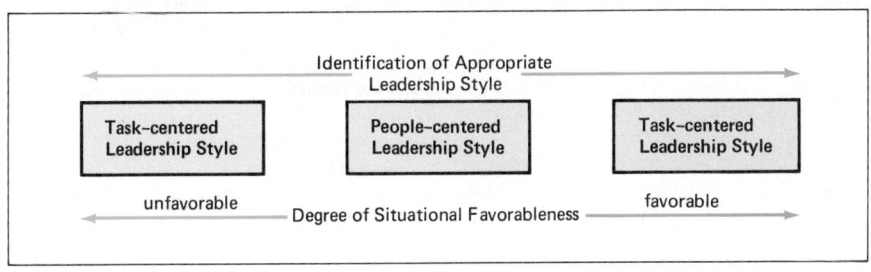

**Figure 14-3
AN ILLUSTRATION OF
FIEDLER'S
CONTINGENCY
THEORY**

mum solution. _Optimizing_ means finding the best balance of factors in a situation rather than attempting to maximize any one factor. For instance, employee satisfaction might have to be partially sacrificed in some situations in order to adapt to the physical requirements of the job. The key is to find the most beneficial balance of the two instead of maximizing employee satisfaction or the adaptation to physical job constraints.

An applied illustration of contingency theory is in order here. Suppose a person is in charge of stocking the shelves at a supermarket near a college campus. One question is, "What is the nature of the task?" If it is (a) coordinative and time-oriented, an autocratic style may be appropriate. If it is (b) analytical and open-ended, a democratic style might be better. Since shelving goods is largely a matter of container handling and keeping the product on the shelf despite rapid turnover, the answer is (a).

Next question: "What types of employees are involved?" If they are (c) status and achievement-oriented, a democratic style is suggested. If they are (d) security and physically oriented, an autocratic style might be the best choice. Suppose that most of the stock personnel are students from a nearby college. In this case the answer may be (c).

A dilemma has arisen. The task itself suggests an autocratic style, but the people involved may respond best to a democratic style. What should the manager do? Contingency thinking involves a consideration of all the possible options. For instance, can the manager change the nature of the work? If so, he or she might be able to match it to the employees' needs and abilities. If the manager determines that only by computerizing and mechanizing the job at prohibitive cost could this be accomplished, the option is ruled out.

Now the manager might ask, "Can I change my people to match the job?" For instance, could all the college students be dismissed and replaced by nonstudents? Or could the college students be indoctrinated again?

Contingency thinking forces the manager to abandon the pursuit of a single best approach. The "best" approach may be determined only after a careful analysis of the task and the people involved.

The Path-Goal Theory of Leadership

Path-goal theory is one of the more recent contributions to the study of leadership.[34] Robert House and his colleagues have done considerable work in this area, and a general leadership theory is emerging. But contradictory evidence and diverse viewpoints have also appeared in the management literature, so the

---

[34] This section is based on, and quotes and adaptations are from, Robert J. House and Terence R. Mitchell, "Path-Goal Theory of Leadership," _Journal of Contemporary Business_ (Autumn 1974), pp. 81–97. Used by permission of _Journal of Contemporary Business_, University of Washington. See also Robert J. House, "Retrospective Comment," in Louis E. Boone and Donald D. Bowen (eds.), _The Great Writings in Management and Organization Behavior_ (Tulsa, Okla.: PennWell Books, 1980), pp. 329–341.

end result of this significant research activity has not yet been determined.[35]

Path-goal theory indicates that effective leadership is dependent on the degree to which one is able to improve the achievement of subordinates' goals, as well as clearly defining the paths to goal attainment for subordinates. House and Mitchell have put it this way:

> The maturational functions of the leader consist of increasing the number and kinds of personal payoffs to subordinates for work-goal attainment and making paths to these payoffs easier to travel by clarifying the paths, reducing road blocks and pitfalls and increasing the opportunities for personal satisfaction en route.

Expectancy theory is the theoretical basis of the path-goal concept of leadership. *Expectancy theory* holds that a person's perception of achieving a prized reward or goal via effective job performance will motivate the individual. But the person must clearly see the relationship between his or her efforts and effective job performance leading to the desired objective. Expectancy theory implies that employee motivation is dependent on leader behavior influencing goal paths and the relative attractiveness of the goals involved.[36]

Two general propositions have emerged for path-goal theory, according to House and Mitchell:

1. Leader behavior is acceptable and satisfying to subordinates to the extent that the subordinates see such behavior as either an immediate source of satisfaction or as instrumental to future satisfaction.

2. Leader behavior will be motivational to the extent that (a) such behavior makes satisfaction of subordinates' needs contingent on effective performance and (b) such behavior complements the environment of subordinates by providing the coaching, guidance, support, and rewards necessary for effective performance."

Path-goal theory indicates that effective leadership is dependent on clearly defining the paths of goal achievement and the degree to which the leader is able to influence subordinates to attain such goals.

Expectancy theory holds that a person's perception of achieving a prized reward or goal via effective job performance will motivate the individual. Expectancy theory forms the basis of path-goal leadership.

---

[35] The literature considering path-goal theory is quite diverse. For a sampling of viewpoints, see Gary Johns, "Task Moderators of the Relationship Between Leadership Style and Subordinate Responses," *Academy of Management Journal* (June 1978), pp. 319–325; Chester Schriesheim and Mary Ann Van Geurow, "The Path-Goal Theory of Leadership: A Theoretical and Empirical Analysis," *Academy of Management Journal* (September 1977), pp. 398–405; Gary Dessler and Enzo R. Valenzi, "Initiation of Structure and Subordinate Satisfaction: A Path Analysis Test of Path-Goal Theory," *Academy of Management Journal* (June 1977), pp. 251–259; John E. Stinson and Thomas W. Johnson, "The Path-Goal Theory of Leadership: A Partial Test and Suggested Refinement," *Academy of Management Journal* (June 1975), pp. 242–252; H. Kirk Downey, John E. Sheridan, and John W. Slocum, Jr., "Analysis of Relationships Among Leader Behavior; Subordinate Job Performance and Satisfaction: A Path-Goal Approach," *Academy of Management Journal* (June 1975), pp. 253–262; and Charles N. Greene, "Questions of Causation in the Path-Goal Theory of Leadership," *Academy of Management Journal* (March 1979), pp. 22–41.

[36] James J. Polyczynski, Robert Graham, Stanford Orma, and LeRoy Cougle, "Increasing Productivity Through Front-Line Supervision and Expectancy Theory," *Pittsburgh Business Review* (June 1978), pp. 9–14. Another interesting article on expectancy is Laurence R. Walker and Kenneth W. Thomas, "Beyond Expectancy Theory: An Integrative Motivational Model from Health Care," *Academy of Management Review* (April 1982), pp. 187–194. Also see Richard W. School, "Differentiating Organizational Commitment From Expectancy as a Motivating Force," *Academy of Management Review* (October 1981), pp. 589–599.

LEADERSHIP THEORY IS A TOPIC OF CONVERSATION IN A VARIETY OF SETTINGS

SOURCE: Reprinted from *The Seattle Business Journal* (October 4, 1982), p. 21, by permission of the Cordovan Corp.

"Possibly you're bored with your work because you're objective oriented rather than process oriented."

House and Mitchell have also identified various strategic leadership functions in path-goal theory: "(1) recognizing and/or arousing subordinates' needs for outcomes over which the leader has some control, (2) increasing personal pay-offs to subordinates for work-goal attainment, (3) making the path to those pay-offs easier to travel by coaching and direction, (4) helping subordinates clarify expectancies, (5) reducing frustrating barriers and (6) increasing the opportunities for personal satisfaction contingent on effective performance."

Two contingency factors are hypothesized for the path-goal concept: (1) the subordinate's personal characteristics, and (2) environmental factors. *Personal characteristics* might include an individual's perception of the locus of control. In other words does he or she see the situation resulting from his or her own behavior or from outside events or random chance? *Environmental* contingency factors include the assigned tasks, the existing authority system, and the group within which the individual primarily works.

The path-goal model first considers leader behavior (directive, supportive, achievement-oriented, or participative, for instance), then considers the contingency factors, their causal results, and finally, the end product—subordinate attitudes and behavior.

Despite the mixed empirical tests of the path-goal concept, clearly this approach will play an important role in future leadership studies. Path-goal theory is making many contributions to our understanding of a very complex subject.

Black and Female Leadership Behaviors

As more and more blacks and women enter management positions, there is an increased effort to develop empirical data about their leadership styles. Until recently there was little but speculation in such matters. Some thought that blacks might not be as autocratic as whites because of the societal environment in which blacks are often raised. Others thought that women, because of their roles as mothers and wives, might make better people-oriented leaders than men.

Not enough research has been done to provide final answers to these questions, but some interesting findings have already been made. One study of black managers found no differences in the way black and white managers perceived themselves.[37] Nor did they find differences in the values of black and white managers. Whether this finding indicates that the blacks were hired because their values were the same as whites', or because their values changed from copying whites on the job, or because such values are simply demanded by the work was not answered by the research. The only difference found was that the black managers were more self-oriented and that the whites were more other-oriented.

Research on women leaders has shown that there is surprisingly little difference between male and female leaders. One study of first-level supervisors found that subordinates saw little difference between men and women leaders in autocratic or democratic activities, despite the stereotype that women are not as aggressive and competitive as men.[38] Another study concluded that "the higher the level of organizational position, the lower the relative degree of acceptance of female managers."[39] While it is often assumed that men will not accept a dominant type of woman as a leader, another study found just the opposite: Male subordinates actually were more satisfied with high-dominance females as superiors than with low-dominance females.[40] Apparently, when a strong man-

[37] John G. Watson and Sam Barone, "The Self-Concept, Personal Values, and Motivational Orientations of Black and White Managers," *Academy of Management Journal* (March 1976), pp. 36–48.
[38] Richard N. Osborn and William M. Vicars, "Sex Stereotypes: An Artifact in Leader Behavior and Subordinate Satisfaction Analysis," *Academy of Management Journal* (September 1976), pp. 439–449.
[39] Giuseppi A. Forgionne and Celestine C. Nwacukwu, "Acceptance of Authority in Female-Managed Organizational Positions," *University of Michigan Business Review* (May 1977), p. 27.
[40] Kathryn M. Bartol, "Male Versus Female Leaders: The Effect of Leader Need for Dominance on Follower Satisfaction," *Academy of Management Journal* (June 1974), pp. 225–233.

A Louis Harris & Associates poll of 602 top managers indicated that women are becoming increasingly accepted in the formerly male-dominated executive suite. Eighty-six percent of the respondents agreed that women executives were doing at least as well as expected in their jobs. Some of the poll's other results were as follows:

	AGREE	DISAGREE
It has been harder to promote women to high-level positions than we thought it would be.	41%	52%
Men don't like to take orders from women.	41%	49%
Women don't like to take orders from other women.	39%	45%

SOURCE: "How Executives See Women In Management," *Business Week* (June 28, 1982), p. 10.

A LOUIS HARRIS REPORT ON WOMEN EXECUTIVES

ager is needed to get the job done, employers prefer firmness whether the superior is a man or a woman.

A Continuing Research Need

Leadership is one of management's most dynamic fields of study. The contingency approach or the path-goal concept is not the final word in leadership theory. While they certainly represent major advances, there is every likelihood that they are merely steps in the evolutionary development of a most complex subject.

Many problems still remain.[41] An overall synthesis of leadership practices and theoretical contributions is a pressing need. Perhaps one of the readers of this textbook will one day make a major breakthrough in leadership theory.

[41] Four interesting articles are Nan Weiner and Thomas A. Mahoney, "A Model of Corporate Performance as a Function of Environmental, Organizational, and Leadership Influences," *Academy of Management Journal* (September 1981), pp. 453–470; Arthur G. Jago, "Leadership: Perspectives in Theory and Practice," *Management Science* (March 1982), pp. 315–336; Jeffrey Pfeffer, "The Ambiguity of Leadership," *Academy of Management Journal* (January 1977), pp. 104–112; and Barbara Karmel, "Leadership: A Challenge to Traditional Research Methods and Assumptions," *Academy of Management Journal* (July 1978), pp. 475–482.

Summary

Leadership is the act of motivating or causing people to perform certain tasks intended to achieve specified objectives. It is the most visible aspect of a manager's job.

All leadership situations involve the use of power, defined as the ability of one person to influence the behavior of another. Five sources of power are available to the leaders: reward, coercive, expert, referent, and legitimate. Some leaders may use only one or two of these power sources; others may employ all five.

Leadership style refers to the selection of a way to lead and how to use available power. The selection of a leadership style is a function of the leader, subordinates, and situation. An important factor concerns the manager's assumption about those being led. The basic assumptions have been described by Douglas McGregor as Theory X and Theory Y. A Theory X leader is an autocrat who believes that subordinates naturally dislike work, so it is the leader's responsibility to direct and control them. A Theory Y leader thinks that work is a rewarding activity for all people, if they are given the opportunity. Theory Y leaders are democratic and

employ a participative leadership style. More comprehensive models have been offered by Rensis Likert and by Robert Tannenbaum and Warren Schmidt, which are also discussed in this chapter.

Leadership theory can be divided into two distinct groupings: the early traditional theories and the more contemporary situational viewpoints. The earliest leadership concept was the Great Man Theory, which held that the emergence of a single person was the cause of any action. Early leadership theorists concentrated on identifying the characteristics of such leaders. Trait theory was the natural extension of the Great Man Theory. Here the objective was to identify and measure the traits or attributes related to leadership behaviors.

Various situational factors have been found to influence leadership style. These include (1) people, (2) the job, (3) management support, and (4) personal characteristics. Recognition of the importance of such factors led to the development of contingency leadership theory. This concept suggests that effective leadership is contingent upon the situation. Leadership behavior should vary according to the circumstances facing the manager. Early studies dealing with contingency theory were conducted at Ohio State University and the University of Michigan. Fred Fiedler is a well-known researcher in this field.

Path-goal theory is one of the latest conceptual entrants in the study of leadership. According to this concept, effective leadership is dependent on the degree to which one is able to improve the achievement of subordinates' goals, as well as clearly defining the paths to goal attainment for subordinates. The work of Robert House and Terence Mitchell is notable in this field.

Chapter 14 concludes with a brief discussion of black and female leadership behaviors and the continuing research needs in leadership theory.

REVIEW EXERCISES

1. Define the following terms: (a) leadership (b) power (c) leadership style (d) Theory X (e) Theory Y (f) Great Man Theory (g) trait theory (h) contingency theory (i) path-goal theory (j) expectancy theory.

2. Discuss the basic points made in the management profile for Chapter 14.

3. Describe the various sources of power available to a leader.

4. Discuss the concept of leadership style.

5. Outline the evolution of leadership theory.

6. What factors can influence the selection of a leadership style?

7. What conclusions were reached in the Ohio State and University of Michigan studies?

8. Assess Fiedler's contribution to leadership theory.

9. Explain Tannenbaum and Schmidt's continuum of manager–nonmanager behavior.

10. Discuss the current status of path-goal theory.

ASSIGNMENTS/ PROBLEMS/ DISCUSSION QUESTIONS

1. Consider the following item from *The Detroit News.* *

TOP EXECUTIVES SHARE EIGHTEEN KEYS TO SUCCESS

Career profiles of executives who have reached the top of large organizations were analyzed for *The Detroit News* by several leading psychologists who study management, managers and power.

Eighteen traits were found to be most commonly shared by successful executives. The executives have

1. Clearly defined goals and career objectives.
2. Moved into position to be discovered by exposing their work to the right superiors and acquiring access to memos and reports of rising superiors.
3. Won sponsors who tapped them for bigger things, such as working for bosses with a history of rapid advancement, and become crucial subordinates to them. They complemented the boss' skills or style without threatening him.
4. Held one job in about every three that was primarily developmental, in order to learn new skills.
5. Gladly accepted "special" assignments, even though the jobs initially didn't seem like promotions or anything special.
6. Kept flexible by never totally committing themselves to a position or program that, if it failed, could undermine their careers.
7. Stressed cooperation rather than competition with other potential executives.

* *The Detroit News* (September 24, 1978), p. 11-A. Reprinted with permission.

8. Worked to keep people with different ideas from becoming personal opponents.
9. Refused to let personal feelings be the basis for any action.
10. Avoided obvious dead-end jobs.
11. Got their way by influencing others to do things voluntarily and cooperatively rather than by intimidation.
12. Began early to develop power through personal and professional relationships, by developing special skills and by consciously developing such personal attributes as presence and grace.
13. Created "grapevines" to keep them aware of things going on.
14. Learned how to neutralize, utilize, convert, avoid, join and nullify the impact of others.
15. Advanced their ideas by displaying self-assurance, decisiveness and confidence, even if they didn't feel it.
16. Often made concessions that were more apparent than real.
17. Learned how to control the flow of vital information.
18. Used power sparingly and gracefully to avoid injuring or antagonizing others.

Relate these "eighteen keys to success" to the material presented in Chapter 14.

2. Board Chairman John F. Welch, Jr., has described his approach to running General Electric's far-flung operations: "You've got to give people their own businesses and their own heads. Maybe they fail a bit, but let them run."† Relate Welch's viewpoint to the material presented in this chapter.

3. It has been suggested that many successful leaders have had a mentor at some critical point in

† "Answer to Ailing Industry: Overhaul at the Very Top," *U.S. News & World Report* (January 17, 1983), p. 39.

their career development. Typically, the mentor has been some senior person in the organization who took an active interest in the subordinate's professional advancement.** Comment on this. Can you identify any examples of this situation?

4. Prepare a report on the leadership style of one of the following:

    a. Margaret Thatcher
    b. Ronald Reagan
    c. Jesse Jackson
    d. Billy Martin
    e. Tom Landry
    f. Martin Luther King, Jr.
    g. Betty Ford
    h. John F. Kennedy

5. Submit a brief outline of your own leadership style.

** See, for example, Abraham Zoleznik, "Managers and Leaders: Are They Different?" *Harvard Business Review* (May–June 1977), pp. 67–78.

A MANAGERIAL INCIDENT

David Mahoney Sets the Leadership Style at Norton Simon, Inc.

David Mahoney impresses a visitor as a leader. The chairman, president, and chief executive officer of Norton Simon, Inc., was born the son of a Bronx construction worker who was unemployed during the Depression. Mahoney has remarked, "I just always knew I never wanted to be poor" in explaining his personal motivation. Today, David Mahoney runs the billion-dollar conglomerate from elegantly furnished Park Avenue offices. But he is still the fighter who parlayed his high school basketball ability into a college education at the University of Pennsylvania's prestigious Wharton School.

As for his leadership style, Mahoney made these observations in an interview a few years ago: "Basically, for all the companies I've worked for, I've had to be a money-maker. There has to be a leader to make things work, somebody who has whatever that intangible quality is." Mahoney adds, "I much prefer consensus, but I don't trust total agreement. If two people agree all the time, one of them is unnecessary."

Leadership of people is the biggest part of Mahoney's job. How does he do it? He uses both positive and punitive tactics. "You fill people's needs for money, security, whatever it is, everybody wants something, after all, even if it's only a good table at the Pump Room." But Mahoney also expressed the other side of the power relationship. "People fear anyone or anything that can cause you a problem. People's fear of me is really their fear of themselves. If they're performing, they don't have anything to fear. There's probably fear in every organization, and it's natural. The first time you disagree with the boss the fear starts. It can't be helped."

SOURCE: Adapted from Michael Korda, *Power* (New York: Ballantine Books, 1975), pp. 33–41. Used with permission of the author and Random House, Inc.

Questions and Problems

1. Describe Mahoney's leadership style.

2. Relate Mahoney's approach to leadership to the material presented in Chapter 14.

3. Do you think you would function effectively as a subordinate in an organization run by David Mahoney?

15.
Communi-
cation

Learning Objectives

AFTER STUDYING THIS CHAPTER YOU SHOULD BE ABLE TO

1. Explain the process of communication.
2. Describe the communication model.
3. Identify the roadblocks to effective communication and the means to avoid them.
4. Discuss the basic concepts of group communication.
5. Understand the importance of channel selection in communication.
6. Relate communication to motivation and leadership.

Key Terms

communication

body language

noise

cognitive dissonance

rationalizing

feedback

empathy

Homan's interaction hypothesis

committee

formal communication channel

multiplexing

climate surveys

informal communication channel

grapevine

I like to listen. I have learned a great deal from listening carefully. Most people never listen.

ERNEST HEMINGWAY

I am a great believer, if you have a meeting, in knowing where you want to come out before you start the meeting. Excuse me if that doesn't sound very democratic.

NELSON ROCKEFELLER

Lee Morgan spends his time running a $9.5 billion corporation. And the board chairman of Caterpillar Tractor Co. knows that interpersonal communication is an important part of this responsibility. So despite a tight schedule and afternoon flights back and forth between Peoria, Caterpillar's headquarters city, and New York, Morgan took time out to see a retired employee with whom he used to walk to work.

The Caterpillar retiree told Morgan that his son hauled parts between two nearby plants. He went on to explain that a supervisor has upped his son's work load from six to seven trips a day. This change caused the young employee to drive too fast, endangering his safety and Caterpillar's reputation in the community.

Morgan assured his acquaintance from years ago that he would check out the situation. The board chairman's discussion with the retiree is indicative of the importance that is placed on effective communication at Caterpillar Tractor.[1]

What Is Communication?

If an employee does not understand his or her job or has a complaint, improving communications and discussing the problems face to face is often useful. Communication can also convey positive information that is useful to management. Effective communication provides important benefits to executives willing to work at improving their performance in this area.

[1] Paul Gulson with Barbara Rudolph, "Playing Peoria—to Perfection," *Forbes* (May 11, 1981), p. 60.

It is also important to realize that communication does not always work. Communicating the wrong information at the wrong time can hurt employee motivation. Giving people information they do not need can interfere with their job performance. Information that is misinterpreted can cause problems that otherwise would not have existed. And bringing people together to communicate does not automatically mean that they will get along better. It may convince them more than ever that their differences are real and cannot be overcome. Communication is the critical factor in some problem situations, but not in others.

COMMUNICATION: A DEFINITION

Communication is the transfer of information via an understandable message from a sender to others.

There are numerous definitions of communication. These range from highly technical ones to generalized versions that suggest all human activities are forms of communication. From a managerial perspective, a reasonable definition is that *communication* refers to the transfer of information via an understandable message from a sender to others.

All communication attempts to transfer some type of information. Some transfers are successful, others are not. The key ingredient is that the information is presented in the form of an understandable message to those with whom the sender wishes to communicate.

TYPES OF COMMUNICATION

Communication in management usually occurs in three ways. It may be spoken, written, or transmitted via nonverbal forms. Spoken communication may be the single most important activity performed by management. Caterpillar's Lee Morgan assigns a high priority to oral communication. Written messages are also a vital aspect of the manager's job in all organizations. The written message may also be one of the most widely studied forms of communication.

Body language is the form of nonverbal communication that employs eye contact, gestures, and posture.

Nonverbal communication—often called *body language*—is also important. This type of communication supplements, amplifies, and clarifies spoken communications. Nonverbal communication includes eye contact, gestures, and posture. All of these can be used to suggest agreement, boredom, anxiety, and so

GOOD NEWS . . . BAD NEWS

The Paperwork Reduction Act of 1980 called for cuts in the paperwork that the government requires individuals and businesses to complete. The federal government reported a 29 percent cut in such activity, over 100 million hours in 1982. That was the good news . . . the bad news was that it took the government five pages of press releases and an eighty-nine-page booklet to report the reduction in required paperwork.

SOURCE: "Government Writes a Book to Herald Cut in Paperwork," *Journal-American* (January 14, 1983), p. 8-A; and "Paperwork: U.S. Pats Itself on Back—With More of the Same," *The Seattle Times* (January 14, 1983), p. 2-A (Both AP stories).

forth. One study reported that a message's verbal content is responsible for 7 percent of attitude change, while vocal characteristics and facial expressions account for 38 percent and 55 percent, respectively.[2]

IMPORTANCE OF COMMUNICATION

The importance of effective communication goes well beyond the application of a managerial technique. The role of communication is to provide an informational system whereby management can plan, organize, motivate, direct, and control the various segments of the organization. Communication is the very lifeblood of the organization. It provides the means for accomplishing the managerial job.[3]

[2] Reported in Clifford Hurston and Gloria Wilson, "Body Talk—The Unspoken Language," *Management World* (July 1978), p. 16.

[3] The importance of information to decision making is discussed in Charles A. O'Reilly III, "Variations in Decision Makers' Use of Informational Sources: The Impact of Quality and Accessibility of Information," *Academy of Management Journal* (December 1982), pp. 756–771.

Managers often use the acronym KISS ("keep it simple, stupid") to summarize an important key to effective written communications. In his book *The Power of Words,* Stuart Chase reported an excellent example of failure to apply the KISS axiom. A plumber in New York had begun to use hydrochloric acid to clean drains but was concerned about possible harmful effects. After writing to the U.S Bureau of Standards in Washington, D.C., to ask their advice, he received the following reply:

> The efficacy of hydrochloric acid is indisputable, but chlorine residue is incompatible with metallic permanence.

The plumber sent a second letter to Washington, thanking the correspondent at the Bureau of Standards for responding and expressing his satisfaction in learning that the bureau agreed with him. He received the following note of alarm by return mail:

> We cannot assume responsibility for the production of toxic and noxious residues with hydrochloric acid, and suggest that you use an alternative procedure.

Again, the plumber responded, noting that he was happy that the Bureau still agreed with him. This time the Bureau response was short and direct:

> Don't use hydrochloric acid; it eats hell out of the pipes.

SOURCE: Stuart Chase, *Power of Words* (New York: Harcourt, Brace and Company, 1955), p. 259. Adapted from *Power of Words,* copyright 1954, 1982 by Stuart Chase. Reprinted by permission of Harcourt Brace Jovanovich, Inc.

"WHAT THEY REALLY MEANT WAS . . ."

**Figure 15-1
THE BASIC
COMMUNICATION
MODEL**

THE BASIC COMMUNICATION MODEL

The simplest communication system is made up of only four parts: a sender, a message, a communication channel, and a receiver. This basic communication model is shown in Figure 15-1. If the sender is a manager, the purpose in communicating is often to get an employee, the receiver, to carry out some desired action. The employee may be told to unload a freight car, for example. The trick is to avoid garbling the message at any point along its route from the sender through the medium to the receiver so that the right freight is unloaded at the right time in the right condition at the right cost.

Communication Roadblocks

Responsibility for effective communication lies with the manager. Whenever communication breaks down, the manager should determine whether he or she is at fault before blaming the channel or, worse yet, the employee. Roadblocks to communication include poor timing, inadequate information, inappropriate

**CAMERAS CAN ALSO
INHIBIT
COMMUNICATIONS**

SOURCE: Reprinted from *The Seattle Business Journal* (October 12, 1981), p. 6, by permission of the Cordovan Corp.

channel, noise, selective perception, premature evaluation, emotions, and be-liefs.[4]

POOR TIMING

The manager must know when to communicate. If an employee fails to take action, it may be because the manager assumed the employee knew when or how to do a job. A loading dock supervisor, for instance, might assume that an employee would know to unload *any* freight delivered to the dock. Yet a dock worker might not do this without specific instructions if, for instance, the freight is in an unusual carton or if it is damaged.

INADEQUATE INFORMATION

Even if the manager communicates when he or she should, the employee may receive inadequate information. Too little information endangers effective communication, but so does too much. The employee whose only job is to remove the freight from a boxcar or truck might not understand the loading instructions if they are included in billing details or in instructions on making claims for damaged goods.

The manager must also scrutinize the symbols used to convey a message. The information must be meaningful to the employee. This can mean anything from using correct grammar, spelling, and punctuation, to avoiding typographical errors in written orders, to clear pronunciation in oral orders.

INAPPROPRIATE CHANNEL

If the manager has properly performed his or her tasks as a sender, the *channel* will determine the effectiveness of the communication. Should the manager write it down, make a phone call, talk face to face, or use some combination? Writing, for instance, enables the receiver to study the message thoroughly. It also provides proof that the message was sent. A phone conversation, on the other hand, is fast and allows for discussion to make the message clear. But even this does not provide the emphasis that can be given to a message by hand gestures or eye contact in a face-to-face communication. The medium must be matched to the message and the receiver.

A basic question concerns whether the message ever reaches the desired receiver. Would publishing a safety slogan in the company newspaper reach the dock laborer? It might if the person reads it or talks to co-workers who read it. But then it might not, and if the message is important or specific enough, it should be sent in a more direct manner.

[4] Another list of barriers appears in Leonard R. Sayles and George Strauss, *Human Behavior in Organizations* (Englewood Cliffs, N.J.: Prentice-Hall, 1966), pp. 238–246. Similar lists appear in a variety of other sources. See, for example, Mary Polfer, "Communications: The Secret of Success in the World of Business," *Pittsburgh State University Business and Economic Review* (February 1979), pp. 3–6.

NOISE

Another problem in communications channels is noise. *Noise* refers to any situation that interferes with or distorts the message being communicated. This may be physical noise, as when a truck engine drowns out the supervisor's oral instructions. Or it may be noise in a more general sense, as when a manager tries to send too many messages over a channel. Phone conversations are effective when brief instructions are given, but lengthy conversations can be too much for this type of channel. By the time the call is over, the receiver may have forgotten what was said earlier in the conversation.

Probably the most complicated link in the communication system is the receiver. The receiver, being a human being, has a less-than-perfect memory. Scientific measures of oral messages have shown that as much as 50 percent of a message will be forgotten just moments after it is received.[5] This is one strong argument for repeating oral instructions.

SELECTIVE PERCEPTION

Perception is a very selective, individual process. How a message will be perceived by a person depends on past experiences, emotions, beliefs, and other personal factors.

Sometimes an employee may resist a message simply because he or she has learned from past experience not to trust a manager. Suppose a manager has promised pay raises to an employee but does not have a good record of delivering on these promises. Whenever the manager talks about salary to this employee, the message will probably be ignored. Some workers may not trust company newspapers if they view them as management propaganda. As a result they may fail to receive important news.

PREMATURE EVALUATION

When a receiver evaluates the content of a message before the communication is completed, the person is said to evaluate it prematurely.[6] This is what the mistrusting employees above were doing. Premature evaluation can work both ways. Suppose the supervisor tells a subordinate something like this: "Jack, you are the hardest working and fastest person on the dock. I've got a special job that only a special person can handle. I'd like you to use the fork-lift truck to move these fragile chemical containers from the warehouse to the dock." In this case the worker's premature evaluation is likely to be positive.

[5] Roger Bellows, Thomas Q. Gilson, and George S. Odione, *Executive Skills* (Englewood Cliffs, N.J.: Prentice-Hall, 1962), pp. 60–61.

[6] A classic discussion of this roadblock appears in Carl R. Rogers and F. J. Roethlisberger, "Barriers and Gateways to Communication," *Harvard Business Review* (July–August 1952), pp. 46–52.

EMOTIONS

But if emotions are brought into perception, the outcome may be different. Suppose Jack was very upset by having just seen another worker burned by acid spills from a chemical carton he had dropped. How receptive would he be to the supervisor's flattery now? The mere mention of "fragile chemical containers" might prompt resistance to the order.

A standard example of the effects of emotions on receptiveness to communications is the employee wanting to see a superior about an increase in pay. "Not today," warns the secretary, "she's in a lousy mood." Most employees would quickly decide to try again some other time when the executive might be in a more receptive mood.

BELIEFS

Beliefs and attitudes affect communication effectiveness, although their influence is not quite so obvious. Beliefs cause people to hear or see in a message only what they want when the information causes them mental conflict. The tension state resulting from information that contradicts currently held beliefs and attitudes is called *cognitive dissonance.* Sometimes a receiver might avoid a message altogether, if he or she thinks it might run counter to his or her beliefs. Hitler, for example, was notorious for avoiding those field commanders who might tell him the war was going badly. Though an extreme personality, Hitler was not rare in doing this; it is a common, natural defense put up by people in a variety of situations.

Cognitive dissonance refers to the discrepancy between existing beliefs and attitudes and new perceptions.

What happens when a disagreeable message cannot be avoided? Return to the story of the dock laborer who had been given a superior performance rating by a supervisor. Suppose now that a new supervisor gives a mixed annual review, pointing out that the person is a quick worker but is sometimes careless.

The employee may accept the message and correct the deficiencies noted. But there is a good chance that the worker may read the message differently. The person may hear only the compliment and immediately reject the criticism. The word *careless* may not even register with this individual.

Then, too, the dock worker may distort the message in the annual review to bring it into line with his belief, a process called *rationalizing.* The worker could reason that carelessness is an unavoidable side effect of fast work.

Rationalizing is the distortion of a message to bring it into line with one's own beliefs.

Avoiding the Roadblocks to Effective Communication

The effective communicator can take a number of actions to avoid the obstacles cited in the previous section.

**Figure 15-2
THE EXPANDED
COMMUNICATION
MODEL**

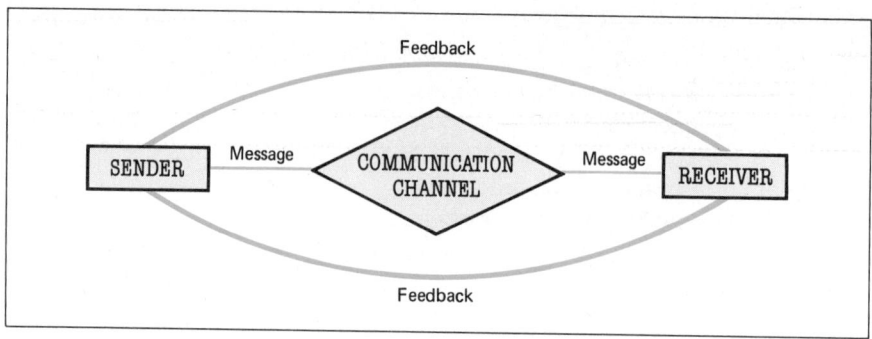

EXPAND THE BASIC COMMUNICATION MODEL TO INCLUDE FEEDBACK

**Feedback is
information transmitted
by a receiver back to
the original sender of a
message.**

Effective communication requires the receiver to feed back information to the sender. *Feedback* refers to information transmitted by a receiver back to the original sender of a message. Many communications experts believe that a true "communication" cannot take place until the sender has received confirmation from the receiver that the message has been understood. The expanded communication model is shown in Figure 15-2.

Managers often feel that two-way communication is unnecessary. However, various studies that have been done comparing one-way and two-way communications[7] generally conclude that information is transferred more accurately when there is feedback. The receiver can better clarify his or her understanding of what the sender means. Also, these studies have found that the receiver has more positive feelings toward the sender when he or she can respond to the message.

Feedback benefits come at a cost.[8] Repeating, discussing, and quizzing take time; and if the appropriate action is delayed too long, the extra accuracy is valueless. Two-way communication appears to be most appropriate in instances when a situation is unclear and the quality of the action is important. But if action must be taken quickly in a situation that is clear-cut, one-way communication may be called for.

IMPROVE LISTENING SKILLS

Communications expert Stuart Chase emphasizes that "Listening is the other half of talking."[9] Clearly, listening should be an inherent part of the total com-

[7] William V. Haney, "A Comparative Study of Unilateral and Bilateral Communication," *Academy of Management Journal* (June 1964), pp. 128–136; and Harold J. Leavitt and Ronald A. H. Mueller, "Some Effects of Feedback on Communications," *Human Relations* (November 1951), pp. 401–410.

[8] Management's problems in obtaining accurate feedback about situations are discussed in Chris Argyris, "Doubleloop Learning in Organizations," *Harvard Business Review* (September–October 1977), pp. 115–125.

[9] Stuart Chase, *Power of Words* (New York: Harcourt, Brace and World, 1954), p. 165.

munication process. But in many cases it is not. For many people listening is that agonizing time period they must survive before they themselves speak.

Paying close attention to what the other person says is one of the simplest ways to improve communication. Keith Davis has offered some suggestions to facilitate good listening practices. His recommendations are listed in Table 15-1.

<table>
<tr><td>

1. *Stop talking!*
    You cannot listen if you are talking.
    Polonius (*Hamlet*): "Give every man thine ear, but few thy voice."

2. *Put the talker at ease.*
    Help the person feel that he or she is free to talk.
    This is often called a permissive environment.

3. *Show the individual that you want to listen.*
    Look and act interested. Do not read your mail while the person talks.
    Listen to understand rather than to oppose.

4. *Remove distractions.*
    Don't doodle, tap, or shuffle papers.
    Will it be quieter if you shut the door?

5. *Empathize with the person.*
    Try to see the other's point of view.

6. *Be patient.*
    Allow plenty of time. Do not interrupt.
    Don't start for the door or walk away.

7. *Hold your temper.*
    An angry person gets the wrong meaning from words.

8. *Go easy on argument and criticism.*
    This puts the person on the defensive. He or she may "clam up" or get angry.
    Do not argue: Even if you win, you lose.

9. *Ask questions.*
    This encourages the speaker and shows you are listening. It helps to develop points further.

10. *Stop talking!*
    This is first and last, because all other commandments depend on it.
    You can't do a good listening job while you are talking.

    Nature gave man two ears but only one tongue, which is a gentle hint that he should listen more than he talks.
</td><td>

Table 15-1 TEN COMMANDMENTS FOR GOOD LISTENING
</td></tr>
</table>

SOURCE: Adapted by permission from Keith Davis, *Human Behavior at Work*, 4th ed. (New York: McGraw-Hill, 1972), p. 396.

PRACTICE EMPATHY

**Empathy is
identification with
another person's
perspective.**

Semanticist (and former U.S. senator) S. I. Hayakawa says: "The meanings of
words are *not* in the words; they are in us."[10] If meaning must be found in something beyond words themselves, then true communication must involve a degree
of *empathy*—the identification with another person's perspective.

Carl R. Rogers has suggested an interesting technique for improving communication through empathy. He suggests moderating arguments or disagreements
by accepting the basic rule that no person can speak until he or she has "restated
the ideas and feelings of the previous speaker accurately and to that speaker's satisfaction."[11]

Effective communication requires that the listener understand exactly what
others mean and the perspective from which they speak. The Rogers proposal
seeks to develop that type of perspective. But regardless of how it is achieved,
empathy is an important ingredient for the efficient functioning of the organizational communication system.

FOLLOW BASIC COMMUNICATION GUIDELINES

Various guidelines have been suggested for improving a firm's communication
practices. All have a place in organizational communication, with most designed
to eliminate one or more of the roadblocks mentioned earlier in this chapter.

Some standard guidelines include

1. *Eliminate ambiguities.* Senders should make their communications as
   precise as possible so as to minimize the number of possible interpretations.
2. *Use proper follow-up.* Some communications require a follow-up from the
   sender. Certain instances require a manager to follow a verbal instruction
   with a written memorandum confirming the spoken details. Managers
   should also monitor a subordinate's response to a communication; if action is delayed or inappropriate, the executive should immediately follow
   up on the matter.
3. *Avoid negativism.* Statements like "It probably won't work anyway, but
   why not try plan B" should be avoided in organizational communication.
   They set the stage for failure. After all, if management does not think the
   action will work, why should the subordinate risk proving the superior
   wrong?
4. *Watch the timing of messages.* The timing of certain communications is
   vital. Management should time communication so as to avoid noise in the
   communication channel.

[10] S. I. Hayakawa, *Language in Thought and Action,* 3rd ed. (New York: Harcourt Brace Jovanovich, 1972), p. 258.
[11] Rogers and Roethlisberger, "Barriers and Gateways," p. 48.

Communication Within a Group

Not all communication is between a single manager and a single subordinate. Much organizational communication involves groups of people, not just individuals. To be successful, group communication requires a special blend of skills. This section considers some of the basic concepts in group communication.

COHESIVENESS

In Chapter 13 motivation was studied from the viewpoint of the group. It was noted that groups have a quality called *cohesiveness,* a net measure of the forces acting to hold the group together. One important factor determining cohesiveness is communication among group members.

A basic proposition of group behavior is *Homan's interaction hypothesis:* People who interact will grow to like each other (assuming they have compatible goals and needs); this mutual liking will lead to more communication, which will lead to more liking, and so on.[12] The net result is high cohesiveness.

How does communication within a group start? Certainly, having a common purpose is a factor.[13] And there is the obvious but often overlooked matter of the physical proximity of the participants. To be clustered around a workbench encourages more group communication than does being stretched out along an assembly line. Member turnover is another factor. Groups with high membership turnover find it difficult to establish regular communication channels.[14] Group size is another factor. Large groups restrict the participation in the communication system.[15]

If a manager wants a work group to be cohesive, then members should be encouraged to communicate with each other. To facilitate communications the manager should arrange people in proximity, allow them to stay in the group for a long time, and keep the group small.

Homan's interaction hypothesis states that people who interact will grow to like each other, assuming they have compatible goals and needs, and this will lead to more interaction (or communication), thus establishing a cycle of cohesiveness.

CONFORMING TO GROUP NORMS

One of the most noticeable patterns of communication in a group is the attempts of the regulars to make deviants conform to group norms.[16] Consider a worker who has the usual amount of communication with the others in the work group. Now suppose that the worker does not agree with the idea of adding an extra five minutes to the coffee break as the others do. The person's peers gradu-

---

[12] George C. Homans, *The Human Group* (New York: Harcourt, Brace, 1950), p. 111.

[13] This is discussed at length by James G. March and Herbert A. Simon, *Organizations* (New York: Wiley, 1958), p. 66.

[14] This was illustrated in research by Elton Mayo and George F. Lombard, *Teamwork and Labor Turnover in the Aircraft Industry of Southern California,* Business Research Report No. 32 (Boston: Graduate School of Business Administration, Harvard University, 1944), p. 8.

[15] Studies showing this can be found in Alexander Paul Hare, *Handbook of Small Group Research* (New York: Free Press, 1976), pp. 229–230.

[16] This pattern is described in *ibid.,* pp. 51–52.

ally express their displeasure about the individual's going back to work on time. They begin to warn that the supervisor will soon expect all of them to go back to work at the official time.

If the deviant worker continues to return to work promptly, the interaction continues to grow as the group threatens to take action against the person. If at this point the renegade decides to accept the group norm, the interaction pattern will quickly return to what it was before the incident. If, instead, the worker persists in breaking the group's informal rule, then the communication might stop almost completely. This means that the group is punishing the deviant by rejecting him or her. A manager can often spot a worker who is in disagreement with fellow workers if he or she has been shut off—or if the person seems to be the center of attention.

COMMUNICATION NETWORKS

Laboratory experiments have uncovered some interesting facts about the relationship between a group's task and its communication patterns.[17] Usually the experimenters restrict group members to the circle, chain, Y, and wheel communication networks, shown in Figure 15-3 and then assign them different kinds of tasks.

For example, each group might be given a simple coordinating task such as this: The group members each have a card with several symbols, one of which appears on every card; the task is to identify the common symbol as quickly as possible. Notice that the Y and wheel have one member who is linked to more than just two others. This centralizes the information flow and permits these arrangements to solve the problem faster than the circle and chain.

When the type of task is changed, the results can be different. The circle has been found to solve arithmetical problems better than the wheel. This is probably because the circle—being more centralized—leads to greater participation

[17] Harold J. Leavitt, "Some Effects of Certain Communication Patterns on Group Performance," *Journal of Abnormal and Social Psychology* (January 1951), pp. 38–50; M. E. Shaw, "Some Effects of Problem Complexity upon Problem Solution Efficiency in Different Communication Nets," *Journal of Experimental Psychology* 47 (1954), 211–217; and Harold J. Leavitt, *Managerial Psychology*, 2nd ed. (Chicago: University of Chicago Press, 1964).

Figure 15-3
BASIC
COMMUNICATION
NETWORKS

Circle   Chain   Y   Wheel

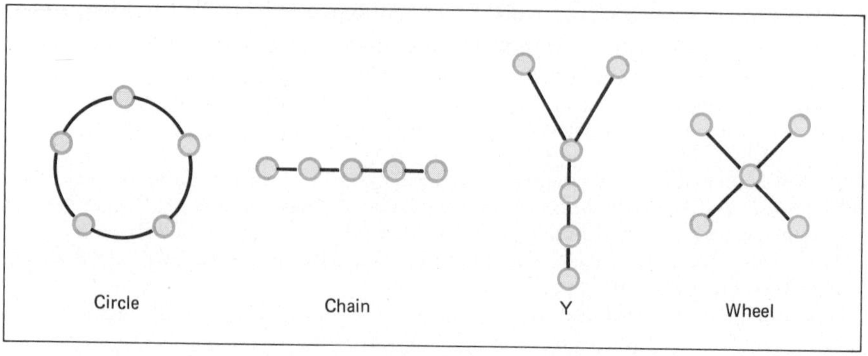

COMMUNICATION NETWORKS CAN ALSO DISTORT MESSAGES

SOURCE: *The New Yorker* (February 8, 1982), p. 39. Drawing by Ziegler; © 1982 The New Yorker Magazine, Inc.

by group members. The combined analytical effort is useful for the more complex arithmetical problem, whereas it does not help in solving the simple, coordinating card problem.

Members of the circle also tend to be more satisfied than the members of the other groups. This is simply due to the fact that they know more about what is going on; the members of the chain, Y, and wheel tend to be less knowledgeable. These experiments have several implications for those interested in choosing communication patterns that will result in high productivity and/or high satisfaction.

COMMITTEES

Committees are a special type of group that typically includes management. *Committees* are groups of people who render decisions or offer advice to management. One study showed that managers spend an average of three and a half hours a week in committee meetings and that 94 percent of large firms and 64 percent of small firms use formal committees.[18]

Often a committee of executives from several departments is formed to solve coordination problems. Of course, these people could be polled by their supervisor for their individual opinions or information, but bringing them together in an advisory or decision-making group has communication benefits.

One benefit is the error-correcting nature of committees.[19] An individual working alone can waste time following up a bad or mistaken idea. But a committee increases the chance that someone will spot the mistake and point it out. Conversely, a committee also offers support for good ideas. An individual alone

Committees are groups of people who render decisions or offer advice to management.

[18] Alan Filley, "Committee Management: Guidelines from Social Science Research," *California Management Review* (Fall 1970), p. 13.
[19] Discussed in Peter M. Blau and W. Richard Scott, *Formal Organizations: A Comparative Approach* (San Francisco: Chandler, 1962), pp. 118–119.

might ignore a good idea, but someone in a group might spot the idea and encourage further work on it.

Other communication benefits of committees include better understanding of the eventual solution and the enthusiasm generated to support it.[20] Being involved in a discussion of a problem gives an individual a better knowledge of its solution than if a decision were made independently by the person's supervisor. The better one understands a decision, the more likely he or she is to support and carry it out correctly.

There are also communication disadvantages in committees. Quite often, the members of committees come from different levels in the organization, and these status differences pose a threat to effective communications.[21] Suppose a marketing manager, a plant manager, and a vice-president of finance are brought together to work out the details for introducing a new product. Then add the company's president. One possible effect of such organizational status differences is that communication may be restricted. Another possibility is the tendency to flatter superiors, to avoid contradictions, and to tell the higher-ranked executives things they want to hear. This distorts the error-correcting and supportive function of the committee.

Finally, even the enthusiasm caused by exchange and involvement can be offset by status differences. Many times committees can be used by a superior to give subordinates a feeling of participation when actually the manager is simply selling a decision already made privately. Nelson Rockefeller's statement at the beginning of this chapter illustrates this situation. Even if the executive's intent is genuine, employees are often suspicious: Whether real or imagined, status differences often can ruin communication in a committee.

Channels of Communication

Communication follows distinct channels. Some are formal channels like the chain of command in a military unit or a financial reporting system for a major corporation. But others are less structured and are often based on interpersonal relations among different employees. These are the informal channels of communication like the office grapevine. Both channels are important delivery vehicles for the firm's communication system. And management must know how to deal with both if that system is to remain viable.

Communications can come from a variety of sources. Henry Mintzberg's observational study of a week's work for five chief executive officers recorded each piece of incoming and outgoing mail as well as verbal contacts. The organizations represented were a consumer goods firm, a technology outfit, a consulting organization, a school system, and a hospital. Figure 15-4 illustrates the diversity of these contacts. Mintzberg put it this way: "The manager does not leave

---

[20] A study showing this can be found in Kurt Lewin, "Forces Behind Food Habits and Methods of Change," *Bulletin of National Resources Council* (1943), 35–65.
[21] Blau and Scott, *Formal Organizations*, pp. 121–124.

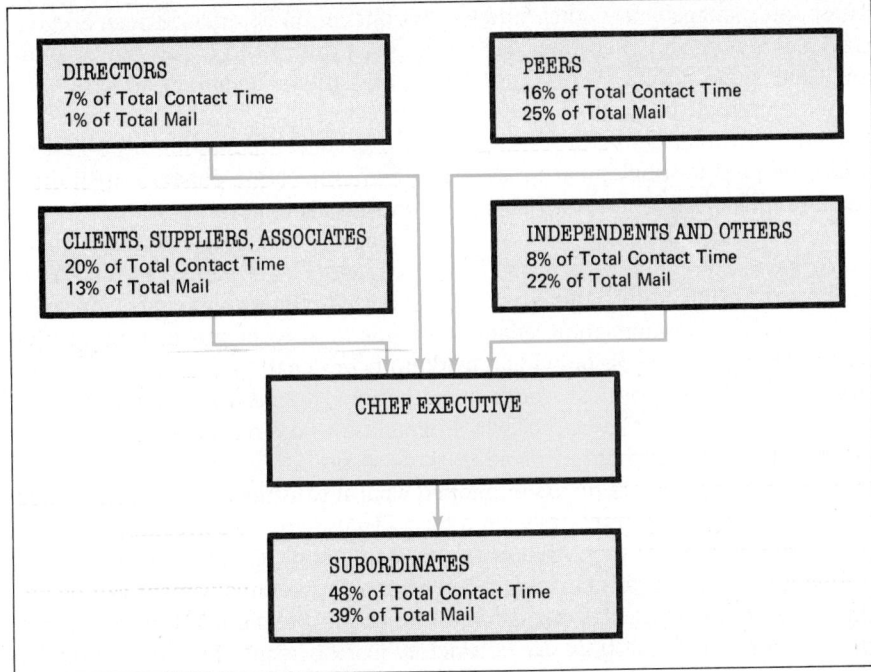

Figure 15-4
THE CHIEF
EXECUTIVE
CONTACTS

SOURCE: Reprinted by permission of the Harvard Business Review. Exhibit from "The Manager's Job: Folklore and Fact" by Henry Mintzberg (July–August 1975). Copyright © 1975 by the President and Fellows of Harvard College; all rights reserved.

meetings or hang up the telephone in order to get back to work. In large part communication *is* his work."[22]

Formal Channels

The formal communication channel follows the chain of command from the president of a company to a vice-president to a division manager to a department manager to a supervisor to a worker. The *formal communication channel* is the pattern of communication within an organization approved and recognized by management. Communication flows both ways along these channels. Noise is a special problem. The more links in a channel, the more opportunity for noise to occur. Direct, person-to-person communication is rare, except for subordinates and their immediate superiors. If it is critical that an undistorted message be transmitted undistorted by noise, then the links should be eliminated by direct communication.

The formal communication channel is the pattern of communication approved and recognized by management.

THE NEED TO MULTIPLEX

Many communications become distorted. This problem is particularly common in upward communication flows, where the natural tendency is for subordinates

---

[22] Henry Mintzberg, "The Manager's Job: Folklore and Fact," *Harvard Business Review* (July–August 1975), pp. 49–61. Part of this article is condensed from *The Nature of Managerial Work* (New York: Harper & Row, 1973).

to support management's edicts and to filter out contradictory evidence. So powerful is this tendency that managers often find it difficult to get an honest opinion from subordinates. Worse still, some executives do not even seek hard, candid appraisals from subordinates.

One way a manager can try to increase the accuracy of communication is by *multiplexing,* the supplementing of formal communication channels with other channels. This can be accomplished in several ways.

Multiplexing is the supplementing of formal communication channels with other channels.

General Electric, American Can, Westinghouse, Pittsburgh National Bank, Ford, Xerox, Prudential, Control Data, Ashland Oil, Union Carbide, A. B. Dick, and Spring Mills, among others, have used climate surveys to multiplex their regular communication channels. *Climate surveys* are communication tools that concentrate on individual work units or departments. Participants are surveyed about their work attitudes and situations; the information is tabulated; and a feedback session is held at which conclusions are reached. Both management and subordinates are involved in these sessions.[23]

Climate survey examines work attitudes and situations within individual work units or departments with the idea of improving communication.

New England Telephone has developed what it calls the *upward communications program.* The firm invites its employees to use *private lines*—company terminology for anonymous written or telephone requests, comments, suggestions, or questions directed to management. The company employs three people full time as a coordinating staff for its communication program. Employees report that the answers to questions are satisfactory in 79 percent of the cases. In addition to getting answers to employee concerns, New England Telephone has also set up various employee task teams to study employee complaints and then forward recommendations to an interdepartmental middle management group. The firm reports that over 85 percent of the task team recommendations are adopted by management. New England Telephone's communication program is successful because it is backed by management action.[24]

There are a variety of other multiplexing techniques. Suggestion systems can prompt employees to offer cost savings suggestions that might be delayed or thwarted by the formal communication channels.[25] Top management sometimes goes on sales calls with marketing representatives to augment the customer information they receive through regular channels. Employees may communicate in a committee differently than if they were reporting to their superior individually. And staff officers can be used to extend the number of viewpoints presented to management. Grievance and auditing procedures are other multiplexing alternatives.

[23] "A Productive Way to Vent Employee Gripes," *Business Week* (October 16, 1978), pp. 170–171.

[24] Bruce Harriman, "Up and Down the Communications Ladder," *Harvard Business Review* (September–October 1974), pp. 143–151. Updated by New England Telephone in 1982.

[25] A good discussion of suggestion systems is contained in Vincent G. Reuter, "Suggestion Systems: Utilization, Evaluation, and Implementation," *California Management Review* (Spring 1977), pp. 78–79.

INFORMATION OVERLOAD

With all the information flowing in from the chain of command and from other channels, the manager can become victim to *information overload*.[26] An overloaded manager might react by backlogging messages during busy periods and then catching up in slow periods. He or she may also have to set up a system of priorities, trying to deal only with information upon which authority to act exists. More important messages could then be forwarded to supervisors, and less important ones to staff or subordinates.

Not all reactions to overload are good ones, and the alert manager should be careful if he or she is to avoid communication problems. An ineffective manager might, for instance, feel so overwhelmed that all work is ignored in an attempt to escape from the pressure. Or the manager might lump messages into categories and give them general responses, such as a form letter. This, of course, runs the risk of alienating the receivers. Then, too, the manager can simply delay any response to a message, assuming that anyone who really wants to talk about an important matter will communicate again—and they probably will, with much irritation and a problem that has grown critical in the meantime.

Some companies have taken actions to alleviate the information overloads that face their managers. United Technologies and Procter & Gamble, for example, have both prohibited memos that exceed one page in length.[27] Another recent example was provided by Alaska Airlines. Faced with an avalanche of applications for thirty to forty flight attendant positions, the company decided to charge an application fee to offset its processing and analysis expenses. Over 5,000 people paid Alaska Airlines $10 each to put in an application.[28]

FORMAL COMMUNICATION CHANNELS SHOULD BE FLEXIBLE

When studying formal communication channels, it is important to consider the relationship between communication and such organizational matters as departmentation, line–staff relations, and the span of management. As far as departmentation is concerned, communication should be flexible; that is, the manager can arrange to increase or decrease communications practically at will. They are not a fixed, constant factor.

Suppose a manufacturing department and a research department both report

[26] Reactions to overload are explored in James G. Miller, "Information Input, Overload, and Psychopathology," *American Journal of Psychiatry* (February 1960), pp. 695–704.
[27] Reported in "How to Be Great," *Time* (November 15, 1982), p. 68. This article is based on Thomas J. Peter and Robert H. Waterman, Jr., *In Search of Excellence* (New York: Harper & Row, 1982).
[28] Carol Picci, "Filing Fee: Company Charges Job Applicants $10," *The Seattle Times* (January 14, 1983), p. 1-B.

to a certain manager. These two departments probably have some dealings with each other that require them to communicate, and yet each also has a separate, specialized job to do: one to produce products, the other to develop products.

The amount of communication that should exist between manufacturing and research depends on how important their coordination is compared with their specialization. If they communicate openly, their coordination may go smoothly, but they may start thinking so much alike that they are not as specialized as they should be. If their communication is limited, they may not work as well together, but they will think and act differently in performing their specific jobs.

The manager can vary the communication pattern between departments to suit a particular purpose. To produce optimal coordination, the departments might be physically located near each other to allow anyone in one department to contact anyone in the other conveniently. To promote specialization, the departments might be located in different buildings, with interaction limited to messengers or committee meetings.

This same lesson applies to line and staff operations. If staff assistants communicate freely with department managers, they will probably come to work closely with them. However, this may interfere with their ability to give objective advice to departments, and so management may want them to remain separate from operating departments. Open communication between staff and operating departments also can create confusion as to who really is in charge. Many managers will not let staff communicate too freely with operating departments simply to preserve their own authority.

Communication is also dramatically affected by changes in a manager's span of management or control. When a manager has many subordinates reporting directly, communication with each is possible but infrequent. The span of control can be narrowed by adding in a couple of supervisors between the manager and subordinates, with only the supervisors reporting directly to the manager. Communication with the supervisors should be effective, but another link has been added to the communication chain. However, the supervisors in turn should be able to have communication with the other subordinates, because there are relatively few of them per supervisor.

One interesting recent development is the computer-based executive information system now used by some fifty companies. This system allows top management to access the firm's primary data bases directly. Westinghouse, Termo Electron Corp., Banco Internacional de Colombia, and Northwest Industries are examples of companies with such capability. Executive information systems permit general management to call up and analyze data without forwarding their requests for information to lower ranked personnel. This system gives top management the ability to immediately query and criticize what is happening at the operational level.

While chief executives may approve of their newfound power, divisional management often worries about excessive querying and top management's second-guessing operational decisions. Few parties, however, will deny that executive information systems have greatly expanded the flexibility of management communications.[29]

Informal Channels

Formal communication channels are planned by managers. They are designed to accomplish the tasks for which these managers have responsibility. But no manager can anticipate every single communication need. As a result, not all communication needs are programmed by management. This unplanned type of communication, which can be helpful to management, is part of the organization's total communication system. The *informal communication channel* refers to communication patterns existing within the organization that are outside of or in addition to management-approved channels.

Much informal communication is not directly related to getting the job done, however. Employees talk to each other for a wide variety of reasons. They can say things to each other that they might be reluctant to say to a superior. Infor-

Informal communication channels are communication patterns that exist outside of or in addition to management-approved channels.

[29] Mary Bralove, "Some Chief Executives Bypass, and Irk, Staffs in Getting Information," *The Wall Street Journal* (January 12, 1983), pp. 1, 20.

OPEN OFFICES: A BOON OR A BUST TO ORGANIZATIONAL COMMUNICATION?

The open office concept—where five-and-a-half-foot-tall partitions and modular furniture replace traditional walled offices—is often promoted partially on the basis of better communication among employees. Research studies are often cited to support this argument. Open offices also offer considerable space and dollar savings. Approximately 10 percent of all U.S. office space employs the open concept. Most managers and employees are content with the new arrangement.

But not all! In fact, there is growing evidence that many workers are dissatisfied with the open offices. A Michigan secretary reports that the new plan has cut her productivity because of the level of employee communication that is generated. Fashion buyers at Paul Harris Stores, Inc., in Indianapolis complained that the open office system was inappropriate for people who were on the phone constantly. The buyers were returned to walled offices with doors. And there was a rebellion among some supervisors at the Department of Health, Education, and Welfare when they discovered that they were to move into new open offices. The supervisors refused, and their superiors abandoned the plan. Regardless of the cost savings and the alleged improvements in communication, it is clear that at least some people object to the open office configuration.

THE MORAL OF THE STORY: More communication is not always improved communication!

SOURCE: "The Trouble with Open Offices," *Business Week* (August 7, 1978), pp. 84–85, 88. Reprinted from the August 7, 1978, issue of *Business Week* by special permission. © 1980 by McGraw-Hill, Inc.

There are two sorts of communication within the firm: formal and informal. While the significance of formal communication processes has long been recognized, the value of understanding and using informal communication was until recently widely underestimated. In the early 1950s, however, Keith Davis began publishing the results of his research on informal communication processes. Through his analysis of the corporate grapevine, he was able to draw some important conclusions as to how management can put the grapevine to best use and most appropriately deal with its negative attributes.

Davis, who was born in 1918, received his MBA from the University of Texas at Austin in 1941 and his Ph.D. from Ohio State University in 1952. From Indiana University, where he served as professor of management from 1951 to 1958, he moved to Tempe, Arizona, to chair Arizona State University's Department of Management from 1958 to 1962. Author of many publications—including numerous scholarly articles as well as the widely read books *Human Behavior at Work* and, with Robert L. Blomstrom, *Business and Society*—Davis continues his professional career at Arizona State, specializing in management, organizational behavior, the grapevine, and social issues that affect management.

The initial work Davis did on the grapevine took the form of a study conducted at one company, a manufacturer of leather goods with approximately 67 management people and 600 other employees. In order to trace the tendrils of the company's grapevine, Davis developed "ecco analysis," a technique for determining the sources of informal communications. In the course of this first study, he identified several characteristics of the grapevine: it was fast; it could be quite selective—so much so that entire groups of employees might be isolated from it; for the most part, it operated within the workplace, not in social settings outside work. Also, somewhat surprisingly, levels of activity on the grapevine seemed to correlate positively with levels of activity in the formal communications system.

mal communication channels also allow employees to reduce the pressures of the job or to relieve boredom. Then, too, employees communicate with each other for social and other interpersonal reasons. Informal conversation can make employees more satisfied with their work environment. This can pay for itself in improved attendance, reduced tardiness, and less frequent job transfers.

THE GRAPEVINE

The grapevine is a term sometimes used by managers to refer to the informal communication channel.

Informal communication often appears to be costly for the organization, and yet in fact it can be beneficial. Managers, who are sometimes leary of the informal communication channel, label it the *grapevine*.[30]

Keith Davis is the acknowledged expert on grapevines within organizations. Davis reports that the four primary features of grapevines are

1. *Speed of transmission.* The grapevine is widely recognized as an extremely fast communication channel.

[30] A general discussion of the grapevine appears in David L. Kurtz and Lawrence A. Klatt, "The 'Grapevine' as a Management Tool," *Akron Business and Economic Review* (Winter 1970), pp. 20–23.

Davis also found here that information is usually transmitted to clusters of individuals. Only a few sources supply many receivers in informal, or grapevine, communication.

While business executives have often viewed the grapevine as a weed to be suffered or eradicated, Davis has taken a different stance. This informal system of communication, he asserts, serves many purposes and should be considered a positive asset. In his view its existence represents "the deep psychological need of people to talk about their jobs and their company as a central life interest." Thus, a withering grapevine indicates a flagging employee esprit de corps. In addition, managers can use the grapevine to communicate matters that would be inappropriate to incorporate into a formal communication—the mood of a given superior, for example. An informal communication system also provides managers with information on employee attitudes and feelings. For all these reasons, Davis maintains, it is to the manager's advantage to cultivate the grapevine carefully.

Rumor, of course, is the part of the vine that sours corporate executives. While Davis emphasizes that his research shows that between 75 and 95 percent of grapevine information is essentially correct, he also acknowledges the negative role that rumor can play. To quash a troublesome rumor, he advocates formal communications of the relevant truth—without direct reference to the rumor itself.

Davis believes managers should view the grapevine as an important ingredient in corporate affairs, one requiring constant monitoring and refinement. In his own words: "To integrate the grapevine's interests with those of the formal organization, they must listen to it, study it, learn who its leaders are, how it operates, and what information it carries."

Sources

Keith Davis, "The Care and Cultivation of the Corporate Grapevine," *Dun's Review* (July 1973), pp. 44–47.

"Cut Those Rumors Down to Size," *Supervisory Management* (June 1975), pp. 2–6.

"Management Communication and the Grapevine," *Harvard Business Review* (September–October 1953), pp. 43–49.

Personal communication, *Dictionary of International Biography*, 1976, s.v., "Davis, Keith."

2. *Degree of selectivity.* Davis' study found that the grapevine can be a discrete communication channel, protecting confidential information. This conclusion differs from the traditional view of grapevine communications.
3. *Locale of operation.* The grapevine functions primarily within the workplace and during work hours.
4. *Relation to formal communication.* Davis concluded that the grapevine usually operates, or does not operate, jointly with the formal channel. The two systems supplement each other.

Four types of informal communication chains are identified by Davis: single strand, gossip, probability, and cluster. They are shown in Figure 15-5. In the *single strand* chain, A passes information to B who repeats it to C and so on. Considerable distortion and filtering can occur in this communication channel. In the case of *gossip*, one sender attempts to communicate a message to everyone. Random communication is the rule in the *probability chain*. A communicates with others randomly, and the chain is then continued on a similar basis. The *cluster chain* may be the most common, according to Davis. Here, A selectively tells some others. But not all of these repeat the message to others. And

Figure 15-5
TYPES OF
GRAPEVINES

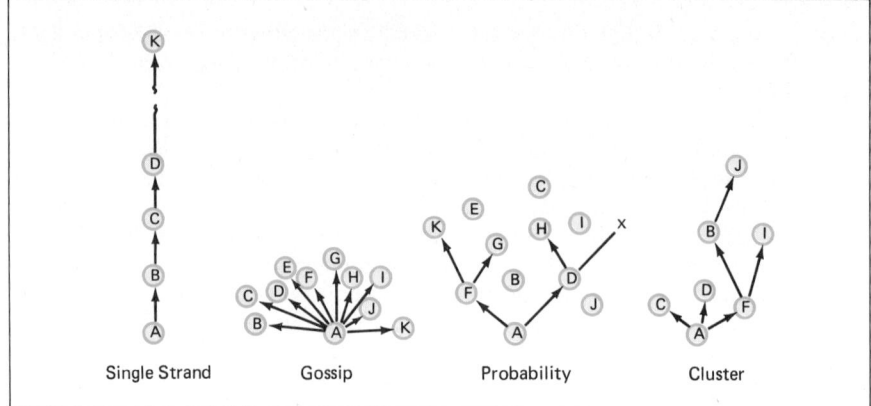

not all of those receiving the information at the third level will pass it on.[31]

New managers sometimes try to destroy the grapevine by forbidding people to communicate this way, disciplining them for it, and even transferring employees. Admittedly, the grapevine sometimes spreads false, anxiety-producing rumors. Management is rightfully concerned about rumor, but attempts to destroy the grapevine are probably inappropriate. In the first place, it is a near impossibility. In the second place, if the grapevine is understood, its accuracy can be improved.

One study revealed that rumors proliferate when people face unclear situations on matters that are important to them.[32] It is not likely that a rumor will be spread as to whether a male superior's wife is pregnant. After all, what does it matter? But if the superior is a female, rumors about her possible pregnancy might abound. If she *were* pregnant, the manager might take an extended leave of absence or even leave her position. This would have a direct impact on her subordinates. Similar situations occur when it is rumored that a supervisor or manager is looking for another position or is about to be promoted or fired.

Management must realize that such matters are important to employees and that it is best to provide them with the facts. The female manager who thinks her pregnancy is strictly a personal matter and refuses to answer questions will probably become the victim of erroneous rumor. Subordinates may begin to resist her authority. She should discreetly provide someone who is active in the grapevine with accurate information insofar as the future management of the department is concerned, the issue about which the employees are really concerned. This will result in the truth being spread as quickly as rumor.

[31] Keith Davis, "Management Communication and the Grapevine," *Harvard Business Review* (September–October 1953), pp. 43–49.

[32] Dorwin Cartwright, Kathleen Barber, Juliet Fleischel, Josephine Gottsdanker, Annette Kaysen, Gloria Leavitt, and Leon Festinger, "A Study of a Rumor: Its Origin and Spread," *Human Relations* (August 1948), pp. 483–485. An excellent discussion of rumor also appears in Keith Davis, *Human Behavior at Work*, 5th ed. (New York: McGraw-Hill, 1976), pp. 268–270.

Rumors are a fact of life in most organizations. But effective communications can alleviate most of their destructive aspects. Here are some classical rumors. *All are untrue*, although many readers will have heard at least one of them.

Eastern Airlines Tristar jets are haunted by the ghosts of dead crew members. The crew members died in a 1972 crash in the Everglades. The rumor circulated in 1975 and some pilots and flight attendants refused to fly Tristars.

Burt Reynolds will pay for your long-distance calls. Burt supposedly won a $2 million lawsuit and decided to celebrate by allowing the public to use his telephone credit card number. Several phony credit card numbers circulated and $110,000 in calls were made before Burt squelched the rumor.

There are people in the Himalayas who live 100 years or more on a diet of berries and goat cheese. Several years ago, photographers and reporters journeyed to the mountains to ask the Hunza tribesmen their ages. The tribesmen answered in a snap: 105, 115, 121, etc. They became famous worldwide. They made it into the encyclopedias. But then a discovery was made. Yes, they looked old. But that's because they suffered from malnutrition. They felt old, but they were actually in their 40s. Moral: Don't eat goat cheese and berries or you'll feel like you're 100.

Soda can tabs can buy time on a kidney machine. An oldie but goodie, it recently cropped up again in California. Supposedly, an aluminum company had agreed to donate one minute of time on a kidney dialysis machine for each tab collected. Hundreds of thousands of the worthless tabs were collected before the hoax was discovered.

Now . . . once and for all . . . none of the above are true!

SOURCE: From Jeffrey Zaslow, "The Great Rumors of Our Time," *The Orlando Sentinel* (November 15, 1981), pp. 1-F, 2-F, 3-F.

THE RUMOR HALL OF FAME

Communication and Motivation

One of the basic practices of a people-oriented style of leadership is the participation of subordinates in decision making. The people-oriented manager uses two-way communication to learn of employee viewpoints. Subordinates' involvement should result in a better decision, but the real payoff may be in areas of motivation.

When employees are involved in a decision, they feel a vested interest in seeing that this decision is correct. As a result they are likely to work harder to implement the decision than if it were merely a managerial directive; two-way communication can be satisfying in and of itself, and it can make subordinates more confident in what they are doing.

Improved production is often a result of employees' participation in decision making, and usually the motivational factors are given credit for the improvement. Still, open communication could account for the improvement for other reasons. When people freely discuss a problem, their understanding of it improves. It could be that increased productivity is a result simply of seeing the problem more clearly and understanding the decision more fully. A large part of the improvement might have occurred even if the motivational factors were not present.

The distinction between the effects of motivation and clarity is rarely made. It is almost impossible to separate the two effects to assess which one, if either, is more important. The manager should not always assume that motivation is most relevant. Executives should avoid efforts to motivate people when that is not the problem but instead put more time into finding ways to make their employees' jobs more understandable.

Communication and Leadership

Managers, as leaders, must know how to communicate with others in their organizations. Leaders must cause communication to happen. But it is also true that communication effectiveness may cause people to become leaders.

Leaders are sometimes leaders simply because they initiate more interaction than do other people. Studies of small groups have shown that some people in a group are prone to communicate with everyone else in the group. Others, however, communicate only with these busy communicators. Simply because they communicate more, the high participators are valued more and are more often seen to be the group leader by its members.[33]

Taking the initiative is only one effect of communication on leadership. People also become leaders because they are in a position that makes them privy to important information. Secretaries sometimes have strong power bases because they are aware of information that others are anxious to get.

This positional effect was evident in the experiments mentioned earlier involving the circle, chain, Y, and wheel communication networks.[34] When their tasks were done, each of these groups was asked to identify a leader. In the wheel the person at the axis was chosen; in the Y the person at the crux was chosen; in the chain the person in the middle was chosen; the group arranged as a circle was unable to select a leader.

[33] This is discussed in John W. Thibaut and Harold H. Kelley, *The Social Psychology of Groups* (New York: Wiley, 1959), p. 39.
[34] See note 17.

Summary

Communication is the transfer of information via an understandable message from a sender to a receiver. While effective communication can solve many management problems, ineffective communication can cre-

ate many additional problems. Communication can occur in three ways: speaking, writing, or nonverbal methods. The basic communication model consists of a sender, message, medium, and receiver. This basic one-way communication format can be expanded to a two-way system by adding feedback to the original model.

There are various roadblocks to effective organizational communication. These include poor timing, inadequate information, inappropriate channel, noise, selective perception, premature evaluation, emotions, and beliefs. Many roadblocks can be avoided by the following management actions:

1. Expand the basic communication model to include feedback.
2. Improve listening skills.
3. Practice empathy.
4. Follow basic communication guidelines.
   a. Eliminate ambiguities.
   b. Use proper follow-up.
   c. Avoid negativism.
   d. Watch the timing of messages.

Not all organizational communications involve single individuals. Much of it is group communications. Basic concepts in group communications include

Cohesiveness: This is the net impact of the forces acting to hold the group together. Homan's interaction hypothesis states that if one assumes compatible goals and needs, communication among people will lead to a mutual liking, and this will generate more communication, and so on.

Conforming to group norms: All groups attempt to enforce group norms by using the communication system against deviants. The end result may be that the group will ostracize those who refuse to abide by group norms.

Communication networks: Four basic communication networks are the circle, chain, Y, and wheel. Each has certain strengths and weaknesses for solving given problems.

Committees: These are a special type of group that generally includes managers. Benefits of committees include error correction, support for good ideas, and the motivational benefits of participation. A disadvantage is possible distortion caused by status differences of members.

Formal channels of communication are the patterns of communication within an organization approved and recognized by management. Since noise is sometimes a problem, management needs to multiplex, or supplement channels with other communication links. Information overload is another problem for management. The need for channel flexibility is also present.

Informal channels of communication are those communication patterns existing within the organization that are outside of or in addition to management-approved formal channels. These are sometimes labeled the *grapevine.* Management should not view the grapevine negatively. It can serve as a useful adjunct to formal communication channels.

Chapter 15 concludes with a brief discussion of the relationship between communication and motivation and between communication and leadership.

REVIEW EXERCISES

1. Define the following terms: (a) communication (b) body language (c) noise (d) cognitive dissonance (e) rationalizing (f) feedback (g) empathy (h) Homan's interaction hypothesis (i) committee (j) formal communication channel (k) multiplexing (l) climate surveys (m) informal communication channel (n) grapevine.

2. What is meant by *communication?*

3. Explain the communication model.

4. What are the roadblocks to effective organizational communication? How might a manager avoid some of these problems?

5. Outline the basic concepts of organizational communication.

6. Discuss formal channels of communication.

7. Discuss informal channels of communication.

8. Review Keith Davis' research on the grapevine.

9. Relate communication to motivation.

10. Relate communication to leadership.

ASSIGNMENTS/ PROBLEMS/ DISCUSSION QUESTIONS

1. Borg-Warner Educational Systems reports that 50 percent of all adult reading material consists of just 824 words! These same words account for 75 percent of all elementary reading material.* If so relatively few words are used, why is communication such a difficult subject?

2. One consultant reports that managers typically evaluate communication within their departments as more effective than those within the total organization.† Discuss the possible reasons for this reported difference.

3. Trace the last rumor you heard at school or at work. Relate what you discover to the discussion of the grapevine in this chapter.

4. Discuss the open office concept and its role in organizational communication.

5. Keep a diary of your communication for one day. Include mail, telephone conversations, and personal contacts. Then prepare a report on what you learned about how you communicate. Compare your communication patterns to the Mintzberg research reported in this chapter.

* Reported in "Reading Uses 824 Key Words," *Detroit News* (January 25, 1978), p. 6-F (UPI story).
† See Donald L. Kirkpatrick, "Communications: Everybody Talks About It, but . . . ," *Personnel Administrator* (January 1978), p. 46.

A MANAGERIAL INCIDENT

Communication Studies Are Common in the Federal Government

The Government's Permanent Conference on Printing decreed in 1921 that, to save money, federal stationery should measure 8 in. by 10½ in., in contrast to the private-industry standard of 8½ in. by 11 in. Bureaucrats have been having second thoughts about the matter ever since.

The Bureau of the Budget reported in 1957 that the savings from switching to a uniform size (i.e., 8½ by 11) would be "marginal." A 1970 study by the Bureau of Standards assessed what it called "paper sizes annoyance factors." A subsequent study by the Bureau of Standards argued that both Government and business should switch to 7¾ in. by 11 in., on the ground that this would be the most esthetically pleasing.

In 1972 the General Services Administration weighed in with yet another report, entitled "Economic Factors Associated with Paper Sizes." It claimed, among other things, that the larger size would reduce by 5% the number of times a secretary needs a second page to finish a letter. Each second page, it went on, costs 4.6¢ (including charges for the secretary's retirement benefits and depreciation of the chair and the typewriter).

Finally, the Congressional Joint Committee on Printing concluded that switching to 8½ in.-by-11 in. stationery would result in a net savings of several million dollars and ordered that the change be made by Jan. 1, 1980. On hearing the news, one straight-faced bureaucrat in the Government Printing Office said of his colleagues' reaction to the news: "Some people think that this issue has been inadequately studied."

SOURCE: Reprinted by permission from *Time*, The Weekly Newsmagazine; copyright Time, Inc., 1979.

Questions and Problems

1. The change to 8½-by-11-inch stationery did go into effect on schedule. Why do you think it took the government fifty-nine years to resolve this matter?

2. Relate this managerial incident to the material found in this chapter.

Case IV-I

LORDSTOWN PLANT OF GENERAL MOTORS: WAS THE WORK FORCE, THE COMPANY, OR THE JOB ITSELF THE CAUSE OF THE VEGA PROBLEM?

INTRODUCTION

In December 1971 the management of the Lordstown Plant was very much concerned about the unusually high rate of defective Vegas coming off the assembly line. For the previous several weeks the lot, which had a capacity of 2,000 cars, had been filled with Vegas waiting for rework before they could be shipped out to the dealers around the country.

The management was particularly disturbed by the fact that many of the defects were not the kinds normally expected in the assembly production of automobiles.[1] There were countless numbers of Vegas with broken windshields, slashed upholstery, broken ignition keys, bent signal levers, broken rear-view mirrors, or carburetors clogged with washers. There were cases in which, as the plant manager put it, "the whole engine blocks passed forty men without any work done on them."

Since then the incident in the Lordstown plant has been much publicized in news media, drawing

---

[1] The normal defect rate requiring rework was fluctuating between 1 and 2 percent at the time.

By Professor Hak-Chong Lee, International Management Institute, Federation of Korean Industries, Seoul, Korea. Copyright 1974 by Hak-Chong Lee. This case was developed for instructional purposes from published sources and interviews with the General Motors Assembly Division officials in Warren, Michigan, and Lordstown, Ohio. The case was read and minor corrections were made by the Public Relations Office of the GMAD. However, the author is solely responsible for the content of the case. The author appreciates the cooperation of General Motors. He also appreciates the suggestions of Professor Anthony Athos of Harvard and Mr. John Grix of General Motors, which improved the case. Adapted and reprinted by permission of the author.

public interest. It has been also frequently discussed in the classroom and in the academic circles. While some people viewed the event as a "young workers' revolt," others reacted to it as simply a "labor problem." Some viewed it as "worker sabotage," and others called it an "industrial Woodstock." This case describes some background and important incidents leading to this much publicized and discussed event.

The General Motors Corp. is the nation's largest manufacturer. The corporation is a leading example of an industrial organization that has achieved organizational growth and success through decentralization. The philosophy of decentralization has been one of the most valued traditions at General Motors from the days of Alfred Sloan in the 1930s through Charles Wilson's and Harlow Curtice's tenures in the 1950s and up to recent years.

Under decentralized management each of the company's car divisions—Cadillac, Buick, Oldsmobile, Pontiac, and Chevrolet—was given maximum autonomy in the management of its manufacturing and marketing operations. The assembly operations were no exception, each division managing its own assembly work. The car bodies built by Fisher Body were assembled in various locations under maximum control and coordination between Fisher Body and each car division.

In the mid-1960s, however, the decentralization in divisional assembly operations was subject to critical review. At the divisional level, the company was experiencing serious problems of worker absenteeism and increasing cost with declines in quality and productivity. They were reflected in the overall profit margins, which declined from 10 percent to 7 percent in the late 1960s. The autonomy of the divided management in body manufacturing and assembly operations, in separate locations in many cases, became questionable under the declining profit situation.

In light of these developments, General Motors

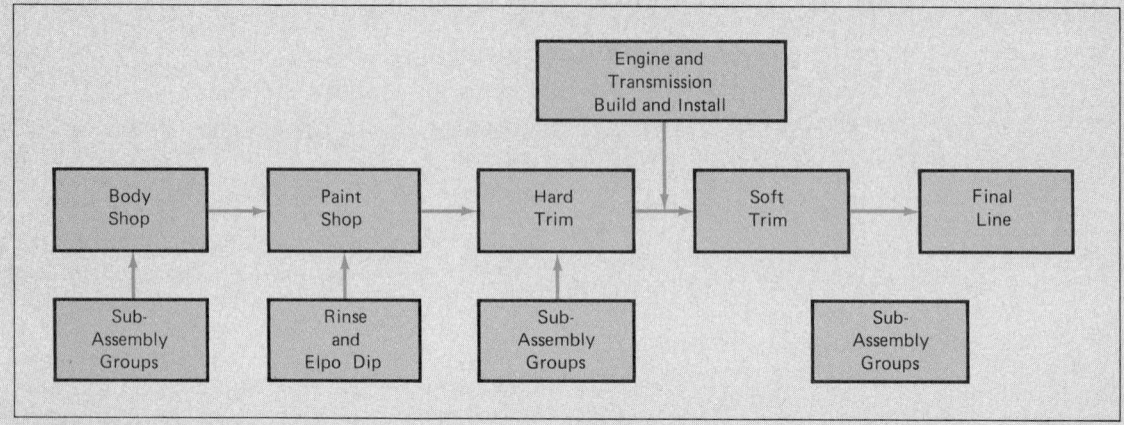

Exhibit 1
GMAD—FLOWCHART OF MAJOR ASSEMBLY OPERATIONS

began to consolidate some of the divided management of body and chassis assembly operations into a single management under the already existing General Motors Assembly Division (GMAD) in order to better coordinate the two operations. GMAD was given an overall responsibility to integrate the two operations in these instances and to see that the numerous parts and components going into the car assembly got to the right places in the right amounts at the right times (see Exhibit 1).[2]

THE GENERAL MOTORS ASSEMBLY DIVISION (GMAD)

GMAD was originally established in the mid 1930s, when the company needed an additional assembly plant to meet the increasing demand for Buick, Oldsmobile, and Pontiac automobiles. The demands for these cars were growing so much beyond the available capacity at the time that the

company began, for the first time, to build an assembly plant on the West Coast that could turn out all three lines of cars rather than an individual line. As this novel approach became successful, similar plants turning out a multiple line of cars were built in seven other locations in the East, South, and Midwest. In the 1960s the demand for Chevrolet production also increased, and some Buick-Oldsmobile-Pontiac plants began to assemble Chevrolet products. Accordingly, the name of the division was changed to GMAD in 1965.

In order to improve the quality and productivity, GMAD increased its control over the operations of body manufacturing and assembly. It reorganized jobs, launched programs to improve efficiency, and reduced the causes of defects that required repairs and rework. With many positive results attained under GMAD management, the company extended the single management concept to six more assembly locations in 1968 that had been run by the Fisher Body and Chevrolet Divisons. In 1971 GMAD further extended the concept to four additional Chevrolet-Fisher Body assembly facilities, consolidating the separate management under which the body and chassis assembly had been operating. One of these plants was the Lordstown plant.

This series of consolidations brought to eighteen the number of assembly plants operated by GMAD. In terms of total production, they were producing about 75 percent of all cars and 67 percent

[2] A typical assembly plant has five major assembly lines—hard trim, soft trim, body, paint, and final—supported by subassembly lines that feed to the main lines such components as engines, transmissions, wheels and tires, radiators, gas tanks, front and sheet metal, and scores of other items. In a typical GMAD assembly plant, the average vehicle on assembly lines has more than 5,500 items, with quality checks numbering 5 million in a sixteen-hour-a-day operation.

of trucks built by GM. Also in 1971 one of the plants under GMAD administration began building certain Cadillac models, thus involving GMAD in the production of automobiles for each of GM's five domestic car divisions as well as trucks for both Chevrolet and the GMC Truck and Coach Division.

THE LORDSTOWN COMPLEX

The Lordstown complex is located in Trumbull County in Ohio, about fifteen miles west of Youngstown and thirty miles east of Akron. It consists of a Vega assembly plant, a van-truck assembly plant, and a Fisher Body metal fabricating plant, occupying about 1,000 acres of land. GMAD, which operates the Vega and van-truck assembly plants, is also located in the Lordstown complex. The three plants are in the heart of the heavy industrial triangle of Youngstown, Akron, and Cleveland. With Youngstown as a center of steel production, Akron the home of the rubber industries, and Cleveland a major center for heavy manufacturing, the Lordstown complex commands a good strategic and logistic location for automobile assembly.

The original assembly plant was built in 1964–1966 to assemble Impalas. But in 1970 it was converted to assemble Vegas after extensive rearrangements. The van-truck assembly plant was constructed in 1969, and the Fisher Body metal fabricating plant was further added in 1970 to carry out stamping operations to produce sheet metal components used in Vega and van assemblies. In October 1971 the Chevrolet Vega and van-assembly plants and Fisher Body Vega assembly plants, which had been operating under separate management, were merged into a single jurisdiction of GMAD.

WORK FORCE AT THE LORDSTOWN PLANT

Over 11,400 employees worked in the Lordstown plant as of 1973. Approximately 6,000 people, of whom 5,500 were on an hourly payroll, worked in the Vega assembly plant. About 2,600 workers, 2,100 of them paid hourly, worked on the van-truck assembly. As members of the United Auto Workers Union, Local 1112, the workers com-

manded good wages and benefits. They started out on the line at about $5.00 an hour, got a ten-cent-an-hour raise within thirty days, and another ten cents after ninety days. Benefits came to $2.50 an hour.[3] The supplemental unemployment benefits virtually guaranteed the worker's wages throughout the year. If the worker was laid off, he got more than 90 percent of his wages for fifty-two weeks. The worker was also eligible for up to six weeks' leave for holidays, excused absence, or bereavement, and up to four weeks' vacation.

The work force at the plant was almost entirely made up of local people, with 92 percent coming from within a 20-mile radius. Lordstown itself is a small rural town of about 500 residents. A sizable city close to the plant is Warren, 5 miles away, which together with Youngstown supplies about two-thirds of the work force. The majority of the workers (57.5 percent) were married, 7.6 percent were homeowners, and 20.2 percent were buying their homes. Of those who did not own their homes (72 percent), over one-half were still living with their parents. The rest lived in rented houses or apartments.

The workers in the plant were generally young. Although various news media reported the average worker age as twenty-four years old, and in some parts of the plant as twenty-two years old, the company records show that the overall average worker age was somewhat above twenty-nine years old as of 1971–1972. The national average was forty-two years old. The work force at Lordstown was the second youngest among GM's twenty-five assembly plants around the country. The fact that the Lordstown plant was the GM's newest assembly plant may partly explain the relatively young work force.

The educational profile of the Lordstown workers indicates that only 22 percent had less than a high school education. Nearly two-thirds—62 percent—were high school graduates, and 16 percent were either college graduates or had attended college. Another 26 percent had attended trade school. The average education of 13.2 years made the Lordstown workers among the best educated in GM's assembly plants.

---

[3] At the time the average GM worker on the line earned $12,500 a year with fringe benefits of $3,000.

THE VEGA ASSEMBLY LINE

Conceived as a major competitor against the increasing influx of foreign cars, which were being produced at a labor rate as low as one-fourth the rate predominant in this country, the Vega was specifically designed with maximum production efficiency and economy in mind. For the initial stages of planning, the Vega was designed by a special task team whose sophisticated techniques included the use of computers in designing the outer skin of the car and making the tapes that form the dies. Computers were also used to match up parts, measure the stack tolerances, measure safety performance under head-on collision, and make all necessary corrections before the first 1971 model car was built. The 2,300-cubic-centimeter, all-aluminum, four-cyclinder engine was designed to give gas economy comparable to that of the foreign imports.

The Vega was also designed with the plant and the people in mind. As GM's newest plant, the Vega assembly plant was known as the "super plant" with the most modern and sophisticated design to maximize efficiency. It featured the newest engineering techniques and a variety of new power tools and automatic devices to eliminate much of the heavy lifting and physical labor. The line gave the workers easier access to the car body, reducing the amount of bending and crawling in and out required of workers at other plants around the country. The unitized body, easily assembled from large components like prefab housing, was lighter and had greater integrity. Most difficult and tedious tasks were eliminated or simplified, on-line variations of the job were minimized, and the most modern tooling and mechanization was used to the highest possible degree of reliability.

It was also the fastest moving assembly line in the industry. The average time per assembly job was thirty-six seconds, with a maximum of 100 cars rolling off the assembly line per hour for a daily production of 1,600 cars from two shift operations. The time cycle per job in other assembly plants averaged about fifty-five seconds. Although the high speed of the line did not necessarily imply greater work loads or job requirements, it was a part of the GM's attempt to maximize economy in

Vega assembly. The fact that the Vega was designed to have 43 percent fewer parts than a full-size car also helped the high-speed line and economy.

IMPACT OF GMAD AND REORGANIZATION IN THE LORDSTOWN PLANT

As stated previously the assembly operations at Lordstown had originally been run by Fisher Body and Chevrolet as two plants. There were two organizations, two plant managers, two unions, and two service organizations. The consolidation of the two organizations into a single operating system under GMAD in October 1971 was a difficult task requiring expensive reorganization and the need to deal with the consequences of manpower reduction, such as work slowdowns, worker discipline, grievances, and so forth.

As duplicating units such as production, maintenance, inspection, and personnel were consolidated, there was a problem of selecting the personnel to manage the new organization. There were chief inspectors, personnel directors, and production superintendents as well as production and service workers to be displaced or reassigned. Unions that had been representing their respective plants also had to go through reorganization. Union elections were held to merge the separate union committees at Fisher Body and Chevrolet into a single-union bargaining committee. This eliminated one full local union shop committee.

At the same time, GMAD launched an effort to bring production efficiency up to the levels found at other assembly plants. It included increasing job efficiency through reorganization and better coordination between the body and chassis assembly and in improving controls over product quality and worker absenteeism. This effort coincided with the plant's early operational stage, a time at which adjustments in line balance and work methods are required. Like other assembly plants, the Vega assembly plant was going through an initial period of diseconomy caused by suboptimal operations, imbalance in the assembly line, and somewhat redundant work force. According to management, line adjustments and work changes were a normal process in accelerating the assembly operations to the peak performance the plant had been designed for after the initial break-in and startup period.

As for job efficiency, GMAD initiated changes in those work sequences and work methods that were not well coordinated under the divided managements of body and chassis assembly. For example, previous to GMAD, Fisher Body had been delivering the car body complete with interior trim to the final assembly line, where often the workers soiled the front seats as they did further assembly operations. GMAD changed this practice so installment of the seats was one of the last operations in building the car. Fisher Body also had been delivering the car with a complete panel instrument frame, and it was difficult for the assembly workers to reach behind the frame to install the instrument panels. GMAD improved the job method so that the box containing the entire instrument panel was installed on the assembly line. Such improvements in job sequences and job methods resulted in savings in time and the number of workers required. Consequently, assembly times were cut down and/or the number of workers were reduced for some jobs.

GMAD also put strict control over worker absenteeism and the causes for defects; the reduction in absenteeism was expected to require fewer relief men, and the improvement in quality and reduced repair work were to require fewer repairmen. In implementing these changes, GMAD instituted a strong policy of dealing with worker slowdowns via strict disciplinary measures, including dismissal. It was rumored that inspectors and foremen passing defective cars would be fired on the spot.

Many workers were laid off as a result of the reorganization and job changes. The union claimed that as many as 700 workers were laid off. Management, on the other hand, put the layoff figure at 375 to which the union later conceded.[4] Although management claimed that the change in job se-

quence and method in some assembly work did not bring a substantial change in the overall speed or pace of the assembly line, the workers perceived the job change as "tightening" the assembly line. The union charged that GMAD brought a return of an old-fashioned line speedup and a "sweat-shop style" of management reminiscent of the 1930s, making the men do more work at the same pay. The workers blamed the "tightened" assembly line for the drastic increase in quality defects. As one worker commented, "That's the fastest line in the world. We have about forty seconds to do our job. The company adds one more thing and it can kill us. We can't get the stuff done on time and a car goes by. The company blames us for sabotage and shoddy work."

The number of worker grievances also increased drastically. Before GMAD took over, there were about 100 grievances in the plant. Since its takeover grievances had increased to 5,000, 1,000 of which were related to the charge that too much work had been added to the job. The worker resentment was particularly great in "towveyor" assembly and seat subassembly areas. The "towveyor" is the area in which engines and transmissions are assembled. Like seat subassembly there is a great concentration of workers working together in proximity. Also, these jobs are typically for beginning assemblers. Thus, the work crew in these areas tend to be younger and better educated.

The workers in the plant were particularly resentful of the company's strict policy in implementing the changes. They stated that the tougher the company became, the more they would stiffen their resistance, even though other jobs were scarce in the market. One worker said, "In some of the other plants where GMAD did the same thing, the workers were older and they took this. But, I've got twenty-five years ahead of me in this plant." Another worker commented, "I saw a woman running to keep pace with the fast line. I'm not going to run for anybody. There isn't anyone in that plant that is going to tell me to run." One foreman said, "The problem with the workers here is not so much that they don't want to work, but that they just don't want to take orders. They don't believe in any kind of authority."

While the workers were resisting management

---

[4] All of the workers who had been laid off were later reinstated as the plant needed additional workers to perform assembly jobs for such optional features to the Vega as vinyl tops, which were later introduced. In addition, some workers were put to work at the van-assembly plant.

orders, there were some indications that the first-line supervisors had not been adequately trained to perform satisfactory supervisory roles. The average supervisor at the time had fewer than three years' experience, and 20 percent of the supervisors had less than one year's experience. Typically, they were young, somewhat lacking in knowledge of the provisions of the union contract and other supervisory duties, and less than adequately trained to handle the workers in the threatening and hostile environment that was developing.

Significantly, the strong reactions of the workers were not due entirely to the organizational and job changes brought about by GMAD alone. Management noted that there were a significant number of worker reactions in areas in which the company hadn't changed anything at all. Management felt that the intense resentment was particularly due to the nature of the work force in Lordstown. The plant was not only made up of young people, but the work force also reflected the characteristics of "tough labor" in the steel, coal, and rubber industries in the surrounding communities. In fact, many of the workers came from families who made their living working in these industries. Management also noted that worker resistance had been much greater in the Lordstown plant than in other plants where similar changes had been made.

A good part of the young workers' resentment also seemed to stem from the unskilled and repetitive nature of the assembly work. One management official admitted that the company was facing a difficult task in getting workers to "take pride" in the product they were assembling. Many of them were benefiting from the company's tuition assistance plan by taking college-level courses in the evening. With this educated background, they obviously found that assembly work was not fulfilling their high work expectations. Also, the job market was tied up at the time, and they could neither find any meaningful jobs elsewhere nor, even if such jobs were found, could they afford to give up the good money and fringe benefits they were earning on their assembly line jobs. This made them frustrated, according to company officials.

Many industrial engineers were questioning whether the direction of management toward as-

sembly line work could continue. As the jobs became easier, simpler, and more repetitive and required less physical effort, there were less need for skill and increased monotony. The worker unrest indicated that they not only wanted to go back to the work pace prior to the "speedup" (pre-October pace) but also wanted the company to do something about the boring and meaningless assembly work. One worker commented, "The company has got to do something to change the job so that a guy can take an interest in the job. A guy can't do the same thing eight hours a day year after year. And it's got to be more than the company just saying to a guy, 'Okay, instead of six spots on the weld, you'll do five spots.'"

As the worker resentment mounted, the UAW Local 1112 decided in early January 1972 to consider possible authorization of a strike against the Lordstown plant to fight the job changes. In the meantime the union and management bargaining teams worked hard on worker grievances. They reduced the number of grievances from 5,000 to a few hundred, and management even indicated that it would restore some of the eliminated jobs. However, the bargaining failed to produce accord on the issues of seniority rights and shift preference, which were related to the wider issues of job changes and layoffs.

A vote was held in early February 1972. Nearly 90 percent of the workers came out to vote, the heaviest turnout in the history of the Local. With 97 percent of the votes supporting it, the workers went on strike in early March.

In March 1972, with the strike in effect, the management of the Lordstown plant was assessing the impact of GMAD and the resultant strike at the plant. It was estimated that the work disruption caused by worker resentment and slowdown had already cost the company 12,000 Vegas and 4,000 trucks, amounting to $45 million.

There had also been an amazing number of complaints from Chevrolet dealers, 6,000 in November alone, about the quality of the Vegas shipped to them. This was more than the complaints concerning all other assembly plants combined.

The strike in the Lordstown plant was expected to affect other plants. The plants at Tonawanda, New York, and at Buffalo were supplying parts for

Vega. Despite the costly impact of the worker resistance and the strike, the management felt that job changes and cost reductions were essential if the Vega were to return a profit to the company. The company had to be operating at about 90 percent capacity to break even. Not only had the plant with highly automated features cost twice as much as estimated, but also the Vega itself ended up weighing 10 percent more than had been planned.

While the company had to do something to increase the production efficiency in the Lordstown plant, the management was wondering whether it couldn't have planned and implemented the organizational and job changes differently in view of the costly disruption of the operations and the organizational stress the plant had been experiencing.

Questions

1. How would you assess the problems at the Lordstown plant?

2. Could a similar situation develop in today's economic environment?

3. What would you suggest that management do about the work force problem at the Lordstown installation?

Case IV-2

NATIONAL DISABILITIES ASSOCIATION OF CHESTER: AN ISSUE OF ORGANIZATIONAL LEADERSHIP

Eldridge Mescon, a general manager of NDA, leaned back in his comfortable chair and gazed at the portrait of his recently married granddaughter. Mescon's thoughts turned to the financial status of NDA and his pending meeting with Richard Clemens. As a fund raiser and grants writer, Clemens had not been effective.

A year ago, when Eldridge accepted the position of general manager, his task seemed simple enough. He felt that his experience as a bank loan officer would enable him to put the organization on a sound financial footing. After retiring from banking, Mescon looked for an ideal job, a job that would allow him to apply the knowledge and expertise gained from over thirty years of experience in banking. When he began at NDA, he thought he had found that ideal job. Unfortunately, he discovered that (1) the association's financial situation was influenced by the fund raiser/grant writer's effectiveness; (2) a big part of the general manager's job was public relations, an area in which he did not excel; and (3) after thirty-eight years in

This case was prepared by George Stevens and Christine Plummer of Arizona State University. Adapted and reprinted by permission of the authors. All names are disguised.

the world of business, he acknowledged that he was a bit of a male chauvinist. To Eldridge all women were inferior, a serious problem considering that five of his six subordinates were women.

Recent staff meetings gave clear indications that all was not well at NDA. Morale seemed to be at an all-time low. Each of the therapists had threatened to quit. One reason for this threat was the frustration they felt over the large case loads and the limited funding for equipment and supplies, which prevented them from providing good quality patient care. In addition, although counseling was sought for patients, none of the therapists had the time or expertise to provide it.

THE ORGANIZATION

The National Disabilities Association of Chester is one of four such nonprofit agencies located in the southeastern corner of Pennsylvania. In Chester, however, it is the only agency in the city that offers therapy to children with physical or mental disabilities. NDA also serves an adult population afflicted with cerebral palsy and related diseases. NDA does have ties to the national organization. Specifically, the national entity provides policy, procedural guidelines, and literature and also conducts the annual fund-raising telethon. NDA of Chester supplies people to work on the local portion of the telethon and is required to give a percentage of its fund-raising to the parent organization.

The staff at NDA of Chester consists of a general manager, a secretary, a person in charge of fund raising and grant writing, and a bookkeeper. In addition, therapy is provided by a physical therapist, speech pathologist, and an occupational therapist. While all the staff are important, the not-for-profit status of NDA gives the fund raiser and grant writer's job special significance. Richard Clemens, the incumbent fund raiser, is responsible for obtaining state and federal monies. State grants do not require matching funds. However, federal monies, awarded in the form of grants, require matching funds to be available before the government releases the grant money. Funding and grant allocations had not gone well, and rumors of the agency's closure persist. A third source of funding existed. Parents were billed for therapy sessions for their children but because the billing system was in a shambles and the clients had modest incomes, most of this money was never collected.

THE MISSION OF NDA

Although the entire staff believed that the association should offer therapy to children with all kinds of physical and mental disabilities, there was less agreement as to how NDA should be run. The therapists and clerical staff felt that the main objective should be to deliver quality therapy sessions to a fixed number of clients. The general manager and fund raiser were interested in serving the maximum number of clients they could solicit in order to qualify for more state and federal monies.

A parents' group, consisting of a small number of parents whose children were treated by the agency, has a different view of the organization's mission. This group believes that more services, such as parental counseling, subsidized therapy, financial help in the purchase of orthopedic equipment, and babysitting services, should be provided. The parents' group, however, does more than ask for money and services. They are a hard-working group, mounting their own fund-raising drive for NDA, volunteering many hours of their time to NDA, and meeting together to exchange information. Often speakers are invited to their meetings so the parents can learn more about the problems affecting their children.

The Board of Directors of NDA serves as the decision-making arm. Not only does the board make policy decisions, it also does all the hiring and firing. The board consists of three members of the community, the general manager, and the president of the parents' group (see Exhibit 1).

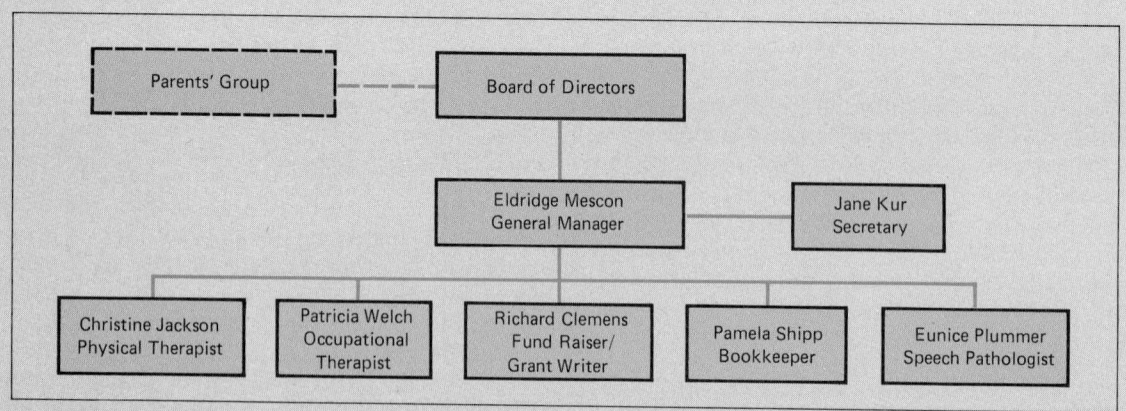

Exhibit 1
NATIONAL DISABILITIES ASSOCIATION—ORGANIZATION CHART

THE COMMOTION

Eleven months had passed since Richard Clemens first arrived at National Disabilities Association. It was now time for Mescon to conduct Clemens' performance review. Before talking to Richard, he planned to talk with other staff members to get their impression of Richard's performance. This review, he realized, would be extremely important because a favorable review meant that Richard would acquire permanent status. As Eldridge contemplated this decision, he heard a commotion outside his office door. The intercom crackled:

"Mr. Mescon, Pamela is here to see you and she seems very upset."

"Well, tell her to come in so that I can find out what is wrong."

"Come in, Pamela. Have a seat. Tell me what happened. Let me get you some water."

"Mr. Mescon, I am mad! I have been working here a long time and I don't need anyone who is new to the agency telling me how to do my job!"

"Hold it. Hold on a minute, will you? What exactly was done or said?"

"What Rich did was to tell me to stop spending so much time out of the office. He claimed no one could keep the books and know what clients owed if she spent so much time shopping in Philadelphia. Boy, did I give him a piece of my mind."

"You and I both know, Pamela, that you have been lax with the books. As the person in charge of billing, you should know what clients owe, but I wouldn't bet on it. Plus, from what I have seen, you spend most of your time doing those exquisite fingernails of yours."

"Eldridge, you are as infuriating as Rich. How can you talk? This place is worse off since you came here. Everyone's talking about the agency's closing down because of lack of funds. Truth is, maybe neither you nor Richard are doing your job. If you were, we wouldn't be worrying about closing."

After Pamela left, Mescon thought about the complaints and allegations she had made. There was some truth in what she said. Things had not gone well during his tenure as general manager. As the situation at NDA worsened, he spent less time at the office. While his comments about Pamela Shipp had been accurate, Eldridge knew that neither he nor Richard had performed at an acceptable level. He knew that, as President Truman liked to say, "the buck stops here" at his desk. He was not accustomed to failure, but if he did not act quickly to turn things around . . . As he sat back, he tried to determine what he should do now.

Questions

1. How would you describe the National Disabilities Association?

2. What are the key problems?

3. How would you describe the NDA staff's overall performance?

4. What might be done to enhance NDA's organizational effectiveness and efficiency?

5. If you were Eldridge Mescon, what would you do?

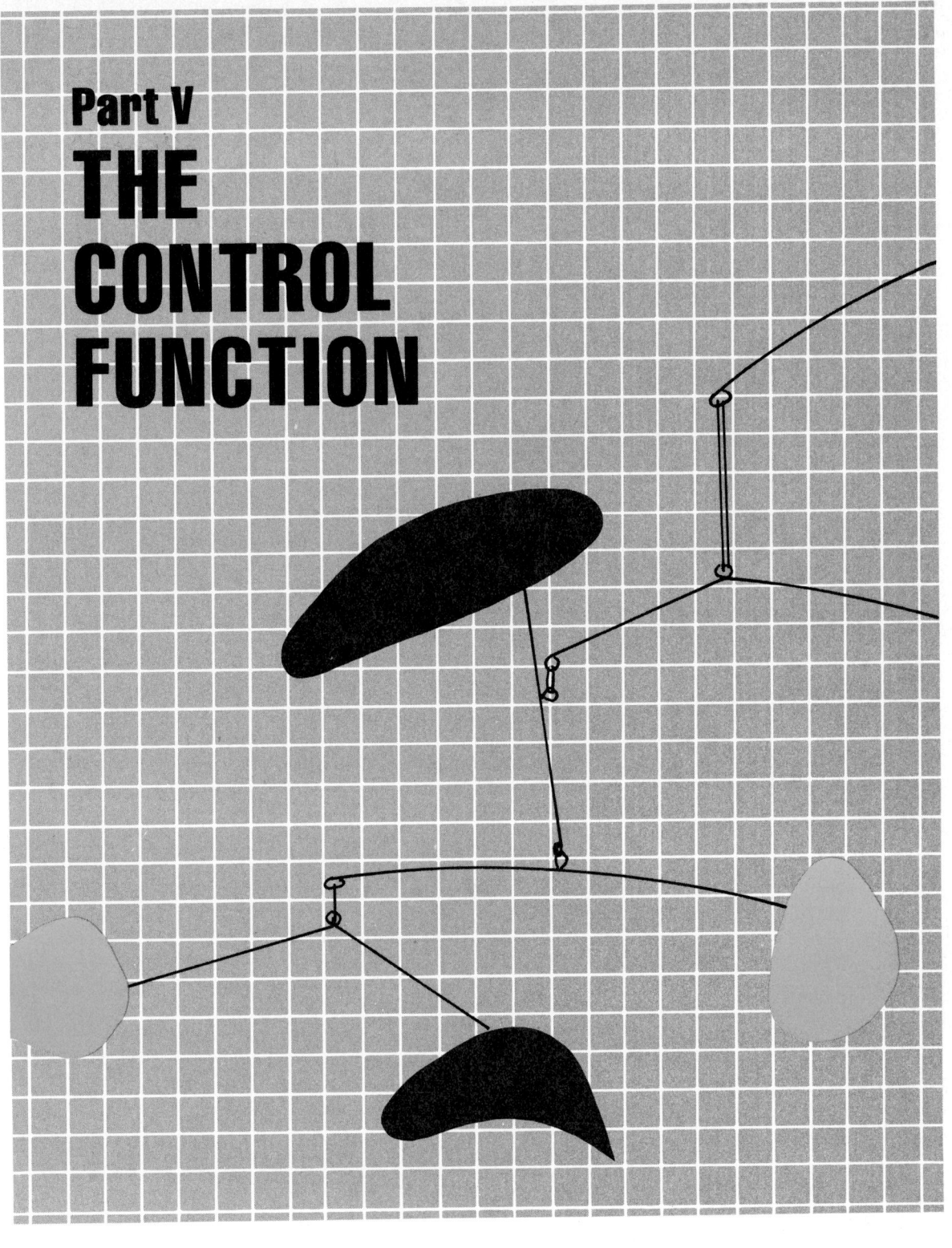

Part V
THE
CONTROL
FUNCTION

16.
Controlling: Evaluating Individual and Organizational Performance

Learning Objectives

AFTER STUDYING THIS CHAPTER YOU SHOULD BE ABLE TO

1. Identify the basic uses of controlling.
2. Explain the steps in the control process.
3. Identify and explain the four basic types of standards.
4. Explain each of the four categories of controls.
5. List the characteristics of effective controls.

Key Terms

controlling

precontrols

steering controls

yes–no controls

postcontrols

management audit

goal displacement

It is not enough to be busy; so are the ants. The question is: What are we busy about?

                    HENRY DAVID THOREAU

Without a yardstick, there is no measurement. And without measurement, there can be no control.

                    PRAVIN P. SHAH

Harding Lawrence was delighted when then President Jimmy Carter signed the Airline Deregulation Act of 1978, ending forty years of federal regulation of the airline industry. Lawrence, chairman and chief executive officer of Braniff Airways, realized that deregulation would make it possible for Braniff to achieve its objective of converting from a relatively small regional airline to a national—and even an international—carrier.

The act allowed carriers to choose new routes subject to some limitations and granted them new powers in reducing air fares. Within twelve months following the passage of the act, Braniff had added eighteen new cities to its route structure in the United States and opened four new routes to Europe and three to the Far East.

But Braniff ran into problems almost immediately following the implementation of its plans to join such giants as Pan Am and TWA as a major international carrier. Fuel costs skyrocketed in 1979, and Braniff was forced to make heavy purchases in the spot market at premiums of twenty cents or more per gallon. Its fuel costs exceeded the industry average by 10 percent, and they were 72 percent higher than the costs of only eight months before. Furthermore, interest rates, an important cost factor in an industry that relies heavily on borrowing to finance expansion, soared to unprecedented rates. To make matters worse, heightened competition in several of the new routes led to price cutting among the airlines, further reducing cash inflows.

Rapid expansion also placed new burdens on the airline's operations. Braniff's on-time performance was by far the worst of the trunk carriers in 1979. On one route—Washington to Boston—nearly nine of every ten Braniff flights showed up at least fifteen minutes late during a single month.

The new routes meant that new personnel had to be hired, trained, and put to work in a very short time period. Braniff cut its flight attendant training period from five to three weeks to cover the added routes, and complaints about quality control—both in personnel qualifications and in adequacy of training—were heard.

Feedback about problems resulting from the unprecedented expansion led Braniff management to reconsider its actions in order to correct the deviations from the organization's overall objectives. The international expansion, which contributed almost half the firm's operating income in 1979, was continued. But domestic service was curtailed as Braniff discontinued service to several U.S. cities in an attempt to control costs and improve passenger service.

The solutions did not work. In 1981 Braniff losses totaled more than $60 million. These losses, coupled with more than $300 million in losses for the 1978–1980 period, proved too great to overcome. Although Braniff fought desperately for life, the end came on May 13, 1982, when the firm filed a bankruptcy petition. Braniff's demise was significant: It was the first major U.S. airline to fail.[1]

What Is Controlling?

The terms *control, controls,* and *controlling* frequently produce visions of the "Big Brother" environment of George Orwell's *1984.* Mind control, police state conditions, and the loss of personal freedom often come to mind in this context to produce a negative connotation of control as a threat to individual freedom and organizational flexibility. As a result the subject of organizational and individual control is often misunderstood and frequently avoided.

But philosophers, theologians, and business practitioners have long recognized that freedom and order are not opposites but actually complement each other.[2] While overcontrol is obviously harmful, the imperfect environment of the 1980s requires various methods to check and balance behavior and performance (see Figure 16-1). Increased organizational complexity makes the need for effective controls even greater. In the same way that automobile tires require periodic checks and balancing, so also do organizations need controls. A well-designed control process provides answers to the important questions "What *is* going on?" and "What *should* be going on?" If the answers to these questions are different, appropriate corrective actions may be taken.

General Motors Corp. was one of the few major manufacturers to earn a profit during the Depression of the 1930s. Although profits dropped from $248 million in 1929 to a low point of $165,000 in 1932, the firm avoided red ink through major cost cuts and sizable layoffs. GM's president, Alfred P. Sloan, Jr., gave the credit to the firm's control systems. In his words, "It would be un-

[1] Daniel F. Cuff, "Major Expansion in the Late 70s Overwhelmed Colorful Braniff," *The New York Times* (May 13, 1982), p. 6-D. See also "Indigestion Brings Financial Woe to Braniff," *Business Week* (October 29, 1979), pp. 184, 188.
[2] E. F. Schumacher, *A Guide for the Perplexed* (New York: Harper & Row, 1977), p. 127.

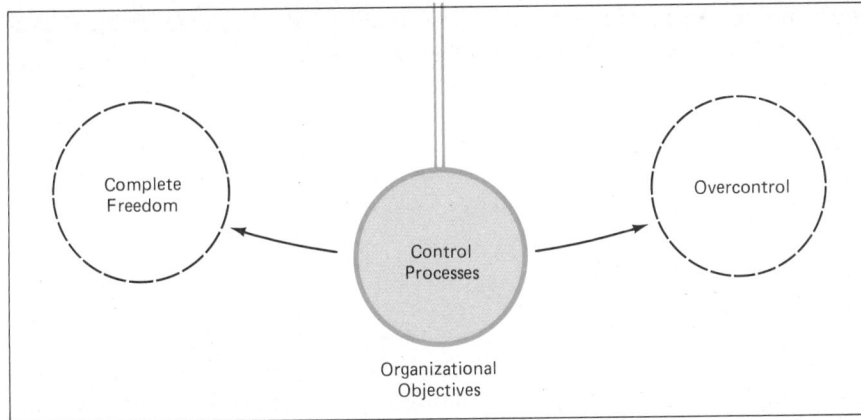

Figure 16-1
CONTROL
PROCESSES AS A
BALANCING FACTOR
IN ACHIEVING
ORGANIZATIONAL
OBJECTIVES

fair to claim any particular prescience on our part; no more than anyone else did we see the Depression coming . . . we had simply learned how to react quickly. This was perhaps the greatest payoff of our system of financial and operating controls."[3]

THE IMPORTANCE OF CONTROLLING

There are many factors that make controlling an important function in today's organizations. First, the need for controlling the activities of individuals and organizations is at the heart of the basic concept of *accountability.* For responsible persons to be held accountable, they must know exactly what their responsibilities are, how their performance will be evaluated, and the standards of effective performance to be used as criteria in the evaluation process. Accountability is virtually impossible without some types of controlling process. And without the ability to require accountability, managers face significant problems in delegating authority to subordinates.

A second factor increasing the importance of controlling is the *rapidity of change.* The fast pace at which environmental and other factors change requires a constant evaluation and reevaluation of the organization's strategic and tactical plans. Controlling systems must be established to assist managers in detecting changes that have significant impact on organizational activities.

A third factor is the growing *complexity* of today's organization. Large, multiproduct, geographically dispersed organizations require consistent and appropriately applied control systems to measure effectiveness. The movement toward decentralized organizational structures in many firms also calls for effective methods for controlling performance.

Another important reason for the development and implementation of controlling systems is that people make *mistakes.* The mistake may be as significant

[3] Reported in Lindley H. Clark, Jr., "The Great Depression Had Its Big Winners Along with the Losers," *Wall Street Journal* (October 26, 1979), p. 34.

as Xerox Corp.'s ill-fated decision to take on IBM in the computer industry or as mundane as the inadequate training of an intracompany mail carrier. Effectively designed control systems should be capable of identifying the wrong decision, forecast, or order so that corrective action can be taken to minimize the damage. Control systems should not be viewed as blame-allocators or as devices for finger-pointing but as an early warning system to spot deviations from organizational objectives.

CONTROLLING: A DEFINITION

Controlling is the process by which managers determine whether organizational objectives are achieved and whether actual operations are consistent with plans.

Controlling is the process by which managers determine whether organizational objectives are achieved and whether actual operations are consistent with plans. Controlling, which involves the measuring and evaluating of performance, was strongly emphasized by the early management writers of the scientific management movement. Taylor, Fayol, Mooney, Urwick, and the Gilbreths focused upon the development of standard methods to facilitate the controlling function.

THE RELATIONSHIP BETWEEN PLANNING AND CONTROLLING

Since controlling is the process by which managers determine whether actual performance is producing the planned results, there is considerable overlap between it and the goal-setting, planning, organizing, and leading functions. Although each managerial function has been discussed separately, each is interrelated, and the interrelationships between planning and controlling are clearly evident. Planning involves the establishment of organizational objectives and the development of strategies, while controlling establishes standards of performance and evaluates actual results with the planned results to determine whether operations are being performed according to plans.

SPECIFIC USES OF CONTROL

Before discussing the control process and the various techniques used by managers in controlling, it is useful to examine the basic uses of control. Eight uses can be identified:

1. *To standardize performance.* This increases efficiency and reduces cost in an organization.
2. *To safeguard company assets.* This reduces the cost of losses from theft, waste, and misuse that run rampant in many organizations today.
3. *To standardize quality.* This is required to meet the specifications of company engineers or customer expectations.
4. *To limit authority.* To establish accountability and provide for needed delegation of authority, controls must establish parameters within which delegated authority can be exercised without higher-level approval.
5. *To measure on-the-job performance.* Individual performance adds up to

collective organizational achievement. Therefore, methods of measuring this performance must be established.

6. *To monitor planning operations.* This type of control is fundamental to the attainment of organizational objectives.

7. *To allow top management to keep the firm's plans and programs balanced.* Master budgets, policy manuals, and financial controls aid in accomplishing this use of control.

8. *To motivate individuals.* Performance measures and the linkage of performance to financial incentives and individual recognition are the final use of control.[4]

As Table 16-1 indicates, different controlling methods may be appropriate for

[4] William T. Jerome III, *Executive Control—The Catalyst* (New York: Wiley, 1961), pp. 31–34.

Table 16-1 EIGHT USES OF CONTROLLING

USE	EXAMPLE OF POSSIBLE CONTROL TECHNIQUE TO BE USED
1. Standardizing performance	Time and motion studies; inspections; written procedures; production schedules
2. Safeguarding company assets	Division of responsibilities; separation of operational, custodial, and accounting activities; system of authorization and record keeping
3. Standardizing quality	Use of such evaluative techniques as specifications, blueprints, and inspections
4. Limiting authority	Policy directives; manuals of various types; internal audits to provide guidance for the exercise of delegated authority
5. Measuring on-the-job performance	Quotas; internal audits; special reports; output reports; time reporting
6. Monitoring planning operations	Sales and production forecasts; budgets; cost standards; scheduling techniques; standards of work measurement
7. Allowing management to keep the firm's plans and programs balanced	The master budget; policy manuals; organizational manuals; financial controls; use of such organizational techniques as committees, task forces, and outside consultants
8. Motivating individuals	Incentive programs; profit sharing; recognition or reward for achievement suggestions

SOURCE: Adapted from William T. Jerome III, *Executive Control—The Catalyst* (New York: Wiley, 1961), pp. 31–34. Copyright © 1982 by John Wiley & Sons, Inc. Reprinted by permission of the publisher.

different purposes. Time and motion studies and production schedules may be most appropriate in standardizing performance; policy directives and internal audits may be used in specifying authority limits.

Achieving Effective Control

Chester I. Barnard, the well-known management writer and former president of New Jersey Bell Telephone Co. (profiled in Chapter 9), recognized that controlling in an organization will necessarily vary from specific techniques focusing upon narrow activities to general methods of analyzing overall performance. In his words:

> Control from the view of effectiveness of the *whole* organization is never unimportant and is sometimes of critical importance.... Thus the executive process, even when narrowed to the aspect of effectiveness of an organization and the technologies of organization activities, is one of integration of the whole, of finding the effective balance between the local and broad considerations, between the general and specific requirements.[5]

At its base the control process is positive. Its basic purpose is to insure the achievement of organizational objectives. *Reconciliation, integration,* and *balance* are terms as descriptive of the controlling process as are *efficiency, error-free, zero-defects, correction, preventive,* and *increased profitability.* A positive overtone pervades the entire control process.

THE CONTROL PROCESS

Since controlling is widely considered a universal management function, a generally accepted process has been developed for its application. The basic steps of the controlling process overlap the general process of management because of the interrelationship of the functions. Planning involves the establishment of organizational objectives, while controlling guides performance to conform to the plan.[6] The four basic steps are as follows:

1. Establish organizational goals that become standards of performance.
2. Monitor the actual performance.
3. Compare the actual performance with the established standards of performance to determine variations.
4. Take corrective action if a variation or deviation exists.

The four-step process is illustrated in Figure 16-2.

[5] Chester I. Barnard, *The Functions of the Executive* (Cambridge, Mass.: Harvard University Press, 1968), p. 238.
[6] Robert J. Mockler, "Developing the Science of Management Control," *Financial Executive* (December 1967), pp. 80–93.

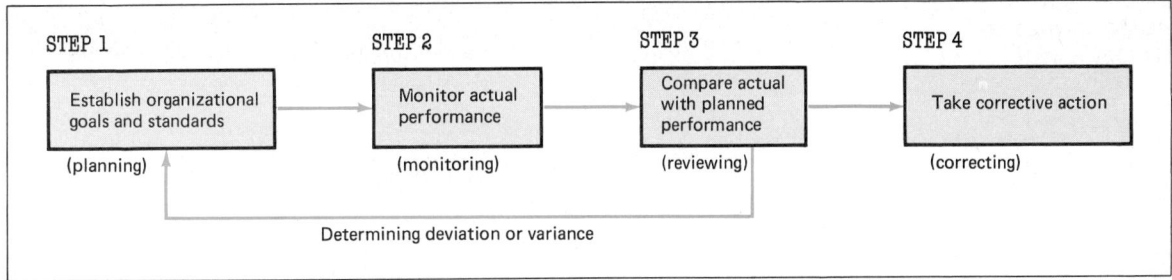

Figure 16-2
**STEPS IN THE
CONTROLLING
PROCESS**

STANDARDS: FIRST STEP IN THE CONTROLLING PROCESS

The controlling process begins with the establishment of organizational goals that become standards of performance. These *standards* serve as reference points against which actual performance can be compared. Without standards, controlling is extremely difficult since no definition of effective performance is available—no indication of adequate quality or efficient energy consumption. Such standards should be defined in as specific terms as possible.[7]

American Airlines employs a number of precise standards for evaluating the performance of its various airport ticket offices. The standards are defined in specific, quantifiable terms. The following list illustrates some of these standards:

1. *Mishandling of baggage.* Baggage mishandlings by airport personnel employed by American Airlines shall not exceed two percent.
2. *Waiting time.* At least 85 percent of all customers at an American Airlines ticket counter shall be waited on within five minutes.
3. *Posted flight-arrival times.* At least 95 percent of all arrival times posted at American Airlines ticket counters will be correct within 15 minutes of the posted time.[8]

Many types of standards can be developed. As Figure 16-3 indicates, four types are commonly used by managers: time, quality, quantity, cost. *Time standards* are used in the allocation of work efforts and in the regulation of production schedules. Managers utilize time standards to forecast work flow and employee output. Financial incentive plans rely heavily on time standards that identify standard output per person during a normal work period.

Quality standards express levels or ranges of acceptable value or worth for a quality control program. Performance evaluations and spot-check inspections are examples of this type of standard. Allowable deviations from standards vary widely, depending on the characteristics of the product. At one extreme is the zero-defects requirements by the National Aeronautics and Space Administration in its space program where a product failure or malfunction could endanger

[7] See Pravin P. Shah, *Cost Control and Information Systems* (New York: McGraw-Hill, 1981).
[8] Standards provided by Paul A. Haney, Manager–News Services, of American Airlines.

**Figure 16-3
FOUR TYPES OF
STANDARDS**

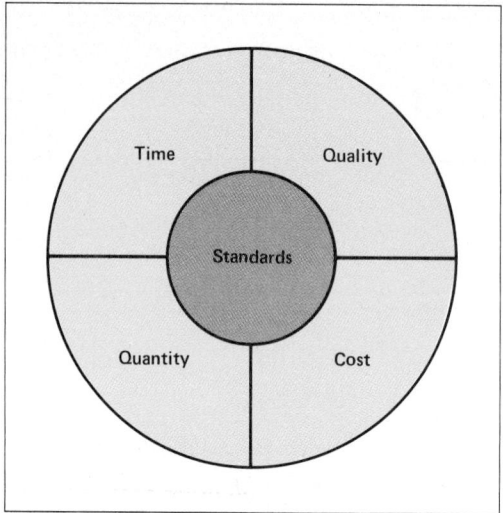

lives. Other products and activities commonly have less stringent quality standards based upon the impact of failure on safety, on meeting contract specifications, and on the loss of customers.

Quantity standards express in numerical terms the expected number of elements to be produced by a specific individual or by a given activity. Units of output or service, numbers of service calls, turnover rates, absenteeism figures, and applications processed are all examples of physical quantity standards.

Each of the three types of standards is interconnected with the others. Extremely high quality standards may adversely affect the amount of output produced in a given time period. But a standard that focuses primarily on quantity may produce increased volume at the expense of quality. The automobile industry contains examples of different standards in use. While high-quality Porsches are handmade at a rate of 67 per day, a high-speed Chevrolet assembly line in Lordstown, Ohio, is capable of producing nearly 100 cars per hour.[9] Standards used by an organization should result from established objectives. In most cases such standards represent compromises between time and quantity, on the one hand, and desired quality levels, on the other.

Cost standards are typically expressed in monetary terms. Budgets are typically developed to reflect cost per unit of output or expenditures required for a particular manufacturing process. Cost standards are directly related to the planning process. Budgets result from organizational plans and provide monetary checkpoints for comparing actual performance with expected performance. Once the basic framework is established, periodic meetings and reports alert managers to the performance of their specific areas of responsibility.

The standards established at the first step in the controlling process—quality,

[9] Joseph T. Straub, *Applied Management* (Cambridge, Mass.: Winthrop, 1979), p. 462.

quantity, time, and cost—must represent the objectives of the organization and must be expressed in meaningful, concrete terms. To be effective they must be clearly communicated to those involved with their use.

MONITORING PERFORMANCE: SECOND STEP IN THE CONTROLLING PROCESS

Once standards have been established, the second step in the controlling process is to monitor actual performance. Monitoring, like the other steps in the controlling process, is a continuous activity in most organizations. It requires the development of reliable methods of measurement and answers to the questions "What, how, and when to measure?"

Clear organizational objectives should identify *what* activities are to be measured. Answers to the question of *how* to measure a given individual or activity depend more on the type of event in question. In some cases continuous monitoring of an entire process is required. On other occasions spot checks and sampling of completed output will be sufficient. The specific activity under consideration also often determines *when* it will be measured. In some control systems, performance is measured only after the completion of an activity. In other cases it is measured continuously during its operation. A commonly used compromise approach is to require that performance be checked, evaluated, and approved at specified points before the next phase is allowed to begin.

The college classroom illustrates these alternative approaches to monitoring performance. Some instructors utilize a single final examination to measure performance. Others rely on mid-term quizzes to test performance prior to completion of the course. Still others may employ monitoring devices on a weekly or even a daily basis. In other cases some instructors require that their students successfully complete specific assignments or achieve a specified minimum grade on test material before continuing with new course material and assignments.

The essence of the monitoring step in the controlling process is to collect data that represent the actual performance of the activity or individual. Clear data are not always easy to collect, and their collection sometimes proves to be very costly. As activities become less technical, representative data are often difficult to develop and even more difficult to interpret. But representative data must be generated at this step to pave the way for the third step of the controlling process.

COMPARING ACTUAL AND PLANNED PERFORMANCE: THIRD STEP IN THE CONTROLLING PROCESS

The third step in the controlling process involves the actual comparison of actual performance with desired performance in an attempt to determine whether significant *deviations* or variations from the plan have occurred. Ideally, such deviations should be anticipated or at least detected sufficiently early for adjustments to be made. If steps one and two are completed satisfactorily, step three is relatively easy. If performance approximates the established standard, no adjustments are necessary and the monitoring process continues. Managers may choose to use the matching of performance to expectations as a motivational and informational tool to encourage people involved in the activity to continue their successful work.

Should performance deviate significantly from plans, management involved with this activity must be alerted for possible corrective action. Several conclusions are possible from such a variation. The most common conclusion is that of a controllable *performance deficiency*—a breakdown in the execution of the process or activity. However, the deviation may have occurred due to a change in the general environment surrounding the process. A third possibility is that the established standards are not realistic. It is essential that management make the correct interpretation of the deviation, since the interpretation will determine the corrective action to be taken. Often a variation is the result of a temporary, uncontrollable factor and does not indicate a problem with the process or the plan. Failure of painted surfaces of a product to match quality standards may be the result of high humidity levels resulting from record-setting rainfalls. Management may choose to interpret such deviations as one-time uncontrollable problems rather than develop a new plan to take into account such unusual situations. To dismantle or alter an effective plan as a result of such unusual occurrences would lead to additional costs and possibly other problems.

FEEDBACK: VITAL PART OF THE CONTROLLING PROCESS

Feedback is the use of information about current performance to determine whether adjustments are necessary in order to meet specified objectives. The importance of a feedback network in the controlling process cannot be overemphasized. The second and third steps in the process involve the collection of data concerning actual performance and their comparison with planned performance. The successful interaction of these steps—as well as the entire controlling process itself—depends on an effective information and feedback network. Many writers even list feedback as a separate step in the controlling process.

Feedback is best viewed as a linking network of communication that ties together the four steps of the controlling process. Feedback should flow upward to decision centers in the organization, as well as downward to the activity centers where needed corrective action can be taken. Control communications should be based on the management by exception principle, and information should be communicated to managers at higher levels only when there is a significant variation from the plan. Written reports, reviews, meetings, and briefing sessions are often used to provide appropriate feedback. International Telephone and Telegraph, the multinational conglomerate with annual sales of several billion dollars, uses one of the most comprehensive reporting systems around to provide feedback concerning its myriad, geographically diverse enterprises. Monthly reports from ITT subsidiaries often exceed fifty pages.[10]

[10] Anthony Sampson, *Sovereign State of ITT* (New York: Stein and Day, 1973).

TAKING CORRECTIVE ACTION: FOURTH STEP IN THE CONTROLLING PROCESS

The investigation and interpretation of any deviations identified in the previous step form the basis for any positive corrective action to be taken at this step. Should the reason for the variations between actual and planned performance be a controllable element of the actual process or of the environment, strategies should be developed and implemented to correct them. If deviations are the result of an uncontrollable element or an unrealistic standard, a different response is required.

The first phase of correcting deviations is to identify the actual cause of the deviation. Great care is required to separate symptoms from causes. The second phase is to implement the corrective action, which may involve a choice among alternative solutions. Sometimes corrective action is obvious and clear-cut. At other times it may be complex and somewhat subjective. It may involve reas-

APPLYING THE STEPS OF THE CONTROL PROCESS TO AUTO PRODUCTION

The steps involved in the control process are illustrated by the automobile assembly plant depicted below. Although the weekly production standard has been set at 2,000 cars, the production manager's weekly report indicates that actual output lagged 200 cars behind the goal. In order to determine the reason for the deviation, feedback is necessary. In this instance feedback is likely to take the form of comparisons of production levels for recent weeks and average numbers of equipment failures. The average number of equipment breakdowns in previous weeks has been three and production goals have been achieved with such a rate. Determination of a "standard" number of equipment failures suggests that the higher equipment failure rate is the problem that must be corrected and that new equipment is necessary to achieve the stated production standard. Until the new equipment arrives, management revises the production standard downward to 1,800 cars to allow for the defective machinery.

The assembly line should produce 2,000 cars a week. **Establish standards**	Production manager's weekly report shows 1,800 cars produced and ten equipment failures. **Check performance**	2,000 cars produced No deviations, continue activity
Until new equipment arrives, expect only 1,800 cars a week. **Reevaluate standards**	**Buy new equipment** **Take corrective action**	Average past rate of equipment failure was three times a week. Compare to standards, find reason for deviation

SOURCE: Adapted by permission from David J. Rachman and Michael H. Mescon, *Business Today*, 3rd ed. (New York: Random House, 1982), p. 132. Copyright © 1982 by Random House, Inc.

signing work, hiring or transferring personnel, purchasing new equipment, increasing marketing efforts, redeveloping plans, modifying objectives, or any number of other actions.

Types of Controls

Precontrols are developed to eliminate the causes of any deviations that might occur in the execution of organizational plans; they are preventive measures.

Controlling processes can be classified in four ways: precontrols, steering controls, yes–no controls, and postcontrols.[11] *Precontrols* are preventive in nature. They involve the development of forward-looking controls to eliminate the cause of any deviations that might occur in the execution of organizational plans. Such controls are established before the activity takes place. The process of using capital budgeting for evaluating capital investments is an example of precontrols. In capital budgeting the present value of the benefits to be received determines whether the return on investment is adequate to justify the investment.

Steering controls predict results; they attempt to detect deviations from predetermined standards, allowing for corrective actions to be taken while the activity is being performed.

Steering controls predict results in an attempt to detect deviations from predetermined standards and to allow corrective action to be taken while the activity is being performed. Steering controls provide for checkpoints that allow corrections to assure that actual results will closely match planned results. Thus, steering controls are particularly important in most organizations.

Yes-no controls allow for a screening process point where specific approval is needed to permit the acitvity to continue.

Yes-no controls allow for a screening process point where specific approval is needed to permit the activity to continue. Quality control inspections, approval of requisitions, safety checks, and legal approval of contracts are common examples of yes–no controls.

Postcontrols measure results following the completion of the activity and compare them with predetermined standards; they are important in the development of precontrols and steering controls for subsequent activities.

Postcontrols measure results following the completion of the activity and compare them with predetermined standards. Final inspections, summary activity reports, and balance sheets are examples of this "after-the-fact" controlling process. Such postcontrols are important in the development of precontrols and steering controls for subsequent activities.

Steering controls are perhaps the most frequently used controls; they are the type of control process typically associated with the controlling function. However, most successful organizations use a combination of all four types in order to maintain an effective, integrated control system. Table 16–2 illustrates each type.

Characteristics of Effective Controls

As the preceding discussion has indicated, control systems will vary from one organization to the next. Different types of controls are used to address the specific needs of different departments, activities, or organizations. In order to be effective, however, they should possess a number of characteristics.[12]

[11] Edgar F. Huse, *The Modern Manager* (St. Paul, Minn.: West, 1979), p. 185.

[12] This list is adapted from discussions in Harold Koontz and Cyril O'Donnell, *Essentials of Management* (New York: McGraw-Hill, 1974), pp. 362–365; and Robert L. Trewatha and M. Gene Newport, *Management: Functions and Behavior* (Dallas: Business Publications, 1979), pp. 260–264.

TYPE	WHEN USED	EXAMPLE	
Precontrols	Prior to start of activity	Proficiency levels for employees trained to perform activity	**Table 16-2 CLASSIFICATION OF CONTROLS**
Steering Controls	During performance of activity	Comparison of employee input per hour with established standards	
Yes–No Controls	During or after performance of activity	Quality control tests of output	
Postcontrols	Following completion of activity	Comparison of actual costs to budgeted costs	

1. *Controls should be understandable.* The individuals with the responsibility for monitoring operations and comparing them with established standards must understand clearly the control systems being used. Misunderstood control systems will be either ignored or misapplied.

2. *Controls must be designed to match the activity under consideration.* The data collected must be relevant to that activity. Sales managers should receive information concerning the performance of salespersons, product sales by territories, customer categories, and order size and competitive data concerning performance, price changes, and new product introductions. Advertising managers should receive information relative to their responsibilities. The marketing vice-president should receive information on these and other marketing activities.

3. *Controls should register deviations quickly.* Ideally, substandard performance should be prevented from occurring through precontrols or should be identified by steering controls as early in the process as possible. Such an early warning control system makes remedial action possible and provides for resumption of activities called for by the established standards.

4. *Controls should be flexible.* Control systems should be flexible enough to accommodate changes in environmental factors. Flexible controls can adjust for the uncertainties of the situation. This flexibility allows the organization to react quickly to changes or to take advantage of new opportunities.

5. *Controls should be economical.* The costs involved in developing and maintaining control systems should reflect the benefits they provide. Spending thousands to save hundreds of dollars is obviously unrealistic. Since control systems should be cost effective, they must focus upon critical areas. The important criterion is the determination of the minimum expenditures required to monitor an activity and insure that it accomplishes the desired goal.

6. *Control systems should indicate corrective action.* An effective control system should not only identify deviations from planned performance quickly but should also prescribe corrective action. Once deviations are

detected, the system should be capable of identifying causes of the variations and suggesting means of correcting them.

7. *Controls should be difficult to manipulate.* Controls should not be subject to misrepresentation. Poorly conceived control systems may be subjected to distortions by managers who attempt to depict more favorable results from their departments than actually occur.

Evaluating Performance

Data generated from a control system provide a basis for evaluating the performance of organizational members. But who should receive the data? Such data might be routed to staff personnel, higher-level line managers, the manager of the unit being measured, or the individuals in the unit being measured. A general rule is that the individual or group who can make the most meaningful use of the data should receive it first.[13] Prompt feedback gives personnel an immediate evaluation of their performance, permits rapid adjustments of deviations from expected performance, and aids in the learning process.

WHO SHOULD EVALUATE PERFORMANCE?

Generally speaking, an individual's performance should be evaluated by the person in the best position to observe his or her performance or the results of that performance. This person is most often the employee's immediate superior. In some organizational settings, the supervisor's evaluation is supplemented by evaluations by the peers or co-workers of the individual.

Evaluations should be conducted as openly as possible with standards of per-

DATA: CRUCIAL INGREDIENT IN PERFORMANCE EVALUATION

SOURCE: "Hagar the Horrible" by Dik Browne (February 12, 1973). Copyright © King Features Syndicate, Inc., 1973. All rights reserved.

[13] Cortlandt Cammann and David A. Nadler, "Fit Control Systems to Your Managerial Style," *Harvard Business Review* (January–February 1976), pp. 65–72.

formance clearly stated. The employee should know the required performance
level in advance of any evaluation. These standards should be related to the primary objectives of the job, and they should be attainable through excellent performance.

Management Audits

Annual audits of financial records by outside independent certified public accounting firms are established practices at most large- and medium-sized organizations. In recent years attention has been given to conducting similar audits in
nonfinancial areas of the organization. The newer audits possess a variety of
titles—management audits, performance audits, operational audits, and internal
audits. Regardless of the specific label used by individual organizations, the
management audit is a professional review and evaluation of an organization's
total activities from the perspective of management.[14]

Management audits are more difficult to conduct than the traditional financial audit since they require a determination of both the specific managerial
characteristics to be measured and the measurement methods to be used. Peter
Drucker argues that since managerial skills must ultimately be measured in
terms of performance the management audit should assess the following areas:
performance in appropriating capital, performance in people-related decisions,
performance in terms of innovations, and performance in planning.[15] A variety
of techniques are utilized by auditors, ranging from personal interviews and
written questionnaires to analysis of such data as turnover rates, departmental
productivity, actual performance to quota, and employee morale surveys, among
others.

Audits may be conducted internally by staff specialists or independent outside
auditors may be employed. Use of outside auditors should reduce the possibility
of bias. The American Institute of Management, a private nonprofit organization, conducts such audits, utilizing a system based upon a 301-item questionnaire. The AIM audit focuses upon such diverse subjects as earnings strength,
research and development, production efficiency, and evaluation of specific executive characteristics. The General Accounting Office (GAO) is responsible for
assisting Congress in assessing federal programs by focusing upon "Three Es" of
government programs—economy, efficiency, and effectiveness. In 1981 the
GAO submitted 976 audit reports. Congressional committees or individual
members of Congress received 720 of these reports, and the remaining 256 went
to the chiefs of federal agencies.

Even though the broad scope of the management audit results in less precise

> **The management audit
> is a professional review
> and evaluation of an
> organization's total
> activities from the
> perspective of
> management.**

[14] William L. Campfield, "Auditing Management Performance," *Financial Executive* (January
1971).
[15] Peter F. Drucker, "A New Scorecard for Management," *Wall Street Journal* (September 24,
1976), p. 16.

In the early 1960s, management found itself in the middle of a major controversy. One of the most outspoken figures in this debate was Douglas McGregor, a professor of industrial management at Massachusetts Institute of Technology. McGregor, whose Ph.D. in psychology was the foundation of a career in industrial relations, upset many a managerial applecart with the 1960 publication of his work *The Human Side of Enterprise*. In this volume he labeled as Theory X a perception of the basic nature of employees that he believed to be common among managers. He then proceeded to formulate Theory Y, another perception of employees that he felt to be the more appropriate foundation for principles of organization and management. The two perceptions about workers, discussed in detail in Chapter 14, produce decidedly contrasting patterns of control.

McGregor was born in Michigan in 1906. He interspersed education with time off for work, completing his Ph.D. at Harvard in 1935. He worked for the Buffalo Grey Auto Stations, a tank-car gasoline concern, for several months in 1927 before taking a promotion to district manager for a retail gasoline merchandising company. After three years in this position, he worked for a year with his father, who headed a welfare mission in Detroit. He left Harvard a couple of years after obtaining his doctorate to assume a position at MIT, where in 1943 he became executive director of the Industrial Relations Section.

Elected president of Antioch College in 1948, McGregor is credited with bringing a more profound sense of purpose to that small college, where the curriculum involves students in off-campus work experiences as well as on-campus classes. By initiating "Goals Discussions," in which all members of the college community—faculty, students, secretaries, and custodial staff, among others—participated, he was able to promote a mutual understanding and sense of di-

results than the other control techniques discussed, it is nevertheless useful in identifying areas of excellence as well as poorly performing parts of the organization. It can aid management in spotting trouble areas by identifying poor communications between responsibility centers; operations experiencing increased unit costs; breakdowns in scheduling; and other sources of deviations from plans.

Effects of Control on the Individual

The behavioral aspects of managerial control systems cannot be overemphasized. At the beginning of the chapter, the occasional problems of negative reactions to control systems by employees were noted. In an impersonal sense, controls are simply methods of insuring that desired results are actually accomplished. But to the individual employee, they may represent the proverbial albatross around his or her neck. Although an effective control system should aid in employee motivation, it is not uncommon for workers to feel threatened by controls.

rection among students, faculty, and staff. In 1954 McGregor returned to MIT as professor of industrial management.

A faith in the validity of applying basic democratic principles to management characterized not only McGregor's tenure as Antioch's president, but also his scholarly endeavors at MIT. He was convinced that the millions of employees in business and industry were not mediocre performers who continually sought methods of minimizing effort—even though this was a common assumption of their superiors. Traditional patterns of controlling and directing these people, McGregor believed, served only to frustrate their potential for contributing to the organization. He emphasized that above-average ingenuity and creativity in solving organizational problems are widely distributed among the work force. McGregor felt that management was responsible for developing the potential for commitment and contribution to organizational objectives that is inherent in each individual.

In his book *The Professional Manager*, published after his death in 1964, McGregor proposed a number of principles for improving organizational effectiveness drawn from research of his own and others. Based upon an elaboration of his Theory Y assumptions, these principles focus on the importance of (1) an interdependent team; (2) self-control; (3) the transactional character of influence; and (4) intrinsic motivation. McGregor's work has had a major influence on both management scholars and industrial practitioners. Businesses throughout the world have begun to introduce management strategies that he and his colleagues advocated to counteract the boredom, close controls, and dehumanizing aspects of mass production lines.

Sources

"Dr. Douglas McGregor, 58, Dies; Ex-President of Antioch College," *New York Times* (October 14, 1964), p. 45.

Douglas McGregor, *The Professional Manager* (New York: McGraw-Hill, 1967).

The National Cyclopedia of American Biography, Vol. 52, s.v., "McGregor, Douglas Murray."

Great care must be taken to communicate the organizational goals and objectives upon which the standards are based. If individuals in the organization feel the standards are relevant and appropriate, they are more likely to possess *positive* attitudes toward the control system. On the other hand, if the standards are perceived to be arbitrary, unrepresentative, and irrelevant, employee reactions are likely to be *negative*. Effective managers attempt to make the control system as meaningful as possible to the employees. Worker participation, clear communication of goals and standards, timely feedback, and realistic appraisal will help foster confidence in the control system.

AVOIDING GOAL DISPLACEMENT

One potential problem in the use of control systems is a phenomenon called *goal displacement*. This occurs when employees view the performance measures used in the control system as more important than the organizational goals upon which they are based.[16] Such behavior is not dysfunctional when the measures

Goal displacement occurs when employees view the performance measures used in the control system as more important than the organizational goals upon which they are based.

[16] Edward E. Lawler III and John Grand Rhode, *Information and Control in Organizations* (Pacific Palisades, Calif.: Goodyear Publishing Co., 1976), pp. 83–94.

are closely related to the goals of the department. Problems arise when they are not. Such problems often occur when performance appraisals are based exclusively on two or three variables. Workers who are evaluated on the bases of absenteeism, output, and amount of spoilage may conveniently ignore areas of safety, equipment maintenance, and other aspects of the job that ultimately can affect departmental objectives but that are not considered by the firm's control system.

AVOIDING OVERCONTROL

Another behavioral response to control systems results from the tendency of some managers to exert excessive control over other people and activities. Any control system creates the potential for misuse and resulting conflict. Care must be taken to prevent situations in which the control system can be used to gain power and coerce others to conform to unrealistic demands. Overcontrol may lead to higher costs, lowered morale, reduced productivity, and employee turnover. Such undesirable occurrences can result when controls are viewed as an end instead of as a means.

Summary

Controlling is the critical managerial function of determining whether organizational objectives are achieved and whether actual performances are consistent with plans. Control is used for such purposes as standardizing performance, safeguarding company assets, standardizing quality levels, limiting authority, measuring on-the-job performance, monitoring planning and programming operations, permitting managers to keep the firm's plans and programs in balance, and motivating individuals within the organization. The control process consists of four basic steps:

1. Establishment of organizational goals, which become standards of performance
2. Monitoring of actual performance
3. Comparison of actual performance to established standards to uncover any variations
4. Implementation of corrective action should significant variations exist

Standards are values used as reference points for comparing actual performance. The four types of standards include time, quality, quantity, and cost.

Controls may be classified in four ways: precontrols, steering controls, yes–no controls, and postcontrols. Effective controls are understandable, designed to match the activity being controlled; they register deviations quickly, are flexible and economical, difficult to manipulate, and indicate the need for corrective action.

The control process has important behavioral implications for the entire organization. Managers can increase the likelihood of positive attitudes on the part of their employees if they communicate the relevance, fairness, and appropriateness of the standards; encourage worker participation; and provide prompt feedback and realistic appraisals. Negative reactions are likely to occur if employees perceive the standards to be arbitrary, unrepresentative, or irrelevant.

REVIEW EXERCISES

1. Define the following terms: (a) controlling (b) pre-controls (c) steering controls (d) yes–no controls (e) postcontrols (f) management audit (g) goal displacement.

2. Explain the relationship between planning and controlling.

3. Identify and briefly explain four factors that increase the importance of the controlling function.

4. List eight uses of control in an organization.

5. Explain the steps in the control process.

6. What are the most common types of standards?

7. Relate the four types of controls to the control process.

8. Identify the characteristics of effective controls.

9. Explain how the determination of the appropriate organizational member to perform performance evaluations should be made.

10. Suggest methods by which the phenomenon of goal displacement can be avoided.

ASSIGNMENTS / PROBLEMS / DISCUSSION QUESTIONS

1. "Not long ago, the Boy Scouts of America revealed that membership figures coming in from the field had been falsified. In response to the pressures of a national membership drive, people within the organization had vastly overstated the number of new Boy Scouts. To their chagrin the leaders found something that other managers have also discovered: Organizational control systems often produce unintended consequences. The drive to increase memberships had motivated people to increase the number of new members reported but had not motivated them to increase the number of Boy Scouts actually enrolled." *

The above incident is a widely publicized example of goal displacement. Consider the following examples and explain how this phenomenon might also occur in each:

   a. Appraisal systems for college instructors
   b. Appraisal systems for students
   c. Quota compensation systems for sales personnel

* Cortlandt Cammann and David A. Nadler, "Fit Control Systems to Your Managerial Style," *Harvard Business Review* (January–February 1976), p. 65.

2. "Attempting to control too many activities is just as great an error as too little control." Discuss.

3. Relate controlling to the following functions:

   a. Planning
   b. Organizing
   c. Leading
   d. Communicating

4. Relate the four types of controls discussed in the chapter to the following examples:

   a. A manufacturer of surfboards
   b. A concert promoter
   c. A heart surgeon
   d. Director of the City Parks Department

5. Discuss the benefits and problems involved in conducting management audits. Who should be responsible for performing such audits?

A Managerial Incident

Mobil Decides to Trim Expenses

1982 was a tough year for many firms throughout the world, and Mobil Corp. was no exception. A major recession and a temporary oil glut forced the firm to seek methods of reducing costs. Mobil decided to seek means of maintaining desired profit levels by creating a temporary position of "cost-containment" manager. The position was filled by Eugene Renna, Mobil's regional vice-president for marketing and refining in the second hemisphere. The *Wall Street Journal* described the position as follows:

Mr. Renna doesn't have authority to cut expenses. All he can do is map out suggestions to heads of corporate units and ask heads of profit centers to report to him on how costs can be trimmed.

"But Tav (Mobil president William Tavoulareas) put out the word that this was serious," Mr. Renna says. "I tell heads of departments to think about what they can do because I'll be reporting back to the executive committee. That kind of framework gets a lot done."

Robert Weeks, head of marketing and refining in the U.S., who closed the Buffalo refinery and other plants, agrees that cost-cutting "was something I didn't dare ignore." Nonetheless, he adds, "a lot of what we cut would have happened with or without

Gene Renna," because of the slowdown in oil markets. . . .

Mr. Renna now is back in his old job, but he continues part-time to monitor and report on cost-cutting to top brass. Asked to quantify how much of Mobil's reductions he was responsible for Mr. Renna says, "I guarantee that (without me) some of the cuts wouldn't have happened as quickly and some of them wouldn't have occurred at all."

SOURCE: Roger Lowenstein, "Mobil Seeks Ways to Trim Its Expenses," *Wall Street Journal* (June 22, 1982), pp. 29, 43. Reprinted by permission of *The Wall Street Journal,* © Dow Jones & Company, Inc., 1982. All rights reserved.

Questions and Problems

1. Relate the actions taken to the model of the control process shown in Figure 16-2. Make any assumptions necessary.

2. What potential problems may have been created among various Mobil departments as a result of its approach? How might the likelihood of the occurrence of such problems have been reduced?

17.
Control Techniques

Learning Objectives

AFTER STUDYING THIS CHAPTER YOU SHOULD BE ABLE TO

1. Identify the five general tools of control and give an example of each.
2. Identify the five steps involved in budget development.
3. List the advantages and disadvantages of using zero-base budgeting.
4. Identify the major types of financial statements and the purpose of each.
5. Distinguish between financial statement analysis and ratio analysis.
6. Identify the major types of ratios.
7. Explain each of the components of the break-even analysis equation.

Key Terms

financial controls

budget

program planning budgeting systems (PPBS)

zero-base budgeting (ZBB)

financial analysis

ratio analysis

breakeven analysis

production control

organizational control

inventory control

quality control

Next to double-entry bookkeeping and
the copying machine, budgets are the
most commonly used management
tools.

PETER DRUCKER

Though my bottom line is black, I am
    flat upon my back,
My cash flows out, and customers pay slow.
The growth of my receivables is almost
    unbelievable;
The result is certain—unremitting woe!
And I hear the banker utter an ominous
    low mutter, "Watch cash flow."

HERBERT S. BAILEY, JR.
(with apologies to
Edgar Allan Poe's
"The Raven")

As the nation's second largest fast-food franchise, Burger King recognized that surpassing the leader—McDonald's—would require a major increase in both sales and profits. A critical component of its plan to achieve these objectives involved the drive-thru concept of purchasing food. But there were problems to overcome, and the organization's control system quickly identified them.

At first glance the drive-thru concept is simple. Drivers order at an outside menu board. They then join a line of cars whose drivers will pick up and pay for their orders at the pick-up window when they are ready. In most units the drive-thru team usually consisted of one or two cashiers who would take the order, run to the sandwich chutes and drink stations, assemble the order, bag it, and hand it to the customer.

Burger King established a standard transaction time of thirty seconds for the drive-thru window, but most units had longer service times. During peak periods drivers wishing to use the drive-thru could not even join the end of the car line, resulting in lost sales. Analysis at a number of units showed that drive-thru transaction times were averaging forty-five seconds. With a forty-five second transaction time, the restaurant could handle a maximum of eighty cars an hour. Because checks averaged $2.44 per order, drive-thru sales were limited to a maximum of $195 per hour. Clearly, a system initially devised to provide customers convenience had become an inconvenience.

Management reasoned that if the transaction time could be shortened to thirty seconds, cars served per hour would increase by 50 percent and maximum sales would rise by almost $100 to $292 an hour. That represents an annual sales increase of over $35,000 per restaurant. Working with franchises, Burger King's operations research department devised a plan to improve the speed of service at the drive-thru. The heart of the new system was the separation of drive-thru work into a series of distinct tasks.

One employee does nothing but take orders. The order taker gives the order to a runner/bagger who assembles the order and places it on an assembly shelf. The third member of the drive-thru team, the cashier, simply makes change and hands the order to a customer. The system allows for additional staffing when demands exceed the ability of the three-person crew to maintain the established standard transaction time.

The operations research department also recognized that customers waited an average of eleven seconds at the order station before being acknowledged. The rubber bell hose was therefore moved ahead of the order station so that the order taker was alerted to a customer's arrival prior to the car's reaching the order station.

Today, all Burger King restaurants with a drive-thru have adopted the efficiency package. These restaurants have increased their average annual sales capacity by over $35,000. If all restaurants in the system, with and without drive-thru windows, increased sales at only half that rate, or $18,000 per unit in annual sales increases, the Burger King system would enjoy additional sales of $52 million annually.[1]

Tools of Control in the Organization

The decisions made by Burger King's managers in response to the feedback they received on the drive-thru concept shows that controls are the key to the design and subsequent modification of the plans implemented to achieve the organization's objectives. Since controls exist at various organizational settings and in a variety of formats, it is understandable that a number of specific tools of control have been developed. The following is a listing of the general kinds of controls:

1. *Financial controls:* concerned with budgets, financial analysis, and break-even analysis
2. *Production controls:* concerned with the scheduling, timing, and routing of a product or project
3. *Organizational controls:* concerned with the determination of working relations, job design, and employee evaluation
4. *Inventory controls:* concerned with the levels of assets held in various stages of inventory
5. *Quality controls:* concerned with the quality of services or products[2]

---

[1] Adapted by permission from William Swart and Luca Donno, "Simulation Modeling Improves Operations, Planning, and Productivity of Fast Food Restaurants," *Interfaces* 11, no. 6 (December 1981), p. 38. Copyright © 1981 The Institute of Management Sciences.

[2] X. Gilbert, "Does Your Control System Fit Your Business?" *European Business* (Spring 1973), pp. 69–76.

FINANCIAL CONTROLS

Budgets, financial analysis of the organization's accounting statements, and the use of breakeven analysis are the primary *financial controls*. Each can make major contributions to the control process.

Budgets—Frequently Used Financial Control Tools

Of all the different financial control techniques, the budget is the best known. Budgets represent in monetary terms the goals and objectives of the organization. A *budget* is simply a financial plan listing in detail the resources or funds assigned to a particular product, division, or project. Inherent in the budget is control through timely feedback. Figure 17-1 indicates the different types of

Financial controls are controls provided by the use of such techniques as budgets, financial analysis, and breakeven analysis.

A budget is a financial plan listing in detail the resources or funds assigned to a particular product, division, or project.

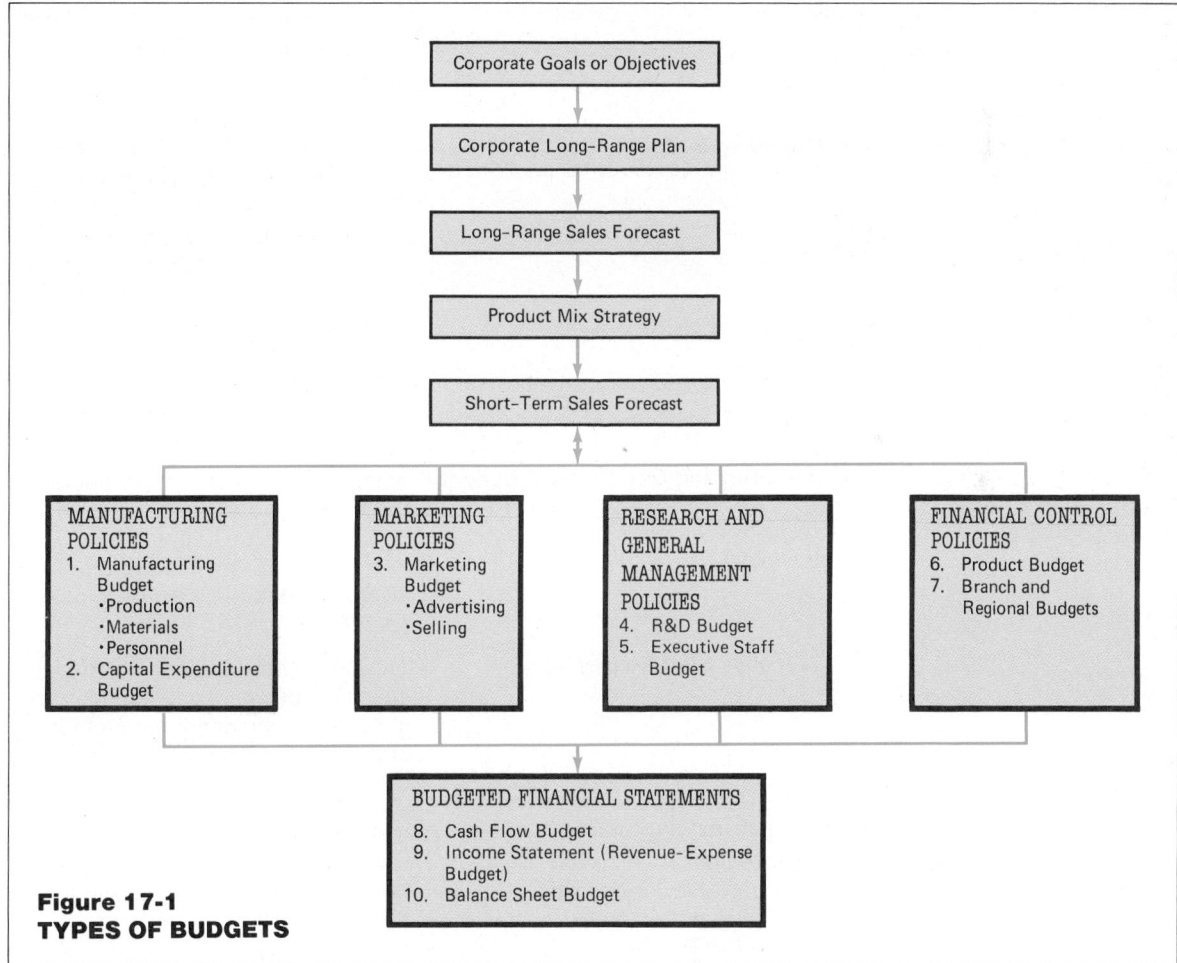

Figure 17-1
TYPES OF BUDGETS

SOURCE: Adapted from *Managerial Finance,* 7th ed., by J. Fred Weston and Eugene F. Brigham. Copyright © 1981 by the Dryden Press, a division of Holt, Rinehart & Winston Publishers. Reprinted by permission of Holt, Rinehart & Winston.

	TYPE	DESCRIPTION
Table 17-1 TEN TYPES OF BUDGETS	1. Manufacturing Budget	This budget, sometimes called the *operations budget,* includes the requirements for production materials, labor, energy, and other elements necessary to accomplish the projected output. Sometimes these budgets are initially expressed in physical terms and translated into monetary terms as the project proceeds.
	2. Capital Expenditures Budget	This budget includes expenditures for new plant and equipment, replacement equipment, improvements to existing facilities, and other expenditures involving long-term commitments.
	3. Marketing Budget	Marketing budgets are typically divided into two parts. The first part is the advertising budget, which includes the plans and required resources to promote the product line. The second part focuses upon the monetary requirements necessary to sell the firm's products. The marketing budget is occasionally combined with other budgets and included in a general operational budget.
	4. Research and Development Budget	This budget reflects the strategies of the firm with relation to research and development expenditures. Future sales and revenue are often closely related to investment in research.
	5. Executive Staff Budget	This specialized budget includes the special expense accounts, compensation, and personnel requirements at higher organizational levels.

budgets that may be used to translate company goals and strategy into action. Not every organization would use all of these budgets, each of which is briefly described in Table 17-1 to illustrate the types of budgets that are available.

DEVELOPING A BUDGET

A comprehensive budgeting process begins with the development of detailed economic, sales, and profit forecasts. These forecasts, designed to meet organizational goals, produce guidelines for use in the budget preparations. Although

TYPE	DESCRIPTION
6. Product Budget	This budget focuses upon a specific product of the firm. Such a budget permits determinations of return on investments in each product.
7. Branch or Regional Budget	This budget is used to establish local or regional cost centers for planning and control purposes.
8. Cash Flow Budget	The cash budget indicates the total amount of funds required and the time at which they are required. This budget forecasts cash receipts and outlays on a monthly, weekly, or even daily basis. It is an extremely important tool for controlling cash and meeting current obligations.
9. Budgeted Income Statement	This budget reflects anticipated *revenue* from sales and other incomes the organization expects to receive during a given time period and compares it with expected *expenses* associated with receiving the revenues.
10. Balance Sheet Budget	This budget reflects expected assets, liabilities, and net worth of an organization at the end of a specific accounting period such as a month or year. Such a budget provides management, lenders, and other interested parties with a forecast of the expected future financial position of the firm. It also provides a standard with which the actual balance sheet for the period can be compared.

some organizations develop budgets at the top management level for distribution throughout the hierarchy, most agree that the departments and individuals responsible for implementation should be able to contribute to the development of the budget. The benefits of the "bottom-up" approach to budget development include the following:

1. Supervisors and personnel in each department are likely to be the most familiar with their own needs.

2. They are less likely to overlook a factor from their own departments that might prove to be a crucial element in budget development.
3. They are more likely to be motivated to accept and meet a budget if they have participated in its development.[3]

Once the preliminary budget proposals are developed by the various departments, they are submitted to a budget committee. This committee, typically composed of middle and top managers with line authority, reviews the proposals and attempts to reconcile the various budgets into a final budget for the coming period. Adjustments to individual budgets are often necessary to eliminate duplication, and committee members may communicate frequently with the managers who submitted the original proposals before a final budget is prepared and adopted. Table 17-2 lists the five stages of budget development.

BUILDING FLEXIBILITY INTO THE BUDGET

A serious drawback to many budgets is their rigidity in the face of changing conditions. Budgets are forward-looking and should provide means of adjustment should changes affect the forecasts upon which they are based. Damage caused by a 1979 hurricane disrupted operations at Litton Industries' Ingalls Shipbuilding Complex in Pascagoula, Mississippi. IBM's introduction of a new series of computer hardware produced major problems for such competitors as Honeywell, Burroughs, and Amdahl. A prolonged 1982 strike adversely affected revenues at Northwest Orient Airlines. In order to avoid control problems resulting from inflexible budgets, organizations often develop flexible budgets. One of the most common, the *variable budget*, is actually a series of different budgets for different levels of output. Since expenses and allowances are computed for different levels of activities, departmental budgets can be easily ad-

[3] Selvin W. Becker and David Green, Jr., "Budgeting and Employee Behavior," *Journal of Business* (October 1962), pp. 392–402.

BUDGETS—NOT A NEW IDEA

Planning is often confused with budgeting. I found that a great many managers, when they speak of "planning," are really talking about their annual budget. One reason is that in most companies budgeting came first and what is called planning was derived from the budgeting process.

We might expect this, for the idea of budgeting goes back to France of the Middle Ages. In those days business people kept their money in a *bougette*, or small leather bag. Budgeting then consisted of counting the money in the bag to see if there was enough to pay expenses. As business grew to include many people, somebody had to keep track of the money, so there arose the *contrerolleur*, the one who kept a record of the *bougettes* in order to control receipts and expenditures. So began the "controller" and "comptroller" as we know them today.

SOURCE: Louis A. Allen, *Making Managerial Planning More Effective* (New York: McGraw-Hill, 1982), p. 8.

STEP	ACTIVITY	
1.	Economic, sales, and profit forecasts are prepared. These forecasts serve as guidelines for managers in preparing the budget for their division or department.	**Table 17-2 STEPS INVOLVED IN BUDGET DEVELOPMENT**
2.	Preliminary budgets are prepared by supervisory and middle management.	
3.	Budget committee reviews preliminary budgets.	
4.	Adjustment of various budgets by committee and budget initiators.	
5.	Finalization and adoption of budget.	

justed by a predetermined formula to reflect more realistically the actual costs related to actual output. Such budgets may be called *flexible budgets, sliding-scale budgets,* or *step budgets.*

PROGRAM PLANNING BUDGETING SYSTEMS (PPBS)

PPBS is a system of budgeting that has been adopted by a number of nonprofit organizations, including the federal, state, and a number of local governments. The system was developed by the Rand Corp. in the late 1950s and introduced in the Department of Defense in the early 1960s. Five basic steps are involved.

1. List and analyze the objectives of the activity.
2. Analyze the result(s) of a given program or activity based on the objectives developed in step 1.
3. Estimate future costs of the program as well as original outlays.
4. Analyze alternatives.
5. Integrate the first four steps into the budgetary process.[4]

PPBS possesses a number of advantages. First, it relates the budget to agency or departmental objectives and requires accountability. Second, it requires a realistic appraisal of future costs and requires managers to justify their decisions. Finally, it brings into sharp focus the relationship between costs and benefits.

> **Program planning budgeting systems (PPBS)** is a system of budgeting that has been adopted by a number of nonprofit organizations. It involves five basic steps.

ZERO-BASE BUDGETING

A favorite assumption of many budget preparers is that last year's budget is a reasonable starting point for the following year's budget request. This assumption inhibits the careful review of the relevance of many activities within the organization. Elimination of this assumption is the essence of zero-base budgeting (ZBB).

   Zero-base budgeting requires that projects, priorities, and objectives be reviewed in every budgeting cycle. First, managers must justify each item in their budget requests as if they were proposing a completely new department. Activities are divided into *decision packages.* Such packages contain sufficient infor-

> **Zero-base budgeting** is the forced periodic justification of any expenditure program, not just incremental changes in such a program.

[4] Robert Anthony and Regina Herzlinger, *Management Control in Nonprofit Organizations* (Homewood, Ill.: Irwin, 1975), p. 129.

mation about an activity for it to be evaluated and compared with other activities on a cost/benefit basis. The decision package also includes a statement of consequences that may occur should the activity not be approved.

The second step requires the evaluation and ranking of all activities in order of benefit to the organization, followed by the actual allocation of resources based upon the final ranking. The decision packages of lowest rank are prime candidates for elimination in periods of cost-cutting if their benefits appear minimal or if they no longer match the objectives of the organization.

A zero-base budgeting process provides greater justification of the continuation or termination of activities, allows greater participation in planning, and gives the budgeting process greater unity. However, the process is more costly and requires more time to complete.

The ZBB concept was originally developed by Texas Instruments, Inc., and received considerable publicity when former President Carter championed it as a method of controlling the costs of government. It has also been utilized by a number of profit-seeking firms ranging from Southern California Edison, Ford Motor Co., and the Bank to Montreal to Playboy Enterprises.[5]

Financial Analysis—An Important Tool of Financial Control

Financial analysis is the use of specific techniques to study a firm's financial documents and control the flow of funds, products, and services both within and outside organizations. Financial statements provide the means for controlling the following:

Financial analysis is the use of specific techniques to study a firm's financial documents and control the flow of funds, products, and services both inside and outside the firm.

1. The *liquidity* of the organization: its ability to meet its current obligations and needs by converting its assets into cash;
2. The general *profitability* of the organization; and
3. The general *financial condition* of the organization.[6]

THREE FINANCIAL STATEMENTS

Three commonly used financial statements are the balance sheet, income statement, and sources and uses of funds statement. The *balance sheet* reflects the financial position of an organization as of a particular date. It is similar to a photograph comparing a firm's assets with its liabilities and net worth at a specific moment in time. Figure 17-2 shows a simplified balance sheet for a manufacturing firm.

The left side of the balance sheet lists the assets of the firm in descending order of liquidity (nearness to cash). These assets represent the items of value owned by the organization; they are uses that management has made of available

[5] Peter A. Phyrr, *Zero-Base Budgeting: A Practical Management Tool for Evaluating Expenses* (New York: Wiley, 1973). See also Stanton C. Lindquist and K. Bryant Mills, "Whatever Happened to Zero-Base Budgeting?" *Managerial Planning* (January–February 1981), pp. 31–35; and Samuel Eilon, "ZBB—Promise or Illusion?" *Omega, The International Journal of Management Science* 9, no. 2 (1981), pp. 107–112.
[6] Fred Weston and Eugene F. Brigham, *Managerial Finance* (Hinsdale, Ill.: Dryden Press, 1978), p. 84.

Figure 17-2
**BALANCE SHEET FOR
ACME
CONSOLIDATED**

Acme Consolidated
Balance Sheet
December 31, 1984

Assets		Liabilities and Net Worth	
Cash	$ 50,000	Accounts Payable	$ 75,000
Marketable Securi-		Notes Payable	125,000
ties	40,000	Accruals	25,000
Accounts Receivable	150,000		
Inventory	200,000		
Total Current Assets	440,000	Total Current Liabilities	225,000
Land	80,000		
Plant & Equipment	900,000	Debentures	200,000
Total Fixed Assets	980,000	Total Long-term Liabilities	200,000
		Common Stock	500,000
		Retained Earnings	495,000
		Net Worth	995,000
		Total Liabilities and	
Total Assets	$1,420,000	Net Worth	$1,420,000

funds. The right side of the balance sheet is the firm's financial structure, indicating the sources of the firm's assets. Liabilities reflect the claims of the firm's creditors—financial institutions that have made long- and short-term loans, suppliers that have provided products and services on credit, and bondholders, among others. Net worth represents the owners' (stockholders' in the case of corporations) claims against the firm's assets, or the excess of all assets over all liabilities.

The *income statement* reflects the performance of the organization over a specific time period. Such statements begin with total sales or revenue generated during a year, quarter, or month and then deduct all the costs related to producing this revenue. Once all costs—costs involved in producing the products, administrative costs, interest, and taxes, for instance—have been subtracted, the remaining net income available to distribute to the firm's owners (stockholders, proprietors, or partners) may be reinvested in the firm as retained earnings. Figure 17-3 shows the 1984 income statement for Acme Consolidated.

As the title of the third basic financial statement indicates, the *sources and uses of funds statement* answers the question, "What has the firm done with the funds it acquired from one accounting period to the next?" Figure 17-4 shows a sources and uses of funds statement for Acme Consolidated.

The statement is prepared by tabulating the changes in an organization's balance sheet from one accounting period to the next and classifying each change as either a source or a use of funds. *Sources of funds* include (1) decreases in asset items, (2) increases in liabilities, and (3) increases in depreciation (since

**Figure 17-3
INCOME STATEMENT
FOR ACME
CONSOLIDATED**

Acme Consolidated Income Statement for Year Ending December 31, 1984		
Sales		$2,700,000
Less: Cost of Goods Sold	$1,800,000	
Depreciation	100,000	
Selling & Administrative Cost	90,000	
	$1,990,000	
Operating Profit		710,000
Other Income	25,000	
Gross Income		735,000
Less: Interest	160,000	
Income Before Taxes		575,000
Less: Taxes (50%)	287,500	
Income After Taxes		$ 287,500

**Figure 17-4
SOURCES AND USES
OF FUNDS
STATEMENT FOR
ACME
CONSOLIDATED**

	Acme Consolidated Comparative Balance Sheet and Sources and Uses of Funds Statement 1983–1984			
Assets	**Dec. 31, 1983**	**Dec. 31, 1984**	**Sources**	**Uses**
Cash	$ 75,000	$ 50,000	$ 25,000	
Marketable Securities	50,000	40,000	10,000	
Accounts Receivable	100,000	150,000		$ 50,000
Inventory	175,000	200,000		25,000
Land	80,000	80,000		
Plant & Equipment	860,000	900,000		40,000
	$1,350,000	$1,420,000		
Liabilities and Net Worth				
Accounts Payable	50,000	75,000	25,000	
Notes Payable	100,000	125,000	25,000	
Accruals	20,000	25,000	5,000	
Debentures	220,000	200,000		20,000
Common Stock	480,000	500,000	20,000	
Retained Earnings	470,000	495,000	25,000	
	$1,350,000	$1,420,000	$135,000	$135,000

depreciation does not involve cash outlays). *Uses of funds* include (1) increases in asset items and (2) decreases in liability items.

In the example shown in Figure 17-4 the firm used its funds to expand accounts receivable and inventory, indicating an increase in sales activity. Another use—expansions in the plant and equipment—also may reflect increased sales and production. A final use was to retire some unsecured bonds (debentures). The source of these funds included a reduction of cash on hand, sale of security holdings, increased trade credit (accounts payable), an increase in bank loans (notes payable), an increase in accruals, an issuance of additional common stock, and retained earnings. This statement is useful for internal control as well as for such outside sources as creditors.

RATIO ANALYSIS—IMPORTANT TOOL OF FINANCIAL ANALYSIS

Ratio analysis is used to extract information from the firm's financial statements in order to evaluate performance in a specific area. Ratios assist the controlling process by interpreting actual performance and making comparisons with what should have happened. The firm's ratios can be compared with those of similar companies to reflect company performance relative to competitors'. These *industry standards* serve as important standards in pinpointing problem areas as well as areas of excellence. Ratios for the current accounting period may also be compared with ratios of previous periods to spot any trends that might be developing. Ratios can be classified according to their specific purpose.

Ratio analysis is used to extract information from the firm's financial statements in order to evaluate performance in a specific area; actual and planned performance ratios are compared with one another and with those of similar companies.

1. *Liquidity ratios* measure a firm's ability to meet its maturing short-term obligations. Examples include the current ratio and the acid-test (or quick) ratio.
2. *Leverage ratios* measure the extent to which the firm is relying on debt financing. Examples include the current liability to net worth ratio and the debt-to-equity ratio.
3. *Activity ratios* measure the effectiveness of the firm's use of its resources. Examples include the inventory turnover rate and the average collection period for receivables.
4. *Profitability ratios* measure the overall financial performance in terms of returns generated on sales and investment. Examples include the gross margin percentage, sales margin, and return on capital.

These ratios relate balance sheet and income statement items to one another and assist management in pinpointing strengths and weaknesses. Table 17-3 shows the formulas used to calculate each ratio.

Breakeven Analysis

Breakeven analysis is a method of determining the minimum sales volume needed to cover all costs at a certain price level. As Figure 17-5 indicates the breakeven point is the point at which the total revenue of a firm is equal to total cost. Total cost includes *fixed costs* (those costs such as lease payments, insurance premiums, or the salaries of top management that remain constant regardless of changes in production) and *variable costs* (those costs such as raw materials and other production inputs that vary with different output levels).

Breakeven analysis is a method of determining the minimum sales volume needed to cover all costs at a certain price level.

The comparison of projected with actual breakeven points for various products or divisions can assist management in recognizing problems in time to take

Table 17-3
COMMONLY USED
FINANCIAL RATIOS

TYPE	FORMULA
1. LIQUIDITY RATIOS	
Current ratio	$\dfrac{\text{Current Assets}}{\text{Current Liabilities}}$
Acid-test ratio	$\dfrac{\text{Cash + Marketable Securities + Accts. Receivable}}{\text{Current Liabilities}}$
2. LEVERAGE RATIOS	
Current liability to net worth ratio	$\dfrac{\text{Current Liabilities}}{\text{Net Worth}}$
Debt-to-equity ratio	$\dfrac{\text{Total Debt}}{\text{Net Worth}}$
3. ACTIVITY RATIOS	
Inventory turnover	$\dfrac{\text{Cost of Goods Sold}}{\text{Inventory}}$
Average collection period	$\dfrac{\text{Receivables}}{\text{Average Daily Sales}}$
4. PROFITABILITY RATIOS	
Gross margin percentage	$\dfrac{\text{Gross Profit}}{\text{Sales}}$
Sales margin	$\dfrac{\text{Net Profit After Taxes}}{\text{Sales}}$
Return on investment	$\dfrac{\text{Net Profit After Taxes}}{\text{Total Assets}}$

corrective action. An increase in costs will increase the breakeven point. The increase may result from changes in fixed costs due to the decision to install new equipment or changes in variable costs such as a price increase for raw materials. In either case additional sales would be required to cover the increased cost if the firm is to break even and possibly earn a profit.

In the example shown in Figure 17-5, fixed costs equal $20,000. The horizon-

Figure 17-5
BREAKEVEN
ANALYSIS

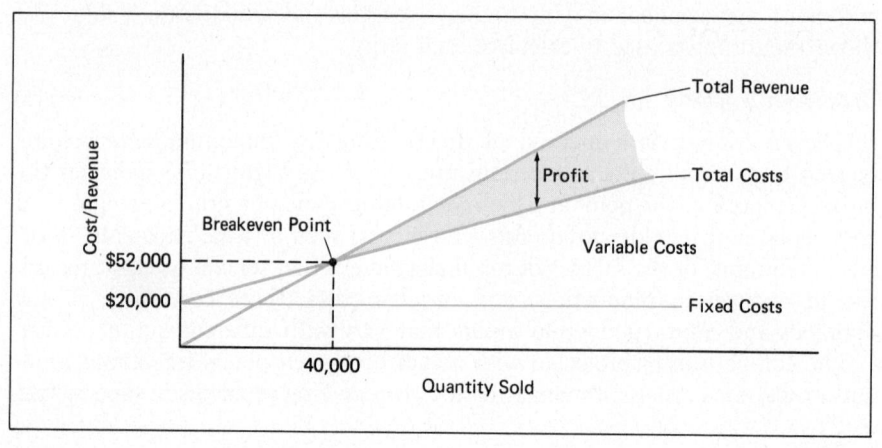

tal line reflects a constant amount of fixed costs regardless of output level. Variable costs are $.80 per unit. The selling price for each unit of output is $1.30. The vertical axis measures revenue and cost, while the horizontal axis measures output in units. The total revenue line reflects the $1.30 selling price multiplied by the number of units sold. The total cost line includes the $20,000 fixed costs and the $.80-per-unit variable costs. The breakeven point is the point of intersection of total revenue and total cost. If production and sales are less than this point, the firm suffers a loss; at levels of production and sales above the breakeven point, the firm earns a profit.

The breakeven point may be determined by analyzing the total fixed costs, the selling price per unit, and the per unit variable costs. By subtracting the variable cost per unit from the product's selling cost, the *contribution margin* indicates the contribution made by each sale to covering the fixed cost. The number of units that must be sold to cover total fixed costs can then be determined by dividing fixed costs by the contribution margin.

$$\text{Breakeven Point} = \frac{\text{Fixed Cost}}{\text{Contribution Margin}}$$

where FC = Total Fixed Costs
P = Price/Unit
V = Variable Cost/Unit
$P - V$ = Contribution Margin

$$BE = \frac{FC}{P - V}$$

$$BE = \frac{\$20,000}{\$1.30 - .80} = \frac{20,000}{.50} = 40,000$$

The breakeven point is 40,000 units, or sales of $52,000 (40,000 × $1.30).

Breakeven analysis is useful in providing managers with a profit or loss estimate at different levels of sales and at different cost estimates. It can also approximate the effect of a change in selling prices on the firm.

PRODUCTION CONTROLS

Production controls are the second general type of control. They were defined earlier as being concerned with the scheduling, timing, and routing of a product or project. Production control employs such tools as Gantt Charts, Program Evaluation and Review Technique (PERT), and Critical Path Method (CPM) in monitoring actual performance and comparing it with expected results. These techniques are discussed in detail in Chapter 19.

ORGANIZATIONAL CONTROL

Organizational control includes both the control exerted by the organizational structure and its planning systems and the control of organizational members.

Production control are concerned with the scheduling, timing, and routing of a product or project.

Organizational controls are controls exerted by the organizational structure and its planning systems and include controls exerted upon organizational members.

At a time when industrial engineering generally took a hard-nosed, dispassionate view of work and workers, Henry Laurence Gantt (1861–1919) was a humanist. Unlike his mentor, Frederick Taylor—considered the developer of scientific management—Gantt believed that workers must be viewed as human beings, not machines, and that managers must learn to lead rather than drive them.

Out of his desire to humanize the management process, Gantt developed several scientific methods of industrial operation whose impact is still felt today. In 1901, while working for Frederick Taylor at the Bethlehem Steel Co., Gantt devised a task-and-bonus system of wage payment that departed from the piece-rate system used by Taylor. It was, said Gantt, "as far as possible removed from the old-fashioned method of fixing piece rates from records of the total time it has taken to do a job." Seeking instead to define exactly what optimum job performance was in standard shop conditions and to create a daily wage base below which the worker could not go, Gantt gave workers a bonus in addition to their regular pay if they completed all the jobs assigned them for that day. When work was left uncompleted, workers still received their full daily rate. In some settings this innovative system resulted in a doubling of production—a fact that convinced Gantt that the success of management programs is tied to a humanistic concern for workers.

As the year passed, Gantt refined his management thoughts, reflecting his efforts in three books and in numerous papers presented to professional organizations. His work in employee relations was crystalized in a presentation to the American Society of Mechanical Engineers in 1908 in which he proposed what

The former types of control were discussed in Chapters 5–8. Management by objective programs, discussed in Chapter 5, serve as important means of control by focusing individual performance on organizational objectives and providing a built-in mechanism for comparing actual and planned performance. Management information systems, the subject of Chapter 18, constitute another critical means of organizational control.

As described in Chapter 16, the basic steps of effective control are similar whether controls apply to organizational members or production or financial processes. Quantifiable standards must be developed for individual performance in order to measure and compare actual performance. Management typically attempts to control individual performance by placing a properly selected, oriented, and trained person in the right job.

1. *Selection.* Employees should be screened and selected on the basis of skills, abilities, and aptitudes compatible with the specific job. Tests and interviews serve as precontrols in recruiting the right person for the right job.
2. *Orientation.* A period of orientation to familiarize the recently hired employee with the nature and duties of his or her job can also serve as an effective precontrol.
3. *Training.* Another effective control is to place new employees in specifically designed job training programs.

was then a revolutionary policy: It was the responsibility of management, said Gantt, to train workers to become more skilled rather than to just drive them to increase their output. He also believed that it was management's role to help employees learn better, more efficient working habits. As a result of this paper Taylor, who supported a much more mechanistic view of workers, severed his long-term personal and working relationship with Gantt. Although Gantt experienced a personal loss, time vindicated his views of human resources management. Years later, after World War I, Gantt's theories became generally accepted as a part of management thought.

During World War I, Gantt volunteered his management services to the government and developed an innovative method for comparing actual to planned work performance. The Gantt Chart, as it came to be known, was a visual method of comparing production output with the time it took to complete a task. For the first time, managers could use a simple visual device to maintain production control. The chart soon became the most widely used control tool in industry and was translated for use by all industrial nations.

In the final years of his life, Gantt extended his humanistic employee relations theories to the concept of industrial service. In his view the ultimate goal of business was to serve the public rather than to create profits. Because of this work, and the work he did throughout his life, Gantt was considered a pioneer in the area of industrial responsibility. He showed that humanism and a systematic approach to production control could work hand in hand.

Sources

Dictionary of American Biography (New York: Charles Scribner & Sons, Inc., 1932), pp. 129–130.

Claude S. George, Jr., *The History of Management Thought*, 2nd ed. (Englewood Cliffs, N.J.: Prentice-Hall, Inc., 1972). Gantt quotation: p. 104.

National Cyclopedia of American Biography, s.v., "Gantt, Henry Laurence."

4. *Performance evaluation.* Individual performance evaluation is an effective use of steering and postcontrols to compare actual performance with measurable goals that have been established as standards for employees.

INVENTORY CONTROL

Inventory control, the fourth type of control, is concerned with the amount of assets that should be held in inventory. Manufacturing firms typically maintain three kinds of inventory: raw materials, work in progress, and finished goods. Each type is affected by different influences. The level of raw materials in inventory is determined by such factors as reliability of supply sources, seasonal nature of production, and anticipated sales. Work in process inventory is affected by the length of the production cycle, while finished goods inventory is a function of sales and the time involved in making shipments to customers. Since a sizable investment is made in inventory, adequate control must be developed to insure that the firm minimizes the cost of the investment, while avoiding the risk of lost sales or interrupted production schedules caused by lack of inventory at a given time.

Controlling inventory is basically a matter of minimizing the total costs of maintaining inventory. A number of sophisticated methods have been developed for determining the optimum levels of inventory for different kinds of organizations. These are discussed in Chapter 19.

Inventory control is concerned with the amount of assets—raw materials, work in progress, and finished goods—that should be held in inventory.

QUALITY CONTROL

Quality control deals with maintaining specified quality levels for a firm's goods or services.

Quality control, the fifth type of control, deals with maintaining the quality of a firm's goods or services. Organizations utilize two basic methods for maintaining the quality of finished products. In organizations where quality level requirements are high and/or where high unit costs are present, individual inspections of each unit of output may be conducted to insure that specifications are met. Other firms will sample a certain percentage of the output in the inspection process. Quality control is also discussed in detail in Chapter 19.

Evaluating Performance

Data generated from a control system can be routed to staff personnel, higher-level line managers, the managers of the unit being measured, or the individuals in the unit being measured. As the previous chapter pointed out, the individual or group who can make the most meaningful use of the data should receive it first in most instances. Such feedback is particularly useful in informing managers and individual employees of their current performance. In cases of deviations from expected performance it is used as a basis for making rapid adjustments and as an aid in the learning process.

PHYSICAL INSPECTION IS A COMMONLY USED QUALITY CONTROL TECHNIQUE

SOURCE: *The New Yorker* (August 10, 1981), p. 83. Drawing by Ross; © 1981 The New Yorker Magazine, Inc.

"Hey, I'm the building inspector. This building O.K.?"

Summary

Controls are important for achieving organizational objectives. They fall into five general categories:

1. *Financial control*, which is concerned with budgets, financial analysis, and breakeven analysis;
2. *Production control*, which is concerned with the scheduling, timing, and routing of a product or project;
3. *Organizational control*, which is concerned with determination of working relations, job design, and employee evaluation;
4. *Inventory control*, which is concerned with the levels of assets held in various stages of inventory; and
5. *Quality control*, which is concerned with the quality of services or products produced by the organization.

Controls are discussed in detail throughout the text. Production control, inventory control, and quality control are major topics in Chapter 19, while organizational controls were first discussed in Chapter 5 and Chapter 9. Consequently, this chapter has placed major emphasis upon budgets, financial analysis, and breakeven analysis as important techniques of financial control.

Perhaps the most widely used device for controlling the activities of an organization is the budget. Budgets are financial plans listing in detail the resources or funds assigned to a particular product, division, or project. Major types include the manufacturing budget, capital expenditures budget, marketing budget, research and development budget, executive staff budget, product budget, branch (or regional) budget, cash flow budget, budgeted income statement, and budgeted balance sheet. Budgets should be flexible enough to allow adjustments for changing conditions. The zero-base budget is an attempt to base resource allocations upon current needs rather than historical actions.

Financial analysis utilizes financial documents of the firm to control its general profitability, its liquidity, and its overall financial condition. Three commonly used financial statements are the balance sheet, income statement, and sources and uses of funds statement. Ratio analysis is used to extract information from these statements and make comparisons between actual and expected performance. The major categories of ratios are liquidity, leverage, activity, and profitability.

Breakeven analysis, the third financial control tool, is a method of determining the minimum sales volume needed to cover all costs at a certain price level. It shows the relationship between sales volume, costs, and profits.

REVIEW EXERCISES

1. Define the following terms: (a) budget (b) program planning budgeting systems (PPBS) (c) zero-base budgeting (ZBB) (d) financial analysis (e) ratio analysis (f) breakeven analysis (g) production control (h) organizational control (i) inventory control (j) quality control.

2. Identify the five general control tools. Give an example of each.

3. List the five steps involved in budget development.

4. What are the major types of budgets?

5. Why is flexibility an important characteristic of budgets?

6. What are the advantages of zero-base budgeting? What problems are involved with this approach?

7. Identify each of the major financial statements. What is the purpose of each statement?

8. Distinguish between financial statement analysis and ratio analysis.

9. Identify the major types of ratios. Give an example of each type.

10. Explain each of the components of the breakeven analysis equation.

ASSIGNMENTS/ PROBLEMS/ DISCUSSION QUESTIONS

1. Secure a copy of the current budget used by your student government association or student newspaper. Compare its development with the steps discussed in the chapter. How flexible is the budget? How might it be made more flexible?

2. Prepare a proposal for instituting zero-base budgeting at your college or university.

3. Refer to the balance sheet and income statement shown in Figures 17-2 and 17-3. Use this data to calculate the following ratios:

   a. Current ratio
   b. Acid-test ratio
   c. Current liability-to-net worth ratio
   d. Debt-to-equity ratio
   e. Gross margin percentage
   f. Sales margin
   g. Return on investment

4. Give an example of a situation in which each of the following types of ratios would be useful:

   a. Liquidity ratio
   b. Leverage ratio
   c. Activity ratio
   d. Profitability ratio

5. What is the breakeven point for a product with a selling price of $50, an average variable cost of $32, and related fixed costs of $252,000?

A MANAGERIAL INCIDENT

Malone and Hyde, Inc.

Everything Joseph Hyde III did from 1973 to 1981 seemed to turn out right for his company, Malone

& Hyde, Inc. The Memphis-based food wholesaler increased sales and profits by 250 percent over the nine-year period. But then Hyde got careless.

A Texas grocery store group asked Malone & Hyde, its supplier, for help when they ran into financial difficulties. Malone & Hyde was promised a $70 million account in return, so Hyde decided to take over the Texas operation. However, he soon discovered that he had acquired some overstated assets. He was eventually forced to liquidate all but six of the twenty-one Texas stores at a loss of $6.5 million.

Hyde had learned an important lesson about control and was determined not to repeat his mistake. He appointed an executive vice-president of finance, Thomas M. Garrott III, and ordered him to develop fail-safe financial controls. Garrott acted quickly. Credit terms were made more restrictive. Accounts receivables were collected a day and a half earlier than previously. A $2.5 million bad debt reserve fund was established. As Garrott ex-

pressed his philosophy of control, "Catch the problem when it's still a skin cancer, not a brain tumor."

The effectiveness of Malone & Hyde's strengthened control system was evident in 1982. The company resumed its previous string of record earnings. As Joseph Hyde put it: "We're not going to have another down year for a long time. A long time."

SOURCE: Thomas Jaffe, "A Self-Inflicted Wound," *Forbes* (February 1, 1982), pp. 81–84.

Questions and Problems

1. Discuss the control techniques that were implemented at Malone & Hyde.

2. What other techniques might be advantageous for the food wholesaler? Defend you answer.

18.

Management Information Systems: Making Control Effective

Facts do not cease to exist because
they are ignored.

ALDOUS HUXLEY

A computer isn't smart enough to make
a mistake.
Computers are dumb.
Fast and efficient and dumb.
No computer ever had an idea.

IBM ADVERTISEMENT

Although the 1980s have been problem-filled years for such organizations as Chrysler, Braniff, and International Harvester, they were years of tremendous growth for Shaklee Corp. During the previous decade, the Emeryville, California, producer of household cleaners, food supplements, and cosmetics increased its sales from $10 million to more than $350 million. But Shaklee managers were concerned about decisions that appeared to be made largely on a subjective and political basis.

A major question facing Shaklee decision makers was whether customers' orders could be filled more rapidly without increasing production or distribution costs. Company planners decided to construct a base of pertinent data for use in making such decisions. The data base consisted of information on plant locations, products made, cost per unit, and production capacity for its three manufacturing facilities and that of its twenty contract manufacturers. It also included details on more than 500 products, 360 customers, and Shaklee's 100 distribution centers. Once the data were collected, a model was developed that allowed Shaklee managers to consider alternative delivery requirements and the effect that each customer response rate would have on transportation costs, the cost of operating distribution centers, and the cost of carrying products in inventory.

The model not only allowed Shaklee to cut delivery time to customers, it also produced an $850,000 savings in operating costs in a single year. In addition, the data base could be utilized to analyze other operating problems and opportunities that might arise. But development costs were considerable. It cost $250,000 and took six months to develop the data base and construct the model. In addition, annual maintenance costs are estimated to total $50,000. However, Shaklee executives are delighted at the expenditure. They estimate that for every dollar spent in the system's development, they will recover $100 over a five-year period.[1]

CONTROLLING AND INFORMATION NEEDS

Sir Arthur Conan Doyle summed up an all-too-common dilemma facing the manager of the 1980s in the form of a remark by the world's most famous detective. In Doyle's book, *The Adventure of the Copper Beeches*, Sherlock Holmes cries impatiently to Watson, "Data! Data! Data! I can't make bricks without clay."[2]

The business environment for the past quarter-century has been characterized by increasing competition, decreasing product life cycles, and the growth of organizations in terms of both human and physical assets. These changes have been accompanied by increasing societal pressures for greater accountability. Decision makers have often been forced to extend planning horizons—and introduce even greater levels of uncertainty. In addition, the typical manager is further removed from action points, increasing communications problems and making effective control more difficult.

Chapters 16 and 17 have focused upon a variety of tools, techniques, and approaches to assist managers in controlling. A key element in both planning and controlling is *information*, and a relatively new discipline has evolved to work toward institutionalizing the planning–controlling process by dealing with the special problems of information gathering, analysis, and reporting. This discipline has been labeled management information systems, or, simply, MIS.

What Is a Management Information System?

Information is increasingly recognized as not only a significant element in the planning–controlling process but also as a major organizational *resource*. If the decision maker defines a problem as a gap between the actual state and a desired state, information is utilized both to identify and to describe the gap. Information will also be utilized in evaluating alternative methods of bridging the gap.

A *management information system* may be defined as a structured, interacting complex of persons, machines, and procedures designed to generate an orderly flow of relevant information, collected from both intra- and extra-organizational sources, for use as the basis for decision making in specified management responsibility areas.[3] The MIS is designed to acquire, store, and convert data into information for decision making. Availability of timely, relevant information is invaluable in performing the planning, control, and operational functions of the organization.

A management information system is a structured, interacting complex of persons, machines, and procedures designed to generate an orderly flow of information.

[1] "'What If' Help for Management," *Business Week* (January 21, 1980), pp. 73–74.
[2] Quoted in C. Richard Roberts and Louis E. Boone, "MIS Development in American Industry: The Apex," *The Journal of Business Strategy* (Winter 1983).
[3] Samuel V. Smith, Richard H. Brien, and James E. Stafford, *Readings in Marketing Information Systems* (Boston: Houghton Mifflin, 1968), p. 7.

DATA VERSUS INFORMATION

In 1983 U.S. organizations spent an estimated $78 billion to develop and operate data processing systems and computer-based information systems.[4] The significant growth in the number of computer installations in both profit and nonprofit organizations has been accompanied by major increases in available data for use by decision makers. In many cases managers complain about an overabundance of data generated by their increasingly sophisticated computer facilities. Daily computer printouts provide thousands of details about production schedules; current inventory positions of raw materials, goods in process, and finished products; output levels by plant, shift, and department; and cost and sales analyses by territory, product, customer, sales division, and order size. Such daily analyses may have been casually requested months ago by the manager in response to a data needs questionnaire, but in many cases they are equally casually ignored. Data and information are not synonymous terms.[5]

Data are facts, statistics, opinions, or predictions categorized on some basis for storage and retrieval. *Information* is data relevant to the manager in making decisions. As Figure 18-1 indicates, a major function of the MIS is the transformation of data into decision-relevant information.

The system shown in Figure 18-1 performs six functions:

1. *Assembly:* the search for and gathering of data
2. *Processing:* the editing and summarization of data
3. *Analysis:* the computation of percentages and ratios, and tests of statistical significance
4. *Storage and Retrieval:* the indexing, filing, and relocating of data
5. *Evaluation:* the determination of information quality, degree of faith the decision maker should have in the accuracy of the data

Data are facts, statistics, opinions, or predictions categorized on some basis for storage and retrieval.

Information is data relevant to the manager in making decisions.

---

[4] Paul H. Cheney and Gary W. Dickson, "Organizational Characteristics and Information Systems: An Exploratory Investigation," *Academy of Management Journal* (March 1982), pp. 170–184.

[5] Louis E. Boone, "Proposed Cure for the Information Explosion," *Business Horizons* (December 1972). See also Reed Sanderlin, "Information Is Not Communication," *Business Horizons* (March–April 1982), pp. 40–42.

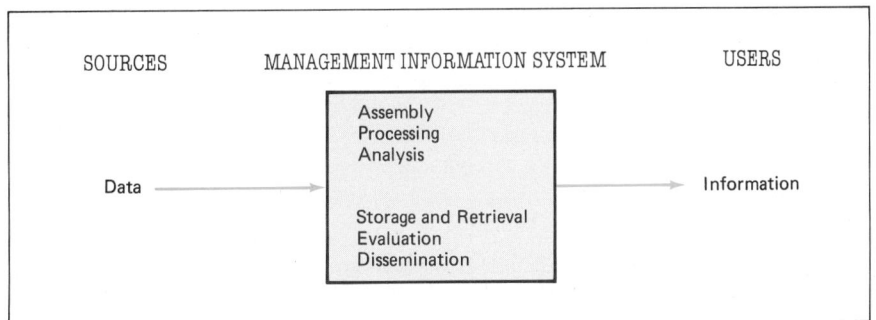

Figure 18-1
THE MANAGEMENT INFORMATION SYSTEM CONCEPT

SOURCE: Adapted from Keith K. Cox and Ben M. Enis, *The Marketing Research Process* (Pacific Palisades, Calif.: Goodyear Publishing Co., 1972), p. 19.

6. *Dissemination:* the routing of useful information to the proper decision maker[6]

Management Information Categories

Management information may be divided into three major categories: strategic planning information, management control information, and operational control information.[7]

Strategic planning information is utilized by managers in deciding upon the objectives of the organization, the resources to be used in attaining these objectives, and the policies developed and used to govern the acquisition, use, and disposition of these resources. External information represents a major part of strategic planning information needs. Relatively unique informational requirements may be present for the strategic planning process.

Management control information is used in determining whether resources are obtained and used effectively and efficiently in the accomplishment of organizational objectives. The control process requires the coordination of efforts of individuals in various departments. Informational inputs often cut across established functional areas.

Operational control information is used in determining whether the specific day-to-day tasks of the organization are being carried out efficiently and effectively. Information used for operational control may include payroll records, inventory listings, and personnel statistics. Such information is typically detailed, highly current, accurate, largely internal, narrow in scope, and in frequent use.

Figure 18-2 compares the three categories on the basis of information scope, source, aggregation level, time horizon, currency, accuracy requirements, and frequency of use. The variations in information characteristics for the different

---

[6] Keith K. Cox and Ben M. Enis, *The Marketing Research Process* (Santa Monica, Calif.: Goodyear Publishing Co., 1972), p. 19.

[7] This widely accepted taxonomy was developed by Robert N. Anthony. See his *Planning and Control Systems: A Framework for Analysis* (Boston: Division of Research, Harvard Business School, 1965), pp. 16–18.

Figure 18-2 INFORMATION NEEDS FOR DIFFERENT CATEGORIES OF MANAGEMENT DECISIONS

Characteristics of Information	Operational Control	Management Control	Strategic Planning
Source	Largely internal ⟶		External
Scope	Well defined, narrow ⟶		Very wide
Level of aggregation	Detailed ⟶		Aggregate
Time horizon	Historical ⟶		Future
Currency	Highly current ⟶		Quite old
Required accuracy	High ⟶		Low
Frequency of use	Very frequent ⟶		Infrequent

SOURCE: G. Anthony Gorry and Michael Scott Morton, "A Framework for Management Information Systems," *Sloan Management Review* (Fall 1971), p. 58. Reprinted by permission of the Sloan Management Review Association. Copyright © 1971 by the Sloan Management Review Association. All rights reserved.

categories are further evidence of the need to tailor information flows to meet the specific needs of managers at different levels in the organization.

Components of the MIS

In order to perform its functions of providing timely, decision-relevant information for the manager, the MIS must have three components: a data bank, an analytical methods bank, and a model bank.[8]

THE DATA BANK

The *data bank* is the foundation of any MIS. It consists of raw data, as assembled, recorded, stored, and retrieved. Data inputs come from both internal and external sources. Internal sources include production and sales reports, invoices, financial data, and reports from such departments as purchasing, engineering, and product development. External sources include government publications, data from suppliers, customer feedback, and data collected from competitors. Table 18-1 illustrates the various sources of data and examples of data from each source.

The data bank consists of raw data, as assembled, recorded, stored, and retrieved.

THE DATA BASE CONCEPT

Although more and more organizations are attempting to develop data banks to serve as repositories for data, all too often the various functional areas develop data networks independently from one another in response to specific needs. Each department or function defines its data requirements, which then may be collected and stored with little coordination with other existing or planned elements. The resulting data system is typically a fragmented, overlapping collection of files that are largely dependent upon the specific systems originally developed at the time of data collection. The result is often too much data in the wrong form that is virtually inaccessible except when using the specific original format.

A data base system is designed to prevent—or correct—these problems. A *data base* is a centralized, manageable repository of the organization's data resources—procedures, computer programs, and specialized personnel. While systems vary widely from one organization to the next, the common interweaving threads are sets of files capable of being read by the organization's computer, sharing of common resources, and centralized authority.[9]

When carried to its logical conclusion, the data base concept includes centralizing the various data resources in files that can be accessed by different decision makers for different uses. The concept is a major milestone in MIS development, making possible access to all portions of the data base across functional

---

[8] This section is based on David B. Montgomery and Glen L. Urban, "Marketing Decision–Information Systems: An Emerging View," *Journal of Marketing Research* (May 1970), pp. 226–234.

[9] Richard L. Nolan, "Computer Data Bases: The Future Is Now," *Harvard Business Review* (September–October 1973), p. 103. See also Fred R. McFadden and James D. Suver, "Costs and Benefits of a Data System," *Harvard Business Review* (January–February 1978), pp. 131–139.

	SOURCE	EXAMPLES	COMMENTS
Table 18-1 SOURCES OF MIS DATA INPUTS	Government	Freedom of Information Act	1974 amendments have led to accelerating use.
		Government Contract Administration	Examination of competitor's bids and documentation may reveal competitor's technology and indicate his costs and bidding philosophy.
		Patent filings	Belgium and Italy publish patent applications shortly after they are filed. Some companies (e.g., pharmaceutical) patent their mistakes in order to confuse their competitors.
	Competitors	Annual reports and 10Ks	FTC and SEC line of business reporting requirements will render this source more useful in the future.
		Speeches and public announcements of competitor's officers	Reveal management philosophy, priorities, and self-evaluation systems.
		Products	Systematic analysis of a competitor's products via back engineering may reveal the competitor's technology and enable the company to monitor changes in the competitor's engineering and assembly operations. Forecasts of a competitor's sales may often be made from observing his serial numbers over time.
		Employment ads	May suggest the technical and marketing directions in which a competitor is headed.
		Consultants	For example, if a competitor has retained Boston Consulting, then portfolio management strategies become more likely.

divisions and at different organizational levels.[10] One survey of the major U.S. manufacturing firms revealed that almost four of every five firms surveyed possess a data base or are currently implementing a data base system.[11]

Effective implementation of the data base concept should result in the creation of an integrated overall information system. Such a system would be made up of information subsystems from such functional areas as marketing, accounting, logistics, and personnel. Rather than duplicating information in the data banks of each subsystem, the integrated system would allow each subsystem to

[10] John G. Burch, Felix R. Strater, and Gary Grudnitski, *Information Systems: Theory and Practice* (New York: Wiley, 1979), pp. 149–150.

[11] Roberts and Boone, "MIS Development in American Industry: The Apex," p. 13.

SOURCE	EXAMPLES	COMMENTS
Suppliers	Banks, advertising agencies, public relations firms, and direct mailers and catalogers, as well as hard goods suppliers	Have a tendency to be more talkative than competitors since the information transmitted may enhance supplier's business. Can be effective sources of information on such items as competitor's equipment installations and on what retail competitors are already carrying certain product lines. Suppliers' biases can usually be recognized.
Customers	Purchasing agents	Generally regarded as self serving. Low reliability as a source.
	Customer engineers and corporate officers	Valued sources of intelligence. One company taught its salespersons to perform elementary service for customers in order to get the salespersons past the purchasing agent and on to the more valued sources of intelligence.
Professional Associations and Meetings	Scientific and technical society meetings, management association meetings	Examine competitor's products, research and development, and management approach as revealed in displays, brochures, scientific papers, and speeches.
Company Personnel	Executives, sales force, engineers and scientists, purchasing agents	Sensitize them to the need for intelligence and train them to recognize and transmit to the proper organizational location relevant intelligence that comes to their attention.

SOURCE: David B. Montgomery and Charles B. Weinberg, "Toward Strategic Intelligence Systems," *Journal of Marketing* (Fall 1979), p. 46. Reprinted by permission.

utilize centrally accumulated data, thereby decreasing overall response time and reducing costs. Figure 18-3 shows the integrated MIS concept with a more detailed description of the accounting and marketing subsystems.

THE ANALYTICAL METHODS BANK

The second component of the MIS, the *analytical methods bank,* has the responsibility for processing and analyzing the data inputs. Such analysis may be limited to development of averages or frequency distributions; in other cases, more sophisticated statistical techniques such as factor analysis or multiple regression may be used in data analysis.

**Figure 18-3
INTEGRATED
MANAGEMENT
INFORMATION
SYSTEM**

SOURCE: Reprinted by permission from James H. Donnelly, Jr., James L. Gibson, and John M. Ivancevich, *Fundamentals of Management* (Homewood, Ill.: Business Publications, Inc., 1981), p. 418. © 1981 Business Publications, Inc.

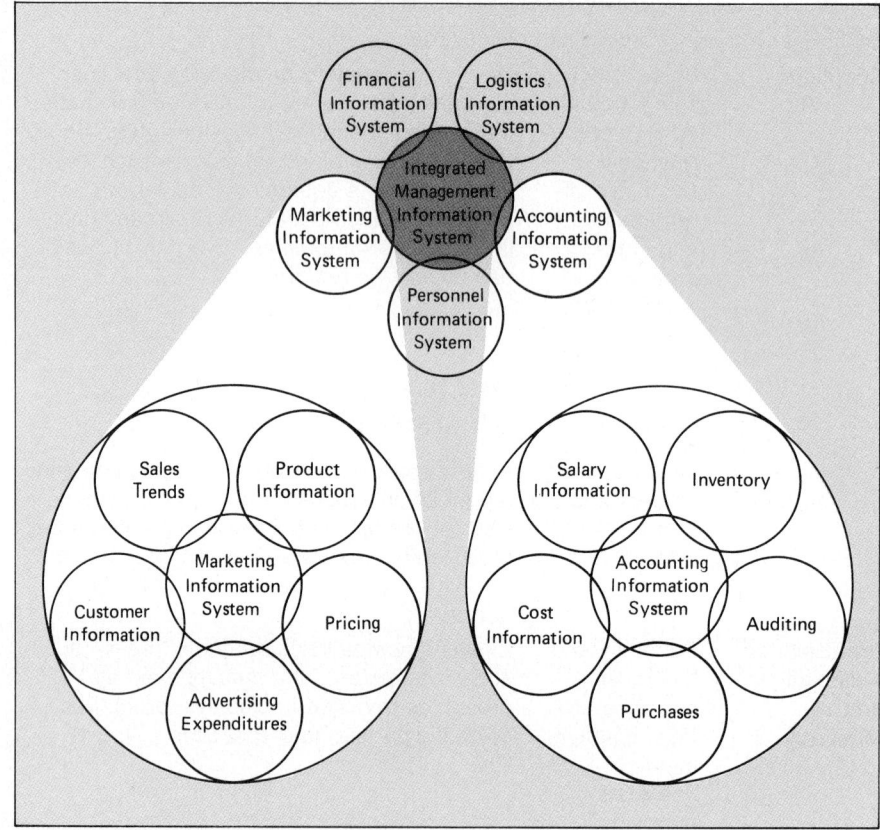

Model bank integrates various models, including linear programming models, simulations, and queuing models, for use in describing, predicting, and possibly controlling organizational behavior.

THE MODEL BANK

As explained in Chapter 8 a variety of mathematical models can be utilized in analyzing and solving problems. Such techniques as linear programming models, simulations, and queuing models have proven useful in analyzing complex problem situations and suggesting possible solutions. The ideal MIS will integrate these models for use in describing, predicting, and possibly controlling.

The Role of the Computer in Management Information Systems

The development of the MIS concept has accompanied the marked advances in computer technology. The recent advances in electronic data processing have made possible the creation of vast data bases and sophisticated analysis and reporting systems. In fact, many people confuse MIS with electronic data processing.

Computers are *only one component* in the organization's information system. The computer is only a tool—although an extremely important tool in many

UTOPIA FOR MIS MODEL BANKS

While models have proven extremely useful in tackling a number of knotty business problems, model builders in many organizations dream of a fully functioning MIS capable of handling a problem like the following:

At 9:32 A.M., a blowout! A blast furnace breaks down in the steel plant. Cold iron will have to be heated to produce the molten iron normally supplied to the refining process from this furnace. Processing time will be almost doubled, reducing the shop's production capacity by 60 percent. The cost per ton of steel will certainly rise sharply as a result of the increased processing time. But how much will it rise?

Using a remote time-shared computer terminal in his office, a manager at Inland Steel Company defines the new conditions resulting from the equipment failure and enters them in a set of models which simulate the steelmaking process and the costs involved. At 11:26 A.M.—less than two hours later the same morning—he estimates the new cost figures and prepares a revised corporate profit projection.

The MIS at Inland Steel has been capable of handling similar problems for over a decade.

SOURCE: Reprinted by permission of the Harvard Business Review. Excerpted from ''Corporate Models: On-Line, Real-Time Systems'' by James B. Boulden and Elwood S. Buffa (July–August 1970). Copyright © 1970 by the President and Fellows of Harvard College; all rights reserved.

instances. However, many valuable information components are not computerized. Special research studies investigating panel members' attitudes to a mockup of a proposed new product, proposed rule changes by a government agency, or the financial report of a major competitor all represent valuable, noncomputerized information.

In some instances the level of computer sophistication actually impedes MIS development. The computer specialists who supervise data processing systems often lack the business background needed to match their systems to the information needs of decision makers. In recent years dozens of major firms have taken steps to fill this void by removing computer management from the hands of technicians and forming steering committees composed of high-ranking executives with the necessary business backgrounds. Such firms as Southern Railway, Security Pacific National Bank in Los Angeles, Massachusetts Mutual Life Insurance Company, Ford Motor Co., and Aetna Life & Casualty utilize the steering committee approach.

At Inland Steel Co., the systems review committee is made up of seven vice-presidents who decide the MIS priorities among corporate sales, finance, and manufacturing.[12]

Figure 18-4 depicts the typical structure of the management information sys-

[12] "Solving a Computer Mismatch in Management," *Business Week* (April 2, 1979), pp. 73–74.

tem and indicates the interactions of the data bank, analytical methods bank, and model bank. It also identifies the boundaries of the organization's information system and relates the impact of the environment on the MIS and the decision maker.

Bases for Comparing Information Systems

Since no two managers have precisely the same information needs, the characteristics of different systems vary considerably. Each MIS reflects an attempt to

**Figure 18-4
INTERACTIONS OF
THE MIS DATA
BANK, ANALYTICAL
METHODS BANK,
AND MODEL BANK**

SOURCE: Adapted from William R. King, *Marketing Management Information Systems* (New York: Petrocelli/ Charter, 1977), p. 69. © 1977 by Litton Educational Publishing, Inc. Reprinted by permission of Van Nostrand Reinhold Company.

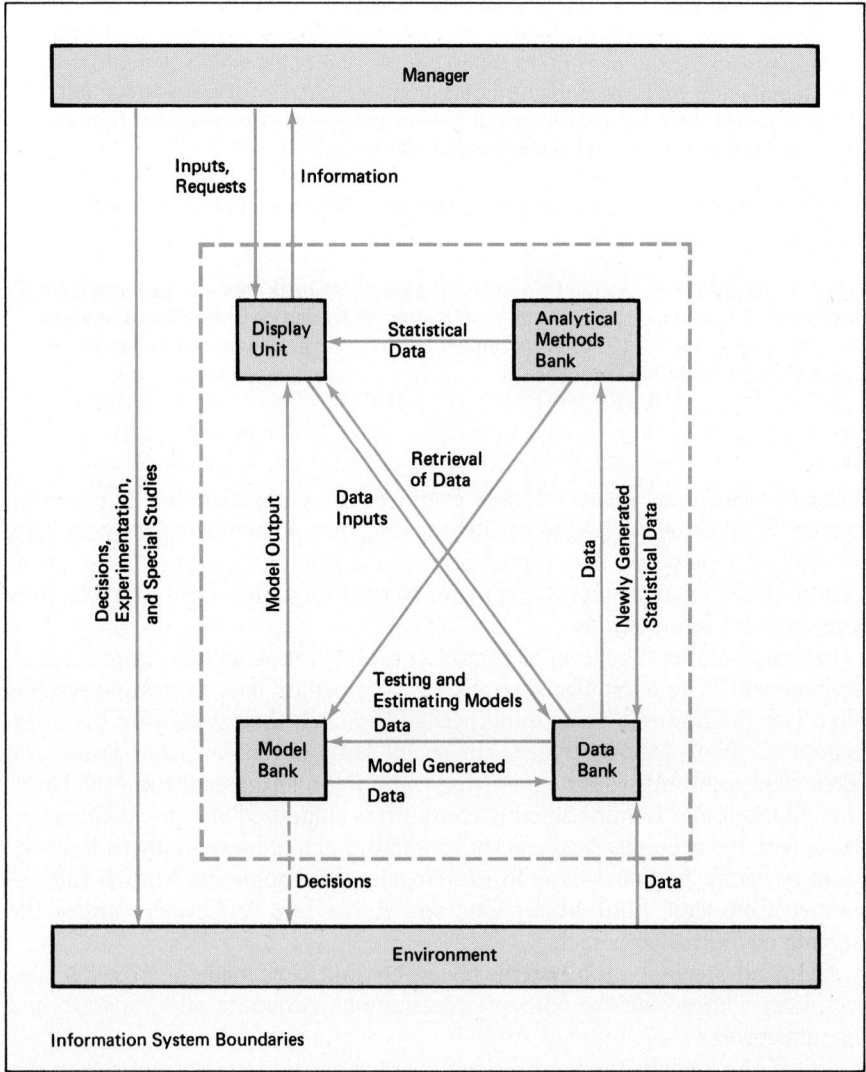

Control systems may be possible without the use of sophisticated computer systems, but the managers at Apple Computer, Inc., are unconvinced. The minicomputer pioneer has even gone so far as to eliminate typewriters and abolish the job title of secretary. It all started in 1980 with a memo circulated by the firm's president:

> Effective immediately! NO MORE TYPEWRITERS ARE TO BE PURCHASED, LEASED, etc. etc. Apple is an innovative company. We must believe and lead in all areas. If word processing is so neat, then let's all use it! Goal: by 1–1–81, NO typewriters at Apple ... We believe the typewriter is obsolete. Let's prove it inside before we try and convince our customers.

Combined with conventional data processing run on a Digital Equipment Corp. minicomputer system, the result is what one executive calls "the most computerized company in the world," a revolutionary development even by the high-tech standards of California's Santa Clara County (a.k.a. Silicon Valley).

There are now no more than 20 typewriters left in the 2,200-employee firm. Instead of typewriters, the several hundred employees involved in composing or disseminating letters, memos, documents, or reports use a typewriter-sized Apple II with built-in keyboard, a pair of add-on disk drives, a video monitor, and Apple Writer, the company's own disk-stored word processing software. Word processing has gained a foothold in many businesses, but never before has a firm so completely done away with typewriters by executive fiat.

Five months after the decision was made to do away with typewriters at Apple Computer, the term "secretary" was abolished and replaced by "area associate" to reflect the more varied responsibilities made possible by personal computers. "We felt we needed a different term," Ann Bowers, vice-president of human resources, explains, "because 'secretary' was so loaded with connotations of typist, errand-runner, and phone answerer. We wanted to expand the area associates' functions so they could use their brains, in additional to their clerical skills."

SOURCE: Reprinted by permission from Steve Ditlea, "An Apple on Every Desk," *INC.* (October 1981), p. 50. © Steve Ditlea.

THE WORLD'S MOST COMPUTERIZED COMPANY?

respond to the specific needs of decision makers, the problems they face, and the approaches they use in planning, controlling, and analyzing and solving problems.

Despite these differences, information systems do possess certain common dimensions that may be analyzed in isolating similarities and differences. These dimensions are

1. Information recency
2. Management access time
3. Information aggregation

4. Analytical sophistication
5. System authority[13]

INFORMATION RECENCY

Information recency refers to the time lapse between the occurrence of an event and the inclusion of data recording that event in the MIS. This may range from a second or two in the recording of retail sales purchases by a cash register-type point of sale terminal linked to the firm's information system to several months in the case of detailed investigations of alternate production site locations. The degree of current, up-to-date information varies among organizations, even for identical data items. Some organizations will record changes in finished goods inventories as they occur; others will record them daily or weekly in a single batch process of aggregate changes.

Holiday Inns, Inc., managers require precise, up-to-the-minute data for their international reservation system. Their Holidex system handles more than 100,000 daily communications for some 2,000 inns in the United States, Canada, and several other countries throughout the world. The system makes possible immediate determination of available accommodations in any inn and automatically makes reservations with printed confirmation to the guest and notification to the inn. Similar sophisticated reservations systems are utilized daily by major airlines.

Determination of appropriate levels of information recency should be based upon the uses to be made of the information. In many cases the cost of continually updating computer data banks is not justified, since managers may be utilizing the data on a weekly or biweekly basis. In these instances a less costly weekly updating may be appropriate. In the case of reservations systems or other instances in which the decision maker must utilize completely current data, the MIS should be designed to meet such requirements.

MANAGEMENT ACCESS TIME

Management access time is the time lapse between the manager's request for certain information and its receipt. It is a measurement of the system's response time for a given request.

INFORMATION AGGREGATION

Information aggregation refers to the detail with which information is maintained in the data bank of the MIS. Data may vary from a highly disaggregated item level recording (performance data for individual employees, inventory

---

[13] Arnold E. Amstutz, "The Marketing Executive and Management Information Systems," in Raymond M. Haas (ed.), *Science, Technology, and Marketing* (Chicago: American Marketing Association, 1967), pp. 69–86.

records by item, or individual sales invoice recording of products sold, customer, salesperson, and order size) to highly aggregated data such as departmental or divisional performance, total sales by product lines, or aggregate inventory positions. A positive correlation exists between aggregation levels and the amount of time delay involved in recording data into the system. Highly disaggregated data tend to be added to the data bank faster than aggregated data, which must accumulate before they are recorded.

ANALYTICAL SOPHISTICATION

Analytical sophistication refers to the complexity of the model bank and the analytical methods bank of the MIS. As Figure 18-5 indicates, the lowest level of analytical sophistication involves the simple retrieval and display of requested data for the manager who must then analyze it. The second level involves the aggregation of data from one or more sources to produce totals or subtotals. The third level consists of arithmetic averaging, while the fourth level logically analyzes data by aggregating it into various classification schemes. Statistical analyses are used at the fifth level to develop forecasts based upon historic data or to employ statistical tests of difference on collected data. Learning, the title of the sixth level of analytical sophistication, involves a system programmed to modify the model structures based upon data inputs received over time. The final level is typical of a relatively small number of highly sophisticated systems capable of evaluating alternate decisions and adjusting simulation models based upon environmental data. This stage provides decision makers with the capability of

Analytical sophistication refers to the complexity of the model and analytical methods banks of the MIS.

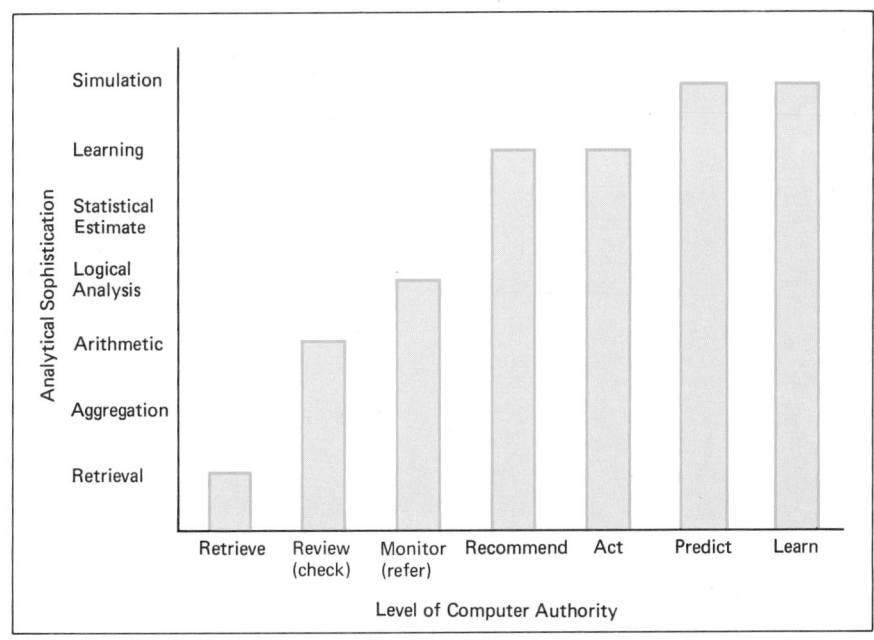

Figure 18-5 RELATIONSHIP BETWEEN DEGREE OF ANALYTICAL SOPHISTICATION AND LEVEL OF COMPUTER AUTHORITY

SOURCE: Arnold E. Amstutz, "The Marketing Executive and Management Information Systems," in Raymond M. Haas (ed.), *Science, Technology, and Marketing* (Chicago: American Marketing Association, 1967).

testing possible strategies in the simulated environment. The MIS is capable of producing scenarios of outcomes to each "What if?" question posed by the system user.

SYSTEM AUTHORITY

System authority refers to the amount of authority delegated to the MIS.

System authority, the final dimension used in comparing information systems of different organizations, is the amount of authority delegated to the MIS. As Figure 18-5 shows, system authority is closely associated with the system's degree of analytical sophistication. Management's willingness to delegate authority increases with the sophistication level of the system. In addition, increased management demands from an MIS require greater levels of analytical sophistication in the system.

At the lowest level, decision makers may restrict authority to retrieval of data from designated locations. The next level calls for system reviews (or checks) of each record for errors. A third level involves monitoring of data and reporting exceptions (as defined by the decision makers) to management. The fourth level of sophistication calls for the system to make recommendations for action. Allowing the system to take action on all but exceptional cases (as defined by management) is the fifth level of system authority. The highest levels of system authority involve permitting the MIS to predict possible outcomes of alternative decisions as a basis for planning and to adapt the system's parameters and models in an evolutionary learning process.

Characteristics of Successful Information Systems

Why are some information systems highly successful while others produce little benefit in return for the costs of development and maintenance? Are the failures due to software programs too limited to utilize the vast capacities of today's computer facilities? Information specialists generally agree that the problems do *not* lie in the technical attributes of the system.[14]

Although the specific functions and outputs of different systems vary to meet specific needs of individual organizations, four characteristics are present in successful systems:

1. *The system is founded on management's conception of the decision environment.*[15] Successful information systems must reflect the priorities of

---

[14] H. C. Lucas, Jr., *Why Information Systems Fail* (New York: Columbia University Press, 1975). See also Daniel Robey, "User Attitudes and Management Information System Use," *Academy of Management Journal* (September 1979), p. 527; Kate Kaiser and Ananth Srinivasan, "User–Analyst Differences: An Empirical Investigation of Attitudes Related to Systems Development," *Academy of Management Journal* (September 1982), pp. 630–646.

[15] These characteristics are suggested by Amstutz in "The Marketing Executive and Management Information Systems." The discussion of each characteristic is based upon his work.

the decision makers who will make use of it. Since it must provide information in the form, amount, and of the type that managers can use, the system must be based on models that reflect management's conception of the environment.

2. *The user-manager must understand and be involved in the construction of the system structure.* The more managers are involved in developing and updating the organization's MIS, the more likely they are to use it to aid their decision making. Managers must understand the structuring of the system; they must make certain that it includes the specific measures and analytical activities they require. Generalized information systems do not exist: each must be designed with the specialized needs and preferences of the ultimate users.

3. *The system is based on disaggregated data files.* The disaggregated data file is the core of the successful information system. New data inputs are added to the data base of existing data as they are received, rather than being combined with existing data. Since information systems tend to increase their levels of sophistication over time, disaggregated data files provide the necessary flexibility to permit a variety of alternative uses, analyses, and combinations of data as needs change. In the early stages of MIS development, it is difficult to anticipate the direction of future advancements. Aggregate data files may prohibit future modifications. Disaggregated data files furnish the flexibility for systems evolution.

4. *System development has proceeded to increasing levels of sophistication through a process of gradual evolution.* MIS sophistication can usually be increased much more readily than the abilities of managers to use it. As managers gain experience in working with well-organized and accessible data, they become increasingly interested in and prepared to use more advanced analytical procedures. The successful system evolves to levels of greater sophistication in response to management's ability and desire to use these expanded capabilities.[16]

---

[16] Hugh J. Watson, Ralph H. Sprague, Jr., and Donald W. Kroeber, "Computer Technology and Information System Performance," *MSU Business Topics* (Summer 1977), pp. 17–24.

SOURCE: "Doonesbury" (December 16, 1982). Reproduced by permission of Universal Press Syndicate. © 1982 by G. B. Trudeau.

MIS SOPHISTICATION LEVELS SHOULD MATCH THOSE OF THE USER-MANAGERS

FIVE DEADLY MIS MISTAKES

1. *Give them more.* Most MIS's are designed on the assumption that the critical deficiency under which most managers operate is the *lack of relevant information.* I do not deny that most managers lack a good deal of information that they should have, but I do deny that this is the most important informational deficiency from which they suffer. It seems to me that they suffer more from an *overabundance of irrelevant information.* . . .

My experience indicates that most managers receive much more data (if not information) than they can possibly absorb even if they spend all of their time trying to do so. . . .

2. *Managers need all the information they want.* Most MIS designers "determine" what information is needed by asking managers what information they would like to have. This is based on the assumption that managers know what information they need and want it.

For managers to know what information they need, they must be aware of each type of decision they should make (as well as do) and they must have an adequate model of each. These conditions are seldom satisfied. Most managers have some conception of at least some of the types of decisions they must make. Their conceptions, however, are likely to be deficient in a very critical way, a way that follows from an important principle of scientific economy: the less we understand a phenomenon, the more variables we require to explain it. Hence, the manager who does not understand the phenomenon he controls plays it "safe" and, with respect to information, wants "everything." The MIS designer, who has even less understanding of the relevant phenomenon than the manager, tries to provide even more of everything. He thereby increases what is already an overload of irrelevant information. . . .

3. *Give managers the information they need and their decision making will improve.* It is frequently assumed that if managers are provided with the information they need, they will then have no problem in using it effectively. The history of OR (operations research) stands to the contrary. For example, give

Constructing an Information System

The first step in the development of the MIS is obtaining the total support of top management.[17] MIS design must be from the top down, and top management must oversee its development and evolution. Systems designed from the bottom up tend to accumulate too much data since subordinates are required to

[17] Phillip Ein-Dor and Eli Segev, "Information-System Responsibility," *MSU Business Topics* (Autumn 1977), pp. 33–40. See also F. Warren McFarlan, "Portfolio Approach to Information Systems," *Harvard Business Review* (September–October 1981), pp. 142–150.

most managers an initial tableau of a typical "real" mathematical programming, sequencing, or network problem and see how close they come to an optimal solution. If their experience and judgment have any value they may not do badly, but they will seldom do very well. In most management problems there are too many possibilities to expect experience, judgment, or intuition to provide good guesses, even with perfect information.

4. *More communication means better performance.* One characteristic of most MIS's which I have seen is that they provide managers with better current information about what other managers and their departments and divisions are doing. Underlying this provision is the belief that better interdepartmental communication enables managers to coordinate their decisions more effectively and hence improves the organization's overall performance. Not only is this not necessarily so, but it seldom is. One would hardly expect two competing companies to become more cooperative because the information each acquires about the other is improved. . . .

5. *A manager does not have to understand how an information system works, only how to use it.* Most MIS designers seek to make their systems as innocuous and unobtrusive as possible to managers with very easy access to the system and assure them that they need to know nothing more about it. The designers usually succeed in keeping managers ignorant in this regard. This leaves managers unable to evaluate the MIS as a whole. It often makes them afraid to even try to do so lest they display their ignorance publicly. In failing to evaluate their MIS, managers delegate much of the control of the organization to the system's designers and operators who may have many virtues, but managerial competence is seldom among them. . . .

No MIS should ever be installed unless the managers for whom it is intended are trained to evaluate and hence control it rather than be controlled by it.

SOURCE: Adapted from Russell L. Ackoff, "Management Misinformation Systems," *Management Science* (December 1967), pp. 147–156. Used with permission.

speculate on the information needs of their superiors. In too many cases, technical staff are given the assignment of building the system. In such cases the typical outcome is expressed in management's complaints of a system that does not fit their information needs.

Design and development of an effective MIS is a complex and time-consuming assignment for most organizations. A period of several months or even a year or more is often necessary to pretest the system before installation, to complete the necessary training for both MIS systems personnel and the user-managers, and to involve users fully in the design of the system. A systematic approach to design and implementation should increase the likelihood of producing a useful, cost-effective MIS.

It should not be surprising that a systems scholar such as Russell Ackoff would conceive of a management information system only in the context of an overall management system. Ackoff, Daniel H. Silberberg Professor of Systems Sciences at The Wharton School of the University of Pennsylvania, offers this conception of an ideal information system:

First, it would be a subsystem of a management system that performs three functions: (1) surveys internal performance and the environment, and uses the output to identify and formulate problems; (2) makes decisions about what to do about them; and (3) controls the implementation and performance of these decisions. The information subsystem of such a system would provide the inputs required by the other subsystems. An effective MIS cannot exist except as an integral part of a larger holistically designed management system. Moreover, it must deal with the principal flow of information into management; that is, from outside the organization, not inside. In addition, it must address the central informational problem of management, the overabundance of irrelevant information, by effectively filtering and condensing all information it receives.

Ackoff, born February 12, 1919, in Philadelphia, decided to follow in the footsteps of his uncle by becoming an architect. Although he did earn an undergraduate degree in architecture in 1941 at the University of Pennsylvania, by that time he had acquired an interest in philosophy. He pursued this interest for a year before World War II intervened. Following military service in the U.S. Army, Ackoff returned to the University of Pennsylvania, where he received a doctorate in philosophy of science in 1947. Operations research professor C. West Churchman—Ackoff's professor and soon-to-be colleague and friend—had a major impact upon his future career. The two men collaborated on four books.

Summary

Management information systems are potentially valuable means of institutionalizing the planning and controlling processes by integrating the various analytical techniques, models, and vast quantities of data. Information systems are structured, interacting complexes of people, machines, and procedures designed to generate an orderly flow of relevant information for decision making. The MIS performs six functions: data assembly, processing, analysis, storage and retrieval, evaluation, and dissemination.

Management information may be divided into three major categories: strategic planning, management control, and operational control information. Each type of information varies in scope, source, time horizon, requirements for accuracy, and frequency of use. Information flows must be tailored to meet the specific needs of managers at different levels in the organization.

The MIS is made up of three primary components. The data bank consists of raw data as assembled, recorded, and stored. The second component, the analytical methods bank, is responsible for processing and analyzing the various data inputs. The model bank consists of the various mathematical models used in analyzing and solving problems.

Although information systems are tailored to meet the needs of each organization, they may be compared on the basis of five dimensions: information recency, management access time, level of information aggregation, degree of analytical sophistication, and relative system authority. Successful information systems possess the following characteristics:

1. The system is founded on management's conception of the decision environment.
2. The user-manager understands and is involved in the construction of the system structure.
3. The system is based on disaggregated data files.
4. System development has proceeded to increasing levels of sophistication through a process of gradual evolution.

Ackoff is currently a member of Wharton's Department of Social Systems Sciences and is active at The Busch Center, which specializes in systems planning, research, and design. To date, he has authored or coauthored sixteen books, including *A Concept of Corporate Planning* (1970), *On Purposeful Systems* (1972), *Redesigning the Future* (1974), *The Art of Problem Solving* (1978), and *Creating the Corporate Future* (1981). He has also published more than 150 articles in books and a wide variety of journals. A charter member and former president of the Operations Research Society of America, founding member and former vice-president of The Institute of Management Sciences, he has received the Silver Medal of the British Operational Research Society and the George E. Kimball Medal of the Operations Research Society of America. In 1967 the University of Lancaster (UK) awarded him an honorary Doctor of Science degree. Ackoff's work in research, consulting, and education has involved more than 250 corporations and 50 government agencies in the United States and abroad.

The scope of Professor Ackoff's activities has proven useful in permitting him to see the flaws as well as the promise of current MIS performance. He describes the major current problems this way:

> The major obstruction to implementation of systems as currently designed is the correct perception by responsible managers that the systems proposed do not address their principal information problems. Data collection, storage, retrieval, and processing do not an information system make. These make for automated clerical systems, not information systems. Filtration and condensation are absolutely necessary. Most managers would prefer an average assistant to the best computerized information system, and for good reason. Until MIS designers understand how much an assistant is used and what he or she does, their systems will continue to be, and be perceived by managers to be, largely irrelevant.

Constructing a successful information system involves gaining the support and involvement of top management. The MIS should be designed from the top down, and users should be involved in its development. The system should be pretested before installation, and both systems personnel and the user-managers should be trained in its use. Such a systematic approach to design and implementation should increase the probability of success.

REVIEW EXERCISES

1. Define the following terms: (a) management information system (MIS) (b) data (c) information (d) data bank (e) analytical methods bank (f) model bank (g) information recency (h) management access time (i) information aggregation (j) analytical sophistication (k) system authority.
2. List the six functions of the management information system.
3. Identify the three major categories of management information.
4. Contrast the three components of the MIS.
5. Explain the role of the computer in an information system.
6. Identify and briefly explain the bases for comparing information systems.
7. Explain the relationship between the analytical sophistication in an MIS and system authority.
8. What characteristics are typically present in a successful information system?
9. Explain the value of disaggregated data files.
10. What is the first step in MIS design? Why is this step so critical?

ASSIGNMENTS/ PROBLEMS/ DISCUSSION QUESTIONS

1. The dispatcher environmental control system of American Airlines has removed pilots from the days when flight crews would assemble hours before a departure to sit down to study winds, temperatures, potential storm areas, and other information such as the plane's takeoff weight. Weather information is received twice daily and the data—winds, weather, anticipated payload for each type of aircraft, and other factors—are used to program the trip.

Evaluate the American Airlines system on the basis of the five MIS characteristics discussed in this chapter.

2. Three major categories of management information were discussed in this chapter. Briefly explain each category, and identify the various groups in your college or university who are likely users of each type.

3. "MIS is just a newfangled term for electronic data processing." Do you agree? Justify your answer.

4. Relate the bases for comparing information systems to the following:

   a. Manager of accounting department
   b. Industrial sales manager responsible for Ohio and eastern Indiana
   c. Manager of manufacturing subsidiary

5. Relate the "five deadly MIS mistakes" to the characteristics of successful information systems. Which characteristic does each mistake disregard?

A MANAGERIAL INCIDENT

MIS Failure at the U.S. Postal Service

A new information system is normally justified as yielding better information that will improve managerial decision making. Unfortunately, implementation problems often prevent the benefits from being achieved. Horror stories about multimillion dollar computer-based information system projects that failed due to a lack of user acceptance are legion. One conspicuous example concerned the implementation of a work measurement information system at the U.S. Post Office.

> The Government Accounting Office reported that this system: was over two years late; cost over 60 million dollars (twice what was expected); required more rather than fewer people; had a higher error rate; had increased operating costs; and produced reports that were not used.

> The system's failure resulted primarily from adverse reactions of the users to the system. Their resistance prevented the achievement of any benefits the new system might have provided. Resistance to the system took the form of intentional input errors (i.e., errors in the transactions made by the employees); projection (i.e., employees criticized the new system for any and all problems arising in their areas); and sabotage (e.g., paper clips were inserted in badge readers to render them inoperable).

SOURCE: Paul H. Cheney and Gary W. Dickson, "Organizational Characteristics and Information Systems: An Exploratory Investigation," *Academy of Management Journal* (March 1982), p. 171. Reprinted by permission. The quotation is from Donald H. Sanders, *Computers and Management* (New York: McGraw-Hill, 1980), p. 340.

Question and Problems

1. Explain the negative reactions to the new system on the part of some postal employees.

2. Suggest procedures whereby managers might minimize similar reactions to a new MIS in other organizations.

Case V-1

THE AMERICAN MACHINE CO.: A NEW SYSTEM IS NEEDED

The American Machine Co., a division of a major corporation, is a heavy machining industry. The company functions as a job-shop and produces a unique product that has sales of $100,000,000 per year.

To retain this leadership position, Joe Bennington, the general manager, has instructed his section managers to install computer control systems where feasible and to reduce manpower. Joe has reasoned that if some headway were made in these areas, the American Machine Co. could keep its market share despite fierce competition from domestic and foreign sources.

Since cycle time, the time required to complete an order, was critical in the marketplace, American Machine had started to modernize its shop area. It was changing from conventional machinery to numerical control equipment. The stock room was going on line, and Materials Requirement Planning had been put into effect. Management was contemplating switching from piece work to day work.

With the shop modernization almost complete, an alternative system for shop loading had to be implemented. The hourly cost of the equipment was $80 for machine time and $12 for labor. Because of these costs, it was essential for American Machine to install an effective method for recording shop input and to provide the shop with a timely measurement so that the optimal use of the special purpose machinery could be made.

Don Hiller, manager of the manufacturing systems, had been given the project of changing the dispatch (piece work system) to a system that could, in time, become an on-line system. The dispatch system, which had been an outgrowth of piece work, was a total manual commitment. As

This case was prepared by John W. Moran and James M. McCulloch at the Graduate School of Business—Rivier College. Adapted and reprinted by permission of the authors.

Exhibit 1
THE AMERICAN MACHINE CO.—SHOP ORDER PRIORITY CARD

Shop Order		F/M
153267/319		7851
151138/139		7901
153002/003		7901
152196		7902
153327/328		7902
153174/175		7905
150610		7906
152197		7908
151140/141		7909
122892/893		7910
152198		7910
123795		7911
152199		7911
153270/71/72		7911
153084/085		7916
151158/159		7918
153189/190		7919
122959/960	CGE	7920
122921/922		7921
153273/74/75		7924
151170/71/72		7926

paper work was received from configuration and documentation control, the dispatchers would log it in on large cards that were keyed to the drawing numbers. The order in which the paperwork was filed depended on the shop order. The general foreman (later the unit manager) gave the supervisor of dispatch a card that listed the shop orders by priority (Exhibit 1). The dispatchers used this card to position the paper work in the files for each station.

The dispatchers were responsible for passing out work and also stamping off operations as they were complete. Since this involved piece work, they turned in the voucher to payroll so that the operators could get paid (Exhibit 2). When operators came to the dispatch window for work, the dispatcher gave them only enough for the day, plus a

Exhibit 2 THE AMERICAN MACHINE CO.—MANUAL PAYROLL VOUCHER

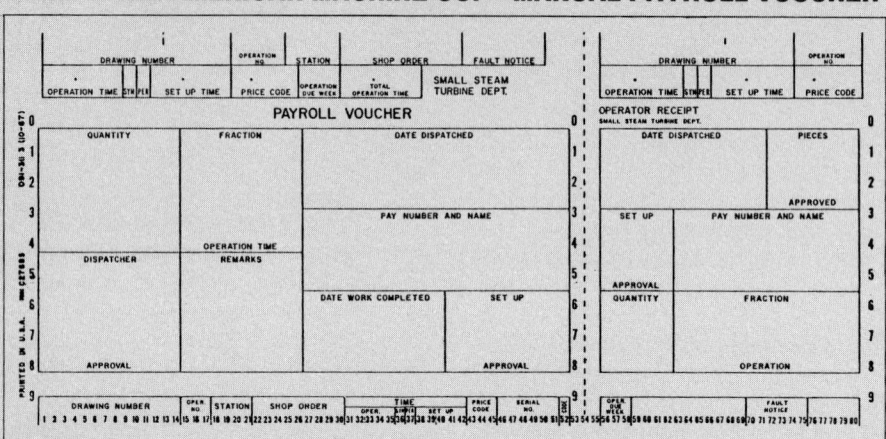

little carryover. No more work was given to the operators until they had turned in what they had taken previously. This method kept the amount of actual work at the machines to a minimum. As an operation was completed, the dispatcher would set up the paper work at the next station in accordance with previously mentioned dispatch system filing methods. The dispatcher would also log in the voucher payments on a sheet by operations, pay numbers, and so forth, so that a record was kept of who received what payments.

Once a week dispatchers would audit all the stations they were responsible for, and thus they knew what was really active at a station. They used this method to take note of what was overdue as well as to define the status of supply jobs. With this information the dispatchers would then expedite their completion. The dispatchers would, on occasion, have to search the shop for lost material and Quality Reports (QRs) so that they could be expedited.

Jobs that were good paying never became lost or missing, only the jobs that nobody wanted to do ended up in this category. These constant search and find missions were the only way the dispatchers could control the amount of lost material and QRs. A meeting was held with the general foreman (unit manager) once a week to outline the process

of the main parts. At this time the company utilized an ABC Inventory Classification System. This was a totally manual-clerical operation and, as such, could not really take advantage of techniques developed for computer applications.

Exhibits 3 and 4 show the organizational structure and work flow of this system.

Questions

1. What changes would you recommend to improve and update this system?

2. Develop a time table for the implementation of the recommendations developed in Question 1.

3. Do you feel that this operation should take advantage of computerized inventory techniques? If so, detail a system that would accomplish the conversion and include a time table for implementation. If not, present arguments against it.

Exhibit 3 THE AMERICAN MACHINE CO.—ORGANIZATIONAL STRUCTURE

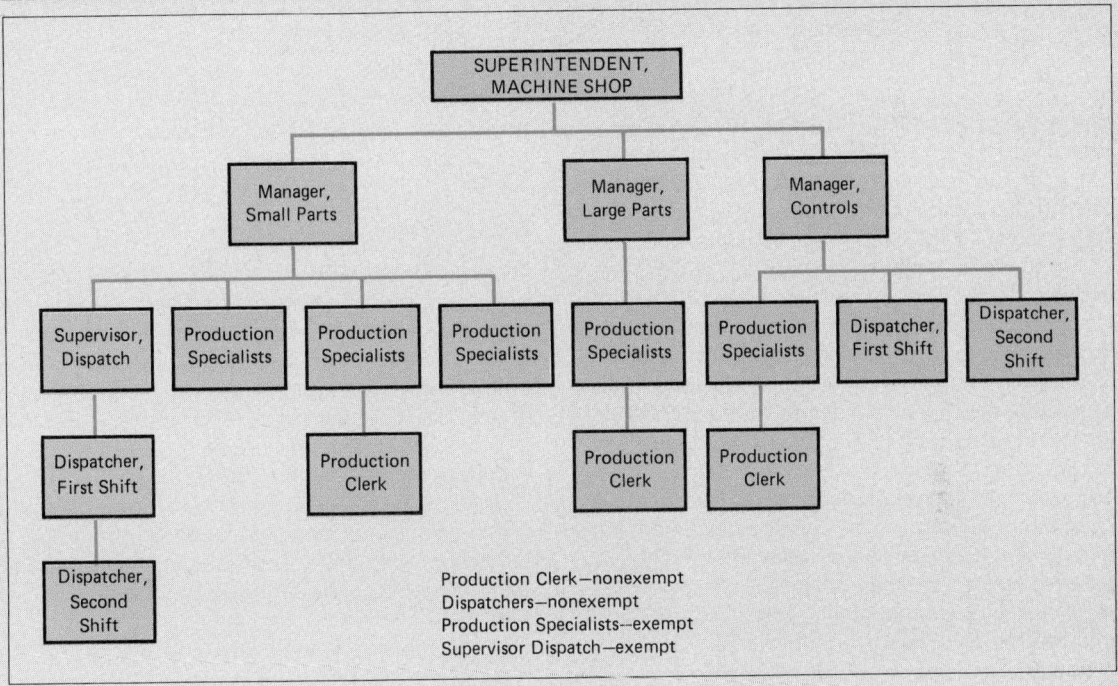

Production Clerk—nonexempt
Dispatchers—nonexempt
Production Specialists—exempt
Supervisor Dispatch—exempt

Exhibit 4 THE AMERICAN MACHINE CO.—WORK FLOW DIAGRAM

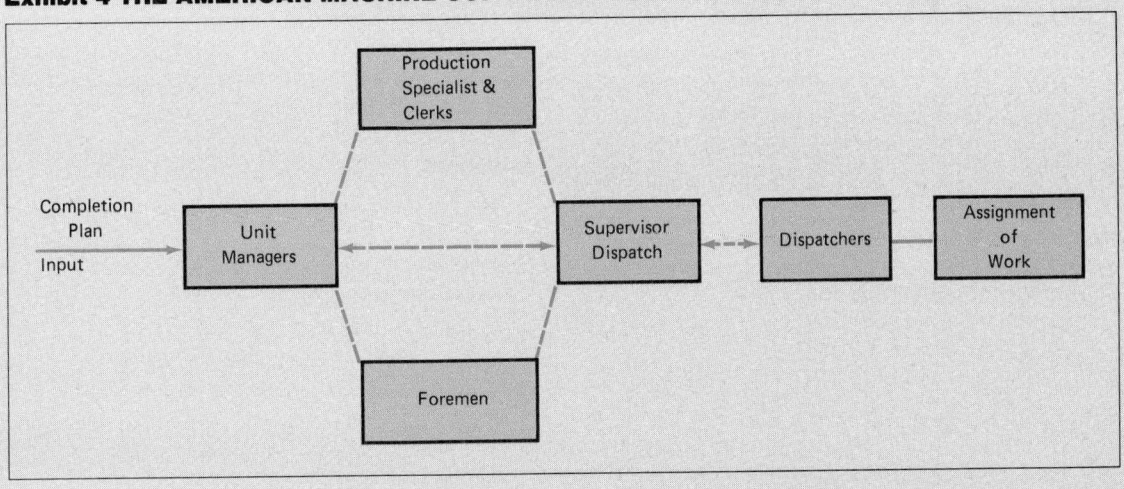

Case V-2

TRANSPO ELECTRONICS, INC.: THE IMPORTANCE
OF THE CONTROL FUNCTION

Transpo Electronics, Inc., was founded in 1978 by Frank Oropeza to produce replacement automotive parts such as voltage regulators, armatures, solenoids, and other parts that wear out. Transpo is the third business venture for Mr. Oropeza. Earlier ventures had been less successful due to their faddish nature. Those previous ventures taught Mr. Oropeza that he needed a business venture that had a basic product with repeat business.

Oropeza and his wife, Ann, mortgaged their house and developed a voltage regulator that is high quality and dependable. In 1978 Oropeza left his engineering position with a *Fortune 500* firm and began the manufacture of voltage regulators in his garage. Oropeza was also the salesman. He believed that his engineering ability enabled him to design, develop, and manufacture products of sufficient quality to enable him to give a money-back guarantee to his customers for trying Transpo products.

Transpo's sales in their first year were $257,000 and profits of $87,000; in the second year sales were $895,000 and profits of $225,000. Estimated third year sales are $1.8 million.

MARKETING

After the initial year of operation, Transpo began using WATS lines to call customers on a regular basis to determine their replacement parts needs. Oropeza's intentions are to continue expansion to the entire United States, with possible considera-

This case was prepared by Professor Terry Campbell. Adapted and reprinted by permission of the author and the University of Central Florida.

tion of international markets. (Exhibit 1 is a portion of the price list of Transpo.)

PRODUCTION

Transpo Electronics, Inc., wants to be known as a quality supplier. To achieve that end Oropeza personally develops the engineering and production rationale for each product. Each of the twenty-two employees is constantly reminded of the strict quality control standards of Oropeza. Less than .01 percent of Transpo products are returned for credit for manufacturing defects.

Transpo's goal is to ship every order complete within twenty-four hours of receiving the order. At times during the third year this goal has been difficult to meet. In general, however, the goal is met.

FINANCE

Oropeza desires no stockholders other than himself and his family. He also wants to avoid debt to the extent possible. Exhibit 2 contains the balance sheet of Transpo Electronics, Inc.

Mr. Oropeza recognizes the increased need for professional management techniques but does not want to sacrifice many of the personal goals noted. To this end Mr. Oropeza has requested your assistance to identify possible problem areas and give suggested alternatives.

Questions

1. Relate this case to Part V of the textbook.

2. What types of control does Oropeza need to establish for his firm?

Exhibit 1
TRANSPO
ELECTRONICS,
INC.—PRICE LIST

Voltage Regulator Price List
Effective 5 Oct. 1979, F.E.T. included
Part Numbers Can Be Mixed For Volume Pricing
NOTE: Delco integrals, trios and remanufactured
voltage regulators do not apply.

LEECE NEVILLE REGULATORS			QUANTITY		
	1-9	10-24	25-49	50-99	100
Replacement					
LN79000	$18.04	$16.93	$15.82	$15.41	$15.13
LN79000P	17.94	16.83	15.71	15.31	15.02
LN79000T	15.87	14.94	14.26	13.67	12.97
LN77973	19.17	18.04	16.94	16.57	16.23
LN77973P	19.07	17.94	16.84	16.47	16.13
LN77973T	17.21	16.24	15.37	14.81	14.39
LN97300	19.41	18.27	17.19	16.77	16.43
LN97300P	19.31	18.17	17.09	16.67	16.33
LN97300T	17.39	16.39	15.59	15.11	14.59
LN78855	18.89	17.37	16.39	15.97	15.67
LN78855P	20.41	18.87	17.87	17.21	16.91
LN79350	18.89	17.37	16.39	15.97	15.67
LN79350P	20.41	18.87	17.87	17.21	16.91
DELCO REMY REGULATORS					
Replacement					
1892812	18.27	16.47	15.69	15.27	14.91
1892812T	17.04	15.49	14.81	14.39	13.77
1892813	19.79	18.73	17.51	17.09	16.67
1892817	18.27	16.47	15.69	15.27	14.91
1892817T	17.04	15.49	14.81	14.39	13.77
1892824	19.33	17.81	16.71	16.21	15.69
1892824T	18.19	16.71	15.69	15.21	14.71
1892832	22.77	20.77	19.49	18.81	18.11
9000590 Super	18.57	16.65	15.49	14.89	13.97
9000591 Super	18.91	16.97	16.04	15.41	14.67
9000593 Super	19.83	17.89	16.93	16.49	15.73
Potted Modules					
9000590	9.37	9.17	8.93	8.74	8.47
9000591	9.49	9.26	9.09	8.83	8.61
9000592	9.81	9.61	9.41	9.17	8.97
9000593	12.67	12.37	12.13	11.83	11.63
PRESTOLITE					
Replacement					
VSH 6201(12V)	17.67	16.37	15.11	14.10	13.07
VSH 6201-1(12V)	18.17	16.87	15.66	14.60	13.57
VSH 6401 (24V)	18.27	17.11	15.89	14.73	13.76
UNIVERSAL VOLTAGE REGULATOR					
VR 1001	9.03	8.71	8.51	8.24	7.84
VR 1002	9.23	8.91	8.71	8.44	8.04
VR 1003	9.17	8.97	8.79	8.53	8.31
VR 1004	9.42	9.22	9.04	8.78	8.56
VR 1005	9.23	8.91	8.71	8.44	8.04
VR 1006	9.42	9.22	9.04	8.78	8.56
VR 1007	9.03	8.71	8.51	8.24	7.84
VR 1008	9.23	8.91	8.71	8.44	8.04
VR 1009	9.23	8.91	8.71	8.44	8.04
VR 1010	9.37	9.17	8.93	8.74	8.47
VR 1011	9.03	8.71	8.51	8.24	7.84
VR 1013	9.49	9.26	9.09	8.83	8.61
VR 1014	9.17	8.97	8.79	8.53	8.31

**Exhibit 1
TRANSPO
ELECTRONICS,
INC.—PRICE LIST
(Continued)**

Original Equipment Remanufactured Regulators to OEM Specifications
Effective 5 Oct. 1979, F.E.T. Included

REGULATOR NO.		QUANTITY			CORE CHARGE
		1-9	10-24	25 up	
DELCO					
1116374	12V	$14.00	$13.50	$12.50	$3.50
1116377	12V	12.50	12.00	11.50	3.50
1116378	12V	14.00	13.50	12.50	3.50
9000551*	12V	34.50	32.50	—	—
9000551* (panel)	12V	28.50	26.50	—	—
9000590	12V	12.50	12.00	11.50	3.00
9000591	24V	14.50	13.50	13.00	3.50
9000592*	30V	16.50	16.00	—	—
9000593*	32V	16.50	16.00	—	5.00
9000597*	24V	34.50	32.50	—	—
9000597* (panel)	24V	28.50	26.50	—	—
1963875*	24V	18.50	17.50	—	—
1963876*	12V	18.50	17.50	—	—
LEECE-NEVILLE					
5013	12V	12.50	12.00	11.50	3.50
5022	12V	13.50	13.00	12.50	3.50
5016	12V	12.50	12.00	11.50	3.50
5062*	32V	17.50	17.00	16.50	4.50
5078*	12V	14.00	13.00	12.50	4.00
B.U.T.E.C. R2/1*	12V	14.50	13.50	—	—
FORD					
GR374	12V	13.50	13.00	12.50	4.00
GR504	12V	13.50	13.00	12.50	4.00

WARRANTY: 90 days

* Due to core shortages, core must be supplied to Transpo with orders.

Transpo Electronics, Inc., and Subsidiary
Consolidated Balance Sheet
March 31, 1980

ASSETS

Current Assets:
Cash in Banks	$ 23,494.69	
Accounts Receivable	142,440.32	
Inventories (Note 1)	186,486.72	
Total Current Assets		$352,421.73

Fixed Assets At Cost (Note 1):
Vehicles	11,203.12	
Furniture & Fixtures	7,607.64	
Equipment	20,744.91	
Total Fixed Assets	39,555.67	
Less: Allowance for Depreciation	(5,831.50)	
Depreciable Value of Fixed Assets		33,724.17

Other Assets:
Patent Rights	185.00	
Deposits	2,800.00	
Total Other Assets		2,985.00
TOTAL ASSETS		$389,130.90

LIABILITIES & STOCKHOLDERS' EQUITY

Current Liabilities:
Accounts Payable	$ 58,111.35	
Payroll Taxes Withheld & Accrued	5,215.95	
Accrued Interest	1,634.00	
Excise Tax Payable	10,767.40	
Note Payable Bank (Note 2)	60,000.00	
Note Payable Banks—Current Portion	3,445.40	
Federal & State Income Tax Payable (Note 3)	49,786.07	
Total Current Liabilities		$188,960.17

Long-Term Liabilities:
Security Deposits	2,150.00	
Loan from Stockholders	77,581.75	
Note Payable Banks—Non-Current Portion	4,987.72	
Total Long-Term Liabilities		84,719.47

Stockholders' Equity:
Common Stock—100 Shares Issued & Outstanding, Par Value $1.00 Per Share	100.00	
Retained Earnings	115,351.26	
Total Stockholders' Equity		115,451.26
TOTAL LIABILITIES & STOCK-HOLDERS' EQUITY		$389,130.90

Exhibit 2
TRANSPO ELECTRONICS, INC.—AND SUBSIDIARY CONSOLIDATED BALANCE SHEET

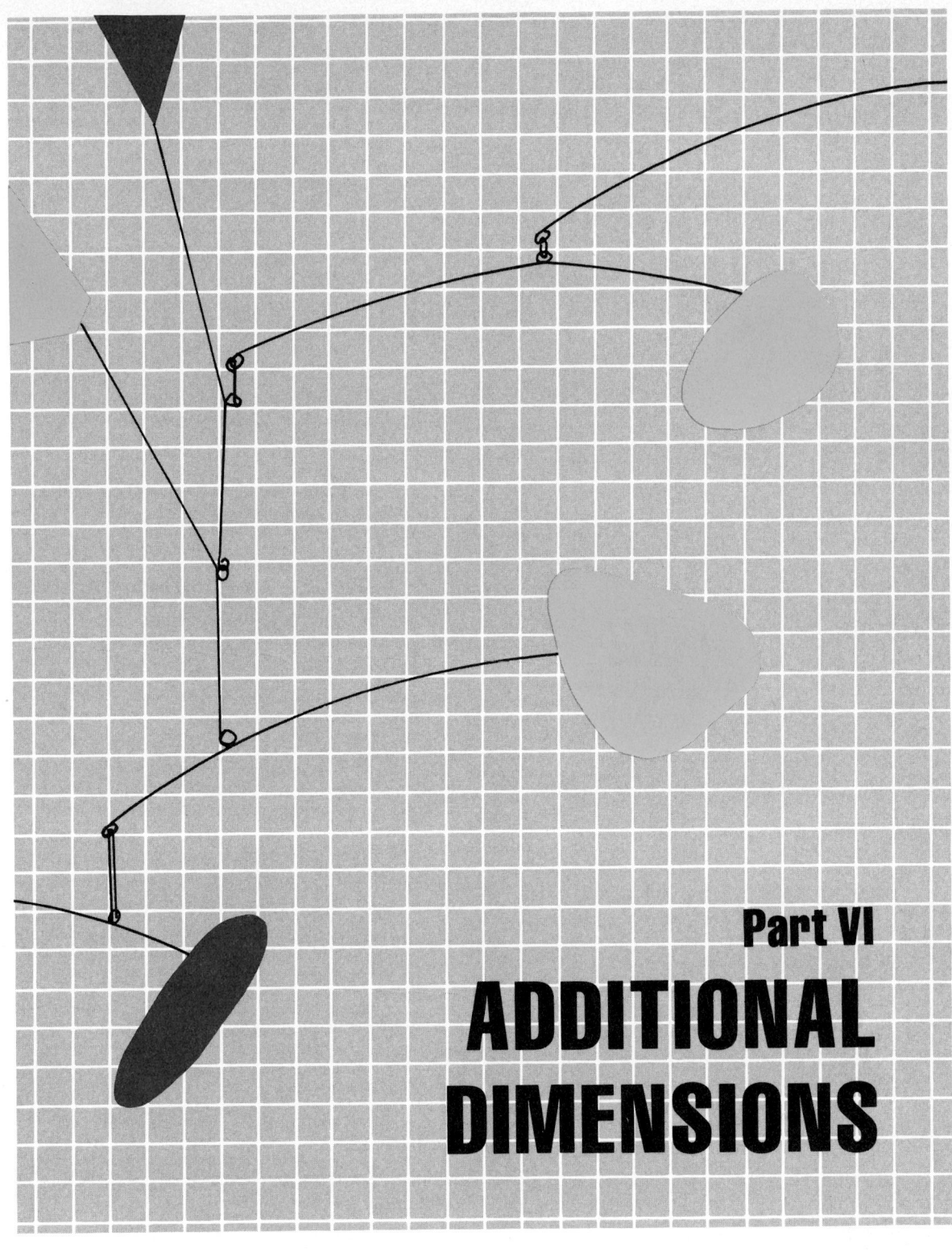

ADDITIONAL
DIMENSIONS

19.
Production Operations Management and Productivity

Learning Objectives

AFTER STUDYING THIS CHAPTER YOU SHOULD BE ABLE TO

1. Describe the importance of the production/operations function and its relationship to other functional areas.
2. Identify the factors to be considered and the steps involved in the site selection decision.
3. List the advantages and disadvantages of the basic types of physical layouts.
4. Outline the aspects of job design.
5. Explain production control.
6. Describe the inventory control systems.
7. Identify the components of an effective quality control program.
8. Explain the concept of productivity and identify the factors influencing recent declines in productivity growth.

Key Terms

production/operations function
automation
technological displacement
materials handling
job design
quality circles
job content
methods improvement
human factors engineering
sociotechnical systems
production control
value analysis
activity scheduling
inventory
economic order quantity (EOQ)
cycle stocks
safety stocks
stockouts
quality control
acceptance sampling
productivity
Theory Z

The reason a lot of people do not recognize opportunity is because it usually
goes around wearing overalls looking
like hard work.

THOMAS ALVA EDISON

The U.S. puts its best young minds to
work in staff jobs and has for years.
Bright people have gotten the message. They avoid line jobs. Japan, on
the other hand, wants its brightest men
in line jobs. After all, that is what manufacturing is all about. Our people understand that while we may rotate them
from line to staff, and vice versa, line
jobs are critical for what you in
America call fast-track executives.

*Chairman of a Japanese
electrical manufacturing
firm*

Sleek, slick—and more trouble than they were worth. And they were
worth a lot. Such was the word on Jaguar. Selling for at least $25,000,
the cars were known for faulty parts and all too frequent breakdowns. Thus, Jaguar buyers often found themselves in the role of the well-heeled chump.

But once Jaguar's parent company, British Leyland Ltd., installed John Egan
as chairman of Jaguar Rover Triumph, things began to change. Mr. Egan's
marching orders were clear: Turn the U.S. operations around or close them
down.

To stop the Leonia, New Jersey–based unit's financial hemorrhaging, Mr.
Egan set corporate sights on the manufacture of a better car—and one produced
more efficiently. To do so he sped up production lines, installed quality controls
modeled on streamlined Japanese precedents and cut the number of employees
from 10,500 in 1980 to 6,900 today.

Several other basic steps emerged as the means to increased productivity.
First, fewer hands doing more jobs translated into greater individual expertise.
"Practice really does make perfect, and the fact that the employees are doing
more work, more often simply means they're better at it."

Secondly, he said, the company began inspecting output before the production run had finished. "Instead, we began checking processes before the line was done, so we wouldn't find mistakes too late."

On Mr. Egan's command, JRT also started to play hard ball with its suppliers, stringently inducing them to deliver superior component parts. "We began to lay down much stronger laws for parts," explained Mike Dale, JRP's vice-president, marketing. "If the failure rate rose above 1.5 percent, the supplier then had to not only replace the parts, but pay for the costs of lost labor time as well."[1]

What Is Production/Operations Management?

The production/ operations function refers to the processes and activities necessary to transform various inputs into goods and/or services.

The *production/operations function* consists of the processes necessary to transform various inputs into goods and/or services. General Motors takes steel, aluminum, glass, plastic, and hundreds of other materials and component parts; puts them together at a Flint, Michigan, assembly line; and the end product is a new Buick. Similarly, Bill Fitch transformed the tremendous individual talents of Robert Parrish, Larry Bird, Nate Archibald, Danny Ainge, and others into a magnificent machine—the Boston Celtics, perennial contenders for the National Basketball Association championship.

In the past the production/operations function was often simply referred to as *production.* This term was usually restricted to the manufacture of tangible items. As the economies of the world's developed nations became increasingly service-oriented, the term evolved to *production/operations management* in order to encompass the creation of intangible services as well as the production of tangible goods. In this chapter *production* and *production/operations* are used interchangeably to refer to the function in either manufacturing or non-manufacturing settings.

What Is Production?

Successful production/operations methods are varied. The inputs can range from basic raw materials to NFL draft choices. And the production processes and activities can range from assembly lines to weight programs and training camps. But the key ingredient in all of these situations is effective management, which is able to put all of the components together and manufacture a quality product or service.

Once the inputs have been determined, the two primary activities of the production/operations function are (1) systems design and (2) production planning and control. These are managerial tasks. Managers determine what system will be used to produce the product or service. While the designs may differ, the un-

[1] Gay Jervey, "Jaguar Pays the Price to Get Back in Hunt," *Advertising Age* (April 12, 1982), p. 4. Reprinted by permission from *Advertising Age.* Copyright Crain Communications, Inc., 1982.

derlying concept is that design is a controllable managerial decision. Thus, University of Michigan head football coach Bo Schembechler relies primarily on the running game for his team. By contrast, Florida State's Bobby Bowden uses a pro-type passing attack.

The football illustration is also applicable to the second production management activity—production planning and control. Sportscasters often ask athletes and coaches about their "game plan" for a coming contest. The football addict is well versed in such "production planning and control," with sequences such as "establish the running game, then attack the seams of their zone." In short, Joe Paterno's game plan for Penn State is not at all unlike the various planning and control sequences used in a Dresser Industries plant.

Relationship of Production to Other Areas

The production/operations function is only one part of the total management system. Admittedly, it is an extremely vital component of any organization, but other activities are also of critical importance. The three major areas of most organizations—whether they produce goods or services or are profit or nonprofit oriented—are production, finance, and marketing. All of these activities must be performed efficiently if the organization is to prosper. A political candidacy, for instance, suffers if the candidate or his or her surrogates are advocating unpopular or misunderstood issues (production); if the candidate is unable to raise campaign contributions (finance); or if a media blitz is seen as unattractive by most voters (marketing). All three areas plus dozens of others like personnel, accounting, and engineering affect the accomplishment of organizational goals.

The Chrysler Corp. is an excellent example of this interrelationship. The ailing auto maker's market share shrunk to about 8 percent during 1979, and many people doubted the continued viability of the company. But Chrysler—under the leadership of board chairman Lee A. Iacocca—took a three-pronged approach to turning the company around. First, a critical cash flow problem was countered by extensive lobbying efforts to get $1.5 billion in federal loan guarantees. Then the company announced a new marketing program known as the "Chrysler Guarantees" designed to get people to try Chrysler models and move the firm's market share to over 10 percent. The new program consisted of a thirty-day or 1,000-mile moneyback guarantee; free scheduled maintenance for two years or 24,000 miles; a two-year membership in a motor club; and a $50 check for people who would test-drive a Chrysler product and then buy it or a specified competing model within thirty days. Meanwhile, Chrysler was also working toward an improved product. Its management credited improved attitudes among employees as the primary reason for a quality improvement of 32 percent during 1979 (as measured by repairs per 100 owners).[2] By 1982, it had increased its market share to 9.9 percent. In 1983, it repaid the government

[2] Edwin G. Pipp, "Chrysler Seeks Over 10 Percent of the Market," *Detroit News* (January 25, 1980), p. 6-C.

loans far ahead of schedule. The Chrysler example clearly illustrates the interrelationships that exist between production and other functional areas within the organization.

The Importance of Production

Diane Von Furstenberg appreciates the importance of the production/operations function. Von Furstenberg came to the United States in 1969 at the age of twenty-two. She knew little about fashion. But today her company's sales are more than $250 million annually.

Diane Von Furstenberg started by learning production at an Italian factory owned by a friend. The factory produced T-shirts, among other things. Von Furstenberg produced some samples and returned to the United States. In 1972, when she was twenty-five, her wraparound dress became an instant success. The wraparound started with a snake print and leopard print; soon nearly everyone was wearing a version of the basic model. As she put it: "We kept producing, producing, producing. . . . We thought we'd never be able to produce enough."

Eventually, of course, the market for wraparound dresses became saturated. Von Furstenberg was stuck with a huge inventory. She was forced to reorganize her company, dismissing about 80 percent of the staff. Today, Diane Von Furstenberg is back on top, having learned the importance of the various aspects of the production function.[3]

Effective production is critical to organizational success, but, as noted in the previous section, the production/operations function must operate within the confines of its interrelationship with other functional areas. The relative importance of the production, or operations, function can be seen by its sheer size compared with that of other functional areas like marketing, finance, accounting, and personnel. In most businesses managers of the production/operations function employ the largest work force and are responsible for most of the controllable assets within the organization.[4] If for no other reason, the size of the production function attests to its relative importance within the overall organizational structure.

Basic Types of Production Systems

There are two basic types of production systems. One is based on continuous flows and the other on intermittent flows. A *continuous flow production system* is a process designed to produce a standardized product that is carried in inventory. Typically, this type of system relies on an assembly line operation. An *in-*

---

[3] The material about Diane Von Furstenberg is based on and quotes from "Designing a Business—In Style," *MBA Executive* (November–December 1979), pp. 1, 8–10. The quote appears on p. 9.

[4] See Charles G. Andrew and George A. Johnson, "The Crucial Importance of Production and Operations Management," *Academy of Management Review* (January 1982), pp. 143–147.

termittent flow production system, by contrast, is used to make products in accordance with purchase specifications contained in separate contracts. No inventory is stored. The firm's production capability is kept ready for contracts that might be obtained. An intermittent production system is often referred to as a *job shop*. A print shop is a common example.[5]

Some industries use both types of production systems. Consider the housing sector, where some homes are custom built according to architectural design (an intermittent flow production system). Others are constructed according to a limited number of building plans in an assembly line style (a continuous flow production system).

PRODUCTION SYSTEMS FOR SERVICES

Most services use an intermittent production system. Doctors, dentists, electricians, plumbers, and accountants often reason that each of the problems they confront is different and that each requires a different approach or production system. In short, the traditional viewpoint has been that services cannot be standardized. Therefore, the use of the continuous flow production system has been deemed inappropriate for most service activities.

But basic productivity questions are changing this scenario. Economic growth is lagging, and there is a real need for greater productivity in the service sector, which is expected to be about 75 percent of the U.S. economy by 1985. Tradition has it that productivity improvements account for about 67 percent of U.S. economic growth. So the only major gains must come from improvements in service productivity.

Theodore Levitt of the Harvard Business School believes that the service sector must, and can, be industrialized in a fashion similar to what occurred in the production of tangible goods. Levitt argues that this is a management responsibility and that society cannot wait for a technological breakthrough to achieve the industrialization. He points out, for example, that Eli Whitney's widely acclaimed 1798 production line used concepts available since the 1300s. Whitney offered a managerial breakthrough, not a technological one.

Levitt says this can be done in services if society concentrates less on greater efforts and more on revisions of the service offering. Avis' "We try harder" philosophy will produce fewer gains than Midas' specialized muffler service, according to Levitt. He argues, "What's required is to apply the analysis and organization that are commonplace in manufacturing to service."[6]

---

[5] Much of the material in this chapter is adapted from James B. Dilworth, *Production and Operations Management: Manufacturing and Nonmanufacturing*, 2nd ed. (New York: Random House, 1983). This includes the following: production systems (pp. 10–11); location factors (pp. 457, 458–461); stages of site location (pp. 463, 466); materials handling (pp. 484–494, 503–505); job design (pp. 521–523); job content, methods, improvement, physical environment, and sociotechnical factors (pp. 520–552); production control (pp. 106–171, 172–199, 270–359); inventory control (pp. 183–186, 188–195, 203–214, 218–230, 239–252); and quality control (pp. 381–419).

[6] Levitt's viewpoints are outlined in "The 'Big Mac' Theory of Economic Progress," *Forbes* (April 15, 1977), pp. 187–188.

Establishing Production/Operations Systems

The first step in establishing a production/operations system is to identify clearly the product or service that is to be produced. But this is only the first step. Various other decisions are required. These include site selection, physical layout, job design, production control procedures, inventory control systems, and quality control requirements. Each step involves a series of management strategy decisions. Operating managers are involved at various stages, playing an integral role in the creation of the overall production system.

PRODUCT/SERVICE PLANNING

Identifying the product or service to be produced requires the best efforts of research and development (R & D) or design people, production experts, and marketers. Conflicts are common among these groups, but cooperation is an absolute necessity. Products and services—whatever their technological merits—must be capable of being produced efficiently and must be sought after by consumers. In recent years many firms have tried to bring their research and development efforts more into line with realistic production and marketing expectations. Du Pont, for instance, has reallocated its R & D budget, moving it away from basic and new-venture research toward "improvements for existing businesses."[7]

Products and services must also meet consumer needs if they are to be successful. Marketing research is essential if the product is to be accepted by consumers. Even Thomas Edison once remarked: "Anything that won't sell, I don't want to invent. Its sale is proof of utility, and utility is success."[8] Production management also plays a role here. Goods and services must be produced efficiently if they are to be priced within the means of buyers. Henry Ford's assembly line was able to reduce production costs to the point where many American households could acquire an automobile during the early 1900s.

PRODUCTION PROCESS DECISIONS

There are a multitude of production process decisions. The most basic one concerns how the various inputs are going to be transformed into outputs. As Figure 19–1 illustrates, this is the conceptual foundation of any production/operations system.

Production process decisions cover a wide range, such as whether to make or buy various inputs, the feasibility of the planned product or service, the exact configuration of the process system, equipment selection, and product routing.

---

[7] Mitchell C. Lynch, "Many Concerns Stress Product Development and Reduce Research," *Wall Street Journal* (October 18, 1977), pp. 1, 19.

[8] Quoted in "The Quintessential Innovator," *Time* (October 22, 1979), p. 72.

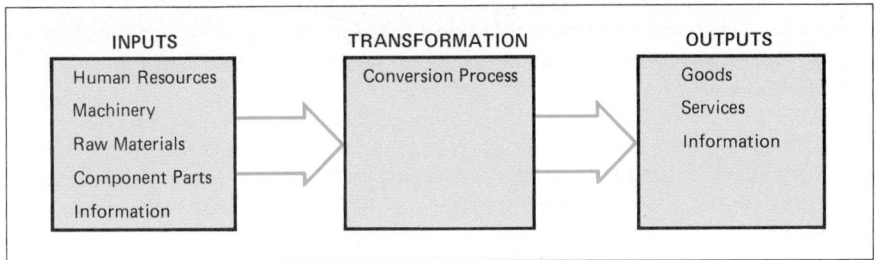

Figure 19-1
THE PRODUCTION/
OPERATIONS SYSTEM

Several factors impact on these decisions. Consider a situation in which economic considerations force the manager to study ways to automate his or her facility in order to make the operation more efficient. In fact, automation is now a commonplace production process decision. Even Chinese egg rolls are sometimes made by a machine in order to keep up with demand for the product.

AUTOMATION—BENEFITS AND COSTS

Mark Twain was a big hit at the *Advertising Age* trade show. So was Johnson & Johnson's "oldest surgeon" at a medical convention. Actually, both were the same mechanical creature on loan from Creative Presentations, Inc. Mechanical figures and robots, in fact, have become commonplace at the trade shows of the 1980s.

Robots are a highly visible aspect of the process of automation. Inventor Benjamin Skora's six-foot-eight-inch, 275-pound robot, Arok, even tells jokes: "You can be replaced by a robot because robots never make mistakes, mistakes, mistakes. . . ."[9] Quasar Industries of Rutherford, New Jersey, plans to mass-produce a $4,000 household robot named Klatu. Quasar's robot has a 250-word vocabulary and can recognize the voice patterns of six different people. The firm claims that Klatu is capable of vacuuming, serving dinner, taking telephone calls, and babysitting.

As helpful as Arok and Klatu might be around the house, the most important use of robots is in automation of the workplace. *Automation* refers to some automatically controlled method of accomplishing a task with minimal involvement of personnel. Texas Instruments, General Electric, and Caterpillar Tractor Co. all use robots. General Motors now has a system of twelve robots capable of painting cars. The GM robots are able to recognize different body styles and can even cover for each other if a robot breaks down. Robot-like mechanical arms have also been used by Detroit's automobile manufacturers to spot-weld during the assembly process.

Automation is having a significant impact on today's factories. General Motors plans to concentrate 90 percent of its machine expenditures in computer-controlled equipment and to reduce employment by 2 to 3 percent annually. Meanwhile, a fully automated factory is already being constructed in

Automation is the method of accomplishing a task by means of automatically controlled equipment, with minimal involvement of personnel.

[9] Donald Morrison, "In Illinois: A Better Robot?" *Time* (August 14, 1978), p. 4.

HERMAN HANDLED A TOUGH ASSIGNMENT AT THREE MILE ISLAND

Herman is probably not the best-looking robot in the world. Nonetheless, the six-foot-by-five-foot robot was called upon by the Nuclear Regulatory Commission to help its experts during the Three Mile Island nuclear accident. Herman's head consists of two television cameras; he has one six-foot arm capable of pulling 500 pounds; and he moves about on tank-like treads. The Union Carbide–developed robot's redeeming virtue is his ability to operate in a radioactive environment. The Three Mile Island incident provided another illustration of the value of automation to modern society.

SOURCE: "Robot 'Herman' Joins Experts at Nuclear Plant," *Wall Street Journal* (April 5, 1979), p. 2. Reprinted by permission of The Wall Street Journal, © Dow Jones & Company, Inc., 1979. All rights reserved.

Japan. One estimate is that between 30 and 40 percent of factory jobs will eventually be replaced by automated robots.[10]

The primary benefits of automation are cost savings and increased productive efficiency. In a mass assembly operation, automation could possibly produce sizable financial benefits both to the company and to consumers through reduced

[10] "Klatu Ready for More Serious Work," *Detroit News* (May 10, 1978), p. 5-C. See also Lee Edson, "Slaves of Industry," *Across the Board* (July–August 1981), pp. 5–12; and "The Robots Are Coming and Japan Leads Way," *U.S. News & World Report* (January 18, 1982), pp. 46–47.

ROBOTS: EFFECTIVE IN PERFORMING ROUTINE, REPETITIVE—AND BORING—TASKS

SOURCE: "Grin and Bear It" by Lichty & Wagner (February 1, 1982). © 1982 Field Enterprises, Inc. Courtesy of Field Newspaper Syndicate.

© Field Enterprises. Inc., 1982

"I don't see how a robot could stand to do this."

prices. Automation also offers the advantage of freeing people from mundane tasks, allowing them to concentrate on potentially more rewarding activities. Possible production gains of 200 percent have made industrial robots a $100 million-plus industry. The Robot Institute of America reports that at least twenty-four major U.S. manufacturers and eleven major distributors are currently active.[11] But automation also carries a high cost in terms of reduced employment opportunities and purchasing power within the community. Admittedly, many of the displaced workers will find jobs in other areas, although retraining may be required. Still, *technological displacement*, as the loss of employment owing to technological changes is called, can be traumatic for the individuals involved. And there is no assurance that their skills will always be transferable to another industry.

Technological displacement is the loss of employment due to technological changes.

Others have raised the question of whether modern technology is beyond management's control. However, a Booz, Allen & Hamilton study supported by General Electric concluded that technology was within management's capability for dealing with it. The study involved twelve "high technology, growth oriented industrial firms."[12]

Site Selection

Volkswagenwerk AG faced a major problem during the mid-1970s. U.S. sales had begun to lag, so the West German firm decided to open a plant to produce the "Rabbit" and other newer, more popular models for the American market. But where should the plant be located?

The Volkswagen decision to initiate U.S. production started one of the most publicized industrial location battles in history. It seemed that everyone wanted the new plant because of its potential benefit to the local economy. Forty-eight states and Puerto Rico offered proposals to the Germans. Volkswagen then conducted thirteen major site selection studies. Eventually, the decision came down to an abandoned tank plant near Cleveland or a partially constructed Chrysler plant at New Stanton, Pennsylvania—thirty miles from Pittsburgh.

The Pennsylvania site was finally picked after Volkswagen was offered an extensive group of incentives, including financing, railroad and highway projects to serve the plant, and employee training programs. Rabbits produced in New Stanton now sell briskly in the U.S. domestic market. The Commonwealth of Pennsylvania has also profited from the Volkswagen decision. The New Stanton plant created directly or indirectly 13,000 to 15,000 new jobs and generated $80 million in additional taxes for Pennsylvania over a five-year period.[13]

The Volkswagen example shows the importance of site selection decisions to both the firm and the community. Production/operations management is

---

[11] See Kathleen K. Wiegner, "The Dawn of Battle," *Forbes* (October 26, 1981), pp. 77–79; and "GE Is About to Take a Big Step in Robotics," *Business Week* (March 8, 1982), pp. 31–32.

[12] "Quick Reflexes," *Nation's Business* (February 1979), p. 88.

[13] Charles B. Camp, "VW Picks New Stanton, Pa., as U.S. Site for Plant," *Wall Street Journal* (June 1, 1976), p. 4.

directly involved in this decision since they are the people who will have operational responsibility for the new facility.

LOCATION FACTORS

Initially, businesses are usually located wherever the entrepreneur happens to reside. Early expansion is typically into nearby or familiar areas. Later, other variables become important. Numerous factors can influence a location decision. These can be categorized as

1. Market-related factors
2. Tangible cost factors
3. Intangible factors

The *market-related* factors involve the location of buyers and the competition. If the company plans to provide a service to senior adults, it should proba-

FACILITIES LOCATION: CRITICAL DECISION FOR RETAILERS

Market-related factors are particularly important for retailing firms. Ron Lubben, president of the Chicago center for the Institute of Store Planning, points out that earlier criteria for selecting retail sites "used to be whether there was decent exposure from the road and if there was a large enough population base."

Such considerations, and other universals, still hold sway, of course. Building or rental costs never stopped being major factors in the location decision: indeed, some professionals contend costs have been even more heavily considered under recent economic conditions.

Central business districts, which drew from the total population base of early cities, still attract very specialized retailers whose goods appeal to only a small percentage of a metropolitan population. Consumer access and transportation needs also remain considerations.

But changing demographics and technology have forced retailers to reevaluate their approach to site selection. Automobile transportation has helped open up new residential areas and led to the development of regional and convenience shopping centers. Specialty stores are nearly as often found in suburban malls as in city centers. . . . Because of the increased number of site choices and a more marketing-oriented approach, retailers are probably more aware than ever of what their primary trade area must look like. Toys "R" Us, the Rochelle, New Jersey–based retailer, requires a market of at least 250,000 people, of which 25 to 28 percent must be children. The market must also be large enough to support four stores, each of which will be located on the path of a major shopping mall. . . .

SOURCE: Janet Neiman, "Retailers Should Know Their Place," *Advertising Age* (November 1, 1982), p. 22-M. Reprinted with permission. Copyright, Crain Communications, Inc., 1982.

bly be located in an area with an aged population. Similarly, some firms prefer to locate in areas where there is limited direct competition. Market proximity is a prime advantage in industry location. For instance, the Delmarva poultry industry (located on the Delaware, Maryland, Virginia peninsula and made popular by the Frank Perdue ads) has a proximity advantage over other poultry-producing areas because of its closeness to the huge consumer markets of the Northeast.

Tangible cost factors include transportation, utilities, labor, taxes, site costs, and construction costs. Other things being equal, management would prefer cheap, nearby transportation; low utility costs; a ready supply of low-cost but skilled labor; a modest tax structure; and minimal site and construction costs. But typically a favorable tangible cost factor is offset by another less favorable factor. The availability of a skilled labor force may be offset by high labor costs, for instance. This situation requires a careful balancing on the part of management. No site meets 100 percent of a firm's ideal standards. So management is forced to balance favorable and unfavorable factors to come up with the site deemed to be most valuable overall.

Intangible factors include local attitude toward industry, zoning and legal regulations, room for growth, climate, schools, churches, hospitals, and recreational opportunities. Some industries have only minimal need to be located near markets, supply sources, or transportation modes; thus, their location decisions are based more on amenity factors such as desirable living conditions for their employees. The population movement to the Sunbelt partially reflects the role of these intangible factors.

THE STAGES OF SITE SELECTION

The process of site selection consists of various stages that follow a generally sequential order. These stages are

1. Select the general area.
2. Select generally acceptable communities.
3. Select sites within the communities.
4. Determine a method of evaluating community–site combinations.
5. Compare sites and select one.

The actual method of evaluating potential sites will vary with the specific circumstances of the decision. One commonly used procedure is a point rating system in which the relevant decision factors are identified and then weighted with a specific number of points. The site alternatives are then graded on each factor, and the one with the highest score is considered the most desirable. If one factor is absolutely essential, then a minimum score should be specified. Sites not meeting this minimum are not considered further.

Physical Layout

All phases of production/operations must be carefully considered in order to design an efficient production facility. A number of alternative layout designs are available. In addition, the necessary inputs at each step of the production/operations process must be considered and a materials handling system must be designed to blend smoothly with the choice of physical layouts.

MATERIALS HANDLING

Materials handling is the physical movement of materials and products within a work facility.

Materials handling refers to the physical movement of materials and products within a work facility. It can range from an overhead crane used in a factory to a robot that delivers and picks up mail in a larger office. In manufacturing operations, the primary pieces of materials handling equipment are conveyors, industrial trucks, and cranes and hoists. Substantial cost and efficiency benefits can stem from effective use of materials handling equipment. Chrysler, for example, was forced to shut its Dodge Main assembly plant in Hamtramck, Michigan, in 1980 because the eight-story factory was outdated. Dodge Main's thirty-two freight elevators were no longer competitive with automated single-floor plants.[14]

BASIC LAYOUTS

There are three basic types of layout: flow lines (or product layouts), process layouts, and fixed position layouts. Each type of layout possesses a number of advantages and disadvantages, and the production/operations manager must consider a number of factors in choosing the most appropriate type. Major influences in the choice of layouts include nature of the product or service, production volume, weight factors, building costs, production mix, and relative fragility of the finished product. Figure 19-2 illustrates each type of layout.

Flow Line

As Figure 19-2 indicates, in *flow lines* the product moves along some type of line along which the various work activities are performed. It is a product-oriented layout common in assembly lines and cafeterias. The flow line layout is also used in military induction centers.

The primary advantages of this type of layout lie in its simplification of production planning and control and the ability to utilize unskilled workers who can quickly learn the tasks involved. In addition, both materials handling and overall processing time are reduced. On the other hand, the flow line layout is only as strong as its weakest link since each step depends upon all other steps. Products cannot flow through the line faster than the slowest task to be performed. In addition, this is a relatively expensive type of layout that typically involves substantial investments in special-purpose equipment. Finally, worker monotony often occurs with the flow line approach.

[14] Barrett Seaman, "In Michigan: Goodbye Dodge Main," *Time* (February 11, 1980).

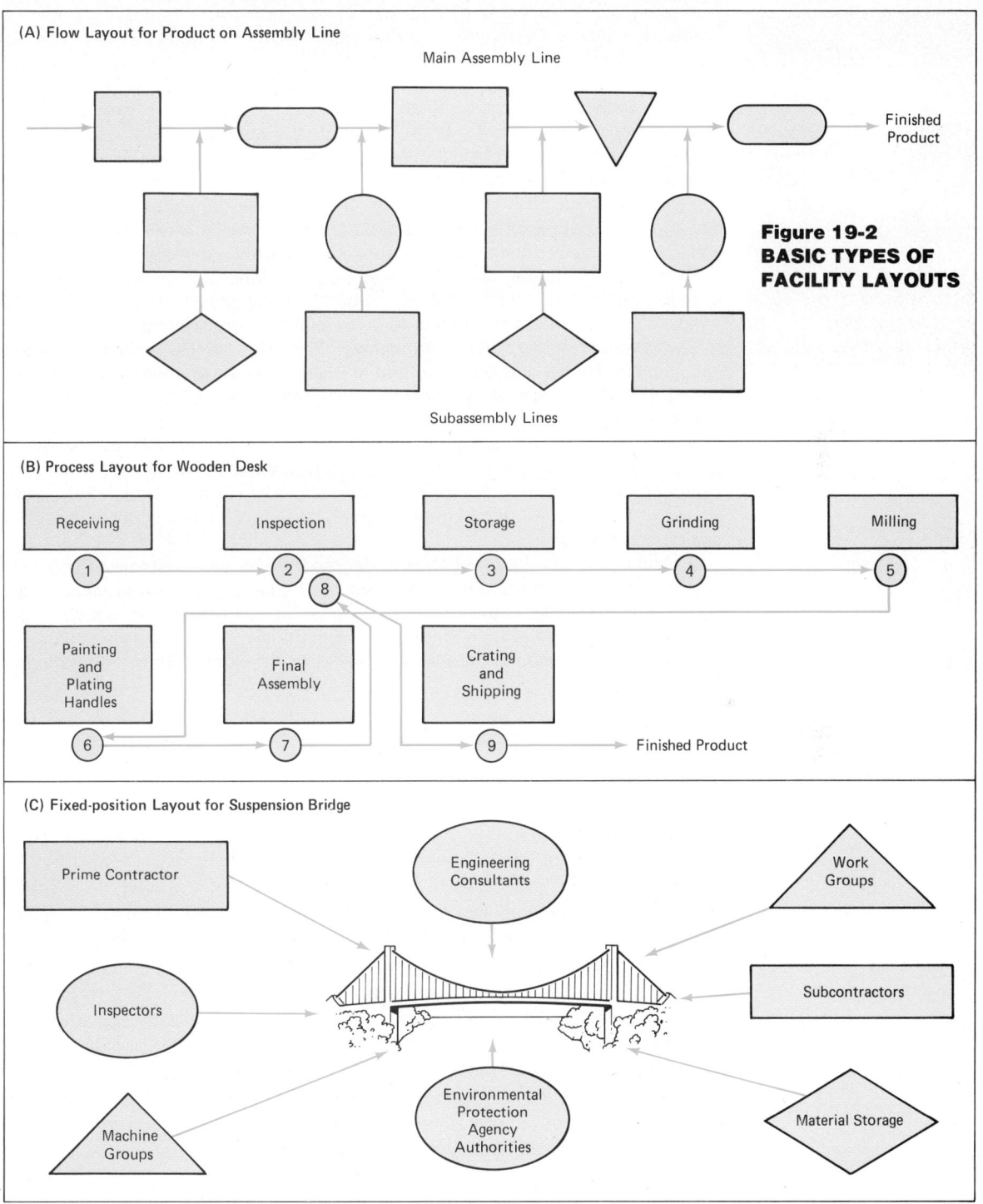

(A) Flow Layout for Product on Assembly Line

Main Assembly Line

Finished Product

Subassembly Lines

Figure 19-2
BASIC TYPES OF
FACILITY LAYOUTS

(B) Process Layout for Wooden Desk

Receiving — 1

Inspection — 2, 8

Storage — 3

Grinding — 4

Milling — 5

Painting and Plating Handles — 6

Final Assembly — 7

Crating and Shipping — 9 — Finished Product

(C) Fixed-position Layout for Suspension Bridge

Prime Contractor

Engineering Consultants

Work Groups

Inspectors

Subcontractors

Machine Groups

Environmental Protection Agency Authorities

Material Storage

Frederick Winslow Taylor was a utilitarian; he sought to achieve "the greatest happiness for the greatest number." Much of his professional life was directed at increasing levels of efficiency in factory shops and yards by refining the relationships between laborer and machine. He hoped to reduce the time workers would expend in drudgery and provide them with greater periods of leisure to enhance their education and their cultural lives. Taylor developed the scientific time study, a method of analyzing and setting standards for the performance of individual tasks in the shop. The time study was central to his principles for production management. Enthusiastically embraced by industrialists in the United States and Europe, these principles prescribed (1) a carefully planned daily task for each worker, (2) standardized tasks and tools, (3) good pay for success, and (4) poor pay for failure. In addition, Taylor urged that "all possible brain work . . . be removed from the shop and centered in the planning department."

Taylor was born in 1856 in Germantown, Pennsylvania. He received his early education in France and Germany and at Phillips Exeter Academy, but his poor eyesight compelled him temporarily to give up attending college.

In his first job at Midvale Steel Co., he found the differential piece-rate system devised by the company's superintendent fascinating, and he was soon working to improve on and extend its utility, particularly in the machine shop. Taylor concentrated on specializing the work responsibilities of each individual. For example, he gave the job of grinding tools, which had been shared by all workers, to one person.

By 1884 Taylor had earned an M.E. degree from Stevens Institute of Technology. In recognition of the efficiency measures he had introduced at Midvale, he was promoted to chief engineer. In this position he was able to conduct scientific time-and-motion studies on a large scale. With the aim of standardizing all points along the production line, he analyzed each job, breaking it down into as many

Process Layout

Sometimes the most appropriate physical layout is based on a department grouping or a division on the basis of each process to be performed. In such instances all equipment and personnel performing the same activity are separated into departments or groups. Figure 19-2 illustrates the *process layout* by describing the various process involved in the production of a wooden desk. Insurance claims offices, colleges and universities, banks, and automobile repair facilities are other examples of this approach to physical layout.

Since the personnel in each department are likely to perform a larger number of tasks than would employees in a manufacturing facility using a flow line layout, the process layout approach has the advantages of flexibility of equipment and personnel and increased worker satisfaction because of the diversity of tasks. In addition, the process layout approach typically requires a smaller investment in equipment because duplication is not necessary unless volume is large. Finally, expertise is developed since the supervisors for each department become highly knowledgeable about their functions.

A major shortcoming of this approach involves costs and reduced efficiency. Backtracking and long movements may occur in materials handling, thereby lowering efficiency in this area. In addition, timing inefficiencies may occur, with basic movements as possible. Then he found the most skilled workers and, with a stopwatch, measured how much time they needed to complete each given task. That amount of time, expanded slightly to allow for unavoidable delays, initial slowness of new workers, and rest periods, became the standard for determining how much work each employee in the shop should produce in a specified time period.

Taylor's success in increasing production at Midvale was phenomenal; the shop output shot up to 300 percent of what it had been. Consistent with Taylor's philosophy that good work should be well rewarded, the pay of his workers moved up by 25 to 100 percent. Efficiency engineering—or *Taylorism*, as his techniques became known—quickly captured the imagination of management everywhere.

Taylor left Midvale in 1890 to assume the position of general manager of the Manufacturing Investment Co.'s paper mills. Later, in 1893, he established his own consulting business, but in 1901 he gave up gainful employment to avoid what he believed to be the dehumanizing effect of too much money. During his retirement he continued his research and authored several books on his findings, among them *Principles of Scientific Management* (1911) and *Shop Management* (1903).

Before his death in 1915, Taylor had applied his creative mind not only to streamlining factory shop and yard production techniques but also to inventing and refining equipment to enhance his efficiency measures. Perhaps the most significant of his numerous inventions were the development of a cutting tool and, in collaboration with J. Mansel White, of a method for heat-treating chrome-tungsten tool steels that effectively doubled their efficiency. For this contribution to industry, he was awarded a gold medal at the Paris Exhibition and the Elliott Cresson medal of the Franklin Institute.

Sources

The National Cyclopaedia of American Biography, Vol. 23. s.v., "Taylor, Frederick Winslow."

Norman M. Pearson, "Public Administration: Fayolism as the Necessary Complement of Taylorism," *American Political Science Review* 39 (February 1945), pp. 66–80.

Paula Smith, "The Masterminds of Management," *Dun's Review* (July 1976), pp. 17–19.

Edwin A. Locke, "The Ideas of Frederick W. Taylor: An Evaluation," *Academy of Management Review* (January 1982), pp. 14–24.

work having to wait between tasks. Since workers must have broad skills, higher wages than those paid to assembly line workers may be necessary to attract qualified employees. Finally, because each job is different, each requires different setups and operator learning. Frequently, the result is lowered productivity.

Fixed Position Layout

Shipbuilding, home construction, and the manufacture of products like airplanes and computers follow a *fixed position layout*. This format is typically used for large or fragile products that cannot be readily moved from place to place.

Since movement of the work item is minimal, it is less likely to be damaged during the production process. A second advantage of this layout approach is that since the item does not go from one department to another, there is more continuity of the assigned work force. This reduces the problems of replanning and the need to instruct people each time a new type of activity is to begin.

One disadvantage of the fixed position layout is that since the same workers are involved in more operations, skilled and versatile workers are required. The necessary combination of skills may be difficult to find, and high pay levels may be necessary. Secondly, movement of people and equipment to and from the work site may be expensive. Finally, equipment utilization may be low because the equipment may be left at a location where it will be needed again in a few days rather than moved to another location where it would be productive.[15]

Table 19-1 summarizes the advantages and disadvantages of each type of layout.

[15] The advantages and disadvantages of the different layouts are described in James B. Dilworth, *Production and Operations Management*, pp. 487–491.

Table 19-1 ADVANTAGES AND DISADVANTAGES OF THE BASIC TYPES OF LAYOUTS	LAYOUT CLASSIFICATION	ADVANTAGES	DISADVANTAGES
	FLOW LINE	1. Reduced materials handling 2. Reduced total processing time 3. Simplified production planning and control systems 4. Simplification of tasks, enabling unskilled workers to learn tasks quickly	1. Facility modification may be required if product changes 2. Product cannot flow through the line faster than the slowest task can be accomplished unless the task is performed at several work stations 3. Large investment for special-purpose equipment 4. Dependence of the whole on each part 5. Worker monotony often occurs
	PROCESS	1. Personnel and equipment flexibility 2. Smaller investment in equipment 3. Expertise developed by supervisors, who become highly knowledgeable about their functions 4. Work more satisfying for people who prefer diversity because of wide variety of tasks	1. Lack of materials handling efficiency 2. Lack of efficiency in timing 3. Complication of production planning and control 4. Higher wages for workers with broad skills result in higher costs 5. Different setups and operator learning required for different jobs result in lowered productivity
	FIXED POSITION	1. Reduced damage and costs of moving the product 2. Reduced need for continual replanning and instruction because of continuity of work force	1. Higher wages for workers with broad skills result in higher costs 2. Moving people and equipment to and from work site may be expensive 3. Equipment utilization may be low

IBM's Tucson, Arizona, plant has an energy management system designed to pay for itself in two years. The heating and cooling needs of the eleven buildings in the complex are controlled by two IBM computers. Even the buildings are turned at angles designed to cut cooling costs. The complex has two wells that supply a self-contained water system. All water used at the plant is recycled. And thirteen storage tanks are used to hold hot and cold water to be employed in heating and cooling. The Tucson facility is considered a prototype of an energy-efficient plant for the 1980s.

SOURCE: "Vast IBM Plant Showcase for Saving Energy," *The Orlando Sentinel* (January 14, 1980), p. 6-D (UPI story).

IBM BUILDS AN ENERGY-EFFICIENT PLANT

COMPUTER-ASSISTED PHYSICAL LAYOUT

Physical layout of production facilities is a very complex managerial task. In recent years considerable effort has been expended on developing computer programs and models that assist management involved in making layout decisions. Programs with identifications such as CRAFT, ALDER, CORELAP, and PREP all have the same basic objective: the most efficient possible physical layout. Further developments in this area are to be expected because of the increased complexity of the production/operations function.

Job Design

While the choices of physical facilities location and the most appropriate process flows are crucial for production/operations management, of equal importance is the careful design of the jobs necessary to perform the activities involved in converting production inputs into finished products and services. *Job design* refers to the process of task delineation necessary to meet various personal, work, organizational, and environmental parameters. The job that is eventually specified should be technically, economically, and behaviorally feasible. Job design consists of several components: job content, methods improvement, the physical environment, and sociotechnical factors.

Job design is the process of task delineation necessary to meet various personal, work, organizational, and environmental parameters.

JOB CONTENT

Job content refers to the work activities that are assigned to a particular job. The early Gilbreth studies identified seventeen therbligs, or motions, involved in work. The Gilbreth research illustrates job content research at its most micro level. Other basic questions concern the degree of job specialization, relative use of machines (see the section on automation), job enlargement, and job enrichment.

Job content refers to the work activities that are assigned to a particular job.

METHODS IMPROVEMENT

Quality circles, which will be discussed shortly, are an excellent example of attempts to improve job methods. Improving the way work is done is an often

Methods improvement involves examining and redesigning aspects of a job or work in order to make them more efficient.

studied subject and has attracted the attention of people like Thomas Edison, Henry Ford, and George Westinghouse. *Methods improvement* involves examining and redesigning aspects of a job or work in order to make them more efficient.

In essence, methods improvement involves the redesign of a job in order to get the work done more efficiently. This may mean that the job is split or expanded. But the overall objective is increased productivity.

THE PHYSICAL ENVIRONMENT

The physical environment has a considerable impact on work effectiveness. In fact, a whole separate field of study—human engineering or ergonomics—has been created to deal with this aspect of production management. *Human factors engineering* applies relevant information about human characteristics and behavior to the design of things people use, how they are used, and the environment in which people live and work.

Human factors engineering applies information about human characteristics and behavior to the design of things people use, how they are used, and the environment in which people live and work.

Human factors engineering is concerned with such subjects as tool design and environmental factors like temperature, noise, and lighting. But safety may be one of its most important topics. Production management always regards an improved safety record as one of its highest priorities.

The Occupational Safety and Health Act of 1970 set up an administrative agency, the Occupational Safety and Health Administration (OSHA), to oversee the protection of the workplace. Most private employers are required to comply with the safety standards set by OSHA. Some 1,200 OSHA inspectors enforce the agency's requirements, and severe financial penalties can be assessed for major violations.

A sociotechnical system is the result of the relationship between the sociopsychological environment in which a task is performed and the technical system required to perform it.

SOCIOTECHNICAL FACTORS

Production management must be concerned with both the technical and social aspects of the job. Hence, job design must consider the overall sociotechnical system in a given work situation. A *sociotechnical system* is the result of the relationship between the sociopsychological environment in which a task is performed and the technical system required to perform it.

As suggested above, the process of job design is extremely complex. It is also one of the most important parts of production/operations management.

Quality circles are volunteer groups of operative employees who periodically brainstorm on how to increase the firm's output, improve quality, or improve the efficiency of the work place.

QUALITY CIRCLES

One of the latest trends in production/operations management is the use of *quality circles*, volunteer groups of employees who meet on a regular basis to identify, discuss, and recommend solutions to problems affecting the firm's output. A typical circle is comprised of five to ten workers who are paid for the time devoted to such meetings. Such programs are designed to provide job satisfaction through participation. In addition, they may result in employees becoming more intimately involved in designing various aspects of their own job activities.

Quality circles are used extensively in Japan and are increasingly common in the United States. General Motors, Ford, American Airlines, and Martin Marietta are examples of U.S. firms using this concept. The sponsoring firm typically expects to recoup its investments through improvements suggested by the circle members, and substantial cost savings have indeed been reported. One quality circle at a Westinghouse plant near Baltimore produced a $22,000 cost saving with the simple idea that one employee report to work fifteen minutes early in order to turn on some wire-bonding machines. The result was that other workers were no longer idle during the machine startup time.[16]

Production Control

One would think that Wendy's, with its 256 kinds of hamburgers, would face a difficult production control problem. However, the multitude of combinations is a product of the number of burgers used in a Wendy's and the eight condiments and cheese that are offered. Wendy's is able to resolve its product control situation by training its cooks to start grilling a hamburger as soon as someone drives up outside. With only five basic products, Wendy's knows that a vast majority of its customers will buy a hamburger.

Wendy's situation may be somewhat simplistic as compared with that faced in many manufacturing operations, but the concept is basically the same. *Production control* is a system designed to produce maximum output with minimal input contributions and at the lowest possible cost. Production control can be thought of as a series of sequential steps:

Production control is a system designed to produce the maximum output with minimal input contributions and at the lowest cost.

1. Aggregate output planning
2. Resource allocation
3. Activity scheduling

An overview of the production control system is presented in Figure 19-3.

AGGREGATE OUTPUT PLANNING

The first step in production control is to forecast the overall output over, say, the next year. Aggregate figures like tons of steel were traditionally used, but computer models now make it possible to forecast specific products rather than some standard measurement of the product mix.

Aggregate output planning has two basic objectives, both applicable within what is often called the *intermediate planning horizon*. The first objective is to assess whether the planned output is feasible. Among other things this step prevents the company from making impossible commitments to buyers. The operation's capacity limit sets the outside parameters for this assessment since the

[16] "The Workers Know Best," *Time* (January 28, 1980), p. 65. See also "Will the Slide Kill Quality Circles?" *Business Week* (January 11, 1982), pp. 108–109.

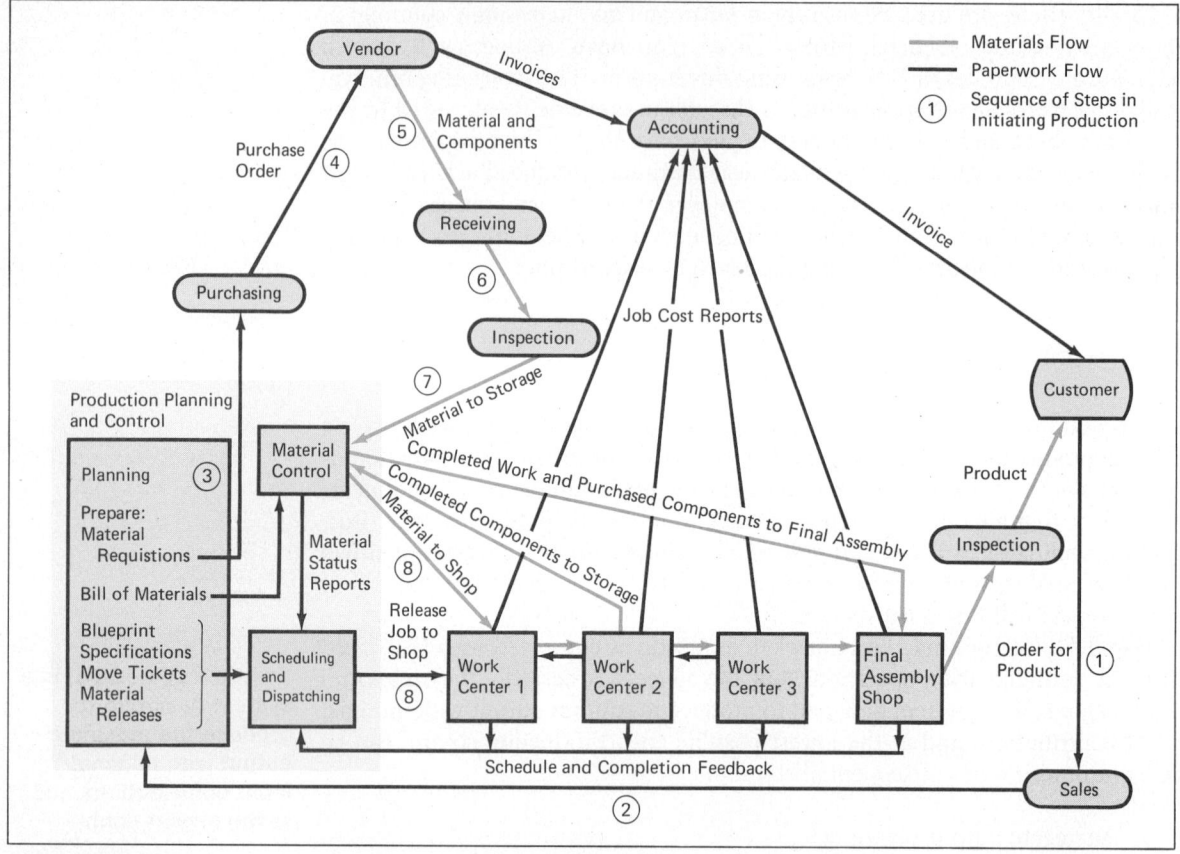

Figure 19-3
OVERVIEW OF
PRODUCTION
CONTROL AND OTHER
ACTIVITIES THAT
MUST BE
COORDINATED TO
PRODUCE A
PRODUCT

SOURCE: Reprinted with permission from James B. Dilworth, *Production and Operations Management*, 2nd ed. (New York: Random House, 1983), p. 282.

building of additional facilities is considered a long-range rather than an intermediate-range project.

The second objective is to optimize the costs and inputs necessary to meet a planned level of output. A given production level can be reached by a variety of methods. The key is to determine the optimal mix of inputs and the like.

Many of the techniques discussed earlier in the planning section are applicable here. Aggregate output planning is basically a forecasting problem and is subject to solution by trial and error, intuition, linear programming, and a variety of other techniques—depending on the particular situation.

RESOURCE ALLOCATION

The model of the production system shown in Figure 19-1 on page 487 reflects the transformation of inputs into outputs by the organization. This transformation process requires the careful allocation of inputs—raw materials, employees, financial resources, component parts, and equipment. Resource allocation is an extremely important and complex subject for the decision maker.

One of the basic resource allocation decisions is whether the firm should manufacture or purchase the input. This is often referred to as the *make-or-buy question*. This decision is typically made on the basis of such factors as production costs, transportation costs, availability, quality control needs, and confidentiality requirements.

Value analysis is a common procedure in the resource allocation stage of production control. *Value analysis* is a formal study of purchases to determine the true needs, relative costs, and alternatives in an effort to minimize overall expenditures. Task forces consisting of production, engineering, and purchasing personnel are a common format for implementing value analysis.

ACTIVITY SCHEDULING

Activity scheduling refers to the sequence and timing of work activities so that this transformation process is completed as efficiently as possible. Scheduling typically consists of two activities. First, *loading* refers to the assignment of a job to some designated plant, work center, or department. Second, *dispatching* refers to the actual scheduling of specific activities within a department such as when a certain cut will be made on a given machine.

Several analytical techniques are useful in activity scheduling. A Gantt Schedule Chart (see Chapter 17) can be employed to monitor the current status of a job. Figure 19-4 shows a Gantt Schedule Chart. In this example the stand is ahead of schedule but the compressor is lagging behind.

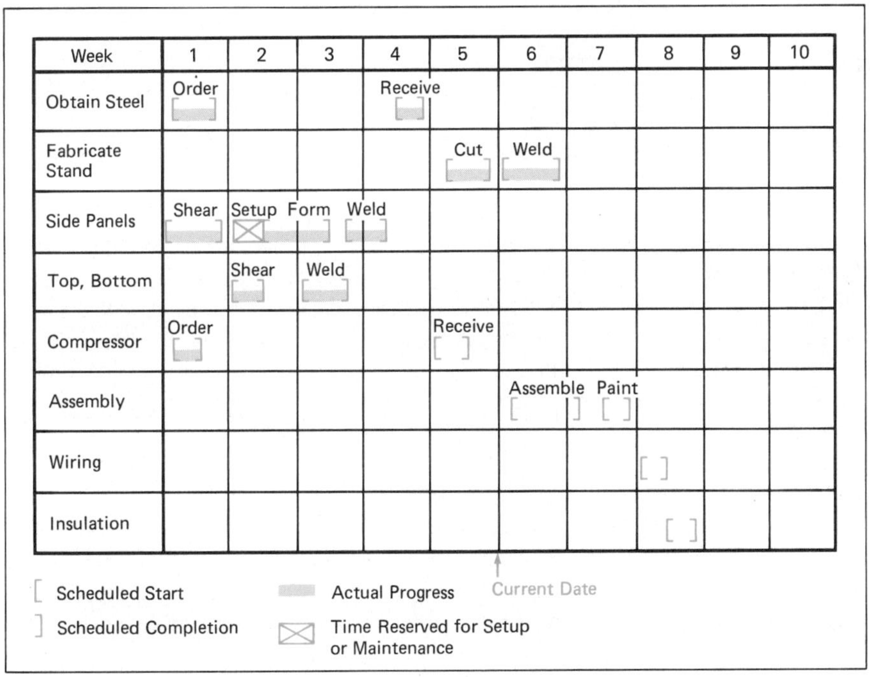

Value analysis is a formal study of purchases to determine needs, relative costs, and alternatives in an effort to minimize total expenditures.

Activity scheduling is the sequential timing of work activities in an effort to maximize efficiency.

**Figure 19-4
A GANTT SCHEDULE CHART**

SOURCE: Reprinted with permission from Dilworth, *Production and Operations Management*, 2nd ed. (New York: Random House, 1983), p. 289.

The Gantt Chart was developed in 1917, and it was not until 1956–1958 that another major activity scheduling breakthrough occurred. Two new techniques, with similar qualities, were developed independently of each other during the 1950s. Both used a network format to assist in scheduling.

CPM (*Critical Path Method*) was created by Du Pont and Remington Rand to improve maintenance and construction scheduling at Du Pont's widespread plants. *PERT* (*Program Evaluation and Review Technique*) was the product of a joint effort by the Navy, Lockheed, and Booz, Allen & Hamilton. The project was the submarine-launched Polaris missile system. While there are differences between CPM and PERT, both may be considered network scheduling techniques.

Consider the following example of the construction of a small warehouse and office designed to store batteries. A transformer must be placed in the attic after

**Figure 19-5
NETWORK
SCHEDULING FOR
THE CONSTRUCTION
OF A BATTERY
WAREHOUSE**

SOURCE: Adapted with permission from Dilworth, *Production and Operations Management*, 2nd ed. (New York: Random House, 1983), p. 341.

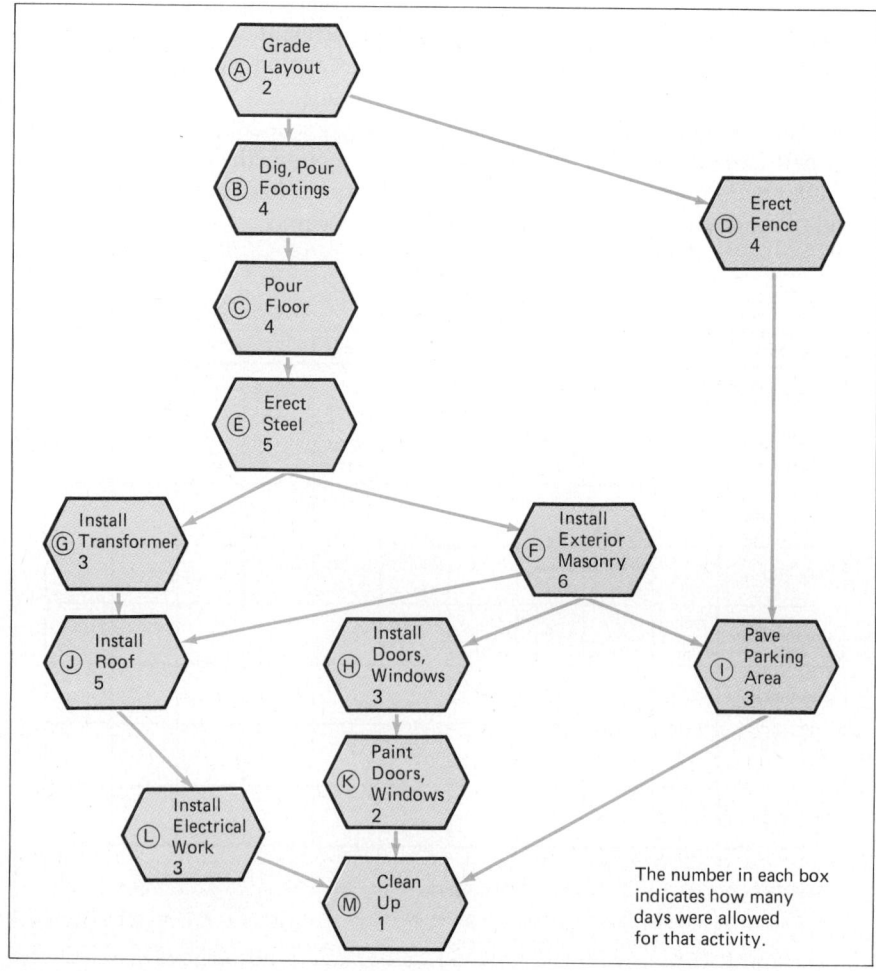

The number in each box indicates how many days were allowed for that activity.

the steel frame is up but before the roof is added. And the roof has to await the exterior wall. Specifications also require that the parking lot must be done after the fence and exterior wall. Figure 19-5 shows the network scheduling technique used for this project.

Inventory Control

The typical manufacturer has two year's worth of profits invested in inventory, according to government statistics. In terms of annual sales, inventory accounts for about 12.5 percent for manufacturers; 11.6 percent for retailers; and 10 percent for wholesalers. Inventory is certainly a major item in most businesses.

DEFINITION AND RATIONALE

Inventory can be defined as any idle resource held for future use. It may take the form of raw materials, partially processed materials, or finished goods that become components of the final product. There are a number of reasons for carrying inventory. These include the following:

Inventory is any idle resource being held for future use.

1. Inventory allows production management to fulfill orders immediately, thus cutting or eliminating lead time.
2. Quantity purchases—some of which will be carried in inventory—spread fixed costs over more units and reduce overall unit costs.
3. The carrying of inventory allows the firm to stabilize production and employment.
4. Inventory protects the company from unexpected surges in sales.
5. Inventory also protects the company from strikes and shortages.
6. Inventory allows a steady materials flow and flexibility in rates of output of various units.

Inventory management can in itself be a complex topic. As a result a variety of inventory control systems has been developed over the years.

TYPES OF INVENTORY CONTROL SYSTEMS

Inventory control systems are typically predicated on the demand situation facing the item. For example, the demand situation may be classified as independent or dependent, based upon whether it is related to the demand for another good. Some of the most common inventory control systems are outlined below.

1. *Fixed quantity system.* Here, the same amount of output is added to inventory every time the inventory reaches some specified reorder level.
2. *Fixed interval system.* In this system, the inventory level is monitored at designated times and then replenished to some predetermined figure.

3. *Minimum-maximum system.* This approach checks inventory levels at certain designated times, but does not reorder unless it is below some specified minimum level.

4. *Budget allocation.* This system is common in retailing. An overall budget figure is provided; within these limits, buyers are free to position their inventories as they see fit.

5. *ABC classification.* This format groups inventory items according to their relative importance. The classification is based on the annual expenditures for such items. A items would be the most critical and would require close control. Other categories (B or C) would receive less attention.

6. *Material Requirements Planning* (MRP). Dependent demand situations call for an alternative inventory control system. *Material Requirements Planning* is such a system. One writer explains the MRP system as follows:

THE VENEER FURNITURE CO.

Veneer Furniture Co. handles several lines of furniture, one of which is the popular Layback Model T chair, which the company purchases from a plant only ten miles from the store. Since the source is so near, Veneer has not bothered to stock a large number of the chairs in its warehouse. Instead, it sends its truck to "pick up a few" when there is none on the showroom floor. Slim Veneer, the owner, has observed that many times when he needs his truck to make a delivery it is tied up making trips to the Layback plant, and he suspects his ordering practices may not be optimal. He has decided to determine by use of the EOQ model the best quantity to obtain in each order.

Mr. Veneer has determined from past invoices that he has sold about 200 chairs during each of the past two years at a fairly uniform rate, and he expects to continue at that rate. He has estimated that preparing an order, paying for the driver and truck and the invoice, and other variable costs associated with each order are about $10, and that it costs him about 1.5 percent per month, or 18 percent per year, to hold items in stock. His cost for the chair is $87, so it costs him 0.18 × $87 = $15.66 to hold a chair for one year. (Of course, a chair does not stay in stock that long, but Slim uses annual usage rates, and the holding cost must be based on the same unit of time as the usage rate. He could use monthly use rate and the cost to hold a chair for a month. Any other time base could be used, so long as it was used for both usage rate and the cost to hold an item.) Veneer's calculations show that

$$\text{EOQ} = \sqrt{\frac{2 \times \text{Order Costs} \times \text{Annual Usage}}{\text{Annual Holding Costs}}} = \sqrt{\frac{2(10)(200)}{15.66}} = \sqrt{255.43} = 15.98 \text{ units}$$

He has therefore told the buyer that each time she orders Layback chairs she should order sixteen of them.

SOURCE: Adapted with permission from James B. Dilworth, *Production and Operations Management: Manufacturing and Nonmanufacturing* (New York: Random House, 1983), pp. 210–211.

"Basically MRP is a technique of working backwards from the scheduled quantities and need dates for end items specified in a master production schedule to determine the requirements for components needed to meet the master production schedule. The technique determines what components are needed, how many are needed, when they are needed, and when they should be ordered so that they are likely to be available when needed."[17]

ECONOMIC ORDER QUANTITY

There are various costs associated with inventory. Some go up with increased inventory levels: the costs of capital, storage space, taxes, insurance, deterioration, and obsolescence. Still others decrease with higher inventory levels: the costs of ordering, setup, production control, and missed sales. In addition, larger inventory purchases may permit quantity discounts. Production management is responsible for balancing these various costs (which can be roughly classified as either holding or order costs) and achieving the best order size—the so-called *economic order quantity* (EOQ).

The graphical determination of EOQ is shown in Figure 19-6. Economic order quantity can also be calculated from the following formula:

Economic order quantity (EOQ) is the optimal order size, based on a balancing of the various costs associated with inventory.

$$EOQ = \sqrt{\frac{2 \times \text{Order Costs} \times \text{Annual Usage}}{\text{Annual Holding Costs}}}$$

Consider the hypothetical situation on the facing page and how an economic order quantity would be calculated at a furniture store.

[17] Dilworth, *Production and Operations Management*, p. 239.

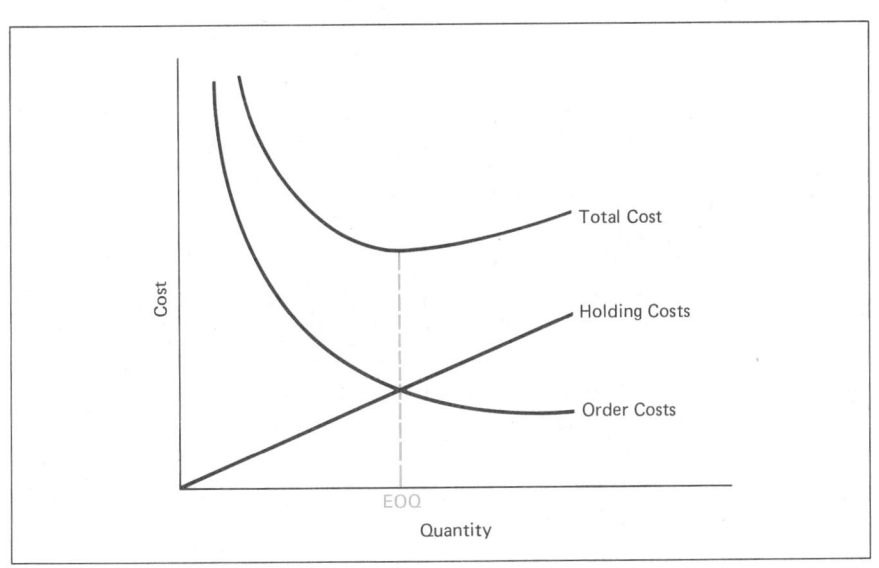

**Figure 19-6
GRAPHICAL
DETERMINATION OF
EOQ**

SAFETY STOCKS

Cycle stock is the amount of inventory expected to be used during a particular cycle.

Safety stock is the inventory kept above the cycle stock to ensure availability in case of unexpectedly high usage.

The inventory control systems discussed earlier deal with replenishment of what is called *cycle stocks*, the amounts that are expected to be used during the cycle established by the particular system. If usage could be predicted accurately every time, there would be no need for inventory beyond the cycle stock. But such is not the case in most instances. So a *safety stock* must be established to protect against unexpected high usage. It can be defined as the inventory kept on hand above the cycle stock—what is available when replenishment orders arrive. Safety stock is particularly important in situations where *stockouts* (a zero inventory situation) are costly in terms of increased production or labor costs, or lost sales.

Production management assumes the major responsibility in matters of inventory control, including the maintenance of adequate safety stocks. Most production processes are contingent upon having adequate, low-cost inventories of both inputs and finished products.

Quality Control

Quality control deals with maintaining specified quality levels for a firm's goods or services.

Quality controls are the processes and associated tasks designed to assure that a product or service meets acceptable standards. Quality controls have three components:

1. The product or service must be designed to be at least the minimum appropriate grade for its use.
2. It should conform to the standards of the design.
3. The consumer should receive the necessary training and service support so that his or her use of the product is satisfactory within reasonable expectations.

Consistently high-quality standards are a major competitive tool for a firm or an industry—in both domestic and international markets. The high cost of product liability litigation is another reason for establishing an effective quality control program.

QUALITY CONTROL INSPECTIONS

Quality control inspections should take place at three different points in the production process: receiving, transformation, and final inspection. Inputs are checked in the receiving stage to see that they comply with established standards. Quality control checks are also set up during the actual transformation process to assure that standards are being met before further work is done. In some cases unacceptable items can be reworked so that they may continue their journey through the transformation process. A final inspection checks the outputs of the transformation process.

QUALITY CONTROL SYSTEMS

Quality control systems can be classified as 100 percent inspection; sampling by attributes; and sampling by variables. A complete—or 100 percent—quality control plan means that all factors involved in the items are examined to assure that they are 100 percent satisfactory. Inspecting a new aircraft illustrates this type of system since the product must be completely reliable.

Sampling by attributes distinguishes acceptable and unacceptable products or groups of products according to whether the items meet minimum standards. Sampling by variables assesses the variations from standards set for specific product characteristics. Both of these systems may be employed for *acceptance sampling*, which refers to some type of random sampling plan used to classify a lot as acceptable, as unacceptable, or as one requiring complete screening of each item to eliminate defective items.

Quality control is the final ingredient of the overall production/operations system. It is production management's grading procedure and an important evaluative component of any organization.

Acceptance sampling is a type of random sampling plan used to classify a lot as acceptable, as unacceptable, or as one requiring complete individual screening.

Productivity

The first census of the United States, conducted in 1790, revealed that over 50 percent of the labor force was engaged in agriculture. Over half of all workers were required to feed the new nation of 3.9 million. In the nearly 200 years since then, vast changes in technology and farm production methods have resulted in crop yields that would have amazed our eighteenth-century ancestors. In 1940 30 million people worked on farms in the United States. Farm production has increased 600 percent over the past four decades, but the number of farm workers has dwindled to fewer than 3.5 million. Today, fewer than 4 percent of the work force feeds a nation of 230 million (and generates surpluses for consumers throughout the world).[18]

Throughout much of its history, growth in other sectors of the U.S. economy roughly paralleled that in agriculture. Technological innovations, a growing work force, and infusions of adequate capital to construct new facilities and equipment for mass production combined to produce productivity increases that sustained economic growth and led to continued improvements in the standards of living of American workers. From the end of World War II through the 1960s, productivity increased at an annual average rate of 3.3 percent. However, during the 1970s, the rate of productivity improvements was only 1.4 percent. In 1979, productivity declined by almost 1 percent.[19]

The recent economic ills of the United States and other economies through-

[18] William W. Bewley, "America's Productivity Decline: Fact or Fiction?" *Financial Executive* (April 1982), pp. 31–32.

[19] Campbell R. McConnell, "Why Is U.S. Productivity Slowing Down?" *Harvard Business Review* (March–April 1979), p. 36.

out the world have focused increased attention on productivity improvements as the answer to inflation, unemployment, and economic growth. On an aggregate basis, increased production with a given bundle of resources results in a richer nation. More is available for profits, for wages, and for use in achieving social goals. Increases in productivity can offset cost increases in such inputs as energy, materials, and human resources. It is a major factor in determining the competitive position of U.S. firms in the international marketplace. The link between productivity growth and improved living standards makes such improvements major objectives at the national level.

Productivity is also vital to the individual organization, since it reflects the efficiency of a department or a firm. Improved efficiency affects a profit-seeking firm's competitive position, its costs, and its profits. Increased productivity allows a nonprofit organization to provide additional services for the same level of resource inputs.

WHAT IS PRODUCTIVITY?

Productivity is a measure of the output of goods and services for a nation, an industry, or a firm.

Productivity can be defined as the relationship between the number of units of goods produced and the number of inputs of human and other resources necessary to produce them. It is a ratio of output to input. When a constant amount of inputs generates increased outputs, an increase in productivity has occurred.

Total productivity considers all inputs necessary to produce a given quantity of outputs. Stated in equation form

$$\frac{\text{Total}}{\text{Productivity}} = \frac{\text{Output (products or services produced)}}{\text{Input (human resources, land, and capital)}}$$

Most productivity ratios focus upon only one of the inputs of the equation: labor productivity or the output per worker per hour. Stated in equation form, *partial productivity* considers the relationship of output to a single major category of input:

$$\frac{\text{Partial}}{\text{Productivity}} = \frac{\text{Output (products or services produced)}}{\text{Partial Input (such as worker hours)}}$$

Since productivity—partial or total—is an estimate of outputs for a given amount of inputs, it is a notoriously poor measure, especially for short-term changes. Over longer periods, however, such estimates do indicate real trends. In recent years such trends have been disturbing.

DECLINES IN THE PRODUCTIVITY GROWTH RATE

Although the United States and other nations actually experienced a *decline* in productivity for a period during the severe recession beginning in 1979, productivity rates have continued to increase throughout the twentieth century. The current concerns involve a decline in the *rate* of productivity growth.

As Figure 19-7 shows, the U.S. output per worker hour is higher than in any other nation. Figure 19-7 compares the gross domestic production per employed worker in Canada, West Germany, the United Kingdom, Italy, and Japan with that of the United States. Although these nations appear to be moving faster than the United States in the drive for productivity, Canada is our closest competitor, with 93 percent as much output per worker, while Japan produces only 68 percent of the U.S. output per worker.

Although productivity in the United States is greater than in other nations, the gap is rapidly closing. A number of factors have influenced the decline in the U.S. rate of productivity growth.

1. *A decline in the capital–labor ratio.* During the 1970s the growth of capital spending dropped from 3.9 percent a year to 1.4 percent. Capital spending results in the creation of new equipment, factories, machinery, and processes. With more and better tools for the work force, more goods can be produced.

2. *Changes in the demographic composition of the labor force.* During the previous decade, some 20 million additional workers joined the U.S. labor force. A great number of them belonged to the baby-boom generation of the 1940s and 1950s and were young, well educated, but unskilled. Not only did the work force expand more rapidly than the nation's capital formation, but the addition of the younger workers to the labor force reduced its average level of skill and experience.

3. *Reduced spending on research and development.* In real terms spending for

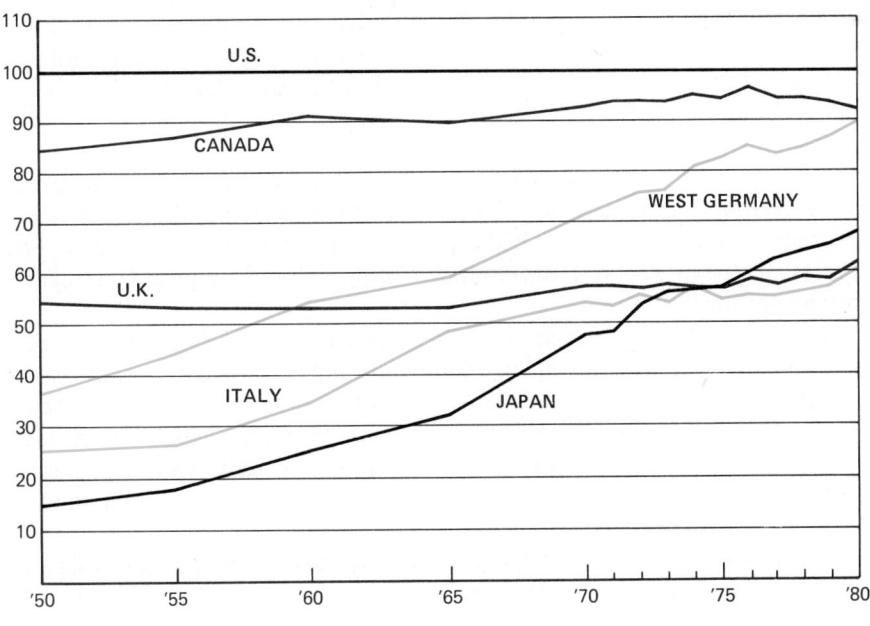

Figure 19-7
GROSS DOMESTIC PRODUCTION PER EMPLOYED PERSON (U.S. = 100)

SOURCE: Reprinted by permission from *Forbes* (July 6, 1981), p. 106. Bureau of Labor Statistics data.

research and development (R&D) has declined since 1970. R&D as a percentage of total gross national product declined from 3 percent in 1964 to 2.3 percent in 1975 to 2.1 percent in 1977.

4. *Interindustry shifts.* In recent decades the U.S. economy has increasingly moved away from basic industries and in the direction of sophisticated electronics, information, and services. Over 50 percent of the work force is now employed in service industries, which typically are more labor-intensive than manufacturing.[20]

5. *Government regulations.* During the past two decades, governmental regulations concerning industrial safety, product specifications, and environmental protection have generated additional costs in equipment and increased paper work. The growth of such regulations may have contributed to reductions in productivity growth rates.

6. *Economic orientation to short-term profits.* The continual search for short-term profits may be at the expense of investments designed to create longer-term profitability. Critics of well-established, publicly held corporations have argued that short-term measures such as quarterly earnings statements and dividend payments may adversely affect fundamental decisions concerning product innovation and technological development. Although empirical evidence is lacking, critics of short-term thinking frequently point to the Japanese economy and its greater emphasis upon longer-term objectives as a case study in productivity management.

JAPANESE PRODUCTIVITY AND THEORY Z

In attempting to explain the major strides in the Japanese economy in the decades since World War II, a number of writers have analyzed the Japanese workers and their special relationships with their employers. UCLA business professor William G. Ouchi (who is profiled in the following chapter) labeled the Japanese approach to management *Theory Z.*

Theory Z is a term coined by Professor William Ouchi to describe the Japanese approach to management. Characteristics of this approach include lifetime employment, employee participation in decision making, slow evaluation and promotion, nonspecialized career paths, and collective responsibility.

The Theory Z approach to management views involved workers as the key to increased productivity. Under this system employment is a lifetime guarantee. No one is ever dismissed or laid off; each worker participates in decision making; and tasks are rotated to avoid boredom, extreme specialization, and rigidity. The contrasts between Theory Z organizations in Japan and the typical U.S. organization are shown in Table 19-2.

Ouchi estimates that perhaps 35 percent of Japan's work force is under lifetime employment, primarily in large companies and government bureaus. "Lifetime employment means that a major firm or government bureau hires once a year, in the spring, when young people graduate from junior high school, high school, and the university. A major firm that hires only 'rookies' takes on a large inventory of new employees all at once, although it typically does not have work

[20] Harold Fearon, William Reif, William Ruch, and William Werther, "Management to the Year 2000," *Arizona Business* (April 1981), p. 4.

JAPANESE ORGANIZATIONS	U.S. ORGANIZATIONS	**Table 19-2 COMPARING JAPANESE AND U.S. ORGANIZATIONS**
Lifetime Employment	Short-term Employment	
Slow Evaluation and Promotion	Rapid Evaluation and Promotion	
Nonspecialized Career Paths	Specialized Career Paths	
Implicit Control Mechanisms	Explicit Control Mechanisms	
Collective Decision Making	Individual Decision Making	
Collective Responsibility	Individual Responsibility	

SOURCE: William G. Ouchi, *Theory Z* (Reading, Mass.: Addison-Wesley, 1981) p. 58. Copyright © 1981 by Addison-Wesley Publishing Co., Inc. Reprinted by permission.

for all of them immediately. Promotions are entirely from within, and a person with one, five, or twenty years at one company will not be hired or even considered by another company. Once hired, the new employee is retained until mandatory retirement at age fifty-five. An employee will not be terminated for anything less than a major criminal offense, and termination is a harsh punishment, since the one who has been fired has no hope of finding employment in a comparable firm and instead must turn either to a minor firm that pays comparatively low wages and offers little security, or else must return to his hometown."[21]

Ouchi argues that the adoption of Theory Z characteristics by U.S. firms would result in productivity increases and improved worker satisfaction. However, a number of major differences between the two countries exist. Japanese business–government relations are frequently so close that the label "Japan, Inc." has been applied to the entire nation. In addition, the markedly dissimilar cultural backgrounds of the two countries produce great differences in worker attitudes. Although a few attempts have been made to apply Theory Z approaches in such U.S. firms as Hewlett-Packard, Dayton-Hudson, Rockwell International, and Intel, little empirical research has been conducted on its impact in non-Japanese organizations.[22]

PRODUCTIVITY IMPROVEMENT

At the federal level, sporadic attempts to deal with the issue of productivity have occurred since 1970 when the National Commission on Productivity was created. In recent years changes in tax laws and investment credits were designed to stimulate additional investment in private industry.

At the individual firm level, a number of organizations have instituted productivity improvement programs. Among them are General Foods, Corning

---

[21] William G. Ouchi, *Theory Z* (Addison-Wesley, 1981), p. 17.

[22] Jeremiah J. Sullivan, "A Critique of Theory Z," *Academy of Management Review* (January 1983), pp. 132–142. See also B. Bruce-Briggs, "The Dangerous Folly Called Theory Z," *Fortune* (May 17, 1982), pp. 41–53.

Glass, Burger King, Hughes Aircraft, and Beatrice Foods.[23] Although the nature of the various programs differ, all of them incorporate three vital ingredients:

1. Measurement of productivity
2. Organizational commitment
3. Feedback on results that are achieved.[24]

While such programs demand commitments of both time and effort by managers and operative employees, they have already proven effective in increasing productivity and improving the firm's competitive position.

[23] Y. K. Shetty, "Key Elements of Productivity Improvement Programs," *Business Horizons* (March–April 1982), pp. 15–22.
[24] Roger G. Schroeder, *Operations Management* (New York: McGraw-Hill, 1981), p. 503.

Summary

Production/operations consists of the process and activities necessary to transform various inputs into goods and/or services. Determination of inputs, systems design, and production planning and control are the primary activities of the production/operations function. While production is only one part of the total management system, it plays a key role in any organization.

There are two basic types of production systems: continuous flow and intermittent flow. The establishment of a production system requires identification of the product or service to be produced, site selection, physical layout, job design, production control procedures, inventory control systems, and quality control requirements. All of these decisions involve a series of component decisions.

Site selection must consider market factors as well as tangible and intangible costs. Physical layout involves decisions concerning materials handling and the basic layout plan (flow lines, process layout, or fixed position layouts) to be used. Job design must consider job content, methods improvement, the physical environment, and sociotechnical factors. Production control involves aggregate output planning, resource allocation, and activity scheduling. Inventory control must be based on decisions as to type of system, economic order quantity, and safety stocks.

The efficiency of a production/operations management system can be expressed in terms of productivity. Productivity is a ratio of outputs to a given quantity of human and other inputs. Although U.S. output per worker hour is the highest in the world, the rate of annual increases in productivity has been declining in recent years. Factors associated with this decline include decline in the capital-labor ratio, changes in the demographic composition of the labor force, reduced spending on research and development, interindustry shifts, government regulations, and economic orientation to short-term profits. Continuing improvements in productivity are required to maintain and improve organizational profitability, increase worker compensation, achieve social goals, and sustain the United States' competitive strength in the international marketplace.

REVIEW EXERCISES

1. Define the following terms: (a) production/operations (b) automation (c) technological displacement (d) materials handling (e) job design (f) quality circles (g) job content (h) methods improvement (i) human factors engineering (j) sociotechnical systems (k) production control (l) value analysis (m) activity scheduling (n) CPM (o) PERT (p) inventory (q) economic order quantity (EOQ) (r) cycle stocks (s) safety stocks (t) stockouts (u) quality control (v) acceptance sampling (w) process control (x) productivity (y) Theory Z.

2. Differentiate between a continuous flow production system and an intermittent flow production system.

3. Identify the various factors that must be considered in the site selection decision and the stages of the selection decision process.

4. What are the major advantages and disadvantages of each of the basic types of physical layout?

5. Discuss the various aspects of job design.

6. Differentiate among the various inventory control systems.

7. Identify the components of an effective quality control program.

8. Distinguish between total productivity and partial productivity.

9. Identify the factors influencing recent declines in the rate of productivity growth.

10. What are the major characteristics of a Theory Z organization?

ASSIGNMENTS/ PROBLEMS/ DISCUSSION QUESTIONS

1. The typical exploratory oil well in the Anadarko Basin of Texas and Oklahoma costs $5,855,000.* Offshore wells are even more expensive. How might this huge expense affect the production process in the petroleum industry?

2. Visit a factory or other production facility. Then prepare a report on what you observed during the visit that relates to one of the following: (a) type of production system (b) site selection (c) physical layout (d) job design (e) production control (f) quality control (g) productivity improvements programs.

3. The number of Americans receiving patents has declined some 25 percent since 1971. But foreign patent holders have increased 14 percent over the same time span.† Comment.

4. Pick a business that interests you. Then develop a study that would identify a new location for this firm. Examples might include a new plant for some locally based company or a new location for a sports franchise.

* From ''Nearly $6 Million to Drill One Well,'' *U.S. News & World Report* (May 14, 1979), p. 24. Source: GHK Corp.
† ''The Productivity Pinch,'' *Time* (August 27, 1979), p. 36.

5. Review the factors influencing the recent declines in the rate of productivity growth. Can any of these factors be eliminated or modified? Should they be changed or modified?

A MANAGERIAL INCIDENT

Brave New World at the Factory

The scene was like an eerie science fiction movie. At midnight in Nagoya, Japan, the new plant of the Yamazaki Machinery Works was deserted. The cavernous, corrugated-metal building was shrouded in darkness. The only worker in the plant was a night watchman, who patrolled the factory with a flashlight. Nonetheless, the Yamazaki Machinery Works was running at full speed, filling the night with screeches and clangs as eight-ton metal castings were milled and moved throughout the plant, untouched by human hands.

In actuality, neither Darth Vader nor Dr. Strangelove had started his own company. The nocturnal scene was merely a routine operation at the $18 million flexible manufacturing lab that Yamazaki, Japan's largest maker of machine tools, put into production (in late 1981). The computer-controlled plant is the closest thing yet to the peopleless factory that futurologists predict will someday be the brave new world of manufacturing.

The plant produces precision components, including columns and bases for lathes and other metalworking implements. To produce its monthly output of 1,400 such parts, older plants that the company runs would have required more than 200 skilled workmen laboring at 68 different pieces of equipment.

There are just 18 machining centers, operating under computer control, at the Yamazaki plant. Human workers are now needed only at the very beginning of the production process. They use cranes to load metal castings onto fixtures which are wheeled into a storage area by a yellow trolley. When the electronic factory is ready for the casting, the metal is automatically rolled from there over to the proper machining center, which selects the right tool from a large drum of some 40 accessories and begins to customize the casting according to computerized blueprints. If a drill bit should suddenly snap in two, the machine senses the problem, selects another one to replace it, and finishes the job. Castings proceed automatically to other machines, and emerge as finished parts in three days, on average, compared with the three months typically required in traditional metalworking shops, where time-consuming setup and alignment are required for each different drilling, milling and grinding operation.

Yamazaki's management is enthusiastic about its new factory, which will operate around the clock, seven days a week, all year long. Says President Teruhiko Yamazaki: "The accuracy is better than humans can do, and the machines never have a blue Monday." To keep the equipment as precisely tuned as possible, workers help resharpen each machining center's drum of ac-

cessory tools every six or seven days. Such tasks, and programming the factory's computers, are all that the plant now requires of employees. There are normally ten to twelve workers in the plant during the day, but just one watchman for the night shift. Employees are pleased about the new machines, convinced they will bring additional growth to Yamazaki (current worldwide sales: $300 million). Although the automated factory meant intracompany transfers for some workers, none were laid off. Through productivity savings, Yamazaki expects to recover the factory's $18 million investment in two years.

SOURCE: "Look, No Hands," *Time* (November 16, 1981), p. 127. Copyright 1981 Time, Inc. All rights reserved. Reprinted by permission.

Questions and Problems

1. What are the major advantages and drawbacks of the automated system described above?

2. Relate the Yamazaki factory to the following production/operations concepts:

   a. Type of production system
   b. Site selection
   c. Physical layout
   d. Job design
   e. Production control
   f. Quality control
   g. Productivity

20.
International and Comparative Management

Learning Objectives

AFTER STUDYING THIS CHAPTER YOU SHOULD BE ABLE TO

1. Explain the importance of using a contingency approach in international management.
2. Outline the sequence of international business development and its related concepts.
3. Identify the environmental differences affecting international management.
4. Identify the basic functions of management and relate them to an international context.

Key Terms

exporting

importing

balance of trade

international business

international manager

MNC

licensing

economic boycott

industrial democracy

comparative management

exchange rate

technocrat

matrix organization

codetermination

systems type leadership

organic type leadership

consensus management

I would not like to be a Russian leader.
They never know when they're being
taped.

    RICHARD NIXON

. . . it is time that we put aside such
labels as "hard hat" and "blue collar"
and gave our skilled workers their
due—craftsman and craftswoman
alike—for the pride they have in their
products, their work place, their company, and their country.

    THOMAS A. MURPHY
    *Former board chairman of General
    Motors*

Lass and Mia Johansson of Södertälje, Sweden, get up early every morning to bicycle to a Saab plant nearly four miles away. The Johanssons
are part of an innovative management plan at Saab. One program has couples
like the Johanssons working together. But they and others are also part of a
broader job enrichment experiment called *line-out.* Groups of workers carry out
a complete production operation as a team. Team members have more flexibility than usual in their work pace. Saab reports less turnover and absenteeism and
better quality control. Employee morale has also been improved.

The plant where Lass and Mia Johansson work has a garden atmosphere featuring plants, flowers, and pleasant rest areas. Saab also provides a tennis court,
sauna, billiards room, lake, and assorted other leisure-time opportunities for its
employees. Management believes that it is important to have a highly satisfied
work force. Of course, in a nation that taxes away $20,000 of a $28,000 salary, it
is foolish to use further wage increases as motivators. Saab management has to
search for other ways to achieve its goals.[1]

One wonders how the Johanssons would react to a Detroit assembly line, with
its emphasis on speed, efficiency, and job specialization. While American automobile manufacturers have studied the Swedish system, job enrichment programs are scarce in assembly line–oriented Detroit.

[1] Robert T. Rahn, "How the Swedes Make the Line Almost Home," *Detroit News Magazine*
(September 17, 1978), pp. 12–14.

A basic theme of modern international management is that the successful executive has adopted a contingency approach to the field. What works in one country may be a disaster in another section of the world. Customs, laws, social structure, tax systems, distribution patterns, employee motivation, buying behavior, and a thousand other factors will differ in each part of the globe.

International managers have to possess an adaptability that is rarely found in other elements of the organization. Flexibility and a willingness to learn about the merits of other systems are the hallmark of managers who function effectively abroad. Many firms routinely assign rising executives to overseas operations in order to give them a broader perspective than they could obtain otherwise. Philip Caldwell's rise through international operations to the head of Ford illustrates this trend. In the 1980s business is truly a worldwide venture that extends to the farthest reaches of the globe. And people who want to lead such organizations must have the ability to relate to a mix of cultures, societies, and business systems.

The Evolution of International Management

Clinton Swan Clothes, Inc., of New York decided to investigate selling its men's suits in Japan, partially in order to alleviate a merchandise surplus. Inquiries were made with the Commerce Department and the Japan Trade Center.[2]

Exporting is the marketing of one's merchandise to other nations.

The firm's decision is typical of the way that most firms get into *exporting*, or the marketing of one's merchandise to other nations. The decision to export is viewed as an alternative to expanding domestic sales. Similarly, another firm might decide to import a product found abroad. *Importing* refers to the purchase and shipment of merchandise from another nation. In some cases there is a profitable opportunity for resale in the domestic market. In other instances the foreign-made items may be used as an ingredient for something produced here in the United States. All nations are involved in exporting and importing, to some degree. The relative status of a nation's exports to its imports is known as its *balance of trade*.

Importing is the purchase and shipment of merchandise from another nation.

Balance of trade is the relationship between a nation's exports and its imports.

MODELING THE EXPORT DECISION

Figure 20-1 shows that a variety of factors affect the pre-export activities of the firm. The decision maker is influenced by attention-evoking factors suggesting export as an appropriate strategy. The manager's perception of these factors is based on the decision maker's personal characteristics and the environment in which he or she operates, as well as on the firm itself.

Attention-evoking factors can be divided into internal and external components. Clinton Swan Clothes' surplus merchandise is an example of an internal factor. Unexpected orders from abroad or government programs to expand exports are examples of external factors.

---

[2] Mike Tharp, "Drive to Bolster Dollar by Increasing Exports Encounters Obstacles," *Wall Street Journal* (September 20, 1978), p. 1.

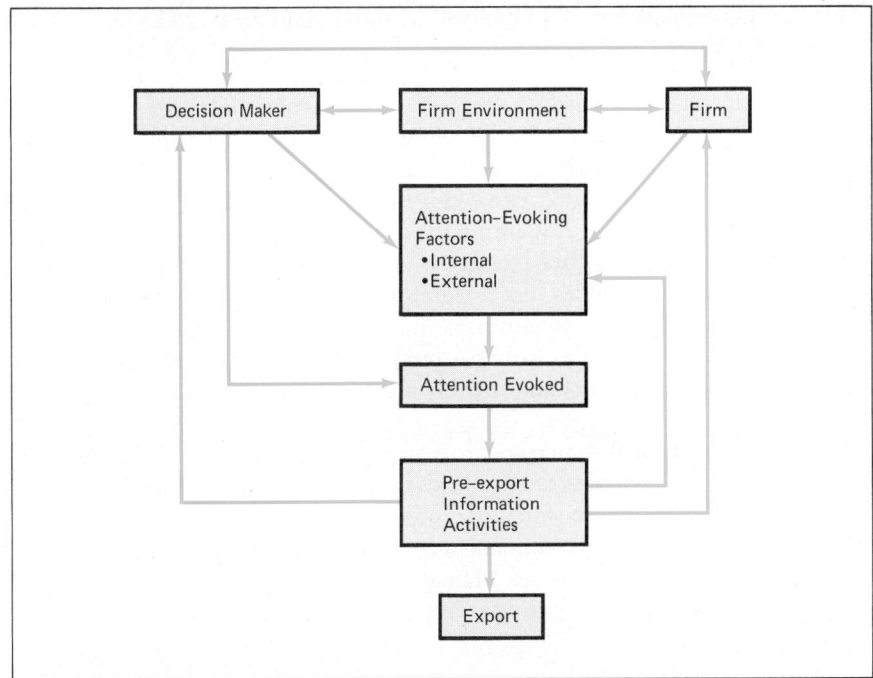

Figure 20-1
FACTORS AFFECTING THE PRE-EXPORT ACTIVITIES OF THE FIRM

SOURCE: Finn Wiedersheim-Paul, Hans C. Olson, and Lawrence S. Welch, "Pre-Export Activity: The First Step in Internationalization," *Journal of International Business Studies* (Spring–Summer 1978), p. 48.

The actual decision to export, then, is preceded by an information-seeking exercise, as when Clinton Swan Clothes contacted the Commerce Department and the Japan Trade Center. But the decision to export is only the first step in the development of international business and the evolution of international management. These processes will be demonstrated in the section that follows.

THE CONCEPTS OF INTERNATIONAL BUSINESS AND INTERNATIONAL MANAGEMENT

Exporting and importing are the basic tasks in what is known as *international business*—a term that can be roughly defined as all economic activities that cross national boundaries. Similarly, the term *international manager* can be used in a variety of ways to refer to any executive involved in international business activities. It might refer to the head of a firm's export or import department, or to a privately employed person engaged in such activities. An international manager might also be someone who works abroad in one of his or her firm's subsidiaries or sales offices. International managers have duties similar to those of domestic managers, except that their functions must be performed in a different environment.

The *multinational company*, often abbreviated *MNC*, is the ultimate level of international business. An MNC is a firm that views itself as essentially global in nature. Its business activities are conducted in numerous national markets and at a variety of different levels ranging from simple export to full-scale foreign companies with comprehensive production and marketing capabilities.

International business refers to all economic activity that crosses national boundaries.

International manager is an executive involved in international business activities.

MNC (multinational company) is a firm that views itself as essentially global in nature, and which conducts business in numerous national markets at a variety of levels.

THE SEQUENCE OF INTERNATIONAL BUSINESS DEVELOPMENT

Licensing is granting the right to produce and/or to distribute a firm's products in another country to an outside firm.

The experience of numerous firms suggests that international business activities tend to follow a standardized developmental sequence (see Figure 20-2). First, firms begin to export, usually through an agent who facilitates the transactions with a foreign buyer. An alternative strategy frequently employed by smaller firms is licensing. *Licensing* is granting the right to produce and/or to distribute the firm's products in another country to an outside firm. As export sales expand, the company concludes that it can justify its own foreign sales subsidiary. In other words it sets up its own overseas marketing arm. The final step is when management actually decides to begin producing the product abroad.[3] Volkswagen's decision to construct an assembly plant in Pennsylvania is illustrative of this step.

Effective international management is required in all phases of the developmental process. Foreign sales agents, heads of sales subsidiaries abroad, and a variety of people working in foreign production facilities can be considered international managers. International management permeates the entire spectrum of international commerce. Management is the mechanism for getting things done in international business, just as in domestic markets.[4]

Environmental Differences Affecting International Management

In Chapter 2 we discussed the importance of environmental factors in the framework for management. As important as these circumstances are to domestic management, they are magnified many times over in the international sphere. A multitude of environmental differences affect international management and its related decision-making process. In fact, the variety and extensiveness of such differences often dominate many discussions of international business and management.

These environmental differences may be divided into political, cultural, and economic differences. Further subclassification is possible, but it will be avoided

[3] This sequence and Figure 20-2 are suggested in Jan Johanson and Jan-Erils Vahlore, "The Internationalization Process of the Firm—A Model of Knowledge Development and Increasing Foreign Market Commitments," *Journal of International Business Studies* (Spring–Summer 1977), p. 24.

[4] An interesting discussion appears in J. Peter Killing, "How to Make a Joint Venture Work," *Harvard Business Review* (May–June, 1982), pp. 120–127.

**Figure 20-2
THE SEQUENCE OF INTERNATIONAL BUSINESS DEVELOPMENT**

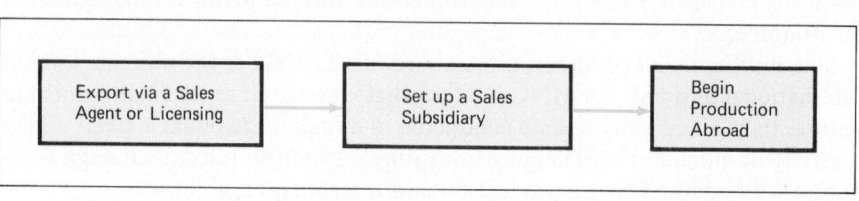

| Export via a Sales Agent or Licensing | Set up a Sales Subsidiary | Begin Production Abroad |

here in order to keep the discussion in its proper perspective. Suffice it to say that political, cultural, and economic differences may include (but are not limited to) the following factors:

1. Political differences
   a. International politics
   b. Foreign policy
   c. National and international legal frameworks
   d. National prejudices and opinions
2. Cultural differences
   a. Alternative value systems
   b. Cultural patterns
   c. Religious preferences and standards
   d. Societal norms
   e. Language barriers
3. Economic differences
   a. Technological differences
   b. Distribution of income and wealth
   c. Demographic factors
   d. Productivity rates
   e. Currency exchange circumstances

A brief explanation of each of these major environmental differences is in order here.

POLITICAL DIFFERENCES

Ben Pon failed when he tried to import Volkswagens in 1949. Too many people remembered that Hitler had ordered Ferdinand Porsche to build a "people's car" that could carry four or five passengers at 60 miles per hour on the new "autobahns" being constructed in Nazi Germany. Hitler further specified that the car average 33 miles per gallon (gasoline was expensive in Nazi Germany) and have an air-cooled engine to avoid frozen radiators. Porsche devised a small car with the engine in the rear, which Hitler called the "KdF" or "Kraft durch Freude." The name translates as "Strength Through Joy"; the car's name was later changed to Volkswagen "Beetle" in the United States. By 1939, American newspaper advertisements were billing the Beetle as a symbol of totalitarian Nazi rule. Given this background it is little wonder that Ben Pon's importing venture—coming only four years after the end of World War II—failed.[5]

Political differences can have a profound impact on international business. Management must recognize the potential problems and risks associated with business activities that must bridge different political systems and philosophies.[6]

---

[5] Michael Grant, "VW Satisfied Basic Needs," *Ypsilanti Press* (June 18, 1978), p. 68 (Copley News Service).

[6] An interesting discussion is presented in R. J. Rummel and David A. Heenan, "How Multinationals Analyze Political Risks," *Harvard Business Review* (January–February 1978), pp. 67–76.

Many nations—the United States included—have viewed international trade as one element of their overall foreign and domestic political policy.

Some governments use international business in a positive way to improve economic conditions at home. These governments actively subsidize management in achieving their objectives abroad, since these revenues eventually flow back to the source nation to support its standard of living and level of employment.[7] Japan is often cited as such a nation.[8]

Economic boycott is a situation where a nation prohibits trade or commerce with another country, typically as an act of political retaliation.

Other countries have threatened to halt international business in order to penalize political adversaries. *Economic boycotts* occur when a nation prohibits trade or commerce with another country, typically as an act of political retaliation. The United States has economically boycotted Cuba and other nations in recent years. The 1982 Argentine invasion of the Falkland Islands prompted the United States to restrict some trade with that South American nation.

Elaborate legal requirements also play an important role in international management decisions. Most of this legislative framework is a derivative of the internal and international political circumstances existing at a particular time. High unemployment might solicit public calls for a nation to impose import restrictions on foreign products.

Bethlehem Steel management makes known its dissatisfaction with the competitive practices of foreign steel suppliers through the advertisement shown on the facing page.

International management must be constantly aware of changing political and legal situations in the nations in which their firms operate. Political differences can affect all the functions performed by international managers, and in some cases these factors can spell the difference between success and failure.

CULTURAL DIFFERENCES

Consider the managerial decision-making process in Israel. In that nation private enterprise controls about 40 percent of the national output, government accounts for 35 percent, and the remaining 25 percent consist of firms owned by the Israeli labor federation, known as *Histadrut*. As an employer Histadrut ranks second only to the government. The union's involvement in operating business enterprises began in the 1920s, when few investors were willing to buy a stake in the desert that became Israel in 1948.

Industrial democracy is a system in which all employees are actively involved in an organization's decision-making processes.

Israel is a mix of private enterprise and socialism. Much of this pattern is derived from the country's unique cultural and historical background. *Industrial democracy*, a system in which all employees are actively involved in an organization's decision-making process, is widely practiced in Israel. While limited in the private sector, industrial democracy is required by law in the government sector. And management in Histadrut firms are appointed by elected union officials.

The ultimate degree of industrial democracy flourishes in a moshav or a kib-

---

[7] The subsidizing of European companies is discussed in Jean Ross-Skinner, "Europe's Subsidy Spree," *Dun's Review* (August 15, 1978), pp. 57–59.

[8] An interesting viewpoint is expressed in Ezra F. Vogel, "Guided Free Enterprise in Japan," *Harvard Business Review* (May–June 1978), pp. 161–170.

Vigorous enforcement of existing trade laws can save jobs for steelworkers -- and for a lot of other Americans, too.

America's existing trade laws were designed to encourage *fair* trade between our nation and others...and also to prevent damage to *any* domestic industry caused by *unfair* trade practices.

One of America's trade laws states that it's illegal for a foreign producer to sell his product in the U.S. at a price *below* his full cost of production.

That's called "dumping." And that's what foreign steel producers have been doing in recent years. "Dumping" their products in the U.S.—in order to keep their plants running, their people employed. What they do, in effect, is export their unemployment to the U.S.

But "dumping" is not just a steel industry problem. That illegal practice affects many American industries and many hundreds of thousands of workers.

One answer: enforce the existing trade laws

Free trade, yes. But *fair*. We don't think any American industry is asking for too much when it demands *fair* play here in our own country. When it asks our government for vigorous and effective enforcement of existing laws.

Trigger pricing

One attempt to achieve fair play for America's steel industry is the trigger price mechanism implemented by the Administration.

Objectives of the mechanism are (1) to monitor the prices of steel imports into the U.S. and (2) to initiate accelerated anti-dumping investigations of imports priced below the trigger price mechanism.

To be effective, the mechanism must reflect the *full* cost of the foreign producer for steel landed in the U.S. If it does not, it will not really eliminate the unfair trade practice of "dumping."

Still needed: U.S. tariffs on steel

Regardless of the ultimate impact of the trigger price mecha-

nism, we believe that existing U.S. tariffs on steel should be retained. These tariffs are an element of moderation in the international arena for steel trade. They must be maintained until such time as fair and nondiscriminatory world trade in steel has been achieved.

Washington must help

Unfair trade practices, such as "dumping," benefit foreign products and foreign workers at the expense of our own. If you believe the U.S. government should enforce U.S. laws to stop such unfair practices, please write your representatives in Washington and tell them so.

Bethlehem Steel Corporation, Bethlehem, PA 18016.

**Fair play in steel trade:
part of the solution to the steel industry puzzle**

Bethlehem
In search of solutions

BETHLEHEM STEEL'S CAMPAIGN AGAINST UNFAIR FOREIGN COMPETITION

SOURCE: Courtesy Bethlehem Steel Corp.

butz, the rural socialist collectives and enterprises that control most of Israel's agricultural output. All who live and work in these situations are Histadrut members. Management positions and most of the jobs are rotated periodically. Executive officers are elected. A *moshav* differs from a kibbutz only in that private family homes and farm plots are permitted. There is no private property in a *kibbutz*. Everyone eats together in a central hall, and children sleep in a dormitory. Everyone shares equally according to a socialist philosophy.[9]

Cultural differences clearly play a big role in the way Israeli managers must operate.[10] Similarly, the well-known Japanese desire to expand exports has been explained by that culture's extreme anxiety over its own economic vulnerability. Over 116 million people inhabit a usable land area only about the size of South

---

[9] Harry Bernstein, "Socialism Marches to a Different Drummer in Israel," *Detroit News* (July 3, 1978), pp. 1-C, 2-C. Another interesting discussion of Israeli management appears in Yoav Vardi, Arie Shirom, and Dan Jacobson, "A Study of the Leadership Beliefs of Israeli Managers," *Academy of Management Journal* (June 1980), pp. 367–374.

[10] An interesting discussion of Israeli management appears in Dale Zand, "Management in Israel," *Business Horizons* (August 1978), pp. 36–46.

Carolina.[11] The Japanese must import a substantial portion of their food supplies and raw materials. The national effort to create exports to pay for such necessities is certainly understandable.

[11] Edwin O. Reischauer, "Better Understanding Key to Japanese Trade," *Marketing in Japan*, prepared by the editors of *Advertising Age and Industrial Marketing*. Population update from U.S. Bureau of Census, *Statistical Abstract of the United States: 1980*, 101st ed. (Washington, D.C.: Government Printing Office, 1980) p. 898.

Table 20-1 NATIONAL CONCEPTS OF COMPETITION	NATURE AND EFFECT OF COMPETITION	TYPICAL AMERICAN VIEWPOINTS	TYPICAL EUROPEAN VIEWPOINTS	TYPICAL JAPANESE VIEWPOINTS
	NATURE OF COMPETITION	Competition is a strong moral force: it contributes to character building.	Competition is neither good nor bad.	There is conflict inherent in nature. To overcome conflicts man must compete; but man's final goal is harmony with nature and his fellow man.
	BUSINESS COMPETITION COMPARED	Business competition is like a big sport game.	Business competition affects the livelihood of people and quickly develops into warfare.	The company is like a family. Competition has no place in a family. Aggressive action against competitors in the marketplace is in order for the survival and growth of the company.
	MOTIVATION	One cannot rely on an employee's motivation unless extra monetary inducements for hard work are offered in addition to a base salary or wage.	A key employee is motivated by the fact that he has been hired by the company.	Same as the European viewpoint.
	REWARD SYSTEM	Money talks. A person is evaluated on the basis of his image (contribu-	An adequate salary, fringe benefits, opportunities for promotion, but no	Same as the European viewpoint.

Among the most important cultural differences affecting management are the varied national viewpoints on competition. The prevailing concept of competition can influence the relative aggressiveness of a manager's actions, the type of people who are hired by firms, leadership styles, motivational practices, and the compensation system that is employed. Table 20-1 shows that the American belief in the virtue of competition is not always shared by other cultures. The table illustrates a type of analysis known as *comparative management*, the cross-cultural study of management practices and techniques. The differences shown

Comparative management is the analysis of cross-cultural studies of management practices and techniques.

NATURE AND EFFECT OF COMPETITION	TYPICAL AMERICAN VIEWPOINTS	TYPICAL EUROPEAN VIEWPOINTS	TYPICAL JAPANESE VIEWPOINTS
	tion) to the company. High tipping in best hotels, restaurants, etc., is expected.	extra incentives —except in sales. Very little tipping (service charge is included in added-value tax).	
EXCESSIVE COMPETITION	Competition must be tough for the sake of the general welfare of society. No upper limit on the intensity and amount of competition is desirable.	Too much competition is destructive and is in conflict with brotherly love and Christian ethic.	Excessive competition is destructive and can create hatred. Only restrained competition leads to harmony and benefits society.
HIRING POLICY	Aggressive individuals who enjoy competition are ideal employees. Individuals who avoid competition are unfit for life and company work.	Diversity of opinion. How competitiveness or aggressive behavior of an individual is viewed varies with national ideology and the type of work. In England it is not a recommendation to describe a job applicant as being "aggressive."	Individuals are hired usually not for specific jobs but on the basis of their personality traits and their ability to become an honorable "company member." Team play and group consensus are stressed.

in Table 20-1 can help explain the difficulties American businesspersons sometimes have in adjusting to international management positions.

Stories of American management's inability to adjust to cultural differences are legend. Dozens of failures have resulted from an international manager's insensitivity to local cultural and societal patterns. A common mistake is to assume that our way of doing things is the correct (or even *only*) way to do them. Consider our penchant for precise legal language with extensive explanations and descriptions of the contemplated act. One American firm was forced to back out of a plan to manage a government-owned manufacturing operation in an African nation. The traditional "whereases" section of the contract noted that the government had been unsuccessful with the operation. It then went on to note the American firm's extensive international management and technical resources. To the host nation, the implication was that American management know-how would save the incompetent Africans. When a local student newspaper began attacking the "foreign imperialism" of the contract language, management had to beat a hasty retreat from a potentially advantageous agreement.[12]

Another story is told about the American executive who was miffed when an Asian businessperson asked to change the American's arrival just ten days before the scheduled date. The American did not realize that his Asian counterpart had asked a religious advisor to suggest a more promising date for an event he consid-

[12] Louis T. Wells, Jr., "Negotiating with Third World Governments," *Harvard Business Review* (January–February 1977), p. 76.

CULTURAL DIFFERENCES CAN HAVE A SIZABLE IMPACT ON INTERNATIONAL BUSINESS PRACTICES

SOURCE: *United Airlines Magazine* (May 1982), p. 20.

In the Arab countries, do not admire an object openly.
You may be the recipient of it.

ered so important. The Asian's action was a compliment that was missed by the American, who was unsophisticated in such cultural differences.[13]

ECONOMIC DIFFERENCES

Economic differences are quite extensive in international business. They can range from minor technological differences to sizable gaps in personal income and wealth. Economic events affect international management in two primary ways:

1. Changing business opportunities
2. The response required by a significant economic event

International management must be quick to recognize shifts in potentially profitable opportunities in worldwide commerce. American business response to the opening of trade with several Communist bloc countries is an example. Perhaps the best illustration has been foreign management's sudden movement into U.S. markets. Americans are good customers for imported products, and they harbor little resistance to foreign-owned firms operating within the United States.

Foreign investment in the United States has soared in recent years. Foreign-owned and -managed companies exist in virtually every segment of the United States economy. A report to Congress by the comptroller general of the United States indicated that European investors were attracted by several features of our business environment.[14]

1. *Profit motive.* Foreign firms are attracted by our large, wealthy market and the favorable acquisition costs of investing in American companies and property.

2. *Favorable labor market.* American labor is viewed as more stable and productive and cheaper than comparative work forces in Europe. Management technology is viewed as more sophisticated than in Europe, where management education has only recently been made available.

3. *Stable business environment.* A variety of factors such as a sizable domestic market and a resilient private enterprise system are indications of a stable business environment.

4. *State development agencies.* Many states maintain business development offices in Europe and openly attempt to solicit investments in their states.

The comptroller general also reported several obstacles to foreign investment:

1. *Foreign investment restrictions.* The United States, like many countries, prohibits foreign investments in what are termed *national interest areas.*

---

[13] This illustration is attributed to Professor Ashok Kapoor of New York University. See David Richlefs, "For the Businessman Headed Abroad, Some Basic Training," *Wall Street Journal* (January 16, 1978), p. 14.

[14] These lists of advantages and disadvantages are found in *Controlling Foreign Investment in National Interest Sectors of the U.S. Economy,* Report to the Congress by the Comptroller General of the United States (Washington, D.C.: General Accounting Office, October 7, 1977), pp. 27–31.

2. *Business regulations.* Two aspects of U.S. business regulations are viewed as distressing. First, the open disclosure requirements (which sometimes apply to the parent European company in addition to the U.S. subsidiary) violate practices common in European firms.

Many American firms have also protested that the *Freedom of Information Act*—allowing private citizens access to some government-held information—violates their right to privacy. The act was originally intended to permit people to study government actions, but it also became a prime source of private data. Standard Oil Co. of California complains that its reports to government agencies contain confidential information. Prudential, Gulf Oil, John Hancock, Chrysler, Metropolitan Life, and Hughes Aircraft, among others, have filed suits over the issue.[15]

Another unfavorable aspect of U.S. business regulation is that U.S. antitrust procedures are viewed as indefinite, since the firm does not always know its legal position before the investment is made. This is in marked contrast to European governments, which make their stance clear in advance of such a decision.

3. *Market complexity.* The size and complexity of the U.S. market are problems to small European companies. Negative stereotypes are also perceived. The complicated American legal framework is another negative factor for foreign investment.

Significant economic events also have a powerful effect on international management. Consider the recent slide of the Canadian dollar as compared with the U.S. dollar. The value of the Canadian dollar declined until the *exchange rate* (the ratio of one currency to another) dropped to less than eighty cents in American monies. This made Canadian products and vacations less expensive for Americans. But it made similar U.S. purchases by Canadians more expensive. The management of both U.S. and Canadian firms had to adjust accordingly. The decline of the Mexican peso relative to the U.S. dollar is another example of how economic events can affect international management.

The exchange rate is the ratio of one currency to another.

The Basic Functions of International Management

In Chapter 1 we noted that managerial functions are usually applicable (as adapted) to all managerial situations, including their international context. Planning, organizing, staffing, leading, and controlling are as important—if not more so—to the international manager as they are to a home-based peer. Only the environmental circumstances differ. Of course, in some cases, these factors can force radical alterations in the way a manager operates.

The importance of environmental constraints is clearly shown in Saudi Arabian planning. The oil-rich but labor-deficient desert kingdom uses loosely structured five-year plans in its economic development process. The Saudis have

[15] "Challenges to Corporate Privacy," *Business Week* (October 9, 1978), pp. 44–46.

decided to concentrate on two export industries—petrochemicals and basic metals.

Saudi planning is quite detailed, often relying on numerous feasibility studies. But, unlike Western planning, they do not relate the planning to larger goals or objectives. These plans are also loose since Saudi planners do not feel compelled to meet deadlines. Revisions and modifications are an expected part of their planning. All Saudi planning is conducted within the framework of Islamic religious and moral concepts. The Saudis go to considerable effort to preserve the traditional values and social structure of their nation.[16] International managers operating in Saudi Arabia (and there are a lot of them) must pay close attention to their host's cultural heritage and to the values prized by the Saudi people. The characteristics of Saudi planning should be appreciated by those seeking to do business there.

PLANNING

As the above example illustrates, planning is important, and in many nations the government plays a significant role in the planning done in international settings. Japan, for instance, has its Ministry of International Trade and Industry (MITI), which plans that nation's economic future.

Technocrats, the staff specialists like engineers, budget analysts, and the like who hold influential positions in the bureaucracy, dominate the planning activities of many foreign countries. International managers must understand the practices and beliefs of these people and interact effectively with them if they are to succeed. National economic planning by technocrats often sets the conditions under which international managers must do their own planning.

Technocrats are specialists within the bureaucracy who dominate national economic planning.

Nowhere is the value of planning in international management better shown than in Chrysler's effort to develop a "world car," one that incorporates European economy and road-handling features with the American penchant for comfort and luxury. Chrysler actually considered such a subcompact car as early as 1969, but decided against the "25-car," which was really a Valiant with a clipped rear end. By 1973 Chrysler engineers were working with their European counterparts at a Chrysler affiliate to develop a world car. The Arab oil boycott and the government mandate on corporate fleet mileages convinced Chrysler management. And on March 21, 1975, the go-ahead was launched, code named "L-car" in the United States and "C2" in Europe. Planners were originally targeting for the 1979 model year, but top management moved the introduction up to 1978.

Chrysler originally hoped to use common components in both American and European models. But because of the new capital costs that would have been involved, they opted for separate projects with the maximum amount of common development possible. The two groups of planners and engineers blended their efforts and on November 21, 1977, the first of the successful Omnis and

[16] Robert D. Crane, "Planning, Islamic Style," *Fortune* (September 25, 1978), pp. 114–116.

Horizons came off the assembly line.[17] The planning effort of managers on both sides of the Atlantic had come to fruition.

ORGANIZING

Organizations also must be adapted to conditions abroad. What works at home is not always appropriate in another nation. For example, French, Italian, Swiss, and Dutch managers prefer a traditional formal organization structure, while German and Scandinavian executives opt for a less rigid structure.[18]

Organizational structures for international business are linked to strategies that the firm attempts to implement.[19] American Motors Corp. is a good illustration of such an organizational adaptation. AMC's cars were commanding only 2 percent of the U.S. market, while its Jeep and AM General buses and military vehicles were selling well. The firm really did not have a viable product in the high-mileage market segment of the automobile industry. Rumors of its eventual withdrawal from the passenger car market were rampant. So AMC sought and obtained a link with Renault, the French government-owned automaker. Renault had some problems of its own. While the French firm annually sold about 1.1 million vehicles worldwide, only 13,000 were sold in the United States. Renault, which now owns 46 percent of AMC, gained access to AMC's U.S. and Canadian dealer network. Similarly, Jeeps were to be sold through Renault dealers in other countries (a plan that has been since developed). And Renaults are now produced at a U.S. plant. In fact, the Renault Alliance produced by American Motors has been a top seller. Both companies were decisive in adapting their organizations to meet changing corporate strategies.[20]

Multinational companies employ five basic organizational structures.[21] Initially, most companies set up an *international division*. This unit resembles a domestic product division except that it serves a worldwide market. A second structure is the *worldwide product division*, where each product unit is given international responsibilities. The *area* or *geographical division* is a third possibility. This format has a separate division for specific parts of the firm's marketplace such as Europe, North America, and South America. A popular new structure is the *matrix organization*, where corporate headquarters is organized functionally while a geographical organization exists at operational levels. A fifth alternative is the *focused market unit*, which sets up a market-oriented

A matrix organization is one in which the corporate headquarters is organized functionally while a geographical organization exists at operational levels.

---

[17] Clark Hallas, "The L-Car," *Detroit News Magazine* (April 2, 1978), pp. 14ff, 20–21, 24–26, 40–41.

[18] "Europe's New Managers," *Business Week* (May 24, 1982), p. 117.

[19] John Hutchinson, "Evolving Organizational Forms," *Columbia Journal of World Business* (Summer 1976), p. 48. See also W. H. Davidson and Philippe Haspeslaugh, "Shaping a Global Product Organization," *Harvard Business Review* (July–August 1982), pp. 125–132.

[20] Ted Kade, "Renault Says 'Oui' to AMC," *Detroit News* (April 1, 1978), pp. 1-A, 5-A.

[21] This discussion is based on Hutchinson, "Evolving Organizational Forms," pp. 48–50. Another excellent article on this general subject is Stanley M. Davis, "Trends in the Organization of Multinational Corporations," *Columbia Journal of World Business* (Summer 1976), pp. 59–71. See also Gerard H. Garnier, "Context and Decision Making Autonomy in the Foreign Affiliates of U.S. Multinational Corporations," *Academy of Management Journal* (December 1982), pp. 893–903.

AREA OF CORPORATE CONCERN	LEVEL OF SUITABILITY					
	INTER-NATIONAL DIVISION	WORLD-WIDE PRODUCT DIVISION	AREA DIVISION	MATRIX	FOCUSED MARKET UNITS
Rapid growth	M	H	M	H	H
Diversity of products	L	H	L	H	H
High technology	M	H	L	H	H
Few experienced managers	H	M	L	L	L
Close corporate control	M	H	L	H	H
Close government relations	M	L	H	M	M
Resource allocation:					
Product considerations should dominate	L	H	L	M	M
Geographic considerations should dominate	M	L	H	M	M
Functional considerations should dominate	L	M	L	H	M
Relative cost	M	M	L	H	M

H = high   M = medium   L = low

Table 20-2 SUITABILITY OF BASIC MNC ORGANIZATIONAL STRUCTURES TO CORPORATE CONCERNS

SOURCE: John Hutchinson, "Evolving Organizational Forms," *Columbia Journal of World Business* (Summer 1976), p. 51. Reprinted with permission from the Summer 1976 issue of the *Columbia Journal of World Business*. Copyright © 1976 by the Trustees of Columbia University in the City of New York.

division to service potential customers regardless of their location. GE's Strategic Business Unit concept is an example.

None of these structures is correct in every case. Circumstances vary, and so should the structure that is employed. Table 20-2 shows the relative suitability of basic MNC organizational structures to specified corporate concerns. For instance, area or geographical divisions would be poorly suited to a high-technology company. Similarly, availability of a limited team of experienced managers might suggest that the international division is the most appropriate organizational structure.

STAFFING

Few international managers encounter the staffing problems of a Russian manager. The USSR has a chronic labor shortage caused by a low birth rate, an aging population, and the loss of 20 million people in World War II. The shortage is so pronounced that a synthetic-alcohol plant started production with 1,400 less than the required number of workers. Only 20 percent of the scheduled work force were on hand when a chemical plant opened. And another estimate has 20 percent of the Soviet metalworking industry's equipment idle at any one time because of the labor problem.[22]

---

[22] Eric Morgenthaler, "Soviet Needs Workers: Shortage Poses Threat to Economic Growth," *Wall Street Journal* (August 17, 1978), pp. 1, 18.

Staffing is a major responsibility of those involved in international management. Traditionally, the chief international manager in an overseas unit and all of his or her key subordinates would be executives posted from corporate headquarters. The *perquisites,* or "perks"—another term for fringe benefits and privileges associated with a position—are often very attractive in overseas assignments. Company-provided housing, automobiles, servants, and vacations back home are common for those given such assignments. U.S. citizens working abroad are also allowed to exclude part of their income for tax purposes. But the cost of living abroad has escalated far faster than it has in North America. As a result most firms are now required to increase an executive's salary considerably for an overseas assignment just to keep the individual even with the domestic standard of living.

International managers can be divided into those who view it as a career position, much the way a diplomat would view his or her current career assignment, and those who are serving a stint in international management to broaden their background so they can assume increased responsibilities at home. This is a common career pattern for successful executives.

Companies are increasingly relying on the nationals of a host country to fill positions in their international organization.[23] Typically, these people have been utilized in operative and lower-level supervisory positions. As they acquire experience in the particular industry, they are given the chance to compete for major executive positions in the firm's international organization.

Foreign nationals have several advantages in this competition:

1. *Training costs may be lower.* Language and cultural sensitivity training can often be eliminated or drastically cut back, thus saving the firm a considerable expenditure.

2. *Executive deployment costs may also be lower.* It is now estimated that it costs $120,000 annually—exclusive of social welfare fringes—to deploy a $50,000-a-year U.S. executive abroad.[24] Use of foreign nationals can provide a considerable savings in most instances.

3. *Culture shock is avoided.* Culture shock is the surprise encountered when an individual is forced to deal with a totally unfamiliar cultural setting. It can render a person managerially useless for a period of time. The foreign national has an awareness of the culture in which he or she will be operating and can adapt more readily.

4. *There is a political advantage.* Some nations require that foreign firms provide a specified degree of employment for local citizens. Extensive use of nationals of the host nation can be of considerable political advantage.

---

[23] This is noted in "Labor Letter," *Wall Street Journal* (September 19, 1978), p. 1. An interesting discussion appears in Ehud Harari and Yoram Zlira, "Training Expatriates for Managerial Assignments in Japan," *California Management Review* (Summer 1978), pp. 56–62.

[24] Estimated by executive recruiter George P. Graighead. See Phillip Greer and Myron Kandel, "Go Abroad to Climb Corporate Ladder," *Detroit News* (October 9, 1978), p. 5-D. Another interesting article is Michael G. Harvey, "The Multinational Corporation's Expatriate Problem: An Application of Murphy's Law," *Business Horizons* (January–February 1983), pp. 71–78.

Toyota Motor Co. has eight plants in Toyota City (population 290,000) in central Japan. The company's presence is everywhere. Some 52,000 people work for Toyota here. The company provides a fantastic array of benefits to its personnel. Here is a partial list:

THE TOYOTA FAMILY

A free hospital.

Food and clothing from the company's retail cooperative.

Subsidized housing including dorms, apartments, and individual homes. In fact, in crowded Japan, Toyota's housing options are considered a major benefit.

A low-interest loan fund.

Seventy-nine sports and cultural clubs.

A 150-acre sports center complete with twelve tennis courts and an indoor swimming pool.

Seven mountain and coastal resorts.

A private high school.

Toyota's company saving plan pays nearly twice the going interest rates.

While many Americans might find the company's paternalistic presence confining, Toyota employees obviously approve. Assembly line turnover is only 3 to 4 percent annually. And most higher ranked employees stay until retirement.

SOURCE: Jim Abrams, "Toyota Eases Workers Down Assembly Line of Life," *The Seattle Times* (June 12, 1982), p. 1-C.

5. *There is a marketing awareness.* Foreign nationals are more likely to be attuned to business opportunities abroad than executives from corporate headquarters. More important, they may help the firm avoid potential marketing errors that might be overlooked by people unfamiliar with the particular marketplace.

LEADING

Effective leadership styles vary according to international settings. Employees and managers of Japanese firms are usually perceived to be satisfied with the participative leadership style in use.[25] West Germany's *codetermination* laws re-

Codetermination refers to the practice of having employee representatives on supervisory boards.

[25] Interesting articles include Richard Tanner Pascale, "Personnel Practices and Employee Attitudes: A Study of Japanese- and American-Managed Firms in the United States," *Human Relations* (July 1978), pp. 597–615; and David Harvey, "The Japanese Way to Industrial Harmony," *Director* (January 1978), pp. 42–44.

For years, the Japanese have been careful students of American business—so careful that they have been able to rebuild their war-shattered economy into one of the mightiest industrial machines in the world. Now, says William Ouchi, professor of the Graduate School of Management at the University of California, Los Angeles, it is time for U.S. business leaders to change places with the Japanese—at least for a while—and study how and why Japan's management style is considered a model of success.

Ouchi became convinced that American firms could learn a lot from their Japanese counterparts after undertaking a study of the managerial practices in Japan in 1973 to determine which practices were applicable to the United States. The results of his study were published in a landmark book titled *Theory Z: How American Business Can Meet the Japanese Challenge,* which was the first book about big business to top the nationwide best seller lists during the 1980s.

In Ouchi's view much of Japan's managerial success, which has been translated into skyrocketing productivity at a time of a serious productivity decline in the United States, is due to the way Japanese industries manage people. "Productivity," says Ouchi, "is a problem that can be worked out through coordinating individual efforts in a productive manner and of giving employees the incentives to do so by taking a cooperative long-range view." Thus, says Ouchi, managerial success is linked to what Western industries perceive as such nontraditional practices as employer–employee trust, lifetime employment, collective decision making, and nonspecialized career paths.

Ouchi points to the fact that more than one out of every three workers in Japanese industry is guaranteed a job until the mandatory retirement age of fifty-five. When times are bad and companies are forced to prune their expenses in order to survive, these workers are able to remain on the payroll for three reasons: the semiannual bonuses that make up a large portion of workers' incomes are cut or deferred; large groups of temporary workers who are considered dispensable are laid off; and the thousands of satellite firms, which act as suppliers to the large firms, absorb the brunt of the market fluctuations, including the layoffs. Because of this system, says Ouchi, lifetime employees have a fierce sense of loyalty to their companies. And since they take on much of their employers' entrepreneurial risk, they also work as hard as they can to make the system pay off.

Ouchi also points to the importance of collective decision making. Unlike U.S.

quire large firms to have employee representatives on supervisory boards. In fact, some German firms have switched to partnership formats from corporate entities in an attempt to avoid codetermination.[26] And in Russia, management personnel in some factories have been imprisoned for allowing poor quality output.[27] Clearly, leadership and motivation incentives are influenced by a variety of factors.

[26] Reported in "World Business," *U.S. News & World Report* (July 10, 1978), p. 47.
[27] Reported in "World Business," *U.S. News & World Report* (April 10, 1978), p. 54.

corporations, where decisions are made at the top with little input from those involved in the production process, Japanese firms seek to build a consensus among employees at various levels of authority to support the policies they themselves have tediously hammered out. Says Ouchi, ''Making a decision in this way takes a very long time, but once a decision is reached everybody affected by it will be likely to support it.''

Japanese managerial success, says Ouchi, is also tied to the system of nonspecialized career paths. Whereas managers in U.S. companies spend entire careers in one specialized area such as production or finance, Japanese executives rotate from department to department and in the process learn all the basic operations of their companies. Ouchi explains the advantages of this system in the following way:

> In the Japanese case virtually every department will have in it someone who knows the people, the problems, and the procedures of any other area within the organization. When coordination is necessary, both sides will be able to understand and cooperate with the other. Perhaps more important is the fact that every employee knows he will continue through his career to move between functions, offices, and geographical locations. The person from another department who is asking for assistance today may be the person who will be his co-worker or even superior tomorrow. Thus there is not only the ability but also the incentive for taking a broad, organization-wide point of view and for cooperating with everyone.

Through these and other management techniques, Japanese companies have succeeded in building a formidable industrial machine. In Ouchi's view, many of these principles cannot be applied to American industry because of the vastly different nature of our society, but others can. And indeed, companies like Hewlett-Packard and Dayton-Hudson have already made some aspects of Japanese management working parts of their systems.

Ouchi is asking American executives not to mimic Japanese industrial success but to learn from it to create uniquely American managerial answers. ''The challenge,'' says Ouchi, ''is to understand and to acknowledge a distinctly American approach to management, to realize that it has stayed the same for two hundred years, and to apply our ingenuity to the development of new organizational and managerial solutions.''

Sources

John Brooks, ''Sake in a Gallo Bottle,'' *The New York Times* (May 5, 1981), p. 2.

Christopher Byron, ''An Attractive Japanese Export,'' *Time* (March 2, 1981), p. 74.

Steve Lohr, ''Japan's Business Secret,'' *Books of the Times* (October 1981), Vol. 4, pp. 444–446.

William Ouchi, *Theory Z: How American Business Can Meet the Japanese Challenge* (New York: Avon Books, 1981). The quotations are on pp. 5, 27, 37, and 164.

''The World of Z,'' *National Magazine* (January 4, 1981), p. 11.

Japanese Versus American Management Styles

A popular international comparison in managerial leadership is to contrast Japanese and American styles.[28] U.S. management is usually classified as a *systems type* leadership. All corporate activities, whether organized functionally or on a

In systems type leadership, all corporate activities are directed toward the achievement of specified objectives.

[28] This comparison is based on and quotes from Charles Y. Yang, ''Management Styles: American Vis-à-Vis Japanese,'' *Columbia Journal of World Business* (Fall 1977), pp. 23–31. Another viewpoint is offered in Richard Tanner Pascale, ''Communications and Decision Making Across Cultures: Japanese and American Companies,'' *Administrative Science Quarterly* (March 1978), pp. 91–109.

MINIMIZING LABOR COSTS IS AN INTERNATIONAL MANAGEMENT PROBLEM

SOURCE: © 1972 *The Wall Street Journal.* Reprinted by permission of Sidney Harris.

"Made in Hong Kong! Made in Hong Kong! How can we compete with their cheap labor?"

Organic type leadership is a style in which the firm is thought of as a collective unit; personnel identify with the organization, rather than with their particular function.

Consensus management is a style in which chief executives rely on various committees, groups, and task forces to reach organization-wide agreement on a particular decision.

decentralized basis, are directed toward the achievement of specified objectives. The various subsystems are linked within a set of constraints such as those set externally or by company policy. Management's role is to design the system and then to make the necessary plans and decisions required to achieve the overall corporate objectives. American managers are viewed as professionals who place the highest priority on efficient decision making.

By contrast, Japanese firms employ an *organic type* of leadership. The firm is thought of as a collective unit, and company personnel identify with the organization rather than with the specific function to which they are assigned, such as accounting, engineering, or marketing. Members are vertically identified within the firm rather than horizontally with other engineers, accountants, and sales executives. The emphasis is on good human relations.

Table 20-3 compares the characteristics of top management in the United States and Japan. The U.S. manager leads through his or her professional decision-making ability, while the Japanese manager acts as a facilitator and social leader. The Japanese executive relies on *consensus management* where various groups, committees, and task forces are formed to reach an organization-wide agreement on a particular decision. The Japanese emphasis on group strength is in marked contrast to the American system. The U.S. manager counts on the firm's hierarchical command system to arrive at decisions. The Japanese firm

SYSTEMS TYPE (U.S.)	ORGANIC TYPE (JAPAN)	
Decision maker	Facilitator	**Table 20-3 CHARACTERISTICS OF TOP MANAGEMENT: A COMPARISON**
Professional	Social leader	
Individual initiative and creativity	Group strength	
Hierarchical command	Free-form command	
Emphasis on functional relationships	Emphasis on human relations	
Management by objectives	Management by consensus	
Decentralization	Centralization	
System adapts to changes	Leader adapts to changes	

SOURCE: Charles Y. Yang, "Management Styles: American Vis-à-Vis Japanese," *Columbia Journal of World Business* (Fall 1977), p. 25. Reprinted with permission from the Fall 1977 issue of the *Columbia Journal of World Business*. Copyright © 1977 by the Trustees of Columbia University in the City of New York.

may have a similar organizational structure, but the Japanese executive reaches decisions and operates through numerous groups of subordinates from throughout the organization. Again, human relations are held in higher regard than decision-making efficiency. For instance, after Matsushita Electric Industrial Co. bought Motorola's television plants and formed Quasar Electronics Co., it took Japanese style consensus management three years to work out a new financial package with its distributors. The independent distributors were involved, along with Quasar financial, sales, marketing, and branch managers.[29]

Which of the two management styles is more effective? Since both have resulted in nearly the same profit performance, it is more meaningful to evaluate the various factors important to profitability. Three such factors can be identified:

1. *Entrepreneurial quality*, defined as "the degree of innovativeness and propensity for risk-taking"
2. *Level of aspiration*, defined as "the confidence that management instills within the organization (internal relations) as well as outside the organization (external relations)"
3. *Executive quality*, defined as "the decision-making ability of executives in terms of the speed and accuracy of decision making as well as the flexibility in adjusting and rectifying decision errors"[30]

The relative performance of U.S. systems type and Japanese organic type leadership is shown in Table 20-4. This evaluation is presented in terms of both the

[29] David P. Garino, "Takeover by Japanese Hasn't Hurt After All, Quasar Workers Find," *Wall Street Journal* (October 10, 1978), p. 16.
[30] Quotes are from Yang, "Management Styles," p. 24.

Table 20-4
COMPARISON OF
THE QUALITY OF
MANAGEMENT IN
THE UNITED STATES
AND JAPAN IN
DIFFERENT
SITUATIONAL
CONFIGURATIONS

	QUALITY OF ENTREPRENEURSHIP	
1. *Evaluation*	INNOVATIVENESS	RISK-TAKING
American management (systems type)	fair	fair
Japanese management (organic type)	poor	poor
2. *Management requirements in past situations*		
American situational configuration prior to the oil crisis: moderate to high economic growth, moderate external influence and technological leader	required	required
Japanese situational configuration prior to the oil crisis: high economic growth, strong external influence and technological follower	not strongly required	not strongly required
3. *Management requirements under the new situational configuration*		
New situational configuration: common to the U.S. and Japan: low economic growth, high external influence and technological leadership	required	required
4. *Modifications needed to cope with the new situation*		
American management Japanese management	minor	minor

SOURCE: Charles Y. Yang, "Management Styles: American Vis-à-Vis Japanese," *Columbia Journal of World Business* (Fall 1977), p. 29. Reprinted with permission from

traditional environment facing each country and the new common set of situational circumstances. Finally, suggestions for both minor and major modifications in each system are noted. The analysis points out that the American systems approach needs to make a significant effort to improve its external level of aspiration, while the Japanese organic approach needs to find new ways to speed up its traditional decision-making process.

EVALUATION AND CONTROL

International managers are also involved in evaluating and controlling operations. Some of this assessment is done locally, some at corporate headquarters. The process is as important to international operations as it is to domestic ones.

| LEVEL OF ASPIRATION | | EFFECTIVENESS OF DECISION MAKING | | |
INTERNAL	EXTERNAL	SPEED	ACCURACY	ADJUSTMENT
poor to fair	poor	good	good	good
good	good	poor	good	poor
required	not strongly required	strongly required	strongly required	strongly required
strongly required	strongly required	not strongly required	required	required
strongly required	strongly required	strongly required	strongly required	strongly required
minor	major	major		minor

Business performance is always monitored. And it seems logical to assume that social performance will increasingly be evaluated.[31]

Table 20-5 shows the nature of the supervision and evaluation process among international units. The data suggest that most international units have a broad span in which to operate. Total centralization of decisions occurs in less than 5 percent of the cases cited. On the other hand, complete decentralization prevailed in less than 2 percent of the firms.

The exact location of the monitoring procedure is not as important as its existence and relative effectiveness somewhere within the managerial structure. The

[31] An interesting discussion is contained in Lee E. Preston, Françoise Rey, and Meinoff Dierkes, "Comparing Social Performance: Germany, France, Canada, and the U.S.," *California Management Review* (Summer 1978), pp. 40–49.

NATURE OF SUPERVISION BY CORPORATE HEADQUARTERS	PERCENTAGE OF RESPONDENTS
Total decentralization. International units are independent and autonomous. Nominal ties only.	1.6
Complete autonomy in internal operations. Loose financial controls only.	15.6
Broad policies and guidelines with responsibilities and authority delegated to international units. Only important policy decisions such as new investments are made at the corporate headquarters.	35.9
International units are moderately controlled. In addition to all important policy decisions, some internal operating decisions are made at corporate headquarters.	31.3
Operational decisions are highly centralized.	10.9
Total centralization. All operating decisions are made at corporate headquarters.	4.7

Table 20-5 CONTROL OF MANAGERIAL DECISIONS IN INTERNATIONAL UNITS BY CORPORATE HEADQUARTERS

SOURCE: Guvenc G. Alpander, "Multinational Corporations: Homebase–Affiliate Relations," *California Management Review* (Spring 1978), p. 51. Copyright © 1978 by the Regents of the University of California. Reprinted from *California Management Review* XX, no. 3, p. 51, Table 3, by permission of the Regents.

evaluative and control procedure should be operational and capable of providing the same degree of feedback that it does at home.

International Management— The Authors' Viewpoint

It is readily apparent that American business is becoming increasingly multinational in scope. Most large U.S. firms already receive a substantial portion of their sales and/or profits from abroad. American management cannot afford the complacency of commercial isolation.

Tomorrow's managers must have a working knowledge of overseas business situations.[32] Many will gain this experience through an international assignment; others will acquire it while completing their regular duties. But regardless of how the knowledge is obtained, it surely *must be obtained.*

The authors suggest that today's business students pay very close attention to the international aspects of all their studies—management, finance, economics, and marketing. You are tomorrow's leaders, and tomorrow's leaders will have to be international leaders!

---

[32] The authors are not alone in this viewpoint. For instance, see the comments of executive recruiter Egan P. S. Zehnder that appear in Greer and Kandel, "Go Abroad to Climb Corporate Ladder," p. 5-D.

Summary

Modern international management has adopted a contingency approach to worldwide operations. What works in one part of the globe may be a failure elsewhere. Adaptability is the key to effective international management.

The evolution of international management normally begins with a company's decision to export (the marketing of its merchandise abroad) or import (the purchase and shipment of some merchandise from another nation). In the macro sense, the relative status of exports to imports is known as the balance of trade. A basic model describing the events leading up to the decision to export is also presented here.

Some basic concepts are developed next. International business is all business activity that crosses international boundaries. An international manager is one who is involved with international business activities. The multinational company (MNC) is the ultimate level of international business. An MNC views itself as global in nature. The sequence of international business development from exporting to sales subsidiaries to foreign production is outlined in this chapter.

Various environmental differences affect international management. These include political, cultural, and economic differences. The importance of these inherent differences is highlighted. Terms like *industrial democracy* and *exchange rates* are also explained in this chapter.

The management functions of planning, organizing, staffing, leading, and controlling are as applicable abroad as they are at home. Each of the functional activities is explained in regard to its place in international management. Chapter 20 concludes with the authors' viewpoint of international management since future worklives will likely involve that dimension.

REVIEW EXERCISES

1. Define the following terms: (a) exporting (b) importing (c) balance of trade (d) international business (e) international manager (f) MNC (g) licensing (h) economic boycott (i) industrial democracy (j) comparative management (k) exchange ratio (l) technocrat (m) matrix organization (n) codetermination (o) systems type leadership (p) organic type leadership (q) consensus management.

2. Review the basic points in the managerial profile of William Ouchi.

3. Why must international managers adopt a contingency approach?

4. What factors are involved in the decision to export?

5. Describe the sequence of international business development.

6. Discuss the various environmental differences affecting international mangement.

7. What features of the U.S. business environment are attractive to foreign investors?

8. What investment obstacles do foreigners perceive to exist in the United States?

9. Describe how the various functions of management operate within an international context.

10. Contrast the Japanese and American styles of management.

Applications

ASSIGNMENTS/ PROBLEMS/ DISCUSSION QUESTIONS

1. A recent report says that managers must be careful when giving business gifts overseas. They suggest avoiding

Clocks in China because *clock* sounds like *funeral* in Chinese.

Red roses in Germany, where they signify romance and would be inappropriate in a business situation.

Black- or purple-colored gifts in Latin America since those colors are associated with penitence.*

Relate these warnings to the material found in Chapter 20.

2. Forty years from now, it is estimated that 20 percent of Japan's population will be over sixty-five. The comparable figures will be 14.2 percent in the United States and 17.2 percent in Europe.†

What impact will its aging population have on Japanese management in future decades?

3. The People's Republic of China has increased agricultural output by allowing workers on collective farms to produce and sell on the open market some of the output from their individual plots of land.** What can be learned from this experiment in private enterprise?

4. Texas Instruments (TI), the large, Dallas-based consumer electronics firm, has a style similar to the Japanese, TI's leading competitors. Texas Instruments prefers to hire new college graduates and train them, rather than hire away experienced professionals from other firms. "People involvement teams" are featured prominently in the TI organization. Few long-service employees are ever fired. Texas Instruments values employee seniority and loyalty. One vice-president even proclaimed: "The TI culture is a religion."‡ Prepare a report on the relative merits of TI's management style.

* "Business Gifts Abroad," *United Airlines Magazine* (May 1982), p. 20; "It's a Gift," *Journal-American* (November 23, 1981), p. 7-B (AP story).

† "World Business," *U.S. News & World Report* (June 28, 1982), p. 42.

** "Revolution Down on the Farm," *Time* (November 23, 1981), p. 51.

‡ See "Under Its Ten-Gallon Hat, a Japanese-Style Culture," *Business Week* (September 18, 1978), pp. 68–69.

5. Do you agree with the trend toward using nationals of the host country to staff overseas positions? Explain.

A MANAGERIAL INCIDENT

A Law That Has a Broad Impact on International Management

The Foreign Corrupt Practices Act became law on December 17, 1977. The bill was the culmination of lengthy congressional and Security and Exchange Commission investigations into alleged bribery and other suspect activities by American firms operating abroad. Over 300 U.S. firms were eventually tied to such matters. Under the Foreign Corrupt Practices Act, substantial fines and even imprisonment are now specified for illegal foreign payments such as bribes, excessive commissions, and so forth.

Since many former abuses were disguised by secret foreign accounts and inaccurate accounting, the new law requires that companies maintain good records and an adequate accounting system. But perhaps most important, the accounting provisions apply to all public companies since the Foreign Corrupt Practices Act is really an amendment to the Securities and Exchange Act. In fact, some legal actions based on the new act have already been initiated even though the allegation had nothing to do with foreign payments.

SOURCE: Charles N. Stabler, ''Foreign-Bribery Act Imposes Tough Rules on the Bookkeeping of All Public Firms,'' *Wall Street Journal* (July 28, 1978), p. 28. Reprinted by permission of The Wall Street Journal, © Dow Jones & Company, Inc., 1978. All rights reserved.

Questions and Problems

1. How does this act affect international management?

2. What is your opinion of the sweeping coverage of the Foreign Corrupt Practices Act?

3. Does this law put U.S. management at an unfair disadvantage when operating abroad?

21.
Social Responsibility and Executive Behavior

Learning Objectives

AFTER STUDYING THIS CHAPTER YOU SHOULD BE ABLE TO

1. Explain the concept of social responsibility.
2. Outline the phases of management's social responsibility.
3. Identify the current status of management ethics.
4. Describe the various levels of social responsibility.
5. Discuss the Sethi model.
6. Explain the five types of industrial democracy.
7. Explain the measurement of social responsibility.

Key Terms

social responsibility

management ethics

externalities

Business Roundtable

industrial democracy

If we find that we have to do things that don't fit our standards of integrity in order to be successful, we back out of business.

> RICHARD M. RINGEON
> *Chief executive officer,*
> *Ball Corp.*

The number one corporate responsibility is to make a profit . . . this sounds like you're not even thinking of society, your fellow man or anybody else. It sounds like you're selfish. But profit is like breathing. If you can't do that, you can forget about doing anything else. Once a corporation learns how to breathe, or make a profit, then it can turn to the other corporate responsibilities, like creating jobs and adding to GNP [gross national product].

> ROBERT MERCER
> *Chief executive officer,*
> *Goodyear Tire and Rubber Co.*

The typical American eats fifteen pounds of chocolate annually. A lot of it comes from Hershey Chocolate Co. The Pennsylvania firm's product has been a consumer favorite for decades. But on March 28, 1979, the seventy-five-year-old enterprise faced one of the biggest crises in its history.

A few minutes away from the largest chocolate factory in the world, the Three Mile Island nuclear power plant experienced a widely publicized radiation leak. The nuclear accident had a potentially far-reaching effect on Hershey. Its plant requires fifty tons of milk a day. And experts cited milk—should it contain radiation contamination—as a major cause of thyroid cancer in children.

The Hershey management quickly instituted new, more stringent controls to cover all milk and other materials coming into the plant from within a seventy-five-mile radius. Although radiation tests indicated no problems, management went a step further by isolating the milk received from a ten-mile radius of the Three Mile Island site. None proved to be contaminated. A Hershey spokesperson summed up the firm's actions this way: "While we have no indication of anything wrong with any product, if we are going to err we want to err on the safe side."[1]

[1] Dennis Montgomery, "Candy Firm Monitoring Atomic Risk," *Detroit News* (April 2, 1979), pp. 3-A, 6-A.

Ralph Currier Davis, professor emeritus of business organization at Ohio State University, says that "the consuming public does not exist to serve the owners and employees of business organizations. Rather, business exists to serve the public." This statement summarizes what Davis calls the *service objective* of business—the obligation of business to supply at competitive prices the goods and services the public requires at the time and place they are needed.

In his classic management volume, *The Fundamentals of Top Management,* published in 1951, Davis states that each business must define its service objective in terms of the economic values of the customers it serves. A manufacturer of washing machines, for example, must understand that people purchase washing machines to free themselves from the physical labor of washing by hand, to save time, and, of course, to wash their clothes. The manufacturer must keep these economic values in mind as it designs its products. Moreover, it must always weigh the economic value of one product over that of another. If a competing brand gives consumers more of what they want, they will buy it. If this happens

Hershey Chocolate's management conducted itself in a highly professional and socially responsible manner. While few executives will ever have to face health threats of this magnitude, Hershey's immediate and comprehensive response to the Three Mile Island incident suggests the ethical standards maintained by most contemporary managers.

What Is Social Responsibility?[2]

Social responsibility has almost as many definitions as there are people willing to define the concept.[3] At its extremes, management's social responsibility can be alternatively described as profit maximization, or as a total corporate immersion in society's problems, as through philanthropy. A reasonable definition of *social responsibility* is those management philosophies, policies, procedures, and actions that have the advancement of society's welfare as one of their primary objectives. This view acknowledges the equivalent importance of traditional profitability objectives and attempts to balance them with socially oriented objectives.

The key to setting contemporary standards of social responsibility is to be able

Social responsibility refers to those management philosophies, policies, procedures, and actions that have the advancement of society's welfare as one of their primary objectives.

[2] An excellent discussion of social responsibility appears in Dan R. Dalton and Richard A. Cosier, "The Four Faces of Social Responsibility," *Business Horizons* (May–June 1982), pp. 19–27; and Kenneth E. Goodpaster and John B. Matthews, Jr., "Can a Corporation Have a Conscience?" *Harvard Business Review* (January–February 1982), pp. 132–141.

[3] Definitions of social responsibility are discussed in Thomas J. Zenisek, "Corporate Social Responsibility: A Conceptualization Based on Organizational Literature," *Academy of Management Review* (July 1979), pp. 359–362.

often enough, the manufacturer will go out of business. "The ultimate control of business in a democracy rests with the customer," says Davis. "He has the right of freedom of choice in the market place."

By labeling the service objective the top priority of business, Davis places business profits in a secondary position. He views profits, wages, salaries, and bonuses as collateral objectives that are earned in direct proportion to the amount of public service the organization provides. When companies place profits above their primary service objectives, they quickly lose sight of what the public wants. They forget that their very existence depends on filling a specific public need.

Even though Davis received his undergraduate degree in 1916 from Cornell University as a mechanical engineer and never earned a Ph.D. (he was granted an honorary Doctorate of Science by Wayne State University in 1964), his theories have had a tremendous impact on the science of management and specifically on the concept of corporate social responsibility.

Sources

Ralph Currier Davis, *The Fundamentals of Top Management* (New York: Harper & Row, 1951). The quotations are on pp. 99 and 786.

"Biography of Ralph C. Davis," Faculty Information Service of the Ohio State University News and Information Service, October 9, 1964.

to tie the idea of corporate involvement in social and public issues to traditional standards of profitability. FMC Corp.—a diversified manufacturer with products ranging from industrial chemicals to airfreight loading equipment—takes this approach in determining how and where it will direct its contributions.[4] FMC has two basic requirements:

1. Its contribution will help areas in which FMC facilities are located, or in which its employees live.
2. The corporation's business environment should be improved by such a donation.

Examples of FMC's specific guidelines to supporting educational institutions include

Give financial support to colleges and universities that supply our manpower needs or are located in communities where we have facilities (provided that the other guidelines mentioned in this list are also met).

Make grants to schools that present the case for the competitive enterprise philosophy and those that present a balanced perspective of our economic system.

Make grants in support of minority programs in fields relevant to the company's businesses.

[4] The discussion about FMC's program is based on and quotes from Robert H. Malott, "Corporate Support of Education: Some Strings Attached," *Harvard Business Review* (July–August 1978), pp. 137–138. The 1982 update was provided by FMC Foundation.

In order to understand the social responsibility climate of the 1980s, it is useful to look briefly at the evolution of this concept in management.

Three Historical Phases of Management's Social Responsibility[5]

Social responsibility in organizations has evolved through three distinct phases or stages. Each required its own unique managerial value system. The phases are

Phase 1. Profit maximizing management

Phase 2. Trusteeship management

Phase 3. "Quality of life" management

Profit maximizing management was based on Adam Smith's concept that people acting in their self-interest would provide or create an invisible hand that would guide the advancement of society. Managers with this orientation believed that their sole goal was to maximize profits. Profit maximization was viewed as a socially responsible action because it created a stronger economy. Applicable business laws were the only requirement to be met by managers of this era—the nineteenth and early part of the twentieth century.

Trusteeship management, a product of the 1920s and 1930s, acknowledged that other groups such as employees, customers, creditors, and the like had claims on the organization that competed with those of the firm's owners. Trusteeship management was responsible to all these contributor groups. In other words the concept of social responsibility was broadened beyond its original narrow base of profit maximization.

Phase 3 can be dated from about 1950. Popular concern with the *quality of life* dictated that management direct some of its efforts and resources to the solution of broader societal issues. Phase 3 goes beyond merely improving the national standard of living by emphasizing quality, not quantity, standards.

The third phase saw an increasing number of managers devoting considerable time and corporate effort to such social responsibilities as developing special programs to improve hiring and promotion opportunities for women and minority employees; developing improved pollution control systems; making concerted efforts to hire handicapped workers; and adopting energy conservation measures. In many instances these actions were undertaken by managers who recognized that these measures were part of their societal responsibilities. In other instances they resulted from government laws and regulations.

[5] This section is based on Robert Hay and Ed Gray, "Social Responsibilities of Business Managers," *Academy of Management Journal* (March 1974), pp. 135–143. Another excellent discussion of the various eras of social responsibility is contained in Patrick E. Murphy, "An Evolution: Corporate Social Responsiveness," *University of Michigan Business Review* (November 1978), pp. 19–25.

The current view of social responsibility is mixed. Most modern managers are devotees of the Phase 2 viewpoint. An increasing number advocate the characteristics of Phase 3. The general trend is in the direction of Phase 3, partly due to growing acceptance of social obligations and partly due to government requirements.

Management Ethics[6]

A few years ago, an investigation at NBC revealed that the network's unit managers (people who travel with television crews to handle business arrangements, often in cash) were sometimes called on to bribe a variety of people who could expedite the work of the crew. This posed several ethical dilemmas for the unit managers. One NBC employee expressed it this way: "The networks won't let you put in for '$200 to bribe a cop.' In order to get your money back, you have to hide it with a phony receipt or doctor up a bill." Later allegations suggested that some network staff also siphoned off company monies for personal use. NBC initiated a thorough investigation that led to several changes in business

[6] Management ethics are discussed in an article such as Kristine Hanson and Robert Solomon, "The Real Business Ethics," *Business and Society Review* (Spring 1982), pp. 58–59; George K. Sand, "Business Ethics: Where Are We Going?" *Academy of Management Review* (April 1981), pp. 269–276; Darrell J. Fasching, "A Case for Corporate and Management Ethics," *California Management Review* (Summer 1981), pp. 62–76; and Harold L. Johnson, "Ethics and the Executive," *Business Horizons* (May–June 1981), pp. 53–59.

SOME PEOPLE CONFUSE SOCIETY'S ETHICAL GAME RULES

SOURCE: *Sales & Marketing Management* (December 1978), p. 93.

"*As far as I'm concerned, it is whether you win or lose and not how you play the game.*"

practices at the network. For example, NBC unit managers—like those at CBS and ABC—are now given company credit cards rather than cash.[7]

The incident at NBC indicates the range and diversity of the ethical problems that face executives. *Management ethics* refers to the moral premises upon which executive decisions are made. Most people view ethical business practices as an inherent part of management's responsibility to society.[8]

Management ethics refers to the moral premises upon which executive decisions are made.

MANAGEMENT ETHICS—THE PUBLIC'S VIEWPOINT

How does the public evaluate the status of management ethics? The Gallup polling organization found that business executives ranked sixteenth in a list of twenty-five occupations ranked according to their perceived adherence to ethical standards. Clergymen, druggists, dentists, medical doctors, engineers, college teachers, policemen, bankers, TV reporters and commentators, journalists, newspaper reporters, funeral directors, lawyers, stockbrokers, and senators were ranked higher. Table 21-1 shows the ranking of all twenty-five occupations.

Another survey focused on the responses by business executives. Managers viewed themselves as less ethical than medical doctors and college professors. However, the executives saw themselves as more ethical than politicians, lawyers, union leaders, and officials of government agencies.[9]

HOW MANAGEMENT ETHICS CHANGE

The *Harvard Business Review* published a 1977 follow-up on a 1961 study about the ethics of U.S. business executives. This comparison produced the following conclusions:

1. There is substantial disagreement among respondents as to whether ethical standards in business today have changed from what they were.
2. Respondents are somewhat more cynical about the ethical conduct of their peers than they were.
3. Most respondents favor ethical codes, although they strongly prefer general precept codes to specific practice codes.
4. The dilemmas respondents experience and the factors they feel have the greatest impact on business ethics suggest that ethical codes alone will not substantially improve business conduct.
5. Most respondents have overcome the traditional ideological barriers to the concept of social responsibility and have embraced its practice as a legitimate and achievable goal for business.

---

[7] "Embezzlement at NBC," *Newsweek* (April 2, 1979), pp. 93–94.

[8] An interesting discussion of the relationship between ethics and social responsibility appears in Phillip M. Van Auken and R. Duane Ireland, "The Ethics of Social Responsibility," *Baylor Business Studies* (August–September–October 1978), pp. 33–40.

[9] Steven N. Brenner and Earl A. Molander, "Is the Ethics of Business Changing?" *Harvard Business Review* (January–February 1977), p. 59.

Honesty and Ethical Standards—Overview

Following is the entire list of occupations tested, ranked according to the total percentage of combined "very high" and "high" ratings:

	VERY HIGH, HIGH	VERY HIGH	HIGH	AVERAGE	LOW	VERY LOW	NO OPINION
Clergymen	63%	24%	39%	28%	5%	1%	3%
Druggists, pharmacists	59	12	47	33	4	1	3
Dentists	52	10	42	38	6	1	3
Medical doctors	50	13	37	38	7	3	2
Engineers	48	9	39	35	4	1	12
College teachers	45	8	37	36	7	1	11
Policemen	44	8	36	41	9	4	2
Bankers	39	5	34	47	8	2	4
TV reporters, commentators	36	6	30	45	10	5	4
Journalists	32	3	29	44	12	3	9
Newspaper reporters	30	5	25	49	12	4	5
Funeral directors	30	6	24	41	12	7	10
Lawyers	25	4	21	41	19	8	7
Stockbrokers	21	3	18	46	6	1	26
Senators	20	2	18	50	19	6	5
Business executives	19	2	17	53	15	4	9
Building contractors	19	3	16	48	20	7	6
Congressmen	15	2	13	47	22	10	6
Local political officeholders	14	2	12	51	20	10	5
Realtors	14	2	12	48	22	8	8
Labor union leaders	14	3	11	29	29	19	9
State political officeholders	12	1	11	50	23	7	8
Insurance salesmen	11	2	9	49	25	11	4
Advertising practitioners	9	1	8	41	27	11	12
Car salesmen	6	2	4	33	36	19	6

SOURCE: *The Gallup Report* (September 1981), Report No. 192 (Princeton, N.J.: The Gallup Poll). Reprinted by permission.

6. Most respondents rank their customers well ahead of shareholders and employees as the client group to whom they feel the greatest responsibility.[10]

The study suggests a variety of factors that influence ethical standards. Some act to raise standards, others tend to lower them. Table 21-2 presents a listing of these influencing factors. The three most frequently cited factors causing higher standards were public disclosure, increased public concern, and government regulation. By contrast, the most often mentioned factors leading to lower standards were a lowering of society's standards, competition, political ethics and climate, and public awareness of unethical acts.

[10] Reprinted by permission from *ibid.*

Table 21-2
FACTORS
INFLUENCING
ETHICAL
STANDARDS

Factors causing higher standards	PERCENTAGE OF RESPONDENTS LISTING FACTOR
Public disclosure; publicity; media coverage; better communication	31%
Increased public concern; public awareness, consciousness, and scrutiny; better informed public; societal pressures	20
Government regulation, legislation, and intervention; federal courts	10
Education of business managers; increase in manager professionalism and education	9
New social expectations for the role business is to play in society; young adults' attitudes; consumerism	5
Business's greater sense of social responsibility and greater awareness of the implications of its acts; business responsiveness; corporate policy changes; top management emphasis on ethical action	5
Other	20

Factors causing lower standards	
Society's standards are lower; social decay; more permissive society; materialism and hedonism have grown; loss of church and home influence; less quality, more quantity desires	34%
Competition; pace of life; stress to succeed; current economic conditions; costs of doing business; more businesses compete for less	13
Political corruption; loss of confidence in government; Watergate; politics; political ethics and climate	9
People more aware of unethical acts; constant media coverage; TV; communications create atmosphere for crime	9
Greed; desire for gain; worship the dollar as measure of success; selfishness of the individual; lack of personal integrity and moral fiber	8
Pressure for profit from within the organization from superiors or from stockholders; corporate influences on managers; corporate policies	7
Other	21

SOURCE: Reprinted by permission of the Harvard Business Review. Excerpt from "Is the Ethics of Business Changing?" by Stephen N. Brenner and Earl A. Molander (January–February 1977). Copyright © 1977 by the President and Fellows of Harvard College; all rights reserved.

NOTE: Some respondents listed more than one factor, so there were 353 factors in all listed as causing higher standards and 411 in all listed as causing lower ones. Categories may not add up to 100 due to rounding errors.

Selected Viewpoints on Management's Social Responsibility

A subject as complex as social responsibility is certain to produce a multitude of views among management theorists, writers, practitioners, and others. One useful classification contains three components:

1. The popular viewpoint
2. The traditional viewpoint
3. Enlightened self-interest[11]

THE POPULAR VIEWPOINT

This viewpoint might be termed the Steiner-Davis argument since it is often associated with George Steiner and Keith Davis, two leading management theorists. The Steiner-Davis view is "that the doctrine of corporate social responsibility has evolved from a changing managerial philosophy which explicitly recognizes the obligations of the corporation to society and eschews the narrow goal of simply increasing profits or earnings."[12] In other words the popular view of social responsibility goes beyond a mere profit orientation.

Management professor Joseph W. McGuire is also associated with the popular viewpoint. He puts it this way:

> A socially responsible company is one in which the ownership utility function does not dominate those of other claimants in all situations and at all times. It is a company where the satisfactions of non-owner claimants are taken into account, and where the totality of organizational satisfactions is widely shared. The more equitable the distribution of organizational satisfactions, the greater the social responsibility of the company.[13]

The popular viewpoint, then, is of the businessperson who realizes the full extent of his or her social responsibilities. Those responsibilities are then built into the decision-making process.

---

[11] Management author Gerald Keim has suggested the popular–traditional dichotomy. The third category, enlightened self-interest, has evolved partially from the views of leading business executives. See Gerald D. Keim, "Managerial Behavior and the Social Responsibility Debate: Goals Versus Constraints," *Academy of Management Journal* (March 1978), pp. 57–69.

[12] *Ibid.*, p. 58.

[13] Joseph W. McGuire, "The Changing Nature of Business Responsibilities," Oklahoma State University's College of Business Administration Honors Lecture (March 8, 1978), p. 10.

THE TRADITIONAL VIEWPOINT

The traditional viewpoint is that expressed by economists relying on Adam Smith's *Wealth of Nations.*[14] The basic premise is that an "invisible hand" of self-interest is the best guide for the business system. Profit maximization is the accepted goal.

Milton Friedman, a recipient of the Nobel Prize for economics, is the best-known advocate of this position. Friedman feels that management's responsibility is to represent the interests of stockholders—not of other groups as a whole. Friedman argues that social issues are best confronted by government, not by private enterprise.[15] Adam Smith's words will ring true for proponents of this viewpoint: "I have never known much good done by those who affected to trade for the public good."[16]

ENLIGHTENED SELF-INTEREST

Enlightened self-interest is a description of how many modern managers view their responsibilities. This third viewpoint merges the popular and traditional concepts by recognizing that being socially responsible is simply good business.

Henry Ford II noted that failure to respond to societal challenges often results in heavy-handed government intervention. Citing an example from his own industry, Ford noted: "Maybe we wouldn't have won any prizes if we had answered auto-safety charges more effectively before the consumerists moved into the area, but we would have saved ourselves—and our customers—some nightmarish regulations."[17]

Du Pont's retired board chairman, Irving S. Shapiro, is a leading proponent of this viewpoint. Shapiro, who spent 30 to 40 percent of his time dealing with public issues, noted:

> I think we're a means to an end, and while producing goods and providing jobs is our primary function, we can't live successfully in a society if the hearts of its cities are decaying and its people can't support their families. We've got to help make the whole system work, and that involves more than just having a safe workplace and providing jobs for the number of people we can hire. It means that just as you want libraries, and you want schools, and you want fire departments and police

[14] Keim, "Managerial Behavior," pp. 57–58.

[15] See Milton Friedman, "The Social Responsibility of Business Is to Increase Its Profits," *New York Times Magazine* (September 13, 1970), pp. 122–126. Friedman's views are discussed in Robert Hay and Ed Gray, "Social Responsibilities of Business Managers," *Academy of Management Journal* (March 1974), p. 141.

[16] Adam Smith quoted in Milton Friedman, "Social Responsibilities: A Subversive Doctrine," *National Review* (August 24, 1965), p. 723.

[17] Ford is quoted in Ted Kade, "Henry Ford II Admits Errors: Questions 'Capitalist Virtues,'" *Detroit News* (April 27, 1979), p. 13-A.

The *Business Roundtable* is one of the most prestigious public issue groups in the United States. Organized in 1972, the Business Roundtable consists of 250 managers, all chief executive officers of their firms. Roger Blough of U.S. Steel, Fred Borch of General Electric, economist Arthur Burns, and former Texas Governor John Connally are some of the names associated with the founding of this important forum.

Roundtable members are divided into various tasks forces. Issues are examined, and the group's positions are announced. The Business Roundtable then seeks to make its views known to Congress, the White House, various government units, and the general public. For instance, the Business Roundtable recently highlighted the importance of socially responsible decisions by issuing a "Statement of Corporate Responsibility."

The Business Roundtable is one of the most effective groups of its kind in Washington. It is widely credited with influencing the outcome of several pieces of legislation. The Roundtable also represents an abrupt departure from the apathy that traditionally characterized business's relations with government.

SOURCE: Walter Guzzardi, Jr., "Business Is Learning How to Win in Washington," *Fortune* (March 27, 1978), p. 53. Material based on the original article which appeared in the March 27, 1978 issue of *Fortune* Magazine and reprinted by special permission; © 1978 Time Inc. The 1982 update is from Kenneth Mason, "The Future of Private Enterprise Initiatives in the 1980s," a presentation given in Washington, D.C., on May 13, 1982.

THE BUSINESS ROUNDTABLE

Business Roundtable is a group of 250 top managers from different organizations who meet to discuss public issues and report their opinions as business representatives.

departments, you also want businesses to help do something about unsolved social problems.[18]

The enlightened self-interest viewpoint is that being socially responsible is also good business practice in that it will lead to greater long-run profits. Management must also make the level of social responsibility compatible with other corporate goals and their own set of business ethics. The different levels of social responsibility are discussed in the section that follows.

Levels of Social Responsibility

A number of levels exist in management's response to social responsibility issues. One way to look at this problem is to focus on the extremes. The most rudimentary position is for management simply to be aware that a social responsibil-

[18] Shapiro is quoted in "Today's Executive: Private Steward and Public Servant," *Harvard Business Review* (March–April 1978), p. 101.

**Figure 21-1
SPECTRUM OF
SOCIAL
RESPONSIBILITY**

SPECTRUM OF SOCIAL RESPONSIBILITY

Low   High

The Organization   Social Responsibility
Acknowledges Some   Considerations Are
Social Responsibility   Integrated Throughout
                                                              the Organization

ity does exist in a given set of circumstances.[19] At the other extreme is the thorough integration of social responsibility considerations into the organization. Intermediate level responses may be viewed as falling somewhere on a spectrum between these two alternatives—as illustrated in Figure 21-1.

Instead of attempting to place the entire organization at some point along the social responsibility continuum, it may prove more useful to focus on specific social responsibility areas. For instance, fair employment practices may be fully integrated throughout the organization and located at the far right in Figure 21-1. Energy saving programs might rank in the middle range, while a special pro-

[19] This is suggested in Kenneth Rowe and John Schlacter, "Integrating Social Responsibility into Corporate Structure," *Public Relations Quarterly* (Fall 1978), pp. 7–12.

**SOCIAL
RESPONSIBILITY
STANDARDS VARY**

SOURCE: *The New Yorker* (May 19, 1980), p. 48. Drawing by C. Barsotti; © 1980 The New Yorker Magazine, Inc.

*"Look, the industry itself has a bad reputation, but within
that framework my reputation is good."*

gram to encourage voluntarism among employees may be just beginning. Such programs would fall to the extreme left in the social responsibility continuum. This focus on levels of social responsibility for a large number of individual social responsibility areas may prove much more insightful than an attempt to categorize the entire organization.

CORPORATE BEHAVIOR: THE SETHI MODEL[20]

Management tends to respond to a dual set of social forces: market and nonmarket. The firm can adapt its competitive strategy to meet marketplace demands and its success may be evaluated by volume and profitability standards. Nonmarket forces—often called *externalities*—have placed an increased burden on management. Traditionally, such externalities as pollution have been dealt with by the whole society. Today, however, business is being asked to play a greater role in the solution of these problems. How has business responded?

Externalities are nonmarket social forces.

University of Texas business professor S. Prakash Sethi has identified three stages in corporate behavior:

1. Social obligation
2. Social responsibility
3. Social responsiveness

Social obligation refers to corporate behavior designed to deal only with legal requirements and competitive market factors. The second stage, *social responsibility,* refers to corporate behavior that complies with contemporary values, norms, and expectations of society. Since many societal standards will later become part of the legal framework for management, stage two may be viewed as prescriptive in nature, rather than proscriptive as was the case in stage one. *Social responsiveness* is the third stage of corporate behavior. Here, management is expected to anticipate various changes and to take appropriate preventive action.[21] As Table 21-3 shows, the Sethi model relates the three stages to various dimensions of corporate behavior.

---

[20] This section is based on S. Prakash Sethi, "A Conceptual Framework for Environmental Analysis of Social Issues and Evaluation of Business Response Patterns," *Academy of Management Review* (January 1979), pp. 63–74. Another interesting article is David W. Fischer, "Strategies Toward Political Pressures: A Typology of Firm Responses," *Academy of Management Review* (January 1983), pp. 71–78.

[21] Roy Ash, former head of Addressograph-Multigraph Corp. and former high government official, offers some interesting guidelines on how management can better affect public policy issues in Roy L. Ash, "A Business Guide to Political Action," *Carroll Business Bulletin* (Winter 1978), pp. 4–8.

Table 21-3 A THREE-STAGE SCHEMA FOR CLASSIFYING CORPORATE BEHAVIOR	DIMENSIONS OF BEHAVIOR	STAGE ONE: SOCIAL OBLIGATION PROSCRIPTIVE
	Response to social pressures	Maintains low public profile, but, if attacked, uses PR methods to upgrade its public image; denies any deficiencies; blames public dissatisfaction on ignorance or failure to understand corporate functions; discloses information only where legally required.
	Activities pertaining to governmental actions	Strongly resists any regulation of its activities except when it needs help to protect its market position; avoids contact; resists any demands for information beyond that legally required.
	Legislative and political activities	Seeks to maintain status quo; actively opposes laws that would internalize any previously externalized costs; seeks to keep lobbying activities secret.
	Philanthropy	Contributes only when direct benefit to it clearly shown; otherwise, views contributions as responsibility of individual employees.

Industrial Democracy

Industrial democracy may be one of management's most confusing terms. It is often used to refer to different organizational and work schemes. The term's meaning also varies from country to country. For example, *industrial democracy* is often used to refer to a range of participative management schemes.[22] Some 250 U.S. firms now have a version of worker participation.[23]

[22] Industrial democracy is discussed in Richard J. Long, "Desires and Patterns of Worker Participation in Decision Making After Conversion to Employee Ownership," *Academy of Management Journal* (September 1979), pp. 611–617; Bernard M. Boss and V. J. Shacketon, "Industrial Democracy and Participative Management: A Case for a Synthesis," *Academy of Management Review* (July 1979), pp. 393–404; and S. Benjamin Prasad, "The Growth of Co-Determination," *Business Horizons* (April 1977), pp. 23–29.

[23] Estimate attributed to Donald Pearson of Eastern Michigan University. See "Donald Pearson Examines Labor Experiments," *Focus EMU* (October 10, 1978), p. 2.

STAGE TWO: SOCIAL RESPONSIBILITY PRESCRIPTIVE	STAGE THREE: SOCIAL RESPONSIVENESS ANTICIPATORY AND PREVENTIVE
Accepts responsibility for solving current problems; will admit deficiencies in former practices and attempt to persuade public that its current practices meet social norms; attitude toward critics conciliatory; freer information disclosures than stage one.	Willingly discusses activities with outside groups; makes information freely available to public; accepts formal and informal inputs from outside groups in decision making; is willing to be publicly evaluated for its various activities.
Preserves management discretion in corporate decisions, but cooperates with government in research to improve industrywide standards; participates in political processes and encourages employees to do likewise.	Openly communicates with government; assists in enforcing existing laws and developing evaluations of business practices; objects publicly to governmental activities that it feels are detrimental to the public good.
Willing to work with outside groups for good environmental laws; concedes need for change in some status quo laws; less secrecy in lobbying than stage one.	Avoids meddling in politics and does not pursue special interest laws; assists legislative bodies in developing better laws where relevant; promotes honesty and openness in government and in its own lobbying activities.
Contributes to noncontroversial and established causes; matches employee contributions.	Activities of stage two, *plus* support and contributions to new, controversial groups whose needs it sees as unfulfilled and increasingly important.

SOURCE: S. Prakash Sethi, ''A Conceptual Framework for Environmental Analysis of Social Issues and Evaluation of Business Response Patterns,'' *Academy of Management Review* 4, no. 1 (January 1979), p. 67. Reprinted with permission of the author.

Sweden—particularly the Volvo and Saab firms—is often noted as the ultimate user of industrial democracy. Yet when the Ford Foundation financed an experiment in which six U.S. automobile assembly line workers were sent to Sweden to work briefly at Saab-Scandia, five of the six reported that they preferred the American system over the highly touted Swedish one.[24]

INDUSTRIAL DEMOCRACY DEFINED

Industrial democracy refers to a range of participative formats that provide employees with varying degrees of involvement in the operation and achievements

Industrial democracy refers to a range of participative formats that provide employees with varying degrees of involvement in the operation and achievements of their firms.

[24] Nancy Foy and Herman Gadon, ''Workers' Participation: Contrasts in Three Countries,'' *Harvard Business Review* (May–June 1976), p. 71.

THE FIVE FACES OF EUROPEAN INDUSTRIAL DEMOCRACY

1. CODETERMINATION: WORKERS ON BOARDS

First instance: 1947 in German coal and steel industries as anti-Nazi device (50% workers).

By 1974, minority representatives on boards (usually 33%) required by law in Germany, Austria, Denmark, Sweden, Holland. Upped to 50% in Germany, 1977 (private companies with 2,000 employees). German formula, roughly, proposed for Britain by Bullock Committee, 1977, but no legislation in sight.

Worker polls (1976) in Britain, Denmark, France showed workers do not feel it very important. Not much interest in form in Scandinavia. Many people everywhere feel it is essentially cosmetic.

EEC proposes two-tier structure: (1) 50% owners–50% workers, (2) 100% management, latter reporting to former, for all Eurocompanies in future.

Generally conceived/perceived as "communications" structure against worker "control" device; no known instance in Europe (yet) of workers on boards blocking management decisions, or seeking to.

In Britain, Germany, much publicized by press (in Britain as "industrial democracy").

Wherever present, achieved by legislative processes, or national law. Opposed by Communists.

2. WORKS COUNCILS

Since World War II, either through legislation or collective bargaining works councils mandatory in all European countries in varying degrees and strengths. Stated functions: to improve company performance, working conditions, security.

In some companies, worker/union-run; in some, management chairs. Usually mostly workers, some stewards; usually members elected democratically from workplace.

In France, where legally mandated, weak discussion groups without power. In Britain, nonmandated, wide variance between weakness and strength. In Holland and Germany, where mandated, powerful and legally protected. In Scandinavia, where mandated, not considered important structures. In Italy, where not mandated, extremely powerful.

Generally, particularly Holland and Germany, growing in influence (and achievements) over factory-level management decision making, performance, and productivity.

Usually achieved, in most countries, through legislative process, or national law.

3. SHOP FLOOR PARTICIPATION

Other names: workplace democracy, quality of work life, job enrichment. Seminal efforts: Britain's Tavistock Institute, Norway's Work Research Institute, notably latter.

Various notions/restructuring processes designed to provide workers with greater participation in decisions affecting day-to-day performance of work.

British Work Research Unit (1974), A.N.A.C.T. in France (1974), Work Research Unit in Sweden (1977).

Unilateral (management only) "job enrichment" activities increasingly unpopular with unions, particularly in Sweden and Holland, as "union-busting"; bilateral, joint union-management participative activities, particularly in Germany, increasingly popular with both unions and managements.

German Humanization of Work Act (1974): $109,000,000 over five years for experimentation in this area. Almost no legislative mandates; almost wholly private/voluntary, wherever found.

4. FINANCIAL PARTICIPATION

Other names: profit sharing with unions/workers.

Except for scarce voluntary plans, nonexistent in Europe outside France, although much discussed/advocated by unions, notably in Sweden.

Under French law (1973), most workers get nothing, the few get pittances; considered a farce.

Swedish Meidner Plan (1976), introduced to Parliament in Fall 1983, proposed giving 20% of all private profits to unions; considered a key reason for voters' ouster (1976) of Social Democrats who endorsed it.

Most proposed financial participation plans suggest laws mandating percentages of all private profits going into centrally administered fund, dominated or controlled by union confederation (e.g., Meidner Plan: Sweden). Most seen as union ploy to dominate economy over long run as profits accrue; in most, payouts to workers small or even nonexistent.

Union advocates call such plans "capitalist alternative to socialism," but voters are not buying hence absence of legal achievements in this face.

Opposed by Communists.

5. COLLECTIVE BARGAINING

Still number one mainstay of industrial democracy in Europe in all countries; notably weak in France and Britain; notably strong in Germany, Holland, Italy, Belgium, and Sweden.

Worth noting: "faces" above, and laws creating same, carefully avoid any intrusion on rights of collective bargaining, or relationship thereto. Such laws, as noted, tend to provide new "social" rights; collective bargaining is (except in Italy and Sweden) economic.

In Italy, where no industrial democracy legislation exists, unions (notably powerful metal workers) have used bargaining to achieve industrial democracy gains won politically elsewhere.

In Sweden, 1977 Democracy At Work law radically opens collective bargaining to matters traditionally considered management prerogative for first time, down to local union levels.

SOURCE: Reprinted by permission of the Harvard Business Review. Exhibit from "Europe's Industrial Democracy: An American Response" by Ted Mills (November–December 1978). Copyright © 1978 by the President and Fellows of Harvard College; all rights reserved.

of their firms. Ted Mills of the American Center for the Quality of Work Life points out that five specific types of industrial democracy have been enacted by law in Europe.[25]

1. Codetermination
2. Works councils
3. Shop floor participation
4. Financial participation
5. Collective bargaining

The term *industrial democracy* has been used to apply to all of these formats.

TYPES OF INDUSTRIAL DEMOCRACY

As it is practiced in Europe, there are five types of industrial democracy. The legally sanctioned forms include *codetermination*, or the inclusion of workers on the board of directors; *works councils*, factory-level joint management–worker committees; *shop floor participation*, a variety of attempts to involve workers in task-related decisions such as in the job enrichment process (described in detail elsewhere); *financial participation*, or profit sharing; and *collective bargaining*, or labor-management negotiations.

THE CURRENT STATUS OF INDUSTRIAL DEMOCRACY

Legislative action on industrial democracy has been primarily limited to Europe. And it was largely a product of the 1970s. Twenty-eight of the thirty-five significant pieces of European industrial democracy legislated were enacted in the 1970s.

Industrial democracy has been widely accepted in Europe despite the misgivings of managers who worry about the possible cost implications. But European style industrial democracy has not spread to the United States, since it lacks majority support within the ranks of American labor, management, or union leadership. The most striking exception was Douglas Fraser's selection to the Chrysler board as a result of contract negotiations between the manufacturer and the United Automobile Workers (UAW). The UAW president, a former metal finisher at the corporation's DeSoto factory, is the first labor representative to become a board member of a large U.S. firm. Fraser made his role clear when he remarked: "I'm going to represent the auto workers and I'm going to speak out

---

[25] The remainder of this section on industrial democracy is based on Ted Mills, "Europe's Industrial Democracy; An American Response," *Harvard Business Review* (November–December 1978), pp. 143–152. Article is adapted from his book *Industrial Democracy in Europe: A 1977 Survey* (American Center for the Quality of Work Life, 1978). Works councils and codetermination are also discussed in Reyer A. Swaak, "Industrial Democracy: An Update," *Personnel Administrator* (April 1978), pp. 34, 40, 45.

in their behalf anytime I believe that the board acts contrary to the interest of the workers."[26]

Americans in management and labor alike are generally individualistic in nature. They have tended to prefer to work out their differences through either individual negotiations or collective bargaining, with minimum government involvement. Also, U.S. labor unions are regarded as far more democratic than their European counterparts. Europe, by contrast, has had a long history of looking to government for the solution of economic and social problems. While industrial democracy is, understandably, a widely discussed topic it has been used only on a limited basis in the United States.

Measuring Social Responsibility

There have been numerous proposals and attempts to measure social responsibility.[27] While these efforts are to be applauded, their findings are often mixed. One of the primary problems seems to be indecision as to *what should be measured.* A closely related issue is *how* to measure such items.

WHAT SHOULD BE MEASURED?

The insurance industry is often cited as a leader in the measurement of social responsibility. Its social reporting program includes the following categories:

1. *Community projects* defined as those in which the company played a significant role or provided substantial support. These include civic and cultural programs, youth activities, student and school activities, and local health programs
2. *Contributions* to federated drives, education programs, urban/civic affairs, and cultural activities
3. *Equal employment opportunity* for women and minority group members, including both initial employment and promotions
4. *Environmental concerns and energy conservation* defined as the existence of policies or procedures concerning the environmental impact of company investments and of policies or procedures directed at energy conservation
5. *Voluntarism* measured according to the number and hours contributed by persons loaned to or given release time for public service work; and the

---

[26] Mark Lett and Charlie Cain, "Historic Contract Puts Fraser on Chrysler's Board," *Detroit News* (October 26, 1979), pp. 1-A, 3-A. Fraser quote from p. 1-A.

[27] The measurement of social responsibility is explored in articles such as James E. Post and Marc J. Epstein, "Information Systems for Social Reporting," *Academy of Management Review* (January 1977), pp. 81–87; James M. Higgins, "A Proposed Social Performance Evaluation System," *Atlanta Economic Review* (May–June 1977), pp. 4–9; and Gordon J. Alexander and Rogene A. Buchholz, "Corporate Social Responsibility and Stock Market Performance," *Academy of Management Journal* (September 1978), pp. 479–486.

THE BUSINESS
COMMITTEE FOR THE
ARTS REPRESENTS
SOCIALLY
RESPONSIBLE
MANAGEMENT
ACTION

percentage of companies having programs to encourage individual involvement

6. *Social investments* that would not otherwise have been made under the company's customary lending standards, or those in which social consideration played a substantial part in the investment decision[28]

After studying the insurance industry's social reporting program, former Commerce Secretary Juanita Kreps once suggested that the federal government establish a "social performance index." Some firms owned by the governments of the United Kingdom and France have "social contracts" that reward the firms for their social contributions. A variety of other proposals have surfaced in recent years.[29] But what are the actual practices of American industry in this critical area?

[28] Adapted from *1978 Special Report of the Life and Health Insurance Business* (Washington, D.C.: Clearinghouse on Corporate Social Responsibility, 1978).

[29] See, for example, Stanley G. Karson, "A 'Social Index' for Business," *Response* (November 1977), p. 2; and Walter F. Abbott and R. Joseph Monsen, "On the Measurement of Corporate Social Responsibility: Self-Reported Disclosures as a Method of Measuring Corporate Social Involvement," *Academy of Mangement Journal* (September 1979), p. 501.

THE ERNST & WHINNEY SURVEY

Ernst & Whinney, a major public accounting firm, has surveyed companies about their involvement in/and disclosure of social responsibility issues.[30] They focused on the nation's 500 largest industrial companies, 50 largest life insurance firms, and 50 biggest banks—as listed in *Fortune* magazine.

Almost 9 of every 10 of *Fortune*'s 500 now make social responsibility disclosures. Some 40 percent of the respondents have a special social responsibility section in their annual reports.

Social responsibility disclosures vary by the categories used in the Ernst & Whinney study. As Figure 21-2 reveals, comments about fair business practice are the most cited disclosure category. Energy rates second.

Some firms supplement their social responsibility disclosures with quantified information—either in monetary or nonmonetary terms. The extent of this supplementary disclosure is shown in Figure 21-3.

The Ernst & Whinney data demonstrate that a socially responsible management philosophy is the norm in American industry. The accounting firm's research provides some benchmarks in this crucial area, even though it is limited to only a select group of major companies and their annual report disclosures. In fact, one analyst suggests that "most U.S. companies participate in more socially responsible activities than are indicated in their annual reports."[31]

---

[30] The remainder of this section is based on Dennis R. Beresford and Scott S. Cowen, "Surveying Social Responsibility Disclosure in Annual Reports," *Business* (March–April 1979), pp. 15–20. The Ernst & Whinney research is also discussed in Abbott and Monsen, "On the Measurement of Corporate Social Responsibility," pp. 501–515.

[31] Beresford and Cowen, "Surveying Social Responsibility Disclosure," p. 19.

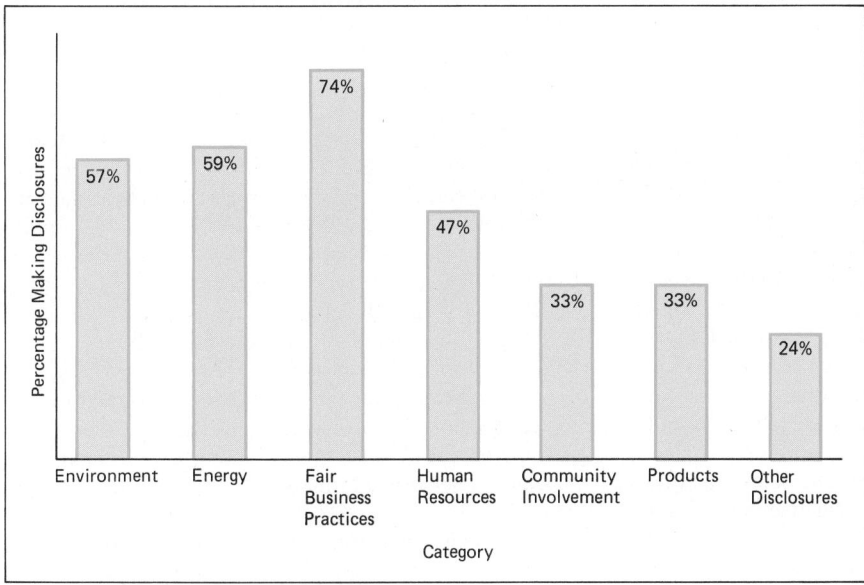

**Figure 21-2
PERCENTAGES OF COMPANIES MAKING SOCIAL RESPONSIBILITY DISCLOSURES BY CATEGORY**

SOURCE: Adapted by permission from Dennis R. Beresford and Scott S. Cowen, "Surveying Social Responsibility Disclosure in Annual Reports," *Business* (March–April 1979), p. 16. Published by Georgia State University.

**Figure 21-3
PERCENTAGES OF
COMPANIES
PROVIDING
QUANTIFIED SOCIAL
RESPONSIBILITY
DISCLOSURES**

SOURCE: Adapted by permission from Beresford and Cowen, "Surveying Social Responsibility Disclosure," p. 17.

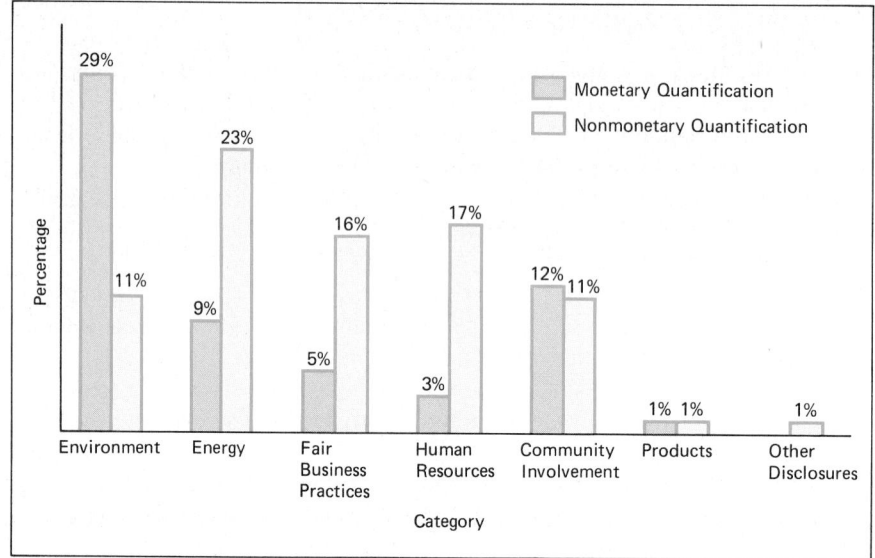

Summary

Social responsibility refers to management philosophies, policies, procedures, and actions that have the advancement of society's welfare as one of their primary objectives. The social responsibility issue has gone through three distinct stages. In stage one, management viewed profit maximization as its primary obligation. Stage two can be called *trustee management,* when executives realized that other groups like employees, customers, and vendors also had claims on the organization. Trustee management was responsible to all these contributor groups. In stage three, concern with the quality of life meant that management had to direct some of its efforts and resources to the solution of societal issues.

Ethical business practice is closely tied to management's social responsibility. Management ethics refers to the moral premises upon which executive decisions are made. The current state of management ethics gets mixed reviews. A Gallup Poll reported that in the public's eyes, executives ranked sixteenth in a list of twenty-five occupations in terms of their honesty and ethical standards. A longitudinal report on management ethics by the *Harvard Business Review* noted that respondents tended to disagree on whether or not business ethics had improved over the years.

Most viewpoints on management's social responsibility can be categorized into one of three groupings: popular, traditional, or enlightened self-interest. The first view is of a management that realizes the full extent of its social responsibilities. The traditional viewpoint is that management exists to serve the firm's stockholders and that profit maximization should be the prevailing corporate objective. Enlightened self-interest attempts to merge the other two concepts by realizing that being socially responsible is simply good business.

Chapter 21 also examines the various levels of social responsibility. Table 21-3 shows the Sethi model, which identifies three stages of corporate behavior: social obligation, social responsibility, and social responsiveness. An open discussion of management's views on public affairs is an approach to social responsibility practiced by the Business Roundtable—a public issue group consisting of 250 chief executive officers.

The term *industrial democracy* refers to a range of participative formats that provide employees with varying degrees of involvement in the operation and achievement of their firms. European style industrial democracy has five formats:

1. Codetermination, the inclusion of workers on the board of directors. Douglas Fraser's selection

to the Chrysler board is a notable example in the United States.

2. Works councils, a factory-level joint management–worker committee.
3. Shop floor participation, a variety of attempts to involve workers in task-related decisions such as the job enrichment process.
4. Financial participation, or profit sharing.
5. Collective bargaining, or labor-management negotiations.

The insurance industry—often cited as one of the leaders in the measurement of social responsibility—uses the following categories to assess its social performance: community projects, contributions, equal employment opportunity, environmental concerns and energy conservation, voluntarism, and social investments.

Chapter 21 concludes by discussing Ernst & Whinney's survey of industry's involvement in/and disclosure of social responsibility issues. The accounting firm's data show that about nine out of every ten corporations of *Fortune*'s 500 list make social responsibility disclosures. Fair business practice is the most often cited disclosure category. Energy places second.

REVIEW EXERCISES

1. Define the following terms: (a) social responsibility (b) management ethics (c) externalities (d) Business Roundtable (e) industrial democracy.

2. Outline the historical phases of the social responsibility issue.

3. Discuss the current status of management ethics.

4. Contrast the popular, traditional, and enlightened self-interest views of social responsibility.

5. Discuss the varying levels of social responsibility.

6. Describe the Sethi model of corporate behavior.

7. Why might a corporation give money to support cultural activities?

8. Differentiate between the five types of industrial democracy.

9. How can society measure management's social responsibility?

10. What does the Ernst & Whinney survey reveal about the level of social responsibility in the United States?

ASSIGNMENTS/ PROBLEMS/ DISCUSSION QUESTIONS

1. Several women's banks have opened in cities like New York, San Francisco, Richmond, Los Angeles, Denver, and San Diego. While they have received considerable acclaim by feminists and others, all have had to deal with the realities of economic life. San Diego's Women's Bank decided its name was a disadvantage, so the bank is now called California Coastal Bank. The (male) president of San Francisco's Western Women's Bank says: "Businessmen will deposit with us, but don't want to use our checks. So we get only a minor part of their business." *

Relate the emergence of feminist banks to the concepts discussed in Chapter 21. What social responsibilities exist for managers of the banks? businesses in the community? government units?

2. First Federal Savings and Loan Association of Cumberland, Maryland, once fired a teller because she refused to contribute to the local United Way. Prior to this incident, the firm had a record of 100 percent participation for twenty-five years. But the teller refused to donate because of moral objections to some of the organizations supported by United Way. The association later issued an apol-ogy and offered to rehire the teller.† What can be learned from this incident?

3. Membership on a firm's board of directors was often treated like an honorary position for people not actually employed by the organization. But both "outside" and "inside" directors (those who are also employees) are increasingly being held responsible for the actions of management and employees. This trend is true of both profit and nonprofit organizations, regardless of size. ** Do you think directors should be the ones who must accept the ultimate social responsibility? If so, under what conditions would your judgment apply?

4. Codetermination gives workers considerable clout in major corporate decisions. For example, the startup of a Volkswagen factory in Pennsylvania was postponed for a long period of time because workers on VW's board feared the loss of German jobs.‡

What is your opinion of the suitability of codetermination to American business?

† "Apology: Bank Offers to Rehire Worker Who Spurned United Way," *The Seattle Times* (December 1, 1981), p. 16-A.

** This trend is discussed in Jane Bryant Quinn, "Risks at the Top," *Newsweek* (October 2, 1978), pp. 16-D, 16-H.

‡ Reported in Victor Lederer, "Decision Making: Should Employees Get in the Act?" *Administrative Management* (September 1978), p. 52.

* "Feminism Takes a Backseat at Women's Banks," *Business Week* (October 4, 1978), pp. 125, 128, 130.

5. Chapter 21 describes some of the steps taken by Hershey's management in response to the Three Mile Island nuclear accident. Another decision was to convert milk bought from local farmers into powder that could be held until all possible radiation content disappeared.

Evaluate the response of Hershey management to the near nuclear disaster.

A MANAGERIAL INCIDENT

The Presidential Task Force on Voluntarism

When budget cuts slashed many of the nation's social programs, President Reagan initiated a forty-four member President's Task Force on Private Sector Initiatives. The group was headed by Armco, Inc., Board Chairman C. William Verity. The task force sought to increase private contributions to offset the budget cuts. An objective of 5 percent of after-tax income was set for individuals, and 2 percent of corporate before-tax income. Voluntarism was also encouraged as part of the program.

American business gives about $3 billion in contributions annually. Only about 35 percent of U.S. corporations make charitable donations. Corporate giving has averaged approximately 1 percent of pretax income annually since World War II. The task force hoped to up this figure considerably. The need was obvious. Many companies and foundations reported a three- to fivefold increase in the number of requests for funding.

Most observers gave this program a mixed review. Voluntarism was up. But few social agencies were able to recoup their budget losses.

SOURCE: Timothy D. Schellhartdt, "Voluntarism, So Far, Fails to Compensate for U.S. Budget Cuts," *The Wall Street Journal* (June 22, 1982), pp. 1, 23; Nancy Way, "Business Philanthropy Moving into High Gear," *Journal-American* (May 18, 1982), p. 1-C.

Questions and Problems

1. Assess the current status of the voluntarism movement.

2. What are management's responsibilities when it comes to voluntarism?

3. If you were a member of the presidential task force, how would you attempt to stimulate private giving?

Case VI-1

ABBOTT MANUFACTURING CO.:
THE PRODUCTIVITY OF THE QUALITY INSPECTION DEPARTMENT

The Abbott Manufacturing Co. is an operating division of the ACO Corp. The company was founded in 1917 by C. K. Abbott, whose ambition was to develop and market refined men's toiletry and grooming aids. The company steadfastly pursued this charge through heavy expenditures in and acquisition of smaller manufacturing plants.

By the late 1940s, the company had established itself in the market as one of the leaders in men's toiletries. The company marketed over twenty national and international products ranging from tubed creams, aerosol shaving creams, aerosol and nonaerosol deodorants, and hair sprays to antiperspirant products and cosmetics.

By the mid 1960s, the Abbott Co. produced over eighty products spanning the entire range of men's and women's toiletry, grooming, and cosmetic aids marketed under the name of the Abbott or Aero Cos. In order to solidify its holdings, the Abbott Co. applied for status under the name of the Aero Corp. in 1965.

Both the Abbott (men's toiletries) and Aero (women's toiletries) divisions were housed in the same manufacturing facility. As new products were introduced into the market, both divisions competed for available production capacity. Finally, it was decided to construct a new plant that would provide adequate capacity for both divisions. The new plant was located in Stowe, Massachusetts. Operations were gradually phased out of the old facility and introduced at the Stowe plant until full-scale processing was reached there in 1970.

THE PRODUCTION PROCESS FOR AEROSOL PRODUCTS

The product lines marketed by the Abbott Co. had progressed through several major product mutations. This development had seen the introduction

This case was prepared by Professor Joel Corman of Suffolk University. Adapted and reprinted by permission of the author and Suffolk University.

of the aerosol product as a major convenience and packaging system that has dramatically changed the face of the toiletries industry. Thus, over 70 percent of the new Abbott Manufacturing Co. was dedicated to the production of aerosol products.

The aerosol filling operation at Abbott Manufacturing Co. employs a "product line" process of continuous product flow from one operation to the next until the unit is complete. Exhibit 1 is an outline of the physical makeup of an aerosol line.

In the first operation, the unfilled aerosol cans are automatically fed into a conveyor system that supports the entire production line. These cans then proceed to a can cleaning operation in which each unit undergoes a series of inversions and air blasts that purify each unit of all foreign material. The next operation is the concentrate filling process, which exactly meters a homogeneous weight quantity of a chemical concentrate to each unit.

Once filled, the unit passes into the valve placer unit, which synchronizes a valve so that can and valve arrive at the same location at the same time. The valve is then placed on top of the aerosol can unit. The valve is secured to the can by a valve crimper, which consists of six metal fingers. These fingers force the valve down onto the can and then expand the metal of the valve to interlock with the metal found in the can's top, thus forming a metal seal.

The units, now sealed from the atmosphere, are given a can code that is designed to identify a finished unit as to the year, day, shift, and location of production. The unit then travels to the propellant filling operation. Again, crimped units are synchronized and fed into the gasser. The gassing nozzle mates with the valve stem, and an exact weight of Freon propellant is injected into each unit.

THE QUALITY CONTROL FUNCTION AT AMC

After gassing, the units move to the actuator placer, which firmly positions the white spray but-

Exhibit 1 ABBOTT MANUFACTURING CO.——AEROSOL LINE

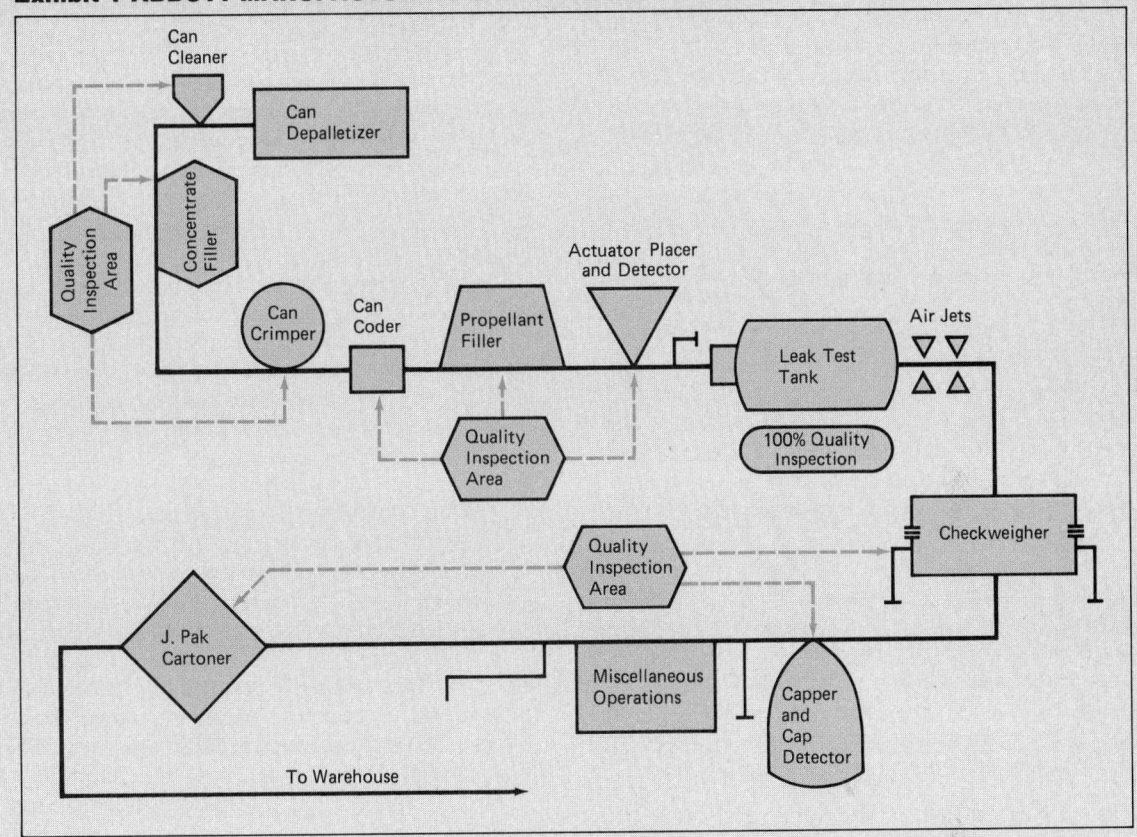

ton on the valve stem and also actuates each unit to insure proper functioning. The appearance of a spray is detected by an electronic eye. The spray from a unit breaks the electronic beam and an accept or reject status for each unit is electronically made. If the unit sprays, it travels to the next operation. However, if the electronic eye fails to detect a spray, the unit is rejected; it exits to a side conveyor, where it is manually actuated.

Acceptable units proceed to enter a leak test area which contains water heated to 160° Fahrenheit. The aerosol units are completely submerged and travel through the tank for one to two minutes. While submerged, a quality inspector visually observes each unit for signs of leakage or can malformation.

Once the aerosol units exit the tank, they are blown by a series of air jets and proceed to pass through an electronic checkweigher, which weighs each unit to verify that it complies with a predetermined net weight. The checkweigher unit employs an electromagnetic current load to determine the "no-go" status of each unit. A unit that is deemed rejectable by the checkweigher unit is guided to a side track for manual recheck weighing.

Acceptable checkweighed units travel a conveyor system until they reach an automatic capper that firmly affixes a cap to each unit. The units then pass through a metal arm height detector that checks for the presence of a cap. If the unit does not contain a cap, the arm does not deflect and the can is blown to a side spur by a series of air jets and later manually capped.

Once the unit receives its topper, it proceeds to

571

an automatic packaging machine, which arranges the units in a predetermined quantity grouping; places the grouping into a carton; glues the top, bottom, and sides; and places a carton code on two sides of each carton. Again, as with the can, the code is decoded to reveal the year, date, shift, location of production, and hour of packaging.

Finished cartons now travel a conveyor system to the warehouse storage area where they are automatically palletized and placed in an appropriate storage bin, awaiting final quality control acceptance.

Each variable filling or placement machine on any AMC aerosol line is monitored and checked each half hour by trained quality control inspectors who insure process compliance to established quality control process and product limits, or acceptance levels. The lead test tank as mentioned before receives 100 percent quality inspection on a continuous basis.

Products may be rejected at any inspection point for violation of the established process, product limits, or acceptance levels. The quality control inspectors are the key factor. They act as a "super consumer" and a production-working extension of management. The final quality level of product received by the consumer is dependent on both the objective and subjective judgment of each inspector.

Rejected products are placed in a segregated area, and each pallet is marked with the date, reason for rejection, and reject number. These units will be screened or sampled by the quality control inspectors in order to ferret out the rejectable units. Again, the final quality level is determined by the alertness and judgment of the inspectors as to whether the rejected product complies with established defect levels.

ORGANIZATION OF AMC'S QUALITY CONTROL FUNCTION

The Quality Inspection Department at the Stowe plant consisted of four men—the manager and three shift supervisors—and fifty-two women who are divided among three production shifts. The personnel who formed this essential group represented a mix of people who worked at the old facility and people who were hired when the new facility was opened.

The department manager handled a myriad of administrative activities and was very often absent from the office. The major contact that he had with employees were the brief morning and afternoon planning sessions with supervisors and the occasional meeting with an employee who had a special problem. The day-to-day running of the department fell basically to the supervisors.

The three supervisors' main duty was to assign the inspectors of various work teams, usually three in size, to the various production lines or function that need processing monitoring. The women were rotated every two weeks so that no one person worked in the same group or at the same location for any length of time. This is done to insure that each inspector receives maximum work orientation and homogeneous personnel blending.

The inspectors, twenty-two on the first shift, eighteen on the second shift, and twelve on the third, varied greatly in age and company service. Each shift had one or more inspectors who transferred from the old Abbott plant. These inspectors acted as the unofficial welcoming committee whenever a new person joined the department. And invariably these senior personnel were assigned the task of training and orientating the member to the normal inspection routines and general procedures.

The senior inspectors commanded the respect of the various people associated with the specific production lines. Their advice as to what procedure or action should be taken was sought by those inside and outside the Inspection Department. When the lines were down from production because of coffee breaks, dinner, or changeover, these inspectors seemed to group together whenever possible to attract a large segment of the newer inspectors.

No matter where they were assigned, the senior inspectors blended together with the remaining portion of the work team. They seemed to direct the exact work tempo and quality level for that shift. They would verbally admonish those within their own work team who failed to comply with what they interpreted to be the quality level of output, and would punish those outside their work team by using a strict enforcement of the quality limits or levels. These senior inspectors would automatically determine the final acceptance level when working with people with less seniority. If the work team contained more than one senior inspector, the one with the most company service became the ultimate authority for that specific work area.

The intellectual backgrounds of the inspectors varied significantly; their education ranged from grade school to college level. The job performed by the inspectors, though not difficult, required a certain ability in mechanical, mathematical, and logical reasoning. Employees seeking a job as an inspector were given an ability test to evaluate their potential in adapting to and understanding the job and its requirements. Although the senior inspectors were never subjected to this test, they were instrumental in its formation. In fact, management eliminated some of the suggestions they made because they were too difficult.

Those who successfully passed the test and were hired by the department were generally very energetic and innovative. They could express their enthusiasm on the job until it exceeded the established level, which was dictated by a particular senior inspector or the entire group. Those new members who did not slow down to an acceptable level found it very difficult to function on line. They often found themselves performing their jobs completely alone, without the assistance or expertise of the more experienced inspectors. At times they were also given the silent treatment, which sometimes reached an intolerable point.

SOME NEW POSITIONS ARE CREATED

Due to the rapidly expanding product lines that were being created by the research and development groups of the ACO Corp., the Quality Inspection Department was projected to increase 100 percent in personnel requirement. The three existing men supervisors were thought to have reached their maximum efficiency and control levels by an upper management planning team. The team recommended the creation of an assistant supervisory position for each shift. These positions would be filled by people who would assume the responsibility of handling day-to-day problems,

thus freeing the existing supervisors to tend to administrative matters.

The management team desired to advertise these jobs outside of the company so as to attract women with college-level education with a major concentration in business or economic theory. They also thought that the injection of new blood into the department would bring new ideas to the quality system. However, this line of thought went completely against the old Abbott philosophy of promoting those loyal and time-tested employees who had the greatest seniority. The existing department manager also knew that the top three senior inspectors were already receiving unofficial congratulations from their working peers.

The Abbott Manufacturing Co. was a nonunion plant that existed as an individual profit and operating division of the ACO Corp. The management planning team decided to modify the old company policy to allow the hiring of three new people for the inspection jobs. They sought to justify their decision by stating that not being bound by a union promotion system, current policies or procedures could be modified to satisfy overall good or the best interest of the Abbott Manufacturing Co.

THE NEW SUPERVISORS ARE REJECTED BY OTHER PERSONNEL

Three women were hired and received a thorough company and department orientation. They were immediately met with strong resentment by the majority of inspectors. They found that the senior inspectors began to challenge their level of authority by completely ignoring it, or loudly questioning a request to implement a quality action.

The new women supervisors found themselves socially isolated. For an hour in the morning and afternoon, they attended the department briefing sessions with the male management and supervisory personnel. The association with the men usually ended there except when the women were faced with a special quality problem that needed further consultation. They received the complete silent treatment from a majority of inspectors. All efforts to strike up a conversation were returned generally with a cold stare or the suggestion, ''I'm too busy to talk.'' Now and then one of the newer members of the department would be observed talking to the women supervisors, but the number of these talks diminished as this person became oriented to the established group or received strong pressure to end the association. The women supervisors basically found themselves alone no matter what shift they were working and no matter what they did to gain acceptance.

The quality level of outgoing products seemed to be lower than ever before. The women supervisors would be making a routine check only to find substandard material frequently going into the warehouse storage area and a quality control inspector watching the material going by without any effort to correct the situation. At times, especially when a senior inspector received a stern verbal warning by the new supervisors, the quality levels were enforced so strictly that entire shifts or days of production were being rejected, causing considerable reworking, screening, and product scrap costs. These wild fluctuations in quality output were now being brought to the attention of management.

Work assignments were in complete disarray as friends sought to work with each other. Situations were encountered where an inspector would be working at a different production location each day. Inspectors began to refuse work assignments or accept them with vehement objections due to the fact that they could not work with their first choice. Absenteeism reached an all-time high. It was not uncommon for several of the senior inspectors per shift to be ill at the same time and for the same length of time.

The problem culminated with the resignation of two of the women supervisors. They were replaced with two senior inspectors who quickly brought calm back to the department. The third supervisor received less resistance on her shift once the two senior inspectors were promoted. Her presence was tolerated by the inspectors, who basically assumed control of their shift as the supervisor became visibly absent.

Questions

1. Discuss how the effectiveness of the firm's quality control process was impacted by organizational changes.

2. Relate this case to the textbook's discussion of operations management and productivity.

3. What major productivity issues have been raised by this case?

Case VI-2

PROFESSOR WALTER STANTON:
EMPLOYEE RESPONSIBILITY AND THE USE OF TIME

In discussing the responsibility of an employee to his or her employer with a group of business students at a southwestern business school, Professor Walter Stanton was surprised at the number of questions he received and the diversity of opinion he found among his students regarding the use of time on and off the job. In order to give some focus to the discussion, he asked the students to write up incidents in their own lives in which this question had arisen. The following are a few of the incidents reported by the students.

JERRY DONALDSON

Last summer I was employed in a service station in my home town in Idaho. Besides selling petroleum products, this station had a Big O Tire and Honda motorcycle franchise. My responsibilities included pumping gas, fixing tires, greasing cars, making minor motorcycle repairs, and assembling new motorcycles, which came in crates from Japan. I also assisted the mechanic and the manager whenever they needed me.

Early in the summer, the manager decided that it would be profitable to stay open twenty-four hours a day. Many tourists traveled through our town during the summer months and they had no place to purchase gas after 10:00 P.M. The manager also thought that the night man could clean up the station, do the necessary motorcycle repairs, and assemble at least two motorcycles each night.

Although I was reluctant to work the 10:00 P.M.-to-7:00 A.M. shift, I finally agreed to rotate every other week with another of the employees.

During the first week of working the night shift, I went over the detailed list of duties for the night man to perform and planned how much time I had to accomplish each assigned job. I tried to use all of the time allotted to each job even if it meant

This case was prepared by Professor Clinton L. Oaks. Adapted and reprinted by permission of the author. Copyright © 1980 by Brigham Young University.

doing the job very slowly. This method allowed me to be busy the whole night and made the time go faster. I also found that if I wasn't busy all the time, I became very bored and drowsy. Therefore, I always tried to stay busy.

About the third week of working the night shift, however, I started to see how fast I could finish all of the assigned tasks. I worked out a whole series of short-cuts for cleaning the station and found that I could do it in an hour less than it had taken me previously. I also found that I could up my efficiency in doing the motorcycle repairs and in assembling new Hondas. I made a game out of pushing myself and found that I could do all the jobs and still have at least two hours left after they were all completed. At first I did not know what to do during the two hours, and they went by very slowly. I have always enjoyed tinkering with my car, however, so I decided that during this spare time I would wash and wax it, work on the tune-up, and make all of the little repairs that it needed. I always felt a little guilty working on my car while I was getting paid, but since I was doing a good job of finishing all the assigned tasks, I felt that I was justified in using any spare time on my own projects.

My boss evidently was pleased with my work because he frequently commended me on doing my job well. Several times I heard him "chewing out" the other employees for not doing a good job. I never told him that I worked on my car, but since I had him get parts for me I was pretty sure he knew what I was doing. He never said anything to me about it.

Toward the end of summer, my boss announced that the corporation that owned this station had decided that it would be beneficial to the company if every employee in the company received a polygraph test at least once a year. They had all of their employees sign a statement that they agreed to take the test.

Early one Saturday morning when I arrived at work, I discovered that the test administrator was at our station and that I was to take the test that morning. I was not alarmed since I had been honest in putting all money that I had received in the till and making a proper receipt out after each sale.

After putting all of the equipment on me and turning on his tape recorder, the man began asking some general questions regarding my honesty. I felt very comfortable telling him I had never stolen any money from the till and that I always accomplished tasks, that were assigned to me. Toward the end of the test he asked, ''Do you make good use of all of your time at work?'' Suddenly, I felt very uncomfortable and could feel my heart start to beat a lot faster.

ALLEN KNIGHT

After I finished my undergraduate work in mathematics and computer science, my wife persuaded me to take a job for a couple of years so that we could pay off some of our bills and get ahead a little before I started on my MBA. She was also concerned that I wasn't spending enough time with my two young sons. Because of the demands of my course work and a part-time job, I usually left early in the morning and often was not home until after they had been put to bed.

One of my professors was instrumental in getting me a job with Nelson Data Processing. I understood before I started that they were a hard-driving firm with a reputation for high-quality work. Once aboard, I found that the company had a large backlog and that management was encouraging everyone to put in overtime, for which they paid a generous hourly rate on top of the employee's salary.

We needed the money and the work was interesting. Before long, I found myself working late almost every night. Barbara, my wife, didn't say much at first, but I could tell she wasn't happy with the way things were working out. Finally one day she said, ''Allen, you were spending more time at home when you were in school than you are now.'' I mumbled something about ''trying to cut it down a little'' and dropped the subject.

The next day at noon, when another employee and I were on our way out to grab a sandwich, I mentioned that my wife was unhappy about all the time I was spending away from home. He said, ''Look, Allen, you don't have to punch a time clock on those extra hours. A lot of the guys just take

their work home with them. Keep track of your time and turn it in just like you do now. I'm not sure what the company policy is, but I have been doing this every so often for several months now, and nobody has ever said anything about it.''

The more I thought about the idea of doing my overtime at home, the better I liked it. I could spend the early evening with the family and then, after the boys were to bed, I could really get some work done. As I had expected,. Barbara was elated when I explained to her what I was going to do.

The first few nights I found it hard to get up to speed again after letting down for dinner and roughhousing with the kids. As I got into the swing of it, however, I found that since there was no distractions, as there often were at the office, I could do a lot more at home in an hour than I was doing at work. Whenever I needed someone to help with the checking or sorting, Barbara was always available and seemed to enjoy working with me. I found that there were some things she could do faster and more accurately than I could. One night after we had finished a particularly long and involved task in about half the time it would ordinarily have taken me, I said, ''Barbara, there ought to be some way to put you on the payroll.'' She laughed and said, ''Why don't you just increase the number of hours put in for yourself to cover it?''

WELDON GATES

I had been working for Patterson Engineering for nearly a year when I decided to come back and get my MBA. About three weeks before school was to start, I gave my supervisor, Jim, who was really a great boss, my two-week notice. Since he and I had talked a number of times about my going on to school as a preparation for a move into management, he was not at all surprised. He asked me to come in his office for a few minutes later that morning to make plans for my departure. I thought he might be concerned about several things I was working on that would be hard to turn over to anyone until I completed my present segment. I wasn't too concerned, however, because I had worked out a careful schedule and I figured I would just have time to do it all in those last two weeks.

When I entered my supervisor's office, he said,

"Weldon, you have done a great job for us, and when you finish your education, we want you to keep us in mind. You said that school started right after the first of next month?" I nodded, and he went on to say, "I imagine that you have a lot of work to do to get packed and moved, don't you?" I replied, "Boy I'll say! Moving is always such a hassle. We want to get out of our apartment by the fifteenth so that we can get our deposit back. I would like to have allowed myself a few more days, but when we figured out what we would need for school this year, we found that the money from these last two weeks was really crucial."

My supervisor smiled and leaned back in his chair. "Yes," he said, "I remember how it was. I think, though, that I can help you out. According to my records, you have accumulated about twelve days' sick leave. Is that right?" "Yes," I answered. "Well, as you know, the firm doesn't pay any sick leave unless you are actually sick. In your case, though, you are going to be sick—sick of moving. I want you to spend this afternoon acquainting Tom with where you are on each one of your projects. Then each morning for the next two weeks I want you to call in sick. If there is any question about it, I'll cover for you."

That night I thought a lot about what Jim had said—but I just didn't feel good about it. Tom was a good man, but it would take someone else at least twice as long to finish the things I was working on as it would take me. One of the projects was the kind that someone new would almost have to start over. The executives at Patterson had really been good to me in terms of the kinds of assignments they had given me—and I had been given a pay raise every six months instead of every year as was typical with new employees.

I went in early the next morning and was right in the middle of my most important project when Jim came by. He frowned when he saw me at my desk. "I thought I told you to take these two weeks off. I don't want to see you in here after today!"

LORRAINE ADAMS

When I was an undergraduate, I worked summers on an electronic composer for Brown Publishing. This is a typewriter with a memory that enables it to type course material in columns and justified (flushed right) margins. Because it is difficult to determine how long it takes to type material into memory and play it back, I often went for four hours without taking the fifteen-minute break we were supposed to have both morning and afternoon. Some of the other girls, who had the same problem, kept track of the breaks they didn't take and then used them as justification for leaving a half hour early or arriving a half hour late, recording their time as if they had left or arrived at the normal time. One girl even saved hers for two weeks and then took an afternoon off to do some shopping. I am sure that this was contrary to company policy, but our supervisor was a very relaxed and friendly woman who never seemed to notice when someone was gone.

Another problem I had with breaks was "What constitutes a break?" If a friend, who wasn't an employee of the company, dropped in for a few minutes, I always thought of that as a break. But what if some other employee who is tired, bored, or worried comes by and spends a few minutes talking about her work, her plans for the weekend, her current boy friend, or some personal problem? Should you count that as a break? One morning our supervisor talked to me for twenty minutes about job opportunities for women with MBAs. Was that a break?

Accounting for my time has always been a problem for me. Last summer, I worked as a department manager in a branch of a large department store in Los Angeles. A number of the department managers would arrive at 8:00, as we were supposed to do, and then take off across the mall to a coffee shop "to make plans for the day." They usually got back just before the store opened at 9:30. I went with them a couple of times and found that if they discussed anything related to their work in the store, it was only an incidental part of their conversation. A couple of these guys would also regularly take up to an hour and a half for lunch and then check out right after five. Since we didn't have to check in and out for breaks or for lunch, their time card would show an eight-hour day. When I said something to one of them about it one day, he answered, "Listen, Lorraine, summer is a slack time around here. You ought to be here during the Christmas rush. We work a lot of hours then that we don't get paid for. The store owes us a chance to relax a little when the heat is off."

ROBERT JEFFRIES

Before I came back to school, I worked for two years for a branch of Jefferson Sporting Goods. Jefferson had five large stores located in different metropolitan areas in the state and did a large volume in men's and women's sports clothes. Our branch wasn't the largest in the chain but would have been second or third.

The store manager, Rand Walker, has been manager since the store was opened. He had previously had soft goods experience with several other stores and really knew that part of the business.

We got along really well. Not long after I came to work, Rand put me in charge of the shoe department. Later he made me manager of the men's clothing department, and a year later, he made me assistant manager. He always saw that I got a substantial raise after each six month review. He seemed to have a lot of trust in me. I noticed, for example, that even before I had been there for a year, he shared a lot of confidential figures with me that he didn't show to any of the other managers.

One day Rand called me into his office. He told me to shut the door so that no one else would hear our conversation. "Bob" he said, "I've got a chance to buy the Blue Hills Pant Depot and I want to know what you think about it." Blue Hills was in a suburb about ten miles north of our store. Rand proceeded to tell me the details of the offer. "It really looks like a good deal as far as I can tell," I said, "but would it be as profitable for you as Jefferson's has been?" (I was assuming he would quit when he bought the store.) "Oh," he said, "I'm not going to quit unless Elliot Jefferson, the owner, tells me to." I was surprised because it looked to me like a clear case of conflict of interest. I knew that Rand had been looking at some outside investments since he had done very well at Jefferson's, but I hadn't thought he would consider buying another clothing store.

I didn't say much after that, trying not to get too involved with what was happening. Many times Rand would come to me to ask my opinion on certain clothing lines. He asked me to give him a list of the top five pant vendors and their salesmen's names and addresses, which I did.

Several weeks later, I asked Rand if he had made a decision on the store. He said he had gone ahead and bought it. He said he put it under his wife's name and that she was going to run it; that way he felt he could justify continuing his work at Jefferson's.

After that, I noticed that Rand spent a lot more time in his office and less time out on the floor. Occasionally, I would drop into his office to see him and find him paying invoices and doing book work for his pant store. I never asked anything about it and, in fact, tried to keep our conversations on problems that needed attention at Jefferson's.

This situation remained unchanged for several months. I concentrated my attention on doing my job and kept my thoughts to myself. Many of the other employees kept asking me about the Pant Depot. They wanted to know, for example, who really owned it, Rand or his wife. I would just tell them I didn't know.

In October, Rand came to me again and said that he was planning on acquiring a second pant store in another suburb about fifteen miles south of our store. A clothing store in that town was going out of business, and he had a chance to rent the building. This really surprised me. I kiddingly asked if he was planning to open a whole chain. He replied that he would like to open several stores similar to the one he had already and that all he needed was to find good locations where he could rent store space cheaply.

On November 1, Rand opened his second store. It immediately became a success, almost equaling the volume of the first.

After that, I seldom saw Rand on the floor. He was either in his office or gone. I found myself trying to cover for him when we would get calls from the home office. This situation made me very uncomfortable. When he did come in, he seemed a lot more absentminded about things in our store.

I wondered how much Elliot Jefferson knew (or suspected) about Rand's involvement in these other stores. I wondered, too, if I should tell the home office why our reports were slow and why our sales had stopped increasing as rapidly as they had when Rand spent full time managing the store.

Questions

1. What lessons do these student reports offer a basic management student?

2. Examine each of these five incidents. What would you have done under similar circumstances? Why?

Part VII
YOUR FUTURE
IN MANAGEMENT

22.
Future Trends in Management

Learning Objectives

AFTER STUDYING THIS CHAPTER YOU SHOULD BE ABLE TO

1. Describe the difficulties in predicting future management and business trends.
2. Explain the need for effective planning for an uncertain future.
3. Understand the major trends and counter-trends that may have an impact on future management decisions.
4. Identify the attributes and style of successful management in the 1980s.

Key Terms

futurology

future shock

contingency plans

information explosion

bottom line

egalitarianism

obsolete manager

I know it is a hell of a challenge but ask
yourselves: If not us, who? If not now,
when?

RONALD REAGAN

Some men see things as they are and
say why. I dream things that never
were and say, why not?

ROBERT F. KENNEDY

Monsanto is known as a company that makes tremendous efforts to alleviate potential problems with its new products. Technology risk reviews—using both employees and outside experts—are conducted to determine whether the new product creates a potential hazard of any kind.

But even this conservative and reasonable approach cannot spot all potential risks. Monsanto spent $100 million developing Cycle-Safe, a recycleable plastic beverage container that was to help eliminate the nation's litter problems. Cycle-Safe bottles could be ground up and made again or could be washed and refilled. Monsanto went to great lengths to be sure this new product would be safe. Experts in both the government and the private sector were consulted. A scientific symposium was held in Boston. FDA and EPA personnel liked the test results profile. So Monsanto launched the new container.

Just a few years later (in 1977), the FDA issued an edict that banned Cycle-Safe. Monsanto believes that this action was largely the result of the intense environmental concerns that permeated society at the time. The company is pursuing legal action.[1] The Cycle-Safe story illustrates how difficult it is to predict the future.

Chapter 22 deals with the topic generally labeled *futurology*, which will have considerable impact on management in the 1980s. Futurology is the discipline of predicting future trends and events, including new developments in technology and government regulation.

Not all predictions prove to be accurate assessments of future events. Many forecasts are substantially off target and must be altered or discarded. Others prove essentially true, but only in a different time frame than originally envisioned. Still others are lost in comparison with larger, more significant trends, or are at least partially offset by countertrends. Twenty-five years ago, a common prediction was that managers in the 1980s would commute to and from work in their personal helicopters. In some cases people will magnify current events and unjustifiably extrapolate them into the future.

> **Futurology is the discipline of predicting future trends and events such as new technological developments.**

[1] John W. Hanley (interviewed by David W. Ewing and Millicent R. Kindle), "Monsanto's 'Early Warning' System," *Harvard Business Review* (November–December 1981), pp. 107–116.

**MARK TWAIN'S
SPECULATION**

Mark Twain once projected with tongue-in-cheek that since the Mississippi River had been shortened by floods by 150 miles between Cairo, Illinois, and New Orleans during the 18th century, it was safe to conclude that the Mississippi would continue to shrink 1.5 miles per year indefinitely. Therefore, in 800 years Cairo, Illinois, and New Orleans, Louisiana, would become a single municipality, with a single city council and a common utility company. All of which shows what a heartening yield in speculation can be extracted from a trifling amount of information.

SOURCE: Reprinted from George S. Odiorne, ''A Management Style for the Eighties,'' *University of Michigan Business Review* (March 1978), p. 2. Reprinted by permission of the publisher, the Graduate School of Business Administration, The University of Michigan.

Predictions of Future Trends Often Go Astray

Prediction is risky business. Generations of business administration students know the story of Sewell Avery's decision to protect Montgomery Ward from a post–World War II depression (that never came) by accumulating cash rather than expanding like its rival, Sears.[2] The two retailers were about the same size in 1946. Today Sears is the nation's largest retailer, more than three times the size of its competitor.

Similar examples are abundant. Underwood—once the big name in office machines but now only part of Olivetti—passed up the electric typewriter. Curtiss-Wright—the equal of Douglas and Boeing combined in 1945—decided to put its money into an improved piston engine instead of jets.[3] When it finally did get into jets, Curtiss-Wright's management poured millions of dollars into ill-fated projects, such as trying to get the government order for an SST engine.[4]

Kemmons Wilson is the person who best symbolizes America's hospitality industry. Wilson fulfilled novelist Sinclair Lewis' earlier prediction that someone would become rich by offering a national chain of standardized hotels. A self-made millionaire builder, Wilson set off on a family vacation in 1951. The family's unpleasant experiences in several motels convinced him that standardized, quality motels would be well received by travelers.

He built the first Holiday Inn on Sumner Avenue in his hometown of Memphis. The phenomenal growth of Holiday Inns is now one of the greatest success stories in United States management history. Kemmons Wilson had the foresight to predict the hospitality industry of the future and the courage to take the management actions necessary to fulfill his vision.

But even a successful manager like Kemmons Wilson can make a business mistake. Wilson admits that one of his worst errors was a decision not to invest in a contract of a young Memphis rock singer—Elvis Presley.[5]

[2] *Forbes* (September 15, 1978), Portfolio 87.
[3] *Forbes* (September 15, 1978), Portfolio 88.
[4] "The Battle of the Lightweights," *Forbes* (May 1, 1978), p. 24.
[5] Kemmons Wilson's story is chronicled in John F. Mariane, "If You Haven't Slept in His Bed, You Must Have Tasted His Tobasco," *Detroit News Magazine* (April 16, 1978), pp. 44–48.

Much can be learned by reviewing earlier predictions. David Sarnoff first attracted attention as the telegraph operator who received the *Titanic's* SOS,[6] and later went on to build RCA into a major corporation. He was an extremely perceptive manager whom *Forbes* once called "one of the most compelling figures in American business life for nearly half a century."[7] Sarnoff selected "Twenty Years from Now: A Forecast" as the title for an after-dinner talk at his Golden Anniversary banquet in September 1956. His selection of "twenty major developments likely to affect all of us" shows how far predictions can go astray.

Management prognosticators must deal with a multitude of factors in at-

[6] *Forbes* (September 15, 1977), Portfolio 32.
[7] "The Future That Never Came," *Forbes* (July 10, 1978), p. 51.

SARNOFF'S TWENTY PREDICTIONS—A FEW HITS, MANY MISSES

1. Nuclear energy would power industry and home life, fuel planes, trains, ships and automobiles.
2. The use of solar rays effectively harnessed worldwide.
3. Global television.
4. Rocket-type vehicles traveling 5,000 mph. Guided missiles to transport mail.
5. A "crescendo" of automation through cheap power that would increase employment and leisure.
6. New materials to meet any imaginable need through chemical breakthroughs.
7. Electroluminescent light would change the appearance of our lives.
8. Computers to do tedious and complicated business and industrial jobs.
9. Every conceivable scientific improvement would combine to greatly expand mankind's food resources and eliminate famine.
10. An avalanche of improvements in preventive medicine through scientific advances, plus an extension of man's life span to near 100 years.
11. An all-automatic home. House chores done electronically.
12. Year-ahead weather forecasts and weather control.
13. The fall of Soviet Communism.
14. The emergence of people's capitalism and the decline of the Marxist and Socialist ideal.
15. An era of relative economic abundance in which the intelligent use of leisure time will be the workingman's most pressing problem.
16. Universal education and a seller's market for brains.
17. Every form of art and entertainment will be readily accessible in the home.
18. Public opinion will be more important in politics because of access to information.
19. A world shrunk by communications and speedy transportation will find it necessary to effect arms controls.
20. The gradual elimination of physical hungers will whet appetites for spiritual salvation among the temporally satisfied.

SOURCE: Reprinted from "The Future That Never Came," *Forbes* (July 10, 1978), p. 52.

Edith Weiner, a principal and executive vice-president of Weiner, Edrich, Brown, Inc., consultants in the management of change and strategic planning, has a somewhat unorthodox view of the energy crisis of the 1970s. "It was the best thing that happened to industry," said Weiner, as she sat in her office high above the streets of Manhattan. "Executives had been talking about the country's energy dependency since the early 1950s but never did anything about it. It took the OPEC stranglehold to make them understand that their old way of doing business—and of planning—simply had no relevance to the future."

According to Weiner the energy crisis taught companies that they could not use straight historical projections to predict the future costs, competition, and health of their business as they did in the past. Instead, they must begin to understand how social, economic, technological, and political forces come together and leave clues as to what the future might bring. "I'm talking about an interdisciplinary approach to anticipating the future," said Weiner. "If you take just one narrow view, your future vision is bound to fail."

Through her firm's Strategic Trend Evaluation Process, Weiner helps executives in some of the nation's largest firms, including Philip Morris, Bristol-Myers, American Express, and Sears, Roebuck & Co., put together these diverse trends and apply them to their businesses. No crystal ball reading is involved. Rather, Weiner and her associate Arnold Brown systematically read over fifty publications each month, ranging from the *Harvard Business Review* to *Mother Jones*, attend numerous conferences and meetings, review research in various fields, and listen to the feedback they get from their client-executives who come together in small groups to discuss their visions of the future. As Weiner points out, this is far more than an academic exercise. "We're interested in seeing executives integrate the information they get here throughout their firms."

Weiner's effect on corporate policy was felt during the early 1970s when, as director of the futures research program for the entire life insurance business—a program that became known as the foremost environmental scanning program in American business—she began spotting changes in the traditional American life

tempting to assess future business trends. These include changes in the environment for decision making, changes in the rate of change itself, structural changes in our industrial society, and variation in the timing of changes. All can have a significant impact on management.

The Changing Nature of Change Itself

Change itself is inconsistent! Executives who have grown accustomed to fast-paced but consistent change within broad overall trends have had to readjust to a dynamic environment in which even our basic managerial premises are questioned. Managerial concepts like zero-base budgeting—the mandatory periodic justification of any expenditure program, not just incremental changes in such a program—has forced managers to rethink some of the basic precepts upon which they act.

But even more basic questions might arise in the future. Can we assume a relatively stable political and social environment in which to conduct future

cycle that she believed would radically affect the life insurance market. "We were looking at a lot of different signals that up until then were treated as discrete bits of information," said Weiner. "Changes in the retirement age, for example, the growth of adult education, the high rate of divorce, serial marriage, and single parent families, and the growth of the day care industry told us that it was time to redefine the life cycle and reevaluate its impact on work, education, the family—and the purchase of life insurance."

As a result of Weiner's recommendations, one of the nation's largest life insurance companies developed the concept of life cycle life insurance, which within two years of its introduction accounted for more than half the company's premium income. "The company realized," said Weiner, "that the days of marketing life insurance policies that remained static throughout the people's lives were over. They also realized that working women with family financial responsibilities were becoming an increasingly large, untapped market."

Through her consulting work, her writings in such prestigious journals as the *Harvard Business Review* and *Planning Review,* her seat on the executive board of the U.S. Association for the Club of Rome, her membership on the board of directors of Union Mutual Life Insurance Co. (to which she was elected at the age of twenty-eight), appearances before Congress and on nationwide TV, Edith Weiner has made a mark on the future of business management even before that future arrived. Despite the complexity of her field, her overall advice to managers boils down to just three messages: Look to the entrepreneurial spirits within the corporation—those independent souls willing to take risks in order to get the job done—for real progress. Look also to the intelligence and sensitivity of all workers at every level of the organization for answers to the problems that have stymied traditional managers, who seem always to be seeking quantifiable results. And finally, look forward in a systematic way. "Managers have to realize," said Weiner, "that trying to piece together clues to the future is not a frivolous exercise. It is the difference between a successful organization and a company that ceases to grow and understand where its real competition will come from."

Sources

Roger Ricklefs, "Firm Helping Bosses Focus on the Future," *The Wall Street Journal* (October 5, 1981), p. 31.

Edith Weiner, biographical sketch provided by Weiner, Edrich, Brown, Inc., 200 E. 33rd Street, New York, N.Y.

business? Can we assume an ongoing source of supply? Can we expect the dollar to remain the pillar of worldwide trade? Can we assume that tomorrow's employees will have the same value system as that of their predecessors? Can we assume ample financial incentives for business risk-taking?

Let's look at the changing nature of change itself. Future-oriented managers must be cognizant of how change is occurring as well as the trends that are expected to dominate business.

CHANGES ARE OCCURRING AT A DIFFERENT RATE THAN IN THE PAST

Alvin Toffler used the term *future shock* to indicate our problems in dealing with sudden changes in our society and technology. Toffler observed that "events are occurring so fast that we forget them before we have had a chance to learn from them."[8] This comment is quite appropriate for the current level of

Future shock is the term Alvin Toffler used to indicate the problems in dealing with sudden changes in society and technology.

[8] Remarks to the World Future Society's Second General Assembly in Washington, D.C. Quoted in *Futurist* (October 1975), p. 228.

management development. Modern managers are hard pressed to stay abreast of the changes that occur about them and of which they are a part. New products are being introduced at an amazing pace; employees, customers, and vendors are all changing; and the effective manager has to keep up if he or she is to succeed.

There has also been a knowledge explosion within management science itself. Aside from numerous changes in the operational environment, the management role is also changing at the same time. Management theories, techniques, and procedures are constantly evolving in response to environmental change. The recent popularity of Theory Z is an example. Even the best-prepared manager is soon outdated unless he or she consciously realizes this evolutionary process and takes corrective action. Further education and executive development program participation are now becoming prerequisites to further advancement for many managers.

THE ENVIRONMENT FOR DECISION MAKING IS CHANGING

Earlier chapters pointed out that managers must make decisions within the constraints prescribed by the societies in which they operate. Modern managers are faced with changing circumstances in which to do business. Both government and private citizens have forced these modifications.

Some local zoning boards are far more restrictive with commercial building permits than they were in the past. OSHA places specific restraints on many parts of the organization. Minimum wage legislation is having a noticeable effect on industries that have historically relied on relatively low-wage (and low-skill) labor. The centralized kitchens of restaurant chains illustrate how some labor-oriented industries are moving toward a greater emphasis on capital investment. Government—at all levels—is having an obvious impact on the types of decisions managers make.

Private groups and individuals also have affected the decision-making setting. What corporate office does not fear the perennial gadfly's questions at the next stockholders' meeting? Environmentalists have suppressed the development of nuclear energy in the United States. Citizen groups picket firms allegedly causing pollution. Every television station and newspaper has investigative reporters ready to pounce on almost any managerial indiscretion. Contemporary decision making is also complicated by the various special interest groups willing to make their opinions heard.

STRUCTURAL CHANGES ARE OCCURRING IN OUR INDUSTRIAL SOCIETY

Our industrial society is experiencing basic structural changes. Consider just a few:

Today, there are more single people and households headed by single parents.

More married women are working than ever before in United States history.

The birthrate has declined significantly in recent years.

These statistics suggest the basic structural changes that are occurring in our industrialized society. Effective managers must be aware of such trends, and they must be adaptive in dealing with them. An increased number of singles means that both employees and consumers may exhibit different value systems than those of their predecessors.

Significant new market opportunities present themselves. Examples include the frozen food products and cookware designed for single person households. More women in the work force—particularly at professional levels—may require adjustments by some male counterparts. In addition, these women will have to seek out their own particular niche and areas of expertise within the organization. More working women also create a need for child-care facilities. Fewer younger people raises the possibility that future managers may face selected labor shortages and a smaller market for certain products. Demographic and societal changes will have a decided effect on how future managers operate.

THE TIMING OF CHANGES VARIES

Many managers are conditioned to constant change. Something is happening every day for these executives. Even change itself can become an accepted, traditional aspect of one's job and environment. But what happens when the timing of such change is altered?

Many decision makers are at a loss when there is no crisis awaiting their attention. Rapid change in some industries has produced a generation of what might be called *crisis managers.* These people become so used to dealing with supposed emergency situations that they cannot adapt to a normal decision-making framework.

Management experts are constantly pointing out that many industries may have slower growth in the future. Managers will no longer be able to count on 10 percent annual sales increases and the like. But slow growth does not eliminate change. In fact, adapting to change may be all the more important since additional volume will probably have to come at the expense of competitors. Heightened competition can be expected under slow growth situations. William Agee, former president of Allied Corp. and chairman of Bendix Corp., puts it this way: "The successful managers of the eighties will be those who can manage a slower rate of growth and react very quickly to changing opportunities."[9]

Future Uncertainty Makes Effective Planning Vital to Managers

An action by General Electric illustrates management's realization that assessments of a wide range of future events can have a significant influence on a firm's success. GE created a Business Environment Studies group in 1967 to ex-

[9] William M. Agee, "Futurism: A Lesson from the Private Sector," *Business Horizons* (June 1978), p. 16.

PREDICTING THE FUTURE HAS BECOME AN INCREASINGLY SOPHISTICATED ACTIVITY

SOURCE: *The Wall Street Journal* (September 22, 1982), p. 29. Reprinted by permission of Cartoon Features Syndicate.

"I never use my crystal ball anymore."

amine various long-run political and social trends and to see how these possibilities could affect the company. General Electric's management later set up a strategic planning system that employed its long-term environmental forecast.[10]

General Electric's management clearly recognized the integral relationship between effective planning and future managerial decision making. Chapter 5 noted the importance of planning in the overall process of managing any organization. The uncertainty of future events demonstrates why planning is so important in modern business.

Contingency plans provide alternative scenarios for use in case of deviations from expected trends.

Plans must be developed to cope with expected long-run trends. But even these are not enough. *Contingency plans* that account for deviations in expected trends and happenings are also a must. Consider the possible contingencies that must be evaluated. Examples might include the further implementation of matrix or project management formats; adoption of new management styles like Theory Z or Yugoslav plant democracy types; and structural changes such as a significant increase in public ownership. While none of these are dominating factors in contemporary management, all must be considered in the future. Contingency planning is what allows some managers to succeed where others fail.

Identifying major trends affecting management is an important, yet difficult, task. A variety of countertrends exist, and these may in time come to replace the basic premises upon which management operates. The need for contingency plans to deal with all eventualities is obvious.

Trends and Countertrends

No list of trends could ever hope to be complete. And when complicated with a multiplicity of countertrends, it is easy to envision the problems faced by current and future managers. This section introduces some trends and countertrends that may influence tomorrow's decision makers.

[10] Ian H. Wilson, "Business Management and the Winds of Change," *Journal of Contemporary Business* (Winter 1978), pp. 46–47.

Let's start by identifying some prevailing trends:

1. Greater government involvement in all phases of business
2. An activist consumerism movement
3. An information explosion induced by increasingly sophisticated computer hardware and software
4. More participative and open organizations as evidenced by open office configurations, MBO procedures, and shared decision making
5. Egalitarianism in an advanced society
6. Increased environmental concerns
7. Bureaucracy, with its emphasis on accumulating staff and responsibilities
8. Emphasis on job enlargement and enrichment

While many others could be identified, most readers might agree that there is evidence to support the trends listed here. But are all these trends as clear-cut as they initially appear?

The answer an obvious "no." There are numerous countertrends, thus confusing management's task of predicting the future events that will affect business. Figure 22-1 suggests some of the trends and countertrends.

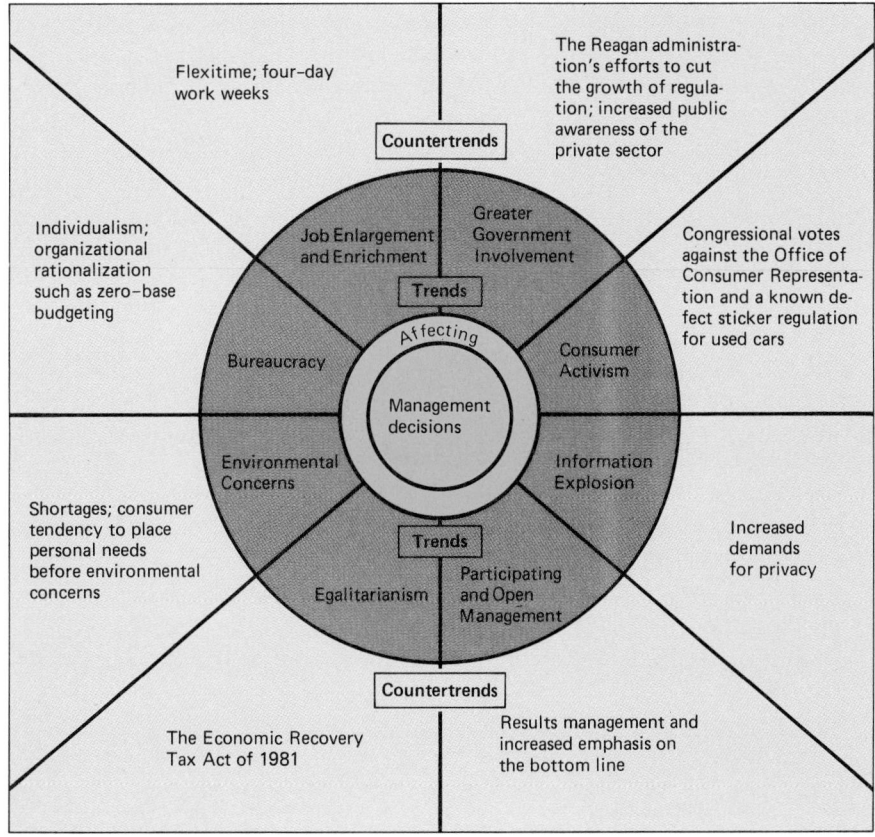

**Figure 22-1
TRENDS AND
COUNTERTRENDS
AFFECTING
MANAGEMENT
DECISIONS**

Growing government interference in business has been a traditional topic of discussion in management circles. But the Reagan administration has sought to moderate this interference by cutting the growth of federal regulations. Public recognition of the importance of the private sector has also greatly increased in recent years.

Similarly, the consumerism movement has begun to meet resistance from both legislators and the general public. The Office of Consumer Representation was voted down in Congress, which also overturned a regulation requiring known defect notices on used cars. Just a few years ago, voting against these items would have been political suicide. Generally, the indictments of consumer advocates no longer carry the weight they once did, as the public tires of claims of new health and safety threats and the cost of added regulations.

The *information explosion*—a diffusion of excessive amounts of data that is often directed to the wrong people—was created by significantly enhanced computing ability. It has led to a situation whereby data storage and retrieval is viewed as a national problem by many. Increased demands for privacy are common today. Chapter 16 also pointed out management's current need to gain systematic control over information if it is to be harnessed and employed in the accomplishment of organizational objectives.

The open, participative management style that we have come to accept as the norm faces a renewed challenge from those who argue that management is responsible for results—the *bottom line*. Even some union officials take the position that management should be concerned with operations and results, and unions with employee welfare. Participative management might then be viewed as an infringement on union prerogatives.

The bottom line refers to the final results of an action or management decision.

Egalitarianism is the premise that the economic stature of all members of society should be as equal as possible. Redistribution of income schemes, progressive income tax rates, public welfare systems, and automatic cost-of-living social security increases are illustrative of this concept. Only recently has anyone dared object to these ideas.

Egalitarianism is the premise that the economic stature of all members of society should be as equal as possible.

The need to provide an adequate incentive for industry is quite prevalent in a nation whose annual productivity gain between 1973 and 1980 was less than 2 percent. By comparison, Japan had a 6.8 percent annual gain, and Belgium posted a 6.2 percent yearly growth.[11] The Economic Recovery Tax Act of 1981 provides such tax relief. The 1981 legislation also provided for individual across-the-board tax cuts that benefited all strata of society rather than just the lowest income groups.

Environmental concerns are popular. When shortages or inconvenience threaten an accepted lifestyle, however, the public is quick to switch allegiance. Many writers have noted that the public typically supports environmental concerns but is not willing to pay for them.

Bureaucracy characterizes many large organizations—both public and private. Some large corporations are every bit as bureaucratic as those government enti-

---

[11] Patricia Capdevielle and Donato Alvarez, "International Comparisons of Trends in Productivity and Labor Costs," *Monthly Labor Review* (December 1981), p. 15.

ties that executives are prone to criticize. A collection of countertrends exists to combat growing bureaucracy. A revival of individualism among younger workers is most promising. Zero-base budgeting and similar techniques call for at least a periodic review of the reasons for engaging in any activity. Such practices could have a considerable impact on future organizations. There seems to be a renewed interest in maintaining lean, viable, and competitive organizations.

Job enrichment and enlargement programs are well documented in American industry. A countertrend seems to argue that the personal satisfaction to be obtained from any job is limited, making increased leisure time desirable. Four-day work weeks mean longer working hours but limit the length of the work week. Again, the emphasis is on making nonworking time more enjoyable.

The Future Manager

This section could just as well have been titled "How Not to Become an Obsolete Manager" because that is really what it concerns. It is easy to become an *obsolete manager,* one who has outstayed his or her usefulness to the organization. Even successful managers can become obsolete managers. All executives assume their posts with a given set of personal strengths, educational qualifications, experience, and so forth. If they succeed it is reasonable to conclude that their abilities were right for the managerial situations that existed. But, over time, these managers can become stale. They may fail to keep up with advancements in managerial techniques; industry trends; changes in their employees, customers, and other stakeholders; or technological advances. In short, they have become obsolete managers trained and experienced in dealing with circumstances that no longer exist.

Future-oriented managers, by contrast, are those who think ahead and take appropriate steps to stay ahead. They keep up with events and changes in philosophy, thought, and theories. They are well read and probably participate in con-

An obsolete manager is one who has outstayed his or her usefulness to the organization.

Retired General Electric board chairman Reginald Jones expects future managers to have a different set of attributes than do current managers:

"More of them will be women, and more will be of ethnic and racial backgrounds that are not being widely utilized today.

"Broader persons intellectually . . . capable of relating their business life to the wider stream of human experience.

"More sensitive to corporate social responsibilities.

"Much greater political sophistication."

SOURCE: Quoted in Perry Pascarella and Daniel D. Cook, "2000 Future Focus Management. Can You Win?" *Industry Week* (January 23, 1978), p. 79.

A TOP EXECUTIVE LOOKS AT FUTURE MANAGERS

tinuing education programs both directly and indirectly related to their work. Future-oriented managers are also good listeners; they realize that much can be learned from even the most casual conversation. Above all, future-oriented managers attempt to broaden their experience, seeking out additional and varied responsibilities that will lead to further professional development.

Management style will also vary in the years ahead. Ten elements of a management style for the 1980s have been identified by George S. Odiorne. Obviously, these are broad generalizations subject to numerous exceptions. But the elements do form a conceptual basis for counseling tomorrow's managers. Odiorne's elements are

1. *Less bureaucratic, more individualistic.* The countertrend identified earlier is predicted to become the accepted operational method of the future.
2. *More systematic.* Wide adoption of the systems approach will be facilitated by the availability of mini- and microcomputers.
3. *Development centered management.* Increased attention will be given to developing the organization's human resources.
4. *Situational management.* Directive and charismatic leadership will be replaced by contingency management.
5. *Management by commitment.* Effective managers will seek personal commitments from their employees and then hold them responsible for their performance.
6. *Achievement motivation.* A high achievement orientation in managers usually means that their organizations accomplish more.
7. *Group management processes.* Team building will be stressed from the board of directors down. Task forces will be used in a more innovative fashion.
8. *Due process in personnel decisions.* Due process protection will become an integral part of most personnel procedures.
9. *Management by information.* Accurate, timely information will be the key to good management communications systems.
10. *Physical aspects of the workplace.* Tomorrow's workplace will be altered by the desire to improve occupational health, safety, and security and employee motivation.[12]

Today's management student has an interesting opportunity to assess history. Simply file this book away on an appropriate bookshelf and then pull it out again in, say, twenty years. It might be informative to see if the ideas presented in this chapter prove any more accurate than the predictions offered by David Sarnoff in 1956.

---

[12] George S. Odiorne, "A Management Style for the Eighties," *University of Michigan Business Review* (March 1978), pp. 3–6. Reprinted by permission of the publisher, the Graduate School of Business Administration, The University of Michigan.

MEGATRENDS—THE
LATEST SET OF
PREDICTIONS

John Naisbitt's recent book *Megatrends* was based on what is called *content analysis,* whereby major societal trends are spotted in the monitoring of 6,000 local newspapers. Naisbitt's research indicates that most changes first occur in one of the five bellwether states, led by California. The second leading trend-setter is Florida. The other three are Washington, Colorado, and Connecticut.

Naisbitt lists ten megatrends impacting American society:

1. The United States has shifted from an industrial society to one of information creation and distribution.
2. The country has also moved from forced technology producing regimental outputs to high tech/high touch systems, or a blend of innovative new technology and a counterbalancing human response.
3. We have shifted from a national economy to a world economy, a trend we are beginning to acknowledge.
4. Management is shifting from short-term to long-term orientation.
5. Centralization is being replaced by decentralization throughout U.S. society.
6. Americans are now relying on self-help approaches rather than institutional help.
7. There is a move from representative democracy to participatory democracy in various sectors of U.S. society—government, business, and the marketplace.
8. Hierarchical organizational structures are being replaced by informal organizations and communications, often called *networking.*
9. Population, wealth, and the economic base have been transferred from the North to the South. Actually, the shift to the South is really a shift to Florida and to the southwestern and western states.
10. Personal choices are now being greatly expanded. Americans now have multiple rather than either/or options in their personal lives.

SOURCE: Reprinted by permission of Warner Books/New York from *Megatrends.* Copyright © 1982 by John Naisbitt.

Summary

Some managers are able to forecast future business trends accurately. But predictions are often inaccurate and may lead to substantial managerial errors, such as when Sewell Avery restrained Montgomery Ward's growth after World War II. A great deal can be learned by reviewing earlier forecasts to see where they went wrong.

Numerous factors can affect future trends in management and business. These include

1. Changes in the environment for decision making
2. Changes in the rate of change itself
3. Structural changes in our industrial society
4. Variation in the timing of changes

These uncertainties make an effective planning function vital to management. General Electric's Business Environment Studies group illustrates this concern with the impact of future political and social trends.

A variety of trends and countertrends affect management decisions. The information explosion is partially offset by the desire for greater privacy, and the bureaucratic tendencies of large organizations are countered by the growing individualism of employees and others.

Figure 22-1 illustrates some of the trends and counter-trends of today that are expected to influence future management decisions.

Even successful executives can become professionally obsolete if they do not keep abreast of developments in management theory and practice, industry trends, changes in employees, customers, and other stakeholders, and technological developments. Effective managers for the coming decade are those who keep up to date, think ahead, and take appropriate action to remain viable leaders. Chapter 22 concludes with some elements of a management style that is

expected to predominate in the 1980s:

1. Less bureaucratic, more individualistic
2. More systematic
3. Development centered management
4. Situational management
5. Management by commitment
6. Achievement motivation
7. Group management processes
8. Due process in personnel decisions
9. Management by information
10. Physical aspects of the workplace

REVIEW EXERCISES

1. Define the following terms: (a) futurology (b) future shock (c) contingency plans (d) information explosion (e) bottom line (f) egalitarianism (g) obsolete manager.

2. Discuss the basic points made in the managerial profile.

3. Given their failure to predict the regulatory environment for Cycle-Safe, should Monsanto discontinue their efforts to assess the future for new products? Why or why not?

4. Why is it difficult to predict future management and business trends?

5. Evaluate the accuracy of David Sarnoff's predictions made in 1956.

6. Why did General Electric create a Business Environment Studies group?

7. Identify the various trends and countertrends that may have an impact on future management decisions.

8. Contrast the future-oriented manager with the obsolete manager.

9. Identify and briefly explain George Odiorne's ten elements of management style for the 1980s.

ASSIGNMENTS/ PROBLEMS/ DISCUSSION QUESTIONS

1. Albert Einstein once remarked: "I never think of the future. It comes soon enough." Would Einstein's observation be an appropriate philosophy for a manager in the 1980s? Comment.

2. Prepare a report on a management decision that was based on an incorrect assessment of the future. What can be learned from this incident?

3. Prepare a report on the current status of futurology as a field of study. What is your evaluation of this discipline?

4. Management expert George S. Odiorne has remarked: "Too often, managerial reactions are responding to the environment of the fading decade when the new one engulfs them. In part, this is because problems and solutions require lead time, and lead time appears to be collapsing on management."* Do you agree with Odiorne's comments? Explain.

5. Peter Drucker has commented that "Forecasting is not a respectable human activity."† What do you think is the basis of this remark?

* George S. Odiorne, "A Management Style for the Eighties," *University of Michigan Business Review* (March 1978), p. 2.

† Quoted in Terry W. Rothermel, "Forecasting Resurrected," *Harvard Business Review* (March–April 1982), p. 139.

A MANAGERIAL INCIDENT

Howard Johnson Looks at the Future

Howard Johnson, son of the food and lodging company founder, faced a unique management problem. Howard Johnson Co., with little debt and substantial cash, had been consistently outpaced by its competition in recent years. Johnson put it this way:

I have to react to a whole new way of eating in the U.S. We face the danger of being thought of as a company that did things so well one way that everyone figures that is the only way we can do it. So we must change not only our business but our image.

An environmental factor—the energy crisis—played havoc with Johnson's expansion plans in the 1970s. "My plans got stalled in the 1974 oil embargo," he explains. "I overreacted, I stopped all expansion, and once you stop, you know how hard it is to get the monster going again. For me the embargo was a shocking thing. Highway travel went down and we saw some startling internal numbers."

Howard Johnson Co. was subsequently acquired by Imperial Group, Ltd. This British firm still faces the task of anticipating future trends in lodging and eating and changing the Howard Johnson image accordingly.

In January 1982, Howard Johnson retired as company chairman, president, and chief executive officer. He was replaced by G. Michael Hostage, former chairman, president, and chief executive officer of the ITT-Continental Bakery Co., who described the challenge before him in this way: "The industry itself is moving forward and in order to catch up we have to move relatively faster than we would have to just keep pace. And that's difficult. . . . Our problems didn't come in a year and it's not very realistic to think they can be resolved in a year."

SOURCES: "To Be and What to Be—That Is the Question," *Forbes* (May 1, 1978), p. 25; "Hostage on Howard Johnson's," *Landmark* III, no. 2 (April 1982), 5.

Questions and Problems

1. Do you agree with Hostage's assessment of the managerial problems facing his firm?

2. What can be learned from Johnson's response to the oil embargo?

3. What management action would you propose for Howard Johnson Co.?

23.
Careers in Management

You can't push anyone up the ladder
unless he is willing to climb himself.

> ANDREW CARNEGIE

It is simple, although not easy, to become a millionaire. Get a part-time job
on Saturdays and do it for 10 years.
Then take that money and invest it at
12 percent, wait 10 more years, and
you're a millionaire. However, most
people don't want to give up their free
time for 10 years. I've been working
Saturdays since I was 16.

> DR. JERRY BUSS
> *Owner of the Los Angeles Lakers,*
> *Kings, Stings, and Forum,*
> *among other things*

Quentin Thomas, the new twenty-nine-year-old vice-president of a major New York bank, often talks in glowing terms about his former employer, the Cleveland Trust—which he left because of inadequate advancement opportunities. Sound strange?

Not at Cleveland Trust. Thomas had participated in the bank's executive career development program, which includes an individual career assessment; information on career opportunities at Cleveland Trust; development of career plans at the bank; and, for those who desire it, an outplacement service[1] that helps the person find a more suitable position with another employer. The bank's program involves employees, supervisors, senior management, and the personnel department. The emphasis is on matching personal career objectives with available career opportunities, whether or not these are at Cleveland Trust.

Thomas had originally been hired in the lending area, where substantial opportunity to advance to bank officer status was thought to exist. But the number of these projected openings was later reduced, and the promotion pace slowed. Thomas entered the bank's career development program and he eventually got the New York job with Cleveland Trust's help.[2] Quentin Thomas' experience at the Cleveland Trust illustrates the importance of having a career plan.

---

[1] Outplacement is explained fully in a later section of Chapter 23.

[2] Quentin Thomas' experience and the Cleveland Trust programs are described in Robert E. Hastings, "Career Development: Maximizing Options," *Personnel Administrator* (May 1978), pp. 58–61.

Effective career development programs are vital to both employers and employees. Companies need to know who will be available for what slots and with what qualifications. For the individual, good career planning allows him or her to work toward goals and achieve success in all endeavors. A successful career usually means that the individual will be satisfied with his or her personal life also. A longitudinal study of a group of male college graduates revealed that career success was related to adaptability to situations, and that this flexibility was as important to one's personal life as it was to one's business life.[3]

A satisfactory career is closely linked with happiness in other areas. An old Chinese proverb says, "Of all the unhappy people in the world, the unhappiest are those who have not found something they want to do."[4]

The Job Search Process

The initial job search is the beginning step in a management career. Some would-be managers view this effort too lightly, rationalizing that since they do not realistically expect to spend a lifetime with a single employer, their initial selection is not that critical. They are anxious to get started on their career.

Most experts conclude that one's initial job search indicates much about how that person will function as an employee. Careful preparation and execution suggest competence in later work. It is an important decision that should not be slighted.

The basic stages of the job search process are as follows:

1. Conduct preparatory research.
2. Identify prospective employers.
3. Initiate employment contacts.
4. Evaluate opportunities.

While the discussion here is specifically oriented to the entry-level job seeker, many of the points are relevant to an experienced person desiring to switch jobs.

PREPARATORY RESEARCH

Whether college students realize it or not, preparatory research begins with their selection of courses. Other factors such as program requirements, reputation of the instructor, and the time sequences for the class are also important variables. But the starting point should be some general scheme of how a course will help the person meet overall career and personal goals. Advisors, counselors, aptitude tests, instructors, family, and friends can all have an input into one's decision.

---

[3] This study is discussed in "Living Well Is More than the Best Revenge," *Forbes* (December 1, 1977), pp. 62–63.
[4] Quoted in *Sparks from the Anvil* (Concordville, Pa.: Clemprint, 1978), p. 13.

But all students should develop a broad plan for their future worklife. Case histories of successful people often show that they have done considerable planning in this area. The process for most people is to determine who they are (what talents or strengths they offer), where they are going (a career plan), and how to get there (a strategy for achieving their career objectives).

IDENTIFYING PROSPECTIVE EMPLOYERS

A well-prepared job seeker should be ready to identify employers that might fulfill his or her employment objectives and be receptive to the skills and potentials offered by the individual. Trade association listings, college placement offices, private and state employment agencies, personal contacts, and the like can be rich information sources for prospective employers.

Job seekers should direct their efforts toward specific employers rather than using a "shotgun" approach and contacting every available employment source. Career decisions are too important to be left to chance, and proper targeting of the job search effort is vital. Once the companies have been listed, the job seeker should attempt to identify the specific individual in the organization who is responsible for hiring entry-level personnel. Perhaps there is more than one person involved.

INITIATING EMPLOYMENT CONTACTS

Initial employment contacts may come in various ways. These include

1. Mailing resumes to prospective employers
2. Responding to advertisements
3. Organizing initial interviews through college placement offices
4. Telephone inquiries
5. Referrals from other people
6. Personal contacts

A key aspect of any initial contact is to provide a resume or vita to a prospective employer. A *resume* is a summary of one's qualifications for employment. It typically contains personal data, education, work experience, and information regarding references. Figure 23-1 shows a brief resume that would be appropriate for initial contacts.

Job applicants are often asked to complete a job application form as part of their initial contact with an employer. The *job application* is a form designed to obtain information that will allow the employer to determine if the job seeker meets basic qualifications and is suitable for further screening. The type of job application used by Random House, Inc., is shown in Figure 23-2. Note that it contains much of the information included in a typical resume for a management position.

A resume is a summary of one's qualifications for employment.

Job application is a form designed to obtain information that will allow the employer to determine if the job seeker meets basic qualifications and is suitable for further screening.

Resume
PAUL DONNELLY

Address: 201 East 50th Street
New York, N.Y. 10022

Phone: 212–987–6543
Age: 23
Social Security Number: 000–00–0001

Education: A.A. Bronx Community College (1981)
B.S.B.A. Pace University (1983)

Studied business administration; overall gradepoint average was 3.01.

Related Work Experience:
Evening Manager (1981 to date)
Lugiono's Family Restaurant
New York, New York

Sales Representative (1979–1981)
Books Unlimited
New York, New York

Financed all college expenses from these jobs.
Employment Objective: An entry-level position that offers opportunity to advance to supervisory and managerial roles in accordance with performance. My long-run objective is top management.

Personal: • avid tennis player
• well read with a preference for politics and historical novels

References: Personal, college, and job references are available upon request.

Interview is a personal meeting in which the employer evaluates a prospective employee and the applicant assesses opportunities offered by the firm.

If the employer decides to consider a candidate further, an interview will be arranged. An *interview* is a personal meeting in which the employer evaluates a prospective employee and the applicant assesses opportunities offered by the firm. In some cases interviews may be arranged directly, such as in the case of a student signing up for a campus interview. Employment interviews can be classified as screening interviews and selection interviews. In a *screening interview*, the employer makes an initial evaluation of a candidate's qualifications, rejecting those who do not meet essential requirements and arranging additional interviews for those deemed worthy of further consideration. A *selection interview* usually follows a screening interview and is longer, more detailed, and typically involves several managers. Actual hiring decisions are made on the basis of selection interviews.

How should one prepare for an interview? The first bit of advice would be *to prepare*. Recruiters often complain of applicants who are totally unprepared for

DATE OF APPLICATION _____

RANDOM HOUSE INC.

EMPLOYMENT APPLICATION

AN EQUAL OPPORTUNITY EMPLOYER

INSTRUCTIONS

1. Type or print in ink.
2. Answer each question fully and accurately. Use additional sheet, if necessary.
3. Do not include information regarding race, color, religion, age or national origin.
4. Read declaration carefully — then sign and date form.

Name	Last	First	Middle	Area Code Telephone ( )

Address	Number	Street	City	State	Zip	Social Security No.

EXPERIENCE

List All Employment - Including Previous RANDOM HOUSE, INC. Employment and U.S. Military Service - Start with Present Employer.

Dates Employed		Employer's Name and Address	Major Duties Performed
From	To		

Starting Position

Starting Salary (Base) $ Per

Terminal Position	Supervisor's Name and Title	Reason For Leaving	Last Salary (Base) $ Per

EDUCATION

Show All Formal Education Including U.S. Military Schools.

Institution and Location	Dates Attended		Graduated		Degree Received	Major and Minor Fields of Study
	From	To	Yes	No		
High School (Last Attended)						
College or University						
Other						

EMPLOYMENT INTERESTS

Describe Type of Position Desired

Date available for employment	Salary expected $ Per

Will you travel? ☐ None ☐ Occasional ☐ Frequent	Will you work nights? ☐ Yes ☐ No

MISCELLANEOUS

Reason for applying at Random House, Inc. - Referred by a Random House, Inc. employee, private employment agency, newspaper advertising, etc.	Are there any types of jobs you are not able to fully perform because of physical or mental injury, disability or disease? ☐ Yes ☐ No. If Yes, explain. Yes *will not* disqualify you from consideration for employment.
If employed, can you submit proof of U.S. Citizenship? ☐ Yes ☐ No If employed, can you submit proof of age? ☐ Yes ☐ No	

Do you have a currently effective agreement with employers or others concerning inventions you have made or may make?
☐ Yes   ☐ No   If Yes, please furnish copy of agreement and indicate the number of months the agreement remains effective after termination.
_____ Months

REFERENCES

List Former Supervisors Not Previously Shown or Others Familiar With Your Work - Exclude Relatives.

Name	Occupation	Address	Telephone
Name	Occupation	Address	Telephone
Name	Occupation	Address	Telephone

Signature of Applicant _____   Date _____

LAST NAME

FIRST

Figure 23-2   SAMPLE APPLICATION FOR EMPLOYMENT

SOME PEOPLE WILL DO ANYTHING FOR A JOB

Chutzpah. Sometimes that's what it takes to find the job you want. Author Henry Miller had it even before he wrote *Tropic of Cancer*. As a young job seeker, he was turned down after an interview with a company personnel director. Upset at the rejection, Miller stormed up to the executive office to protest. The president, after listening to Miller's outburst, decided to hire him—as the new personnel manager.

One modern-day Miller, also rejected by a personnel office, went directly to the president's office where he was stopped by the Stonewall Jackson of a secretary. Undaunted, he left the office and telephoned for the president. "I have this truckload of fish to deliver," he told the hesitant secretary. "Nobody's at his home and the fish are melting fast." The secretary, not wanting the responsibility for a load of spoiled fish, relented. An amused president hired the bright, young and very persistent fishmonger as a management trainee.

If you've reached the point of mass-mailing your resumes at bulk rates, take a tip from two New Yorkers. One invested that postage money in a sandwich board, painted "For Hire" on it, along with his qualifications, then passed out resumes as he literally pounded the pavement. An advertising agency personnel manager spotted him on the evening news and the resourceful young man traded his board for a job. Meanwhile a taxi driver, excellently located in Manhattan, taped a resume to the cab window in full view of his passengers.

The point: Be sure to inject a healthy amount of zest and imagination into the job-hunting process. It's a good way to keep yourself psyched—and it may bring some new opportunities rolling your way.

SOURCE: Reprinted with publisher's permission from *Ford's Insider: A Continuing Series of College Newspaper Supplements*, © 1980, 13–30 Corp., Knoxville, Tenn. 37902.

their interviews. Interviewees should be familiar with the company they are interviewing, its products and operations, as well as the positions for which they are interviewing. Much of this information is readily available from published sources, such as the recruiting brochures that firms provide college placement offices.

Since good interviewers allocate about two-thirds of their interview time to the comments of the job candidate, the job seeker should be well prepared to talk about himself or herself—personal background, education, job skills, and career ambitions. Different employers look for different things. Charles Revson, the cosmetics industry genius, valued intelligence more than industry experience. He once remarked, "If a man's smart, he'll learn the business in a year. If he's not smart, I don't want him."[5] When Hughes Aircraft questioned forty interview specialists about the most vital job applicant characteristics, six primary qualifications emerged:

[5] Quoted in Allan G. Mottus, "Execs Guilty of Shortsighted Talent Search," *Product Marketing* (February 1978), p. 39.

1. Specific ability
2. Ambition
3. Maturely directed energy
4. Ability to communicate
5. General intelligence and knowledge
6. Integrity[6]

Interviewees should realize that prospective employers often have biases in hiring decisions. For instance, many believe that the current generation is unwilling to work as hard as their generation did. The second and third items of the Hughes Aircraft survey indicate that employers value the work ethic highly. There is some empirical evidence to back the contention that the *work ethic*, a belief in the inherent value of work in a society, has declined.[7] Job seekers should demonstrate their "willingness to work" in an interview situation and elsewhere. The sample resume in Figure 23-1 indicated that Paul Donnelly earned all of his college expenses, signifying his basic acceptance of the traditional work ethic and a desire to succeed.

Work ethic is a belief in the inherent value of work in a society.

EVALUATING OPPORTUNITIES

The final step in the job search process is to evaluate carefully the opportunities that the candidate uncovers in his or her job search. A natural inclination is to accept the first offer and ignore other possibilities, especially in the case of persons who have engaged in an incomplete job search. One approach is to set some arbitrary time deadline for the employment decision. Employers can be informed of the decision date and alternate opportunities can be carefully analyzed before a final decision is reached.

Not all job seekers will be flooded with employment opportunities. In fact, many will be fortunate enough to get *one*. But advance preparation and an orderly, sequential job search should increase the probability of securing a better position than would otherwise be the case.

Employment Trends in Management

A working knowledge of projected employment trends is vital in career planning. The competition for desirable jobs is tough, and it is expected to become even tougher. According to Bureau of Labor Statistics estimates, between 1978 and 1990 the 13.5 million college graduates entering the labor force will find only 10.2 million job openings. Those who do not find jobs commensurate with their training will remain unemployed or be forced to accept positions not tradition-

[6] Ross Whitehead, "Interviewing—The Test Most Managers Flunk," *Industry Week* (September 18, 1978), p. 89.
[7] See Rogene A. Buchholz, "The Work Ethic Reconsidered," *Industrial & Labor Relations Review* (July 1978), p. 459.

The Academy of Management evolved from a 1936 dinner meeting arranged at the University of Chicago by a faculty member, William N. Mitchel, and Professor Charles L. Jamison of the University of Michigan. The two founders proposed setting up a professional society for management academics. Today, the academy represents 5,500 management professors and professional practitioners in thirty-seven countries. The Academy of Management conducts scholarly meetings, publishes research contributions, and generally serves as a conduit for those interested in the development of the management discipline.

John W. Slocum, Jr., currently Distinguished Professor of Organizational Behavior and Administration at Southern Methodist University, is the 1983–1984 president of the Academy of Management. Slocum, a Ph.D. from the University of Washington, is the co-author of four books on management. He has also written sixty articles on management-related subjects. Professor Slocum is an active consultant and teaches in executive development programs throughout the world.

When asked to comment on the state of management education, the Academy of Management president responded:

> Everyone knows that the business environment is changing. Consider the following events that have occurred in the past twenty-five years: (1) travel to the moon; (2) doubling of the world's population; (3) genetic manipulation; (4) development of solid state physics; (5) huge growth in wealth, consumption, education, travel, housing and mobility; and (6) development of energy resources. Not everyone fully appreciates how these events, among others, have affected business. To deal with these issues, future managers will have to study international economic conditions, law, religion, ethics, and a host of other subjects. Studying these different subjects will enable managers to deal more effectively with their environment. Twenty years ago, most managers spent relatively little time on external affairs. Today, top managers estimate that they spend up to 50 percent of their time on managing the environmental forces that affect their business. Unfortunately, these managers are being asked to make important decisions in shorter periods of time and with less information than ever before because the forces in the environment are constantly changing. The effective manager needs the ability to integrate technical skills with astute administrative skills in areas of social responsibility, corporate planning, and business–

ally sought and filled by college graduates. This has already begun to happen. Between 1969 and 1978, only about three out of four college graduates entering the labor force found traditional college graduate jobs. By contrast, nine out of ten found traditional employment in the period 1962–1969.[8]

COLLEGE—A GOOD INVESTMENT

Education is an important advantage in the labor force. The average male college graduate earns 33 percent more than someone with just a high school diploma. And those with five or more years of college education earn 14 percent

[8] "RE Job Outlook for College Graduates Through 1990," *Occupational Outlook Quarterly* (Winter 1979), pp. 6–7; *Occupational Outlook Handbook, 1982–1983 Edition* (Washington, D.C.: Government Printing Office, Bureau of Labor Statistics, 1982), p. 14.

government relations. At some organizations, the ability of the manager to handle these sensitive areas is among the key criteria for promotion.

How have these changes affected business education? The manager in the fifties and sixties learned technical skills, assumed that people made rational decisions, established fairly structured organizations, relied on the organization to clarify people's roles and job duties, and expected a long tenure with the firm. The manager of the eighties will have to learn how to deal with ambiguity and conflict, temporary assignments, contingency plans, interdisciplinary team assignments to handle novel decisions (e.g., putting a man on the moon, test tube babies, and the like).

While noting that no comprehensive list can be prescribed, Professor Slocum suggested that a manager of 1990s will need to possess the following traits:

First, a thorough knowledge of the economic and technical characteristics of the business.

Second, the ability to lead others to achieve the objectives of the company. The business leader will not only have to inspire people through charisma but also be an influential spokesperson on public issues.

Third, the ability to formulate a strategy for the company. This includes the ability to take on a global perspective in decision-making so that capital and products can be made where the cost is the least, but decisions can be changed as social and political factors dictate.

Fourth, top managers must be able to think clearly about many complex issues and communicate with a wide range of people and external groups. Managers will find it necessary to communicate better with the media.

Fifth, the top manager must be profit conscious. The firm's vitality and viability depend on its economic performance and its ability to sustain, protect and improve its profitability. This profitability must be balanced by attention to social and political demands being made upon the firm.

Sixth, a high moral tone must be established.

With contributors like John W. Slocum, Jr., it is clear that the discipline will prepare future managers to be thoroughly versed in management theory, concepts, and practices. The organization he represents—the Academy of Management—provides a major impetus for further contributions to the field.

Source

Based on information supplied by John W. Slocum, Jr., and used by permission.

more than holders of bachelor's degrees. According to the Bureau of Labor Statistics, the lifetime earning potential in 1972 dollars of a male with five years or more of college is $825,000; with four years of college $710,000; and with a high school diploma $480,000. Unemployment rates also vary with education. Those with more years of schooling are less likely to be unemployed.[9] By most standards education is an excellent investment for a future manager.

INDUSTRY TRENDS

Figure 23-3 shows the expected growth in employment for major industries to 1990. Services are expected to lead all industries, with only agriculture ex-

[9] See *Occupational Outlook Handbook, 1978–1979 Edition* (Washington, D.C.: Government Printing Office, Bureau of Labor Statistics, 1978), p. 26.

**Figure 23-3
EMPLOYMENT
GROWTH BY
INDUSTRY**

SOURCE: *Occupational Outlook Handbook, 1982–
1983 Edition*, Bulletin 2200
(Washington, D.C.: Government Printing Office, Bureau
of Labor Statistics, 1982),
p. 17.

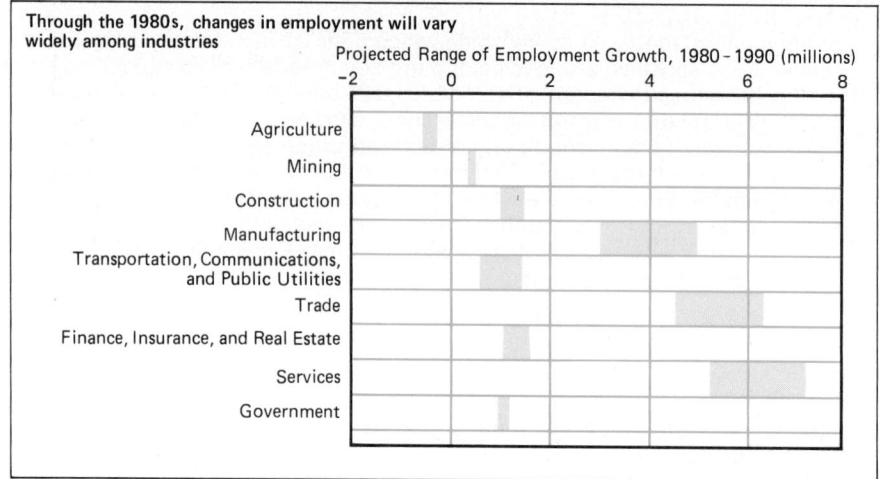

periencing an absolute decline. Potential job applicants should be aware of overall industry trends in making their career decisions.

TRENDS IN MANAGEMENT JOBS

Figure 23-4 shows the expected employment growth by occupational groups to
1990. The number of managerial jobs is expected to increase by 21 percent during the ten-year period.

   Projections for specific management-related jobs are shown in Table 23-1. Individuals planning a career in management should be familiar with the employment trends in each area of work.

**Figure 23-4
EMPLOYMENT
GROWTH BY
OCCUPATIONAL
GROUP**

SOURCE: *Occupational Outlook Handbook, 1982–
1983 Edition*, Bulletin 2200
(Washington, D.C.: Government Printing Office, Bureau
of Labor Statistics, 1982),
p. 18.

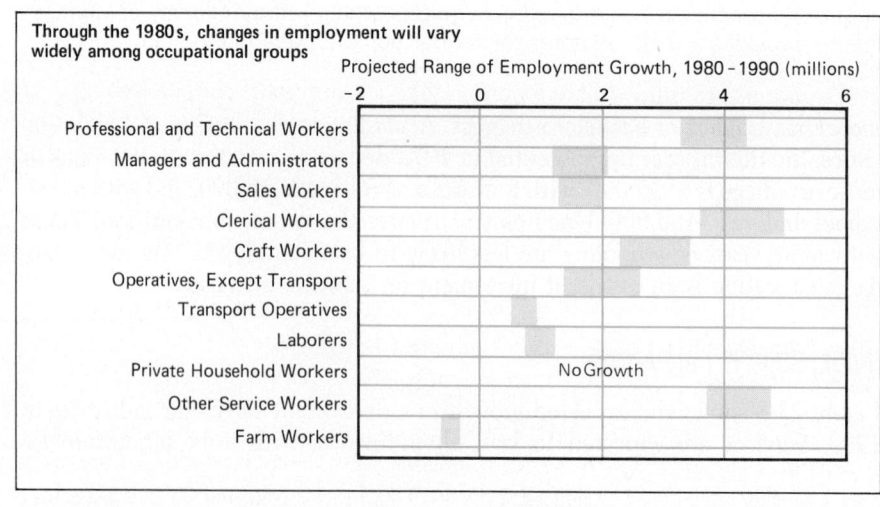

POSITION	APPROXIMATE 1980 EMPLOYMENT	PROJECTION RELATIVE TO A 17.1 AVERAGE GROWTH FOR ALL OCCUPATIONS	Table 23-1 PROJECTED EMPLOYMENT GROWTH FOR SELECTED OCCUPATIONS: 1980–1990
Accountants and Auditors	900,000	Faster than average	
Bank Officers and Managers	400,000	Faster than average	
Blue Collar Work Supervisors	1,300,000	About as fast as the average	
City Managers	3,300	About as fast as the average	
Credit Managers	55,000	More slowly than the average	
Hotel Managers and Assistants	84,000	Faster than average	
Industrial Engineers	115,000	Faster than average	
Occupational Safety and Health Workers	80,000	About as fast as the average	
Personnel and Labor Relations Specialists	178,000	About as fast as the average	
Public Relations Workers	87,000	About as fast as the average	
Purchasing Agents	172,000	About as fast as the average	

SOURCE: Adapted from *Occupational Outlook Handbook, 1982–1983 Edition*, Bulletin 2200 (Washington, D.C.: Government Printing Office, Bureau of Labor Statistics, 1982), pp. 23–26, 28–30, 33–34, 38–47, 63, 193–195, 390–391.

Strategies for Career Advancement

It is important to differentiate among career development, career planning, and career management. *Career development* may be defined as the methods and procedures for effectively employing and shifting personnel within the organizational framework.[10] It consists of two distinct elements: career planning and career management.

Career development refers to the methods for effectively employing and shifting personnel within the organization.

THE TWO ELEMENTS OF CAREER DEVELOPMENT

Career planning refers to the personal determination of one's career path. This process includes such factors as selecting an occupation and an employer, and

Career planning is the personal determination of one's career path.

[10] The definitions of career development, career planning, and career management are similar to those found in Thomas Gutteridge, "Organizational Career Development and Planning," *Pittsburgh Business Review* (March 1978), p. 9.

THE DUAL CAREER PROBLEM

Dual careers have become a major issue for most career management programs. Dual careers refer to a couple who both have long-term professional career interests rather than a supplemental employment/income perspective.* When both spouses are developing careers, it is difficult to transfer someone even if it is a career advancement. In fact, the increased number of dual career couples has altered traditional approaches to career management.

A Merrill Lynch Relocation Management, Inc., survey of major corporations found that 90 percent of dual career couples wanted spouse job assistance in any type of geographical move. As a result industry is beginning to offer such services. The Merrill Lynch survey is shown below:

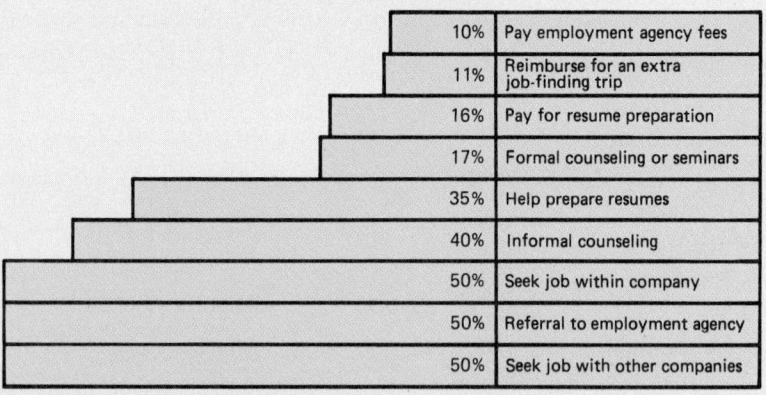

Some Services Offered To Transferred Employees' Spouses
(By 603 major companies)

10%	Pay employment agency fees
11%	Reimburse for an extra job-finding trip
16%	Pay for resume preparation
17%	Formal counseling or seminars
35%	Help prepare resumes
40%	Informal counseling
50%	Seek job within company
50%	Referral to employment agency
50%	Seek job with other companies

SOURCE: Merrill Lynch Relocation Management, Inc. Reprinted by permission.

Consultants specializing in the placement of transferred spouses are now widely used. For instance, when Nabisco Brands decided to hire food scientist Leslie Buteau, they hired such a firm to find a position for her husband. James Buteau now works at nearby Dictaphone Corp.† It seems clear that dual careers are going to be an increasingly important element of career management programs in the 1980s.

* This difference is noted in Carol B. Gilmore and William R. Fannin, "The Dual Career Couple: A Challenge to Personnel In the Eighties," *Business Horizons* (June 1982), pp. 36–41.
† Earl C. Gottschalk, Jr., "Firms Increasingly Help Spouses of Transferred Employees Find Jobs," *The Wall Street Journal* (January 21, 1982), Section 2, p. 25.

Career management is the firm's attempt to match employee goals with organizational opportunities.

the like. Self-development programs are also important. Career planning approaches the subject from the perspective of the individual.

By contrast, *career management* takes an organizational perspective. It involves a program for matching employee goals with organizational opportunities. It involves recruiting, hiring, placement, training, evaluation, compensation, and job assignment and a comprehensive review of career path alternatives.

Many companies have established active career development programs. Sears, Bank of America, AT&T, General Motors, General Foods, and General Electric have long been active in career management.[11] While levels and approaches vary, all of these firms and many more have to some degree made a commitment to career development.

THE NEED FOR A CAREER DEVELOPMENT APPROACH

Firms institute a career development program for a variety of reasons. Major factors include

1. The relative shortage of qualified managers.
2. A need to make more effective use of the organization's human resources.
3. Inclusion as part of an overall affirmative action and equal opportunity program.
4. Management's desire to fulfill a socially responsible obligation to the firm's employees.

A MODEL OF THE CAREER DEVELOPMENT PROCESS

The career development process is shown in Figure 23-5. Inputs come from individuals and the organization. There is a need for an assessment that matches

[11] See Betty Ann Duval and Roslyn S. Courtney, "Upward Mobility: The G.F. Way of Opening Employee Advancement Opportunity," *Personnel* (May–June, 1978), pp. 43–53; James Walker, "Human Resource Planning: An Odyssey to 2001 and Beyond," *Pittsburgh Business Review* (March 1978), p. 3; and Phillip G. Benson and George C. Thorton III, "A Model Career Planning Program," *Personnel* (March–April 1978), p. 34.

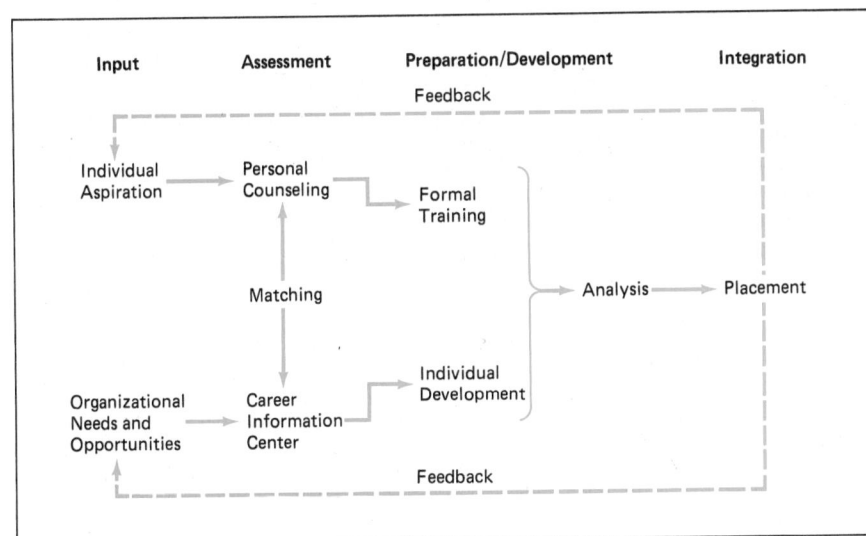

Figure 23-5
CAREER DEVELOPMENT PROCESS

SOURCE: John C. Arpin and Darlene K. Gerster, "Career Development: An Integration of Individual and Organizational Needs," *Personnel* (March–April 1978), p. 25. © 1978 by AMACOM, a division of American Management Associations. All rights reserved. Reprinted by permission of the publisher.

employee career objectives with the needs of the organization. Superior–subordinate counseling and an effective system for identifying internal opportunities are
labeled preparation/development. The intent here is to give the person an adequate background for further advancement. Finally, the integration stage attempts to place the individual in a position that meets both personal and
organizational objectives.

CAREER PLANNING AND GETTING AHEAD

From an individual perspective, a career plan is a blueprint for the person's professional and personal development. Individuals should prepare a written plan of
where they want their careers to go and the various intermediate steps involved.
Frank Kutcher, Jr., president of Foote & Davis, requires all his executives to develop such a plan. Kutcher has his own plan, and once quit an excellent position
heading another firm's finance, planning, and acquisitions activities because his
career scenario was to broaden his background in another industry and a larger
company.[12]

Many of the planning concepts developed in Chapter 5 are applicable to
career plans. Plans should be written with definite dates and expected accomplishments. Career plans should also be reviewed periodically to spot factors that
need updating or to take corrective action if one falls behind the schedule desired.

But how *does* one get ahead? Research suggests that students and managers
sometimes disagree in their perceptions of what allows a person to advance in
corporate life.[13] So it is important for entry-level employment candidates to
know how management ranks the factors leading to promotion. One survey
asked chief executive officers to identify the importance of various factors in
leading to promotion at their firms; next, they were asked to determine how important these factors *should* be. Basically, the survey compared the way executives perceived the situation to be and how they thought it ought to be. Table
23-2 presents some selected responses. Overall, the respondents believed that
high concern for both people and production was vital to career success.[14]

REACHING FOR TOP MANAGEMENT

Like the young .230 hitting shortstop of the minor league team, all beginning
managers like to imagine their rise to the top. The young shortstop may eventually become an all-star with the Los Angeles Dodgers, and the new trainee in
the Midwest regional sales office may become the president of a major U.S. cor-

---

[12] Frank E. Dutcher, Jr., "Needed: A Personal Marketing Plan," *Sales & Marketing Management*
(February 6, 1978). Another excellent article is John F. Veiga, "Do Managers on the Move Get
Anywhere?" *Harvard Business Review* (March–April, 1981), pp. 20–22, 26, 28, 30, 34, 36, 38.

[13] W. J. Heisler, "Promotion: What Does It Take to Get Ahead?" *Business Horizons* (April 1978),
pp. 57–63.

[14] *Ibid.*, p. 59; see also Robert R. Blake and Jane S. Mouton, "The Managerial Grid" (Houston:
Gulf Publishing Co., 1964).

poration. Both have a long way to go, but both have the right to aspire to the top slots in their chosen profession.

TOP MANAGEMENT RECEIVES TOP PAY

The rewards of top management are significant. However, the financial compensation should be viewed in the proper context. Top management is the highest achievement in the field of business and deserves the high levels of compensation given outstanding performance in any field. Top management of firms employing thousands of people usually make considerably less than well-known entertainers and athletes.

What determines one's level of compensation? A study of the 148 highest paid U.S. executives revealed that

1. Executive compensation is *not* linked substantially to
   a. Level of responsibility
   b. Performance
2. Executive compensation *is* substantially linked to
   a. The industry in which the person works
   b. The corporate power structure
   c. Relative bargaining power[15]

Boards of directors set top executive salaries, and chief executives are usually actively involved in the selection of board members. The end result is that many top executives play at least an indirect role in determining their own salaries. Sometimes this influence can have interesting results. When the Charter Co.— an oil, insurance, and communications firm—needed to conserve cash, its founder and chairman, Raymond K. Mason, cut his $249,000 salary to zero![16]

Top executives are also expert negotiators and bargainers, and this ability can have a sizable impact on their salaries. The tough negotiating involved in these situations is illustrated by the deal Michel Bergerac struck when he moved to Revlon from ITT. Charles Revson, Revlon's head, had incurable cancer, and like many self-made successes, he had given little attention to selecting and preparing a successor. Bergerac accepted the Revlon position for a $300,000 annual salary and a $1.5 million bonus upon promotion to the head of the firm. He was guaranteed a $1.2 million additional payment if Charles Revson had not left the top position in a year.[17] He now makes about $1.1 million per year and has a contract that lasts until 1992.[18]

---

[15] William Steve Albrecht and Phillip Thin, "The Million Dollar Man," *Business Horizons* (August 1978), pp. 9–14.

[16] Mason's salary cut is described in "The Cream at the Top," *Newsweek* (May 17, 1982), p. 76.

[17] The Bergerac negotiations are reported in Paul W. Strum, "Choosing the Next Boss—Why So Many Bosses Do It Badly," *Forbes* (October 2, 1978), p. 44.

[18] The Bergerac update is from "Revlon: A Painful Case of Slow Growth and Fading Glamour," *Business Week* (April 14, 1982), p. 118.

**Table 23-2
SELECTED VIEWS OF
PROMOTIONAL
FACTORS FOR A
SAMPLE OF CHIEF
EXECUTIVE
OFFICERS**

Percentage of respondents indicating item is at least "somewhat important"

ITEM	ACTUAL RANKING OF FACTORS	IDEAL RANKING	% DIFFERENCE
1. Comes up with new ways to handle problems	100	99	−1
2. Is cooperative, has the spirit of teamwork	100	99	−1
3. Has a good record of accomplishments	100	99	−1
4. Is able to operate with a minimum of direction	100	99	−1
5. Is able to argue logically	100	99	−1
6. Is able to meet deadlines	99	98	−1
7. Is tactful in making suggestions to superiors	98	82	−16
8. Is able to sell his or her ideas	98	99	+1
9. Is able to develop subordinates	97	99	+2
10. Is willing to make a geographical move when necessary	96	90	−6
11. Has a pleasant personality	95	84	−11
12. Is willing to work more than forty hours a week	94	92	−2
13. Is in good physical shape	93	87	−6
14. Is in a position that provides an opportunity to deal with higher-level managers	92	76	−16
15. Doesn't complain about rules and procedures	84	64	−20
16. Is a college graduate	80	63	−17

ENTREPRENEURSHIP—THE ALTERNATIVE TO CORPORATE LIFE

An *entrepreneur* is one who accepts the risks associated with establishing and operating a commercial venture. This definition has often fit Stephen Huse, even when he was a student at Indiana University's School of Business.[19] Huse ran a cookware sales outfit employing seven sales representatives out of his married student housing unit. A daughter's bedroom doubled as the firm's warehouse, and Huse's sales personnel covered campuses all over Indiana.

After graduation, a short stint with a corporation (Huse became its top sales

[19] The Stephen Huse story is told in Joseph M. Waldman, "Making It Big in the Fast Food Industry," *Business Horizons* (June 1978), pp. 65–72. The 1982 update is provided by Noble Roman's.

Percentage of respondents indicating item is at least "somewhat important"

ITEM	ACTUAL RANKING OF FACTORS	IDEAL RANKING	% DIFFERENCE
17. Has a clean-cut appearance	80	52	−28
18. Has worked for superiors who have reputations for being good managers	79	63	−16
19. Has a good academic record	76	68	−8
20. Makes it clear that he or she wants a promotion	68	57	−11
21. Looks like a manager	57	38	−19
22. Works for a superior who is promotable	55	31	−24
23. Has a sponsor at a higher level	53	18	−35
24. Is willing and able to play organizational politics	44	24	−20
25. Is not considerably younger or older than others in the level to which he or she is to be promoted	38	20	−18
26. Is a graduate of a high-prestige college	27	11	−16
27. Goes strictly by the book	26	18	−8
28. Is married	24	14	−10
29. Has a similar social background to those already at the top	22	6	−16
30. Belongs to the same club or lodge as those already at the top	8	2	−6

SOURCE: Adapted from W. J. Heisler, "Promotion: What Does It Take to Get Ahead?" *Business Horizons* (April 1978), p. 60.

producer) convinced Huse that he was better suited to be his own boss. He became a partner in an Arby's franchise. Later, he took over two Little Caesar's Pizza units. But a disagreement with Little Caesar's eventually led him to set up his own pizza chain—Noble Roman's.

Today, Noble Roman's and its affiliated companies have sales exceeding $17 million annually and employ 1,150 people. Huse also is a partner in a chain of fourteen Arby's outlets and is involved in airplane leasing, real estate development, farming, and two video arcade/billiards centers.

Huse is a classic example of a person who was very successful in corporate life but who was more comfortable running his own enterprise. So he became an entrepreneur.

Many management and business administration courses and textbooks are criticized for ignoring the entrepreneurship alternative to corporate life. For the most part, this is a valid criticism. Running one's own business is certainly an option that should be considered in a career plan. Entrepreneurship offers exciting opportunities, the contentment of running one's own business, and the chance for substantial financial payoffs. But this option is also full of risks (after all, it is the entrepreneur's money or that of his or her investors which is at stake), long hours, and often long odds at success. Yet Stephen Huse withstood the twelve-to-sixteen-hour days and six-to-seven-day weeks during the first-year startup period of his first Arby's franchise and went on to become an outstanding success. For him, the risks paid off.

Students interested in the entrepreneurship alternative should structure their academic program to include a course in small business management, and they should diversify their educational program to provide at least an introduction to the functional activities involved in running a business.

SWITCHING JOBS

A job switch is different from a promotion or transfer, since it involves moving from one firm to another. There are two types of managers who are candidates for a job switch—those who are actively seeking a new opportunity and those who are not. Many executives reach a point at which a job switch is desirable and even necessary to their future career development. For instance, reduced opportunities in Cleveland Trust's lending area caused Quentin Thomas to look elsewhere. People actively seeking other opportunities can employ a variety of methods in their job search. Experienced managers also have the advantage of extensive professional contacts upon which to draw. Business acquaintances often prove invaluable in seeking a new position.[20]

When Opportunity Knocks

A second category of potential job switch candidates includes those not actively seeking new employment. In the past, if a company needed a person to fill a certain slot, the responsible managers typically relied on their own array of friends and associates, the so-called "old boy" network.[21] The eventual pick was often a service or college friend of the hiring executive. The "old boy" network was often justifiably criticized as being a leading cause of discriminatory hiring behavior against blacks and women. But this has changed!

Headhunter is a term used to describe an executive search firm.

Increasingly, executives are being secured through executive search firms, or *headhunters,* as they are known in management circles. Executive search firms are private organizations hired to recruit acceptable candidates for executive em-

[20] Job changes are discussed in Raymond E. Hill and Edwin L. Miller, "Job Change and the Middle Seasons of a Man's Life," *Academy of Management Journal* (March 1981), pp. 114–127.
[21] The discussion of executive research firms is based on Herbert E. Meyer, "The Headhunters Come Upon Golden Days," *Fortune* (October 9, 1978), pp. 100–102, 104, 106, 110.

ployment. A $1 billion business that has quadrupled in size between 1978 and 1981, executive search firms moved 80,000 executives into jobs averaging $50,000 during 1981.[22] The recruiter Heidrich & Struggles estimates that 47 percent of all executive jobs are now filled by headhunters.[23]

Executive search firms tend to deal with mature, seasoned managers. While some executives forward resumes to headhunters for inclusion in their elaborate data banks (some of which contain over 100,000 names), others are contacted initially by the search firms.

Headhunters work for the employer, not the job candidate. They will typically bill the client for 30 percent of the hiree's first year's salary. Most executive search companies follow a similar pattern. They begin by working with the client to develop a profile of who they want to hire. Particular attention is paid to the operational style of the company. One executive, accustomed to a plush Park Avenue office, quickly accepted an excellent financial offer by a West Coast firm, but quit at 4:00 P.M. of the first day because of the metal desk and linoleum environment of the California firm.

Once the profile has been completed, the search firm develops a preliminary list of up to six qualified candidates that is submitted to the employer. After the client has interviewed likely candidates and made a choice, the headhunter often acts as mediator in attempting to arrange the actual employment of the individual.

Although executive search firms may be somewhat removed from the early stages of one's career plan, they may be an integral part at a later stage. Headhunters are used by over 90 percent of the nation's largest 500 companies, and there is every likelihood that their importance will grow in the future.

A FINAL COMMENT

Regardless of who makes the initial contact, the essential decision concerns the necessity for a job switch. Many people procrastinate in such a decision because of an innate fear of new surroundings and of a new way of doing things. Personal factors such as a spouse's attitudes, educational opportunities for children, or lifelong ties to a specific geographical area all play an important role in such a decision. But unless one's personal situation dictates otherwise, a job switch is in order in situations where a person is stymied from achieving the next step in his or her career development plan.

Obstacles to Achieving Managerial Career Objectives

All managers should have clearly defined career objectives. Expectations of major job accomplishments are a feature of good career planning. But immediate and/or sustained success is not typically the case. Most managers will plateau out somewhere in the middle management ranks, and competitive, time,

---

[22] James Kennedy, *Executive Recruiter News*, 1982.
[23] Walter Kiechel III, "The Care and Feeding of Contacts," *Fortune* (February 8, 1982), p. 122.

and other work pressures can have a damaging impact on a manager's health. And dismissal—many times for reasons beyond the manager's control—is always a threat.

THE CAREER PLATEAU

Most younger people, anxious to begin their careers, have a difficult time visualizing a point when their career advancement will cease. College students often assume that if there is a position beyond which further promotion is unlikely, surely it is at the corporate vice-presidential level. Of course, this is not the case for most individuals.

A career plateau is a stage in one's career from which further advancement is not expected

A *career plateau* is a stage in one's career development from which further advancement is not expected.[24] The higher one climbs, the fewer opportunities exist at the next level. While a major corporation may have as many as 1,000 supervisory positions, middle management positions may number only a hundred or so, and top management positions may number fewer than twenty. As promotion occurs the number of opportunities for further promotions declines. In fact, it is estimated that each level of management has 30 percent fewer jobs than the position just below it.[25]

Career plateaus can vary. Some are encountered at high levels, some at low levels. Some plateaued executives continue to be effective at their plateau, others experience frustration at their inability to achieve further promotions. A study of AT&T managers found that there is no relationship between career plateaus and personal happiness. Many plateaued executives are content because of family and hobbies.[26] Another study involving fifty-five senior executives in nine separate organizations led to the development of the Ference–Stoner–Warren model of managerial careers. This concept, depicted in Figure 23-6, provides an excellent means for studying the plateaued manager.

The two parameters of the model are the person's current level of performance and his or her future likelihood of advancement. "*Learners*" (comers) are those just learning a position, such as a new hiree or a freshly promoted manager. They offer good potential, even if their current productivity is low. "*Stars*" are excellent current performers who show every likelihood of continued advancement. They are often referred to as being on a "fast track" (to higher executive positions). The plateaued executives are identified as "*deadwood*" (low current performance, low likelihood of future promotions) and "*solid citizens*" (high current performance, low likelihood of future promotions). The "dead-

---

[24] Except as noted this section is based on and quotes from Thomas P. Ference, James A. F. Stoner, and E. Kirby Warren, "Managing the Career Plateau," *Academy of Management Review* (October 1977), pp. 606–612. Another excellent article is John F. Veiga, "Plateaued Versus Nonplateaued Managers: Career Patterns Attributes and Path Potential," *Academy of Management Journal* (September, 1981), pp. 566–578.

[25] Terri Minsky, "More People Face Career Plateaus, A Relief for Some, Shock for Others," *The Wall Street Journal* (August 2, 1981), Section 2, p. 15.

[26] "Labor Letter," *The Wall Street Journal* (March 16, 1982), p. 1.

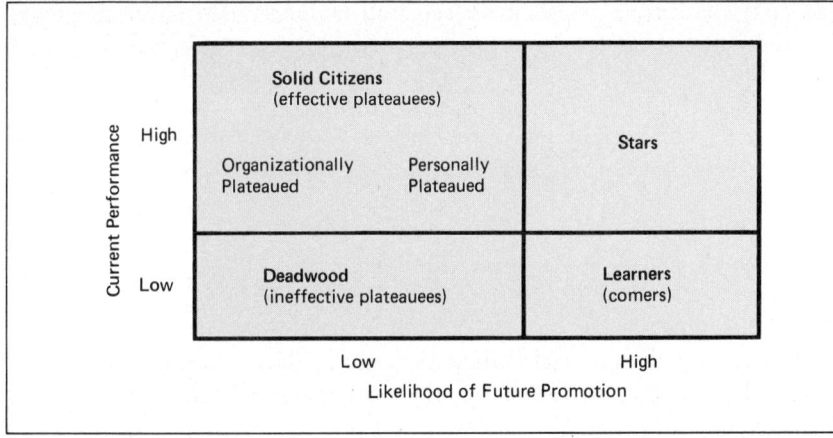

**Figure 23-6
THE FERENCE–
STONER–WARREN
MODEL OF
MANAGERIAL
CAREERS**

SOURCE: Thomas P. Ference, James A. F. Stoner, and E. Kirby Warren, "Managing the Career Plateau," *Academy of Management Review* (October 1977), p. 603.

wood" managers are simply not doing the job. "Solid citizens" can be *organizationally* plateaued (they have the ability to do higher-level jobs but there is a lack of openings) or *personally* plateaued (the organization perceives them to lack the ability or the desire to perform higher-level jobs).

More research and managerial effort are needed in order to develop meaningful ways to increase the efficiency of plateaued executives. But three major implications are apparent from the Ference–Stoner–Warren model:

1. Management must prevent effectively performing plateaued executives from slipping into the "deadwood" category.
2. A contingency approach is required in dealing with the various career stages.
3. More techniques are needed for dealing with the "solid citizens." Little management effort has been devoted to this type of plateaued executive.

It would appear that the starting point for most aspiring managers is simply to realize that career plateaus do occur and that plateauing is not synonymous with failure. The Ference–Stoner–Warren study puts it this way: "Plateauing indicates only arrival at a presumably permanent position in the organizational hierarchy; it does not necessarily imply cessation of personal growth and development."

MANAGERIAL HEALTH CONSIDERATIONS

Maintenance of good health is a prerequisite to managerial effectiveness. Successful executives know that their time is too valuable to be hindered by poor health, so they must try to remain physically fit.

Management has a number of built-in health dangers. Lengthy business luncheons can lead to excessive intakes of calories and alcohol. Long hours and tight schedules make exercising and proper eating difficult. The sedentary life found in the executive environment can lead to inadequate physical activity. Stress, the tensions created by job-related factors and the workplace, is another consideration.

While unhealthy practices may not lead to immediate physical disability or death, they can drain an executive's vitality and, eventually, productivity. As a person strives to achieve career goals, it is often easy to forget the role of good health in the continuation of career progress. Like education and the cultivation of effective work habits, health is an environmental factor that can have a major impact on one's career. Some basic rules for maintaining executive health are shown below.

1. Have a periodic physical examination and medical consultation.
2. Maintain proper dietary habits and the optimal weight recommended by a physician.
3. Exercise regularly in a manner prescribed by a physician.
4. Provide for adequate sleep and relaxation.
5. Eliminate or reduce the consumption, if any, of tobacco, alcohol, and unnecessary (and not medically recommended) drugs.

DISMISSAL—TENURE IS NOT PART OF THE GAME

Dismissal is involuntary separation from one's job.

Dismissal, involuntary separation from one's job, is a natural part of executive life. Just as major league managers and football coaches are "hired to be fired," managers—at all levels—must face this possibility.

College professors have tenure. Bureaucrats have the civil service. Operative employees have seniority in a bargaining unit. Even sports figures, authors, and entertainment personalities have contracts for job security, in some instances. But the executive usually lacks protection against an immediate firing. "Clean out your desk and vacate the building by 5:00 P.M." is an edict heard by thousands of managers each year.

Management's job security must rest with the abilities and experience of individuals. No one is protecting an executive's position, so the manager must have confidence in his or her own abilities. Becoming an expert in what one does is the best security available.

OVERCOMING DISMISSAL

Dismissals can result from a variety of causes. Nonperformance or ineffective performance is not the only possibility. Some dismissals are beyond the control of the manager. Examples include a plant closing, discontinuation of a product line, acquisition by another firm, or a personality conflict between the dismissed executive and his or her immediate superior.

If the individual can accept a firing as a normal career event, the first battle is won. Thousands upon thousands of executives have been fired before, and the majority of them have gone on to rewarding careers in other organizations.

A firing should be viewed as a new opportunity—another chance to achieve

"*I'm going to have to let you go, Clayton.
I want to put a file cabinet here.*"

SENIORITY DOES NOT COUNT FOR MANAGERS . . . EVEN WHEN IT COMES TO FILE CABINETS

SOURCE: *The Saturday Evening Post* (May–June, 1982), p. 30. Reprinted with permission from the Saturday Evening Post Society, a division of BFL & MS, Inc. © 1982.

one's utmost potential. Successful people are those who are confident in their own abilities and who are anxious to proceed with the next stage in their career development. These people overcome rejection and go on with their lives. Richard Nixon's comeback after being defeated for the presidency in 1960 and the California governorship in 1962; the late Hubert Humphrey, beaten in 1960 and 1968, yet the "Happy Warrior" rallying to become one of the Senate's most respected members; and Ronald Reagan's election after losing in his first bids for the presidential nomination—these are classic illustrations of the importance of strong belief in oneself.

Outplacement—Finding a New Position for the Dismissed Executive

One of the newest aspects of employment termination is the use of *outplacement firms,* consultants who help a fired employee adjust to unemployment and then help him or her find a new job.[27] A handful of outplacers (also known as *dehiring firms*) are serving clients like Exxon, United Airlines, Motorola, Sears, Consolidated Edison, and Phillip Morris. Employers pay the outplacers' fee of 12 to 15 percent of the dismissed executive's annual salary—the ultimate management fringe benefit.

Outplacement firms help a fired employee adjust to unemployment, and then help him or her find a new job.

[27] This section is based on Herbert E. Meyer, "The Flourishing New Business of Recycling Executives," *Fortune* (May 1977), pp. 328–330, 334, 336, 338; and Jane Bryant Quinn, "Getting Fired, Successfully," *Newsweek* (October 30, 1978), pp. 18-D, 18-H.

Much can be learned from the procedures used by outplacers. The dehiring companies prefer to meet the executive who has decided to terminate someone before the actual firing takes place. The outplacer wants to know why the person is being dismissed (the typical reason is personality conflicts, according to out-placement sources) and as much information as possible about the individual in order to assist with his or her eventual placement in another firm. The employer is advised to keep the terminated manager on the payroll rather than providing a lump sum severance payment. In most cases the payroll cost until the person finds another job and the outplacement fee combined are less than the typical executive's severance pay.

Outplacers also offer advice on the mechanics of firing. Typically, employers are counseled to limit the appointment to ten minutes during which the superior announces the decision and the reasons for it, informs the former employee of his or her severance package, and then tells the person that an outplacement consultant has been hired to assist in locating a new position. Dismissed employ-ees are usually in at least a mild state of shock when they are taken to another office and introduced to their outplacer. The first few days after a firing are criti-cal, and outplacement firms advise employers to fire someone on Monday rather than just prior to a weekend or a holiday.

Fired executives are encouraged to ventilate their feelings to their outplacer. Extremely angry executives are urged not to file legal cases or to criticize their former employer publicly but to get on with their career. Those who are de-pressed are provided with counseling assistance.

The executives are asked to complete lengthy questionnaires that serve as a data source for the manager's resume. Outplacers consider even the smallest de-tails. Some advise candidates to tint graying hair, avoid bow ties, and never use cream in coffee (since most top management prefers black coffee). Meanwhile, candidates work with outplacers to develop a comprehensive job prospect file. Finally, when the candidate is thoroughly prepared for the job search, contacts are made with people who might help the executive land a new job.

Outplacement results are impressive. About 80 to 97 percent of the fired exec-utives are employed within six months, and 80 to 88 percent are paid what they made before, or more. As a general rule, the higher one's former position, the longer it takes to find a suitable new position.

Retirement and Other End-of-Career Options

Count von Bismarck had a problem. He needed an acceptable way of replacing some aging generals. So he invented the premise that people should be forced to retire at age sixty-five. The Bismarck concept became the accepted one in Eu-rope and the United States and remained so for years.

Bismarck would be shocked at retirement practices of the 1980s. General Motors employees average 60 at the time of their retirement. The average re-tirement age is sixty at Exxon and 61 at Bendix. In fact, about 63 percent of those who retire do so before they are sixty-five. At the same time, the United

States population is aging. In 1900 there were three million people over sixty. Now there are thirty-three million, about 15 percent of all Americans. Life expectancy has increased more than twenty-five years during this time span.[28] The increased number of older Americans has created a significant social and economic power group, sometimes referred to as *gray power.*

Mandatory retirement has been a major public debate in recent years. The 1967 Age Discrimination in Employment Act banned discrimination for persons between forty and sixty-five. This was recently extended by Congress to prohibit mandatory retirement before seventy years of age with a few exceptions.[29] It is estimated that approximately 11.6 percent of the noninstitutionalized population over sixty-five continued to work in March 1982.[30]

All workers, including the various levels of management, must face the retirement issue in light of their own circumstances. Many people choose to continue working; others seek to retire at an earlier age. But regardless of the age that is selected, a common problem is what is termed *retirement shock*—the personal adjustment problems caused by going from full-time work to full-time leisure. Many people experience difficulty in making the adjustment; and personal, interpersonal, psychological, and health maladies are common. As a result, the concept of gliding or phased retirement is common in such European countries as the Netherlands, Sweden, France, and the United Kingdom. *Phased retirement* means that a person is gradually provided additional leisure time as he or she approaches the planned retirement age. This can be done by granting additional vacation time, such as at Gillette-France, or by switching the person from full-time to part-time work. A Swedish law, for instance, allows employees to pick the number of hours (seventeen is the minimum per week) they want to work when they are in the sixty–seventy-year age bracket.[31]

In the United States, some retired executives offer their expertise to SCORE (Service Corps of Retired Executives), a volunteer group that assists small businesses, or work for civic and philanthropic causes.

Various other retirement options exist, which range from continued work to a complete leisure-oriented retirement. While it may be difficult for entry-level job candidates to concern themselves with retirement, it is an event that must be faced. And careful career planning should include the script for the final act.

Retirement shock refers to the personal adjustment problems caused by going from full-time work to full-time leisure.

Phased retirement means that a person is gradually provided additional leisure time as he or she approaches the planned retirement age.

---

[28] Dana Stevenson, "Working Past 65—If You Want to—And If They'll Let You," *Detroit News Magazine* (March 12, 1978), p. 49. The 1982 update provided by JRB Communications, Inc. Another excellent article is James B. Shaw and Lisa L. Grubbs, "The Process of Retiring: Organizational Entry in Reverse," *Academy of Management Review* (January 1981), pp. 41–47.

[29] See "New Retirement Rules: Their Impact on Business, Workers," *U.S. News & World Report* (November 7, 1977), pp. 71–73; "Now the Revolt of the Old," *Time* (October 10, 1977), pp. 18–28; and "The Ax for Forced Retirement," *Business Week* (September 19, 1977), pp. 38–39.

[30] Bureau of Labor Statistics.

[31] Bernhard Terret, "Gliding Out: The European Approach to Retirement," *Personnel Journal* (July 1978), pp. 368–370. See also Allan T. Otten, "Many Swedes 60 and Older Cut Working Hours Before Retirement Under Government Program," *The Wall Street Journal* (July 6, 1982), p. 42.

Career Planning for Women and Minorities

Special attention should be devoted to the subject of career planning for women and minorities. A brief introduction to these vital issues is included here.

WOMEN IN MANAGEMENT

The simple truth is that women are still very much a minority in management circles. Recent growth in the labor force has come primarily from women, yet they continue to cluster in a limited number of lower-paying occupations. Forty percent of all employed women work in ten jobs: secretary, retail sales, bookkeeper, domestic worker, elementary school teacher, waitress, typist, cashier, sewer/stitcher, and nurse. Eighty percent or more of the jobs in these occupational groups are held by women.[32]

While the overall numbers may still be small, more women are entering management positions. The latest Department of Labor statistics show that between 1960 and 1982 the number of women in management grew 175 percent while the number of men in managerial positions increased by only 37 percent.[33] Twenty percent of all management jobs are held by women today, up from about 12 percent a decade ago.[34]

New career opportunities in management have led more and more women to seek out education in business-oriented disciplines. Many colleges now report that a third of their undergraduate business administration students are women. It appears that successful women will soon not be lonely figures in the top management suite.

Women face some unique career problems.[35] Several types of bias influence female employment: (1) cultural bias (such as job stereotyping); (2) management bias; (3) covert discrimination; (4) female bias (women sometimes discriminate against other women); and (5) systems bias (society assumes a traditional view of men and women that works against professional careers for women).[36]

American business is now working to integrate women managers into what was once an all-male execuutive hierarchy. A variety of training methods have been employed.[37] CBS has a director of career development programs for

---

[32] C. Glyn Williams, "Women in the American Economy," *Business and Economic Review* (October 1978), p. 15.

[33] "When Women Take Over as Bosses," *U.S. News & World Report* (March 22, 1982), p. 77.

[34] "Newsgram®," *U.S. News & World Report* (June 21, 1982), p. 12.

[35] Excellent articles include George F. Bites and Holly A. Pryatel, "Myths, Management, & Women," *Personnel Journal* (October 1978), pp. 574–577; and Benson Rosen, Mary Ellen Templeton, and Karen Kichline, "The First Few Years on the Job: Women in Management," *Business Horizons* (November–December 1981), pp. 26–29.

[36] These biases are discussed in Patricia C. Elliott, "The Progress of Women in Business," *New Mexico Business* (December 1977), pp. 7–11.

[37] Some of these are described in Laurie Larwood, Marion M. Wood, and Sheila Davis Interlied, "Training Women for Management: New Problems, New Solutions," *Academy of Management Review* (July 1978), pp. 584–593.

women. And more and more successful female executives are volunteering to counsel younger women in matters of career planning.[38]

MINORITIES IN MANAGEMENT

Blacks and other minorities aspiring to management positions often face problems similar to those faced by women. They are sometimes the victims of assorted forms of discrimination. They often lack business-oriented educational backgrounds, they do not have a role model to guide them, and so forth. Minorities, male and female, are clearly disadvantaged when it concerns efforts to achieve managerial positions.

Progress has been slow for blacks. About 2.3 percent of all United States management was black in 1960. In 1982—more than two decades later—this had increased to only 6.2 percent.[39] While affirmative action programs have succeeded in opening some doors to the management hierarchy, blacks still have a long way to go before achieving proportionate representation in management.

More and more minorities are now entering business careers, and this trend seems likely to continue. Various companies have made concentrated efforts to hire minorities. Admittedly, most of these hirings have been at entry-level slots, but these people will soon progress according to merit in these companies. So it is reasonable to expect the percentage of blacks and other minorities in management to escalate rapidly in the years ahead.

A good career plan is essential for blacks; aside from the usual considerations, blacks should anticipate obstacles not encountered by whites. But, white or black, there is no substitute for a carefully prepared career plan.

[38] "Women Finally Get Mentors of Their Own," *Business Week* (October 23, 1978), pp. 74, 79, 80.

[39] George Stevens and Penny Marquette, "Room at the Top," *MBA* (August–September 1978), p. 42. The 1982 update is from the Bureau of Labor Statistics.

Summary

Effective career development has a number of facets. The initial job search is where a management career begins, and the basic steps of the job search process are as follows:

1. Conduct preparatory research.
2. Identify prospective employers.
3. Initiate employment contacts.
4. Evaluate opportunities.

Competition for desirable jobs is intense, and career planning should take into account employment trends. Services are expected to experience more growth than other industries. Overall, management jobs are expected to increase some 20.8 percent during 1978–1990.

Career development refers to the methods and procedures for effectively employing and shifting personnel within the organizational framework. There are two separate aspects:

1. Career planning (personal career planning)
2. Career management (the company's programs to match people and jobs)

Many firms have established career development programs on at least some level of the organization. Another avenue of career development—entrepreneurship—is also introduced.

The rewards for reaching top management are impressive. Research indicates that executive compensation is not substantially linked to the level of responsibility or performance, but to the industry, corporate power structure, and relative bargaining power.

Successful career development sometimes calls for job switching. In the past, many executive positions were filled through the "old boy" network of friends and associates. But, increasingly, management positions are filled by executive search firms, known as *headhunters*.

A variety of obstacles to achieving career objectives are discussed. All managers eventually reach some type of career plateau, from which future advancement is not expected. The management pyramid offers fewer and fewer opportunities as one moves upward, causing more and more managers to plateau. But persons will reach their career plateaus at different levels in the or-

ganizational hierarchy. Some executives are effective performers at the plateaued level, others are not.

Maintenance of health and reducing stress are important. And dismissal is always a threat to executives. But more companies are providing outplacement assistance to dismissed employees.

The concept of retirement—the final stage in the career development process—has changed considerably in recent years. Legislation has had a profound impact. From the managerial viewpoint, the objective should be to avoid or reduce retirement shock, the personal adjustment problems caused by going from full-time employment to full-time leisure. The concept of gliding or phased retirement, as practiced in Europe, is one alternative end-of-career option.

Career planning for women and minorities is extremely important. In the past these people have been subject to considerable bias and reduced career opportunities. But this situation is changing, and industry is moving to integrate women and minorities into management.

REVIEW EXERCISES

1. Define the following terms: (a) resume (b) job application (c) interview (d) work ethic (e) career development (f) career planning (g) career management (h) entrepreneur (i) "old boy" network (j) headhunter (k) career plateau (l) dismissal (m) outplacement firms (n) retirement shock (o) phased retirement.

2. Discuss the primary conclusions of the longitudinal study of career and personal success.

3. Outline the basic stages of the job search process.

4. Identify the major employment trends in management.

5. Explain the career development process.

6. What determines the level of executive compensation?

7. Explain the concept of career plateauing. Is its occurrence indicative of failure to attain career goals?

8. How should managers view dismissal?

9. Describe the major end-of-career options available to managers.

10. Discuss career planning for women and minorities.

Applications

ASSIGNMENTS / PROBLEMS / DISCUSSION QUESTIONS

1. Try the following exercise suggested by Alvin Toffler in his book *Future Shock:*

Write a "future autobiography" . . . by setting down a scenario of your career and life five or even 10 years after college. What do you see yourself doing? How far have you risen beyond an entry-level job? How have you accomplished this rise? What section of the country do you live in? What size community? Are you married? With children? How have you managed with a career and a family? Are you happy with your job? With your life? Watch out for the fleeting thoughts of fantasy that tend to clutter reality. Throw out all of the "if onlys" (you get thinner, better-looking or inherit your uncle's business). Deal, rather brutally and honestly, with what is *likely* to happen to you.

Put this autobiography on the shelf to study again in a few months from now. Better yet, do the exercise with a friend or two, read each other's work and discuss it. In these pages, you'll find many clues about your own philosophy of life and priorities for working.*

2. The way you act today may influence your future career advancement. Complete the career control questionnaire below to determine if you are in control of your own career.

3. John T. Molloy is a consultant and best-selling author on the subject of the role of apparel in a person's success. His advice includes the following:

Dark-blue or gray clothing implies power and prestige.

Leaders should wear something that makes them stand out.

Beige raincoats show more class than black ones do.

*Reprinted from *Ford's Insider: A Continuing Series of College Newspaper Supplements,* © 1978, 13–30 Corporation, 505 Market Street, Knoxville, Tenn. 37902. *Future Shock* by Alvin Toffler, © 1970 by Random House, Inc.

CAREER CONTROL QUESTIONNAIRE

Self-enhancing actions	FREQUENTLY +5 pts.	OCCASIONALLY +3 pts.	RARELY +1 pt.	Self-defeating actions	FREQUENTLY −5 pts.	OCCASIONALLY −3 pts.	RARELY 0
1. Making visible accomplishments				1. Prolonging conflict			
2. Supporting important others				2. Putting down			
3. Demonstrating expertise				3. Exploiting others			
4. Giving respect				4. Making visible errors			
5. Being understanding				5. Being intolerant			
6. Acting sincerely				6. Staying aloof			
7. Being friendly				7. Being unfair			
8. Being tactful				8. Blaming others			
9. Keeping informed				9. Being uncooperative			
10. Assuming responsibility				10. Being inconsistent			

Scoring: 90–100 pts. Complete control
80–89 Partially in control
70–79 Losing control
Under 70 Out-of-control

SOURCE: Ed Roseman, "Evaluate Your Actions: Advance Your Career," *Product Marketing* (September 1978), p. 22. Reprinted with permission.

Women executives should wear appropriate things to work.

Gaudy ties have a lower-class look.

Businesswomen: Carry an attaché case instead of a purse.

Bow ties show unpredictability.†

Do you agree with this advice? Defend your answer.

4. Eaton Corp. assigns a fired executive an office and a secretary. Hubert Hubben, Eaton's vice-president, Management Resources, describes his firm's policy this way: "Outplacement is nothing more than this: Your job in the next three months is to find yourself a job. Don't change your lifestyle. Follow the same rigors as before; don't become a built-in babysitter; don't down that first martini until 5:30 in the afternoon."** What is your evaluation of Eaton's policy?

5. Many corporations are now providing top managers with what have been called "Golden Parachutes," or elaborate severance pay contracts

† Reprinted from *U.S. News & World Report* (September 25, 1978), p. 62. Copyright © 1978 U.S. News & World Report, Inc.
** Charles R. Day, Jr., "Is Job Loyalty a Worthless Virtue?" *Industry Week* (August 21, 1978), p. 45.

that can be implemented if they lose their jobs as a result of a takeover.‡ What argument can be advanced both for and against such compensation provisions?

‡ "Golden Parachutes" are discussed in Ann M. Morrison, "Those Executive Bailout Deals," *Fortune* (December 13, 1982), pp. 82–87.

A MANAGERIAL INCIDENT

J. Paul Lyet Came a Long Way from Brewerytown

As chief executive of Sperry Rand Corp. J. Paul Lyet ascribed his success to "sheer luck." But he put his success in perspective by adding, "The rewards come if you worked hard. . . . If your objective is to get your head above the pack and be seen, one way is to work like hell."

A poor boy from a rundown neighborhood of North Philadelphia known as Brewerytown, Lyet was motivated by a burning ambition to get ahead. He puts it simply: "I wanted not to be poor." In pursuit of success, he worked by day and studied at the University of Pennsylvania's Wharton Evening School of Accounting and Finance. After stints as a suitcase wrapper, a rent collector, and a real estate broker, and gradual pay increases to a salary of $18 a week, he decided to go into accounting. Soon he was assigned to audit corporations. One of his superiors remarked that he had never met anybody who had the eagerness to learn that Lyet did.

Lyet asked questions, weighed answers, and learned the details of every company he audited. He was already training himself to become a generalist by asking questions and making judgments about things outside his field.

For all his success as an auditor, Lyet was still only making $120 a week. When he failed to receive a raise he expected, he decided to accept an offer from New Holland, a manufacturer of farm implements, to become its comptroller. New Holland grew rapidly. When it was acquired by Sperry, the purchasing management soon found that Lyet was one of the firm's hidden assets. He knew the business and had all the answers. He was, in the words of one observer, "always prepared." When a company is merged or bought, the new owners are looking for someone who can tell them what the business they have purchased really consists of. They are naturally not inclined to trust the company's own top management, who may feel compelled to give glowing accounts of the company's operations in support of their decision to sell. Also, the acquirer wants to find loyal people. Hard-working people at the middle management level can fill this void. Careers can be made or destroyed at this critical point in a company's life. Lyet's was made. Sperry took notice of him.

When Sperry itself was acquired by Remington Rand, Lyet was once again one of the management assets. He was soon assigned to master the rapidly accumulating problems of the company's Univac division as part of a task force of company talent. Once again, Lyet did well, proving that one of the quickest routes to success is to plunge into a high-visibility, high-risk task when it is offered.

Lyet was on the fast track and soon was given the task of running Sperry Rand. But even when he had almost reached his goal, he was put through the ordeal of making a presentation to a hostile group of executives, including the chief executives of the company, who, in Lyet's words, "cut me down right at the ankles." It was a test, and J. Paul Lyet passed.

SOURCE: Adapted from Michael Korda, *Success! How Every Man and Woman Can Achieve It*. Copyright © 1977 by Success Research Corporation. Reprinted by permission of Random House, Inc.

Questions and Problems

1. Was Lyet's successful career really the result of luck?

2. What does this case suggest about effective career planning?

Case VII-1

AMERICAN BANK: THE CAREER OF PAT ALLEN CRAWFORD

Nearly a decade ago, Pat Allen Crawford, vice-president in the Retail Banking Division of American Bank, discussed her thirteen-year business career at the bank and her experiences as a working mother with two children. A women whose career had been launched prior to the enactment of equal employment legislation, she had earlier experienced some resistance to her managerial aspirations. On the basis of her experiences, she offered advice to women with serious business career interests.

THE BANK

American Bank is a full-service commercial bank offering a broad range of banking and financial services for consumers, businesses, financial institutions and governments throughout the world. It is organized to deliver financial services to key business markets instead of historic geographic markets.

American Bank is divided into a number of departments. These include a Multinational Business Division, which delivers financial services to those corporations whose operations are based worldwide; the National Division, which extends a full range of banking service through a staff based in New York to corporate customers whose primary markets are in the United States; an International Banking Division, which manages the bank's overseas branches, representative offices, banking subsidiaries, and affiliates; the domestic Retail Banking Division, which manages personal consumer banking and retail credit services in the

This case was prepared for class discussion. It is not intended to portray either effective or ineffective administrative practices. The case was written by Sandra Ekberg-Jordan, former director of the Graduate Program for Women, Pace University, New York, and Leon Winer, professor, Pace University, New York. This case is one in a series of case studies that was supported by a grant from First National City Bank. Adapted and reprinted by permission of the authors and Pace University. All names and dates were disguised at the request of the company.

greater New York City area; and the Trust and Investment Division, which operates trust and investment businesses in the world.

WOMEN EMPLOYEES

In the mid-1970s, American Bank reported that "the number of women in managerial and professional positions, as well as those holding titles as officials, [had] more than doubled since 1964." In the fall of 1975, the Personnel Department offered the following analysis of the percent of female officers at various levels and college trainees.

	PERCENT WOMEN
Vice-president and equivalent	2.3
Assistant Vice-president and equivalent	5.8
Assistant cashier and equivalent	18.0
Total officers	12.0
College trainee hires	21.2

PAT ALLEN CRAWFORD

A 1961 graduate of Duke University with a B.A. degree in English literature, Pat Allen Crawford taught speech and journalism at a private school in Maryland before arriving in New York City with her husband, Jim, a lawyer.

Pat decided not to pursue a teaching career, and when she reached New York, she began looking into job opportunities in business. With a background in English literature, she first thought about the publishing industry, but soon found that the only positions she was offered were secretarial. Her husband then suggested she consider applying to American Bank, which was within walking distance of their apartment.

When Pat talked to the Personnel Department at the bank, she was told of an opening in the National Division. The position—one of four identical ones—was in the area of customer services and paid $4,500 annually. Responsibilities focused on taking care of the bank's out-of-town clients and included ordering theater tickets, arranging for hotel services, and having money transferred. Pat felt this job promised to be more interesting than any of the others she had been interviewed for and she accepted the bank's employment offer.

FIRST YEARS WITH THE BANK

In the next three years, the banking area in which Pat worked experienced considerable growth, and by 1965 it was staffed by eight women, all of whom were college graduates. Each woman was assigned a different geographical area of the country. Over time, each woman became more deeply involved in investigation work, which entailed reviewing credit ratings of the companies within her area of the country.

Soon after she started working at the bank, Pat felt some resentment concerning the training program and the career opportunities offered to male employees, none of which was available at that time to women. In the early 1960s the bank hired young men with the same educational background as women, then gave them course work in accounting procedures and credit analysis, thus preparing them for positions with greater responsibility and higher salaries than were open to women.

Several men in Pat's area were aware of the women's interest in learning about financial procedures, and one of them ran an informal, early morning basic credit program especially for these women. Pat was among two or three women who took advantage of the pre-workday training.

In reviewing her career with the bank, Pat recalled a growing sense of frustration, which she shared with her female colleagues. As the women became more knowledgeable, they came to be relied upon to help new male college recruits learn the ropes. They would then watch the men be promoted while they remained in their same positions. Although the women raised the issue of promotion with management on several occasions, Pat said they made no headway. In the early 1960s, it was bank policy that women could not travel, and as the clients served by the National Division were located outside of New York, women could not be given higher positions. At the same time, Pat said she and her colleagues had become a source of embarrassment to the bank. Although the women knew the work of the division thoroughly and had done everything to prepare themselves for promotion, the bank would not change their titles or responsibilities. Pat's salary was under $10,000 and she knew it was lower than it would have been had she been a man and been promoted as rapidly as men were.

Finally, in 1967, one of Pat's accounts invited her on a one-day trip to visit the corporation's new headquarters several hundred miles from New York City. When she presented the invitation to management, she was told she could not go. Policy prohibited it. At that point Pat decided to resign. The bank offered her assignments in other areas, but she said, "No," and refused all offers.

After a few months of staying home, Pat went to work for a former associate who was setting up his own business, a hedge fund. This position lasted for six months, at which point she gave birth to her first son, resigned from her job, and stayed home for a year.

RETURN TO THE BANK

About the same time that Pat was celebrating her son's first birthday, she received a call from Arthur Jones, a member of the bank's Personnel Department, who asked if she would like to work on a bank project on a part-time basis. Pat accepted. After two weeks of work, she decided she didn't like working part time. The project director needed additional help, so she began working full time.

When the project was completed, Arthur Jones received a promotion and was named director of the Corporate Planning Department. He invited Pat to work with him as assistant in charge of Staff Department Planning and Budgeting. Pat agreed but also asked that she be given an officer's title.

Arthur agreed that she deserved the title but said, "Why does it matter? It doesn't interfere with your ability to deal with people in the bank. Nobody cares whether you are an officer or not. You deal with the chairman and the president and they don't care."

Pat's response was, "It makes a difference to me. It is far more important with my peer group than with the people I work for." She said Arthur Jones seemed to understand the feeling and he was successful in persuading management to name her an assistant cashier.

A week before Pat received her promotion, she learned that she was pregnant, a fact she temporarily kept to herself. Although she had always told Arthur she planned to have another child, when she did break the news to him—soon after being given her title—he was very upset, saying he had to promise many of the bank's top managers that this would not happen.

When Pat had stayed home with the first son, she decided she did not like being at home, and it was her intention to work throughout her second pregnancy and to return to work shortly after her next child was born. The bank's official policy, however, called for a woman's leaving her job when she was five months pregnant. It was a policy that both Pat and Arthur chose to ignore.

About one month before Pat's second child was due, she called the Benefits Department to find out what medical coverage she had. The people she spoke with became very upset when they learned she was still working, and the manager of the department went to her boss and said she had to leave as her continued employment was in violation of company policy. Not only that, the manager felt particularly concerned over her remaining as she was in a visible position and it was obvious to everyone else around that policy was being violated.

Pat recalled that Arthur had handled the situation calmly. He told the manager the following: "As soon as Pat has finished working on the five-year plan that is her project, she will leave." It took Pat another month to complete the project and as she delivered the finished report to the president, she felt labor pains. Her second son was born the next day, and Pat stayed home with him for six weeks.

While she was working in Corporate Planning, Pat had begun thinking about the three kinds of positions existing in the bank: (1) credit/lending; (2) people management; and (3) expertise in a particular subject matter. She evaluated her work experience and decided that her future career direction lay in the people-management area. "Because I had not had an opportunity to get specialized credit training, I decided to try to get a people-management job."

When Pat returned from her maternity leave,

she was given a promotion by the president. Her new area of responsibility was to include the implementation of the Manpower Planning Process, which the president felt should not be part of the bank's five-year planning process but rather an ongoing operation. In 1971 she was given assistant vice-president rank.

MANAGEMENT RESPONSIBILITIES

In Pat's view her first real management assignment came in 1973 and resulted from a reorganization in the Personnel Department. Pat was given responsibilities for a new department called Personnel Policy Development, Communications and Implementation and Employee Programs. In this position she was able to bring about considerable change in the bank's personnel policies so that they were less restrictive toward women. The bank eliminated previous policies barring women from working in the bank alone or coming into the bank on Saturdays or Sundays. Pat also hoped to change policies regarding maternity leave so that it would be treated like normal illness but was not able to do so at the time.

As part of her responsibilities for employees, Pat organized an employee discount store, which achieved sales of over $50,000 a year. As the result of her performance record, Pat was promoted to vice-president in 1973. The following April she was offered a new assignment and was asked to implement a special transfer program that had been designed particularly for employees whose jobs were being discontinued. She accepted the short-term assignment and by September had been able to place more than 100 people.

RETAIL BANKING DIVISION

In September Pat was offered a transfer to the Retail Banking Division as a personnel manager. Working with a staff of eleven, Pat was responsible for advising all line managers on corporate personnel policy and practice.

In July 1975 Pat was again promoted, this time to the position of officer in charge of a cluster of six branch banks, the position she held when this case was prepared. A line position was the kind of job she said she had wanted, and had asked for, for two years.

Pat expressed the belief that it was important for women to let management know they wanted significant assignments. In her view companies often placed men in assignments that were not related to their previous experience, yet companies expressed reluctance at offering women similar career changes.

Pat shaped her own strategy, which was to try to change management's perception of the job she wanted. In her view being manager of a cluster of branches was more involved with people management than it was with traditional banking. She felt her experience as a personnel manager was good preparation for the kinds of skills her new position entailed.

By the time Pat was placed in charge of the cluster of branches, she was earning three times what she had been earning in 1970 and she felt her salary was comparable to a man's. But being vice-president carried with it some problems as well as rewards. Pat said that when she entertained customers, they frequently wanted to pay. She found that as a vice-president, she was allowed to use the bank's dining room, where cash was not accepted, which she felt solved some problems. She suggested that women might consider maintaining a club membership to avoid problems. It was her feeling that if a woman let a man pay for the meal, it changed the nature of the relationship.

One of the annoyances she had experienced was in following the bank's tradition of using a nearby private club to hold meetings. In 1975 the club still maintained its sexist policy of not allowing women to use certain dining rooms or to sit in the general lounge area. One day when Pat was conducting business there, she sat down with a client in the lounge so that some papers could be signed. The club's doorman quickly came over to the man and told him that Pat had to leave. While Pat fumed the man roared with laughter and Pat resolved to go through channels at the bank to try to bring about either a change in the club's policy or a change in the location of future meetings.

FAMILY RESPONSIBILITIES

In talking about her family life, Pat said her work called for a 9:00 A.M. to 7:00 P.M. day in the office.

In addition, as a branch officer Pat felt that it was necessary to take work home each night, and she usually spent an hour or more a night catching up. So that her family could have time together on weekends, Pat made it a point not to go to the office Saturdays or Sundays, although she would often take additional work home with her.

As a lawyer Pat's husband worked the same weekday hours that she did, although she admitted Jim tended to view her working at home somewhat less favorably than he did his own homework.

Pat admitted her workday was a long one and said, "I think the thing that makes the biggest difference is having small children. They are a constant pull. When I come home, there is dinner to be cooked. My children have been fed, but they need to be bathed and be read to. Then I cook dinner for my husband and myself and clean up. I consider this work, too."

Pat considered herself fortunate in having been able to employ the same woman to care for her children throughout their lives. When her sons were too little to attend school, they spent the day at their sitter's apartment, which was close to the Crawfords' home. When the children reached school age, the sitter began coming to their home in the afternoon. Pat felt she had been lucky with her child-care arrangements.

"Both the woman who takes care of my children and the boys themselves are unbelievably healthy," she said. "My housekeeper has been ill only once in seven years. That day my husband went to work in the morning and I went in the afternoon."

When asked about what insight she would offer women thinking about careers in business, Pat mentioned the following:

1. Every woman has to make her own decision as to what kind and how much of a commitment she is willing to make. Pat said, "I work because I personally need the gratification. I'm willing to put a lot of energy into it. I think anything a wife and mother does, no matter how well, is expected of her. It's not something I ever gave myself extra credit for. It's probably related to the fact that I had worked for six years before having a child. I found I was not happy staying around the

home. You can't complete anything with a young child around. You can only work in spurts.''

2. Women within companies have to help management realize that there are going to be some women who want responsibility as well as some who do not. Pat often found herself challenging a commonly expressed view that if women had a choice, they would elect not to work. As evidence of men's reluctance to accept the idea that a woman might choose to work, Pat reported that although her husband had been a lawyer before she joined the bank, after she had been working for the bank for as many as ten years she would hear people say, ''Pat's only working because Jim is in law school.''

3. In 1975 women still had to be willing to prove themselves. ''I don't think women are promoted as frequently as men are as a matter of course. Rather, they have to have done something outstanding.'' Pat recalled that practically every man she had dealt with had said at some point, ''But you're different.'' She felt this was an indication that men still clung to the old myth, especially the belief that women won't stay with a company very long or that women would move.

4. Women are sometimes led to expect things they shouldn't expect regarding job responsibility because men who are their supervisors are afraid to tell them they are not doing the job. Pat felt the men were afraid women might cry. Her response was, ''So what? Some men cry. I've seen it frequently in personnel jobs.''

5. Anyone who has decided to promote a woman must make a stronger commitment to his/her superior. When the woman leaves, her superior is often called in to explain ''why'' she left. Pat did not think that would be the case with a man.

6. Anyone who seeks advancement within any corporate structure must be willing to determine what type of career goal she is seeking and then plot a calm, considered course for reaching the goal. No one, man or woman, should sit back and expect advancement to come to him or her. Women should not be reluctant to seek out a mentor. Men have been doing it for centuries. Politics is a fact of life and should be handled discreetly and well.

Questions

1. What lessons can be learned from Crawford's career?

2. Are Crawford's career planning suggestions still valid for women today?

3. What is the current status of various inequities raised in this case?

Case VII-2

CAREER DEVELOPMENT AT HI-TECH CORP.:
THE FRED MIDDLETON CASE

Fred Middleton, thirty-two years of age, was senior product development specialist at HI-TECH Corp. There was general agreement among Fred's superiors, immediate associates, and others in the organization that Fred was exceptionally well versed in his technical specialty. His graduate degree, received from a prestigious university, gave credence to this strong reputation as a technical expert. He made it a point to stay abreast of the latest research and technological developments in his field. Fred was constantly aware of competitors' new products and market thrusts.

FRED MIDDLETON'S STRENGTHS

One of Fred Middleton's unique qualities was his blend of technical expertise with a sense of the market opportunities for HI-TECH Corp.'s products. He avidly read trade papers, professional journals, general business magazines, and newspapers to stay abreast of specific product developments and the potential market applications for those new developments.

Another striking characteristic of Fred Middleton was his high energy level. He was capable of working long hours without losing his effectiveness. In fact, some of his co-workers sometimes wished Fred would relax a bit and take things more in stride. Fred was also quick to make judgments about people and events in the company. He was a critical thinker and at times used devastating force in reacting to those about him. He was seen as outspoken, aggressive, and even abrasive by certain associates.

FRED MIDDLETON'S WEAKNESSES

Although Fred had high verbal ability, he had difficulty putting things in writing. Fred was action-oriented and could not see wasting time writing

This case was prepared by Professor Philip C. Shaak of the Graduate School of Business Administration of Rutgers University. Adapted and reprinted by permission of the author. All names have been disguised.

long memos and reports. He was quick-tempered and at times lost his patience with HI-TECH's policies, procedures, and practices.

One particular event crystalized Fred's antipathy to the corporate norms of behavior. One day Fred drove his car to a company facility located about ten miles from the facility in which his office was located. These visits to the other facility were quite frequent, and Fred made it a practice to park in the visitors' parking lot rather than in the more distant employees' parking lot. After spending several hours in the building working on a particularly important project, Fred walked to his car and found a large sticker glued to his windshield noting that the car was improperly parked. A company guard had placed the sticker on the windshield because employee cars were not allowed in the visitors' parking lot.

Fred was livid when he saw the sticker. He returned to his office and spent over an hour relating the incident over and over to anyone who would listen. He berated one person after another for "... this stupid horse ..." and hurled other invectives at the people responsible for the policies regarding parking lots.

MIDDLETON'S ROLE AT HI-TECH

Fred occupied a senior staff role in HI-TECH, offering his views and technical expertise to all levels in the organization. He had no subordinates but contacted people at all levels in the organization, exchanging information and offering technical advice on some of the company's most sophisticated product developments. He was generally regarded as a major individual contributor to the company, even though he frequently lost patience with people when they could not grasp things as quickly as he could.

In the course of pursuing his job as he perceived it, Fred tried to bring about improvements in the way things were done. He challenged priorities of work, questioning why certain things were being done and why other things were not being done. To some, he was a chronic irritant. Just when action plans were agreed upon, Fred would come along and be the spoiler. From Fred's viewpoint, he was serving as the constructive critic. The reaction from others often ranged from annoyance to total exasperation. On balance, however, people generally saw Fred as a positive force in the company.

A CAREER PLANNING DILEMMA

When thinking about career planning, Fred found himself facing a dilemma. He felt that if he stayed with HI-TECH Corp. his promotional opportunities would be reasonably good by company standards but very slow by his personal standards. After six years with HI-TECH, Fred felt he knew the promotional patterns in the corporation quite well, and they did not match his self-concept of career growth.

While HI-TECH Corp. was growing, it was not a high-flyer in the industry. Top management was concerned with steady, solid, and sustained growth. It tended to be conservative in character, deliberate in approach, and very much concerned with corporate integrity in the marketplace. Over-promises to customers about product performance were anathema to top management. Promises to customers about delivery dates for products ordered were to be based on authentic estimates of what could realistically be delivered by the plant rather than what the sales representative would like to see happen. The customer was provided full service, which meant abiding not only by the letter, but also by the spirit, of the sales contract.

Although this mode of operation made sense to Fred, he often felt frustrated about getting things done. He felt top managers at HI-TECH Corp. were not risk-takers. They took things too cautiously for Fred, and delayed making critical decisions. Fred was bothered by what he saw as their myopic view of management. He was convinced the company missed major growth opportunities by their sluggish response to changing market conditions and failure to pour resources into researching areas he perceived as clear growth opportunities. One thought Fred harbored was that he would someday get high enough in the organization to influence the decision-making process if he stayed with HI-TECH long enough.

On several occasions Fred openly shared his views about the company and his lack of progress with his boss, Bert Anderson. Bert was concerned about losing Fred but was not certain what action he could take. There were no foreseeable promotions in his department for someone of Fred's stature; he had already achieved the top position of senior specialist at a young age. However, Bert saw Fred as a very bright person and did not want to lose him.

Questions

1. Is Fred Middleton a good candidate for promotion to management? Why or why not?

2. What could HI-TECH do to retain a skilled specialist like Fred Middleton?

3. Relate this case to the discussion of careers that appears in the text.

Glossary*

Acceptance sampling is a type of random sampling plan used to classify output as acceptable, as unacceptable, or as requiring complete individual screening. (19)

Accountability is the act of holding the subordinate liable for performing those activities for which he or she has been delegated the necessary authority and responsibility. (9)

Activity scheduling is the sequential timing of work activities in an effort to maximize efficiency. (19)

Affirmative action programs are designed to increase opportunities for females and minorities through recruitment, training, and promotion so they are fairly represented in the work force. (10)

Analog model is a physical representation of a real object or situation that does not have the same appearance as that which it represents. (8)

Analytical methods banks process and analyze data inputs. (18)

Analytical sophistication refers to the complexity of the model and analytical methods banks of the MIS. (18)

Apprenticeship training is a combination of on-the-job training and off-the-job instruction. (10)

Authority is the legitimate power a manager possesses to act and make decisions in carrying out responsibilities. (9)

Automation is the method of accomplishing a task by means of automatically controlled equipment, with minimal involvement of personnel. (19)

Balance of trade is the relationship between a nation's exports and its imports. (20)

Behavioral school is an approach to management thought that emphasizes effective employee motivation as a primary determinant of organizational and managerial effectiveness. (2)

Body language is the form of nonverbal communication that employs eye contact, gestures, and posture. (15)

Bottom line reflects company profitability on the income statement. (1, 22)

Boundary separates the system and its environment; it can help to clarify issues in analyzing a particular problem. (3)

Bounded rationality is Herbert Simon's term for boundaries or limits that exist in any problem situation that necessarily restrict the manager's picture of the world and thus his or her ability to make decisions. (7)

Brainstorming is a technique used to bring forth many alternative solutions; it involves a group of people brought together for the purpose of exchanging ideas. (7)

Breakeven analysis is a method of determining the minimum sales volume needed to cover all costs at a certain price level. (17)

Budget is a financial plan listing the resources or funds assigned to a particular program, project, product, or division. (5, 17)

* The numbers in parentheses refer to the chapters in which each term is defined.

Bureaucracy refers to a management approach based on a formal organizational structure with set rules and regulations. (2)

Business Roundtable is a group of top managers from different organizations who meet to discuss public issues and report their opinions as business representatives. (21)

Career development refers to the methods for effectively employing and shifting personnel within the organization. (23)

Career management is the firm's attempt to match employee goals with organizational opportunities. (23)

Career planning is the personal determination of one's career path. (23)

Career plateau is a stage in one's career from which further advancement is not expected. (23)

Cash cows are products or businesses with high market share but low growth prospects. They generate considerable inflows of funds for the firm. (6)

Change agent is a person who initiates a change; this can be an outside person such as an auditor or consultant. (11)

Climate survey examines work attitudes and situations within individual work units or departments with the idea of improving communication. (15)

Closed systems are sets of interacting elements operating without any exchange with the environment in which they exist. (3)

Coaching is a management development technique in which junior executives work closely with a senior manager, called a *mentor* or *sponsor.* (10)

Codetermination refers to the practice of having employee representatives on supervisory boards. (20)

Cognitive dissonance refers to the discrepancy between existing beliefs and attitudes and new perceptions. (15)

Commitment principle states that an organization should plan for a period of time in the future sufficient to fulfill the commitments resulting from current decisions. (5)

Committees are groups of people who render decisions or offer advice to management. (15)

Communication is the transfer of information via an understandable message from a sender to others. (15)

Comparative management is the analysis of cross-cultural studies of management practices and techniques. (20)

Compressed work week is one in which workers spend fewer days on the job but work approximately the same number of hours. (9)

Consensus management is a style in which chief executives rely on various committees, groups, and task forces to reach organization-wide agreement on a particular decision. (20)

Contingency plans provide alternative scenarios for use in case of deviations from expected trends. (22)

Contingency theory, often called situational management, is an approach to management that emphasizes adjusting managerial actions and styles to the specific circumstances of the situation confronting the organization. (2) It further states that effective leadership style is contingent upon the situation: Different styles of leadership are best for different situations. (14)

Controlling is the process by which managers determine whether organizational objectives are achieved and whether actual operations are consistent with plans. (1, 16)

CPM (Critical Path Method) is a method of scheduling activities for a complex project; it estimates the least possible time for completion of the entire project by projecting the time needed to complete the essential activities which comprise the critical path. (19)

Cycle of events refers to the process by which the open system receives inputs from its environment, transforms them, and generates output. (3)

Cycle stock is the amount of inventory expected to be used during a particular cycle. (19)

Data are facts, statistics, opinions, or predictions categorized on some basis for storage and retrieval. (18)

Data bank consists of raw data, as assembled, recorded, stored, and retrieved. (18)

Decision making involves making a choice among alternative courses of action. (7)

Decision tree is a branched model helpful in identifying alternative courses of action; probability estimates are made for each alternative, indicating the courses of action with the highest payoffs. (8)

Delegation is the assignment of authority and responsibility to subordinates. (9)

Delphi method is a forecasting technique that uses the combined knowledge of several experts in a given field. (6)

Departmentalization is the subdividing of activities and responsibility areas into units within the organization. (9)

Differentiation is achieved as the open system develops specialized functions among its various components; as the system grows in response to its environment, it differentiates into increasingly complex components. (3)

Dismissal is involuntary separation from one's job. (23)

Dogs are products or businesses with low market shares and poor growth prospects. (6)

Dynamic homeostasis is the process whereby the open system maintains equilibrium over a period of time. (3)

Economic boycott is a situation in which a nation prohibits trade or commerce with another country, typically as an act of political retaliation. (20)

Economic order quantity (EOQ) is the best order size,

based on a balancing of the various costs associated with inventory. (19)

Effectiveness is a measure of the extent to which a decision alternative meets the stated objective regardless of the costs involved. (7)

Efficiency in decision making is a comparison of the costs involved in generating an expected return or other stated objective. (7)

Egalitarianism is the premise that the economic stature of all members of society should be as equal as possible. (22)

Empathy is identification with another person's perspective. (15)

Entrepreneur refers to a person who takes financial and other risks to start a business entity. (2, 23)

Equal employment opportunity is the right of all persons to work and to advance on the basis of merit, ability, and potential without any form of discrimination because of race, color, religion, sex, or national origin. (10)

Equifinality is the principle that open systems can achieve their objectives through different courses of action. (3)

Equity theory has been offered to explain the human tendency to balance work efforts or inputs with the rewards received. (13)

Exception principle states that managers should permit their subordinates to make routine, recurring decisions and that only unusual or highly important problems should be referred to higher levels in the organization. (9)

Exchange rate is the ratio of one currency to another. (20)

Expectancy theory holds that a person's perception of achieving a prized reward or goal via effective job performance will motivate the individual. Expectancy theory forms the basis of the path-goal leadership theory. (12, 14)

Exporting is the marketing of one's merchandise to other nations. (20)

Externalities are nonmarket social forces, such as pollution. (21)

External objectives refer to service to customers and to society as a whole. (4)

Feedback is information transmitted by a receiver back to the original sender of a message. (3, 7, 15)

Feedback mechanisms, characteristic of open systems, inform the organization of deviations from objectives and may lead to adjustments in activities. (15)

Financial analysis is the use of specific techniques to study a firm's financial documents and control the flow of funds, products, and services both inside and outside the firm. (17)

Financial controls are budgets, financial analysis, and breakeven analysis. (17)

Flexitime is a work scheduling system that allows em-

ployees to set their own work hours within constraints specified by the organization. (9)

Forecasts are estimates or predictions of future events or outcomes for a specified future period. (6)

Formal communication channel is the chain of command within a company; it is the pattern of communication approved and recognized by management. (15)

Fringe benefits are nonmonetary benefits such as insurance, retirements plans, paid vacations, holidays, and the like. (10)

Future shock is the term Alvin Toffler used to describe our problems in dealing with rapid changes in our society. (22)

Futurology is the discipline of predicting future trends and events such as new technological developments. (22)

Game theory is a technique for determining the strategy that is likely to produce maximum profits in a competitive situation; this technique uses probability theory to test the possible effects on profits or market share of various competitive moves. (8)

Gantt schedule chart is a chart used to monitor the progress or status of a job. (19)

Goal displacement occurs when employees view the performance measures used in the control system as more important than the organizational goals upon which they are based. (16)

Goals are the concrete aims of the organization. They are more specific than objectives. (4)

Grapevine is a term sometimes used by managers to refer to the informal communication channel. (15)

Great Man theory states that only an exceptional person is capable of playing a prominent leadership role. (14)

Hawthorne effect refers to the positive impact on employee motivation of factors other than money and job security, as revealed by the Hawthorne studies. (13)

Hawthorne studies were a series of investigations that revealed money and job security are not the only sources of employee motivation. They led to the development of the human relations approach to employee motivation. (13)

Headhunter is a term used to describe the executive search firm, a private employment and placement agency for managerial positions. (23)

Hierarchy of objectives describes the relationship among the various levels of objectives, from broad corporate objectives to those of the individual worker. (4)

Homan's interaction hypothesis states that people who interact will grow to like each other, assuming they have compatible goals and needs, and that this will lead to more interaction (or communication), thus establishing a cycle of cohesiveness. (15)

Human factors engineering applies information about

human characteristics and behavior to the design of things people use, to the way they are used, and to the environment in which people live and work. (19)

Human relations approach to management aims to improve and increase employees' production by boosting their morale. (13)

Human relations model suggests that management should be responsible for establishing an environment that best utilizes all the human resources for improved performance. (13)

Human relations school is a management school based on the belief that better treatment of subordinates would make them more productive. (13)

Human resources management is the organizational function of planning for human resources needs, recruitment, selection, development, compensation, and evaluation. (10)

Iconic model is a physical replica or a scale representation that looks like the object it represents. (8)

Importing is the purchase and shipment of merchandise from another nation. (20)

Industrial democracy refers to a range of participative formats that provide employees with varying degrees of involvement in the operation and achievements of their firms. (20, 21)

Industrial revolution was the mid-eighteenth century movement of English manufacturing to a factory system (where products are produced in a centralized location) from a cottage system (where production was contracted to family living/work units). (2)

Informal communication channels are communication patterns that exist outside of or in addition to management approved formal channels. (5)

Informal group leader is a leader in a group who functions as a social–emotional task leader. (13)

Information is relevant data employed by the manager in making decisions. (18)

Information aggregation refers to the amount of detail with which information is maintained in the data bank; the higher the degree of aggregation, the more complex that data tends to be, and the longer it usually takes for it to be added to the data bank. (18)

Information explosion is the diffusion of excessive amounts of data that are often directed to the wrong people. (22)

Information recency depends on the lapse of time between the occurrence of an event and the inclusion of data recording that event in the MIS. (18)

Inputs are human and other resources that are necessary to operate and maintain the system or subsystem. (3)

Institutional decisions involve long-term planning and policy formulation with the aim of assuring the organization's survival as a productive part of the economy and society. (7)

Internal objectives are designed to satisfy groups within the organization. (4)

International business refers to all economic activity that crosses national boundaries. (20)

International manager is an executive involved in international business activities. (20)

Intervention refers to the changes that are introduced either to individuals or the organization. (11)

Interview is a personal meeting in which the employer evaluates a prospective employee and the applicant assesses opportunities offered by the firm. (23)

Inventory is any idle resource being held for future use. (19)

Inventory control is concerned with the amount of assets that should be held in inventory: raw materials, work in progress, and finished goods. (17)

Job analysis is the systematic study of jobs, consisting of identifying the requirements of the person assigned to the job and the elements and characteristics of the job. (10)

Job application is a form designed to obtain information that will allow the employer to determine if the job seeker meets basic qualifications and is suitable for further screening. (23)

Job content refers to the work activities that are assigned to a particular job. (19)

Job description is a written statement describing the objectives of a job, the work to be performed, the skills needed, the responsibilities involved, the relationship of the job to other jobs, and its work conditions. (10)

Job design is the process of task delineation necessary to meet various personal, work, organizational and environmental parameters. (19)

Job enlargement is the rearranging of jobs to increase their complexity. (11)

Job enrichment is a rearrangement of jobs in which the employee is involved in some job-oriented decisions. (11)

Job evaluation is a comparison of different jobs on such bases as responsibilities and education, skill, and physical requirements to determine the relative worth of a job. (10)

Job rotation is a management development technique in which managers are assigned to different departments to familiarize them with various operations of the organization. (10)

Job sharing refers to the division of one job assignment among two or more persons. (9)

Job specification is a written description of the special qualifications required of a person who fills a particular job, including skills, education, and previous experience. (10)

Laboratory training refers to the use of unstructured

small group discussions to induce interactions that will produce behavior change in the participants. (11)

Leadership is the act of motivating people to perform certain tasks intended to achieve specified objectives. (14)

Leadership style is the way a person uses available power in order to lead others. (14)

Leading is the act of motivating or causing people to perform certain tasks intended to achieve specific objectives. It is the act of making things happen. (1)

Licensing is granting the right to produce and/or to distribute a firm's products in another country to an outside firm. (20)

Linear programming is a mathematical technique that is used to find the best solution to a given problem from a set of feasible solutions; linear programming employs a model designed to optimize outputs when resources are scarce. (8)

Line-out refers to workers who carry out a complete production operation as a team. (19)

Locus of control refers to a person's perception of the controlling factor in their own destiny. (12)

Long-range objectives refer to objectives extending for a period longer than one year. (4)

Management is the use of people and other resources to accomplish objectives. (1)

Management access time is the time lapse between the manager's request for certain information and its receipt. (18)

Management audit is a professional review and evaluation of an organization's activities from the perspective of management. (16)

Management by objectives (MBO) is a process whereby the superior and subordinate managers of an organization identify goals common to each, define areas of responsibility in terms of expected results, and use these measures as guides for operating the unit and assessing the contribution of each member of the organization. (4)

Management ethics refers to the moral premises upon which executive decisions are made. (21)

Management information system (MIS) is a structured, interacting complex of persons, machines, and procedures designed to generate an orderly flow of information; this information is used as the basis of decision making in specified management responsibility areas. (18)

Managerial decisions are related to issues of the coordination and support of the core activities of the organization; managerial decisions focus primarily upon the integration of the organization's differentiated or specialized components. (7)

Materials handling is the physical movement of materials and products within a work facility. (19)

Matrix approach attempts to integrate the activities of several specialists from different departments in the organization for specific projects. (9)

Matrix organization is one in which the corporate headquarters is organized functionally while a geographical organization exists at operational levels. (9, 20)

Methods improvement involves examining and redesigning aspects of a job or work in order to make them more efficient. (9)

Mission is the unique and fundamental purpose that sets a firm apart from other firms of its type and that identifies the scope of its operation in product and market terms. The mission is a general, enduring statement of company intent. (6)

Model is a representation, or abstraction, of a real object, situation, or system. (8)

Model bank integrates various models, including linear programming models, simulations, and queuing models, for use in describing, predicting, and possibly controlling organization behavior. (18)

Motion study refers to the determination of the best set and numbers of motions to accomplish a specified task. (2)

Motivation is behavior directed toward the satisfaction of some need. (12)

Multinational company (MNC) is a firm that views itself as essentially global in nature and that conducts business in numerous national markets at a variety of levels. (20)

Multiplexing is the supplementing of formal communication channels with other channels. (15)

Negative entropy is the ability of a system to repair itself, survive, and grow; by continuing to import resources from its environment and transform them into outputs, the open system fights against disorder, or entropy, and achieves negative entropy. (3)

Noise refers to any situation that interferes with or distorts the message being communicated. (15)

Nonprogrammed decisions are those that deal with unusual or novel problems. (7)

Objectives are the desired outcomes that management hopes to attain. (4)

Obsolete manager is one who has outstayed his or her usefulness to the organization. (22)

Office of the chief executive is a top management arrangement that involves the use of several executives who share the responsibilities for directing the firm. (9)

"Old boy" network is one where jobs are offered to the relatives or friends of the hiring (or other) executive. (23)

On-the-job training consists of learning the specifics of a job in the actual work environment. (10)

Open systems emphasize the interdependence of the system with its environment; they allow for the evolution of structure over time and for interaction with the environment. (3)

Operant behavior is voluntary behavior. (12)

Operations research is the application of mathematical techniques to managerial decision making; models are used to describe and understand problems and their possible solutions. (8)

Organic type leadership is a style in which the firm is thought of as a collective unit; personnel identify with the organization, rather than with their particular function. (20)

Organization chart is a blueprint of the organization indicating lines of authority within it. (9)

Organization controls are controls exerted by the organizational structure and its planning systems and include controls exerted upon organization members. (17)

Organization development (OD) is an effort by management to increase organization effectiveness by planned intervention in the organization's processes. (11)

Organizing is the process of arranging people and physical resources to carry out plans and accomplish organizational objectives. (1, 9)

Outplacement firms help a fired employee adjust to unemployment and then help him or her find a new job. (23)

Outputs are the products of the system; direct outputs are those for which the system was originally established; indirect outputs are those that have an impact on an organization's physical, economic, or social environments. (3)

Path-goal theory indicates that effective leadership is dependent on clearly defining the paths of goal achievement and the degree to which the leader is able to influence subordinates to attain such goals. (14)

Performance gap refers to the difference between the predicted or expected level of performance and the actual level. (7)

PERT (Program Evaluation and Review Technique) is a scheduling technique for minimizing production delays by coordinating all aspects of the production task. (19)

Phased retirement means that a person is gradually provided additional leisure time as he or she approaches the planned retirement age. (23)

Planning is the process of setting objectives for the future and developing courses of action to accomplish them. (1, 15)

Plans are detailed expressions of actions necessary to accomplish stated organizational objectives. (5)

Policies are general guidelines for decision making. (5)

Postcontrols measure results following the completion of the activity and compare them with predetermined standards; they are important in the development of precontrols and steering controls for subsequent activities. (16)

Power is the ability of one person to influence the behavior of another. (14)

Precontrols are developed to eliminate the causes of any deviations that might occur in the execution of organizational plans; they are preventive measures. (16)

Probability is the likelihood of occurrence of some uncertain event or condition. (8)

Problems are barriers to the achievement of organizational goals. (7)

Procedures are guides to action that specify in detail the manner in which activities are to be performed. (5)

Production refers to the processes and activities necessary to transform various inputs into goods and/or services. (19)

Production controls are concerned with the scheduling, timing, and routing of a product or project; they monitor actual performance and compare it with expected results. (17, 19)

Productivity is a measure of the output of goods and services for a nation, an industry, or a firm. (2)

Professional management refers to persons who are hired for their training and skills in managerial techniques but who were not involved in establishing the enterprise. (2)

Program is a large-scale, single-use plan involving numerous interrelated activities. (5)

Program planning budgeting system (PPBS) is a system of budgeting that has been adopted by a number of nonprofit organizations. It involves five basic steps. (17)

Programmed decisions are those involving simple, common, frequently occurring problems that have well-established and understood solutions. (7)

Project is a single-use plan that is a component of a program or that is on a smaller scale than a program. (5)

Promotion is movement to a position with higher pay, more responsibility, and added status. (10)

Qualitative forecasting provides subjective estimates or predictions of future events or outcomes based upon such inputs as customer surveys, sales force estimates, predictions of key executives, and/or expectations of other industry experts. (6)

Quality circles are volunteer groups of operative employees who periodically brainstorm on how to increase the firm's output. (19)

Quality control deals with maintaining specified quality levels for a firm's goods or services. (17, 19)

Quantitative forecasting provides estimates or predictions of future events or outcomes based upon such statistical techniques as trend extensions, statistical correlation, computer simulations, econometrics, and/or mathematical programming. (6)

Question marks are products or businesses with low market share in a high growth market. They typically require more cash than they are able to generate. Managers must make a go/no go decision regarding them or pursue other alternatives if they decide not to go with the business. (6)

Queuing models attempt to solve problems caused by waiting lines by determining the appropriate balance between the cost of providing extra service and the cost of having people, machines, or materials wait. (8)

Ratio analysis is used to extract information from the firm's financial statements in order to evaluate performance in a specific area; actual and planned performance ratios are compared with one another and with those of similar companies. (17)

Rationalizing is the distortion of a message to bring it into line with one's own beliefs. (15)

Reference groups are those sets or categories of people with which a person identifies. (13)

Reflex behavior is involuntary behavior. (12)

Reinforcement is the process by which behavior is modified by either positive or negative factors. (12)

Responsibility is the obligation of the manager to carry out assigned duties. (9)

Resume is a summary of one's qualifications for employment, containing personal data, education, and work experience. (23)

Retirement shock refers to the personal adjustment problems caused by going from full-time work to full-time leisure. (23)

Rules are statements of actions that must be taken or not taken in a given situation. (5)

Safety stock is the inventory kept above the cycle stock to ensure availability in case of unexpectedly high usage. (14)

Salary refers to compensation for white-collar workers based on a unit of time. (10)

Satisficing is the term Herbert Simon has used to describe the way modern managers must, necessarily, make decisions with incomplete information, by choosing from among a minimum of likely alternatives. (7)

Scalar principle states that authority and responsibility should flow in a clear, unbroken line from top management to supervisory levels. (9)

Scientific management is a school of management popularized during the early 1900s that is based upon the application of the scientific method to the workplace and other management activities. (2)

Scientific method is a systematic and logical approach to the identification and solution of problems facing the decision maker. (8)

Self-concept is the image a person has of who he or she is; it is shaped over time by many internal and external forces. (12)

Sensitivity training is a process of group dynamics that influences a T-group participant's behavior. (11)

Separation refers to a resignation, a layoff, a dismissal, or a retirement. (10)

Short-range objectives refer to objectives to be obtained within a period of one year or less. (4)

Simulation is a process for replicating the major aspects of an existing system or process that is too complex to be expressed in mathematical terms; elements are described by probability distributions, then combined in various ways so their effect on the model can be studied. (8)

Single-use plans are predetermined courses of action developed for nonrepetitive situations. (5)

Social objectives are objectives designed with the larger interests of society in mind. (4)

Social responsibility refers to those management philosophies, policies, procedures, and actions that have the advancement of society's welfare as one of their primary objectives. (21)

Sociotechnical system is the result of the relationship between the sociopsychological environment in which a task is performed and the technical system required to perform it. (19)

Span-of-management concept refers to the optimum number of subordinates a person can effectively manage. (9)

Specialization is the concentration on one or on a small number of activities in order to increase efficiency. (9)

Staff planning groups assist managers by developing a planning system, helping to develop corporate and divisional plans, and gathering and evaluating information. (5)

Stakeholders are the persons whom the organization is dedicated to serve. (1)

Standing plans are predetermined courses of action developed for repetitive situations. (5)

Stars are products or businesses that are high-growth market leaders. They generate considerable funds that more than offset the funds needed to finance the additional investments and working capital needed for continuing growth. (6)

Steering controls predict results; they attempt to detect deviations from predetermined standards, allowing for corrective actions to be taken while the activity is being performed. (16)

Stockouts occur when all inventory has been used or sold; they are very costly in terms of increased production or labor costs, or lost sales. (19)

Strategic business units (SBUs) are divisions composed of key businesses within multiproduct companies with specific managers, resources, objectives, and competitors. SBUs may encompass a division, a product line, or a single product. (6)

Strategic planning is the process of determining the major objectives of an organization and the adoption of courses of action and the allocation of resources necessary to achieve those objectives. (5, 6)

Suboptimization occurs when attempts to optimize the operations of one component result in less than optimal operations of the overall organization. (3)

Survey research and feedback refer to action research involving attitude surveys and the resulting feedback to employees. (11)

Symbolic, or mathematical, model uses equations or groups of equations to express the relationships among factors in a given process or system being modeled. (8)

Synectics approach is the technique widely used to generate alternative solutions; by synectics, the manager examines analogous methods and perceptions of other fields in order to gain insight into management problems. (7)

Synergy is a term used to describe the idea that a system is more than the sum of its individual parts. (3)

System is an organized group of parts, components, or subsystems linked together according to a plan in order to achieve specific objectives. (3)

System authority refers to the amount of authority delegated to the MIS. (18)

Systems type leadership is a style in which all corporate activities are directed toward the achievement of specified objectives. (20)

Tactical planning focuses on short-term implementation of current activities and the allocation of resources for those activities. (5, 6)

Team building is a process designed to improve the effectiveness of a work group with emphasis on work procedures and interpersonal relationships. (11)

Technical decisions are decisions that concern the process whereby inputs are changed into outputs. (7)

Technocrats are specialists within the bureaucracy who dominate national economic planning. (20)

Technological displacement is the loss of employment due to technological changes. (19)

Technology is the science of applying information and knowledge to problem-solving situations. (2)

T-groups consist of those executives undergoing a laboratory training experience. (11)

Theory X proposes that subordinates dislike work and require an autocratic style of leadership. (14)

Theory Y advocates a democratic style of leadership in which employees are encouraged to participate in the decision-making process. (14)

Theory Z is a term coined by Professor William Ouchi to describe the Japanese approach to management. Characteristics of this approach include lifetime employment, employee participation in decision making, slow evaluation and promotion, nonspecialized career paths, and collective responsibility. (20)

Therbligs is the term coined by the Gilbreths to refer to the seventeen basic hand motions they identified in the course of their studies of motions. (2)

Trait theory concerns the identification and measurement of traits or attitudes that are associated with a leader's behavior. (14)

Transfer is a lateral movement to another position that usually does not include a pay increase or added responsibilities. (10)

Transformations are the operations involved in converting inputs into outputs. (3)

Unity-of-command concept states that each organizational member should report to only one supervisor for any single function. (9)

Value analysis is a formal study of purchases to determine needs, relative costs, and alternatives in an effort to minimize total expenditures. (19)

Vestibule training is designed to build skills by allowing the individual to perform the work in a training area under the supervision of a trainer before being assigned to the actual work area. (10)

Wage refers to a method of payment based on a calculation of the number of hours worked or the number of units produced by an employee. (10)

Work ethic is a belief in the inherent value of work in a society. (23)

Yes–no controls allow for a screening process point where specific approval is needed to permit the activity to continue. (16)

Zero-base budgeting is the forced periodic justification of any expenditure program, not just incremental changes in such a program. (17)

Additional Acknowledgments and Credits

CHAPTER 1:
Frost quote is from Barbara Rowes, *The Book of Quotes* (New York: Ballantine Books, 1978), p. 18. The Caldwell quote is from Clark Hallas, "Caldwell: The Kind Who Gets Things Done," *Detroit News* (November 19, 1978), p. 2-E.

CHAPTER 2:
The Coolidge quote is from Laurence J. Peter, *Peter's Quotations* (New York: Morrow, 1977), p. 84. Nixon is quoted in Barbara Rowes, *The Book of Quotes* (New York: Ballantine Books, 1978), p. 140.

CHAPTER 4:
Bryant quote is from *Time* (December 28, 1981).

CHAPTER 6:
The Wood quote is from Alfred D. Chandler, Jr., *Strategy and Structure* (Cambridge, Mass.: MIT Press, 1962), p. 325.

CHAPTER 8:
Taylor quote in testimony before the Special House Committee. Chesterton quote from Laurence J. Peter, *Peter's Quotations* (New York: Morrow, 1977), p. 408.

CHAPTER 9:
Ripley quotation is from "Thoughts on the Business of Life," *Forbes* (July 5, 1982), p. 196.

CHAPTER 10:
Disney quote from "Thoughts on the Business of Life," *Forbes* (July 5, 1982), p. 196.

CHAPTER 11:
Sevareid quote from Barbara Rowes, *The Book of Quotes* (New York: Ballantine Books, 1979), p. 242. Agee quote from Hugh D. Menzies, "The Boardroom Battle at Bendix," *Fortune* (January 11, 1982), p. 64.

CHAPTER 13:
John Paul II's quote is reported in "The Pope Gets to Work," *Newsweek* (September 28, 1981), p. 59. Schwab quote from "Thoughts on the Business of Life," *Forbes* (June 7, 1982), p. 212.

CHAPTER 14:
Haig quote is from *Time* (December 28, 1981), p. 44. Ford quote from Laurence J. Peter, *Peter's Quotations* (New York: Morrow, 1977), p. 296. Napoleon quote from ad for Boyden Associates, Inc., which appeared in *The Wall Street Journal.*

CHAPTER 15:
Hemingway quote is from "Thoughts of the Business of Life," *Forbes* (May 10, 1982), p. 332. Rockefeller quoted in *The Imperial Rockefeller* by Joseph E. Persico. Quote reprinted from "Other Comments," *Forbes* (June 21, 1982), p. 22.

CHAPTER 16:

Thoreau quote from Louis A. Allen, *Making Managerial Planning More Effective* (New York: McGraw-Hill, 1982), p. 251. Shah quote from Pravin P. Shah, *Cost Control and Information Systems* (New York: McGraw-Hill, 1981), p. 127.

CHAPTER 17:

Drucker quote from *An Introductory View of Management* (New York: Harper & Row, 1977), p. 431. Bailey quote from *Publisher's Weekly* (January 13, 1975). Reprinted by permission of Herbert S. Bailey, Jr.

CHAPTER 19:

Japanese executive quote from Arch Patton, "Industry's Misguided Shift to Staff Jobs," *Business Week* (April 5, 1982), p. 12.

CHAPTER 20:

Nixon quote is from Barbara Rowes, *The Book of Quotes* (New York: Ballantine Books, 1978), p. 147. Murphy quote is from Thomas A. Murphy, Speech to the Golden Anniversary Meeting of the Akron Rubber Group, Inc., February 15, 1978.

CHAPTER 21:

Ringeon quote from James Peltz, "Ball Corp. Executive Stresses Integrity," *Journal-American* (January 9, 1983), p. 2-B (AP story). Mercer quote from "Goodyear President Visits," *Focus EMU* (April 3, 1979), p. 5.

CHAPTER 22:

President Reagan ordering the cabinet to make budget cuts. Quoted in "Reaganomics: Turbulent Takeoff," *Time* (December 28, 1981), p. 64. Kennedy quote from Laurence J. Peter, *The Peter Plan* (New York: Morrow, 1976).

CHAPTER 23:

Carnegie is cited in Terri Minsky, "More People Face Career Plateaus, A Relief for Some, Shock for Others," *The Wall Street Journal* (August 2, 1982), Section 2, p. 15. Buss quote is from "Buss Outlines Route to $Millions," *The Seattle Times* (March 21, 1982), p. 5-B.

PHOTO CREDITS

Pages 10, 82, 148, 176, 256, 257, 350: UPI. Page 46: Wide World Photos. Pages 31, 35, 444, 494: Courtesy of Stevens Institute of Technology. Page 54: Courtesy of Maria Von Bertalanffy. Page 59: The Bettman Archive. Page 64: Camera Clix. Page 104: Courtesy of International Management Magazine. Page 109: Courtesy Potlatch Corporation. Page 126: Courtesy of UCLA Graduate School of Management. Page 226: Courtesy of New Jersey Bell. Page 242: Fogg Art Museum. Page 290: Courtesy of Harvard University. Page 312: © Karen Zebulon. Page 326: Courtesy of the Baker Library, Fogg Art Museum. Page 328: Western Electric Company. Page 390: Arizona State News Bureau. Page 424: Antioch College. Page 469: © Frank Ross, Photography. Page 534: Courtesy William Ouchi. Page 564: Courtesy of Business Committee for the Arts, Inc.

Name Index

Subject Index

649

problems and constraints in, theories of, 338
reinforcement theory and, 317–18
summary of, 321
see also behavior theories; Hawthorne studies
Motorola, 113, 261
multinational companies (MNCs), 519
  organizational structures in, 530–31
  see also international management
multiplexing, 386

Nabisco, 316
National Aeronautics and Space Administration (NASA), 54, 415–16
National Commission on Productivity, 511
National Disabilities Association of Chester (case study), 403–5
National Football League (NFL), 317
National Insurance Co. (case study), 298–300
National Labor Relations Act (1935) (Wagner Act), 251
Navy, U.S., 502
NBC, 549–50
needs, 35–36, 309–14
  for achievement, 313
  for affiliation, 313
  ego, 310
  McClelland's identification of, 313–14
  Maslow's hierarchy of, 309–12
  motivational tools and, 312
  physical, 309
  for power, 313
  satisfied, 312
  security, 309
  self-actualization, 310
  social, 309–10
negative entropy, 62
Neiman-Marcus, 42
Netherlands:
  phased retirement in, 623
  technology and productivity in, 45
network scheduling techniques, 502–3
New England Telephone, 386
New Harmony, Indiana, 27
Newhouse newspaper chain, 23–24
New York City Emergency Medical Service, 205
New York Times, 73–74
Nissan Motors, 58
Noble Roman's, 615–16
nonprofit organizations, 4, 12–13
Northwestern Mutual Life Insurance Co., 128–29
Northwest Industries, 388
Northwest Orient Airlines, 436
Norton Simon, Inc., 135, 369
Nuclear Regulatory Commission, 488

objectives, 72–97
  customer services, 84
  direction provided by, 81

external, 84–85
goals and missions vs., 80–81
hierarchy of, 87
internal, 84–85
long-range, 84
as motivators, 82
number of, 83–84
organizational effectiveness and, 81–82
in planning, 102, 106
profits as, 83–84
purpose of, 80
realism in, 89
short-range, 84
social, 84–85
as standards, 81–82
strategic planning and, 125
studies on, 86–87
summary of, 94–95
see also management by objectives
obsolete managers, 593
Occidental Life Insurance Co., 235
Occupational Safety and Health Act (1970), 251, 338, 498, 588
Occupational Safety and Health Administration (OSHA), 43, 498
Ocean Pacific, 110
OD, *see* organizational development
officials, 346
Ohio State University, studies of leadership at, 359–60
"old boy" network, 616
Olin Corp., 140–41
Olivetti group, 44–45
on-the-job training, 259
open systems, 59, 61–64
  characteristics of, 62–64
  closed systems thinking in, 62
  cycle of events in, 62
  defined, 61
  differentiation in, 63
  dynamic homeostasis in, 62–63
  equifinality in, 64
  feedback mechanisms in, 62
  negative entropy in, 62
operant behavior, 317
operational control information, 454–55
operations control, 103, 106–7
operations management, *see* production/operations management
operations research, 27, 177–79
  see also models; quantitative techniques in decision making
optimizing, 361–62
organic type leadership, 536–38
organization, 215–39
  authority relationships in, 225–32
  Barnard's concept of, 226–27, 414
  charts for, 222–23
  chief executive officers in, 229–31
  coordination in, 224–25
  defined, 218–19
  departmentalization in, 219–20
  division of work in, 219–24

in international management, 530–31
line and staff relationships in, 231–33
linking pin theory and, 225
managers and, 218
span-of-management and, 221–22
strategy as prerequisite of, 218
summary of, 237–38
unity-of-command concept and, 220–21
work schedules and, 235–37
organizational control, 443–45
organizational design, 233–35
  classical, 233
  matrix, 234–35
  modern, 233–34
  neoclassical, 233
  see also departmentalization
organizational framework of management, 38–41
  entrepreneurs in, 39–40
  professional management in, 40–41
  succession in, 41
organizational structures, 443
  change and, 283–84
  of MNCs, 530–31
  not-for-profit, 4, 12–13
  profit-oriented, 4
  tall vs. flat, 222–24
  see also departmentalization
organization development (OD), 284–95
  contemporary approaches to, 287–95
  current status of, 293–95
  defined, 285
  emergence of, 287
  goals of, 285
  job enrichment/job enlargement as, 289–92
  management by objectives and, 289
  Managerial Grid®, and, 287–89
  precedents for, 285–86
  summary of, 295
  team building approach to, 292–93
organization size, 114
organizing, 5, 7–8
  defined, 6, 218
orientation, 258–59, 444
outplacement firms, 621–22
outputs, 58–59

Pan American Airlines, 175–76
Paperwork Reduction Act (1980), 372
path-goal theory of leadership, 362–64
  contingency factors in, 364
Paul Revere Life Insurance, 90
Peabody Coal Co., 250
performance:
  actual vs. planned, 417–18
  data on, 164–65
  planning and, 105
performance appraisal, 263–65, 417, 422–23, 446
  data for, 422, 446
  forced distribution scales, 264–65
  formal systems for, 263

cost and, 182
data bases and, 181
decision trees, 198–200
disadvantages of, 182
equipment replacement and, 201
feedback, 189
game theory, 197–98
implementation and, 190
in inventory control, 200–201
lead time and, 182
linear programming, 192–96
model construction in, 187–88
oversimplification from, 182
probability theory and, 191–92
problem formulation in, 187
problems simplified by, 181
queuing (waiting-line) models, 197
reality misrepresented by, 182
resource allocation and, 192, 201
in scheduling and sequencing
  work flows, 201
scientific method in, 179–80
simulation models, 196–97
solution testing, 188–89
strategic planning vs., 128
summary of, 202
systematic focus of, 180–81
waiting-line, 197
waiting-line regulation and, 201
quantity standards, 416
Quasar Electronics Co., 487, 537
queuing models, 197
question marks, 134–35

Ralston Purina Co., 84–85
Rand Corp., 137, 437
Random House, Inc., 220, 601, 603
ratio analysis, 441
rationalizing, 377
rational-legal authority, 30
Rawlins Electric Co. (case study),
  301–4
RCA, 90, 230, 585
  planning at, 106–7
Reagan, Ronald, 229, 265, 569, 583,
  621
Reaganomics, 43
recruitment, 252–54
reference checks, 256
reference groups, 333–34
referent power, 345
reflex behavior, 317
reinforcement, 317–18
Relay Assembly Test Room study,
  327–29
reliability, in testing, 258
Remington Rand, 502
Renault, 530
Republic Steel, 58
research and development (R&D),
  509–10
resignations, 268–70
resource allocation, 500–501
  decision making and, 155

linear programming and, 192, 201
responsibility, 226
resumes, 601, 602
retirement, 268–70, 622–23
  phased, 623
retirement shock, 623
reward power, 345
rewards:
  in equity theory, 333
  intrinsic vs. extrinsic, 319–20
  of management career, 14–15
risk, 128, 162–63
Robot Institute of America, 489
robots, 487–89
Rockwell International, 511
Rolls Royce, 99–100
ROLM Corp., 102
Romac Industries, 340–41
rules, 112, 147

Saab, 517, 559
safety regulations, 43, 251, 498
safety stocks, 506
Safeway Stores, 120–21
Saga Corp., 38–40
Sageview, City of (case study), 68–72
salaries, 266–68
satisficing, 149
Saudi Arabia, planning management
  in, 529
scalar principle, 227–28
Schwinn Bicycle Co., 58
scientific management, 27, 28, 30–34
  basic features of, 31–32
  principles of, 31
scientific method, 179–80
Scott Paper Co., 111
screening interviews, 254–55, 602
Sea-Land Industries, Inc., 128–29
Sea Ray Boats, 185
Sears, Roebuck, 218, 222–24, 584, 611
Securities and Exchange Commission (SEC), U.S., 543
security needs, 309
selection process, 252–59, 444
  orientation in, 258–59
  physical examinations in, 257–58
  recruitment in, 252–54
  reference checks in, 246
  screening interviews in, 254–55
  testing in, 258
self-actualization needs, 310
self-concept, 311
sensitivity training programs, 286
separations, 268–70
Service Corps of Retired Executives
  (SCORE), 589
service staff, 233
Sethi model of corporate behavior,
  557–59
Shaklee Corp., 451–52
Shell Oil, 234
Sherman Antitrust Act (1890), 43
Sherwin-Williams, 294–95

silent monitor, 27
simulation models, 196–97
site selection, production, 489–91
  importance of, 489–90
  intangible factors in, 491
  market-related factors in, 490–91
  stages of, 491
  tangible cost factors in, 491
situational management, see contingency theory
sliding-scale budgets, 436–37
social needs, 309–10
social obligations, 557–59
social responsibility of management,
  332, 544–69
  defined, 546
  enlightened self-interest and, 554–55
  Ernst & Whinney survey of, 565
  externalities and, 557
  levels of, 555–59
  management ethics and, 549–52
  measurement of, 563–65
  popular viewpoint on, 553
  profit maximizing management
    and, 548
  quality of life management and, 548–49
  Sethi model and, 557–59
  summary of, 566–67
  traditional viewpoint on, 554
  trusteeship management and, 548–59
  see also industrial democracy
social responsiveness, 557–59
Society of Manufacturing
  Engineers, 236
sociotechnical systems, 498
Soviet Union:
  management science in, 21
  managers imprisoned in, 534
  staffing problems in, 531
  Vilnius furniture plant in, 307
span-of-management concept, 46,
  221–22, 388
specialization, 219, 388
sponsors, 261
staff authority, 231–32
staffing, see human resources
  management
staff planning groups, 115–16
staffs:
  advisory, 232
  defined, 231–32
  personnel managers as, 245–46
  purposes of, 232–33
  service, 232
stakeholders, 13
Standard Brands, Inc., 241
Standard Oil Co. of California, 528
Standard Oil Co. of New Jersey, 218
standing plans, 111–12
  policies, 111
  procedures, 111
  rules, 112
steering controls, 420
step budgets, 436–37

658

The milestones are continued from inside the front cover.

MILESTONES IN THE DEVELOPMENT OF MANAGEMENT THOUGHT

1947
Kurt Lewin proposes a model of individual change.

1948
Lester Coch and **John R. P. French, Jr.,** conduct their classic study on resistance to change.

1950s
Emergence of the **Human Relations School**.

Herbert A. Simon conducts his pioneering work on decision theory.

1951
Kurt Lewin emphasizes environmental factors as determinants of behavior.

1952
IBM introduces the first widely available electronic data processing system.

1953
Keith Davis describes the importance of the informal organization and coins the term "grapevine."

1954
Peter Drucker popularizes management by objectives (MBO) in his book *The Practice of Management*.

1956–1958
PERT and **CPM** are developed.

1959
Frederick Herzberg publishes the two-factor theory of motivation.

1960
Douglas McGregor describes Theory X and Theory Y managers.